Gay KEY WEST

 gayspringbreakkeywest.com

 kampkeywest.com

 keywestpride.org

 tropicalheatkw.com

 womenfest.com

 headdressballkeywest.com

 gaykeywestfl.com

The Florida Keys
Key West
Close To Perfect - Far From Normal

(305)294-4603 | gaykeywestfl.com

do you speak SONOMA?

{ **Sonomads:** *n.* People who embrace the wanderlust of Sonoma Wine Country.

Speak a little Sonoma and you'll feel like a local.

Because you're more than a visitor, you're a new friend.

Learn by immersion and win a savory Sonoma County experience!

SonomaCounty.com/gay   1-800-576-6662

SONOMA
COUNTY

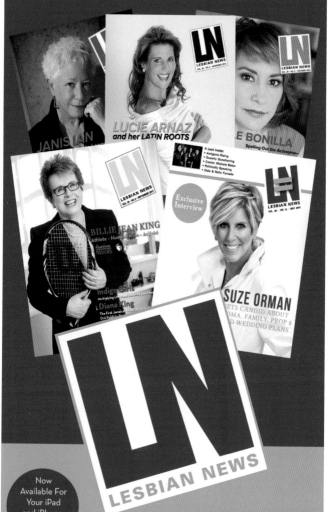

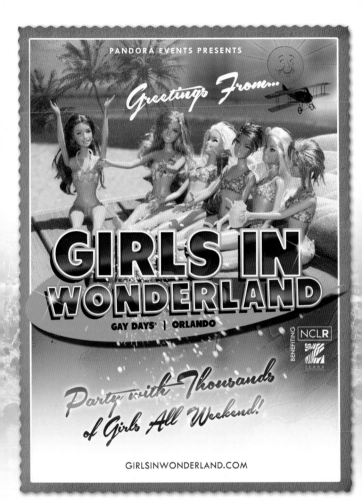

PANDORA EVENTS PRESENTS

Greetings From...

GIRLS IN WONDERLAND

GAY DAYS® | ORLANDO

BENEFITING · NCLR · ZEBRA

*Party with Thousands
of Girls All Weekend!*

GIRLSINWONDERLAND.COM

Traveller Codes

Most of the codes used in this book are self-explanatory. Here are the few, however, that aren't.

➤—This symbol marks an advertiser. Please look for their display ad near this listing, and be sure to tell them you saw their ad in the *Damron Women's Traveller*.

Popular—So we've heard from the business and/or a reader.

Mostly Women—80-90% lesbian crowd.

Mostly Gay Men—Women welcome.

Lesbians/Gay Men—Roughly 50/50 mix of lesbians and gay men.

LGBT—Lesbian, Gay, Bisexual, and Transgendered.

Gay/Straight—A little bit of everything.

Gay-Friendly—LGBT folk are definitely welcome but are rarely the ones hosting the party.

Neighborhood Bar—Regulars and a local flavor, often has a pool table.

Dancing/DJ—Usually has a DJ at least Friday and Saturday nights.

Transgender-Friendly—Transsexuals, cross-dressers, and other transgendered people welcome.

Live Shows—From an open mic to live music.

Multiracial—A good mix of women of color and their friends.

Beer/Wine—Beer and/or wine. No hard liquor.

Nonsmoking—No smoking anywhere inside premises.

Private Club—Found mainly in the US South where it's the only way to keep a liquor license. Call the bar before you go out and tell them you're visiting. They will advise you of their policy regarding membership. Usually have set-ups so you can BYOB.

Wheelchair Access—Includes rest room.

WiFi—Wireless Internet access.

the Damron Women's Traveller*

Publisher	**Damron Company**
President	**Gina M. Gatta**
Editor-in-Chief & Art Director	**Erika O'Connor**
Design Consultant	**Mary Burroughs**

Board of Directors

Gina M. Gatta, Edward Gatta, Jr., Louise Mock

How to Contact Us

Mail:	PO Box 422458, San Francisco, CA 94142-2458
Email:	info@damron.com
Web:	www.damron.com
Fax:	415/703-9049
Phone:	415/255-0404 & 800/462-6654

Table of Contents

United States

Table of Contents

International

Tours & Events

ALABAMA

Statewide

PUBLICATIONS

Ambush Mag 504/522–8049 • LGBT newspaper for the Gulf South (TX through FL)

Birmingham

ACCOMMODATIONS

Hampton Inn 2021 Park Pl N (at 21st St N) 205/322–2100 • gay-friendly • also restaurant & lounge • WiFi • wheelchair access

BARS

The Garage Cafe 2304 10th Terrace S (at 23rd St S) **205/322–3220** • 11am-close, from 3pm Sun-Mon • gay-friendly • great sandwiches • live music

Our Place 205/715–0077 • 4pm-midnight, till 2am Fri-Sat • mostly gay men • neighborhood bar • videos • gay-owned

Wine Loft 2200 1st Ave N 205/323–8228 • 5pm-close, clsd Sun-Mon • gay-friendly • wine bar • light food served

NIGHTCLUBS

Al's on 7th 2627 7th Ave S (at 27th St) 205/321–2812 • lesbians/ gay men • neighborhood bar • dancing/DJ • drag shows • theme nights • 18+ • private club

The Quest Club 416 24th St S (at 5th Ave S) 205/251–4313 • 24hrs • mostly gay men • karaoke • dancing/DJ • 19+ Wed-Sun • drag shows • private club • patio • wheelchair access • cover charge

Steel Urban Lounge 2300 1st Ave N (at 23rd St) 205/324–0666 • 6pm-close, from 8pm wknds • gay-friendly • upscale lounge • dancing/DJ

CAFES

Chez Lulu 1909 Cahaba Rd 205/870–7011 • lunch & dinner Tue-Sun, Sun brunch, clsd Mon • plenty veggie • also bakery • live shows

Birmingham

LGBT PRIDE:
June. web: www.centralalabamapride.org.

ANNUAL EVENTS:
April/May - Birmingham International Center 205/252-7652, web: www.bic-al.org
Alabama Shakespeare Festival 800/841-4273, web: www.asf.net.
August - Birmingham Shout: Gay & Lesbian Film Festival of Alabama 205/324-0888, web: www.bhamshout.com.

CITY INFO:
800/458-8085 or 205/458-8000, web: www.birminghamal.org.

ATTRACTIONS:
Alabama Jazz Hall of Fame 205/254-2731, web: www.jazzhall.com.
Birmingham Zoo & Botanical Gardens 205/879-0409, web: www.birminghamzoo.com.Civil Rights Museum 205/328-9696, web: www.bcri.org.

Sloss Furnaces Nat'l Historic Landmark 205/324-1911, web: www.slossfurnaces.com.
Vulcan Statue at 20th St S & Valley Ave, atop Red Mountain, www.visitvulcan.com.

BEST VIEW:
Overlook Park.

WEATHER:
Hot and humid in the 80°s and 90°s during the summer, mild in the 50°s to low 40°s during the winter.

TRANSIT:
Yellow Cab 205/222-2222, web: www.birminghamyellowcab.com.
Birmingham Airport shuttle 205/591-5550, www.birminghamdoortodoor.com.
Birmingham Transit Authority 205/521-0101, web: www.bjcta.org

RESTAURANTS

Bottega Cafe & Restaurant 2240 Highland Ave S (btwn 22nd & 23rd) 205/939–1000 • 5:30pm-10pm, clsd Sun • some veggie • full bar • wheelchair access

The Bottletree 3719 3rd Ave S (at 37th St S) 205/533–6288 • 3pm-close, from 11am wknds • vegetarian/ vegan • also bar • also live music venue

Highlands Bar & Grill 2011 11th Ave S (at 20th St) 205/939–1400 • 5:30pm-10pm, clsd Sun-Mon • wheelchair access

John's City Diner 112 21st St N (btwn 1st & 2nd Ave N) 205/322–6014 • lunch weekdays & dinner Mon-Sat, clsd Sun • seafood & steak • full bar • wheelchair access

Rojo 2921 Highland Ave S (at 30th St) 205/328–4733 • 11am-10pm, clsd Mon, wknd brunch • Latin & American cuisine

Silvertron Cafe 3813 Clairmont Ave S (at 39th St S) 205/591–3707 • 11am-9pm, from 8am Sat • also full bar • more gay Mon

Taj India 2226 Highland Ave S 205/939–3805 • lunch & dinner • Indian • plenty veggie

ENTERTAINMENT & RECREATION

Terrific New Theatre 2821 2nd Ave S (in Dr Pepper Design Complex) 205/328–0868

Tragic City Rollers • Birmingham's female roller derby league • visit www.dixiederbygirls.com for events

EROTICA

Alabama Adult Books 801 3rd Ave N (at 8th) 205/322–7323

Dothan

NIGHTCLUBS

Dothan Dance Club 2563 Ross Clark Circle (at Hwy 52 West) 334/792–5166 • 11pm Fri, from 6pm Sat-Sun, clsd Mon-Th • gay/ straight • drag shows • cabaret • private club • gay-owned

Huntsville

BARS

Partners 256/539–0975 • 5pm-2am, from 6pm Sat , from 2pm Sun • lesbians/ gay men • dancing/DJ • food served • live entertainment • karaoke • wheelchair access • lesbian-owned

ENTERTAINMENT & RECREATION

Dixie Derby Girls • Huntsville's female roller derby league • visit www.dixiederbygirls.com for events

Mobile

INFO LINES & SERVICES

Pink Triangle AA Group 251/479–9994 (AA#), 251/438–7080 (CHURCH) • 7pm Tue, Th & Sat • call for locations

ACCOMMODATIONS

Berney Fly B&B 1118 Government St 251/405–0949 • gay-friendly • full brkfst • pool • jacuzzi • nonsmoking • WiFi • wheelchair access

BARS

Flipside Bar & Patio 54 S Conception St 251/431–8869 • open 4pm • lesbians/ gay men • neighborhood bar • non-smoking

Gabriel's Downtown 55 S Joachim St (off Government) 251/432–4900 • 7pm-close • lesbians/ gay men • videos • karaoke • patio • private club

Midtown Pub 153 S Florida St (at Emogene) 251/450–1555 • noon-2am • lesbians/ gay men • neighborhood bar • dancing/DJ • karaoke • food served

NIGHTCLUBS

B–Bob's Downtown 213 Conti St (at Joachim) 251/433–2262 • 6pm-close, from 7pm Sat • mostly men • dancing/DJ • also gift shop • wheelchair access

RESTAURANTS

True Midtown Kitchen 1104 Dauphin St 251/434–2002 • lunch & dinner, brunch only Sun • full bar • soul food

Montgomery

ACCOMMODATIONS

The Lattice Inn 1414 S Hull St (at Clanton) 334/262–3388 • mixed gay/ straight • pool • nonsmoking • WiFi • wheelchair access

NIGHTCLUBS

Club 322 322 N Lawrence St 334/263–4322 • 8pm-close, clsd Mon • lesbians/ gay men • dancing/DJ • drag shows

Tuscaloosa

NIGHTCLUBS

Icon 516 Greensboro Ave • 9pm-2am, clsd Sun-Mon • mostly gay men • dancing/DJ • drag shows

ALASKA

Statewide

ENTERTAINMENT & RECREATION

Out in Alaska PO Box 82096, Fairbanks 99708 **877/374-9958, 907/374-9958** • adventure travel throughout Alaska for LGBT travelers

Anchorage

INFO LINES & SERVICES

AA Gay/ Lesbian 336 E 5th Ave (at Community Center) **907/929-4528** • 6pm Mon

Gay/ Lesbian Helpline 1300 East St **907/258-4777, 888/901-9876 (OUTSIDE ANCHORAGE)** • 6pm-11pm • ask about women's events: usually every Sat except summers when everyone's outdoors

Identity, Inc 336 E 5th Ave **907/929-4528** • LGBT community center • newsletter

ACCOMMODATIONS

A Wildflower Inn B&B 1239 I St (at 13th) **907/274-1239, 877/693-1239** • gay/ straight • close to hiking trails & scenic vistas • fun hosts • nonsmoking • WiFi • gay-owned

Alaska Heavenly Lodge 34950 Blakely Rd (at Mile 49 Sterling Hwy), Cooper Landing **907/595-2012, 866/595-2012** • gay-friendly • hot tub • cedar sauna • nonsmoking

Alaska's North Country Castle B&B 14600 Joanne Cir **907/345-7296** • gay-friendly • ocean & mtn views • full brkfst • nonsmoking

Anchorage Jewel Lake B&B 8125 Jewel Lake Rd **907/245-7321, 877/245-7321** • gay/ straight • full brkfst • kids ok • WiFi • nonsmoking • gay-owned

Arctic Fox Inn 327 E 2nd Ct **907/272-4818, 877/693-1239** • gay/ straight • also apts • gay-owned

City Garden B&B 1352 W 10th Ave (at N St) **907/276-8686** • gay-straight • beautiful views of Mt McKinley • 10-minute walk to downtown area • nonsmoking • gay-owned

Copper Whale Inn 440 L St (at 5th Ave) **907/258-7999, 866/258-7999** • gay/ straight • located downtown • WiFi • nonsmoking • gay-owned • wheelchair access

Gallery B&B 1229 G St (at 12th) **907/274-2567** • gay/ straight • kids/ pets ok • wheelchair access • lesbian-owned

Inlet Tower Hotel & Suites 1200 L St (at 12th) **907/276-0110, 800/544-0786** • gay/ straight • kids/ pets ok • WiFi • wheelchair access • also bar & restaurant

Renfro's Lakeside Retreat 27177 Seward Hwy, Seward **907/288-5059, 877/288-5059** • gay-friendly • WiFi • furnished modern log cabins on Kenai Lake • seasonal • gay-owned

BARS

Bernie's Bungalow Lounge 626 D St (at W 5th Ave) **907/276-8808** • gay-friendly • cocktail lounge • patio • food served

Kodiak Bar 225 E 5th Ave (btwn Cordova & Barrow) **907/258-5233, 907/865-8978** • 3pm-2:30am, till 5am Fri-Sat • lesbians/ gay men • food served • DJ nights

Mad Myrna's 530 E 5th Ave (at Fairbanks) **907/276-9762** • 4pm-2:30am, till 3am Fri-Sat • lesbians/ gay men • neighborhood bar • dancing/DJ • karaoke • food served • drag shows

Raven 708 E 4th Ave **907/276-9672** • 1pm-2:30am, till 3am wknds • lesbians/ gay men • neighborhood bar • wheelchair access

RESTAURANTS

Bear Tooth Theatre Pub & Grill 1230 W 27th Ave **907/276-4200** • movie theater, pub & grill all in one

China Lights 12110 Business Blvd, Eagle River **907/694-8080** • 11:30am-10pm, till 10:30pm wknds

Club Paris 417 W 5th Ave **907/277-6332** • 11am-midnight, from 4pm Sun • perhaps the finest restaurant in town

Garcia's 11901 Business Blvd #104 (next to Safeway), Eagle River **907/694-8600** • 11am-midnight, from noon wknds • Mexican

Ginger 425 W 5th Ave (at D St) **907/929-3680** • lunch Mon-Fri, dinner nightly, bar from 3pm • Pacific Rim/ Asian

Marx Brothers Cafe 627 W 3rd Ave **907/278-2133** • 5:30pm-10pm, clsd Sun-Mon • great food & views

Simon & Seafort's 420 L St (btwn 4th & 5th) **907/274-3502** • lunch weekdays, dinner nightly • seafood & prime rib • full bar • great views

Snow City Cafe 1034 W 4th Ave (at L St) **907/272-2489** • 7am-3pm, till 4pm wknds

ENTERTAINMENT & RECREATION

Out North Contemporary Art House 3800 DeBarr Rd **907/279-3800** • community-based & visiting-artist exhibits, screenings & performances

BOOKSTORES

Title Wave Books 1360 W Northern Lights Blvd **907/278-9283, 888/598-9283** • 10am-8pm, till 9pm Fri-Sat, 11am-7pm Sun • largest independent bookstore in Alaska

RETAIL SHOPS

The Sports Shop 570 E Benson Blvd **907/272-7755** • 10am-7pm, till 6pm Sat, noon-5pm Sun • women's outdoor clothing, adventure gear & equipment

PUBLICATIONS

Anchorage Press 907/561-7737 • alternative paper • arts & entertainment listings

EROTICA

Le Shop 305 W Diamond Blvd (at C St) **907/522-1987** • 8am-1am

Fairbanks

ACCOMMODATIONS

All Seasons B&B Inn 763 7th Ave (at Barnette St) **907/451-6649, 888/451-6649** • gay-friendly • full brkfst • nonsmoking • WiFi • wheelchair access

Billie's Backpackers Hostel 2895 Mack Blvd **907/479-2034, 907/799-6120** • gay-friendly • kids ok • food served • women-owned

Anchorage

LGBT PRIDE:
June. web: alaskapride.org.

ANNUAL EVENTS:
January - Anchorage Folk Festival, web: www.anchoragefolkfestival.org.
February - World Ice Art Championship 907/451-8250, web: www.icealaska.com.
March - Iditarod Sled Dog Race 907/376-5155, web: www.iditarod.com.
June - Mayor's Marathon 907/786-1325, web: www.mayorsmarathon.com.
August - Alaska State Fair 907/745-4827, web: www.alaskastatefair.org.
October - Quyana Alaska (native dance celebration) 907/274-3611, web: www.nativefederation.org.

CITY INFO:
907/276-4118, web: www.anchorage.net.

ATTRACTIONS:
Alaska Museum of Natural History, 907/274-2400, web: www.alaskamuseum.org.
Alaska Native Heritage Center 907/330-8000, web: www.alaskanative.net.

Alaska Wildlife Conservation Center (in Portage) 907/783-2025, web: www.alaskawildlife.org.
Portage Glacier.
Wolf Song of Alaska Museum 907/622-9653, web: www.wolfsongalaska.org.

BEST VIEW:
The 11-mile-long paved Tony Knowles Coastal Trail along Cook Inlet offers spectacular views of several mountains, including Denali (Mt McKinley).

WEATHER:
Anchorage's climate is milder than one might think, due to its coastal location. It is cold in the winter (but rarely below 0°F), and it warms up considerably in June, July, and August. Winter sets in around October. Expect more rain in late summer/ early fall.

TRANSIT:
Yellow Cab 907/222-2222, web:akyellowcab.com.
Alaska Shuttle 907/338-8888, 907/694-8888, web: www.alaskashuttle.net.
Rideline (bus) 907/343-6543, www.muni.org/transit1/rideline.cfm.

CAFES

Hot Licks Ice Cream 3453 College Rd
907/479-7813 • seasonal

Haines

ACCOMMODATIONS

The Guardhouse Boarding House 15 Fort
Seward Dr **907/766-2566, 866/290-7445** •
lesbians/ gay men • in former jail of Fort
William H. Seward • great views of Lynn Canal
• bald eagle-watching • nonsmoking • WiFi •
lesbian-owned

Homer

ACCOMMODATIONS

Sadie Cove Wilderness Lodge Kachemak
Bay State Park **907/235-2350, 888/283-7234** •
gay-friendly • 5 cabins • tree planted for every
guest to offset carbon emissions • built from
hand-milled driftwood • 3 full meals a day •
nonsmoking

Spit Sister B&B Homer Spit Rd (at Harbor
View Boardwalk #5, at Spit Sister Cafe)
907/235-4921 (SUMMER), 907/299-7748 • gay/
straight • full brkfst • kids/ 1 small pet ok •
private deck overlooks Homer Harbor •
nonsmoking • WiFi • cafe downstairs •
women-owned

CAFES

Spit Sister Cafe Homer Spit Rd (at Harbor
View Boardwalk #5) **907/235-4921 (SUMMER),
907/299-6868/ 6767 (WINTER)** • 5am-4pm •
gay/ straight • WiFi • also B&B • women-
owned

ENTERTAINMENT & RECREATION

Alaska Fantastic Fishing Charters
800/478-7777 • deluxe cabin cruiser for big-
game fishing (halibut)

Juneau

ACCOMMODATIONS

**Pearson's Pond Luxury Suites &
Adventure Spa** 4541 Sawa Circle
907/789-3772, 888/658-6328 • gay-friendly •
B&B resort & spa • hot tub • nonsmoking

The Silverbow Inn 120 Second St
907/586-4146, 800/586-4146 • gay-friendly •
full brkfst • also restaurant & bakery •
alternative cinema • gallery • kids ok •
nonsmoking • WiFi

RESTAURANTS

Hangar on the Wharf 2 Marine Way Ste 106
907/586-5018 • lunch & dinner • full bar •
great fish & chips

Ketchikan

ACCOMMODATIONS

Anchor Inn by the Sea 4672 S Tongass Hwy
907/247-7117, 800/928-3308 • gay-friendly •
nonsmoking • WiFi

ENTERTAINMENT & RECREATION

Southeast Sea Kayaks 3 Salmon Landing
907/225-1258, 800/287-1607 • trip planning •
tours • wilderness kayaking

McCarthy

ACCOMMODATIONS

McCarthy Lodge & Ma Johnson's Hotel
907/554-4402 • gay-friendly • full brkfst • also
restaurant • kids ok • inside Wrangell St Elias
nat'l park • nonsmoking

Palmer

ACCOMMODATIONS

Alaska Garden Gate B&B 950 S Trunk Rd
907/746-2333 • gay/ straight • full brkfst • hot
tub • kids/ pets ok • WiFi • lesbian-owned

Seward

ENTERTAINMENT & RECREATION

Puffin Fishing Charters PO Box 606, 99664
907/224-4653, 800/978-3346 • gay/ straight •
day fishing trips

Sitka

ENTERTAINMENT & RECREATION

Esther G Sea Taxi 215 Shotgun Alley
907/738-6481, 907/747-6481 • marine
wildlife tours • transportation service

ARIZONA

Apache Junction

ACCOMMODATIONS

Susa's Serendipity Ranch 4375 E
Superstition Blvd **480/288-9333** • women
only • guesthouses on 15-acre ranch • 2 RV
hookups • hot tub • nonsmoking • pets ok •
lesbian-owned

Bisbee

ACCOMMODATIONS

Casa de San Pedro B&B 8933 S Yell Ln (at
Hwy 92 & Palominas Rd), Hereford
520/366-1300, 888/257-2050 • gay-friendly •
full brkfst • pool • hot tub • nonsmoking •
WiFi • wheelchair access • gay-owned

Copper Queen Hotel 11 Howell Ave 520/432–2216 • gay-friendly • restored landmark hotel • kids ok • pool • nonsmoking • restaurant • wheelchair access

David's Oasis Camping Resort 5311 W Double Adobe Rd, McNeal 520/979–6650 • lesbians/gay men • 21+ • pool • BYOB bar on wknds • WiFi • gay-owned

Eldorado Suites 55 OK St 520/432–6679 • gay-friendly • territorial architecture •WiFi • kitchens • nonsmoking

Sleepy Dog Guest House 212A Opera Dr 520/432–3057, 520/234–8166 (CELL) • gay-friendly • reclaimed miner's cabin • patio • great views • very dog-friendly • lots of stairs • WiFi

BARS

St Elmo's 36 Brewery Ave 520/432–5578 • 10am-2am • gay-friendly • live bands Fri-Sat

Bullhead City

includes Laughlin, Nevada

Flagstaff

ACCOMMODATIONS

Abineau Lodge 1080 Mountainaire Rd 928/525–6212, 888/715–6386 • gay/ straight • huskies on premises • cedar sauna • full brkfst • nonsmoking • WiFi • gay-owned

The Historic Hotel Monte Vista 100 N San Francisco St (at Aspen) 928/779–6971, 800/545–3068 • gay-friendly • live shows • full bar • nonsmoking

Inn at 410 410 N Leroux St 928/774–0088, 800/774–2008 • gay-friendly • full brkfst • WiFi • wheelchair access • gay-owned

Motel in the Pines 80 W Pinewood Blvd (exit 322), Pinewood 928/286–9699, 800/574–5080 • gay-friendly • 20 miles from Flagstaff • wheelchair access

Starlight Pines B&B 3380 E Lockett Rd (at Fanning) 928/527–1912, 800/752–1912 • gay/ straight • full gourmet brkfst • kids ok (call for details) • nonsmoking • WiFi • gay-owned

BARS

Charly's Pub & Grill 23 N Leroux St (at Weatherford Hotel) 928/779–1919 • 8am-2am • gay-friendly • food served • some veggie • live shows nightly • patio • wheelchair access

Monte Vista Lounge 100 N San Francisco St (at Hotel Monte Vista) 928/774–2403 • noon-2am, from 11am Fri-Sun • gay-friendly • dancing/DJ • live bands • karaoke

CAFES

Macy's European Coffee House 14 S Beaver St 928/774–2243 • 6am-8pm • food served • vegetarian/ vegan bakery

RESTAURANTS

Cafe Olé 119 S San Francisco St (at Butler) 928/774–8272 • lunch & dinner, clsd Sun • Mexican • plenty veggie • beer/ wine • wheelchair access

Granny's Closet 218 S Milton Rd 928/774–8331 • lunch & dinner • also sports bar

Pasto 19 E Aspen (at San Francisco) 928/779–1937 • lunch & dinner, clsd Sun • Italian • beer/ wine • wheelchair access

Golden Valley

EROTICA

Pleasure Palace Adult Bookstore 4150 US Hwy 68 (at Houck Rd) 928/565–5600

Grand Canyon

ACCOMMODATIONS

Grand Canyon Lodge North end of Hwy 67, North Rim 877/386–4383 • gay-friendly • at the North Rim of the Grand Canyon

Grand Canyon Lodges 928/638–2631 • gay-friendly • the only "in-park" lodging at the South Rim

Jerome

ACCOMMODATIONS

The Cottage Inn Jerome 928/634–0701, 928/649–6759 • gay/ straight • full brkfst • kids/ pets ok • gay-owned

Mile High Grill & Inn 309 Main St 928/634–5094 • gay-friendly • cool hotel • also restaurant • lesbian-owned

RESTAURANTS

Quince Grill & Cantina 363 S Main St 928/634–7087 • 8am-5pm, 7am-9pm Th-Sun • wheelchair access

Kingman

ACCOMMODATIONS

Kings Inn Best Western 2930 E Andy Devine Ave 928/753–6101, 800/750–6101 • gay-friendly • pool • food served • kids/ pets ok • WiFi • wheelchair access

Lake Havasu City

INFO LINES & SERVICES

Lake Havasu City AA 877/652–9005

ACCOMMODATIONS

Nautical Inn 1000 McCulloch Blvd N 928/855–2141, 800/892–2141 • gay-friendly • beachfront hotel • full restaurant & bar • WiFi • pool

Lake Powell

ACCOMMODATIONS

Dreamkatchers Lake Powell B&B 435/675–5828 • gay/ straight • spa on deck • full brkfst • WiFi • gay-owned

Phoenix

see also Scottsdale & Tempe

INFO LINES & SERVICES

1 Voice LGBT Community Center 4442 North 7th Ave 602/712–0111 • noon-7pm, clsd Sun

Lambda Phoenix Center 2622 N 16th St (at Virginia Ave) 602/635–2090 • space for many 12-step programs

ACCOMMODATIONS

Clarendon Hotel & Suites 401 W Clarendon Ave (at 3rd Ave) 602/252–7363 • gay/ straight • boutique hotel in midtown • pool • WiFi • wheelchair access • gay-owned

FireSky Resort & Spa 4925 N Scottsdale Rd, Scottsdale 480/945–7666, 800/528–7867 • gay-friendly • pool • garden courtyard spa • WiFi • wheelchair access

Hotel San Carlos 202 N Central Ave 602/253–4121, 866/253–4121 • gay-friendly • boutique hotel • rooftop pool • restaurant • WiFi

Maricopa Manor B&B Inn 15 W Pasadena Ave 602/274–6302, 800/292–6403 • gay/ straight • pool • hot tub • WiFi • wheelchair access • gay-owned

Orange Blossom Hacienda 3914 E Sunnydale Dr (btwn Recker & Hunt Hwy), Gilbert 480/755–4346, 877/589–8465 • gay-friendly • pool • gay-owned

The Saguaro 4000 N Drinkwater Blvd 480/308–1100 • gay-friendly • hip boutique hotel • pool • gym • nonsmoking • WiFi

Scottsdale Thunderbird Suites 7515 E Butherus Dr (at Scottsdale Rd), Scottsdale 480/951–4000, 800/951–1288 • gay-friendly • full brkfst • pool • nonsmoking • WiFi • kids/pets ok • also full bar • wheelchair access

ZenYard 830 E Maryland Ave 602/845–0830, 866/594–0242 • gay/ straight • private suites w/ kitchens • saltwater pool

BARS

Anvil 2303 E Indian School Rd 602/956–2885 • 1pm-2am • mostly gay men • dancing/DJ • leather • male revue

Apollo's 5749 N 7th St (S of Bethany Home) 602/277–9373 • 11am-2am • mostly gay men • neighborhood bar • karaoke • drag shows • WiFi • patio

Bar 1 3702 N 16th St (at E Clarendon) 602/266–9001 • 10am-2am • mostly gay men • neighborhood bar • karoke • WiFi

BS West 7125 E 5th Ave (in the Kiva Center), Scottsdale 480/945–9028 • 2pm-2am • lesbians/ gay men • dancing/DJ • shows • karaoke • wheelchair access

Cash Inn Country 2140 E McDowell Rd (at 22nd St) 602/244–9943 • 2pm-close, from noon wknds • mostly women • dancing/DJ • country/ western • karaoke • WiFi • wheelchair access

Cruisin' 7th 3702 N 7th St (near Indian School) 602/212–9888 • 6am-2am, from 10am Sun • mostly gay men • transgender-friendly • drag shows • karaoke • wheelchair access

Ice Pics 3108 E McDowell Rd (at 32nd St) 602/267–8707 • 10am-2am, from 2pm Sun • mostly men • video bar

Kobalt 3110 N Central Ave 602/264–5307 • 11am-2am • lesbians/ gay men • karaoke • live shows

Oz 1804 W Bethany Home Rd (at 19th) 602/242–5114 • 6am-2am • lesbians/ gay men • neighborhood bar • WiFi • wheelchair access

Plazma 1560 E Osborn Rd (at N 16th St) 602/266–0477 • 2pm-close, from noon wknds • lesbians/ gay men • neighborhood bar • karaoke • videos

Rainbow Cactus 15615 N Cave Creek Rd (btwn Greenway Pkwy & Greenway Rd) 602/867–2463 • 3pm-2am • lesbians/ gay men • neighborhood bar

The Rock/ La Roca 4129 N 7th Ave (at Indian School) 602/248–8559 • 2pm-2am, from 11am wknds • lesbians/ gay men • neighborhood bar • dancing/DJ • karaoke • live shows

Roscoe's on 7th 4531 N 7th St (at Minnezona) 602/285–0833 • 2pm-2am, from 10am wknds • lesbians/ gay men • sports bar • food served

Stacy's @Melrose 4343 N 7th Ave 602/264-1700 • 4pm-2am • lesbians/gay men • dancing/DJ

The Zoan 4301 N 7th Ave (at Indian School Rd) 602/265-3233 • 5pm-2am, from 10am Th-Sun • mostly women • dancing/DJ • multiracial • karaoke • live /drag shows • wheelchair access • women-owned

Zorfs 1028 E Indian School Rd (at N 10th Pl) 602/277-7729 • 2pm-2am, from 10am Sun • mostly gay men • neighborhood bar • drag shows • food served • karaoke • gay-owned

NIGHTCLUBS

Bar Smith 602/229-1265 • 9pm-2am, till 3am Sat, clsd Sun • gay/ straight • full menu

Club Zarape 1730 McDowell Rd 602/253-0689 • 9:30pm-close Fri-Sat • mostly men • drag shows • mostly Latino

Karamba 1724 E McDowell (at 16th St) 602/254-0231 • 9pm-close, clsd Mon-Wed • mostly gay men • dancing/DJ • drag shows • Latin wknds • wheelchair access

CAFES

Copper Star Coffee 4220 N 7th Ave (at Indian School) 602/266-2136 • 6am-9pm, till 11pm Fri-Sat • coffee in a converted gas station • WiFi

RESTAURANTS

DeFalco's Italian Deli 2334 N Scottsdale Rd 480/990-8660 • best sandwiches in AZ

Phoenix

LGBT PRIDE:
April. 602/277-7433, web: www.azpride.org.

ANNUAL EVENTS:
April - Phoenix Film Festival 602/955-6444, web: www.phoenixfilmfestival.com.
April - Phoenix Improv Festival 480/389-4852, web: www.phoeniximprovfestival.com.
October - Rainbows Festival 602/277-7433, web: www.phoenixpride.org/events/rainbows-festival.

CITY INFO:
Arizona Office of Tourism 866/275-5816, web: www.arizonaguide.com.
Greater Phoenix Convention & Visitors Bureau 877/225-5749, web: www.visitphoenix.com.

ATTRACTIONS:
Arizona Golf Association 602/944-3035, web: www.azgolf.org.
Castles & Coasters Park on Black Canyon Fwy & Peoria 602/997-7575, web: www.castlesncoasters.com.
Desert Botanical Garden in Papago Park 480/941-1225, web: www.dbg.org.
Heard Museum 602/252-8848, web: www.heardmuseumshop.com.
Hiking trails in Papago Park, Squaw Peak & Camelback Mtns.
Phoenix Zoo 602/273-1341, web: www.phoenixzoo.org.

BEST VIEW:
South Mountain Park at sunset, watching the city lights come on.

WEATHER:
Beautifully mild and comfortable (60°s-80°s) October through March and April. Hot (90°s-100°s) in summer. August brings the rainy season (severe monsoon storms) with flash flooding.

TRANSIT:
Yellow Cab 602/252-5252, web: www.aaayellowaz.com.
Super Shuttle 602/244-9000, web: www.supershuttle.com.
Phoenix Transit 602/253-5000, www.valleymetro.org.

Alexi's 3550 N Central Ave #120 (in Valley Bank Bldg) 602/279-0982 • lunch Mon-Fri, dinner nightly, clsd Sun • full bar • patio • wheelchair access

AZ/88 7553 E Scottsdale Mall, Scottsdale 480/994-5576 • 11:30am-1am (food till 12:30am)

Barrio Cafe 2814 N 16th St 602/636-0240 • lunch Tue-Fri, dinner Tue-Sun, Sun brunch, clsd Mon • Mexican • live music • lesbian-owned

Coronado Cafe 2201 N 7th St 602/258-5149 • lunch Mon-Sat, dinner Tue-Sat, clsd Sun

Dottie's True Blue Cafe 4151 N Marshall Way, Scottsdale 480/874-0303 • 7:30am-3pm, clsd Mon • plenty veggie • great brkfst • gay-owned

Durant's 2611 N Central Ave 602/264-5967 • lunch Mon-Fri, dinner nightly

FEZ 3815 N Central Ave (S of Clarendon) 602/287-8700 • 11am-midnight, from 8:30am wknds • Moroccan influence • full bar • patio

Green 2240 N Scottsdale Rd #8, Tempe 480/941-9003 • 11am-9pm, clsd Sun • new American vegetarian/vegan

Harley's Bistro 4221 N 7th Ave (N of Indian School) 602/234-0333 • lunch Tue-Fri, dinner nightly, clsd Mon • lesbians/gay men • Italian

Los Dos Molinos 8684 S Central Ave 602/243-9113 • lunch & dinner, clsd Sun-Mon • Mexican homecooking

MacAlpines's Soda Fountain 2303 N 7th St 602/262-5545 • 11am-7pm, till 8pm Fri-Sat, great milkshakes

Malee's 7131 E Main, Scottsdale 480/947-6042 • lunch & dinner • Thai • plenty veggie • full bar

Mi Patio 3347 N 7th Ave 602/277-4831 • 10am-10pm • Mexican

Persian Garden Cafe 1335 W Thomas Rd (at N 15th Ave) 602/263-1915 • lunch & dinner, dinner only Sat, clsd Sun-Mon • plenty vegan• WiFi

Portland's 105 W Portland St (at Central Ave) 602/795-7480 • lunch Tue-Fri, dinner Mon-Sat, clsd Sun • also wine bar

Restaurant Mexico 423 S Mill Ave, Tempe 480/967-3280 • 11am-9pm, till 10pm Fri-Sat, clsd Sun

Rose & Crown 628 E Adams St 602/256-0223 • 11am-2am • British pub

Switch 2603 N Central Ave 602/264-2295 • 11am-midnight, from 10am wknds • full bar • WiFi

Ticoz 5114 N 7th St (N of Camelback) 602/200-0160 • 11am-midnight • Latin cuisine • full bar • WiFi

Vincent on Camelback 3930 E Camelback Rd (at 40th St) 602/224-0225 • dinner Mon-Sat, clsd Sun • Southwestern • wheelchair access

ENTERTAINMENT & RECREATION

Arizona Roller Derby • Arizona's female roller derby league • visit www.azrollerderby.com for events

Lesbian Social Network 480/946-5570 • 7:30pm-10pm Fri • popular informal social evenings of games, videos & discussions • smoke- & alcohol-free • call for location

Soul Invictus 1022 NW Grand Ave (near W Van Buren St) 602/214-4344 • queer-friendly art gallery & cabaret

Stray Cat Theatre 132 E 6th St (at Performing Arts Ctr), Tempe 480/634-6435 • provocative, off-the-beaten-path productions

BOOKSTORES

Changing Hands 6428 S McClintock Dr, Tempe 480/730-0205 • 10am-9pm, from 9am Sat, till 6pm Sun • new & used • LGBT section

RETAIL SHOPS

Off Chute Too 4111 N 7th Ave (at Indian School Rd) 602/274-1429 • 9am-9pm, till 10pm Fri-Sat, 10am-6pm Sun • LGBT gift shop in Melrose District

PUBLICATIONS

Echo Magazine 602/266-0550, 888/324-6624 • bi-weekly LGBT newsmagazine

Ion Arizona Magazine 602/308-4662 • entertainment guide for the AZ gay community

'N Touch Magazine 602/373-9490 • LGBT newsmagazine

Women's Community Connection 480/946-5570 • monthly newspaper w/ events & lesbian resources

GYMS & HEALTH CLUBS

Pulse Fitness 18221 N Pima Rd #H-130, Scottsdale 480/907-5900

EROTICA

Adult Shoppe 111 S 24th St (at Jefferson) 602/306-1130 • 24hrs • several locations

Castle Megastore 300 E Camelback (at Central) 602/266-3348 • 11am-11pm, tll 2am Fri-Sat

Fascinations 10242 N 19th Ave #1-7
602/943-5859 • many locations

Zorba's Adult Book Shop 2924 N
Scottsdale Rd (N of Thomas), Scottsdale
480/941-9891 • 24hrs • video rentals &
arcade

Prescott

ACCOMMODATIONS

The Motor Lodge 503 S Montezuma St (at
Leroux) 928/717-0157 • gay-friendly •
nonsmoking • WiFi • gay-owned

Sedona

ACCOMMODATIONS

A Woman's Way PO Box 127, 86339
928/254-1897 • women only • "healing
sanctuary" • retreats

Apple Orchard Inn 656 Jordan Rd
928/282-5328, 800/663-6968 • gay-friendly •
full brkfst • hot tub • pool • hiking • scenic
views • nonsmoking • wheelchair access

El Portal Sedona 95 Portal Ln
928/203-9405, 800/313-0017 • gay-friendly •
suites in a 1910 adobe hacienda •
nonsmoking • food served • WiFi • wheelchair
acccess

**The Lodge at Sedona—A Luxury B&B
Inn** 125 Kallof Pl 928/204-1942,
800/619-4467 • gay/ straight • full gourmet
brkfst • pool • nonsmoking • WiFi •
wheelchair access

Sedona Rouge Hotel & Spa 2250 W Hwy
89-A 928/203-4111, 866/312-4111 • gay-
friendly • pool • nonsmoking • WiFi •
restaurant & bar • wheelchair access

Southwest Inn at Sedona 3250 W Hwy
89-A 928/282-3344, 800/483-7422 • gay-
friendly • pool • spa • workout room • WiFi •
nonsmoking

CAFES

Old Town Red Rooster Cafe 901 N Main
St, Cottonwood 928/649-8100 • 10am-4pm,
8am-2pm Sun

RESTAURANTS

Judi's 40 Soldiers Pass Rd 928/282-4449 •
lunch & dinner, clsd Sun • some veggie • full
bar

RETAIL SHOPS

Sedona Green Gallery & Gifts 273 N Hwy
89A #K (btwn Jordan & Mesquite)
928/239-5353 • 10-15% discount to self-
identifying gay & lesbian customers

Tucson

INFO LINES & SERVICES

AA Gay/ Lesbian 3269 N Mountain Ave
520/624-4183 • many mtgs

**Wingspan, Southern Arizona's LGBT
Community Center** 430 E 7th St
520/624-1779, 800/553-9387 • 11am-2pm,
resources, youth support (3pm-8pm Mon-Fri)

ACCOMMODATIONS

Armory Park Guesthouse 219 S 5th Ave
520/206-9252 • gay-friendly • renovated 1896
residence w/ 2 detached guest units • gay-
owned

Catalina Park Inn 309 E 1st St (at 5th Ave)
520/792-4541, 800/792-4885 • gay/ straight •
full brkfst • nonsmoking • kids 10+ ok • WiFi •
gay-owned

Desert Trails B&B 12851 E Speedway Blvd
520/885-7295, 877/758-3284 • gay-friendly •
adobe hacienda on 3 acres bordering Saguaro
Nat'l Park • far from the madding crowd •
swimming • smoking outside only

Hotel Congress 311 E Congress St
520/622-8848, 800/722-8848 • gay/ straight •
historic hotel • WiFi • also cafe, full bar & club

La Casita Del Sol 407 N Meyer Ave (btwn
Church Ave & Franklin Ave) 520/623-8882 •
gay/ straight • 1880s adobe guesthouse •
nonsmoking • WiFi • gay-owned

Natural B&B & Retreat 520/881-4582,
888/295-8500 • gay/ straight • full brkfst •
nonsmoking • nontoxic/ nonallergenic • some
shared baths • kids ok • WiFi • massage
available • gay-owned

Royal Elizabeth B&B Inn 204 S Scott Ave
(at Broadway) 520/670-9022, 877/670-9022 •
gay/ straight • full brkfst • pool • hot tub • kids
ok • nonsmoking • WiFi • gay-owned

BARS

Club Congress/ The Tap Room 311 E
Congress (at Hotel Congress) 520/622-8848
• 11am-2am • gay-friendly • neighborhood
bar • dance club from 9pm • karaoke • live
bands

IBT's (It's About Time) 616 N 4th Ave (at
University) 520/882-3053 • noon-2am •
lesbians/ gay men • dancing/DJ • live shows •
karaoke • wheelchair access

New Moon 915 W Prince Rd (at Fairview)
520/293-7339 • 4pm-close, clsd Mon •
lesbians/ gay men • dancing/DJ • food served •
karaoke • WiFi

Woody's 3710 N Oracle Rd (at W Thurber Rd) **520/292-6702** • 11am-2am • mostly gay men • karaoke • video/ sports bar • wheelchair access

CAFES

Revolutionary Grounds 606 N 4th Ave (at E 5th St) 520/620-1770 • 8am-8pm, from 9am Sun • plenty veggie/vegan/ gluten free • WiFi • also leftist bookstore

RESTAURANTS

Blue Willow 2616 N Campbell Ave (at Grant) **520/327-7577** • 7am-9pm, from 8am wknds • brkfst served all day

Cafe Poca Cosa 110 E Pennington St **520/622-6400** • 11am-9pm, till 10pm Fri-Sat, clsd Sun-Mon • Mexican-influenced bistro • patio

The Grill on Congress 100 E Congress St (at Scott) **520/623-7621** • 24hrs • plenty veggie • full bar

ENTERTAINMENT & RECREATION

The Loft Cinema 3233 E Speedway Blvd **520/795-0844, 520/322-5638** • Tucson's independent art house • pizza, beer & wine

Tucson Roller Derby 520/390-1454 • Tucson's female roller derby league • visit tucsonrollerderby.com for events

BOOKSTORES

Antigone Books 411 N 4th Ave (at 7th St) **520/792-3715** • 10am-7pm, till 9pm Fri-Sat, 11am-5pm Sun • LGBT/ feminist • gifts • wheelchair access

EROTICA

Hydra 145 E Congress (at 6th) **520/791-3711** • vinyl • leather • toys • shoes • lingerie

Tucson

LGBT PRIDE:
June & Oct 520/622-3200, web: www.tucsonpride.org.

ANNUAL EVENTS:
February - La Fiesta de los Vaqueros (rodeo & parade) 520/741-2233, web: www.tucsonrodeo.com.
April - Int'l Mariachi Music Conference 520/838-3913, web:www.tucsonmariachi.org.

WEATHER:
350 days of sunshine a year. Need we say more?

TRANSIT:
Yellow Cab Tucson 520/594-9494, web: www.aaayellowaz.com.
Arizona Shuttle 800/888-2749, web: www.arizonashuttle.com.
Sun Tran 520/792-9222, web: www.suntran.com

CITY INFO:
520/624-1817, web: www.visittuc-son.org.

BEST VIEW:
From a ski lift heading up to the top of Mount Lemmon.

ATTRACTIONS:
Arizona-Sonora Desert Museum 520/883-1380, web: www.desert-museum.org.
Arizona State Museum 520/621-6302, web: www.statemuseum.arizona.edu.
Biosphere 2 520/838-6200, web: www.b2science.org.
Catalina State Park 520/628-5798.
Colossal Cave 520/647-7275, web: www.colossalcave.com.
Mission San Xavier del Bac, 520/294-2624, web: www.sanx-aviermission.org.
Old Tucson.
Saguaro National Park 520/733-5153, web: www.nps.gov/sagu.

ARKANSAS

Crosses

CAFES

Crosses Grocery & Cafe 4223 Hwy 16 (E of Elkins, outside Fayetteville) 479/643–3307 • 6am-8:30pm • on the Pig Trail • gay-owned

Eureka Springs

ACCOMMODATIONS

A Byrds Eye View 36 N Main (at Douglas) 479/253–0200, 888/210–8401 • gay/ straight • in heart of downtown • porch • nonsmoking • WiFi • gay-owned

The Grand TreeHouse Resort 350 W Van Buren (at Pivot Rock Rd) 479/253–8733 • gay/ straight • outdoor showers up in trees • WiFi • gay-owned

Heart of the Hills Inn 5 Summit St (on Historic Loop) 479/253–7468, 800/253–7468 • gay/ straight • historic inn near downtown • full brkfst • private decks • nonsmoking • gay-owned

Lookout Lodge 3098 E Van Buren 479/253–9335, 877/253–9335 • gay-friendly • private entrances • kids/ pets ok • WiFi • nonsmoking

Mount Victoria 28 Fairmount St 479/253–7979, 888/408–7979 • gay-friendly • full brkfst & dinner • WiFi

Out on Main 269 N Main St (at Magnetic Rd) 479/253–8449 • gay/ straight • 3-room cottage • full kitchen • nonsmoking • WiFi • gay-owned

Palace Hotel & Bath House 135 Spring St 479/253–7474, 866/946–0572 • gay-friendly • historic bathhouse open to all • nonsmoking • WiFi

Pond Mountain Lodge & Resort 479/253–5877, 800/583–8043 • gay/ straight • mountaintop inn on 150 acres • cabins • pool • nonsmoking • jacuzzis • wheelchair access • lesbian-owned

Red Bud Manor Inn 7 Kingshighway 479/253–9649, 866/253–9649 • gay-friendly • full brkfst • WiFi • indoor hot tub • women-owned

Roadrunner Inn 3034 Mundell Rd 479/253–8166, 888/253–8166 • gay-friendly • lake views • reservations advised • guestrooms & log cabins • WiFi

Texaco Bungalow 77 Mountain St 888/253–8093 • gay/ straight • art deco service station rentals • gay-owned

Tradewinds 141 W Van Buren (at 23 N) 479/363–6189 • gay/ straight • motel reminiscent of the motor inns of the '40s & '50s, mention Damron and receive 20% off BnB Suite rate • pool • pets ok • WiFi • gay-owned

BARS

Chelsea's Corner Cafe 10 Mountain St (at Center St) 479/253–6723 • 11am-2am, till 10pm Sun • gay-friendly • dancing/DJ • patio • also restaurant • live shows • WiFi • women-owned

Eureka Live 35 N Main 479/253–7020 • 11am-1:30am, clsd Mon-Tue • gay/ straight • dancing/DJ • food served • karaoke

Henri's Just One More 19 1/2 Spring St 479/253–5795 • noon-2am, clsd Tue • gay/ straight • gay night Wed from 5pm • bar menu • live shows • WiFi

Pied Piper Pub & Inn 82 Armstrong (at Main St) 479/363–9976, 866/363–9976 • noon-midnight • gay-friendly • popular Reuben sandwich, fish & chips • also hotel

CAFES

Mud Street Cafe 22G S Main St 479/253–6732 • 8am-3pm, clsd Tue-Wed

RESTAURANTS

Autumn Breeze 190 Huntsville Rd (1/2 mile off Hwy 62) 479/253–7734 • 5pm-9pm, clsd Sun, hrs vary in winter • cont'l • nonsmoking

Caribe Restaurant & Cantina 309 W Van Buren 479/253–8102 • 4pm-9pm, clsd Tue, from noon wknds • also bar

Cottage Inn 450 Hwy 62 W 479/253–5282 • 5pm-9pm, clsd Mon-Wed • Mediterranean • full bar

Ermilio's 26 White St 479/253–8806 • 5pm-9pm • Italian • plenty veggie • full bar

Gaskins Cabin Steak House 2883 Hwy 23 N (Hwy 187) 479/253–5466 • 5pm-9pm, till 8pm Sun, clsd Mon-Tue • full bar • reservations suggested

ENTERTAINMENT & RECREATION

Diversity Pride Events 479/253–2555 • produces events during Valentine's & Spring, Summer, Fall Diversity Wknds & more

Fayetteville

INFO LINES & SERVICES

AA Gay/ Lesbian 568 W Sycamore 479/443–6366 (AA#)

ACCOMMODATIONS

Hilton Garden Inn Bentonville 2204 SE Walton Blvd (Exit 85, off I-540), Bentonville 479/464-7300, 877/782-9444 • gay-friendly • pool • kids ok • WiFi • wheelchair access

NIGHTCLUBS

Club Push 21 N Block Ave 479/443-4600 • 9pm-2am, clsd Sun-Tue • lesbians/ gay men • dancing/DJ • karaoke • drag shows • 18+

Speakeasy 509 W Spring St (at West St) 479/443-3279 • 5pm-2am, clsd Sun-Tue • mostly gay men • dancing/DJ • wheelchair access

CAFES

The Common Grounds 412 W Dickson St (at West) 479/442-3515 • 7am-midnight • full bar • also restaurant • lots of veggie

RESTAURANTS

Bordinos 310 W Dickson St 479/527-6795 • dinner nightly, lunch Tue-Fri, clsd Sun • full bar

Hugo's 25 1/2 N Block Ave 479/521-7585 • 11am-10pm, clsd Sun

BOOKSTORES

Hastings Bookstore 2999 N College Ave (Fiesta Square Shopping Center) 479/521-0244 • 9am-10pm, till 11pm Fri-Sat, 9am-11pm Sun

Fort Smith

BARS

Kinkead's 1004 1/2 Garrison Ave 479/226-3144 • 5pm-2am, from 7pm Fri-Sat, clsd Mon • gay/ straight • neighborhood bar • dancing/DJ • draw shows • karaoke • WiFi • gay-owned

Helena

ACCOMMODATIONS

The Edwardian Inn 317 Biscoe 870/338-9155, 800/598-4749 • gay-friendly • 60 miles from Memphis • full brkfst • nonsmoking • WiFi

Hot Springs

ACCOMMODATIONS

The B Inn 316 Park Ave (at Cental Ave) 501/547-7172 • gay/ straight • WiFi • kids/ pets ok • gay-owned

Park Hotel of Hot Springs 211 Fountain St (at Central Ave) 501/624-5323, 800/895-7275 • gay/ straight • WiFi

The Rose Cottage 218 Court St (at Exchange St) 501/623-6449 • gay-friendly • historic Victorian row house • kids/ pets ok • jacuzzi

Little Rock

ACCOMMODATIONS

Legacy Hotel & Suites 625 W Capitol Ave (at Gaines) 501/374-0100, 888/456-3669 • gay-friendly • nat'l historic property in downtown area • kids ok • WiFi • wheelchair access

BARS

Discovery 1021 Jessie Rd (btwn Cantrell & Riverfront) 501/664-4784 • 9pm-5am Sat only • gay/ straight • dancing/DJ • drag shows • male dancers • videos • 18+ • private club • wheelchair access

Miss Kitty's 307 W 7th St (at Center St) 501/374-4699 • 9pm-2am Fri-Sat • lesbians/ gay men • karaoke

Trax 415 Main St, North Little Rock 501/244-0444 • 5pm-2am • mostly gay men • neighborhood bar • also restaurant • country/ western • bears • leather • older crowd • WiFi • wheelchair access

Triniti Nightclub 1021 Jessie Rd (btwn Cantrell & Riverfront) 501/664-2744 • 9pm-5am Fri only • lesbians/ gay men • dancing/DJ • drag shows • male dancers • videos • 18+ • private club • wheelchair access

RESTAURANTS

Bossa Nova 2701 Kavanaugh Blvd (at Ash St) 501/614-6682 • lunch & dinner, Sun brunch, clsd Mon • Brazilian • plenty veggie

Juanita's 614 President Clinton (at River Market) 501/372-1228 • 11am-close, clsd Sun • Mexican • reservations recommended • live music

La Hacienda 3024 Cantrell Rd 501/661-0600 • lunch & dinner • Mexican

Lilly's Dim Sum, Then Some/ B-Side 11121 N Rodney Parham Rd 501/716-2700 • 11am-9pm, till 10pm Fri-Sat, clsd Sun • contemporary Asian • plenty veggie • lesbian-owned

Vino's Pizza 923 W 7th St (at Chester) 501/375-8466 • 11am-close • beer/ wine

ENTERTAINMENT & RECREATION

The Weekend Theater 1001 W 7th St (at Chester) 501/374-3761 • plays & musicals on wknds • gay-owned

BOOKSTORES

Wordsworth Books & Co 5920 R St
501/663-9198 • 9am-7pm, till 6pm Fri-Sat,
noon-5pm Sun • independent

RETAIL SHOPS

A Twisted Gift Shop 1007 W 7th St (at
Chester) 501/376-7723 • noon-midnight •
gift shop

Inz & Outz 6115 W Markham #103
501/296-9484 • 10am-8pm, noon-6pm Sun •
pride items • books • gifts • wheelchair access

Texarkana

BARS

The Chute 714 Laurel St 870/772-6900 •
7pm-2am Th-Sat • lesbians/ gay men •
dancing/DJ • karaoke • drag shows

CALIFORNIA

Amador City

ACCOMMODATIONS

Imperial Hotel 14202 Hwy 49 (at Water St)
209/267-9172 • gay-friendly • B&B • brick
Victorian hotel • nonsmoking • full brkfst •
restaurant & bar

Anaheim

see Orange County

Arcata

INFO LINES & SERVICES

Queer Humboldt PO Box 45, 95518-0045
707/834-4839 • "Humboldt County's online
resource for the LGBT community" • includes
links & events calendar • check out
www.queerhumboldt.org

BARS

The Alibi 744 9th St 707/822-3731 •
lesbian/gay men • cocktail lounge w/ live
music • neighborhood bar • also restaurant
(8am-midnight) • young crowd

CAFES

Cafe Mokka 495 J St (at 5th) 707/822-2228
• from noon • coffee & soups (bread bowls) •
live music • also Finnish sauna & hot tubs

North Coast Co-op 811 I St 707/822-5947 •
6am-9pm • co-op store w/ bakery, deli &
espresso cafe • WiFi

RESTAURANTS

Wildflower Bakery & Cafe 1604 G St
707/822-0360 • 8am-8pm, till 9pm Th-Sat •
popular • vegetarian • organic beer & wine

BOOKSTORES

Northtown Books 957 H St 707/822-2834 •
10am-7pm, till 9pm Fri-Sat, noon-5pm Sun •
LGBT section • carries The L Word paper

Bakersfield

INFO LINES & SERVICES

Gay AA 1001 34th St 661/322-4025 (AA#),
661/324-0371 (ALANO CLUB #) • 7:30pm Mon

ACCOMMODATIONS

The Padre Hotel 702 18th St 661/427-4900
• gay/straight • sleek hotel with nightclubs,
bar, cafe, and fine dining room

BARS

The Mint 1207 19th St (at M) 661/325-4048
• 6am-2am • gay/ straight • alternative • live
music

NIGHTCLUBS

The Casablanca Club 1825 N St (at 19th St)
661/324-0661 • 9pm-2am, clsd Mon-Wed •
gay/ straight • neighborhood bar • dancing/DJ
• live entertainment • cabaret • drag shows •
videos • wheelchair access

Berkeley

see East Bay

Big Bear Lake

ACCOMMODATIONS

Alpine Retreats 433 Edgemoor (at Big Bear
Blvd) 909/725-4192, 909/878-4155
(RESERVATIONS) • gay/ straight • 3 cottages •
fireplaces • nonsmoking • kids ok • gay-owned

Grey Squirrel Resort 39372 Big Bear Blvd
909/866-4335, 800/381-5569 • gay/ straight •
20 cabins & 30 private rental homes • pool •
some nonsmoking • WiFi • lesbian-owned

Knickerbocker Mansion Country Inn 869
Knickerbocker Rd 909/878-9190,
877/423-1180 • gay/ straight • log mansion
on lake • full brkfst • jacuzzi • hiking •
nonsmoking • WiFi • wheelchair access • gay-
owned

Rainbow View Lodge 2726 View Dr (at
Hilltop), Running Springs 909/867-1810 •
gay/ straight • cottages w/ themed decor • kids
ok • nonsmoking • women-owned

Big Sur

ACCOMMODATIONS

Eagle's Nest 46274 Pfeiffer Ridge 831/667–2587, 888/742–9321 • gay-friendly • deck w/ views of Pfeiffer Ridge & ocean • full kitchen • WiFi • nonsmoking • gay-owned

Lucia Lodge 62400 Hwy 1 831/688–4884, 866/424–4787 • gay-friendly • oceanview cabins • also restaurant & lounge • WiFi

Cambria

ACCOMMODATIONS

El Colobri 5620 Moonstone Beach Dr 805/924–3003 • gay-friendly • WiFi • pets ok

Sea Otter Inn 6656 Moonstone Beach Dr 805/927–5888, 800/966–6490 • gay-friendly • pool • nonsmoking • WiFi • wheelchair access

BARS

Mozzi's Saloon 2262 Main St 805/927–4767 • 1pm-2am, from 11am Sat-Sun • gay-friendly cowboy bar • live music

Carmel

see also Monterey

ACCOMMODATIONS

Best Western Carmel Mission Inn 3665 Rio Rd 831/624–1841, 800/348–9090 • gay-friendly • near Monterey Bay • pool • pets ok • also restaurant & lounge • nonsmoking

Cypress Inn Lincoln & 7th 831/624–3871, 800/443–7443 • gay-friendly • pets very welcome • owned by Doris Day • WiFi • also restaurant & lounge

RESTAURANTS

Flaherty's Seafood Grill & Oyster Bar 6th Ave (btwn Dolores and San Carlos) 831/625–1500 • open daily 11am • wheelchair access

Rio Grill 101 Crossroads Blvd 831/625–5436 • lunch & dinner daily, Sun brunch • "Creative American" • full bar

Chico

INFO LINES & SERVICES

Stonewall Alliance Center 358 E 6th St (at Flume) 530/893–3336 • HIV testing & counseling • also recorded info • meetings • events

Chino

RESTAURANTS

Riverside Grill 5258 Riverside Dr (at Central) 909/627–4144 • 8am-9pm

Clearlake

includes major towns of Lake County

ACCOMMODATIONS

Blue Fish Cove Resort 10573 E Hwy 20, Clearlake Oaks 707/998–1769 • gay-friendly • lakeside resort cottages • kitchens • kids ok • pets ok by arrangement • boat launch facilities & rentals

Edgewater Resort 6420 Soda Bay Rd (at Hohape Rd), Kelseyville 707/279–0208, 800/396–6224 • "gay-owned, straight-friendly" • cabin • camping & RV hookups • lake access & pool • boat facilities • WiFi • kids/pets ok • lesbian-owned

Featherbed Railroad B& B 2870 Lakeshore Blvd, Nice 707/274–8378 • gay-friendly • pool • full brkfst • WiFi • pets ok

Sea Breeze Resort 9595 Harbor Dr, Glenhaven 707/998–3327 • gay/ straight • lakefront cottages • swimming • nonsmoking • WiFi • wheelchair access • gay-owned

Cloverdale

see also Healdsburg

ACCOMMODATIONS

Vintage Towers B&B 302 N Main St (at 3rd) 707/894–4535, 888/886–9377 • gay-friendly • Queen Anne mansion • full brkfst • nonsmoking

RESTAURANTS

Hamburger Ranch & Bar-B-Que 31195 N Redwood Hwy 707/894–5616 • 7am-9pm • beer & wine • patio

Concord

see East Bay

Costa Mesa

see Orange County

Cupertino

ACCOMMODATIONS

Cypress Hotel 10050 S De Anza Blvd 408/253–8900, 800/499–1408 • gay-friendly • pool • pets ok • WiFi • nonsmoking • also gym & restaurant

Davis

see also Sacramento

INFO LINES & SERVICES

LGBT Resource Center University House Annex **530/752-2452** • 9am-5pm, clsd wknds • info • referrals • meetings • library • WiFi • wheelchair access

CAFES

Mishka's Cafe 610 2nd St **530/759-0811** • 7:30am-11pm

BOOKSTORES

The Avid Reader 617 2nd St **530/758-4040** • 10am-10pm • general independent • readings

East Bay

includes major cities of Alameda and Contra Costa Counties: Alameda, Antioch, Berkeley, Concord, Danville, Fremont, Hayward, Lafayette, Newark, Oakland, Pleasant Hill, Richmond, San Leandro, Walnut Creek

INFO LINES & SERVICES

East Bay AA **510/839-8900** • variety of LGBT-friendly mtgs

Lighthouse Community Center 1217 A St (near 2nd St), Hayward **510/881-8167** • LGBT support groups & social events

East Bay

ANNUAL EVENTS:

October - Community Celebration for the Days of the Dead 510/238-2200, web: www.museumca.org.

CITY INFO:

Berkeley Convention & Visitors Bureau 800/847-4823, web: www.visitberkeley.com.
Oakland Convention & Visitors Bureau 510/839-9000, web: www.oaklandcvb.com.

ATTRACTIONS:

The Claremont Hotel & Restaurant, Berkeley 510/843-3000, web: www.claremontresort.com.
Emeryville Marina Public Market.
Jack London Square, Oakland, web: www.jacklondonsquare.com.
Oakland Museum of California 510/238-2200,
web: www.museumca.org.
The Paramount Theater, Oakland 510/465-6400, web: www.paramounttheatre.com.
UC Berkeley.

BEST VIEW:

Claremont Hotel, Tilden Park, various locations in the Berkeley and Oakland Hills. Or from the top of Sather Tower on the UC Berkeley campus.

WEATHER:

While San Francisco is fogged in during the summers, the East Bay remains sunny and warm. Some areas even get hot (90°s-100°s). As for the winter, the temperature drops along with rain (upper 30°s-40°s in the winter). Spring is the time to come – the usually brown hills explode with the colors of green grass and wildflowers.

TRANSIT:

Yellow Cab (Berkeley) 510/524-1999, web: www.yellowcabexpress.com.
Veteran's Cab (Oakland) 510/848-5555, web: www.veteranstaxicab.com.
Bayporter Express 877/467-1800, web: www.bayporter.com.
AC Transit 510/891-4706, web: www.actransit.org.
BART (subway) 510/465-2278, web: www.bart.gov.
Ferry, web: www.eastbayferry.com.

Pacific Center for Human Growth 2712 Telegraph Ave (at Derby), Berkeley **510/548-8283** • 10am-10pm Mon-Fri • wheelchair access

Rainbow Community Center of Contra Costa County 3024 Willow Pass Rd #500 (btwn Parkside & Esperanza), Concord **925/692-0090** • 10am-5pm Mon-Fri

ACCOMMODATIONS

Hotel Durant 2600 Durant Ave, Berkeley **510/845-8981, 800/238-7268** • gay/ straight • nonsmoking • WiFi • restaurant on premises

Washington Inn 495 10th St (at Broadway), Oakland **510/452-1776** • gay/ straight • historic boutique hotel • full brkfst • nonsmoking • also restaurant • wheelchair access

Waterfront Hotel 10 Washington St, Oakland **510/836-3800, 888/842-5333** • gay-friendly • pool • bar & restaurant • WiFi • wheelchair access

BARS

The Alley 3325 Grand Ave (btwn Lake Park & Elwood Aves), Oakland **510/444-8505** • 4pm-2am • gay/ straight • camptastic sing-along piano bar from 9pm • more gay Th • also restaurant

Bench & Bar 510 17th St, Oakland **510/444-2266** • 4pm-2am • popular • mostly gay men • dancing/DJ • drag shows • theme nights • wheelchair access

Cafe Van Kleef 1621 Telegraph Ave (at Broadway), Oakland **510/763-7711** • 4pm-2am, clsd Sun • gay-friendly • eclectic crowd & live-music scene—from cabaret to blue grass to jazz • more

Club 21 2111 Franklin St (at 21st St), Oakland **510/268-9425** • mostly gay men • dancing/DJ • mostly Latino/a • theme nights • videos

The New Easy 3255 Lakeshore Ave, Oakland **510/338-4911** • 3:30pm-2am, from 2pm Sat • gay-friendly • cool lounge • food served

White Horse 6551 Telegraph Ave (at 66th), Oakland **510/652-3820** • 3pm-2am, from 1pm wknds (also Sun beer bust) • lesbians/ gay men • dancing/DJ • karaoke • wheelchair access

World Famous Turf Club 22519 Main St (at A St), Hayward **510/881-9877** • 4pm-2am, from noon Sat-Sun • lesbians/ gay men • dancing/DJ • drag shows • sports bar • huge patio • BBQs • live music • WiFi • near BART • wheelchair access

NIGHTCLUBS

Club 1220 1220 Pine St (at Civic Dr), Walnut Creek **925/938-4550** • 4pm-2am • lesbians/ gay men • dancing/DJ • theme nights • karaoke • WiFi • wheelchair access

CAFES

The Actual Cafe 6334 San Pablo Ave (at Alcatraz), Oakland **510/653-8386** • 7am-9pm, till 10pm wknds • food served • events

Au Coquelet Cafe 2000 University Ave, Berkeley **510/845-0433** • 6am-2am • WiFi

Bittersweet 5427 College Ave (in Rockridge District), Oakland **510/654-7159** • 9am-7pm, till 9pm Fri-Sat

Caffe Strada 2300 College Ave (btwn Way & Durant), Berkeley **510/843-5282** • 6am-midnight • students • great patio • wheelchair access

Cole Coffee 6255 College Ave (btwn 62nd & 63rd Sts), Oakland **510/985-1958** • 7am-7pm • hip hideaway in lovely Rockridge

Raw Energy 2050 Addison St (btwn Shattuck & Milvia), Berkeley **510/665-9464** • 7:30am-7pm, 11am-4pm Sat, clsd Sun • organic juice cafe • gay-owned

RESTAURANTS

Arizmendi Bakery & Pizzeria 4301 San Pablo Ave (at 43rd St), Emeryville **510/547-0550** • 7am-7pm, till 3pm Mon, clsd Sun • excellent pastries, breads & pizzas

Banh Cuon Tay Ho 344-B 12th St (at Webster), Oakland **510/836-6388** • 10am-9pm, till 8pm Sun, clsd Mon

Cactus Taqueria 5642 College Ave (at Shafter, in Rockridge), Oakland **510/658-6180** • 11am-10pm, till 9pm Sun

César 4039 Piedmont, Oakland **510/883-0222** • noon-11pm • Spanish tapas • full bar

Connie's Cantina 3340 Grand Ave (btwn Lake Park Ave & Mandana Blvd), Oakland **510/839-4986** • 10:30am-9pm, clsd Sun • popular • delicious homemade Mexican food • plenty veggie • patio • woman-owned

Dopo 4293 Piedmont Ave (btwn Glenwood & Echo), Oakland **510/652-3676** • lunch Mon-Th, dinner nightly, clsd Sun • Italian • worth the wait

Le Cheval 1007 Clay St, Oakland **510/763-8495** • 11am-9:30pm, from 5pm Sun • popular • Vietnamese • wheelchair access

Lois the Pie Queen 851 60th St (off Martin Luther King Jr Hwy), Oakland **510/658-5616** • 8am-2pm, 7am-3pm wknds • popular • Southern homecooking & killer desserts

Mama's Royal Cafe 4012 Broadway (at 40th), Oakland **510/547-7600** • 7am-2:30pm, from 8am wknds • popular • come early for excellent wknd brunch • beer/ wine • wheelchair access

Rockridge Cafe 5492 College Ave (at Forest), Oakland **510/653-1567** • 7:30am-3pm • popular • great brkfsts • plenty veggie

Zachary's Chicago Pizza 5801 College Ave, Oakland **510/655-6385** • 11am-10pm • popular • pizza that is worth the crowds & the long wait!

BOOKSTORES

Black Oak Books 2618 San Pablo Ave, Berkeley **510/486-0698** • 11am-7pm • independent • new & used

Diesel, A Bookstore 5433 College Avenue, Oakland **510/653-9965** • 10am-9pm, till 10pm Fri-Sat, till 6pm Sun • independent

Laurel Book Store 4100 MacArthur Blvd (at 39th Ave, 2 blks from High St), Oakland **510/531-2073** • 10am-7pm, till 6pm Sat, 11am-5pm Sun • general • LGBT section • readings • wheelchair access • lesbian-owned

Pendragon Books 5560 College Ave (at Oceanview), Oakland **510/652-6259** • 9am-10pm, from 10am Sun • used books • magazines • great to browse while waiting for a table in Rockridge

RETAIL SHOPS

See Jane Run Sports 5817 College Ave, Oakland **510/428-2681** • 11am-7pm, 10am-6pm Sat-Sun • women's athletic apparel

EROTICA

Good Vibrations 2504 San Pablo Ave (at Dwight Wy), Berkeley **510/841-8987** • 10am-9pm, till 10pm Fri-Sat • clean, well-lighted sex toy store • workshops & events • wheelchair access

Good Vibrations 3219 Lakeshore Ave, Oakland **510/788-2389** • 10am-9pm • clean, well-lighted sex toy store • workshops & events • wheelchair access

Lingerie Etc 2298 Monument Blvd (at Buskirk), Pleasant Hill **925/676-2962** • 9am-midnight

Elk

RESTAURANTS

Queenie's Roadhouse Cafe 6061 S Hwy 1 **707/877-3285** • 8am-3pm, clsd Tue-Wed • fabulous all-day brkfsts • some veggie • lesbian-owned

Eureka

ACCOMMODATIONS

Abigail's Elegant Victorian Mansion 1406 C St (at 14th St) **707/444-3144** • gay-friendly • sauna • nonsmoking

Carter House Inns 301 L St **707/444-8062, 800/404-1390** • gay-friendly • enclave of 4 unique inns • full brkfst • nonsmoking • kids ok • restaurant • wine shop • wheelchair access

Trinidad Bay B&B 560 Edwards St (at Trinity), Trinidad **707/677-0840** • gay-friendly • nonsmoking • WiFi • kids ok • full brkfst • gay- & straight-owned

BARS

Lost Coast Brewery 617 4th St (btwn G & H Sts) **707/445-4480** • 11am-1am • gay-friendly • food served till midnight • beer/ wine • WiFi • wheelchair access • women-owned

The Shanty 213 3rd St (at C St) **707/444-2053** • noon-2am • gay/ straight • neighborhood bar • lesbian-owned

NIGHTCLUBS

Where's Queer Bill **707/832-4785** • monthly queer events • check wheresqueerbill.com for info

CAFES

North Coast Co-op 25 4th St (at B St) **707/443-6027** • 6am-9pm • co-op store w/ bakery, deli & espresso cafe

Ramone's Cafe & Bakery 209 E St (Old Town) **707/445-2923** • 7am-6pm

RESTAURANTS

Chalet House of Omelettes 1935 5th St (at U St) **707/442-0333** • 6am-3pm, brkfst & lunch • wheelchair access

Folie Douce 1551 G St, Arcata **707/822-1042** • dinner only, clsd Sun-Mon • bistro • beer/ wine • reservations recommended • wheelchair access

BOOKSTORES

Booklegger 402 2nd St (at E St)
707/445–1344 • 10am-5:30pm, 11am-4pm
Sun • mostly used • wheelchair access •
women-owned

PUBLICATIONS

The "L" Word PO Box 272, Bayside 95524
• lesbian newsletter for Humboldt County •
available at Eureka Natural Foods &
Booklegger in Eureka • also at the co-op &
North Town Books in Arcata

EROTICA

Good Relations 223 2nd St **707/441–9570,
888/485–5063** • lingerie • toys • books
• videos • wheelchair access • queer-owned/
run

Fort Bragg

ACCOMMODATIONS

The Cleone Gardens Inn 24600 N Hwy 1
707/964–2788, 800/400–2189 (N CA ONLY) •
gay-friendly • country garden retreat on 2.5
acres • hot tub • WiFi • nonsmoking •
wheelchair access

The Weller House Inn 524 Stewart St (at
Pine) **707/964–4415, 877/893–5537** • gay-
friendly • 1886 Victorian • full brkfst • jacuzzi •
nonsmoking • WiFi

RESTAURANTS

Cowlick's 250B N Main St **707/962–9271** •
delicious homemade ice cream, including
mushroom ice cream (in-season)—it's actually
quite good!

Purple Rose 24300 N Hwy 1 **707/964–6507**
• 5pm-9pm, clsd Sun-Mon • Mexican •
wheelchair access

ENTERTAINMENT & RECREATION

Skunk Train California Western foot of
Laurel St **707/964–6371, 866/457–5865** •
scenic train trips

Fremont

see East Bay

Fresno

INFO LINES & SERVICES

Community Link **559/266–5465** • info •
LGBT support, including LGBT youth group •
also publishes Newslink

Fresno AA **559/221–6907** • call or check
website (www.fresnoaa.org) for meetings

ACCOMMODATIONS

The San Joaquin Hotel 1309 W Shaw Ave
(at Fruit) **559/225–1309, 800/775–1309** • gay-
friendly • pool • WiFi • wheelchair access

BARS

The Phoenix 4538 E Belmont Ave (at Maple)
559/252–2899 • 4pm-2am • mostly gay men •
country/western • bears • leather • multiracial
• videos • older crowd • popular beer busts •
patio • gay-owned

Red Lantern 4618 E Belmont Ave (at Maple)
559/251–5898 • 2pm-2am • mostly gay men •
neighborhood bar • country/western • Latin
night Sat very popular • food Sun • patio •
WiFi • wheelchair access

NIGHTCLUBS

Club Legends 3075 N Maroa Ave
559/222–2271 • 7pm-2am, from 9pm Sat,
from 4pm Sun • lesbians/gay men •
dancing/DJ • drag shows

North Tower Circle 2777 N Maroa Ave (at E
Princeton Ave) **559/229–4188** • 8pm-2am •
lesbians/gay men • dancing/DJ • drag shows

RESTAURANTS

Don Pepe's 4582 N Blackstone Ave (at
Gettysburg) **559/224–1431** • 9am-9pm •
Mexican

Irene's Cafe 747 E Olive Ave (in Tower
District) **559/237–9919** • 8am-9pm • some
veggie • good hamburgers • beer/wine

Sequoia Brewing Company 777 E Olive
Ave (in Tower District) **559/264–5521** • 11am-
10pm, till midnight Fri-Sat, till 9pm Sun •
microbrewery w/ restaurant • live music

Veni Vidi Vici 1116 N Fulton (S of Olive Ave,
in Tower District) **559/266–5510** • California
fine dining • nightclub later

EROTICA

Suzie's Adult Superstores 1267 N
Blackstone Ave **559/497–9613** • 24hrs

Garden Grove

see Orange County

Grass Valley

see also Nevada City

Gualala

ACCOMMODATIONS

Breakers Inn 39300 S Hwy 1 707/884-3200 • gay/ straight • oceanfront • women-owned

North Coast Country Inn 34591 S Hwy 1 707/884-4537 • gay-friendly • B&B overlooking Mendocino coast • hot tub • nonsmoking

BOOKSTORES

The Four-Eyed Frog 39138 Ocean Dr (in Cypress Village) 707/884-1333 • 10am-6pm, till 5pm Sun • independent

Half Moon Bay

ACCOMMODATIONS

Mill Rose Inn 615 Mill St 650/726-8750, 800/900-7673 • gay-friendly • classic European elegance by the sea • full brkfst • hot tub • nonsmoking • WiFi • kids 10+ ok

RESTAURANTS

Moss Beach Distillery 140 Beach Wy (at Ocean) 650/728-5595 • lunch & dinner, Sun brunch • popular • steak & seafood • some veggie • patio • even own ghost • wheelchair access

Pasta Moon 315 Main St (at Mill) 650/726-5125 • lunch & dinner • Italian • full bar • live shows • wheelchair access

Sam's Chowder House 4210 N Cabrillo Hwy (S of Pillar Point Harbor) 650/712-0245 • lunch & dinner • great loster rolls and views

Hayward

see East Bay

Healdsburg

see Russian River & Sonoma County

Huntington Beach

see Orange County

Idyllwild

ACCOMMODATIONS

The Rainbow Inn 54420 S Circle Dr 951/659-0111 • gay/ straight • full brkfst • kids ok • nonsmoking • patio • fireplaces • WiFi • also conference center • gay-owned

Strawberry Creek Inn B&B 26370 Hwy 243 (at S Cir Dr) 951/659-3202, 800/262-8969 • gay-friendly • relaxing getaway w/ sundeck, garden & hammocks • nonsmoking • wheelchair access • gay-owned

RESTAURANTS

Cafe Aroma 54750 North Circle 951/659-5212 • 7am-10pm • great ambience & food • live music most nights

Irvine

see Orange County

Joshua Tree Nat'l Park

ACCOMMODATIONS

The Desert Lily PO Box 139, 92252-0800 760/366-4676, 877/887-7370 • gay-friendly • artist-owned adobe-style B&B on 5 acres • also cabins • clsd July-Aug • woman-owned

Desert Wonderland & The Tile House 805/452-4898 • gay/ straight • in high desert near Joshua Tree Nat'l Park • gay-owned

Joshua Tree Highlands Houses 760/366-3636 • gay/ straight • private, fully equipped rentals • near Joshua Tree Nat'l Park • nonsmoking • kids/ pets ok • WiFi • wheelchair access • gay-owned

Kate's Lazy Desert 58380 Botkin Rd, Landers 845/688-7200 • gay-friendly • love shack owned by Kate Pierson of the B-52s • WiFi • nonsmoking

Sacred Sands HC1 Box 1071 A, 63155 Quail Springs Rd (at Desert Shadows), Joshua Tree 760/424-6407 • gay/ straight • private outdoor living • spa • nonsmoking • WiFi • gay-owned

Spin & Margie's Desert Hideaway 64491 29 Palms Hwy 760/366-9124 • gay-friendly • hacienda-style B&B • suites w/ private patios

Starland Retreat Yucca Valley 760/364-2069 • mostly gay men & radical faeries, but women very welcome • membership-only rustic rural camp • hot tub • nudity permitted

RESTAURANTS

The Crossroads Cafe & Tavern 61715 29 Palms Hwy 760/366-5414 • 7am-8pm, till 9pm Fri-Sat, clsd Wed

Kernville

ACCOMMODATIONS

Riverview Lodge 2 Sirretta St 760/376-6019 • gay/ straight • riverfront resort • jacuzzi • kids/ pets ok • nonsmoking • gay-owned

La Mirada

RESTAURANTS

Mexico 1900 11531 La Mirada blvd
562/941-2016 • lunch & dinner • Mexican

Laguna Beach

see Orange County

Lake Tahoe

see also Lake Tahoe, Nevada

ACCOMMODATIONS

Alpine Inn & Spa 920 Stateline Ave (Lake Ave/ Hwy 50), South Lake Tahoe **530/544-3340, 800/826-8885** • gay/ straight • motel • just steps from casino • swimming • lesbian & gay & straight-owned

Black Bear Inn 530/544-4451, **877/232-7466** • gay/ straight • full brkfst • hot tub • fireplaces • nonsmoking • WiFi • gay-owned

The Cedar House Sport Hotel 10918 Brockway Rd, Truckee **530/582-5655, 866/582-5655** • gay-friendly • full bar • WiFi • kids/ pets ok

Holly's Place 800/745-7041, 530/544-7040 • gay/ straight • cabins • fireplaces • kitchens • hot tubs • nonsmoking • kids/ dogs ok • WiFi • women-owned

Spruce Grove Cabins 3599-3605 Spruce Ave, South Lake Tahoe **530/544-0549, 800/777-0914** • gay-friendly • full kitchens • near Heavenly Ski Resort • hot tub • dog-friendly • nonsmoking

Tahoe Valley Lodge 2241 Lake Tahoe Blvd (at Tahoe Keys Blvd), South Lake Tahoe **530/541-0353, 800/669-7544** • gay-friendly • motel • pool • nonsmoking • WiFi

RESTAURANTS

Driftwood Cafe 1001 Heavenly Vlg Way #1A **530/544-6545** • 7am-3pm • homecooking • some veggie • wheelchair access

Passaretti's 1181 Emerald Bay Rd/ Hwy 50, South Lake Tahoe **530/541-3433** • 11am-9pm • Italian • beer/ wine

Lancaster

includes Palmdale

Livermore

see East Bay

Long Beach

INFO LINES & SERVICES

AA Gay/ Lesbian 2017 E 4th St (at Cherry, at Gay & Lesbian Center) **562/434-4455** • 7pm Mon • lesbians/ gay men

The Gay & Lesbian Center of Greater Long Beach 2017 E 4th St (at Cherry) **562/434-4455** • 9am-9pm, by appt Sat • activities & support groups • also newsletter

ACCOMMODATIONS

Beachrunners' Inn 231 Kennebec Ave (at Junipero & Broadway) **562/856-0202, 866/221-0001** • gay/ straight • B&B • near beach • hot tub • nonsmoking

Dockside Boat & Bed Dock 5, Rainbow Harbor (at Pine Ave Pier) **562/436-3111** • gay-friendly • spend the night on a yacht • views of the Queen Mary

Hotel Current 5325 E Pacific Coast Hwy **562/597-1341, 800/990-9991** • gay/ straight • swimming • WiFi • wheelchair access

Hotel Maya 700 Queensway Dr **562/435-7676** • gay/ straight • luxury boutique resort hotel w/ waterfront Fuego restaurant • pets ok

The Varden Hotel 335 Pacific Ave (at 3rd St) **562/432-8950, 877/382-7336** • gay/ straight • urban boutique hotel • nonsmoking • WiFi • wheelchair access

BARS

The Brit 1744 E Broadway (at Cherry) **562/432-9742** • 10am-2am • mostly gay men • neighborhood bar • patio • wheelchair access

The Broadway 1100 E Broadway (at Cerritos) **562/432-3646** • 10am-2am • lesbians/ gay men • neighborhood bar • karaoke Fri-Sat • wheelchair access

The Crest 5935 Cherry Ave (at South) **562/423-6650** • 2pm-2am, from noon wknds • mostly gay men

The Falcon 1435 E Broadway (at Falcon) **562/432-4146** • 8am-2am, from 7am wknds • mostly gay men but women very welcome • neighborhood bar • wheelchair access

Flux 17817 Lakewood Blvd (at Artesia), Bellflower **562/633-6394** • noon-2am • lesbians/ gay men • neighborhood bar • patio • theme nights

Liquid Lounge 3522 E Anaheim St **562/494-7564** • gay/ straight • neighborhood bar • food served • karaoke Fri-Sat • live music • patio • gay-owned

Mineshaft 1720 E Broadway (btwn Gaviota & Hermosa) **562/436–2433** • 11am-2am • popular • mostly gay men • bears

Paradise Piano Bar & Restaurant 1800 E Broadway Blvd (at Hermosa) **562/590–8773** • 3pm-1am, from 10am Sat-Sun • lesbians/gay men • live entertainment

Pistons 2020 E Artesia (at Cherry) **562/422–1928** • 2pm-2am • mostly gay men • bears • leather • patio

Que Será 1923 E 7th St (at Cherry) **562/599–6170** • 9pm-2am Tue, from 5pm Wed-Sat, from 3pm Sun, clsd Mon • gay/straight • dancing/DJ • alternative • live music • cover after 9pm

Silver Fox 411 Redondo (at 4th) **562/439–6343** • 4pm-2am, from noon wknds • popular happy hour • mostly gay men • karaoke Wed & Sun • videos • wheelchair access

Sweetwater Saloon 1201 E Broadway (at Orange) **562/432–7044** • 10am-2am • popular days • mostly gay men • neighborhood bar • wheelchair access

NIGHTCLUBS

The Basement Lounge 149 Linden Ave (at E Broadway) **562/901–9090** • gay/straight • dancing/DJ • live shows • also restaurant

Club Ripples 5101 E Ocean (at Granada) **562/433–0357** • noon-2am • popular • mostly gay men • more women Fri • dancing/DJ • theme nights • multiracial • food served • karaoke • videos • young crowd • patio

Executive Suite 3428 E Pacific Coast Hwy (at Redondo) **562/597–3884** • 1pm-2am, from noon wknds • popular • lesbians/gay men • dancing/DJ • Latin night Th • women's night Sat • wheelchair access

The Powder Room 525 E Broadway (at Bliss 525) **562/495–7252** • 7pm-10pm Th only • mostly women • live music • fashion

Unzipped 5101 E Ocean Blvd (at Ripples Bar) **562/433–0357** • 7pm-2am Fri only • popular • mostly women • dancing/DJ • multiracial • food served • videos • live entertainment • karaoke • go-go girls • patio

Long Beach

LGBT PRIDE:
3rd wknd in May. 562/987-9191, web: www.longbeachpride.com.

ANNUAL EVENTS:
June - AIDS Walk, web: www.aidswalklb.org.
Aug - Long Beach Jazz Festival, web: www.longbeachjazzfestival.com.
September - Q Films LGBT film festival, web: www.qfilmslongbeach.com.

CITY INFO:
800/452-7829, web: www.visitlongbeach.com.

ATTRACTIONS:
Belmont Shores area on 2nd St, south of Pacific Coast Highway— lots of restaurants & shopping, only blocks from the beach.
Long Beach Downtown Marketplace, 10am-4pm Fri.
The Queen Mary 562/435-3511, web: www.queenmary.com.
"Planet Ocean" mural at 300 E Ocean Blvd.

BEST VIEW:
On the deck of the Queen Mary, docked overlooking most of Long Beach. Or Signal Hill, off 405. Take the Cherry exit.

WEATHER:
Quite temperate: highs in the mid-80°s July through September, and cooling down at night. In the winter, January to March, highs are in the upper 60°s, and lows in the upper 40°s.

TRANSIT:
Long Beach Taxi Co-op 562/529-3556, web: www.longbeachyellowcab.com.
Long Beach Transit & Runabout (free downtown shuttle) 562/591-2301, web: www.lbtransit.com.

Cafes

Hot Java 2101 E Broadway Ave **562/433–0688**
• 6am-11pm, till midnight Fri-Sat • also soups,
sandwiches, salads • WiFi

The Library 3418 E Broadway **562/433–2393**
• 6am-midnight, till 1am Fri-Sat, from 7am
wknds

Restaurants

212 Degrees Bistro 2708 E 4th St
562/439–8822 • 8am-2pm, clsd Mon •
Mexican-inspired

Cafe Sevilla 140 Pine St **562/495–1111** •
dinner only, Sun brunch • Spanish • also
music & dancing

Hamburger Mary's 740 E Broadway (at
Alamitos) **562/436–7900** • 11am-2am •
lesbians/ gay men • full bar • dancing/DJ • Th
women's night

Omelette Inn 318 Pine Ave **562/437–5625** •
7am-4pm

Open Sesame 5215 E 2nd St **562/621–1698**
• lunch & dinner • Middle Eastern

Original Park Pantry 2104 E Broadway (at
Junipero) **562/434–0451** • 6am-10pm, till
11pm Fri-Sat • int'l • some veggie • wheelchair
access

Two Umbrellas Cafe 1538 E Broadway
(btwn Gaviota & Falcon) **562/495–2323** •
8am-2pm, clsd Mon • gay-owned

Utopia 445 E 1st St **562/432–6888** • lunch
Mon-Fri, dinner nightly, clsd Sun • seafood,
California cuisine • plenty veggie

Bookstores

Open 2226 E 4th St (btwn Cherry & Junipero,
in heart of Retro Row) **562/499–6736** • 11am-
7pm, till 8pm Sat, till 6pm Sun, clsd Mon •
general • also films, art & events

Retail Shops

Hot Stuff 2121 E Broadway (at Junipero)
562/433–0692 • noon-8pm, 10am-6pm Sat-
Sun • cards • gifts • adult novelties • serving
community since 1980 • gay- & lesbian-owned

So Cal Tattoo 339 W 6th St, San Pedro
310/519–8282 • woman-owned tattoo &
piercing shop • reservations recommended

Erotica

The Crypt on Broadway 1712 E Broadway
(btwn Cherry & Falcon) **562/983–6560** •
10am-midnight • leather • toys

The RubberTree 5018 E 2nd St (at
Granada) **562/434–0027** • 11am-9pm, till
10pm Fri-Sat, noon-7pm Sun • gifts for lovers
• women-owned

Los Angeles

Los Angeles is divided into 8
geographical areas:
LA—Overview
LA—West Hollywood
LA—Hollywood
LA—West LA & Santa Monica
LA—Silverlake
LA—Midtown
LA—Valley
LA—East LA & South Central

LA—Overview

Info Lines & Services

Alcoholics Anonymous 323/936–4343 &
735–2089 (EN ESPAÑOL), 800/923–8722 • call or
check web (www.lacoaa.org) for meetings

Crystal Meth Anonymous 877/262–6691 •
call or check website (www.crystalmeth.org) for
meetings in LA County

LA Gay & Lesbian Center 1625 N Schrader
Blvd (McDonald/Wright Building)
323/993–7400 • 9am-9pm, till 1pm Sat, clsd
Sun • wide variety of services

**LA Gay & Lesbian Center's Village at Ed
Gould Plaza** 1125 N McCadden Pl (at Santa
Monica) 323/860–7302 • 9am-9pm, clsd Sun
• cybercenter • cafe • theaters

Entertainment & Recreation

Bikes and Hikes LA 8743 Santa Monica
Blvd 323/796-8555, 888/836–3710 • bike/hike
tour company

The Celebration Theatre 7051 Santa
Monica Blvd (at La Brea) 323/957–1884 •
LGBT theater • call for more info

The Ellen DeGeneres Show • you know
you want to dance w/ Ellen! • check out
ellen.warnerbros.com for tickets

The Gay Mafia Comedy Group •
lesbians/ gay men • improv/ sketch comedy •
gay-owned

The Getty Center 1200 Getty Center Dr,
Brentwood 310/440–7300 • 10am-6pm, till
9pm Fri-Sat, clsd Mon • LA's shining city on a
hill & world-class museum • of course, it's still
in LA so you'll need to make reservations for
parking (!)

Griffith Observatory enter on N Vermont St
(in Griffith Park) 213/473–0800 • noon-10pm,
from 10am wknds, clsd Mon

Highways 1651 18th St (at the 18th Street
Arts Center), Santa Monica 310/315–1459 •
"full-service performance center"

IMRU Gay Radio KPFK LA 90.7 FM • 7pm Mon

LA Sparks 310/426-6033, 877/447-7275 (LA AREA ONLY) • check out the Women's Nat'l Basketball Association while you're in Los Angeles

Outfest 213/480-7088 • LGBT media arts foundation that sponsors the annual LGBT film festival each July • see listing in Film Festival Calendar

Vox Femina 310/922-0025 • women's chorus

Women on a Roll 310/578-8888 • "largest lesbian organization in California" • offering sporting, cultural & social events, as well as worldwide travel, for women

PUBLICATIONS

Adelante Magazine 323/256-6639 • bilingual LGBT magazine

Los Angeles

LGBT PRIDE:

June. Christopher St West 323/969-8302, web: www.lapride.org.
June-July. Los Angeles Black LGBT Pride 323/285-4225, web: www.atbla.com.

ANNUAL EVENTS:

June - AIDS LifeCycle 323/308-4000, web: www.aidslifecycle.org. AIDS benefit bike ride from San Francisco to LA.
July - Outfest 213/480-7088, web: www.outfest.org. Los Angeles' lesbian/ gay film & video festival.
August - Centre Court, web: www.lataweb.com. LA Tennis Association's int'l tournament.
October - AIDS Walk-a-thon 213/201-9255, web: www.aidswalk.net.
October - Gay Days at Disneyland, web: web: www.gaydaysanaheim.com.

CITY INFO:

Los Angeles Convention & Visitors Bureau, 800/228-2452, web: www.discoverlosangeles.com.
West Hollywood Convention & Visitors Bureau, 800/368-6020, web: www.visitwesthollywood.com.

TRANSIT:

LA Yellow Cab 877/733-3305, web: www.layellowcab.com.
LA Express 800/427-7483.
Super Shuttle 310/782-6600.
Metro Transit Authority 323/466-3876, web: www.mta.net. Includes subway.

ATTRACTIONS:

3rd St outdoor mall in Santa Monica.
Chinatown, near downtown.
City Walk in Universal Studios.
The Getty Center 310/440-7300, web: www.getty.edu.
Grauman's Chinese Theatre on Hollywood Blvd 323/461-3331, web: www.chinesetheatres.com.
Griffith Observatory 213/473-0800, web: www.griffithobs.org.
Melrose Ave, hip commercial district in West Hollywood.
Theme Parks: Disneyland, Knotts Berry Farm, or Magic Mountain.
Watts Towers (Simon Rodia State Historical Park), 1765 E 107th St (not far from LAX), 213/847-4646, web: www.wattstowers.us.
Westwood Village premiere movie theaters & restaurants.
Venice Beach.

BEST VIEW:

Drive up Mulholland Drive, in the hills between Hollywood and the Valley, for a panoramic view of the city, and the Hollywood sign.

WEATHER:

Summers are hot, dry, and smoggy with temperatures in the 80°s-90°s. LA's weather is at its finest — sunny, blue skies, and moderate temperatures (mid 70°s) — during the months of March, April, and May.

Essential Gay & Lesbian Directory
310/841–2800, 866/718–GAYS • business directory serving the LGBT community

▶**Lesbian News (LN)** 310/548–9888, 800/458–9888 • nat'l w/ strong coverage of Southern CA • see ad front color section

Odyssey Magazine 323/874–8788 • dish on LA's club scene

LA—West Hollywood

INFO LINES & SERVICES

Visit West Hollywood 8687 Melrose Ave, Ste M38 (at San Vicente) 800/368–6020, 310/289–2525 • Re-discover West Hollywood! When was the last time you visited? Website offers hotel packages and special events

ACCOMMODATIONS

Andaz West Hollywood 8401 Sunset Blvd (at Kings Rd) 323/656–1234, 800/233–1234 • gay/ straight • on the Sunset Strip • rooftop pool • nonsmoking • WiFi • wheelchair access

Chamberlain 1000 Westmount Dr (near Holloway) 310/657–7400, 800/201–9652 • gay/ straight • boutique hotel • fitness center • rooftop pool • bistro restaurant & lounge

The Elan Hotel Los Angeles 8435 Beverly Blvd (at Croft) 323/658–6663, 866/203–2212 • gay/ straight • hip & trendy • kids ok • wheelchair access • gay-owned

The Grafton on Sunset 8462 W Sunset Blvd (at La Cienega) 323/654–4600, 800/821–3660 • gay/ straight • pool • sundeck • panoramic views • located in heart of Sunset Strip • wheelchair access

Hotel Le Petit 8822 Cynthia St (at Larrabee) 310/854–1114 • gay-friendly • all-suite hotel • hot tub • pool • kids ok • wheelchair access

Le Parc Suite Hotel 733 N West Knoll Dr (at Melrose) 310/855–8888, 800/578–4837 • gay-friendly • all-suite hotel • pool • tennis courts • kids/ pets ok • also restaurant • wheelchair access

The London West Hollywood 1020 N San Vicente Blvd 866/282–4560 • gay-friendly • luxury hotel • pool • WiFi • also Gordon Ramsay's restaurant

Mondrian 8440 Sunset Blvd 323/650–8999, 800/697–1791 • gay-friendly • home of trendy Skybar & Asia de Cuba restaurant

Ramada Plaza Hotel—West Hollywood 8585 Santa Monica Blvd (at La Cienega) 310/652–6400 • gay-friendly • modern art deco • pool & poolside WiFi • kids ok • wheelchair access

Sunset Marquis Hotel & Villas 1200 Alta Loma Rd (1/2 block S of Sunset Blvd) 310/657–1333 • gay/ straight • full brkfst • sauna • hot tub • pool • WiFi • kids ok • wheelchair access

BARS

The Abbey 692 N Robertson Blvd (at Santa Monica) 310/289–8410 • 8am-2am • lesbians/gay men • popular • also restaurant • patio • wheelchair access

Comedy Store 8433 Sunset Blvd (at La Cienega) 323/650–6268 • 8pm-2am • gay-friendly • legendary stand-up club

Fiesta Cantina 8865 Santa Monica Blvd (at San Vicente) 310/652–8865 • noon-2am • lesbians/gay men • raucous Mexican restaurant & bar

Here Lounge 696 N Robertson Blvd (at Santa Monica) 310/360–8455 • 4pm-2am • lesbians/gay men • more women Fri for Truck Stop • swanky & stylish • DJ nightly

Improv 8162 Melrose Ave (at Crescent Heights) 323/651–2583 • gay-friendly • stand-up comedy • also restaurant

Micky's 8857 Santa Monica Blvd (at San Vicente) 310/657–1176 • noon-2am, after-hours wknds • mostly gay men • dancing/DJ • videos • younger crowd • food served • patio • gay-owned

Revolver Video Bar 8851 Santa Monica Blvd (at Larrabee St) 310/694–0430 • 4pm-2am, from noon wknds • popular • mostly gay men • a WeHo institution

NIGHTCLUBS

Eleven Restaurant & Nightclub 8811 Santa Monica Blvd (at Larrabee St) 310/855–0800 • lunch & dinner • more gay for the bar atmosphere till 2am

The Factory 652 N La Peer Dr (at Santa Monica) 310/659–4551 • check www.factorynightclub.com for events • mostly gay men • dancing/DJ • videos

Girl Bar 692 N Robertson (at The Abbey) 310/659–4551, 877/447–5252 • Wed night • popular • women only • dancing/DJ • visit girlbar.com for info

Juicy Club LA 8911 Santa Monica Blvd (at San Vicente, at Rage) 310/659–4551 • 9pm-3am 1st Sat • LA's newest monthly Girl night • dancing/DJ

Rage 8911 Santa Monica Blvd (at San Vicente) 310/652–7055 • noon-2am, lunch Tue-Sun, dinner nightly • popular • mostly gay men • dancing/DJ • live shows • videos • 18+ wknds • wheelchair access

Ultra Suede 661 N Robertson Blvd (at Santa Monica) 310/659-4551 • 10pm-2am Wed-Sat • gay/ straight • dancing/DJ • theme nights

CAFES

Champagne French Bakery & Cafe 8917-9 Santa Monica Blvd 310/657-4051 • 6:30am-9pm, till 11pm Fri-Sat • coffees & pastries as well as brkfst, lunch & dinner • some outdoor seating

Grind House Cafe 1051 N Havenhurst Dr 323/650-7717 • 6:30am-10pm • coffeehouse • WiFi • occasional live music

Urth Caffe 8565 Melrose Ave (btwn Robertson & La Cienega) 310/659-0628 • 6:30am-midnight • organic coffees, teas & treats • food served • plenty veggie & vegan • patio

RESTAURANTS

AOC 8022 W Third St (at Crescent Heights Blvd) 323/653-6359 • dinner nightly • wine bar • eclectic • upscale

Basix Cafe 8333 Santa Monica Blvd (at Flores) 323/848-2460 • 7am-11pm • outdoor seating

The Bayou 8939 Santa Monica Blvd (at Robertson) 310/273-3303 • 6pm-2am • full bar • gay-owned

Bite 8807 Santa Monica Blvd (at San Vicente) 310/659-3663 • 11:30am-11:30pm • plenty veggie • beer/ wine • wheelchair access

Bossa Nova 685 N Robertson Blvd (at Santa Monica) 310/657-5070 • 11am-midnight • Brazilian • beer/ wine • patio • wheelchair access

Cafe La Boheme 8400 Santa Monica Blvd (btwn Benecia Ave & Fox Hills Dr) 323/848-2360 • 5pm-10pm Fri-Sat, till 11pm Sun-Th • American eclectic/ California • full bar • patio w/ fireplace • wheelchair access

Canter's Deli 419 N Fairfax (btwn Melrose & Beverly) 323/651-2030 • 24hrs • hip after-hours • Jewish/ American • some veggie • full bar • wheelchair access

Cecconi's 8764 Melrose Ave 310/432-2000 • 8am-midnight, classic Italian

Falcon 7213 Sunset Blvd (btwn Poinsettia & Formosa) 323/850-5350 • dinner Wed-Sat • gay/ straight • California/ cont'l fusion • full bar & lounge

Hamburger Mary's Bar & Grill 8288 Santa Monica Blvd 323/654-3800 • 11am-1am, till 2am Fri-Sat • lesbians/ gay men • transgender-friendly • karaoke • drag shows

Hedley's 640 N Robertson Blvd 310/659-2009 • lunch & dinner, also wknd brunch, clsd Sun night & Mon

The Hudson 1114 N Crescent Heights Blvd 323/654-6686 • 4pm-2am, from 10am Sat-Sun

Il Piccolino Trattoria 350 N Robertson Blvd (btwn Melrose & Beverly) 310/659-2220 • lunch & dinner, clsd Sun • full bar • patio • wheelchair access

Joey's Cafe 8301 Santa Monica Blvd 323/822-0671 • 8am-10pm • a little bit coffeehouse, a little bit diner • popular at lunch

Kokomo Cafe 7385 Beverly Blvd (between La Brea Ave & Fairfax Ave) 323/933-0773 • 8am-4pm • diner • wheelchair access

Koo Koo Roo 8520 Santa Monica Blvd (at La Cienega Blvd) 310/657-3300 • 11am-11pm, till 10pm Sun • lots of healthy chicken dishes • plenty veggie • beer/ wine • wheelchair access

Lola's 945 N Fairfax Ave (at Santa Monica) 323/654-5652 • 5:30pm-1am • great martinis

Louise's Trattoria 7505 Melrose Ave (at Gardner) 323/651-3880 • 11am-10pm • Italian • great foccacia bread • beer/ wine • patio

Lucques 8474 Melrose Ave (at La Cienega) 323/655-6277 • lunch Tue-Sat, dinner nightly • French • full bar • patio • wheelchair access

Marix Tex Mex 1108 N Flores (btwn La Cienega & Fairfax) 323/656-8800 • 11:30am-11pm, from 11am wknds • lesbians/ gay men • some veggie • great margaritas • patio • wheelchair access

Nyala 1076 S Fairfax (at Whitworth Dr) 323/936-5918 • many Ethiopian, Nigerian & other African restaurants to choose from on this block

Real Food Daily 414 N La Cienega (btwn Beverly & Melrose) 310/289-9910 • 11:30am-10pm, till 11pm Fri-Sat, Sun brunch 10am-3pm • organic vegan • beer/ wine • patio • wheelchair access

St Felix 8945 Santa Monica Blvd (at Hilldale) 310/275-4428 • 4pm-2am • small plates

Tart 115 S Fairfax Ave (at Farmer's Daughter Hotel) 323/937-3930, 800/334-1658 • 7am-midnight • Southern

Taste 8454 Melrose Ave (at La Cienega) 323/852-6888 • lunch & dinner, wknd brunch • upscale eclectic • full bar

Versailles 1415 S La Cienega (at W Pico) 310/289-0392 • lunch & dinner • Cuban

BOOKSTORES

Book Soup 8818 W Sunset Blvd (at Larrabee) **310/659-3110** • 9am-10pm, till 7pm Sun • LGBT section

RETAIL SHOPS

665 Leather 8722 Santa Monica Blvd (at Huntley Dr) **310/854-7276** • noon-8pm, till 10pm Fri-Sat • custom leather & neoprene • also accessories & toys

Marginalized Tattoo 4228 Melrose Ave (at Vermont) **213/422-4801** • featuring Dave Davenport (aka "Dogspunk"), named best gay tattoo artist

GYMS & HEALTH CLUBS

24 Hour Fitness 8612 Santa Monica Blvd, West Hollywood **310/652-7440** • recently renovated • tres gay

The Easton Gym 8053 Beverly Blvd (at Crescent Hts) **323/651-3636** • gay-friendly

The Fitness Factory 650 N La Peer Dr (at Santa Monica) **310/358-1838** • 6am-9pm, till 8pm Fri, 7am-5pm Sat, 8am-1pm Sun

EROTICA

Circus of Books 8230 Santa Monica Blvd (at La Jolla) **323/656-6533** • 6am-2am

Hustler Hollywood 8920 Sunset Blvd (at San Vicente) **310/860-9009** • 10am-2am • chic erotic department store • also cafe

Pleasure Chest 7733 Santa Monica Blvd (at Genesee), N Hollywood **323/650-1022** • 10am-midnight, till 1am Th-Sat

LA—Hollywood

ACCOMMODATIONS

Hilton Garden Inn 2005 N Highland (at Franklin) **323/876-8600** • gay-friendly • also restaurant & lounge • pool • jacuzzi • kids ok • WiFi • wheelchair access

Hollywood Hotel – The Hotel of Hollywood 1160 N Vermont Ave (at Santa Monica) **323/315-1800, 800/800-9733** • gay-friendly • full brkfst • pool • nonsmoking • WiFi • wheelchair access

The Redbury 1717 Vine St (at Hollywood) **323/962-1717, 877/962-1717** • gay/straight • WiFi • spacious flats • restaurant & bar

BARS

Boardner's 1652 N Cherokee Ave **323/462-9621** • 4pm-2am • gay/ straight • "a Hollywood legend & best-kept secret since 1942" • dancing/DJ • food served • theme nights

Faultline 4216 Melrose Ave (at Vermont) **323/660-0889** • 5pm-2am, from 2pm wknds, clsd Mon-Tue • popular • mostly gay men • cruisy • leather • bears • videos • patio

NIGHTCLUBS

Arena/ Circus Disco 6655 Santa Monica Blvd (at Seward, Circus behind Arena) **323/810-6993** • 9pm-2am Tue-Wed & Fri-Sat • popular • gay men • dancing/DJ • theme nights • multiracial • strippers

Avalon 1735 Vine St (at Hollywood Blvd) **323/462-8900** • gay/ straight • one of LA's best dance music clubs • call for events

Booby Trap • monthly • mostly women • cute girls • dive bar

Mr Black LA 1737 N Vine St (at Hollywood Blvd, at Bardot) **323/462-8900** • Tue only • lesbians/ gay men • dancing/DJ

Push Party 6510 Santa Monica Blvd (at Wilcox, at Dragonfly) • 9pm-2am every other Sat • mostly women • dancing/DJ • multiracial • hip hop, electro, reggae

TigerHeat 1735 Vine (at Avalon) **323/467-4571** • 9:30pm-3am Th only • gay/ straight • dancing/DJ • transgender-friendly • live shows • videos • 18+ • cover charge

RESTAURANTS

101 Coffee Shop 6145 Franklin Ave **323/467-1175** • 7am-3am • diner

La Poubelle 5907 Franklin Ave (at Bronson) **323/465-0807** • 5:30pm-midnight • French/ Italian • some veggie • full bar • wheelchair access

Musso & Frank Grill 6667 Hollywood Blvd (near Las Palmas) **323/467-5123** • 11am-11pm, clsd Sun-Mon • the grand-dame diner/ steak house of Hollywood • great pancakes, potpies & martinis!

Off Vine 6263 Leland Wy (at Vine) **323/962-1900** • lunch & dinner, wknd brunch • beer/ wine

Prado 244 N Larchmont Blvd (at Beverly) **323/467-3871** • lunch & dinner, dinner only Sun • Caribbean • some veggie • wheelchair access

Quality 8030 W 3rd St (at Laurel) **323/658-5959** • 8am-3:30pm • homestyle brkfst • some veggie • wheelchair access

Rockwell Table & Stage 1714 N Vermont Ave (at Prospect, enter in alley) **323/669-1550** • 11am-midnight, brunch wknds

Roscoe's House of Chicken & Waffles 1514 N Gower (at Sunset) **323/466-7453** • 8:30am-midnight, till 4am Fri-Sat

BOOKSTORES

Skylight Books 1818 N Vermont Ave (at Melbourne Ave) **323/660–1175** • 10am-10pm • way cool independent in Los Feliz • great fiction & alt-lit sections

GYMS & HEALTH CLUBS

Gold's Gym 1016 N Cole Ave (near Santa Monica & Vine) **323/462–7012** • 5am-midnight, 7am-9pm Sat-Sun • gay-friendly

LA—West LA & Santa Monica

ACCOMMODATIONS

Casa Malibu 22752 Pacific Coast Hwy, Malibu **310/456–2219** • gay-friendly • on the beach • WiFi

The Georgian Hotel 1415 Ocean Ave (btwn Santa Monica & Broadway), Santa Monica **310/395–9945, 800/538–8147** • gay-friendly • food served • wheelchair access

Hotel Angeleno 170 N Church Ln (at Hwy 405) **310/476–6411, 866/264–3536** • gay/straight • boutique hotel w/ landmark circular shape • pool • gym • nonsmoking • WiFi

Hotel Erwin 1697 Pacific Ave (at Venice Way), Venice Beach **310/452–1111, 800/786–7789** • gay/straight • rooftop lounge & restaurant • gym • nonsmoking • WiFi

Hotel Palomar **310/475–8711, 800/472–8556** • gay/straight • pool • wheelchair access

The Inn at Venice Beach 327 Washington Blvd (at Via Dolce), Marina Del Rey **310/821–2557, 800/828–0688** • gay-friendly • 43-room European-style inn • kids ok • WiFi • wheelchair access

The Linnington **310/422–8825** • lesbians/gay men • B&B • jacuzzi • kids ok • lesbian-owned

The Malibu Beach Inn 22878 Pacific Coast Hwy, Malibu **310/456–6444** • gay-friendly • balconies with views of the Pacific Ocean • onsite dining • WiFi

Shutters on the Beach 1 Pico Blvd, Santa Monica **310/458–0030, 800/334–9000** • gay-friendly • swimming • WiFi

W Los Angeles 930 Hilgard Ave (at Le Conte) **310/208–8765, 800/421–2317** • gay-friendly • suites • also restaurant • gym • day spa • pool

BARS

The Dolphin 1995 Artesia Blvd (at Green Ln), Redondo Beach **310/318-3339** • 7pm-2am, more women Mon • lesbians/ gay men • neighborhood bar • dancing/DJ Fri-Sat • karaoke Sun, Tue & Th • patio • wheelchair access

CAFES

The Novel Cafe 2507 Main St, Santa Monica **310/396-7700** • 7am-1am, from 8am Sat, 8am-midnight Sun • coffeehouse • used bookstore

RESTAURANTS

12 Washington 12 Washington Blvd (at Pacific), Marina Del Rey **310/822-5566** • 5pm-10pm, till 11pm Fri-Sun • cont'l

Axe 1009 Abbot Kinney, Venice **310/664-9787** • lunch & dinner, clsd Mon • healthy • plenty veggie

Baja Cantina 311 Washington Blvd (at Sanborn), Marina Del Rey **310/821-2252** • 10:30am-1am, also brunch wknds • full bar

Border Grill 1445 4th St (at Broadway), Santa Monica **310/451-1655** • lunch & dinner from famous "Two Hot Tamales" chefs • Mexican

➤**Cantalini's Salerno Beach Restaurant** 193 Culver Blvd (at Vista del Mar), Playa del Rey **310/821-0018** • lunch Mon-Fri, dinner nightly • Italian • homemade pastas • beer/ wine • live music Sun nights

Cora's Coffee Shoppe 1802 Ocean Ave (N of Pico Blvd), Santa Monica **310/451-9562** • 7am-3pm, from 7am wknds, clsd Mon • organic

Drago 410 N Canon, Beverly Hills **310/786-8236** • lunch Mon-Sat, dinner nightly • Sicilian Italian • wheelchair access

Gjelina 1429 Abbot Kinney Blvd, Venice **310/450-1429** • pizzas & small plates • beer/ wine only

Golden Bull 170 W Channel Rd (at Pacific Coast Hwy), Santa Monica **310/230-0402** • 4:30pm-10pm, till 11pm wknds, Sun brunch • American • full bar

Hamburger Habit 11223 National Blvd (at Sepulveda) **310/478-5000** • popular • 10am-11pm, till midnight Fri-Sat

Joe's 1023 Abbot Kinney Blvd, Venice **310/399-5811** • lunch Tue-Fri, dinner nightly, wknd brunch, clsd Mon • French/ Californian

Real Food Daily 514 Santa Monica Blvd (btwn 5th & 6th), Santa Monica **310/451-7544** • 11:30am-10pm • organic vegan • beer/ wine • wheelchair access

Seed Bistro 11917 Wilshire Blvd **310/477-7070** • lunch Mon-Fri, dinner nightly, clsd Sun • vegan

Wokcano 1413 5th St, Santa Monica **310/458-3080** • 11am-12:30am, till 1:30am Fri-Sat • sushi bar & Chinese cafe

ENTERTAINMENT & RECREATION

Santa Monica Pier Ocean Ave (at Colorado Ave), Santa Monica

Will Rogers State Beach Pacific Coast Hwy (at Temescal Canyon Rd) • gay beach

BOOKSTORES

Diesel, A Bookstore 23410 Civic Center Way, Malibu **310/456-9961** • 10am-7pm, till 9pm Fri-Sat, till 6pm Sun • independent

EROTICA

Pleasure Island 18426 Hawthorne Blvd (btwn Artesia & 190th), Torrance **310/793-9477** • 11am-midnight, till 2am Fri-Sat

LA—Silverlake

BARS

4100 Bar 4100 Sunset Blvd (at Manzanita) **323/666-4460** • 8pm-2am • gay/ straight • neighborhood bar

Cavern Club Theater 1920 Hyperion Ave (at Casita Del Campo) **323/969-2530,** **323/662-4255** • wide variety of shows • Wed-Sat nights

Cha Cha Lounge 2375 Glendale Blvd (at Silverlake) **323/660-7595** • 5pm-2am • gay-friendly • hipster lounge • gay-owned

Club Nur 2810 Hyperion Ave (at Rowena, at MJ's) **323/660-1503** • Th only • lesbians/ gay men • Middle Eastern night • dancing/DJ

Eagle LA 4219 Santa Monica Blvd (at Hoover) **323/669-9472** • 4pm-2am, from 2pm wknds • popular • mostly gay men • leather • wheelchair access

Good Luck Bar 1514 Hillhurst Ave (nr Hollywood Blvd) **323/666-3524** • 7pm-2am, from 8pm wknds • gay-friendly • stylish dive bar

Silverlake Lounge 2906 Sunset Blvd (at Silver Lake Blvd) **323/663-9636** • 3pm-2am • gay/ straight • rock 'n' roll club • drag shows wknds

NIGHTCLUBS

A Club Called Rhonda 213/482-2313 • gay/ straight • monthly party • "house, disco, & polysexual hard partying" • check www.rhondasays.net for info

The Echo 1822 W Sunset Blvd (at Glendale Blvd) 213/413-8200 • gay/ straight • dancing/DJ • live shows

Full Frontal Disco 4356 W Sunset Blvd (at Fountain) 213/626-2285 • last Sun only • gay/ straight • dancing/DJ • transgender-friendly

RESTAURANTS

Casita Del Campo 1920 Hyperion Ave 323/662-4255 • 11am-midnight, till 2am Fri-Sat • popular • Mexican • patio

Cha Cha Cha 656 N Virgil Ave (at Melrose) 323/664-7723 • lunch & dinner • lesbians/ gay men • Caribbean • plenty veggie • wheelchair access

Cliff's Edge 3626 Sunset Blvd (at Griffith Park Blvd) 323/666-6116 • dinner only, wknd brunch • plenty veggie • romantic • outdoor seating

El Conquistador 3701 W Sunset Blvd (at Lucille) 323/666-5136 • lunch Tue-Sun, dinner nightly • Mexican • beer/ wine • patio

The Good Microbrew & Grill 3725 Sunset Blvd (at Lucille) 323/660-3645 • 11am-10pm, till 11pm Fri, 9am-10pm wknds • plenty veggie

Home 1760 Hillhurst Ave, Los Feliz 323/669-0211 • 9am-10pm, patio

The Kitchen 4348 Fountain Ave (at Sunset Blvd) 323/664-3663 • 5pm-1am, from 11am Sat, till 10pm Sun • cozy diner • gay-owned

Michelangelo Pizzeria Ristorante 2742 Rowena 323/660-4843 • lunch & dinner

Square One Dining 4854 Fountain Ave (at Vermont Ave) 323/661-1109 • 8am-3pm • great brkfst

Vermont Restaurant & Bar 1714 N Vermont Ave 323/661-6163 • lunch Mon-Fri, dnner nightly, clsd Sun • gay-owned

RETAIL SHOPS

Syren 2809 1/2 W Sunset Blvd 213/289-0334 • noon-10pm, clsd Mon • leather & latex

EROTICA

Romantix Adult Superstore 3147 N San Fernando Rd 323/258-2867 • 24hrs

LA—Midtown

ACCOMMODATIONS

Luxe City Center 1020 S Figueroa St 213/748-1291 • gay/straight • urban oasis amidst skyscrapers and renowned landmarks ,

O Hotel 819 S Flower St 213/623-9904 • gay/ straight • restaurant • WiFi

The Standard, Downtown LA 550 S Flower St 213/892-8080 • gay/ straight • pool • restaurant • WiFi

BARS

Cafe Club Fais Do-Do 5257 W Adams Blvd (btwn Fairfax & La Brea) 323/931-4636 • 8pm-2am • gay-friendly • live music • also Cajun restaurant

NIGHTCLUBS

Bordello 901 E 1st St (at S Vignes St) 213/687-3766 • gay-friendly • burlesque shows • also restaurant

The Catwalk 801 W Temple St (at N Figueroa, at Vertigos bar) 213/977-0888 • 1st Fri only • mostly women • dancing/DJ

Coco Bongo 3311 S Main St 818/233-5322 • 9pm-2am, clsd Mon-Wed • mostly women • dancing/DJ • Latino/a • drag shows • go-go dancers • 18+

Jewel's Catch One Disco 4067 W Pico Blvd (at Norton) 323/734-8849 (HOTLINE), 323/737-1159 • call for hours, clsd Wed-Th • gay/ straight • dancing/DJ • theme nights • wheelchair access

Mustache Mondays 336 S Hill St (at W 4th St, at La Cita bar) 213/687-7111 • 9pm Mon only • lesbians/ gay men • dancing/DJ • transgender-friendly • queer fashionistas

RESTAURANTS

Bar & Kitchen LA 819 S Flower St (at O Hotel) 213/784-3048 • traditional american cuisine with local Californian farm to table influences

Border Grill Downtown 445 S Figueroa St (at 5th St) 213/486-5171 • lunch & dinner, late-night cocktails • wheelchair access • owned by celebrity chefs Mary Sue Milliken & Susan Feniger

Cassell's 3266 W 6th St (at Vermont) 213/480-5000 • 10:30am-4pm, clsd Sun • great burgers

Doughboys Cafe 8136 W 3rd St 323/852-1020 • 7am-10pm

LA—Valley

includes San Fernando & San Gabriel Valleys

BARS

Cobra 10937 Burbank Blvd (1 block E of Vineland), North Hollywood 818/760-9798 • 9pm-2am, till 3am Fri-Sat, clsd Sun-Wed • popular • mostly gay men • dancing/DJ • wheelchair access

The Other Door 10437 Burbank Blvd (2 blocks E of Cahuenga), North Hollywood 818/508-7008 • 3pm-1:30am, from 1pm Fri-Sun • popular • gay/straight • neighborhood bar • dancing/DJ • live bands • wheelchair access

Oxwood Inn 13713 Oxnard (at Woodman), Van Nuys 818/997-9666 (PAY PHONE) • 4pm-2am, 5pm-8pm Mon-Tue, clsd Sun • mostly women • neighborhood bar • dancing/DJ • karaoke • patio • one of the oldest lesbian bars in US • women-owned

NIGHTCLUBS

C Frenz 7026 Reseda Blvd (at Sherman Way), Reseda 818/996-2976 • 3pm-2am, till 3am Sat • popular • lesbians/gay men • neighborhood bar • dancing/DJ • multiracial • strippers • karaoke • patio • wheelchair access • gay-owned

Rain 12215 Ventura Blvd, Studio City 818/755-9596 • 9pm-2am Fri-Sat • gay/straight • dancing/DJ

CAFES

Aroma 4360 Tujunga Ave, Studio City 818/508-0677 • 6am-11pm, from 7am Sun • coffeehouse w/ small bookstore

RESTAURANTS

Firefly Studio City 11720 Ventura Blvd, Studio City 818/762-1833 • 5pm-2am, till midnight Sun, great beer braised mussels, full bar

EROTICA

Romantix Adult Superstore 21625 Sherman Wy (at Nelson), Canoga Park 818/992-9801

Manhattan Beach

see also LA—West LA & Santa Monica

ACCOMMODATIONS

Sea View Inn at the Beach 3400 Highland Ave 310/545-1504 • gay-friendly • ocean views • pool • courtyard • nonsmoking • WiFi

RESTAURANTS

The Local Yolk 3414 Highland Ave (at Rosecranz) 310/546-4407 • 6:30am-2pm • WiFi • wheelchair access

Marin County

includes Corte Madera, Mill Valley, San Anselmo, San Rafael, Sausalito, Tiburon

INFO LINES & SERVICES

AA Gay/ Lesbian 415/499-0400 • check www.aasf.org for meeting times

Spectrum LGBT Center of the North Bay 30 N San Pedro Rd # 160, San Rafael 415/472-1945 • drop-in hours: 11am-5pm Mon-Fri • wheelchair access

ACCOMMODATIONS

Acqua Hotel 555 Redwood Hwy, Mill Valley 415/380-0400, 888/662-9555 • gay-friendly • nonsmoking • pets/ kids ok • WiFi • wheelchair access

Casa Madrona Hotel & Spa 801 Bridgeway, Sausalito 415/332-0502, 800/288-0502 • overlooks SF skyline

Larkspur Hotel 160 Shoreline Hwy, Mill Valley 415/332-5700, 866/823-4669 • gay-friendly • pool • nonsmoking

The Lodge at Tiburon 1651 Tiburon Blvd, Tiburon 415/435-3133, 800/762-7770 • gay-friendly • pool • nonsmoking • kids/ pets ok • WiFi • also restaurant & bar

Waters Edge Hotel 25 Main St, Tiburon 415/789-5999 • gay/ straight • boutique hotel • kids ok • nonsmoking • WiFi • wheelchair access

RESTAURANTS

Guaymas 5 Main St (at ferry dock), Tiburon 415/435-6300 • gourmet Mexican • great views of the Bay

Terrapin Crossroads 100 Yacht Club Dr, San Rafael 415/524-2773 • 4pm-10pm, from 11am wknds, clsd Mon • a healthy down-home all-American eatery, taproom & lounge

BOOKSTORES

Book Passage 51 Tamal Vista Blvd, Corte Madera 415/927-0960, 800/999-7909 • 9am-9pm • beloved independent which draws the biggest names to read • also cafe • WiFi

RETAIL SHOPS

Cowgirl Creamery 80 4th St (at Tomales Bay Foods), Pt Reyes Station 415/663-9335 • 10am-6pm Wed-Sun • handmade cheeses • picnic lunches to go • women-owned

Mendocino

ACCOMMODATIONS

Agate Cove Inn 11201 N Lansing St 707/937-0551, 800/527-3111 • gay-friendly • full brkfst • fireplaces • nonsmoking

The Alegria Quartet & Oceanfront Inn Cottages 44781 Main St 707/937-5150, 800/780-7905 • gay-friendly • located in the village • ocean views • nonsmoking • WiFi • kids ok

Blair House & Cottage 45110 Little Lake St (at Ford St) 707/937–1800, 800/699–9296 • gay-friendly • in former "home" of Jessica Fletcher of Murder, She Wrote • nonsmoking

Brewery Gulch Inn 9401 N Hwy 1 707/937–4752, 800/578–4454 • gay/ straight • oceanview B&B made of eco-salvaged redwood • full brkfst • jacuzzi • nonsmoking • WiFi

Dennen's Victorian Farmhouse 7001 N Hwy 1 (at Hwy 128) 707/937–0697, 800/264–4723 • gay-friendly • nonsmoking • full brkfst • WiFi

Glendeven Inn 8205 N Hwy 1 (1.7 miles S of Mendocino), Little River 707/937–0083, 800/822–4536 • gay-friendly • charming farmhouse on the coast • full brkfst & wine bar • nonsmoking

Hill House Inn 10701 Palette Dr 707/937–0554, 800/422–0554 • gay/ straight • New England–style inn • also restaurant

The Inn at Schoolhouse Creek 7051 N Hwy 1, Little River 707/937–5525, 800/731–5525 • gay/ straight • B&B w/ cottages & suites • full brkfst • hot tub • fireplaces • WiFi • kids/pets ok • wheelchair access

John Dougherty House 571 Ukiah St (at Kasten St) 707/937–5266, 800/486–2104 • gay-friendly • jacuzzi • gay-owned

Little River Inn Resort & Spa 7901 N Hwy 1, Little River 707/937–5942, 888/466–5683 • gay-friendly • resort • ocean views, restaurant & bar • nonsmoking • WiFi

MacCallum House Inn 45020 Albion St (at Lansing) 707/937–0289, 800/609–0492 • gay/ straight • nonsmoking • WiFi • wheelchair access • kids ok • also popular restaurant & full bar w/ cafe

Orr Hot Springs 13201 Orr Springs Rd, Ukiah 707/462–6277 • gay-friendly • hostel-style cabins, private cottages & campsites • clothing-optional • kids ok • mineral hot springs • pool • no food provided • reservations required

Packard House 45170 Little Lake St (at Kasten St) 707/937–2677, 888/453–2677 • gay-friendly • full brkfst • jacuzzi • nonsmoking • WiFi • gay-owned

Sallie & Eileen's Place 707/937–2028, 888/757–5223 • women only • cabin • hot tub • kitchens • fireplaces • kids/ pets ok • nonsmoking • lesbian-owned

Sea Gull Inn 44960 Albion St 707/937–5204, 888/937–5204 • gay-friendly • in the heart of historic Mendocino • nonsmoking • kids ok • WiFi • wheelchair access

Stanford Inn by the Sea 44850 Comptche-Ukiah Rd (at Coast Hwy 1) 707/937–5615, 800/331–8884 • gay-friendly • full brkfst • hot tub • pool • organic vegetarian restaurant • nonsmoking • WiFi • kids/ pets ok • wheelchair access

Stevenswood Resort & Spa 8211 N Hwy 1 707/937–2810, 800/421–2810 • gay/ straight • resort w/ forest spas & hot tubs • WiFi • wheelchair access • gay-owned

RESTAURANTS

Cafe Beaujolais 961 Ukiah St 707/937–5614 • lunch& dinner • reservations recommended • some veggie • wheelchair access

BOOKSTORES

Gallery Bookshop Main & Kasten St S 707/937–2665 • 9:30am-6pm, till 9pm Fri-Sat • independent • also children's bookstore

Menlo Park

see Palo Alto

Mill Valley

see Marin County

Modesto

see also Stockton

ACCOMMODATIONS

Rodeway Inn 936 McHenry Ave (at Roseburg Ave) 209/523–7701 • gay-friendly • pool • WiFi

BARS

Brave Bull 701 S 9th St 209/529–6712 • 7pm-2am, clsd Mon • lesbians/ gay men • dancing/DJ • Latino/a (Latin Night Th w/ drag show & strippers) • drag shows Sun • karaoke Wed

Tiki Lounge 932 McHenry Ave (at Roseburg Ave) 209/577–9969 • 5:30pm-2am • lesbians/ gay men • neighborhood bar • multiracial • transgender-friendly • karaoke

CAFES

Deva Cafe 1202 J St 209/572–3382 • 7am-3pm, 8am-noon Sun • live music • patio • wheelchair access

Queen Bean 1126 14th St 209/521–8000 • 7am-8pm, till 11pm wknds

RESTAURANTS

Minnie's Restaurant 107 McHenry Ave **209/524-4621** • lunch Tue-Fri, dinner Tue-Sun, clsd Mon • full bar

RETAIL SHOPS

Mystical Body 121 McHenry Ave **209/527-1163** • noon-8pm, clsd Sun-Mon • body piercing

EROTICA

Suzie's Adult Superstores 115 McHenry Ave (at Needham) **209/529-5546** • 8am-midnight

Monterey

ACCOMMODATIONS

Asilomar Conference Grounds 800 Asilomar Blvd, Pacific Grove **831/372-8016, 888/635-5310** • gay-friendly • Arts & Crafts-style buildings designed by Julia Morgan • pool • WiFi

Gosby House Inn 643 Lighthouse Ave (at 18th), Pacific Grove **831/375-1287, 800/527-8828** • gay-friendly • B&B • full brkfst • some shared baths • nonsmoking • kids ok • wheelchair access

Monterey Fireside Lodge 1131 10th St **831/373-4172, 800/722-2624** • very gay-friendly • fireplaces • nonsmoking rooms available • kids ok • WiFi

The Monterey Hotel 406 Alvarado St **831/375-3184, 800/966-6490** • gay-friendly • turn-of-the-century boutique hotel • WiFi

NIGHTCLUBS

Franco's Club 10639 Merritt St, Castroville **831/633-2090** • 10pm-2am Sat only • lesbians/gay men • dancing/DJ • Latino/a

RESTAURANTS

Old Fisherman's Grotto 39 Fisherman's Wharf #1 **831/375-4604** • 11am-10pm

Tarpy's Roadhouse 2999 Monterey Salinas Hwy (at Canyon Dr) **831/647-1444** • lunch & dinner, Sun brunch • patios & gardens • full bar

ENTERTAINMENT & RECREATION

Ag Venture Tours PO Box 2634, 93942 **831/761-8463** • customized wine-tasting, agriculture & sight-seeing tours of Monterey and Sata Cruz countries

Morro Bay

see San Luis Obispo

Napa Valley

ACCOMMODATIONS

Beazley House B&B Inn 1910 First St, Napa **707/257-1649, 800/559-1649** • gay-friendly • historic inn • full brkfst • nonsmoking • very pet-friendly • WiFi • wheelchair access

Brannan Cottage Inn 109 Wapoo Ave (at Lincoln Ave), Calistoga **707/942-4200** • gay-friendly • B&B in Victorian cottage • full brkfst • 1 block from downtown • nonsmoking • WiFi

The Chablis Inn 3360 Solano Ave (Redwood Rd at Hwy 29), Napa **707/257-1944, 800/443-3490** • gay-friendly • stylish motel • pool • hot tub • kids/ pets ok • nonsmoking • wheelchair access

The Chanric Inn 1805 Foothill Blvd, Calistoga **707/942-4535, 877/281-3671** • gay/straight • pool & spa • nonsmoking • WiFi • gay-owned

Chateau de Vie 3250 Hwy 128, Calistoga **707/942-6446, 877/558-2513** • gay/ straight • chateau w/ gardens • full brkfst • pool • pets ok • WiFi • gay-owned

The Inn on First 1938 1st St, Napa **707/253-1331, 866/253-1331** • gay/ straight • pets ok • WiFi • gay-owned

Luxe Calistoga 1139 Lincoln Ave (at Myrtle), Calistoga **707/942-9797** • gay-friendly • on historic main street • nonsmoking • wheelchair access

Meadowlark Country House 601 Petrified Forest Rd, Calistoga **707/942-5651, 800/942-5651** • gay-friendly • full brkfst • clothing-optional mineral pool, sauna & hot tub • nonsmoking • WiFi • gay-owned

Napa River Inn 500 Main St (at 5th), Napa **707/251-8500, 877/251-8500** • gay-friendly • luxury boutique hotel w/ spa • located in historic Napa Mill • gay-owned

Yountville Inn 6462 Washington St, Yountville **707/944-5600, 888/366-8166** • gay-friendly • alongside Hopper Creek • spa • nonsmoking

RESTAURANTS

Barolo Italian Kitchen & Cocktails 1457 Lincoln Ave, Calistoga **707/942-9900** • dinner only • Southern Italian cuisine • WiFi • wheelchair access gay-owned

Brannan's 1374 Lincoln Ave (at Washington), Calistoga **707/942-2233** • lunch & dinner, brunch wknds • full bar • live jazz wknds • gay-owned

Cindy's Backstreet Kitchen 1327 Railroad Ave, St Helena 707/963–1200 • 11:30am-9:30pm

Redd 6480 Washington St, Yountville 707/944–2222 • lunch Mon-Sat, dinner nightly, Sun brunch • American • reservations required

SolBar 755 Silverado Trail (at the Solage Hotel), Calistoga 707/226–0850 • soul-food

Tra Vigne 1050 Charter Oak Ave (Hwy 29), St Helena 707/963–4444 • 11:30am-10pm • Northern Italian • also wine bar • reservations recommended

ENTERTAINMENT & RECREATION

Cameo Cinema 1340 Main St, St Helena 707/963–9779 • Cameo exists to entertain, inspire, educate and connect the community through the "art of storytelling"

Harbin Hot Springs 18424 Harbin Springs Rd, Middletown 707/987–2477, 800/622–2477 (CA ONLY) • gay-friendly • nonprofit retreat & workshop center • massage • some sundecks clothing-optional

Lavender Hill Spa 1015 Foothill Blvd (at Lincoln Ave), Calistoga 707/942–4495, 800/528–4772 • 9am-9pm

BOOKSTORES

Copperfield's Books 1330 Lincoln Ave, Calistoga 707/942–1616 • 9am-7pm, till 9pm Fri-Sat, 10am- 6pm Sun

Nevada City

ACCOMMODATIONS

The Flume's End B&B 317 S Pine St 530/265–9665 • gay/ straight • creekside Victorian • full brkfst • women-owned

CAFES

Java John's 306 Broad St 530/265–3653 • 6:30am-5pm

RESTAURANTS

Friar Tuck's 111 N Pine St (at Commercial) 530/265–9093 • dinner from 5pm • American/ fondue • live shows • full bar • wheelchair access

Newport Beach

see Orange County

Oakland

see East Bay

Orange County

includes Anaheim, Costa Mesa, Garden Grove, Huntington Beach, Irvine, Laguna Beach, Newport Beach, Santa Ana

INFO LINES & SERVICES

AA Gay/ Lesbian Laguna Beach 714/556–4555 (AA#) • call or visit www.oc-aa.org for meeting times

The Center Orange County 1605 N Spurgeon St, Santa Ana 714/953–5428 • 9am-5pm Mon-Fri or by appt or event

ACCOMMODATIONS

Best Western Plus Plus Laguna Brisas Spa Hotel 1600 S Coast Hwy (at Bluebird), Laguna Beach 949/497–7272, 888/296–6834 • gay/ straight • resort hotel • free brkfst • pool • 99 steps to the beach • nonsmoking • WiFi • wheelchair access

Best Western Raffles Inn & Suites 2040 S Harbor Blvd, Anaheim 714/750–6100, 800/308–5278 • gay-friendly • pool • WiFi • walk to Disneyland

Casa Laguna Inn & Spa 2510 S Coast Hwy, Laguna Beach 949/494–2996, 800/233–0449 • gay-friendly • inn & cottages overlooking the Pacific • pool • kids/pets ok • nonsmoking • WiFi • gay-owned

Fairfield Inn Placentia 710 W Kimberly Ave, Placentia 714/996–4410, 800/308–5286 • gay-friendly • pool • WiFi • wheelchair access

Holiday Inn & Suites Anaheim 1240 S Walnut, Anaheim 714/535–0300, 800/308–5312 • gay-friendly • walk to Disneyland • pool • restaurant • WiFi • wheelchair access

The Hotel Hanford 3131 S Bristol St (at Baker St), Costa Mesa 714/557–3000, 877/426–3673 • gay-friendly • pool • WiFi • wheelchair access

Laguna Cliffs Inn 475 N Coast Hwy, Laguna Beach 949/497–6645, 800/297–0007 • gay-friendly • hot tub • pool • kids ok • easy beach access • WiFi • wheelchair access

The St Regis Monarch Beach One Monarch Beach Resort, Dana Point 949/234–3426 • gay-friendly • restaurant • pool • nonsmoking • wheelchair access

Surf & Sand Resort 949/497–4477, 888/869–7569 • gay-friendly • restaurant & spa • WiFi • wheelchair access

BARS

Club Bounce 1460 S Coast Hwy, Laguna Beach 949/494–0056 • 2pm-2am • lesbians/ gay men • dancing/DJ Fri-Sat • karaoke

Club Cherry 416 W 4th St (at Velvet), Santa Ana 714/232-8727 • Wed only • mostly women • dancing/DJ • also restaurant

Frat House 8112 Garden Grove Blvd (at Beach Blvd), Garden Grove 714/373-3728 • 3pm-2am • lesbians/gay men • dancing/DJ • multiracial • drag shows & strippers • young crowd • wheelchair access

Ibiza Bar & Nightclub 18528 Beach Blvd 714/963-7744 • noon-2am, from 4pm Mon, from 2pm Sun • gay-friendly • neighborhood bar • dancing/DJ • wheelchair access • gay-owned

Tin Lizzie Saloon 752 St Clair (at Bristol), Costa Mesa 714/966-2029 • 11:30am-2am • mostly gay men • neighborhood bar • wheelchair access

Velvet Lounge 416 W 4th St, Santa Ana 714/232-8727 • 11:30am-2am • lesbians/gay men • dancing/DJ • girls night Wed • also restaurant

NIGHTCLUBS

Bravo 1490 S Anaheim Blvd, Anaheim 714/533-2291 • more gay Th & Sat • gay/straight • dancing/DJ • goth & electronica Sun • Latin music Wed & Fri-Sat

Club Lucky Presents 949/551-2998 • check www.clubluckypresents.com for weekly parties in OC

El Calor 2916 W Lincoln Ave (at E Beach Blvd), Anaheim 714/527-8873 • 8pm-2am • gay-friendly • dancing/DJ • mostly Latino/a • drag shows

Lions Den 719 W 19th St (at Pomona Ave), Costa Mesa 949/645-3830 • 9pm-2am, clsd Mon • gay/straight • only lesbian/gay Fri for Fiesta Latino (Latino/a • drag shows) • dancing/DJ • karaoke Wed • size-acceptance club Sat (www.butterflylounge.com)

CAFES

Avanti Cafe 259 E 17th St (at Westminster), Costa Mesa 949/548-2224 • 11am-10pm, till 8pm Sun • brkfst, lunch & dinner • "hella fierce rockin' world food" • veggie & vegan • beer/wine

The Koffee Klatch 1440 S Coast Hwy (btwn Mountain & Pacific Coast Hwy), Laguna Beach 949/376-6867 • 7am-11pm, till midnight Fri-Sat • brkfst & lunch • desserts • WiFi

Zinc Cafe 350 Ocean Ave (at Broadway), Laguna Beach 949/494-6302 • 7am-4pm, also market till 6pm • vegetarian • beer/wine • patio • wheelchair access

RESTAURANTS

Cafe Zoolu 860 Glenneyre St, Laguna Beach 949/494-6825 • 5pm-10pm, clsd Mon • beer/wine • wheelchair access

The Cottage 308 N Coast Hwy (at Aster), Laguna Beach 949/494-3023 • brkfst, lunch & dinner • homestyle cooking • some veggie

Dizz's As Is 2794 S Coast Hwy (at Nyes Pl), Laguna Beach 949/494-5250 • open 5:30pm, clsd Mon • full bar • patio

Madison Square & Garden Cafe 320 N Coast Hwy, Laguna Beach 949/494-0137 • 8am-3pm, clsd Tue • dog-friendly

Nirvana Grille 303 Broadway St, Laguna Beach 949/497-0027 • dinner nightly • seasonal rooftop deck

Three Seventy Common 370 Glenneyre St, Laguna Beach 949/494-8686 • dinner only • upscale American bistro & martini bar

ENTERTAINMENT & RECREATION

San Onofre State Beach on I-5, S of San Clemente (exit at Basilone Rd), Laguna Beach

West St Beach Laguna Beach

EROTICA

Pink Kitty 17955 Sky Park Cir, Ste A, Irvine 949/660-4990 • 10am-6pm • gay-owned

Oroville

CAFES

Mug Shots 2040 Montgomery St 530/538-8342 • 6am-6pm, 8am-3pm Sun • WiFi • gay-owned

Pacifica

RESTAURANTS

Nicks Seafood Restaurant 100 Rockaway Beach Ave 650/359-3900 • 11am-10pm, from 8am wknds • live jazz wkds

Palm Springs

INFO LINES & SERVICES

AA Gay/ Lesbian 760/324-4880 (AA#) • call for meeting schedule

The Center 611 S Palm Canyon #201 760/416-7790 • programs & services • 12-step meetings

ACCOMMODATIONS

Ace Hotel Palm Springs 701 E Palm Canyon Dr 760/325-9900 • gay/straight • pool • restaurant • WiFi

Caliente Tropics Resort 411 E Palm Canyon Dr **760/327-1391, 888/277-0999** • gay/ straight • hot tub • pool • nonsmoking resort • kids ok • very pet-friendly • wheelchair access • gay-owned

Calla Lily Inn 350 S Belardo Rd (at Baristo) **760/323-3654, 888/888-5787** • gay-friendly • pool • "a tranquil oasis" • nonsmoking • WiFi

Calmada Boutique Hotel 3569 Calmada Rd, Pioneertown **760/228-3141** • gay/straight • pool • WiFi • resort 30 min from Palm Springs

Casitas Laquita 450 E Palm Canyon Dr (near Camino Real) **760/416-9999, 877/203-3410** • lesbian resort • pool • nonsmoking • small pets ok • WiFi • wheelchair access • lesbian-owned

The Horizon Hotel 1050 E Palm Canyon Dr **760/323-1858, 800/377-7855** • gay-friendly • pool • jacuzzi • WiFi

Hotel Zoso 150 S Indian Canyon Dr **760/325-9676** • gay-friendly • 4-acre resort • pool • WiFi • also bar & Nick & Stef's restaurant • also spa

Queen of Hearts Resort 435 E Avenida Olancha **760/322-5793, 888/275-9903** • women • pool • full kitchens • WiFi • lesbian-owned

Rendezvous 1420 N Indian Canyon Dr **760/320-1178, 800/485-2808** • gay-friendly • '50s chic • pool • WiFi

Ruby Montana's Coral Sands Inn 210 W Stevens Rd (at N Palm Canyon) **760/325-4900, 866/820-8302** • gay/ straight • resort • pool • kitschy 1950s chic • kids/ pets ok • WiFi • wheelchair access • lesbian-owned

The Saguaro 1800 East Palm Canyon Dr **760/323-1711** • gay-friendly • hip boutique hotel • pool • food served • WiFi

The Skylark 1466 N Palm Canyon Dr (at Monte Vista) **760/322-2267, 800/793-0063** • gay/ straight • Pool • kitchens • pets ok • WiFi

Palm Springs

LGBT Pride:
November, web: www.pspride.org.

Annual Events:
Spring - Kraft Nabisco Golf Tournament (aka "Dinah Shore"), web: www.kncgolf.com. One of the biggest gatherings of lesbians on the continent. If you're more interested in the party than the golf, get the info at www.thedinah.com.

Spring - White Party, web: www.jeffreysanker.com. Popular circuit party.

City Info:
Palm Springs Visitors Bureau 760/778-8418 or 800/347-7746, web: www.visitpalmsprings.com.

Attractions:
Joshua Tree National Park, web: www.nps.gov/jotr.

Palm Springs Aerial Tramway to the top of Mt San Jacinto, on Tramway Rd, web: www.pstramway.com.

Palm Springs Art Museum 760/322-4800, web: www.psmuseum.org.

Best View:
Top of Mt San Jacinto. Driving through the surrounding desert, you can see great views of the mountains. Be careful in the summer—always carry water in your vehicle, and be sure to check all fluids in your car before you leave and frequently during your trip.

Weather:
Palm Springs is sunny and warm in the winter, with temperatures in the 70ºs. Summers are scorching (100º+).

Transit:
American Cab 760/416-2594.
Desert Valley Shuttle 800/413-3999.
Sun Line Transit Agency 760/343-3451 or 800/347-8628, web: www.sunline.org.

Bars

DiGS 36–737 Cathedral Canyon Dr (at 111), Cathedral City **760/321-0031** • 2pm-2am, from 10am Sun • lesbians/ gay men • neighborhood bar • karaoke • country/ western • patio

Georgie's Alibi 369 N Palm Canyon Dr **760/325-5533** • 11am-close, from 10am Sun • mostly gay men • neighborhood bar • food served • patio

Hunter's Video Bar 302 E Arenas Rd (at Calle Encilia) **760/323-0700** • 10am-2am • popular • mostly gay men • dancing/DJ • video bar • go-go boys Fri • theme nights

Score 301 E Arenas Rd **760/327-0753** • 6am-2am • mostly gay men • neighborhood bar • game bar

Studio One 11 67–555 E Palm Canyon Dr (at E Eagle Canyon Way), Cathedral City **760/328-2900** • 3pm-2am • mostly gay men • dancing/DJ • karaoke • piano bar

Toucan's Tiki Lounge 2100 N Palm Canyon Dr (at Via Escuela) **760/416-7584** • noon-2am • lesbians/ gay men • dancing/DJ • live shows • drag shows • male & female go-go dancers wknds

Cafes

Palm Springs Koffi 515 N Palm Canyon Dr (at Alejo) **760/416-2244** • 5:30am-8pm • WiFi

Restaurants

Azul 369 N Palm Canyon Dr **760/325-5533** • 11am-2am • tapas lounge • full bar upstairs

Billy Reed's 1800 N Palm Canyon Dr (at Vista Chino) **760/325-1946** • 7am-9pm, till 10pm Fri-Sat • some veggie • full bar • also bakery • wheelchair access

Blue Coyote Grill 445 N Palm Canyon Dr **760/327-1196** • 11am-10pm, till 11pm Fri-Sat • Southwestern

Bongo Johnny's 214 E Arenas Rd **760/866-1905** • 8am-10pm, till 11pm Fri-Sat • burgers & sandwiches

Cafe Palette 315 E Arenas **760/322-9264** • 11am-10pm • live shows • also delivers

The Chop House 262 S Palm Canyon Dr **760/320-4500** • from 5pm • fine steaks and chops • reservations recommended

Copley's 621 N Palm Canyon Dr (btwn E Tamarisk Rd & E Granvia Valmonte) **760/327-9555** • 6pm-10pm • contemporary American • full bar

The Crazy Coconut Bar & Grill 166 N Palm Canyon Dr **760/327-8175** • 11am-10pm, till Th-Sat • burgers & fries • karaoke

Davey's Hideaway 292 E Palm Canyon Dr **760/320-4480** • from 5pm • steak, seafood & pasta • piano • patio • full bar

El Gallito 68820 Grove St (at Palm Canyon), Cathedral City **760/328-7794** • 10am-9pm • homemade Mexican • beer/ wine

Hamburger Mary's 415 N Palm Canyon Dr **760/778-6279** • 11am-close • full bar

Jake's 664 N Palm Canyon Dr **760/327-4400** • lunch & dinner, wknd brunch, clsd Sun night & Mon • American bistro

Las Casuelas 368 N Palm Canyon Dr (btwn Amado & Alejo) **760/325-3213** • 11am-10pm • Mexican

Matchbox 155 S Palm Canyon Dr (in Mercado Plaza, 2nd level) **760/778-6000** • 4pm-11pm, till 1am Fri-Sat • pizza

Nature's Health Food & Cafe 555 S Sunrise Way #301 **760/323-9487** • 8am-7pm, 9am-5pm wknds • vegan/ vegetarian

Peppers Thai Cuisine 396 N Palm Canyon Dr **760/322-1259** • lunch & dinner

Pinocchio in the Desert 134 E Tahquitz Canyon Way **760/322-3776** • 7:30am-2pm • outdoor seating

Pomme Frite 256 S Palm Canyon Dr **760/778-3727** • dinner nightly, lunch wknds, clsd Tue • Belgian beer & French food

Rio Azul 350 S Indian Canyon Dr **760/992-5641** • dinner nightly, open for lunch wknds • Mexican

Shame on the Moon 69–950 Frank Sinatra Dr (at Hwy 111), Rancho Mirage **760/324-5515** • 5pm-9:30pm • cont'l • plenty veggie • full bar • patio • reservations recommended • wheelchair access

Sherman's Deli & Bakery 401 E Tahquitz Canyon Wy **760/325-1199** • 7am-9pm • kosher-style deli

Spencer's Restaurant 701 W Baristo Rd **760/327-3446** • 9am-2:30pm & 5pm-10pm • Sun brunch • upscale contemporary • reservations recommended

Tootie's Texas Barbeque 68-703 Perez Rd, Cathedral City **760/202-6963** • 11am-8pm, clsd wknds • the name says it all

Towne Center Cafe 44491 Town Center Wy, Palm Desert **760/346-2120** • 6am-8pm • Greek diner

Trio 707 N Palm Canyon Dr **760/864-8746** • dinner nightly • also lounge

Wang's in the Desert 424 S Indian Canyon Dr (at E Saturnino Rd) **760/325-9264** • from 5:30pm • Chinese • full bar

Zin American Bistro 198 S Palm Canyon (at Arenas) 760/322–6300 • lunch & dinner

ENTERTAINMENT & RECREATION

Desert Dyners PO Box 5072, 92263-5072 760/202–6645 • lesbian social club • membership required • hosts mixers, dances, dinners & golf • singles & couples welcome

BOOKSTORES

Q Trading Company 606 E Sunny Dunes Rd (at Indian Canyon) 760/416–7150, 800/756–2290 • 10am-6pm • LGBT • also cards, gifts, videos, etc

RETAIL SHOPS

GayMartUSA 305 E Arenas Rd (at Indian Canyon) 760/416–6436 • 10am-midnight

Mischief 210 E Arenas Rd (at Indian Canyon) 760/322–8555 • 11am-7pm, 10am-11pm Fri-Sat

Off Ramp Leathers 650 E Sunny Dunes Rd #3 760/778–2798 • custom motorcycle leathers

PUBLICATIONS

Desert Daily Guide/ DDG Media Group 760/320–3237 • LGBT weekly, travel, activity & lodging info for Palm Springs

Odyssey Magazine 323/874–8788 • dish on L.A. & Palm Springs' club scene

GYMS & HEALTH CLUBS

WorkOUT Gym 2100 N Palm Canyon Dr #C100 760/325–4600 • 6am-9pm, 7am-8pm Sat, till 6pm Sun • gay-owned

World Gym Palm Springs 1751 N Sunrise Way (at Vista Chino) 760/327–7100 • 5am-10pm, 6am-8pm wknds • mostly gay men • day passes available • steam & sauna • club-quality sound system • wheelchair access • gay-owned

EROTICA

Gear Leather & Fetish 650 E Sunny Dunes #1 (at S Calle Palo Fierro) 760/322–3363 • noon-7pm, till 9pm Fri-Sat

Palmdale

see Lancaster

Palo Alto

ACCOMMODATIONS

Creekside Inn 3400 El Camino Real (at Page Mill Rd) 650/493–2411, 800/492–7335 • gay/straight • pool • kids ok • WiFi • nonsmoking • restaurant & lounge • wheelchair access

Hotel Avante 860 E El Camino Real, Mountain View 650/940–1000, 800/538–1600 • gay/ straight • in heart of Silicon Valley • pool • WiFi

BOOKSTORES

Books Inc 855 El Camino Real 650/321–0600 • 9am-8pm • LGBT section

Pasadena

BARS

The 35er 626/356–9315 • 3pm-1am, from 12:30pm Fri-Sun • gay/ straight • great neighborhood bar • food served

The Boulevard Bar 3199 E Foothill Blvd (at Sierra Madre Villa) 626/356–9304 • 4pm-2am, from 3pm Fri-Sun • mostly gay men • neighborhood bar • karaoke

RESTAURANTS

Kings Row 20 E Colorado Blvd 626/793–3010 • 4pm-midnight, till 2am wknds • gastropub

Lanna Thai 400 S Arroyo Pkwy 626/577–6599 • 11am-10:30pm • Thai • full bar • wheelchair access

ENTERTAINMENT & RECREATION

The Huntington 1151 Oxford Rd, San Marino 626/405–2100 • art collection • botanical gardens

Paso Robles

ACCOMMODATIONS

Asuncion Ridge Vineyards & Inn 805/461–0675 • gay-friendly • WiFi • gay-owned

Hotel Cheval 1021 Pine St 805/226–9995, 866/522–6999 • gay-friendly • WiFi

ENTERTAINMENT & RECREATION

River Oaks Hot Springs Spa 800 Clubhouse Dr 805/238–4600 • 9am-9pm, clsd Mon

Petaluma

RESTAURANTS

Brixx 16 Kentucky St (in Lanmart Bldg) 707/766–8162 • dinner from 4pm • popular • handmade pizzas & paninis • live bands Sat

BOOKSTORES

Copperfield's Books 140 Kentucky St (btwn Western & Washington, downtown) 707/762–0563 • 9am-9pm, 10am-6pm Sun

Placerville

ACCOMMODATIONS

Albert Shafsky House B&B 2942 Coloma St (at Spring St/ Hwy 49) 530/642-2776, 877/262-4667 • gay-friendly • full brkfst • nonsmoking • WiFi • kids ok • lesbian-owned

Rancho Cicada Retreat 10001 Bell Rd, Plymouth 209/245-4841, 877/553-9481 • mostly gay men • secluded riverside retreat in the Sierra foothills w/ 2-person tents & cabin • swimming • nudity • gay-owned

Pleasant Hill

see East Bay

Pomona

BARS

Alibi East & Back Alley Bar 225 S San Antonio Ave (at 2nd) 909/623-9422 • noon-2am, till 3am Fri • mostly gay men • dancing/DJ • karaoke • smoking patio

The Hookup 1047 E 2nd St (at Pico) 909/620-2844 • noon-2am • lesbians/ gay men • neighborhood bar • food served • karaoke • beer bust Sun • wheelchair access • gay-owned

NIGHTCLUBS

340 340 S Thomas St 909/865-9340 • 7pm-2am , clsd Mon-Wed • lesbian/ gay men • also restaurant • dancing • drag shows

Redding

NIGHTCLUBS

Club 501 1244 California St (at Center & Division, enter rear) 530/243-7869 • 6pm-2am, from 3pm Th-Sun lesbians/ gay men • dancing/DJ • young crowd

Redondo Beach

see also Los Angeles—West LA & Santa Monica

ACCOMMODATIONS

Best Western Sunrise Hotel 400 N Harbor Dr 310/376-0746, 800/334-7384 • gay-friendly • pool • hot tub • kids ok • WiFi

Riverside

see also San Bernardino

NIGHTCLUBS

Menagerie 3581 University Ave (at Orange) 951/788-8000 • 4pm-2am • lesbians/ gay men • dancing/DJ • karaoke • drag shows Th • wheelchair access

VIP Nightclub & Restaurant 3673 Merrill Ave (at Magnolia) 951/784-2370 • 5pm-2am • lesbians/ gay men • dancing/DJ • karaoke • drag shows • food served • 18+

Russian River

includes Cazadero, Forestville, Guerneville, Monte Rio, Occidental & Sebastopol

INFO LINES & SERVICES

AA Meetings in Sonoma County 707/544-1300 (AA#), 800/224-1300 • call for meeting times

Russian River Chamber of Commerce & Visitors Center 16209 First St (on the plaza), Guerneville 707/869-9000 • 10am-5pm, till 4pm Sun

Sonoma County Tourism Bureau 800/576-6662

ACCOMMODATIONS

Applewood Inn 13555 Hwy 116 (at Mays Canyon), Guerneville 707/869-9093, 800/555-8509 • gay-friendly • full brkfst • pool • nonsmoking • WiFi • wheelchair access • also restaurant

boon hotel & spa 14711 Armstrong Woods Rd, Guerneville 707/869-2721 • gay/ straight • resort w/ full-service spa • kids/ pets ok • pool • nonsmoking • jacuzzi • WiFi • gay-owned

Fern Grove Cottages 16650 River Rd, Guerneville 888/243-2674 • gay-friendly • pool • kids/ pets ok • nonsmoking • WiFi

Guerneville Lodge 15905 River Rd (at Hwy 116), Guerneville 707/869-0102 • gay/ straight • WiFi • nonsmoking • gay-owned

Highland Dell Resort 21050 River Blvd (at Bohemian Hwy), Monte Rio 707/865-2300 • gay-friendly • WiFi • full bar & restaurant

Highlands Resort 14000 Woodland Dr, Guerneville 707/869-0333 • lesbians/ gay men • country retreat on 4 wooded acres • hot tub • swimming • clothing-optional pool

Inn at Occidental 3657 Church St, Occidental 707/874-1047, 800/522-6324 • gay-friendly • full brkfst • wheelchair access

r3 Hotel 16390 4th St (at Mill), Guerneville 707/869-8399 • lesbians/ gay men • pool • nudity ok • also restaurant • full bar • wheelchair access • gay-owned

Rio Villa Beach Resort 20292 Hwy 116 (at Bohemian Hwy), Monte Rio 707/865-1143, 877/746-8455 • gay-friendly • kids ok • nonsmoking • WiFi • gay-owned

Village Inn & Restaurant 20822 River Blvd, Monte Rio 707/865–2304 • gay/ straight • historic inn • nonsmoking • also restaurant & full bar • WiFi • wheelchair access • gay-owned

West Sonoma Inn & Spa 14100 Brookside Ln (at Main St), Guerneville 707/869–2470, 800/551–1881 • gay/ straight • 6-acre resort • pool • spa • some jacuzzis • nonsmoking • WiFi • wheelchair access

The Woods Resort 16484 4th St (at Mill St), Guerneville 707/869–0600, 877/887–9218 • mostly gay men • swimming • WiFi • wheelchair access • gay-owned

Bars

Mc T's Bullpen 16246 First St (at Church), Guerneville 707/869–3377 • 10am-2am • gay/ straight • karaoke • bands • patio • WiFi • wheelchair access

Rainbow Cattle Co 16220 Main St (at Armstrong Woods Rd), Guerneville 707/869–0206 • 6am-2am • gay/ straight • neighborhood bar • DJ Bruce Sat

Whitetail Winebar 16230 Main St, Guerneville 707/604–7449 • 4pm-10pm, 3pm-11pm Fri-Sat, till 9pm Sun, clsd Tue • lesbian-owned

Cafes

Coffee Bazaar 14045 Armstrong Woods Rd (at River Rd), Guerneville 707/869–9706 • 6am-8pm • cafe • soups • salads • sandwiches • WiFi

Coffee Catz 6761 Sebastopol Ave (at Hwy 116), Sebastopol 707/829–6600 • 7am-6pm, till 8pm Th, till 10pm Wed & Fri-Sat • live shows • WiFi • wheelchair access

Roasters Espresso Bar 6656 Front St (Hwy 116), Forestville 707/887–1632 • 6am-6pm, from 7am Sat-Sun • WiFi

Russian River

Annual Events:

May - Women's Weekend, web: web:russianriverwomensweekend.org.

August - Lazy Bear Weekend, thousands of bears take over the River, web: www.lazybearweekend.com.

September - Jazz & Blues Festival, web: web:www.russianriverfestivals.com.

City Info:

Russian River Chamber of Commerce & Visitors Center 707/869-9000, web: www.russianriver.com.

Sonoma County Tourism Bureau 800/576–6662, web:www.sonomacounty.com.

Transit:

Bill's Taxi Service 707/869-2177. As far as public transit goes, this area is easiest to reach by car.

Attractions:

Armstrong Redwood State Park.

Bodega Bay, web: www.bodegabay.com.

Fort Ross.

Healdsburg.

Jenner & Goat Rock Beach.

Mudbaths of Calistoga.

Wineries of Napa and Sonoma Counties, web: www.napavalley.com & www.sonomacounty.com.

Best View:

Anywhere in Armstrong Woods, the Napa Wine Country, and on the ride along the picture-postcard-perfect coast on Highway 1.

Weather:

Summer days are sunny and warm (80°s-90°s) but usually begin with a dense fog. Winter days have the same pattern but are a lot cooler and wetter. Winter nights can be very damp and chilly (low 40°s).

Restaurants

Aioli 6536 Front St, Forestville 707/887–2476 • 9am-5pm, from 10am Sat • gourmet deli • beer/ wine • outdoor seating

boon eat + drink 16248 Main St (at Hwy 116), Guerneville 707/869–0780 • lunch & dinner, clsd Tue-Wed • American

Cape Fear Cafe 25191 Main St, Duncans Mills 707/865–9246 • 9am-2:30pm & 5pm-9pm (clsd Wed & Th off-season)

Chef Patrick 16337 Main St (at Hwy 116), Guerneville 707/869–9161 • dinner nightly

Farmhouse Inn Restaurant 7871 River Rd, Forestville 707/887–3300, 800/464–6642 • dinner, clsd Tue-Wed

Garden Grill 17132 Hwy 116, Guerneville 707/869–3922 • 8am-8pm • great burgers & sandwiches • some veggie • patio

Main Street Station 16280 Main St (at Church St), Guerneville 707/869–0501 • 11am-7pm • Italian restaurant & pizzeria • cabaret dinner shows nightly

Mom's Apple Pie 4550 Gravenstein Hwy N, Sebastopol 707/823–8330 • 10am-6pm • pie worth stopping for on your way to & from Russian River!

River Inn Grill 16141 Main St, Guerneville 707/869–0481 • 8am-3pm • local favorite • wheelchair access

Tahoe Chinese Restaurant 6492 Mirabel Rd, Forestville 707/887–9772 • lunch & dinner Mon-Fri, dinner only Sat-Sun • some veggie

Underwood Bar & Bistro 9113 Graton Rd, Graton 707/823–7023 • lunch & dinner, clsd Mon

Willow Wood Market Cafe 9020 Graton Rd, Graton 707/823–0233 • 8am-9pm, from 9am Sat, brunch 9am-3pm Sun

Entertainment & Recreation

Pegasus Theater Co 4444 Wood Rd (at Rio Nido Lodge, at Canyon Two Rd) 707/583–2343 • classic to contemporary plays

Bookstores

River Reader 16355 Main St (at Mill), Guerneville 707/869–2240 • 10am-6pm (extended summer hours) • wheelchair access

Retail Shops

Guerneville 5 &10 16252 Main St, Guerneville 707/869–3404 • 10am-6pm • old-fashioned five & dime • lesbian-owned

Sonoma Nesting Company 16151 Main St, Guerneville 707/869–3434 • antiques & home decorating

Sacramento

Info Lines & Services

Gay AA 916/454–1100 • 24hr helpline

Sacramento Gay & Lesbian Center 1927 L St 916/442–0185 • noon-6pm Mon-Fri

Accommodations

Citizen Hotel 926 J Street 916/447–2700 • gay-friendly • bar & restaurant • wheelchair access

Governors Inn 210 Richards Blvd (at I-5) 916/448–7224, 800/999–6689 • gay-friendly • pool • hot tub • nonsmoking • WiFi

The Greens Hotel 1700 Del Paso Blvd (at Arden) 707/365–5905 • gay/ straight • pool • WiFi • wheelchair access

Inn & Spa at Parkside 2116 6th St (at U St) 916/658–1818, 800/995–7275 • gay/ straight • full brkfst • jacuzzi • WiFi • also full-service spa • wheelchair access • gay-owned

Bars

The Depot 2001 K St 916/441–6823 • 4pm-2am, till 4am Fri-Sat, from noon wknds • mostly gay men • neighborhood bar • transgender-friendly • live shows • videos • wheelchair access

Dive Bar 1016 K St 916 /737–5999 • 4pm-2am • gay/ straight • super cool water tank

Hush 2001 K St (at the Depot) 916/441–6823 • monthly women's dance party • videos • wheelchair access

Nightclubs

Badlands 2003 K St 916/448–8790 • 6pm-2am • mostly gay men • dancing/DJ • wheelchair access

Faces 2000 K St (at 20th St) 916/448–7798 • 4pm-2am • popular • lesbians/ gay men • dancing/DJ • 3 bars w/ various theme nights • karaoke • videos • patio • wheelchair access • cover

Head Hunters Video Lounge & Grill 1930 K St (at 20th St) 916/492–2922 • dinner Tue-Sun, Sun brunch, bar open till 2am • lesbians/ gay men • theme nights • more women Sun 2pm-9pm

Cafes

Mondo Bizarro 1827 I St 916/443–6133 • 7am-7pm, from 8am Sun • live music • WiFi

N Street Cafe 2022 N Street 916/491–4008 • 6am-6pm, 8am-3pm Sat-Sun • WiFi • wheelchair access

RESTAURANTS

Chops 1117 11th St (at L St, across from State Capitol Building) **916/447-8900** • lunch Mon-Fri, dinner nightly • steak & seafood • full bar

Ernesto's 1901 16th St **916/441-5850** • Mexican

Hads Steak & Seafood 1925 J St **916/446-3118** • 11am-9pm, till 10pm Th-Sat, from 5pm Sat, clsd Sun-Mon • lesbian-owned

Hamburger Patties 1630 J St (at 17th) **916/441-4340** • 11am-10pm, from 10am wknds • full bar • karaoke • drag shows • wheelchair access

Hot Rod's Burgers 2007 K St **916/443-7637** • 11am-2am, till 3am Fri-Sat

Ink Eats & Drinks 2730 N St (at 28th) **916/456-2800** • lunch, dinner, late-night brkfst, wknd brunch • full bar • DJ wknds

Jack's Urban Eats 1230 20th St (at Capitol Ave) **916/444-0307** • 11am-8pm, from 5pm wknds

Paesanos 1806 Capitol Ave (at 18th) **916/447-8646** • 11:30am-9:30pm, from noon wknds • Italian • funky artwork • patio • full bar • also 8519 Bond Rd, 916/690-8646

Pizza Rock 1020 K St **916/737-5777** • 11am-10pm, till midnight Wed-Th, till 3am Fri-Sat

Rick's Dessert Diner 2322 K St (btwn 23rd & 24th) **916/444-0969** • 10am-midnight, till 1am wknds, from noon Sun • coffee & dessert

Thai Palace 3262 J St (33rd St) **916/447-5353** • lunch & dinner

Zócalo 1801 Capitol Ave (at 18th St) **916/441-0303** • 11am-10pm • Mexican • full bar

ENTERTAINMENT & RECREATION

Lavender Library, Archives & Cultural Exchange of Sacramento 1414 21st St **916/492-0558** • 4:30pm-8pm Th-Fri, noon-6pm wknds, clsd Mon-Wed

RETAIL SHOPS

Side Show Studios 5635 Freeport Blvd Ste 6 (at Fruitridge) **916/391-6400** • 10am-10pm • tattoo studio • art gallery • reception w/ live music 2nd Sat • lesbian-owned

PUBLICATIONS

Outword Magazine 916/329-9280 • statewide LGBT newspaper w/ Northern & Southern CA editions

EROTICA

G Spot 2009 K St (at 20th) **916/441-3200** • gay-owned

Kiss-N-Tell 4201 Sunrise Blvd (at Fair Oaks) **916/966-5477** • clean, well-lighted erotica store • also 2401 Arden Wy, 916/920-5477

San Bernardino

see also Riverside

INFO LINES & SERVICES

AA Gay/ Lesbian 897 Via Lata, Colton **909/825-4700** • call or visit www.inlandempireaa.org for times

EROTICA

Bearfacts Book Store 1434 E Baseline St **909/885-9176**

San Clemente

see Orange County

San Diego

INFO LINES & SERVICES

Live & Let Live Alano Club 1730 Monroe Ave **619/298-8008** • 10:30am-10pm, from 8:30am wknds • various LGBT meetings (see www.lllac.org)

San Diego LGBT Community Center 3909 Centre St (at University) **619/692-2077** • 9am-10pm, till 7pm Sat, clsd Sun

Women's Resource Center (WRC) 3909 Centre St (at University, in SD LGBT Community Center) **619/692-2077** • variety of resources • health care referrals • social services • community activities

ACCOMMODATIONS

Balboa Park Inn 3402 Park Blvd (at Upas) **619/298-0823, 800/938-8181** • gay-friendly • theme rooms • nonsmoking

Beach Area B&B/ Elsbree House 5054 Narragansett Ave (at Sunset Cliffs Blvd) **619/226-4133, 800/607-4133** • gay-friendly • near beach • nonsmoking

The Bristol Hotel 1055 First Ave **619/232-6141, 800/662-4477** • gay/ straight • hotel • kids ok • restaurant & bar • great collection of pop art • WiFi • wheelchair access

Handlery Hotel & Resort 950 Hotel Circle N 619/298-0511, 800/676-6567 • gay-friendly • pool • hot tub • nonsmoking • kids ok • WiFi • wheelchair access

Inn at the Park 525 Spruce St (btwn 5th & 6th) 619/291-0999, 877/499-7163 • gay-friendly • 1926 hotel • kids ok

Keating House 2331 2nd Ave (at Juniper) 619/239-8585, 800/995-8644 • gay-friendly • Victorian on Bankers Hill • full brkfst • nonsmoking • kids ok • WiFi

Kings Inn Hotel 1333 Hotel Circle S (Bachman St) 619/297-2231, 800/785-4647 • gay/ straight • pool • WiFi • wheelchair access

Lafayette Hotel & Suites 2223 El Cajon Blvd (btwn Louisiana & Mississippi) 619/296-2101, 800/468-3531 • gay-friendly • swimming • kids ok • also restaurant • internet access • nonsmoking • WiFi • wheelchair access

Ocean Inn 1444 N Hwy 101, Encinitas 760/436-1988, 800/546-1598 • gay-friendly • 30 min from downtown San Diego • WiFi • wheelchair access

Porto Vista Hotel 1835 Columbia St 619/544-0164 • gay-friendly • unique European boutique hotel • food served • WiFi

San Diego

LGBT Pride:
July. 619/297-7683, web: www.sdpride.org.

Annual Events:
February - Hillcrest Mardi Gras, web: www.hillcrestmardigras.com.
May- FilmOut San Diego, web: www.filmoutsandiego.com.
August - Hillcrest CityFest Street Fair, web: www.hillcrestassociation.com.

City Info:
San Diego Convention & Visitors Bureau, web: www.sandiego.org.
SanDiego.com, web: www.sandiego.com.

Transit:
Yellow Cab 619/444-4444.
San Diego Cab 619/226-8294.
Silver Cab/Co-op 619/280-5555.
Super Shuttle 800/974-8885, web: www.supershuttle.com.
San Diego Transit System 619/238-0100, web: www.sdmts.com. San Diego Trolley (through downtown or to Tijuana).

Attractions:
Coronado Island (& Hotel Del Coronado), web: www.coronado.ca.us.
Fleet Space Center 619/238-1233, web: www.rhfleet.org.
Hillcrest, web: www.hillquest.com.
Gaslamp Quarter, web: www.gaslamp.org.
Mingei Int'l Museum 619/239-0003, web: www.mingei.org.
La Jolla, web: www.lajollabythesea.com.
The Old Globe Theatre 619/234-5623 (box office), web: www.oldglobe.org.
San Diego Museum of Art 619/232-7931, web: www.sdmart.org.
San Diego Wild Animal Park 760/747-8702, web: www.sandiegozoo.org/wap.
San Diego Zoo 619/231-1515, web: www.sandiegozoo.org.
Sea World 800/257-4268, web: www.seaworld.com.

Best View:
Cabrillo National Monument on Point Loma or from a harbor cruise.

Weather:
San Diego is sunny and warm (upper 60°s-70°s) year-round, with higher humidity in the summer.

The Sofia Hotel 150 W Broadway
619/234-9200, 800/826-0009 • gay/ straight •
kids/ pets ok • wheelchair access

Sunburst Court Inn 4086 Alabama St (at
Polk) 619/294-9665, 866/217-5490 • gay/
straight • all-suite inn • nonsmoking • WiFi •
gay-owned

Bars

Bourbon Street 4612 Park Blvd (at Adams)
619/291-4043 • 4pm-2am • popular • mostly
gay men • mostly women Sun • live shows &
karaoke in front bar • lounge w/ DJ • patio

The Brass Rail 3796 5th Ave (at Robinson)
619/298-2233 • 7pm-2am, from 2pm Fri-Sun,
clsd Tue • lesbians/ gay men • dancing/DJ •
Latin night Sat • wheelchair access

El Camino 2400 India St (at Kalmia, in Little
Italy) 619/685-3881 • dinner nightly, Sun
brunch • kitschy Mexican • live music • full bar

Fiesta Cantina 142 University Ave
619/298-2500 • noon-2am, from 10am wknds
• lesbians/ gay men • Mexican restaurant &
bar

Gossip Grill 1440 University Ave (at Normal)
619/260-8023 • 2pm-close • mostly women •
also restaurant • patio • wheelchair access •
gay-owned

Kickers 308 University Ave (at 3rd Ave, at
Urban Mo's) 619/491-0400 • Th only •
lesbians/ gay men • dancing/DJ • country/
western • dance lessons • wheelchair access

Ladies Night at Bourbon Street 4612 Park
Blvd (at Adams) 619/291-4043 • 8pm Sun
• mostly women

Lis(t)en 1220 University Ave (at the Range)
619/269-1222 • 7pm-midnight Th only •
women's live music

No 1 Fifth Ave (no sign) 3845 5th Ave (at
University) 619/299-1911 • noon-2am •
mostly gay men • neighborhood bar • videos
nights • patio

Redwing Bar & Grill 4012 30th St (at
Lincoln, North Park) 619/281-8700 • 11am-
2am • mostly gay men • neighborhood bar •
patio

Soul Kiss • mostly women • dancing/DJ •
multiracial • weekly hip hop parties • check
soulkisssd.com for details

SRO Lounge 1807 5th Ave (btwn Elm & Fir)
619/232-1886 • 10am-2am • mostly gay men
• cocktail lounge • transgender-friendly

Nightclubs

Inferno/ Hot Flash San Diego 3796 5th Ave
(at Robinson, at Brass Rail) • mostly women
• dancing/DJ • 1st Sat only

Numbers 3811 Park Blvd (at University)
619/294-7583 • popular • mostly gay men •
ladies night Sat • dancing/DJ • karaoke •
theme nights • patio • wheelchair access

Repent 1051 University Ave (at Vermont, at
Rich's) 619/295-2195 (club #) • 10pm Th only
• mostly women • dancing/DJ

Rich's 1051 University Ave (at Vermont)
619/295-2195 • popular • open Wed-Sun •
mostly gay men • ladies night Th • dancing/DJ
• theme nights

Cafes

Babycakes 3766 5th Ave (at Robinson)
619/296-4173 • 9am-11pm, till midnight Fri-
Sat • beer/ wine • patio

The Big Kitchen 3003 Grape St (at 30th)
619/234-5789 • 8am-2pm • wheelchair
access • women-owned

Claire de Lune 2906 University Ave
619/688-9845 • 6am-10pm, till midnight Fri-
Sat

Espresso Roma UCSD Price Center #76 (at
Voight), La Jolla 858/450-2141 • 7am-10pm,
8am-4pm wknds

Extraordinary Desserts 2929 5th Ave
619/294-2132 • also store in Little Italy: 1430
Union, 619/249-7001 • the name says it all

Gelato Vero 3753 India St 619/295-9269 •
7am-midnight • great desserts (yes, the gelato
is truly delicious) & coffee

Twiggs 4590 Park Blvd (at Madison Ave,
University Heights) 619/296-0616 • 7am-
11pm

Restaurants

Adams Avenue Grill 2201 Adams Ave (at
Mississippi) 619/298-8440 • brkfst, lunch &
dinner • bistro • plenty veggie • beer/ wine •
wheelchair access • gay-owned

Arrivederci 3845 4th Ave 619/299-6282 •
lunch & dinner

Bai Yook Thai 1260 University Ave
619/296-2700 • lunch & dinner, dinner only
Sun

Baja Betty's 1421 University Ave (at Normal
St) 619/269-8510 • 11am-midnight, till 1am
Fri-Sat • popular • lesbians/ gay men •
Mexican • some veggie • patio • wheelchair
access

Bamboo Lounge 1475 University Ave (at
Herbert St) 619/291-8221 • 4pm-midnight,
till 1am wknds • sushi

Bangkok Thai Bistro 540 University Ave
619/269-9209 • 11am-10pm, till 11pm Fri-Sat

Brian's American Eatery 1451 Washington St 619/296-8268 • 6:30am-10pm, 24hrs Fri-Sat • beer/ wine

Cafe 222 222 Island Ave 619/236-9902 • 7am-2pm • great brkfst

Celadon 3671 5th Ave (at Pennsylvania) 619/297-8424 • lunch & dinner • upscale Thai

Cody's La Jolla 8030 Girard Ave (at Coast Blvd S), La Jolla 858/459-0040 • brkfst & lunch daily • contemporary California cuisine • live music

The Cottage 7702 Fay (at Klein), La Jolla 858/454-8409 • 7:30am-3pm, dinner June-Sept

Crazee Burger 4201 30th St (at Howard) 619/282-6044 • 11am-9pm, till 11pm Fri, till 10pm Sat • handcrafted burgers

Crest Cafe 425 Robinson (btwn 4th & 5th) 619/295-2510 • 7am-midnight • some veggie • wheelchair access

Hash House A Go Go 3628 5th Ave 619/298-4646 • brkfst, lunch & dinner, clsd Mon • great brkfst

Hillcrest Brewing Company 1458 University Ave 619/491-0400 • first gay brewery in California

Inn at the Park 525 Spruce St (btwn 5th & 6th) 619/296-0057 • popular • dinner nightly • piano bar

Jimmy Carter's Mexican Cafe 3172 5th Ave (at Spruce) 619/295-2070 • 7am-9pm

Kous Kous 3940 4th Ave, Ste 110 (beneath Martinis on Fourth) 619/295-5560 • 5pm-11pm • Moroccan

Lips 3036 El Cajon Blvd 619/295-7900 • 5pm-close, Sun gospel brunch, clsd Mon • "the ultimate in drag dining" • Bitchy Bingo Wed • celeb impersonation Th • DJ wknds

Luna Grill 350 University 619/296-5862 • 11am-10pm • near East & Mediterranean • plenty veggie/ vegan

Martinis Above Fourth 3940 4th Ave, Ste 200 (btwn Washington & University) 619/400-4500 • open 5pm, from 4pm Fri-Sat, clsd Sun • also cabaret lounge • outdoor bar • gay-owned

The Mission 3795 Mission Blvd (at San Jose), Mission Beach 858/488-9060 • 7am-3pm

Ono Sushi 1236 University Ave (at Richmond) 619/298-0616 • lunch wknds, dinner nightly

The Prado 1549 El Prado (in Balboa Park) 619/557-9441 • lunch & dinner • Latin/ Italian fusion

The Range 1220 University Ave 619/269-1222 • lunch & dinner, brkfst wknds

Roberto's 3202 Mission Blvd 858/488-1610 • open 24hrs • the best rolled tacos & guacamole • multiple locations

Rudford's 2900 El Cajon Blvd (at Kansas St) 619/282-8423 • 24hrs • popular homestyle cooking

Saigon on Fifth 3900 5th Ave, Ste 120 619/220-8828 • 11am-3am • Vietnamese

South Park Abbey 1946 Fern St (at Grape St) 619/696-0096 • 3pm-1:30am, from 9am Sat-Sun, till midnight Sun-Mon, clsd Tue

Terra 3900 block of Vermont St (at 10th Ave) 619/293-7088 • lunch & dinner, clsd Mon for dinner

Urban Mo's 308 University Ave (at 3rd) 619/491-0400 • 9am-2am, 10am-midnight Sun • popular • lesbians/ gay men • some veggie • 3 full bars (Club Mo's) • patio • wheelchair access

Veg N Out 3442 30th St (North Park) 619/546-8411 • 11am-9pm, from noon Sun • vegetarian/ vegan

Waffle Spot 1333 Hotel Circle S (at King's Inn) 619/297-2231 • 7am-2pm

West Coast Tavern 2895 University Ave 619/295-1688 • lunch & dinner • upscale • also lounge

ENTERTAINMENT & RECREATION

Diversionary Theatre 4545 Park Blvd #101 (at Madison) 619/220-0097 (BOX OFFICE #), 619/220-6830 • LGBT theater

Ocean Beach I-8 West to Sunset Cliffs Blvd • very dog-friendly

BOOKSTORES

Traveler's Depot 1655 Garnet Ave (btwn Jewell & Ingraham) 858/483-1421 • 10am-6pm, 11am-5pm wknds • guides, maps & more

RETAIL SHOPS

Auntie Helen's 4028 30th St (at Lincoln) 619/584-8438 • 10am-6pm, 11am-5pm Sun-Mon • thrift shop benefits PWAs • wheelchair access

Babette Schwartz 421 University Ave (at 5th Ave) 619/220-7048 • 11am-9pm, till 5pm Sun • campy novelties & gifts • gay-owned

Flesh Skin Grafix 1155 Palm Ave, Imperial Beach 619/424-8983 • tattoos • piercing

Mankind 3425 5th Ave (at Upas St) 619/497-1970 • 11am-10pm, noon-6pm Sun • books, sex toys & videos

Obelisk Shoppe 1037 University Ave (btw 10th & Vermont) **619/297-4171** • 10am-9pm, till 10pm wknds • LGBT • wheelchair access

PUBLICATIONS

Blade California 562/314-7674

The Bottomline 3314 4th Ave 619/291-6690 • bi-weekly • news, entertainment & listings • covers San Diego & Palm Springs

San Diego LGBT Weekly 1850 5th Ave (at Fir) 619/450-4288

San Diego PIX 1010 University Ave 877/727-5446

EROTICA

The Crypt 3847 Park Blvd (at University) 619/692-9499

Pleasures & Treasures Adult/ Leather Shop 2525 University Ave (at Arnold) 619/822-4280 • 11am-11pm, till 6pm Sun • gay-owned

Romantix Adult Superstore 1407 University Ave (at Richmond) 619/299-7186

The Rubber Rose 917 E St. (btwn 9th & 10th) 619/296-7673 • noon-8am, till 6pm Sun-Mon • women-owned sexuality shop

SAN FRANCISCO

San Francisco is divided into 7 geographical areas:
SF—Overview
SF—Castro & Noe Valley
SF—South of Market
SF—Polk Street Area
SF—Downtown & North Beach
SF—Mission District
SF—Haight, Fillmore, Hayes Valley

SF—Overview

INFO LINES & SERVICES

AA Gay/ Lesbian 1821 Sacramento St 415/674-1821 • check www.aasf.org for meeting times

The Center for Sex & Culture 1349 Mission St (btwn 10th & 11th St) 415/902-2071 • very queer-friendly classes, workshops, gatherings, events, readings & more

Crystal Meth Anonymous 415/835-4747

GLBT Hotline of San Francisco 415/355-0999 • 5pm-9pm Mon-Fri • peer-counseling • info

LYRIC (Lavender Youth Recreation/ Information Center) 127 Collingwood (btwn 18th & 19th) 415/703-6150 • peer-run support line for LGBT youth under 24

The San Francisco LGBT Community Center 1800 Market St (at Octavia) 415/865-5555 • noon-10pm, from 9am Sat, clsd Sun • cybercenter • cafe • classes • child care & more

Women's Building 3543 18th St (btwn Valencia & Guerrero) 415/431-1180 • 9am-5pm Mon-Fri, till 6pm Sat • social/ support groups • housing & job listings • beautiful murals

BARS

Thursday Ladies Night with "Betty's List" 415/777-1508 • Th only • mostly women • check bettyslist.com for location

NIGHTCLUBS

Trannyshack • occasional drag events, check trannyshack.com for info

RESTAURANTS

Beach Chalet Brewery & Restaurant 1000 Great Hwy (at Fulton St) 415/386-8439

ENTERTAINMENT & RECREATION

Baker Beach Lincoln Blvd at Bowley, in the Presidio • popular nude beach

Bay Area Derby Girls • SF Bay Area's female roller derby league • visit www.bayareaderbygirls.com for events

Betty's List 415/503-1375 • online & email info service for LGBT community • events • check out www.bettyslist.com • lesbian-owned

Brava! 2781 24th St (btwn York & Hampshire) 415/641-7657 • theater w/ culturally diverse performances by women • wheelchair access

Castro Theatre 429 Castro (at Market) 415/621-6120 • art house cinema • many LGBT & cult classics • live organ evenings

Cruisin' the Castro Tours tour meets at the rainbow flag at Harvey Milk Plaza (corner of Castro & Market) 415/255-1821 • "a TOP city tour & walking w/ pride since 1989! Diverse, fun, informative & NO hills"

Femina Potens 415/864-1558 • nonprofit art & performance promoting women & transfolk in the arts

Frameline 415/703-8650 • LGBT media arts foundation • sponsors annual SF Int'l LGBT Film Festival in June

The Intersection for the Arts 925 Mission St #109 **415/626–2787** • San Francisco's oldest alternative arts space (since 1965!) w/ plays, art exhibitions, live jazz, literary series, performance art & much more

Local Tastes of the City Tours **415/665–0480, 888/358–8687** • explore history & culture of local neighborhoods as "we eat our way through San Francisco"

The Marsh 1062 Valencia (at 22nd St) **415/826–5750, 415/282–3055** • queer-positive theater

➤**National AIDS Memorial Grove** Golden Gate Park (on corner of Middle Drive East & Bowling Green Dr) **415/765–0497, 888/294–7683** • located in a lush, historic dell in Golden Gate Park • guided tours available 9am-noon every 3rd Sat • wheelchair access

QComedy Gay Comedy Showcase **415/533–9133** • see website for locations • popular • lesbians/ gay men • cover charge (sliding scale) • see www.qcomedy.com for location

San Francisco Pride 1800 Market St, PMB #Q31 94102 **415/864–3733** • one of the world's biggest

Steve Silver's Beach Blanket Babylon 678 Beach Blanket Babylon Ave (formerly Green St) (btwn Powell & Columbus, in Club Fugazi) **415/421–4222** • the USA's longest running musical revue & wigs that must be seen to be believed • very popular • 21+ except Sun

Thanks Babs, the Day Tripper **702/370–6961** • tours & getaways • full service concierge for San Francisco & Bay Area • it's like having a lesbian aunt in Northern California!

Theatre Rhinoceros 1360 Mission St #200 **800/838–3006, 415/552–4100** • LGBT theater

Victorian Home Walks **415/252–9485** • custom-tailored walking tours w/ San Francisco resident • gay-owned

Yerba Buena Center for the Arts 701 Mission St (at 3rd St) **415/978–2787** (BOX OFFICE) • annual season includes wide variety of contemporary dance, theater & music • also film theater & gallery

PUBLICATIONS

BAR (Bay Area Reporter) **415/861–5019** • the weekly LGBT newspaper

Bay Times **415/503–1386** • popular • good Bay Area resource listings

SF—Castro & Noe Valley

ACCOMMODATIONS

24 Henry & Village House 24 Henry St (btwn Sanchez & Noe) **415/864–5686, 800/900–5686** • B&B • mostly gay men • some shared baths • nonsmoking • WiFi • gay-owned

Andrew Whelan House **415/621–7736** • gay/ straight • Victorian home & garden • shared baths • nonsmoking • WiFi • gay-owned

Castro Suites 927 14th St (at Noe) **415/437–1783** • gay/ straight • furnished apts • kitchen • nonsmoking • WiFi • gay-owned

Edwardian San Francisco 1668 Market St (btwn Franklin & Gough) **415/864–1271, 888/864–8070** • gay-friendly • hot tub • jacuzzi • some shared baths • nonsmoking

Inn on Castro 321 Castro St (btwn 16th & 17th) **415/861–0321** • lesbians/ gay men • B&B known for its hospitality & friendly atmosphere • full brkfst • nonsmoking • WiFi • gay-owned

The Parker Guest House 520 Church St (at 17th) **415/621–3222, 888/520–7275** • popular • mostly gay men • guesthouse complex w/ gardens • steam spa • nonsmoking • WiFi • gay-owned

The Willows Inn 710 14th St (at Church) **415/431–4770, 800/431–0277** • lesbians/ gay men • "amenities, comfort, great location" • nonsmoking • WiFi • lesbian & gay-owned

BARS

13 Licks 456 Castro St (at Q Bar) **415/864–2877** • 9pm-2am Tue only • popular • mostly women • neighborhood bar • dancing/DJ • sidewalk patio • wheelchair access

440 Castro 440 Castro St **415/621–8732** • noon-2am • popular • mostly gay men • neighborhood bar • leather • bears • women genuinely welcome

Beaux 2344 Market St (at Castro) **415/863–4027** • 2pm-2am • mostly men • dancing/DJ

Blackbird 2124 Market St **415/503–0630** • 3pm-2am • gay/ straight • neighborhood bar • gay-owned

The Cafe 2369 Market St (at Castro) **415/861–3846** • 5pm-2am, from 3pm Sat-Sun • popular • lesbians/ gay men • dancing/DJ • young crowd

San Francisco

LGBT PRIDE:
June. 415/864-0831, web: www.sfpride.org.

ANNUAL EVENTS:
June - San Francisco Int'l Lesbian/Gay Film Festival 415/703-8650, web: www.frameline.org.

September - Folsom Street Fair 415/861-3247, web: folsom-streetevents.org. Huge SM/leather street fair, topping a week of kinky events.

October - Castro Street Fair 415/841-1824, web: www.castrostreetfair.org. Arts and community groups street fair.

CITY INFO:
San Francisco Convention & Visitors Bureau 415/391-2000, web: www.sanfrancisco.travel.

BEST VIEW:
After a great Italian meal in North Beach, go to the top floor of the North Beach parking garage on Vallejo near Stockton, next to the police station. If you're in the Castro or the Mission, head for Dolores Park, at Dolores and 20th St. Other good views: Golden Gate Bridge, Kirby Cove (a park area to the left, just past the Golden Gate Bridge in Marin), Coit Tower, Twin Peaks, Bernal Hill.

WEATHER:
A beautiful summer comes at the end of September and lasts through October. Much of the city is cold and fogged-in June through September, though the Castro and Mission are usually sunny. The cold in winter is damp, so bring lots of layers. When there isn't a drought, it also rains in the winter months of November through February.

TRANSIT:
Yellow Cab 415/333-3333, web: www.yellowcabsf.com.
Luxor Cab 415/282-4141, web: www.luxorcab.com.
Quake City Shuttle 415/255-4899, web: www.quakecityshuttle.com.
511, web: 511.org. Covers all Bay Area transit (also traffic).
Muni 415/673-6864, web: www.sfmuni.org.
Bay Area Rapid Transit (BART) 415/989-2278, subway, web: www.bart.gov.

ATTRACTIONS:
Alcatraz 415/981-7625, web: www.nps.gov/alca/index.htm.
Asian Art Museum 415/ 581-3500, www.asianart.org.
Cablecars.
California Academy of Sciences (adults only on Th eves) 415/ 379–8000, web: www.calacademy.org.
Chinatown.
Coit Tower.
Exploratorium 415/561-0360, web: www.exploratorium.edu.
Fisherman's Wharf & Pier 39 (take the F Car from the Castro down Market & along the Embarcadero to get there).
Golden Gate Park.
Haight & Ashbury Sts.
Japantown.
National AIDS Memorial Grove 415/765-0497, web: www.aidsmemorial.org.
North Beach.
Mission San Francisco de Assisi.
SF Museum of Modern Art 415/357-4000, web: www.sfmoma.org.
Twin Peaks.

Harvey's 500 Castro St 415/431-4278 •
11am-11pm, 9am-2am wknds • popular •
lesbians/ gay men • neighborhood bar •
occasional drag performers • also restaurant •
wheelchair access

Hi Tops 2247 Market St 415/551-2500 •
noon-2am, from 10am Sun • lesbians/ gay
men • food served

The Lookout 3600 16th St (at Market)
415/431-0306 • 3:30pm-2am, from 12:30pm
wknds • mostly gay men • bar food • DJ most
nights

Martuni's 4 Valencia St (at Market)
415/241-0205 • 4pm-2am • gay/ straight •
piano bar & lounge • great martinis

The Mint 1942 Market St (at Buchanan)
415/626-4726 • noon-2am • lesbians/ gay
men • popular karaoke bar nights • also sushi
restaurant • food served till 11pm (till
midnight wknds)

The Mix 4086 18th St 415/431-8616 • 3pm-
2am, from 8am wknds • mostly gay men •
neighborhood bar • heated patio

Moby Dick 4049 18th St (at Hartford) •
2pm-2am, from noon wknds • mostly gay men
• neighborhood bar • videos

Pan Dulce 2369 Market St (at the Cafe)
415/861-3846 • 9pm-2am Th only • lesbians/
gay men • dancing/DJ • Latino/a • "The
Castro's Biggest Latino Party!"

Pilsner Inn 225 Church St (at Market)
415/621-7058 • 10am-2am • popular •
mostly gay men • neighborhood bar • great
patio

Q Bar 456 Castro St 415/864-2877 • 4pm-
2am, from 2pm wknds • popular • mostly gay
men, more women Tue • neighborhood bar •
dancing/DJ • sidewalk patio • wheelchair
access

Swirl 572 Castro St (at 19th) 415/864-2262 •
1pm-8pm, till 9pm Fri-Sat wine bar & wine
store

Cafes

Cafe Flore 2298 Market St (at Noe)
415/621-8579 • 7am-2am • popular •
lesbians/ gay men • some veggie • full bar •
great patio • WiFi

Duboce Park Cafe 2 Sanchez St (at
Duboce) 415/621-1108 • 7am-8pm • outdoor
seating

Eureka! Cafe 451 Castro St 415/355-9110 •
8am-8pm, from 9am wknds * wheelchair
access

Orbit Room Cafe 1900 Market St (at
Laguna) 415/252-9525 • 4pm-2am, till
midnight Sun • also bar

Samovar Tea Lounge 498 Sanchez St (at
18th St) 415/626-4700 • 10am-10pm • tea
culture from around the world

Restaurants

Anchor Oyster Bar 579 Castro St (at 19th)
415/431-3990 • 11:30am-10pm, from 4pm
Sun • lesbians/ gay men • beer/ wine •
women-owned

Catch 2362 Market St 415/431-5000 • lunch
& dinner, wknd brunch • seafood • live music

Chow 215 Church St (at Market)
415/552-2469 • 8am-11pm, till midnight
wknds • popular • patio

Cove Cafe 434 Castro St 415/626-0462 •
8am-9pm, till 10pm Fri-Sat • some veggie •
wheelchair access

Eric's Chinese Restaurant 1500 Church St
(at 27th St) 415/282-0919 • 11am-9pm •
popular

Eureka Restaurant & Lounge 4063 18th St
(at Hartford) 415/431-6000 • dinner nightly •
lounge upstairs

Firewood Cafe 4248 18th St (at Diamond
St) 415/252-0999 • 11am-11pm • rotisserie
chicken, pastas, oven-fired pizzas, salads

Hot Cookie 407 Castro St 415/621-2350 •
11am-1am • hot cookies!

It's Tops 1801 Market St (at Octavia)
415/431-6395 • 8am-3pm daily, 8pm-3am
Wed-Sat • classic diner • great hotcakes

Kasa Indian Eatery 4001 18th St (at Noe)
415/621-6940 • 11am-10pm, till 11pm Fri-Sat
• plenty veggie

La Mediterranée 288 Noe (at Market)
415/431-7210 • 11am-10pm, till 11pm Sat-
Sun • beer/ wine

Mama Ji's 4415 18th St 415/626-4416 •
9:30am-9:30pm, great Dim sum in the Castro

Orphan Andy's 3991 17th St 415/864-9795
• 24hrs • diner • gay-owned

Pesce 2223 Market St 415/928-8025 •
simply prepared fare served Venetian Cichéti
style n• full bar • wheelchair access

Poesia Osteria Italiana 4072 18th St (at
Collingwood) 415/252-9325 • dinner nighly •
Italian • great food & full bar

The Sausage Factory 517 Castro St
415/626-1250 • 11:30am-midnight • lesbians/
gay men • pizza & pasta • some veggie • beer/
wine

Sparky's 242 Church St (at Market) **415/626-8666** • 24hrs • popular late night • diner • some veggie

Takara Sushi 4243 18th St (at Diamond) **415/626-7864** • lunch & dinner, clsd Tue • lesbians/ gay men • cont'l/ Japanese

Thailand Restaurant 438-A Castro St **415/863-6868** • 11am-10pm • plenty veggie

Woodhouse Fish Co 2073 Market St (at 14th) **415/437-2722** • noon-9:30pm • New England clam shack-style seafood

Zuni Cafe 1658 Market St (at Franklin) **415/552-2522** • lunch & dinner, clsd Mon • popular • upscale cont'l/ Mediterranean • full bar

Entertainment & Recreation

Castro Country Club 4058 18th St (at Hartford) **415/552-6102** • alcohol- & drug-free space • cafe

GLBT History Museum 4127 18th St (at Castro) **415/621-1107** • 11am-7pm, noon-5pm Sun, clsd Tue • one of the world's largest collections of GLBT archival materials

Pink Triangle Park near Market & Castro • "in remembrance of LGBT victims of the Nazi regime"

Bookstores

Aardvark Books 227 Church St **415/552-6733** • 10:30am-10:30pm • mostly used • good LGBT section

Books, Inc 2275 Market St **415/864-6777** • 10am-10pm • LGBT section • readings • wheelchair access

Retail Shops

HRC Action Center & Store 575 Castro St **415/431-2200** • 10am-8pm, till 7pm Sun • Human Rights Campaign merchandise & info

Kenneth Wingard 2319 Market St (btwn Castro & Noe) **415/431-6900** • modern & affordable home furnishings, decor & clothing

Rolo 2351 Market St **415/431-4545** • 11am-8pm, till 7pm Sun • designer labels

See Jane Run Sports 3910 24th St (at Noe) **415/401-8338** • 11am-7pm, 10am-6pm Sat, 11am-6pm Sun • women's athletic apparel

Under One Roof 541 Castro **415/503-2300** • 11am-7pm, till 2pm Mon, noon-6pm Sun • 100% donated to AIDS relief • wheelchair access

Gyms & Health Clubs

SF Fitness Castro 2301 Market St **415/348-6377** • day passes available

SF—South of Market

Accommodations

Holiday Inn Civic Center 50 8th St (at Market) **415/626-6103, 877/252-1169** • gay-friendly • pool • small pets ok • WiFi • wheelchair access

The Mosser Hotel 54 4th St (btwn Market & Mission) **415/986-4400, 800/227-3804** • gay/ straight • 1913 landmark hotel • some shared baths • nonsmoking • kids ok • also restaurant • SF cuisine • full bar

The Westin San Francisco Market Street 50 3rd St **415/974-6400, 888/627-8561** • gay-friendly • hip hotel w/ spectacular views • sauna • kids ok • nonsmoking

Bars

Club OMG 43 6th St **415/896-6453** • 6pm-2am • gay bollywood events • gay/ straight • dancing/DJ

The Eagle Tavern 398 12th St (at Harrison) **415/626-0880** • noon-2am • mostly gay men • popular • leather • occasional women's leather events • live music • patio

Hole in the Wall Saloon 1369 Folsom (btwn 9th & 10th) **415/431-4695** • noon-2am • mostly gay men • neighborhood bar • leather

Nightclubs

Asia SF 201 9th St (at Howard) **415/255-2742** • 10pm-close Wed-Sat • popular • gay/ straight • dancing/DJ • mostly Asian American • theme nights • go-go boys • cover charge • also Cal-Asian restaurant w/ en-drag dinner service

BeatBox 314 11th St **415/500-2675** • gay/ straight • dancing/DJ • theme nights

Bootie SF 375 11th St (at Harrison, at DNA Lounge) **415/626-1409 (DNA INFO LINE)** • 9pm-3am Sat, • gay-friendly • dancing/DJ • mashups, bootlegs, bastard pop • cover charge

Cat Club 1190 Folsom St (at 8th) **415/703-8965** • gay/ straight • dancing/DJ • hosts many one-night clubs & events

The Crib SF 715 Harrison St (at 3rd) • 9:30pm-2am Th only • lesbians/ gay men • dancing/DJ • younger crowd • 18+ • cover

Endup 401 6th St (at Harrison) **415/646-0999 (INFO LINE), 415/357-0827** • gay/ straight • dancing/DJ • multiracial • theme nights • popular Sun mornings

Fever 401 6th St (at Harrison, at Endup) • 11pm-11am Fri only • mostly gay men • dancing/DJ

Go BANG! 399 9th St (at The Stud) • 1st Sat only • lesbians/ gay men • underground 70s-80s disco

Honey Soundsystem 1535 Folsom St (at Holy Cow) • Sun only • mostly men • dancing/DJ collective • bears

The Stud 399 9th St (at Harrison) 415/863-6623 • 5pm-2am • popular • lesbians/ gay men • dancing/DJ • theme nights

UHAUL SF 314 11th St (at Beatbox) • mostly women • dancing/DJ • check site for event dates

RESTAURANTS

Ame 689 Mission St (at 3rd St, in St Regis Hotel) 415/284-4040 • lunch & dinner • full bar • reservations recommended

Ananda Fuara 1298 Market St (at 9th) 415/621-1994 • 8am-8pm, till 3pm Wed, clsd Sun • vegetarian

Anchor & Hope 83 Minna St (at 2nd St) 415/501-9100 • lunch Mon-Fri, dinner nightly • seafood

Butter 354 11th St (btwn Folsom & Harrison) 415/863-5964 • 6pm-2am, clsd Mon • "white trash bistro" • full bar • theme nights

Don Ramon's Mexican Restaurant 225 11th St (btwn Howard & Folsom) 415/864-2700 • lunch Tue-Fri, dinner nightly, clsd Mon • some veggie • full bar

Dottie's True Blue Cafe 28 6th St 415/885-2767 • 7:30am-3pm, clsd Tue-Wed • plenty veggie • great brkfst • gay-owned

Fringale 570 4th St (btwn Bryant & Brannan) 415/543-0573 • lunch Tue-Fri & dinner nightly • French bistro • wheelchair access

Rocco's Cafe 1131 Folsom St (at 7th) 415/554-0522 • brkfst & lunch daily, dinner Wed-Sat only

The Slanted Door 1 Ferry Building #3 415/861-8032 • popular • Vietnamese • full bar • reservations recommended

Ted's 1530 Howard St (at 11th) 415/552-0309 • 6am-6pm, 8am-5pm wknds • excellent deli sandwiches

Tu Lan 8 6th St (at Market) 415/626-0927 • lunch & dinner, clsd Sun • Vietnamese • some veggie • dicey neighborhood but delicious (& cheap) food

RETAIL SHOPS

Dandelion 55 Potrero Ave (at Alameda St) 415/436-9500, 888/548-1968 • 10am-7pm, till 6pm Fri-Sat, noon-5pm Sun • gay-owned

Mr S Leather & Fetters USA San Francisco 385 8th St (at Harrison) 415/863-7764, 800/746-7677 • 11am-7pm • erotic goods • custom leather • latex

Stompers 323 10th St (at Folsom) 415/255-6422, 888/BOOTMAN • 11am-6pm, noon-4pm Sun, clsd Mon

GYMS & HEALTH CLUBS

SF Fitness 1001 Brannan St (at 9th) 415/348-6377 • popular • day passes available

EROTICA

Good Vibrations 899 Mission St (at 5th St) 415/513-1635, 800/289-8423 • 10am-9pm, till 10pm Fri-Sat • popular • clean, well-lighted sex toy store • wheelchair access

SF—Polk Street Area

ACCOMMODATIONS

Inn On Broadway 2201 Van Ness Ave (at Broadway) 415/776-7900, 800/727-6239 • gay-friendly • motel • close to Fisherman's Wharf • kids ok • WiFi • wheelchair access • lesbian, gay & straight-owned

The Monarch Hotel 1015 Geary St (at Polk) 415/673-5232, 800/777-3210 • gay-friendly • Edwardian boutique-style hotel • kids ok • nonsmoking rooms available

Nob Hill Motor Inn 1630 Pacific Ave (at Van Ness Ave) 415/775-8160, 800/343-6900 • gay-friendly • hotel • kids ok • nonsmoking • WiFi • wheelchair access

The Phoenix Hotel 601 Eddy St (at Larkin) 415/776-1380, 800/248-9466 • gay-friendly • 1950s-style motor lodge • popular • fave of celebrity rockers • pool • kids ok • WiFi

Radisson Hotel Fisherman's Wharf 250 Beach St (at Hyde) 415/392-6700 • gay-friendly • pool • WiFi • wheelchair access

San Francisco City Center Hostel 685 Ellis St (at Larkin) 415/474-5721 • gay-friendly • shared & private rooms available • free brkfst • kids ok • nonsmoking • WiFi

BARS

The Cinch 1723 Polk St (at Clay) 415/776-4162 • 9am-2am • mostly gay men • neighborhood bar • patio • lots of pool tables & no attitude • DJ Th-Sat • drag shows Fri & Sun • WiFi • wheelchair access

Edinburgh Castle 950 Geary St (at Polk) **415/885-4074** • 5pm-2am • mostly straight Scottish pub w/ single malts & authentic fish & chips • live bands

Gangway 841 Larkin St (btwn Geary & O'Farrell) **415/776-6828** • 8am-2am • mostly gay men • dive neighborhood bar

Lush Lounge 1092 Post (at Polk) **415/771-2022** • 3pm-2am, from noon wknds • gay/ straight • wheelchair access

NIGHTCLUBS

Divas 1081 Post St (at Larkin) **415/474-3482** • 7am-2am • mostly gay men • neighborhood bar • dancing/DJ • multiracial • transsexuals, transvestites & their admirers • drag shows

CAFES

La Boulange de Polk 2310 Polk St (at Green St) **415/345-1107** • 7am-7pm • French bakery & cafe • outdoor seating • Parisian down to the attitude

RESTAURANTS

Lemongrass 2348 Polk St (at Union) **415/929-1183, 415/346-1818** • 11am-10pm, till 10:30pm Fri-Sat • Thai • beer served

Rex Cafe 2323 Polk St **415/441-2244** • dinner from 5:30pm, brunch 10am-3pm wknds • American • full bar

Street 2141 Polk St (btwn Broadway & Vallejo) **415/775-1055** • dinner, clsd Mon • incredible hamburgers

BOOKSTORES

Books Inc Opera Plaza 601 Van Ness Ave (at Turk) **415/776-1111** • 8:30am-9pm • independent • LGBT section • many readings

EROTICA

Glass Kandi 569 Geary St (at Taylor) **415/931-2256** • 4pm-9pm, noon-9pm Sat, till 7pm Sun • glass dildos • women-owned

Good Vibrations 1620 Polk St (btwn Sacramento & Clay) **415/345-0400** • 11am-7pm, till 8pm Th, till 9pm Fri-Sat • clean, well-lighted sex toy store

SF—Downtown & North Beach

ACCOMMODATIONS

Adante Hotel 610 Geary St (at Jones) **415/673-9221, 888/423-0083** • gay/ straight • in Union Square/ Theater District • kids ok • nonsmoking • wheelchair access

Andrews Hotel 624 Post St (btwn Taylor & Jones) **415/563-6877, 800/926-3739** • gay-friendly • Victorian hotel • also restaurant • Italian • nonsmoking • WiFi

Argonaut Hotel 495 Jefferson St (at Hyde) **415/563-0800, 800/790-1415** • gay-friendly • boutique hotel in Fisherman's Wharf • pets ok • nonsmoking • wheelchair access

Dakota Hotel/ Hostel 606 Post St (at Taylor) **415/931-7475** • gay-friendly • near Union Square • kids ok • WiFi

Executive Hotel Vintage Court 650 Bush St (at Powell) **415/392-4666, 888/388-3932** • gay-friendly • nonsmoking • WiFi • also world-famous 5-star Masa's restaurant • French • wheelchair access

Galleria Park Hotel 191 Sutter St (at Kearny) **415/781-3060, 800/792-9639** • gay/ straight • boutique hotel • kids ok • WiFi • nonsmoking • wheelchair access

Grand Hyatt San Francisco 345 Stockton St (at Sutter) **415/398-1234** • gay-friendly • restaurant & lounge • gym

Halcyon Hotel 649 Jones St (at Post) **415/929-8033, 800/627-2396** • gay-friendly • kids/ pets ok • nonsmoking • WiFi • gay & straight-owned/ run

Handlery Union Square Hotel 351 Geary St **415/781-7800, 800/995-4874** • gay-friendly • steps from Union Square • pool • WiFi • wheelchair access

Harbor Court Hotel 165 Steuart St (btwn Howard & Mission) **415/882-1300, 866/792-6283** • gay-friendly • in the heart of the Financial District • gym • pool • pets ok • WiFi • wheelchair access

Hilton San Francisco Financial District 750 Kearny St (at Clay) **415/433-6600, 800/424-8292**

Hotel Adagio 550 Geary St (at Shannon) **415/775-5000, 800/228-8830** • gay-friendly • hotel • kids ok • wheelchair access

Hotel Bijou 111 Mason St (at Eddy) **415/771-1200, 800/771-1022** • gay/ straight • nonsmoking • kids ok • WiFi • wheelchair access

The Hotel California 580 Geary St (at Jones) **415/441-2700, 800/227-4223** • gay-friendly • also popular Millennium gourmet vegetarian restaurant & bar • nonsmoking

Hotel Carlton 1075 Sutter (at Larkin) **415/673-0242, 800/922-7586** • gay-friendly • also Saha restaurant (Arabic-fusion)

Hotel Diva 440 Geary (at Mason) **415/885-0200, 800/553-1900** • gay-friendly • hip hotel • also gym • nonsmoking • WiFi

Hotel Fusion 140 Ellis St (at Powell St) 415/568-2525, 866/753-4244 • gay/ straight • nonsmoking • kids ok • WiFi • wheelchair access

Hotel Griffon 155 Steuart St (at Mission) 415/495-2100, 800/321-2201 • gay/ straight • WiFi • also restaurant • bistro/ cont'l • wheelchair access

Hotel Mark Twain 345 Taylor St (at Ellis) 415/673-2332, 877/854-4106 • gay-friendly • also Fish & Farm restaurant • wheelchair access

Hotel Metropolis 25 Mason St (at Eddy) 415/775-4600, 877/628-4412 • gay-friendly • near Union Square shopping • WiFi

Hotel Monaco 501 Geary St (at Taylor) 415/292-0100, 866/622-5284 • gay-friendly • nonsmoking rooms available • pets ok • also Grand Cafe restaurant (French)

Hotel Nikko San Francisco 222 Mason St (at Ellis) 415/394-1111, 866/645-5673 • gay-friendly • pool • health club & spa • nonsmoking • also restaurant • wheelchair access

Hotel Palomar 12 4th St (at Market) 415/348-1111, 866/373-4941 • gay/ straight • boutique hotel • dogs ok • WiFi

The Hotel Rex 562 Sutter St (at Powell) 415/433-4434, 800/433-4434 • gay-friendly • full bar • wheelchair access

Hotel Triton 342 Grant Ave (at Bush) 415/394-0500, 800/800-1299 • gay/ straight • designer theme rooms • kids/ pets ok • WiFi • wheelchair access

Hotel Union Square 114 Powell St (at Ellis) 415/397-3000, 800/553-1900 • gay-friendly • 1930s art deco lobby • WiFi

Hotel Vitale 8 Mission St (at Steuart) 415/278-3700, 888/890-8688 • gay-friendly • 4-star, full-service waterfront luxury hotel • rooftop spa • restaurant & bar • nonsmoking • WiFi • wheelchair access

Hotel Zetta 55 5th St 415/543-8555 • gay/straight • WiFi • gym & restaurant on-site

Hyatt Regency San Francisco 5 Embarcadero Center (at California) 415/788-1234, 800/233-1234 • gay-friendly • luxury waterfront hotel • WiFi

The Inn at Union Square 440 Post St (at Powell) 415/397-3510, 800/288-4346 • gay-friendly • complimentary breakfast and wine and cheese daily • WiFi

JW Marriott Hotel San Francisco 500 Post St (at Mason) 415/771-8600, 888/236-2427 • gay-friendly • hotel • kids ok • nonsmoking • WiFi • wheelchair access

Kensington Park Hotel 450 Post St 415/788-6400 • gay-friendly • on Union Square • nonsmoking • WiFi • also Farallon Restaurant

King George Hotel 334 Mason St (at Geary) 415/781-5050 • gay/ straight • kids ok • WiFi • wheelchair access

Larkspur Hotel 524 Sutter St (at Powell) 415/421-2865, 866/823-4669 • gay-friendly • B&B-inn on Union Square • afternoon tea • wine hour • WiFi

Luz Hotel 725 Geary St (at Leavenworth) 415/928-1917 • gay/ straight • clothing-optional jacuzzi • gay-owned

Nob Hill Hotel 835 Hyde St (btwn Bush & Sutter) 415/885-2987, 877/662-4455 • gay/ straight • European-style hotel • jacuzzi • nonsmoking • kids ok • also restaurant • wheelchair access

Petite Auberge 863 Bush St (at Taylor) 415/928-6000, 800/365-3004 • gay-friendly • B&B • kids ok • nonsmoking

Prescott Hotel 545 Post St (btwn Taylor & Mason) 415/563-0303, 866/271-3632 • gay-friendly • small luxury hotel • nonsmoking • WiFi

Sir Francis Drake Hotel 450 Powell St (at Sutter) 415/392-7755, 800/795-7129 • gay-friendly • 1928 landmark • also restaurant & Starlight Room • WiFi

The Stratford Hotel 242 Powell St (at Geary) 415/397-7080, 866/688-0038 • gay-friendly • near Union Square

Union Square Plaza Hotel 432 Geary St (at Mason) 415/776-7585, 800/841-3135 • gay-friendly • 1 block from Union Square

Vertigo Hotel 900 Sutter St (at Leavenworth) 415/885-6800, 888/444-4605 • gay/ straight • boutique hotel • nonsmoking • WiFi • wheelchair access

Bars

Aunt Charlie's Lounge 133 Turk St (at Taylor) 415/441-2922 • 10am-midnight, till 2am Fri- Sat • mostly gay men • neighborhood bar • drag shows wknds

Bourbon & Branch 501 Jones St (at O'Farrell) 415/931-7292 • gay/ straight • in Prohibition-era speakeasy • drinks are worth the price • reservations required

CAFES

Caffe Trieste 601 Vallejo St 415/392–6739 • get a taste of the real North Beach (past & present)

Sugar Cafe 679 Sutter St (at Taylor) 415/441–5678 • 10am-2am, from 8am wknds • cafe by day, cocktails by night • food served • WiFi

RESTAURANTS

Ar Roi 643 Post St (at Jones) 415/771–5146 • lunch & dinner, clsd Sun • Thai

The Buena Vista 2765 Hyde St (at Beach) 415/474–5044 • 9am-2am, from 8am wknds • the restaurant that introduced Irish coffee to America

Cafe Claude 7 Claude Ln (near Bush & Kearny) 415/392–3515 • 11:30am-10:30pm, from 5:30pm Sun • live music Th-Sat • as close to Paris as you can get in SF • beer/ wine

Canteen 415/928–8870 • dinner nightly, brkfst wknds

Le Colonial 20 Cosmo Pl (btwn Taylor & Jones) 415/931–3600 • dinner nightly, wknd brunch • Vietnamese • full bar

Golden Era 572 O'Farrell St 415/673–3136 • 11am-9pm, clsd Tue • vegetarian/ vegan

Mario's Bohemian Cigar Store Cafe 566 Columbus Ave (at Union) 415/362–0536 • 10am-close • great foccacia sandwiches • some veggie • beer/ wine • WiFi

Millennium 580 Geary St (at Jones) 415/345–3900 • dinner only • Euro-Mediterranean • upscale vegetarian

ENTERTAINMENT & RECREATION

Rrazz Room 222 Mason (at Nikko Hotel) 415/394–1189, 800/380–3095 • gay/ straight • cabaret w/ world-class performers • wheelchair access

Sunday's A Drag@The Starlight Room 450 Mason St (at Sutter) 415/395–8595 • Sun brunch • noon & 2:30pm drag shows

BOOKSTORES

Book Passage 1 Ferry Bldg #42 415/835–1020 • 10am-8pm, from 8am Sat, 10am-7pm Sun-Mon • independent

City Lights Bookstore 261 Columbus Ave (at Pacific) 415/362–8193 • 10am-midnight • historic beatnik bookstore • many progressive titles • LGBT section • whole floor for poetry

RETAIL SHOPS

Dragonfly Ink 760 Market St #854 (btwn 3rd & 4th St) 415/550–1445 • tattoo studio • woman-owned

Tomboy Tailors 50 Post St 415/652–8440 • a bespoke clothier in San Francisco that caters to butch/boi lesbians, female-to-male transgender individuals & people of any identity who like to don tailored menswear or tailored womenswear

SEX CLUBS

Power Exchange 220 Jones St 415/487–9944 • play space open to hetero, gay, bi, trans, men & women

SF—Mission District

includes Bernal Heights

ACCOMMODATIONS

Elements 2515 Mission St (at 21st St) 415/647–4100, 866/327–8407 • gay/ straight • hostel w/ private or shared rooms • brkfst included • WiFi • also restaurant & cafe

The Inn San Francisco 943 S Van Ness Ave (btwn 20th & 21st) 415/641–0188, 800/359–0913 • gay-friendly • Victorian mansion • hot tub • some shared baths • kitchens • fireplaces • patio • nonsmoking • WiFi

Noe's Nest B&B 1257 Guerrero St (btwn 24th & 25th Sts) 415/821–0751 • gay-friendly • WiFi • nonsmoking • kids ok

BARS

El Rio 3158 Mission St (at Cesar Chavez) 415/282–3325 • 5pm-close Mon-Th, from 3pm wknds • popular • gay/ straight • frequent women's events • neighborhood bar • multiracial • live shows • patio

Esta Noche 3079 16th St (at Mission) 415/861–5757 • 1pm-2am • mostly gay men • dancing/DJ • mostly Latino/a • transgender-friendly • live shows • salsa & disco in a classic Tijuana dive

Lexington Club 3464 19th St (btwn Mission & Valencia) 415/863–2052 • 5pm-2am, from 3pm Fri-Sun • popular • mostly women • neighborhood bar • hip young crowd • lesbian-owned

Lone Palm 3394 22nd St (at Guerrero) 415/648–0109 • 4pm-2am • gay/ straight • a bar for grown ups (we know you're out there)

Nihon 1779 Folsom St (at 14th St) 415/552–4400 • 6pm-close, clsd Sun • gay/ straight • whiskey lounge • dancing/DJ • also Japanese restaurant

Phone Booth 1398 S Van Ness Ave (at 25th) 415/648-4683 • 1pm-2am • lesbians/ gay men • neighborhood/dive bar

Pop's Bar 2800 24th St (btwn York & Bryant) 415/401-7677 • 1pm-2am • gay/ straight • neighborhood dive bar • photobooth • wheelchair access

Truck Bar 1900 Folsom St (at 15th) 415/252-0306 • 4pm-2am, clsd Mon (winter) • mostly gay men • neighborhood bar • food served • gay-owned

Wild Side West 424 Cortland, Bernal Heights (at Wool) 415/647-3099 • 1pm-2am • gay/ straight • neighborhood bar • patio • magic garden • wheelchair access

Zeitgeist 199 Valencia St (at Duboce) 415/255-7505 • 9am-2am • divey biker bar & beer garden • food served

Nightclubs

Hard French 3158 Mission (at El Rio) • 3pm-8pm 1st Sat only • lesbians/ gay men • soul dance party • food served

The Make-Out Room 3225 22nd St (at Mission) 415/647-2888 • 6pm-2am • gay/ straight • dancing/DJ

Mango 3158 Mission (at El Rio) 415/339-8310 • 3pm-8:30pm 4th Sat March-Nov • women only • dancing/DJ • multiracial • food served • cover

Mighty 119 Utah St (at 15th) 415/762-0151 • gay-friendly • dancing/DJ • call for events

Stay Gold 161 Erie St (at Mission, at Public Works) • 10:30pm last Wed only • lesbians/ gay men • dancing/DJ

Sundance Saloon 550 Barneveld Ave (at space550, 2 blocks off Bayshore Blvd at Industrial) 415/820-1403 • 5pm-10:30pm Sun (lessons at 5:30pm) & 6:30pm-10:30pm Th (lessons at 7pm) • lesbians/ gay men • dancing/DJ • country/ western • gay-owned • cover

Cafes

Dolores Park Cafe 501 Dolores St (at 18th St) 415/621-2936 • 7am-8pm • outdoor seating overlooking Dolores Park • live music Fri

Farleys 1315 18th St (at Texas St, Potrero Hill) 415/648-1545 • 6:30am-9:30pm, from 7:30am wknds • coffeehouse • live music some nights

The Revolution Cafe 3248 22nd St (btwn Mission & Bartlett) 415/642-0474 • 9am-1am • live music

Tartine Bakery 600 Guerrero St (at 18th St) 415/487-2600 • 8am-7pm, from 9am Sun • French bakery w/ a line out the door

Restaurants

Aslam's Rasoi 1037 Valencia St (at 21st) 415/695-0599 • 5pm-11pm • Indian & Pakistani

Boogaloos 3296 22nd St (at Valencia) 415/824-4088 • 8am-3pm • worth the wait

Delfina 3621 18th St (at Dolores) 415/552-4055 • 5:30pm-10pm • popular • excellent Tuscan cuisine • full bar • reservations required • patio (summers)

El Farolito 2779 Mission St (at 24th) 415/824-7877 • popular • 10am-3am • delicious, cheap burritos & more

Farina 3560 18th St (at Guerrero) 415/565-0360 • dinner nightly, Sun brunch • Italian

Just For You 722 22nd St (at 3rd St) 415/647-3033 • 7:30am-3pm • popular • lesbians/ gay men • Southern brkfst • some veggie • women-owned

Luna Park 694 Valencia St (at 18th) 415/553-8584 • lunch & dinner, wknd brunch

Maverick 3316 17th St (btwn Mission & Valencia) 415/863-3061 • dinner nightly, also wknd brunch • upscale American • great wine selection

Medjool 2522 Mission St (at 21st St) 415/550-9055 • 5pm-10pm, till 11pm Fri-Sat, clsd Sun • tapas • plenty veggie • also cafe, lounge & rooftop bar • wheelchair access

Moki's Sushi & Pacific Grill 615 Cortland Ave (at Moultrie) 415/970-9336 • dinner nightly

Pauline's Pizza Pie 260 Valencia St (btwn 14th & Duboce) 415/552-2050 • 5pm-10pm, clsd Sun-Mon • popular • lesbians/ gay men • gourmet pizza • beer/ wine

Picaro 3120 16th St (at Valencia) 415/431-4089 • 5pm-10pm, from 9:30am wknds • Spanish tapas bar • beer/ wine • wheelchair access

Pork Store Cafe 3122 16th St (at Valencia) 415/626-5523 • 8am-4pm daily & 7pm-3am Fri-Sat • popular • American/ diner food • great brkfsts • also 1451 Haight St, 415/864-6981

Range 842 Valencia St (btwn 19th & 20th Sts) 415/282-8283 • dinner nightly • popular • California contemporary • full bar

Slow Club 2501 Mariposa (at Hampshire) 415/241–9390 • lunch Mon-Fri, dinner Mon-Sat, wknd brunch • full bar • wheelchair access

ENTERTAINMENT & RECREATION

Dolores "Beach" Church & 19th St (at the top corner of Dolores Park) • popular "beach" in Dolores Park • crowded on sunny days

Women's Building 3543 18th St (btwn Valencia & Guerrero) 415/431–1180 • check out some of the most beautiful murals in the Mission District

BOOKSTORES

Dog Eared Books 900 Valencia St (at 20th) 415/282–1901 • 10am-10pm, till 8pm Sun • new & used • good LGBT section

Modern Times Bookstore 2919 24th St (at Alabama) 415/282–9246

RETAIL SHOPS

Black & Blue Tattoo 381 Guerrero St (at 16th St) 415/626–0770 • noon-7pm • queer-, gender-fluid-, trans- & POC-friendly • women-owned

Body Manipulations 3234 16th St (btwn Guerrero & Dolores) 415/621–0408 • noon-7pm, from 2pm Mon-Th • piercing (walk-in basis) • jewelry

The Scarlet Sage 1173 Valencia St (near 23rd St) 415/821–0997 • 11am-6pm • spiritual & metaphysical emporium • lesbian-owned

EROTICA

Good Vibrations 603 Valencia St (at 17th St) 415/522–5460, 800/289–8423 • 11am-7pm, till 8pm Th, till 9pm Fri-Sat • popular • clean, well-lighted sex toy store • wheelchair access

SF—Haight, Fillmore, Hayes Valley

ACCOMMODATIONS

The Chateau Tivoli B&B 1057 Steiner St (at Golden Gate) 415/776–5462, 800/228–1647 • gay-friendly • historic San Francisco B&B • nonsmoking • WiFi

Hayes Valley Inn 417 Gough St (at Hayes) 415/431–9131, 800/930–7999 • gay/ straight • European-style pension • shared baths • close to opera & symphony • nonsmoking • WiFi

Hotel Del Sol 3100 Webster St (at Greenwich) 415/921–5520, 877/433–5765 • popular • gay/ straight • pool • nonsmoking • wheelchair access • WiFi

Hotel Drisco 2901 Pacific Ave (at Broderick) 415/346–2880, 800/634–7277 • gay-friendly • 1903 hotel in Pacific Heights • kids ok • nonsmoking

Hotel Kabuki 1625 Post St (at Laguna) 415/922–3200, 800/533–4567 • gay-friendly • in the heart of Japantown • wheelchair access

Hotel Majestic 1500 Sutter St (at Gough) 415/441–1100, 800/869–8966 • gay-friendly • one of SF's earliest grand hotels • also restaurant • full bar • kids ok • WiFi • nonsmoking • wheelchair access

Hotel Tomo 1800 Sutter St (at Buchanan) 415/921–4000, 888/822–8666 • gay-friendly • in Japantown • restaurant & bar • nonsmoking • WiFi

Inn at the Opera 333 Fulton St (at Franklin) 415/863–8400, 866/729–7182 • gay-friendly • nonsmoking • WiFi • wheelchair access

Jackson Court 2198 Jackson St (at Buchanan) 415/929–7670 • gay-friendly • 19th-c brownstone mansion • nonsmoking • kids ok • WiFi

The Laurel Inn 444 Presidio Ave (at Sacramento) 415/567–8467, 800/552–8735 • gay-friendly • hotel • in Pacific Heights • nonsmoking • kids/pets ok

Metro Hotel 319 Divisadero St (at Haight) 415/861–5364 • gay-friendly • European-style pension • WiFi

Queen Anne Hotel 1590 Sutter St (at Octavia) 415/441–2828, 800/227–3970 • gay-friendly • wood-burning fireplaces • kids ok • nonsmoking • WiFi • gay-owned • (mention Damron for discount)

San Francisco Fisherman's Wharf Hostel Fort Mason, Bldg 240 (at Franklin) 415/771–7277 • gay/ straight • hostel • shared baths • kids ok • cafe & kitchen • WiFi • nonsmoking • wheelchair access

Shannon-Kavanaugh Guest House 722 Steiner St (at Hayes) 415/563–2727 • gay-friendly • 1-bdrm garden apt in SF's famous "Postcard Row" • kids/ pets ok • nonsmoking • wheelchair access • gay-owned

Stanyan Park Hotel 750 Stanyan St (at Waller) 415/751–1000 • gay-friendly • restored Victorian hotel listed on the Nat'l Register of Historic Places • kids ok • completely nonsmoking • WiFi • wheelchair access

Bars

Rickshaw Stop 155 Fell St (btwn Van Ness & Franklin) 415/861-2011 • Wed-Sat only, Cockblock 2nd Sat • popular hipster bar, nightclub (live bands) & restaurant+

Trax 1437 Haight St (at Masonic) 415/864-4213 • noon-2am • mostly gay men • neighborhood bar

Nightclubs

Cockblock 155 Fell St (at Rickshaw Shop) • 10pm-2am 2nd Sat • queer dance party for lezzies, the happy gays, you & your friends • multiracial

Underground SF 424 Haight St (at Webster) 415/864-7386 • 5:30pm-2am, clsd Mon • gay/ straight • dancing/DJ • alternative • theme nights • call for events • more gay Sat

Cafes

Blue Bottle Coffee Company 315 Linden St (at Gough St) 415/252-7535 • 7am-5pm, from 8am wknds • popular • organic coffee & treats from kiosk in front of artists' workshop— wonderful hidden treat

Restaurants

Absinthe Brasserie & Bar 398 Hayes St (at Gough) 415/551-1590 • lunch & dinner, bar till 2am Fri-Sat, clsd Mon

Alamo Square Seafood Grill 803 Fillmore (at Grove) 415/440-2828 • dinner only

Burma Superstar 309 Clement St 415/387-2147 • lunch & dinner • Burmese food that will rock your world

Cheese Steak Shop 1716 Divisadero St (btwn Bush & Sutter) 415/346-3712 • 9am-10pm, from 11am Sun, from 10am Mon • best cheese steak outside Philly • also veggie versions

Eliza's 2877 California (at Broderick) 415/621-4819 • lunch Mon-Wed, dinner nightly • excellent Chinese food

Ella's 500 Presidio Ave (at California) 415/441-5669 • brkfst & lunch Mon-Fri, popular wknd brunch

Garibaldi's 347 Presidio Ave (at Sacramento) 415/563-8841 • lunch weekdays, dinner nightly • Mediterranean • full bar • wheelchair access • gay-owned

Greens Fort Mason, Bldg A (near Van Ness & Bay) 415/771-6222 • lunch Tue-Sat, dinner Mon-Sat, Sun brunch • gourmet vegetarian • spectacular view of the Golden Gate Bridge

Little Star Pizza 846 Divisadero St (btwn Fulton & McAllister Sts) 415/441-1118 • 5pm-10pm, till 11pm Fri-Sat, clsd Mon • Chicago-style deep dish pizza

Memphis Minnie's BBQ 576 Haight St 415/864-7675 • 11am-10pm, till 9pm Sun, clsd Mon

Nopa 560 Divisadero St (at Hayes) 415/864-8643 • dinner 6pm-1am, bar from 5pm • urban rustic

Park Chow 1238 9th Ave (btwn Irving & Lincoln) 415/665-9912 • 11am-10pm, brunch from 10am wknds • popular • eclectic & affordable

Patxi's Chicago Pizza 511 Hayes St (at Octavia St) 415/558-9991 • 11am-10pm, clsd Mon • Chicago-style deep dish pizza • also thin crust

Pluto's Fresh Food for a Hungry Universe 627 Irving St (btwn 7th & 8th Aves) 415/753-8867 • 11am-10pm • design your own sandwiches

Suppenküche 601 Hayes (at Laguna) 415/252-9289 • dinner, Sun brunch • German cuisine served at communal tables • beer/ wine • gay-owned

Thep-Phanom 400 Waller St (at Fillmore) 415/431-2526 • 5:30pm-10:30pm • popular • excellent Thai food (worth the wait!) • beer/ wine

Bookstores

Bibliohead Bookstore 334 Gough St (at Hayes) 415/621-6772 • eclectic used books • queer section • lesbian-owned

The Booksmith 1644 Haight St 415/863-8688 • cool independent • big-name author readings

Retail Shops

Cold Steel America 1783 Haight St 415/621-7233 • noon-8pm • piercing & tattoo studio

Flight 001 525 Hayes St (btwn Octavia & Laguna) 415/487-1001, 877/354-4481 • 11am-7pm, till 6pm Sun • way cool travel gear

Timbuk 2 Store 506 Hayes St 415/252-9860 • 11am-7pm, noon-6pm Sun, messenger-style bags & backpacks

Gyms & Health Clubs

Kabuki Springs & Spa 1750 Geary Blvd (at Fillmore) 415/922-6000 • 10am-9:45pm • traditional Japanese bath w/ extensive menu of spa sevices

hope
healing
remembrance

Honor a Life Touched by AIDS by Engraving a Name in the Circle of Friends

NATIONAL
·AIDS·
MEMORIAL
GROVE

In 1996, Congress and the President of the United States designated the AIDS Memorial Grove as a national memorial to commemorate all lives touched by AIDS. Located in San Francisco's Golden Gate Park, the National AIDS Memorial Grove is a place of natural beauty and serenity, and home to the Circle of Friends.

The Circle of Friends, engraved in a flagstone terrace near the eastern entrance to the Grove, is surrounded by redwood trees and flowering dogwoods. It is a special place – a place of remembrance. Like the Vietnam Veterans Memorial, the Circle of Friends offers a testament to the individual lives touched by AIDS, making permanent a personal message of love and loss.

By engraving a name in the Circle of Friends, your own, that of someone you honor, love, or miss, you tell the world that this global tragedy must never be forgotten, and that everyone lost to AIDS will be remembered always.

Names are inscribed in November annually, prior to our World AIDS Day national observance on December 1st.

For more information, please call 415-765-0497, or visit www.aidsmemorial.org.

San Jose

INFO LINES & SERVICES

AA Gay/ Lesbian 274 E Hamilton Ave, Ste D, Campbell **408/374-8511** • 24hr helpline • check www.aasanjose.org for meetings

Billy DeFrank LGBT Community Center 938 The Alameda **408/293-3040** • 3pm-9pm, from 10am Wed, clsd Sat-Mon • wheelchair access

ACCOMMODATIONS

Hotel De Anza 233 W Santa Clara St **408/286-1000, 800/843-3700** • gay-friendly • art deco gem • nonsmoking • Italian restaurant • wheelchair access

Moorpark Hotel 4241 Moorpark Ave **408/864-0300, 877/740-6622** • gay-friendly • hotel in heart of Silicon Valley • pool • also bar & restaurant • wheelchair access

BARS

Brix 349 S 1st St (at San Salvadore) **408/947-1975** • 6pm-2am, from 4pm Sun • lesbians/ gay men • neighborhood bar • dancing/DJ • multiracial • transgender-friendly • karaoke • videos • wheelchair access

Mac's Club 39 Post St (btwn 1st & Market) **408/288-8221** • noon-2am • mostly men • neighborhood bar • patio

Renegades 501 W Taylor St (at Coleman Ave) **408/275-9902** • 2pm-2am • mostly gay men • neighborhood bar • leather • patio

NIGHTCLUBS

Hush 65 Post St (at 1st, at Splash) **408/292-2222** • monthly women's dance party

Splash 65 Post St (at 1st) **408/292-2222** • 4pm-2am ,from 3pm Sun • mostly gay men • dancing/DJ • karaoke • videos • gay-owned

RESTAURANTS

Eulipia Restaurant & Bar 374 S 1st St (at San Carlos) **408/280-6161** • dinner only, clsd Mon • eclectic new American • full bar

Pasta Pomodoro 1205 The Alameda (at Race) **408/292-9929** • Italian

Vin Santo 1346 Lincoln Ave **408/920-2508** • dinner nightly, clsd Mon • Northern Italian • wine bar

ENTERTAINMENT & RECREATION

Tech Museum of Innovation 201 S Market St (at Park Ave) **408/294-8324** • 10am-5pm • IMAX Dome Theater • a must-see for digital junkies

EROTICA

Leather Masters 969 Park Ave (at Race St) **408/293-7660** • noon-8pm, clsd Sun-Mon • handmade leather clothes • rubber/ fetishwear • electrical/ medical gear, etc

Pleasures from the Heart 1565 Winchester Blvd, Campbell **408/871-1826** • 11am-10pm, 1pm-7pm Sun • intimate apparel, toys & gifts • women-owned

San Luis Obispo

INFO LINES & SERVICES

GALA/ Gay & Lesbian Alliance of the Central Coast 1060 Palm St (at Santa Rosa St) **805/541-4252** • 8am-noon & 1pm-5pm , clsd wknds

Women's Community Center 1124 Nipomo St **805/544-9313** • counseling • support • referrals

ACCOMMODATIONS

The Madonna Inn 100 Madonna Rd **805/543-3000, 800/543-9666** • gay-friendly • one-of-a-kind theme rooms • food served • pool

The Palomar Inn 1601 Shell Beach Rd, Shell Beach **888/384-4004** • gay/ straight • motel • nonsmoking • WiFi

Sycamore Mineral Springs Resort 1215 Avila Beach Dr **805/595-7302, 800/234-5831** • gay-friendly • hot mineral spring spa • integrative retreat center • also award-winning restaurant

BARS

Fuel Dock 900 Main St, Morro Bay **805/772-8478** • gay-friendly • live music on Sun

Gaslight Lounge 2143 Broad St **805/543-4262** • gay-friendly dive bar

Legends 899 Main St, Morro Bay **805/772-2525** • gay-friendly

The Library 723 Higuera St **805/542-0199** • gay-friendly • dancing/DJ • wheelchair access

CAFES

Linnaea's Cafe 1110 Garden St (near Marsh) **805/541-5888** • 6:30am-11pm • plenty veggie • WiFi • live entertainment

Outspoken Cafe 1422 Monterey St (at California) **805/788-0885** • 7am-5pm, clsd wknds • cafe & juice bar • lesbian-owned

West End Espresso & Tea 670 Higuera St #A (at Nipomo) **805/543-4902, 805/544-3581** • 6:30am-7pm, till 9pm Th, till 8pm Fri-Sat • outdoor seating

Restaurants

Big Sky Cafe 1121 Broad St (btwn Higuera & Marsh Sts) **805/545-5401** • 7am-10pm, 8am-9pm Sun-Th • plenty veggie/ vegan

High Street Deli 350 High St **805/541-4738** • 7am-7pm, 8am-3pm Sun

Novo 726 Higuera St **805/543-3986** • lunch & dinner • great outdoor seating

Vieni Vai 690 Higuera St **805/544-5282** • lunch & dinner, Sun brunch • Italian

Entertainment & Recreation

Pirate's Cove Beach 404 Front St, Avila Beach • gay/ straight • nude beach

Bookstores

Coalesce Bookstore 845 Main St, Morro Bay **805/772-2880** • 10am-5:30pm, 11am-4pm Sun • LGBT section • women-owned

Volumes of Pleasure 1016 Los Osos Valley Rd, Los Osos **805/528-5565** • 10am-6pm, clsd Sun-Mon • wheelchair access • lesbian-owned

Publications

GALA News & Reviews **805/541-4252** • news & events for Central California coast

San Rafael

see Marin County

San Ramon

see East Bay

Santa Ana

see Orange County

Santa Barbara

see also Ventura

Info Lines & Services

Pacific Pride Foundation 126 E Haley St #A–11 **805/963-3636** • 9am-5pm Mon-Fri

Accommodations

Canary Hotel 31 W Carrillo **805/884-0300, 866/999-5401** • gay-friendly

Inn of the Spanish Garden 915 Garden St (at Carrillo) **805/564-4700, 866/564-4700** • gay/ straight • luxury hotel • pool • nonsmoking • kids ok • wheelchair access

Old Yacht Club Inn 431 Corona Del Mar Dr **805/962-1277, 800/676-1676** • gay-friendly • only B&B on beach • full brkfst • nonsmoking • WiFi

The Orchid Inn at Santa Barbara 420 W Montecito St **805/965-2333, 800/427-2156** • gay/ straight • 1900s Queen Anne Victorian • full brkfst • nonsmoking • WiFi • wheelchair access • gay-owned

Bars

Reds Wine Bar 211 Helena Ave **805/966-5906** • 2pm-10pm, till 2am Th-Sat, clsd Mon • food served • live music • WiFi

Nightclubs

Wildcat Lounge 15 W Ortega St **805/962-7970** • gay/ straight • more gay Sun • popular • dancing/DJ

Cafes

Our Daily Bread 831 Santa Barbara St **805/966-3894** • 6am-5:30pm, 7am-4pm Sat, clsd Sun • bakery/ cafe

Restaurants

Joe's Cafe 536 State St **805/966-4638** • 7:30am-11pm

The Natural Cafe 508 State St **805/962-9494** • 11am-9pm

Opal Restaurant & Bar 1325 State St (at Sola St) **805/966-9676** • lunch (Mon-Sat) & dinner nightly • full bar

Sojourner Cafe 134 E Canon Perdido (at Santa Barbara) **805/965-7922** • 11am-10pm, till 11pm Th-Sat • plenty veggie • beer/ wine • wheelchair access

Entertainment & Recreation

Santa Barbara Mission 2201 Laguna St **805/682-4713** • the "queen of the missions" • take a self-guided tour btwn 9am-4:30pm daily & find out why

Bookstores

Chaucer's Books 3321 State St (at Las Positas Rd, Loreto Plaza) **805/682-6787** • 9am-9pm, till 6pm Sun • popular •

Erotica

The Riviera Adult Superstore 4135 State St (at Hwy 154 intersection) **805/967-8282** • 10am-midnight • pride items • community resources

Santa Clara

Accommodations

Avatar Hotel 4200 Great America Pkwy **408/235-8900, 800/586-5691** • gay/ straight • nonsmoking • WiFi • wheelchair access

Biltmore Hotel & Suites 2151 Laurelwood Rd (at Montague Expwy) **408/988-8411, 800/255-9925** • gay-friendly • pool • also restaurant & gym • nonsmoking • WiFi

NIGHTCLUBS

A Tinker's Damn (TD's) 46 N Saratoga Ave
(at Stevens Creek) **408/243–4595** • 3pm-2am,
from 1pm wknds • mostly gay men •
dancing/DJ • drag shows

Santa Cruz

INFO LINES & SERVICES

AA Gay/ Lesbian 5732 Soquel Dr, Soquel
831/475–5782 (AA#) • call or visit
www.aasantacruz.org for meetings

The Diversity Center 1117 Soquel Ave (at
Cayuga) **831/425–5422** • open daily • call for
events • WiFi

ACCOMMODATIONS

Chaminade Resort & Spa 1 Chaminade Ln
(at Soquel Ave) **831/475–5600, 800/283–6569**
• gay-friendly • pool • nonsmoking •
wheelchair access

Dream Inn 175 W Cliff Dr **831/426–4330,
866/774–7735** • gay/ straight • restaurant •
pool & hot tub • WiFi • wheelchair access

BARS

Mad House 529 Seabright Ave (at Murray St)
831/425–2900 • 4pm-2am, clsd Mon • gay/
straight • more gay Th • local bar • drag shows
• gay-owned

NIGHTCLUBS

Blue Lagoon 923 Pacific Ave **831/423–7117**
• 3:30pm-2am • gay-friendly • dancing/DJ •
alternative • transgender-friendly • videos •
live bands • wheelchair access

RESTAURANTS

Betty Burgers 505 Seabright Ave (at Murray)
831/423–8190 • 10am-10pm • retro burger
joint • outdoor seating • some veggie

Cafe Limelight 1016 Cedar St (at Locust St)
831/425–7873 • lunch & dinner, clsd Mon •
European • transgender-friendly • wheelchair
access • gay-owned

Cilantros Mexican Restaurant 1934 Main
St (in Town Center strip mall), Watsonville
831/761–2161 • lunch & dinner

Crêpe Place 1134 Soquel Ave (at Seabright,
across from Rio Theater) **831/429–6994** •
11am-midnight, from 9am Sat-Sun • live
music • full bar • garden patio • wheelchair
access

Saturn Cafe 145 Laurel St (at Pacific)
831/429–8505 • 10am-3am • vegetarian diner
• lesbian-owned

Silver Spur 2650 Soquel Dr **831/475–2725** •
6am-3pm, clsd Sun

ENTERTAINMENT & RECREATION

Bonny Doon Beach Hwy 1 at Bonny Doon
Rd (at milepost 27.6, N of Santa Cruz) • gay/
straight • park in paved parking lot • nude side
of beach to the north

BOOKSTORES

Bookshop Santa Cruz 1520 Pacific Ave
831/423–0900 • 9am-10pm • cafe •
wheelchair access

GYMS & HEALTH CLUBS

Kiva Retreat House Spa 702 Water St (at
Ocean) **831/429–1142** • noon-11pm, till
midnight Fri-Sat • check for women-only &
men-only hours

EROTICA

Frenchy's Cruzin Books & Video 3960
Portola Dr (at 41st Ave) **831/475–9221** •
arcade, adult novelties, lingerie & DVDs

Santa Rosa

see Sonoma County

Saratoga

RETAIL SHOPS

Vine Life 14572-A Big Basin Way
408/872–1500 • 11am-5pm • wine, cards &
gifts

Sausalito

see Marin County

Sebastopol

see also Russian River & Sonoma County

Sonoma County

see also Russian River

INFO LINES & SERVICES

AA Meetings in Sonoma County
707/544–1300 (AA#), 800/224–1300 • call or
visit www.sonomacountyaa.org for meetings

Sonoma County Tourism Bureau
707/522–5800, 800/576–6662

ACCOMMODATIONS

An Inn 2 Remember 171 W Spain St (at
First St W), Sonoma **707/938–2909** • gay-
friendly • located in Wine Country • whirlpool
baths & fireplaces • free use of bikes •
nonsmoking • WiFi

Beltane Ranch 11775 Sonoma Hwy (Hwy
12), Glen Ellen **707/996–6501** • gay-friendly •
1892 New Orleans-style ranch house

Best Western Dry Creek Inn 198 Dry Creek Rd, Healdsburg **707/433-0300, 800/222-5784** • gay/ straight • near wineries • pool, gym steam & sauna • pets ok • WiFi

Camellia Inn 211 North St (at Fitch), Healdsburg **707/433-8182, 800/727-8182** • gay-friendly • Italianate Victorian • full brkfst • pool • nonsmoking • WiFi

The Gaige House 13540 Arnold Dr, Glen Ellen **707/935-0237, 800/935-0237** • gay-friendly • boutique hotel in the Wine Country • pool • WiFi

Grape Leaf Inn 539 Johnson St, Healdsburg **707/433-8140, 866/433-8140** • gay-friendly • Queen Anne Victorian • full brkfst • WiFi

Hyatt Vineyard Creek Hotel 170 Railroad St (at Third St), Santa Rosa **707/284-1234** • gay-friendly • resort • pool • kids/ pets ok • WiFi • seafood restaurant • wheelchair access

Madrona Manor 1001 Westside Rd, Healdsburg **707/433-4231, 800/258-4003** • gay-friendly • full brkfst • pool • nonsmoking • some rooms ok for kids • also restaurant • wheelchair access

Magliulo's Rose Garden Inn 681 Broadway (at Andrieux), Sonoma **707/996-1031** • gay-friendly • WiFi • wheelchair access

Sonoma Chalet 18935 5th St W, Sonoma **707/938-3129, 800/938-3129** • gay-friendly • B&B inn & cottages • hot tub

Sonoma's Best Guest Cottages 1190 E Napa St (at 8th St E), Sonoma **707/933-0340, 800/291-8962** • gay-friendly • vacation cottages • kids/ pets ok • WiFi

CAFES

A' Roma Roasters 95 5th St (Railroad Square), Santa Rosa **707/576-7765** • 6am-close, from 7am Sat-Sun • lesbians/ gay men • live music wknds • wheelchair access • lesbian-owned

Coffee Catz 6761 Sebastopol Ave #300 (in Gravenstein Station), Sebastopol **707/829-6600** • 7am-6pm, till 10pm Wed (open mic), till 10pm Fri-Sat (live bands) • garden • WiFi

Screamin' Mimi's 6902 Sebastopol Ave (intersection of Hwy 12 & 116), Sebastopol **707/823-5902** • espresso drinks & homemade ice cream

Sonoma's Best 1190 E Napa St (at 8th St E), Sonoma **707/996-7600** • 7am-6pm, 8am-5pm Sun • local products—cheese, wine, olive oils & more—all under one roof

RESTAURANTS

Estate 400 W Spain St, Sonoma **707/933-3663** • lunch & dinner, Sun brunch, clsd Mon • Italian

Fig Cafe & Wine Bar 13690 Arnold Dr, Glen Ellen **707/938-2130** • dinner nightly, Sun brunch

Mom's Apple Pie 4550 Gravenstein Hwy N, Sebastopol **707/823-8330** • pie worth stopping for on your way to & from Russian River!

Singletree Inn 165 Healdsburg Ave, Healdsburg **707/433-8263** • 7am-3pm • good brkfsts • famous BBQ sandwiches (including tofu) • some veggie • local wines • outdoor seating • lesbian-owned

Slice of Life 6970 McKinley St, Sebastopol **707/829-6627** • 11am-9pm, from 9am Sat-Sun, clsd Mon • vegan & vegetarian

Syrah Bistro 205 5th St (at Davis), Santa Rosa **707/568-4002** • dinner nightly • California/ French

ENTERTAINMENT & RECREATION

Out In The Vineyard 707/495-9732 • tours of the wine country • gay-owned

River's Edge Kayak & Canoe Company 707/433-7247 • river excursions • lesbian-owned

RETAIL SHOPS

Grower's Collective Tasting Room 707/996-1364 • noon-5:30pm, clsd Tue-Th, open wknds only in winter

Milk & Honey 123 N Main St, Sebastopol 707/824-1155 • 11am-7pm • transgender-friendly • goddess- & woman-oriented crafts • cafe

EROTICA

Secrets Santa Rosa 3301 Santa Rosa Ave (at Todd), Santa Rosa **707/542-8248**

Springville

ACCOMMODATIONS

Great Energy PO Box 473, 93265 **559/539-2382** • lesbians/ gay men • retreat in foothills of Sierra Nevada mtns • pool • hiking • kids ok • woman-owned

Stockton

see also Modesto

NIGHTCLUBS

Paradise Club 10100 N Lower Sacramento Rd (near Grider) **209/477-4724** • 6pm-2am, from 3pm Sun • lesbians/ gay men • dancing/DJ • live shows • young crowd

EROTICA

Suzie's Adult Superstores 3126 E Hammer Ln **209/952-6900** • 24hrs

Sunnyvale

see also San Jose

ACCOMMODATIONS

Wild Palms Hotel 910 E Fremont Ave (at Wolfe Ave) **408/738-0500, 800/538-1600** • gay-friendly • pool • hot tub • kids ok • WiFi • wheelchair access

Temecula

NIGHTCLUBS

Aloha J's 27497 Ynez Rd **951/506-9889** • gay/ straight • more gay Wed • dancing/DJ • also restaurant

Club Velocity 27725 Jefferson Ave Ste 101 (at Johnny G's) **951/506-0399** • 9pm Sun only • lesbians/ gay men • dancing/DJ • also Wed at Aloha J's

Tiburon

see Marin County

Twentynine Palms

see Joshua Tree Nat'l Park

Ukiah

BARS

Perkins St Lounge 228 E Perkins St **707/462-0327** • 3pm-2am • gay-friendly • dancing/DJ • live shows • karaoke

Upland

NIGHTCLUBS

Oasis 1386 E Foothill Blvd #H (at Grove) **909/920-9590** • 6pm-2am Wed-Sat, from 8pm Sun • mostly gay men • dinner served Wed-Sun • dancing/DJ • drag shows • wheelchair access

EROTICA

Sensations Love Boutique 1656 W Foothill Blvd (at Mountain) **909/985-1654**

Vacaville

INFO LINES & SERVICES

Solano Pride Center 1125 Missouri St #203-D, Fairfield **707/398-3463** • call for meeting times

Vallejo

includes Benicia

BARS

Town House Cocktail Lounge 401-A Georgia St (at Marin) **707/553-9109** • 1pm-midnight, from 10am Sat-Sun • gay/ straight • neighborhood bar • gay-owned

BOOKSTORES

Bookshop Benicia 856 Southampton Rd, Benicia **707/747-5155** • 10am-7pm, till 6pm wknds • wheelchair access

Ventura

see also Santa Barbara

INFO LINES & SERVICES

AA Gay/ Lesbian 805/389-1444 (AA#), 800/990-7750

BARS

Paddy McDermott's 2 W Main St (at Ventura) **805/652-1071** • 2pm-2am • lesbians/ gay men • dancing/DJ • food served • live shows • karaoke • beer busts

EROTICA

Three Star Books 359 E Main St **805/653-9068** • 24hrs

Victorville

BARS

Ricky's 13728 Hesperia Rd #12 **760/951-5400** • 6pm-2am, clsd Mon • gay/ straight • dancing/DJ • food served • karaoke • wheelchair access

Walnut Creek

see East Bay

Yosemite Nat'l Park

ACCOMMODATIONS

The Ahwahnee Hotel Yosemite Valley Floor **866/875-8456** (RESERVATIONS) • gay-friendly • pool • non-smoking • also restaurant

Highland House B&B 3125 Wild Dove Ln (at Jerseydale Rd), Mariposa **209/966-3737** • gay-friendly • B&B near Yosemite & Sierra Nat'l Forest • kids ok

The Homestead 41110 Rd 600, Ahwahnee 559/683-0495, 800/483-0495 • gay-friendly • cottages, suite & 2-bdrm house nestled under the oaks on 160 acres • close to restaurants, golf, hiking & biking • kitchens • fireplaces • nonsmoking • WiFi • kids ok

June Lake Villager 2640 Hwy 158 (2.5 miles W of Hwy 395), June Lake 760/648-7712, 800/655-6545 • gay-friendly • 20 minutes from Yosemite • jacuzzi • nonsmoking • kids/pets ok • women-owned

Queen's Inn by the River 41139 Hwy 41, Oakhurst 559/683-4354 • gay/ straight • private patios & decks • some fireplaces • garden w/ river view • nonsmoking • WiFi • wheelchair access • lesbian-owned

Tenaya Lodge at Yosemite 1122 Hwy 41, Fish Camp 559/683-6555, 888/514-2167 • gay-friendly • resort w/ spa services • restaurant • pets ok • pool

Yosemite View Lodge 11136 Hwy 140, El Portal 209/379-2681, 888/742-4371 • gay-friendly • 3 pools • lounge & 2 restaurants • wheelchair access

Yosemite's Apple Blossom Inn B&B 559/642-2001, 888/687-4281 • gay-friendly • B&B • 20 minutes from south entrance of Yosemite Nat'l Park • hot tub • kids/ pets ok nonsmoking • wheelchair access

COLORADO

Aspen

ACCOMMODATIONS

Aspen Mountain Lodge 311 W Main St 970/925-7650, 800/362-7736 • gay-friendly • full brkfst • après-ski wine & cheese • kids/pets ok • hot tub • pool • nonsmoking

Hotel Aspen 110 W Main St 970/925-3441, 800/527-7369 • gay-friendly • mountain brkfst • après-ski wine & cheese • hot tub • pool • nonsmoking • kids/ pets ok

Hotel Lenado 200 S Aspen St 970/925-6246, 800/321-3457 • gay-friendly • full brkfst • hot tub • full bar

St Moritz Lodge 334 W Hyman Ave 970/925-3220, 800/817-2069 • gay-friendly • pool • hot tub/ steam • nonsmoking • WiFi • gay-owned

RESTAURANTS

Jimmy's 205 S Mill St (at Hopkins) 970/925-6020 • 5:30pm-11pm, Sun brunch • also bar from 4:30pm • patio

Syzygy 308 E Hopkins Ave 970/925-3700 • seasonal • 6pm-10pm, bar till 2am • some veggie • live jazz • wheelchair access

BOOKSTORES

Explore Booksellers & Bistro 221 E Main St (at Aspen) 970/925-5336, 800/562-7323 • 10am-10pm • also gourmet vegetarian restaurant • WiFi • wheelchair access

Beaver Creek

ACCOMMODATIONS

Beaver Creek Lodge 26 Avondale Ln (at Village Rd) 970/845-9800, 800/525-7280 • gay-friendly • nonsmoking • also restaurant w/ mtn views & fire pits • pool • WiFi • wheelchair access

Boulder

INFO LINES & SERVICES

Out Boulder 2132 14th St (at Pine) 303/499-5777 • LGBT resource center

ACCOMMODATIONS

The Briar Rose B&B 2151 Arapahoe Ave (at 22nd St) 303/442-3007, 888/786-8440 • gay-friendly • full organic brkfst • nonsmoking • WiFi

CAFES

Walnut Cafe 3073 Walnut St (at 30th) 303/447-2315 • 7am-3:30pm • popular • plenty veggie • patio • wheelchair access • women-owned

ENTERTAINMENT & RECREATION

Boulder Area Bicycle Adventures 303/918-7062 • bike tours of Boulder & annual LGBT ride in June • lesbian-owned

RETAIL SHOPS

Enchanted Ink 1200 Pearl St #35 (at Broadway) 303/440-6611 • tattoos, piercing, henna • lesbian-owned

Colorado Springs

(includes Manitou Springs)

INFO LINES & SERVICES

Colorado Springs Pride Center 719/471-4429 • noon-5pm • call for events • WiFi

ACCOMMODATIONS

Blue Skies Inn B&B 402 Manitou Ave (at Mayfair), Manitou Springs 719/685-3899, 800/398-7949 • gay/ straight • Civil Unions • full brkfst • gazebo hot tub • WiFi • kids ok • wheelchair access

Blue Skies Inn B&B 402 Manitou Ave (at Mayfair), Manitou Springs **719/685-3899, 800/398-7949** • gay/ straight • Civil Unions • full brkfst • gazebo hot tub • WiFi • kids ok • wheelchair access

Old Town Guesthouse 115 S 26th St **719/632-9194, 888/375-4210** • gay-friendly • full brkfst • nonsmoking • WiFi • wheelchair access

Pikes Peak Paradise 236 Pinecrest Rd, Woodland Park **719/687-6656, 800/728-8282** • gay-friendly • mansion w/ view of Pikes Peak • full brkfst • hot tub • fireplaces • nonsmoking • pets/kids ok • WiFi • gay-owned

Two Sisters Inn—A B&B 10 Otoe Pl (at Manitou Ave), Manitou Springs **719/685-9684** • gay-friendly • kids over 10 years ok • full brkfst • women-owned

BARS

Club Q 3430 N Academy Blvd (at N Carefree) **719/570-1429** • 6pm-2am, till 4am Sat, clsd Mon • mostly men • ladies night Sun • neighborhood bar • dancing/DJ • karaoke • live entertainment • strippers • food served • 18+ • wheelchair access • gay-owned

CAFES

Spice of Life an Ingredients Emporium 727 Manitou Ave, Manitou Springs **719/685-5284** • 7am-6pm • WiFi

RESTAURANTS

Dale Street Bistro Cafe 115 E Dale (at Nevada) **719/578-9898** • lunch & dinner, brunch wknds • some veggie • full bar

EROTICA

First Amendment Adult Bookstore 220 E Fillmore St (at Nevada) **719/630-7676**

Denver

INFO LINES & SERVICES

Gay/ Lesbian AA 303/322-4440

The GLBT Center of Colorado (The Center) 1301 E Colfax **303/733-7743** • 10am-8pm Mon-Fri, from noon Sat • extensive resources & support groups • wheelchair access

ACCOMMODATIONS

The Brown Palace 321 17th St (at N Broadway) **303/297-3111, 800/321-2599** • gay-friendly • sun in every room • WiFi • restaurant & spa

Capitol Hill Mansion B&B 1207 Pennsylvania St (at 12th) **303/839-5221, 800/839-9329** • gay-friendly • B&B • full brkfst • hot tub • nonsmoking • kids ok • WiFi

Castle Marne B&B 1572 Race St (at 16th Ave) **303/331-0621, 800/926-2763** • gay-friendly • 1889 mansion on Nat'l Register of Historic Places • hot tubs on private balconies • WiFi

The Curtis-a DoubleTree by Hilton 1405 Curtis St **303/571-0300, 800/525-6651** • gay-friendly • hip hotel • WiFi • also restaurant

Hotel Monaco 1717 Champa St (at 17th) **303/296-1717, 800/990-1303** • gay-friendly • gym • spa • nonsmoking • WiFi • also Italian restaurant • pets ok

The Oxford Hotel 1600 17th St **303/628-5400, 800/228-5838** • gay-friendly • health club & spa • also 2 restaurants, art deco lounge • WiFi

BARS

Aqua Lounge 1417 Krameria (btwn 14th & Colfax) **720/287-0584** • 4pm-2am • lesbians/ gay men • piano bar • WiFi

Barker Lounge 475 Santa Fe Dr (at 5th St) **303/778-0545** • noon-2am • mostly gay men • neighborhood bar • patio w/ bar • dogs welcome

The Beauty Bar **720/542-8024** • 5pm-2am , from 7pm Sat, clsd Sun-Mon • gay/ straight • dancing/DJ • shows

Black Crown Piano Lounge 1446 S Broadway **720/353-4701** • 4pm-midnight, till 2am Fri-Sat, from 11am Sat-Sun • mostly gay men • tapas menu • game room

Broadways 1027 Broadway (at 11th Ave) **303/623-0700** • 2pm-2am, from noon Sat-Sun • lesbians/ gay men • neighborhood bar • cool mix of folk • karaoke • WiFi

Charlie's 900 E Colfax Ave (at Emerson) **303/839-8890** • 11am-2am • popular • mostly gay men • country bar & house music room • dancing/DJ • country/ western • wheelchair access

The Compound/Basix 145 Broadway (at 2nd Ave) **303/722-7977** • 7am-2am • popular • mostly gay men • neighborhood bar • dancing/DJ Fri-Sat

Dazzle 930 Lincoln St (btwn 9th & 10th Aves) **303/839-5100** • from 4pm Sun-Th, from 11am Fri, also Sun brunch • gay-friendly • jazz club & restaurant • live music

Decatur St Bar 800 Decatur St **303/825-4521** • mostly women • neighborhood bar • live music • food served • WiFi

Denver Eagle 3600 Blake St (at 36th) **303/291-0250** • 4pm-2am, from 2pm Sun, clsd Mon • mostly men • bears • never a cover charge • wheelchair access • gay-owned

Eden 3090 Downing St (at 31st Ave) **303/832-5482** • 4pm-2am, from 11am Sun (brunch till 4pm) • mostly women • robust tapas menu • live shows

El Chapultepec 1962 Market St (at 20th) **303/295-9126** • 9am-2am • popular • gay-friendly • live jazz & blues since 1951 • 1-drink minimum per set • cover

El Potrero 4501 E Virginia Ave, Glendale **303/388-8889** • gay/ straight • Mexican restaurant from 3pm• Latino gay bar late, clsd Mon-Tue

R&R Denver 4958 E Colfax Ave (at Elm St) **303/320-9337** • 3pm-2am, from 1pm Fri, from 11am wknds • lesbians/ gay men • neighborhood bar

X Bar 629 E Colfax Ave **303/832-2687** • 3pm-2am, from noon Sun • lesbians/ gay men • dancing/DJ

NIGHTCLUBS

Beta Nightclub 1909 Blake St (btwn 19th & 20th) **303/383-1909** • gay/ straight • more gay Th • dancing/DJ • cover charge

Climax Sunday at Club Vinyl 1082 Broadway **303/832-8628** • 4pm-2am Sun • dancing/DJ • great rooftop patio

Denver

LGBT PRIDE:
June. 303/733-7743, web: www.denverpridefest.org.

ANNUAL EVENTS:
July- 2nd weekend, Rocky Mountain Regional Rodeo (gay rodeo), web: cgra.us.

August/September - AIDS Walk, web: coloradoaidsproject.org.

September/October- Great American Beer Festival, web: www.gabf.org.

CITY INFO:
303/892-1112, web: www.denver.org.

BEST VIEW:
Lookout Mountain (at night especially) or from the top of the Capitol rotunda.

WEATHER:
Summer temperatures average in the 90°s and winter ones in the 40°s. The sun shines an average of 300 days a year with humidity in the single digits.

ATTRACTIONS:
16th Street Mall (pedestrian mall in Lower Downtown or LoDo).

Black American West Museum 720/242-7428, web: www.black-americanwestmuseum.org.

Denver Art Museum 720/865–5000, web: denverartmuseum.org.

Denver Botanic Gardens 720/865-3500, web: www.botanicgardens.org.

Denver Center for the Performing Arts 303/893-4100, web: www.denvercenter.org.

Denver Zoo 303/376-4800, web: www.denverzoo.org.

Downtown Aquarium 303/561-4450.

Elitch Gardens 303/595-4386, web: www.elitchgardens.com.

LoDo (Lower Downtown).

Molly Brown House 303/832-4092, web: www.mollybrown.org.

TRANSIT:
Yellow Cab 303/777-7777, web: www.yellowtrans.com.

Metro Taxi 303/333-3333, web: www.metrotaxidenver.com.

Super Shuttle 800/258-3826, web: www.supershuttle.com.

RTD 303/299-6000, web: www.rtd-denver.com.

First Friday/ Babes Around Denver 3500 Walnut St (at 35th, at Tracks) 303/475–4620 • 6pm-2am, 1st Fri only • mostly women • dancing/DJ

Hip Chicks Out • mostly women • roving monthly • check www.hipchicksout.com

La Rumba 99 W 9th Ave (at Broadway) 303/572–8006 • gay-friendly • salsa dancing & lessons Th & Sat • more gay for Lipgloss Fri (Brit-pop & indie music) • cover

Lannie's Clocktower Cabaret 16th St Mall at Arapahoe (in historic D&F Tower) 303/293–0075 • gay-friendly • upscale cabaret w/ variety of acts weekly, including drag & burlesque

Lipstick 989 Sheridan Blvd 303/482–1003 • 9pm-2am Th-Sat • lesbians/gay men • dancing/DJ

Tracks 3500 Walnut St (at 36th) 303/863–7326 • 9pm-2am, clsd Sun-Wed • gay/ straight • women's night 1st Fri • dancing/DJ • drag shows

Cafes

City, O City 206 E 13th Ave (at Sherman) 303/831–6443 • 7am-2am, from 8am wknds, vegetarian/ vegan • also bar

Common Grounds 1550 17th St 303/296–9248 • 6:30am-10pm, till 9pm Sun

Jelly Cafe 600 E 13th Ave (at Pearl) 303/831–6301 • 7am-3pm • a whole lotta Jelly filled fun

The Market at Larimer Square 1445 Larimer Sq (btwn 14th & 15th) 303/534–5140 • 6am-11pm, till midnight Fri-Sat, till 10pm Sun

Paris on the Platte 1553 Platte St (at 15th) 303/455–2451 • 7am-2am, soups, salads, sandwiches • live music • WiFi

Restaurants

Annie's Cafe & Bar 3100 E Colfax (at St Paul) 303/355–8197 • 7am-10pm, from 8am Sat • popular • diner • popular • some veggie

The Avenue Grill 630 E 17th Ave (at Washington) 303/861–2820 • 11am-11pm, till midnight Fri-Sat, till 10pm Sun

Banzai Sushi 6655 Leetsdale Dr (E of Colorado Blvd) 303/329–3366 • lunch Mon-Fri, dinner nightly

Barricuda's 1076 Ogden St (at E 11th) 303/860–8353 • 10am-2am • also dive bar

Beatrice & Woodsley 38 S Broadway 303/777–3505 • one of America's top restaurants • reservations suggested

Benny's Restaurante y Tequila Bar 301 E 7th Ave (at Grant St) 303/894–0788 • lunch & dinner • patio

The Corner Office Restaurant & Martini Bar 1405 Curtis St (at Curtis Hotel) 303/825–6500 • 6am-midnight, till 2am Fri-Sat • groovy Sun disco brunch

Devil's Food 1020 S Gaylord St (at E Tennessee) 303/733–7448 • 7am-10pm, till 4pm Sun-Mon • yummy desserts

Duo 2413 W 32nd Ave (at Zuni) 303/477–4141 • dinner nightly, wknd brunch • hip, organic, creative American • full bar

Euclid Hall Bar & Kitchen 1317 14th St 303/595–4255 • 11:30am-1am-, till 2am Fri-Sat • American tavern focuses on high quality and innovative pub food

Fruition 1313 E 6th Ave 303/831–1962 • 5pm-10pm, till 8pm Sun • contemporary French

Hamburger Mary's/ Club M 700 E 17th Ave (at Washington St, across from JR's bar) 303/832–1333 • 11am-2am, from 10am Sun • popular • gay/ straight • dancing/DJ • karaoke • drag shows

Il Vicino 550 Broadway 303/861–0801 • 11am-10pm • pizza

Las Margaritas Uptown 1035 E 17th Ave (at Downing) 303/830–2199 • 11am-1am • popular • Mexican • some veggie • also bar • outdoor dining • gay-owned

Racine's 650 Sherman St (at 6th Ave) 303/595–0418 • brkfst, lunch, dinner, late night & Sun brunch • some veggie • full bar

Steuben's 523 E 17th Ave 303/830–1001 • 11am-11pm, till midnight Fri, 10am-midnight Sat • American comfort food served up hip • patio • full bar

Sunny Gardens 6460 E Yale Avenue 303/691–8830 • Chinese • plenty veggie/ vegan

Thai Pot Cafe 1550 S Colorado Blvd (at E Florida) 303/639–6200 • lunch & dinner

Tom's Home Cookin' 303/388–8035 • 11am-3pm, clsd Sat-Sun • Southern comfort food • wheelchair access • gay-owned

Vesta Dipping Grill 1822 Blake St (near 18th St) 303/296–1970 • 5pm-10pm Sun-Th, till 11pm Fri-Sat • upscale

WaterCourse Foods 837 E 17th Ave (at Clarkson) 303/832–7313 • 7am-9pm, till 10pm Fri-Sat • vegetarian/ vegan

Wazee Supper Club 1600 15th St (at Wazee) 303/623–9518, 303/825–3199 (PIZZA DELIVERY) • 11am-2am, noon-midnight Sun • classic comfort food • full bar • wheelchair access

ENTERTAINMENT & RECREATION

Rocky Mountain Rainbeaus 303/863–7739 • all-inclusive, all-levels, high-energy square dance club

Rocky Mountain Rollergirls 720/984–3132 • Denver's female roller derby league • visit www.rockymountainrollergirls.com for events

BOOKSTORES

Tattered Cover Book Store 2526 Colfax Ave (at Elizabeth St) 303/322–7727, 800/833–9327 • 9am-9pm, 10am-6pm Sun • independent • cafe • also 1628 16th St, 303/436–1070 • wheelchair access

PUBLICATIONS

Out Front Colorado 303/778–7900 • statewide bi-weekly LGBT newspaper • since 1976

GYMS & HEALTH CLUBS

Pura Vida Fitness & Spa 2955 E 1st Ave #200 303/321–7872

EROTICA

The Crypt on Broadway 8 Broadway (at Ellsworth) 303/733–3112 • 11am-11pm • leather, clubwear & more

Durango

ACCOMMODATIONS

Leland House B&B 721 E 2nd Ave 970/385–1920 • gay-friendly • full brkfst • nonsmoking • WiFi • wheelchair access

Mesa Verde Far View Lodge 1 Navajo Hill, Mesa Verde National Park 602/331–5210, 800/449–2288 • gay-friendly • camping • RV hookups • inside nat'l park at 8250' elevation • full brkfst • nonsmoking • WiFi

Rochester Hotel 721 E 2nd Ave 800/664–1920 • gay-friendly • popular • newly renovated 1892 house decorated in Old West motif • full brkfst • nonsmoking • kids/pets ok • wheelchair access

RESTAURANTS

Palace Restaurant 505 Main Ave (at 5th St) 970/247-2018 • 11am-10pm, clsd Sun in winter, full bar • patio • gay-owned

Estes Park

ACCOMMODATIONS

Stanley Hotel 333 Wonderview Ave 800/976–1377, 970/577–4000 • gay-friendly • pool • restaurant • WiFi • the inspiration for Stephen King's The Shining

Fort Collins

INFO LINES & SERVICES

Women's Resource Center 424 Pine St #201 970/484–1902 • 9am-5pm Mon-Fri • "helping women lead healthy lives"

ACCOMMODATIONS

Archer's Poudre River Resort 33021 Poudre Canyon Hwy, Bellvue 970/881–2139, 888/822–0588 • gay-friendly • cabins, tents, RV hookups • lesbian-owned

BARS

Choice City Shots 124 LaPorte Ave (at College) 970/221–4333 • 6:30pm-midnight, till 1:30am Th-Sat • lesbians/gay men • neighborhood bar • karaoke Th • wheelchair access • lesbian- & gay-owned

Grand Junction

RESTAURANTS

Leon's Taqueria 505 30th Rd 970/242–1388 • 11am-9pm

Hotchkiss

ACCOMMODATIONS

Leroux Creek Inn & Vineyards 12388 3100 Rd 970/872–4746 • gay-friendly • Southwestern-style adobe on 54 acres • full brkfst

RESTAURANTS

North Fork Valley Restaurant & Thirsty Parrot Pub 140 W Bridge St 970/872–4215 • 11am-8pm • American/Mexican

Pueblo

BARS

Pirate's Cove 105 Central Plaza (off 1st & Union) 719/543–2683 • 4pm-2am, call for Sun hrs, clsd Mon • lesbians/gay men • neighborhood bar • wheelchair access

Stratton

ACCOMMODATIONS

Claremont Inn & Winery 800 Claremont St (off exit 419, I-70) 719/348–5125, 888/291–8910 • gay/ straight • 2 hours from Denver • full brkfst • commitment ceremonies • WiFi • gay-owned

Vail

RESTAURANTS

Larkspur Restaurant & Market 458 Vail Valley Dr (in the Golden Peak Lodge) 970/754–8050 • lunch & dinner • fine dining • also bar • patio • ski-in/ out • wheelchair access

Sweet Basil 193 E Gore Creek Dr 970/476–0125 • lunch & dinner • some veggie • full bar • wheelchair access

Westcliffe

RESTAURANTS

Westcliffe Wine Mine 109 N 3rd St (at Main St) 719/783–2490 • call for hours • older crowd • wheelchair access • lesbian-owned

CONNECTICUT

Bethel

CAFES

Molten Java 213 Greenwood Ave 203/739–0313 • 6am-9pm, till 10pm Fri-Sat, 8am-8pm Sat-Sun • live entertainment • lesbian-owned

RESTAURANTS

Bethel Pizza House 206 Greenwood Ave 203/748–1427 • 11am-11pm, till mid Fri-Sat

Bridgeport

RESTAURANTS

Bloodroot Restaurant & Bookstore 85 Ferris St (at Harbor Ave) 203/576–9168 • lunch Tue & Th-Sat, dinner Tue-Sat, brunch only Sun, clsd Mon • feminist vegetarian • patio • wheelchair access • women-owned

EROTICA

Romantix Adult Superstore 410 North Ave 203/332–7129

Bristol

EROTICA

Amazing Superstore 167 Farmington Ave 860/582–9000

Colebrook

ACCOMMODATIONS

Rock Hall Luxe Lodging 19 Rock Hall Rd 860/379–2230 • gay/ straight • resort-style lodging in an Addison Mizner manor house & estate • pool • nonsmoking • WiFi

Danbury

ACCOMMODATIONS

Maron Hotel & Suites 42 Lake Ave Extension (off I-84) 203/791–2200, 866/811–2582 • gay-friendly • kids/ pets ok • WiFi • wheelchair access

BARS

Triangles Cafe 66 Sugar Hollow Rd, Rte 7 203/798–6996 • 5pm-1am, till 2am Fri-Sat • popular • lesbians/ gay men • 1st & 3rd Fri ladies night • dancing/DJ • live shows • karaoke • patio • gay-owned

RESTAURANTS

Sesame Seed 68 W Wooster St 203/743–9850 • lunch & dinner, clsd Sun, Mediterranean/ Italian • funky decor • plenty veggie

Thang Long 56 Padanaram Rd (near North Street Shopping Center) 203/743–6049 • lunch & dinner • Vietnamese • bring your own bottle

Enfield

EROTICA

Bookends 44 Enfield St/ Rte 5 860/745–3988

Hartford

INFO LINES & SERVICES

Hartford Gay & Lesbian Health Collective 1841 Broad St (at New Britain Ave) 860/278–4163 • 9am-5pm, till 9pm Th, clsd wknds

True Colors 30 Arbor St (at Capital Ave) 860/232–0050, 888/565–5551 • support & mentoring for LGBT youth

ACCOMMODATIONS

Butternut Farm 1654 Main St, Glastonbury 860/633–7197 • gay/ straight • 18th-c house furnished w/ antiques • full brkfst • WiFi

Inn at Kent Falls 107 Kent Cornwall Rd, Kent 860/927–3197 • gay/ straight • 1 hr from Hartford • pool • kids ok • nonsmoking • WiFi • wheelchair access • gay-owned

The Mansion Inn 139 Hartford Rd (at Main St), Manchester 860/646–0453 • gay-friendly • B&B • full brkfst • in-room fireplaces

BARS

Chez Est 458 Wethersfield Ave (at Main St) **860/525–3243** • 3pm-1am, till 2am Fri-Sat • popular • lesbians/gay men • dancing/DJ • food served • karaoke • drag shows

Polo 678 Maple Ave (btwn Preston & Mapleton) **860/278–3333** • 9pm-1am, till 2am Fri-Sat, clsd Sun-Wed • lesbians/gay men, Th ladies night • dancing/DJ • karaoke • drag shows

CAFES

Tisane Tea & Coffee Bar 537 Farmington Ave (at Kenyon) **860/523–5417** • 8am-1am, till 2am Sat • food served • karaoke • WiFi • also bar • women's night 1st Sun

RESTAURANTS

Arugula 953 Farmington Ave, West Hartford **860/561–4888** • lunch & dinner, clsd Mon • Mediterranean • reservations recommended • wheelchair access

Firebox 539 Broad St **860/246–1222** • 11:30am-10:30pm, 4:30pm-8:30pm Sun • contemporary American • also farmers market Th (April-Oct)

Peppercorns Grill 357 Main St **860/547–1714** • lunch Mon-Fri, dinner nightly, clsd Sun • Northern Italian

Pond House Cafe 1555 Asylum Ave, W Hartford **860/231–8823** • lunch & dinner Tue-Sat, wknd brunch • bring your own bottle • patio • wheelchair access

Trumbull Kitchen 150 Trumbull St (at Pearl St) **860/493–7417** • lunch Mon-Sat, dinner nightly • global cuisine/tapas

ENTERTAINMENT & RECREATION

Real Art Ways 56 Arbor St **860/232–1006** • contemporary art • cinema • performance • also lounge • WiFi

RETAIL SHOPS

MetroStore 493 Farmington Ave (at Sisson Ave) **860/231–8845** • 8:30am-8pm, till 5:30pm Tue, Wed & Sat, clsd Sun • magazines • travel guides • DVD rentals • leather & more

PUBLICATIONS

Metroline **860/233–8334** • regional newspaper & entertainment guide • covers CT, RI & MA

EROTICA

Very Intimate Pleasures 100 Brainard Rd (exit 27, off I-91) **860/246–1875**

Mystic

ACCOMMODATIONS

House of 1833 B&B Resort 72 N Stonington Rd **860/536–6325, 800/367–1833** • gay-friendly • full brkfst • pool • kids ok • nonsmoking • WiFi • gay-owned

The Mare's Inn B&B 333 Colonel Ledyard Hwy, Ledyard **860/572–7556** • gay-friendly • full brkfst • nonsmoking • wheelchair access • lesbian-owned

Mermaid Inn of Mystic 2 Broadway **860/536–6223, 877/692–2632** • lesbians/gay men (all welcome) • B&B w/ village location & river views • full brkfst • kids ok • nonsmoking • WiFi • lesbian-owned

The Old Mystic Inn 52 Main St (at Rte 27), Old Mystic **860/572–9422** • gay-friendly • full brkfst • nonsmoking • WiFi • gay-owned

New Haven

INFO LINES & SERVICES

New Haven Pride Center 14 Gilbert St, West Haven **203/387–2252** • events • meetings • resources • library • movies • wheelchair access

ACCOMMODATIONS

Linden Point House 30 Linden Point Rd, Stony Creek **203/481–0472** • gay-friendly • WiFi • kids/pets ok

Omni New Haven Hotel at Yale 155 Temple St (at Chapel) **203/772–6664, 800/843–6664** • gay-friendly • WiFi • wheelchair access

BARS

168 York St Cafe 168 York St **203/789–1915** • 3pm-1am, till 2am Fri-Sat • lesbians/gay men • also restaurant • dinner Mon-Sat, Sun brunch • patio • gay-owned

The Bar 254 Crown St (at College) **203/495–8924** • 11:30am-1am, from 5pm Mon-Tue • gay/straight • more gay Tue • dancing/DJ • pizza • wheelchair access

Partners 365 Crown St (at Park St) **203/776–1014** • 5pm-1am, till 2am Fri-Sat, from 8pm Mon-Tue & Sat-Sun • lesbians/gay men • dancing/DJ • karaoke

NIGHTCLUBS

Gotham Citi Cafe 169 East St **203/498–2484** • 9pm-4am, clsd Sun-Wed • gay/straight • more gay Sat • 18+ • dancing/DJ • drag shows • wheelchair access

Connecticut • USA

CAFES

Atticus Bookstore/ Cafe 1082 Chapel St (at York St) 203/776-4040 • 7am-9pm

RESTAURANTS

116 Crown 116 Crown St 203/777-3116 • upscale tapas • great mixed drinks

Beachhead 3 Cosey Beach Ave, East Haven 203/469-5450 • 4pm-close, from 1pm Sun • seafood • Italian • patio • live music

Bentara 76 Orange St 203/562-2511 • lunch Mon-Sat, dinner nightly • Malaysian • plenty veggie

Claire's Corner Copia 1000 Chapel St (at College St) 203/562-3888 • 8am-9pm, till 10pm Fri-Sat • vegetarian • WiFi • wheelchair access

Mezcal 14 Mechanic St (at Lawrence) 203/782-4828 • lunch Tue-Sun, dinner nightly • authentic Mexican

Miya Sushi 58 Howe St (at Chapel St) 203/777-9760 • lunch & dinner, clsd Sun-Mon

Soul de Cuba 238 Crown St 203/498-2822 • lunch & dinner • full bar

EROTICA

Very Intimate Pleasures 170 Boston Post Rd, Orange 203/799-7040

New London

BARS

Frank's Place 9 Tilley St (at Bank) 860/442-2782 • 4pm-1am, till 2am Fri-Sun • mostly gay men • dancing/DJ • live shows • food served • karaoke • patio • wheelchair access

O'Neill's Brass Rail 52 Bank St 860/443-6203 • noon-1am, till 2am Fri-Sat • mostly gay men • karaoke • drag shows • WiFi

Norwalk

INFO LINES & SERVICES

Triangle Community Center 16 River St (at Elm St) 203/853-0600 • activities • newsletter • call for info

Westport

ENTERTAINMENT & RECREATION

Sherwood Island State Park Beach left to gay area

Rehoboth Beach

INFO LINES & SERVICES

Camp Rehoboth Community Center 37 Baltimore Ave 302/227-5620 • 9am-5:30pm Mon-Fri, 10am-4pm wknds • drop-in community center • support groups • magazine w/ extensive listings • HIV testing & counseling

Gay & Lesbian AA 302/856-6452 • noon Th

Narcotics Anonymous 37 Baltimore Ave (at Camp Rehoboth center) 302/227-5620 • 5:30pm Sun

ACCOMMODATIONS

At Melissa's B&B 36 Delaware Ave (btwn 1st & 2nd) 302/227-7504, 800/396-8090 • gay/ straight • 1 block from beach • nonsmoking • WiFi • women-owned

Bellmoor Inn 6 Christian St (at Delaware) 866/227-5800, 800/425-2355 • gay-friendly • upscale inn & spa • pool

Bewitched & BEDazzled B&B 67 Lake Ave (at Rehoboth Ave) 302/226-3900, 866/732-9482 • gay/ straight • hot tub • nonsmoking • WiFi • wheelchair access • lesbian-owned

Breakers Hotel & Suites 105 2nd St (at Olive) 302/227-6688, 800/441-8009 • gay-friendly • pool • kids/ pets ok • wheelchair access

Cabana Gardens B&B 20 Lake Ave (at 3rd St) 302/227-5429 • gay/ straight • lake & ocean views • deck • pool • nonsmoking • gay-owned

Canalside Inn Canal at 6th 302/226-2006, 866/412-2625 • gay/ straight • pool • hot tub • WiFi • nonsmoking • wheelchair access • gay-owned

The Homestead at Rehoboth B&B 35060 Warrington Rd (at Old Landing Rd) 302/226-7625 • gay-friendly • small dogs ok • nonsmoking • WiFi • wheelchair access • lesbian-owned

Lazy L at Willow Creek 16061 Willow Creek Rd (at Hwy 1), Lewes 302/644-7220 • gay/ straight • full brkfst • pool • hot tub • very pet friendly • WiFi • lesbian-owned

The Lighthouse Inn B&B 20 Delaware Ave (at 1st St) 302/226-0407 • seasonal • gay/ straight • also apt (weekly rental) • nonsmoking • kids/ pets ok • gay-owned

Rehoboth Guest House 40 Maryland Ave (btwn 1st & 2nd Sts) 302/227-4117, 800/564-0493 • lesbians/gay men • near boardwalk & beach • nonsmoking • WiFi • gay-owned

Silver Lake Guest House 20388 Silver Lake Dr (at Robinson Dr) 302/226-2115, 800/842-2115 • lesbians/gay men • near Poodle Beach • nonsmoking • lakefront • ocean views • WiFi • gay-owned

Summer Place Hotel 30 Olive Ave (at 1st) 302/226-0766, 800/815-3925 • gay/straight • also apts • near beach

BARS

The Blue Moon 35 Baltimore Ave (btwn 1st & 2nd) 302/227-6515 • 6pm-2am, clsd Jan • popular • lesbians/gay men • live music • drag shows • also restaurant

Dogfish Head Brewings & Eats 320 Rehoboth Ave (at 4th) 302/226-2739 • gay-friendly • micro-brewery • wood-grilled food • live music wknds

Double L Bar 622 Rehoboth Ave (at Church) 302/227-0818 • 4pm-2am • open year round • mostly gay men • dancing/DJ • leather • bears • patio

Finbar Pub & Grill 316-318 Rehoboth Ave (at 4th) 302/227-1873 • from 3pm, from noon Fri-Sun, clsd Mon-Tue • gay-friendly • popular happy hour

Frogg Pond 3 S 1st St (near Rehoboth Ave) 302/227-2234 • 11am-1am • gay-friendly • neighborhood bar • food served • karaoke • live music

Rigby's Bar & Grill 404 Rehoboth Ave (at State St) 302/227-6080 • 3pm-1am, from 10am Sun

NIGHTCLUBS

Ladies 2000 856/869-0193 • seasonal parties • call hotline for details

CAFES

The Coffee Mill 127B Rehoboth Ave 302/227-7530 • 7am-11pm, till 5pm (off-season) • WiFi • lesbian-owned

Lori's Cafe 39 Baltimore Ave (at 1st) 302/226-3066 • seasonal, call for hours • also sandwiches • courtyard • lesbian-owned

RESTAURANTS

Aqua Grill 57 Baltimore Ave 302/226-9001 • seasonal • deck • full bar

Back Porch Cafe 59 Rehoboth Ave 302/227-3674 • lunch & dinner • Sun brunch • seasonal • live shows • full bar • wheelchair access

Big Sissies Bar & Grill 37385 Rehoboth Ave 302/226-7600 • 3pm-1am

Buttery 102 2nd St, Lewes 302/645-7755 • lunch, dinner, Sun brunch • fine dining in elegant Victorian • reservations suggested

Cafe Sole 44 Baltimore Ave 302/227-7107 • lunch daily, dinner Wed-Sun • casual • patio • also full bar

Cloud 9 234 Rehoboth Ave (at 2nd) 302/226-1999 • 4pm-2am • popular bar • fusion bistro • also bar • wheelchair access

The Cultured Pearl 301 Rehoboth Ave (2nd flr) 302/227-8493 • dinner only • pan-Asian/ sushi • cocktail lounge

Dos Locos 208 Rehoboth Ave (across from Fire Company) 302/227-3353 • 11:30am-10pm, till 11pm Fri-Sat • popular • Mexican • full bar

Eden 23 Baltimore Ave 302/227-3330 • dinner Tue-Sun • seasonal • wine list & martini bar • wheelchair access

Espuma 28 Wilmington Ave 302/227-4199 • 5pm-10pm, clsd Mon • modern Mediterranean • full bar

Fins 243 Rehoboth Ave 302/226-3467 • dinner nightly, lunch Sat-Sun • fish house • raw bar

Go Fish! 24 Rehoboth Ave 302/226-1044 • 11:30am-9:30pm (in-season) • authentic British fish & chips

Hobos Restaurant & Bar 56 Baltimore Ave 302/226-2226 • from 11am (in-season)

Iguana Grill 52 Baltimore Ave 302/727-5273 • lunch & dinner (summers) • Southwestern • full bar • patio

JD's Filling Station 329 Savannah Rd, Lewes 302/644-8400 • 8am-2:30pm & 5pm-9pm, clsd Tue for dinner

Jerry's Seafood 108 2nd St, Lewes 302/645-6611 • lunch & dinner daily • "home of the crab bomb"

Mariachi 302/227-0115 • 11am-9pm, till 11pm Fri-Sat • Mexican-Latin American • wheelchair access

Planet X Cafe 35 Wilmington Ave 302/226-1928 • seasonal, lunch, dinner, Sun brunch • organic global cuisine • kitschy decor housed in converted Victorian

Purple Parrot Grill 134 Rehoboth Ave 302/226-1139 • lunch & dinner daily, brunch Sun • karaoke & drag shows wknds • wheelchair access

Seafood Shack 42 1/2 Baltimore Ave (at 1st St) **302/227–5881** • patio seating • live music wknds

ENTERTAINMENT & RECREATION

Cape Henlopen State Park Beach 42 Cape Henlopen Dr, Lewes **302/645–8983** • 8am-sunset

Gordon Pond State Park/ North Shores S end of Cape Henlopen State Park (at jetty S of watch tower) • popular women's beach • 20-minute walk from boardwalk • by car follow the shoreline road to State Park entrance

Poodle Beach S of boardwalk at Queen St • popular gay beach

Rehoboth Beach

LGBT PRIDE:
Every day, but Wilmington has their pride here in September.

ANNUAL EVENTS:
July - Fireworks 302/227-2772, web: www.rehomain.com/down-town-happenings/july-4th-fire-works.htm.

October - Rehoboth Beach Autumn Jazz Festival, web: www.rehobothjazz.com.

October - Sea Witch Halloween Festival, web: www.beach-fun.com.

November - Rehoboth Beach Independent Film Festival 302/645-9095, web: www.rehobothfilm.com.

CITY INFO:
Rehoboth Beach-Dewey Beach Chamber of Commerce 302/227-2233 & 800/441-1329, web: www.beach-fun.com..

WEATHER:
You're not far from DC, but you're on the coast. So, yes, it does get hot and muggy in the summers (90s for temps and humidity), but you can take a dip in the ocean. In the winter, a lot of businesses close as the temperatures drop along with the occasional snow flurries.

ATTRACTIONS:
Anna Hazzard Museum, 302/226-1119. Photos & memorabilia from when Rehoboth was a Christian resort.

DiscoverSea Shipwreck Museum, Fenwick Island, 302/539-9366, web: discoversea.com.

Dolphin- & whale-watching July-Oct. Boat tours leave from Fisherman's Wharf in Lewes, DE. 302/645-8862, web: www.fish-lewes.com/sightseeing.html.

Main Street 302/227-2772, web: www.rehomain.com.

Rehoboth Beach Boardwalk with 2 amusement parks (Funland, web: www.funlandRehoboth.com, & Playland).

Tanger Outlets, web: www.tanger-outlet.com. 130 designer stores with no sales tax.

BEST VIEW:
Watching the sun rise over the bay at Dewey Beach or eating a swanky sunset dinner at Victoria's (www.boardwalkplaza.com/rehoboth-beach-hotel-dining) on the Boardwalk

TRANSIT:
Seaport Taxi 302/645-6800.

Jolly Trolley 302/227-1197 (seasonal tour & shuttle), web: www.jollytrolley.com.

Cape May-Lewes Ferry (80-minute ferry ride between N Cape May, NJ & Lewes, DE), 800/643-3779, web: www.capemaylewesferry.com.

BOOKSTORES

Proud Bookstore 149 Rehoboth Ave (at Village of the Sea Shops) 302/227-6969

RETAIL SHOPS

Leather Central 36983 Rehoboth Ave 302/227-0700 • leather uniforms, toys, accessories

PUBLICATIONS

Letters from Camp Rehoboth 302/227-5620 • newsmagazine w/ events & entertainment listings

GYMS & HEALTH CLUBS

Midway Fitness 34823 Derrickson Dr 302/645-0407

Wilmington

NIGHTCLUBS

Crimson Moon Tavern 1909 W 6th St (at Union St) 302/654-9099 • 6pm-2am, from 7pm Sat, clsd Sun-Tue • mostly gay men • dancing/DJ • videos

RESTAURANTS

Eclipse 1020 Union St 302/658-1588 • lunch Mon-Fri, dinner nightly • upscale

The Green Room 11th & Market St (at Hotel Dupont) 302/594-3154 • brkfst, lunch & dinner, Sun brunch • full bar • live music

Mrs Robino's 520 N Union St (at Pennsylvania) 302/652-9223 • 11am-9pm, till 10pm Fri-Sat • family-style Italian • full bar • wheelchair access

DISTRICT OF COLUMBIA

Washington

INFO LINES & SERVICES

Triangle Club 202/659-8641 • site for various 12-step groups • call for times

ACCOMMODATIONS

Beacon Hotel & Corporate Quarters 1615 Rhode Island Ave NW (at 17th) 202/296-2100, 800/821-4367 • gay-friendly • restaurant & bar • wheelchair access

The Carlyle Suites Hotel 1731 New Hampshire Ave NW (btwn R & S Sts) 202/234-3200, 800/964-5377 • gay/ straight • WiFi • gym • also restaurant & bar • popular gay Sun brunch • wheelchair access

Donovan House 1155 14th St NW (at Massachusetts Ave NW) 202/737-1200 • gay/ straight • stylish hotel • rooftop bar

Embassy Suites Hotel at the Chevy Chase Pavilion 4300 Military Rd NW (at Wisconsin) 202/362-9300 • gay-friendly • pool • gym • wheelchair access

Grand Hyatt Washington 1000 H St NW 202/582-1234 • gay-friendly • pool • also restaurant & lounge • nonsmoking • WiFi • wheelchair access

Hamilton Crowne Plaza Hotel 14th & K St, NW 202/682-0111, 800/263-9802 • gay-friendly • offers a special women's floor, catering to the female business traveler • kids/ pets ok • wheelchair access

Hotel George 15 E St NW 202/347-4200, 800/546-7866 • gay-friendly • WiFi • pets ok

Hotel Helix 1430 Rhode Island Ave NW 202/462-9001, 800/706-1202 • gay-friendly • full-service boutique hotel • also Helix Lounge • nonsmoking • WiFi • wheelchair access

Hotel Monaco Washington DC 700 F St NW (at 7th) 202/628-7177, 800/649-1202 • gay-friendly • boutique hotel • kids/ pets ok • WiFi • wheelchair access

Hotel Palomar 2121 P St NW (at 21st St) 202/448-1800, 866/866-3070 • gay-friendly • in Dupont Circle • gym • WiFi • pool • restaurant • wheelchair access

Hotel Rouge 1315 16th St NW (at Rhode Island) 202/232-8000, 800/738-1202 • gay-friendly • • kids/ pets ok • also restaurant & bar • WiFi • wheelchair access

Kalorama Guest House 2700 Cathedral Ave NW (off Connecticut Ave) 202/328-0860, 800/974-9101 • gay/ straight • near Nat'l Zoo & Washington Cathedral • nonsmoking • WiFi

Morrison-Clark Historic Hotel & Restaurant 1015 L St NW (at Massachusetts Ave NW) 202/898-1200, 800/322-7898 • gay-friendly • hotel in 2 Victorian town houses • very popular restaurant • WiFi

The River Inn 924 25th St NW (at K St) 202/337-7600, 888/874-0100 • gay-friendly • suites w/ kitchen • gym • WiFi • also Dish + Drinks restaurant • wheelchair access

Savoy Suites Hotel 2505 Wisconsin Ave NW (near Georgetown) 202/337-9700, 800/944-5377 • gay-friendly • also restaurant • WiFi • wheelchair access

Topaz Hotel 1733 N St NW (at Massachusetts Ave NW) 202/393-3000, 800/775-1202 • gay-friendly • boutique hotel • kids/ pets ok • also restaurant & bar • WiFi • wheelchair access

BARS

The Black Cat 1811 14th St NW (at the Black Cat) **202/667-4490** • gay/ straight • many queer events • live music • dance parties • also cafe

DC Eagle 639 New York Ave NW (btwn 6th & 7th) **202/347-6025** • 4pm-2am, till 3am Fri-Sat, 2pm-2am Sun • popular • mostly gay men • leather • wheelchair access

DIK Bar/ Windows 1637 17th St NW (at R St NW, upstairs) **202/328-0100** • 4pm-2am • mostly gay men • aka Dupont Italian Kitchen • dancing/DJ • karaoke • older crowd

The Fireplace 2161 P St NW (at 22nd St) **202/293-1293** • 1pm-2am, till 3am Fri-Sat • mostly gay men • neighborhood bar • multiracial • videos • wheelchair access

JR's 1519 17th St NW (at Church) **202/328-0090** • 2pm-2am, till 3am Fri, 1pm-3am Sat, 1pm-2am Sun • popular • mostly gay men • neighborhood bar • food served • videos • young crowd

Lace Restaurant & Lounge 2214 Rhode Island Ave NE **202/832-3888** • lunch & dinner, clsd Mon, club from 6pm-3am Fri-Sat, till midnight Sun • upscale women's bar • mostly African American • lesbian-owned

Larry's Lounge 1840 18th St NW (at T St) **202/483-1483** • 4pm-1am, till 2am Fri-Sat • lesbians/ gay men • neighborhood bar • patio • wheelchair access • gay-owned

Mova 2204 14 St NW **202/797-9730** • 5pm-3am • mostly gay men

Mr Henry's Capitol Hill 601 Pennsylvania Ave SE (at 6th St) **202/546-8412** • 11:30am-11:30pm • gay-friendly • multiracial • also restaurant • nonsmoking • wheelchair access

Nellie's Sports Bar 900 U St NW (at 9th) **202/332-6355** • 5pm-midnight, 3pm-2am Fri, from 11am wknds • mostly gay men

Number Nine 1435 P St NW (at 15th St NW) **202/986-0999** • 5pm-close • lesbians/ gay men • neighborhood bar

Phase 1 525 8th St SE (btwn E & G Sts) **202/544-6831** • 7pm-2am, till 3am Fri-Sat (clsd Mon-Tue winter) • mostly women • oldest lesbian bar in the US! • neighborhood bar • dancing/DJ • karaoke • shows • multiracial • wheelchair access

POV Roof Terrace Bar 515 15th Street NW (at Alexander Hamilton Pl) **202/661-2400** • 11am-2am • gay-friendly • pricey cocktails • superior views of the White House & Lincoln Memorial • tapas served

Wisdom 1432 Pennsylvania Ave SE **202/543-2323** • 6pm-12:30, till 3am Fri-Sat, till 10pm Sun • clsd Mon • gay/ straight • bar food served

NIGHTCLUBS

Bachelors Mill 1104 8th St SE (downstairs at Back Door Pub) **202/546-5979** • 11pm-3am Th-Sat only • lesbians/ gay men • popular • dancing/DJ • mostly African American • live shows • karaoke • wheelchair access

Bare 1639 R St NW (at 17th, at Cobalt) **202/232-4416** • 10pm 3rd Sat only • mostly women • dancing/DJ

Chief Ike's Mambo Room 1725 Columbia Rd NW (at Ontario Rd) **202/332-2211** • 4pm-2am, till 3am Fri, 6pm-3am Sat gay-friendly • dancing/DJ • food served• wheelchair access

Cobalt/ 30 Degrees Lounge 1639 R St NW (at 17th) **202/232-4416** • 5pm-2am, till 3am Fri-Sat • mostly gay men • dancing/DJ • live shows • drag shows • videos

Delta Elite 3734 10th St NE (at Perry St NE, in Brookland) **202/529-0626** • midnight-4am Fri-Sat only • ladies night Fri • dancing/DJ • mostly African American

Mixtape • 2nd Sat only • alternative queer dance party • venue changes, check mixtapedc.com for info

Phase 1 of Dupont 1415 22nd St NW (btwn O & P Sts) **202/544-6831** • 9pm-2am Th, till 3am Fri-Sat, clsd Sun-Wed• lesbians/ gay men • young crowd • wheelchair access • cover

She Rex 1725 Columbia Rd NW (at Ontario Rd, at Chief Ike's) **202/332-2211** • 2nd Fri only • mostly women • dancing/DJ • queer party featuring all music by women • wheelchair access

Town Danceboutique 2009 8th St NW (at U St NW) **202/234-8696** • 9pm-4am Fri-Sat • popular • mostly gay men • dancing/DJ • bears Fri • drag shows • 18+ Fri

CAFES

Cosi 1647 20th St NW **202/332-6364** • 7am-11pm, till midnight Fri-Sat, 8am-10pm Sun • full bar from 4pm • popular • make your own s'mores • WiFi

Hello Cupcake 1361 Connecticut Avenue NW **202/861-2253** • 10am-7pm, till 9pm Fri-Sat, 11am-6pm Sun • cupcakes!

Jolt 'n' Bolt 1918 18th St NW (at Florida) **202/232-0077** • 7am- 8:30pm • popular • patio

Soho Tea & Coffee 2150 P St NW (at 21st St) 202/463-7646 • 7am-1am, till 2am wknds• WiFi • food served • patio • wheelchair access

RESTAURANTS

18th & U Duplex Diner 2004 18th St NW (at Ave U) 202/265-7828 • 6pm-11pm, till 12:30am Tue-Wed, till 1:30am Fri-Sat • American comfort food • full bar

2 Amys Pizza 3715 Macomb St NW 202/885-5700 • lunch & dinner Tue-Sun, dinner only Mon • wheelchair access

Acadiana 901 New York Ave NW 202/408-8848 • lunch Mon-Fri, dinner nightly, brunch Sun • Cajun • great bourbon selection • reservations recommended

Annie's Paramount Steak House 1609 17th St NW (at Corcoran) 202/232-0395 • 10am-11:30pm, till 1am Th & Sun, 24hrs Fri-Sat • popular • full bar • wheelchair access

Banana Cafe & Piano Bar 500 8th St SE (at E St) 202/543-5906 • 11am-10:30pm, till 11pm Fri-Sat • Puerto Rican/ Cuban food • some veggie • famous margaritas • gay-owned

Bar Pilar 1833 14th St NW (at Swann St) 202/265-1751 • dinner nightly, Sun brunch • new American

Beacon Bar & Grill 1615 Rhode Island Ave NW (at 17th, at Beacon Hotel) 202/872-1126 • brkfst, lunch & dinner • popular Sun brunch • patio

Washington

LGBT PRIDE:

June. 202/719-5304, web: www.capitalpride.org.

May. Black Lesbian/ Gay Pride, web: www.dcblackpride.org.

ANNUAL EVENTS:

March - Women's History Month at various Smithsonian Museums 202/633-5330, web: www.smithsonianeducation.org.

October - Reel Affirmations Film Festival, web: www.reelaffirmations.org.

CITY INFO:

DC Convention & Tourism Corporation. 202/789-7000, web: www.washington.org.

WEATHER:

Summers are hot (90°s) and MUGGY (the city was built on marshes). In the winter, temperatures drop to the 30°s and 40°s with rain and sometimes snow. Spring is the time of cherry blossoms

ATTRACTIONS:

Ford's Theatre 202/347-4833, web: www.fords.org.

Jefferson Memorial.

JFK Center for the Performing Arts 800/444-1324, web: www.kennedy-center.org.

Lincoln Memorial.

National Gallery 202/737-4215, web: www.nga.gov.

National Museum of Women in the Arts 202/783-5000, web: www.nmwa.org.

National Zoo 202/633-4800, web: nationalzoo.si.edu.

Smithsonian 202/633-5330, web: www.smithsonianeducation.org.

Vietnam Veteran's Memorial.

United States Holocaust Memorial Museum 202/488-0400, web: www.ushmm.org.

BEST VIEW:

From the top of the Washington Monument..

TRANSIT:

Yellow Cab 202/544-1212, web: www.dcyellowcab.com.

Washington Flier 703/661-6655 (from Dulles or Ronald Reagan National).

Super Shuttle 800/258-3826.

Metro Transit Authority 202/637-7000, web: www.wmata.com.

Busboys & Poets 2021 14th St NW (at V St) **202/387-7638** • 8am-midnight, till 2am Fri-Sat, 10am-midnight Sun • also bookstore • live jazz & poetry • WiFi • wheelchair access

Cafe Japoné 2032 P St NW (at 21st) **202/223-1573** • 6pm-1:30am, till 2:30am Fri-Sat • mostly Asian American • full bar • live jazz Wed • karaoke

Cafe La Ruche 1039 31st St **202/965-2684** • dinner, Sun brunch • French • patio

Cafe Saint Ex/ Gate 54 1847 14th St NW **202/265-7839** • lunch, dinner, Sun brunch • modern American • also Gate 54 club downstairs • popular Th dance party • gay-friendly

Dupont Italian Kitchen & Bar 1637 17th St NW (at R St) **202/328-3222, 202/328-0100** • 11am-11pm, bar 4pm-2am • some veggie • wheelchair access

Floriana 1602 17th St NW (at Q St NW) **202/667-5937** • dinner nightly • Italian • full bar • patio • gay-owned

Food For Thought 1811 14th St NW (at the Black Cat) **202/667-4490** • 8pm-1am, 7pm-2am Fri-Sat • gay-friendly • mostly vegan/veggie • also live music • readings • indie/punk • young crowd • wheelchair access

Guapo's 4515 Wisconsin Ave NW (at Albemarle) **202/686-3588** • lunch & dinner • Mexican • some veggie • full bar • wheelchair access

Jaleo 480 7th St NW (at E St) **202/628-7949** • lunch & dinner • tapas • full bar • Sevillanas dancers Wed • wheelchair access

Java Green Eco Cafe 1020 19th St NW **202/775-8899** • 8am-8pm, 10am-6pm Sat, clsd Sun • organic cafe • plenty veggie/ vegan

Level One 1639 R St NW (at 17th) **202/745-0025** • dinner nightly, wknd brunch

Logan Tavern 1423 P St NW **202/332-3710** • lunch & dinner, wknd brunch • American comfort food • also bar • gay-owned

Occidental Grill 1475 Pennsylvania Ave NW (btwn 14th & 15th) **202/783-1475** • lunch Mon-Sat, dinner nightly, clsd Sun • upscale • political player hangout

Perry's 1811 Columbia Rd NW (at 18th) **202/234-6218** • 5:30pm-10:30pm, till 11:30pm wknds, popular drag Sun brunch • contemporary American & sushi • full bar • roof deck

Pizza Paradiso 2003 P Street NW **202/223-1245** • 11am-11pm, till midnight wknds • Gluten-Free Crust

Posto 1515 14th St NW **202/332-8613** • dinner nightly • terrific Italian

Rasika 633 D St NW **202/637-1222** • lunch Mon-Fri, dinner Mon-Sat, clsd Sun • Indian • wheelchair access

Rice 1608 14th St NW (at 'Q') **202/234-2400** • lunch & dinner • Thai

Rocklands 2418 Wisconsin Ave NW (at Calvert) **202/333-2558** • 11am-10pm, till 9pm Sun • BBQ & take-out

Sala Thai 1301 U St NW (at 13th) **202/462-1333** • lunch & dinner • some veggie

Smoke & Barrell 2471 18th St NW **202/319-9353** • beer, bbq & bourbon

Soul Vegetarian Exodus 2606 Georgia Ave NW **202/328-7685** • 11am-9pm, till 3pm Sun (brunch) • all-vegan menu • no frills

Thaitanic 1326 14th St NW (at Rhode Island Ave) **202/588-1795** • lunch & dinner • Thai • plenty veggie

Zaytinia 701 9th Street NW (at G St) **202/638-0800** • lunch & dinner • Greek/Mediterranean • plenty veggie

ENTERTAINMENT & RECREATION

Anecdotal History Tours 301/294-9514 • gay-friendly • variety of guided tours • by appt only

Bike & Roll Washington DC 1100 Pennsylvania Ave NW (off 12th St, at Old Post Office Pavilion) **202/842-2453** • 9am-6pm • tour the nation's capital on bike!

Capital Bikeshare 877/430-2453 • look for the red bikes at parking stations around the city • join for 24hrs or longer

Hillwood Museum & Gardens 4155 Linnean Ave NW (at Tilden St NW) **202/686-5807** • 10am-5pm Tue-Sat • Fabergé, porcelain, furniture & more • reservations required

National Museum of Women in the Arts 1250 New York Ave **202/783-5000, 800/222-7270**

Phillips Collection 1600 21st St NW (at Q St) **202/387-2151** • clsd Mon • America's first museum of modern art • near Dupont Circle

Washington Mystics 202/266-2277, 877/324-6671 • check out the Women's Nat'l Basketball Association while you're in DC

BOOKSTORES

G Books 1520 U St NW, BSMT (btwn 15th St & U St) **202/986-9697** • 4pm-10pm • used gay books, mags, movies • pride items • gay-owned

Kramerbooks & Afterwords Cafe & Grill 1517 Connecticut Ave NW (at Q St) 202/387-1400 • 7:30am-1am, 24hrs wknds • also cafe & bar • live music • wheelchair access

RETAIL SHOPS

HRC Action Center & Store 1633 Connecticut Avenue NW 202/232-8621 • 10am-9pm, till 10pm wknds • Human Rights Campaign merchandise & info

Leather Rack 1723 Connecticut Ave NW (btwn R & S Sts) 202/797-7401

Pulp 1803 14th St NW 202/462-7857 • 11am-7pm, till 5pm Sun • cards • gifts • music

Universal Gear 1529 14th St NW (btwn P & Q) 202/319-0136 • 11am-10pm, till midnight Fri-Sat • casual, club, athletic & designer clothing

PUBLICATIONS

Metro Weekly 202/638-6830 • LGBT newsmagazine • extensive club listings

Washington Blade 202/747-2077 • LGBT newspaper

GYMS & HEALTH CLUBS

Washington Sports Club 1835 Connecticut Ave NW (at Columbia & Florida) 202/332-0100

EROTICA

Pleasure Place 1063 Wisconsin Ave NW, Georgetown (btwn M & K Sts) 800/386-2386 • 10am-10pm, till midnight Wed-Sat, noon-7pm Sun • wheelchair access

FLORIDA

Statewide

PUBLICATIONS

Ambush Mag 504/522-8047 • LGBT newspaper for the Gulf South (TX through FL)

HOTSPOTS! Magazine 954/928-1862 • "South Florida's largest gay publication"

She Magazine, "The Source for Women" 954/354-9751 • "The hippest & hottest source for women of the rainbow community"

Boynton Beach

see also West Palm Beach

Bradenton

see Sarasota

Clearwater

see also Dunedin, New Port Richey, Port Richey & St Petersburg

ACCOMMODATIONS

Holiday Inn Select 3535 Ulmerton Rd (Rte 688 W) 727/577-9100, 888/465-4329 • gay-friendly • pool • restaurant & lounge • wheelchair access • WiFi

BARS

Pro Shop Pub 840 Cleveland St (at Prospect) 727/447-4259 • 1pm-2am • popular • mostly gay men • neighborhood bar • bears • gay-owned

RETAIL SHOPS

Skinz 2027 Gulf to Bay Blvd (aka State Rd 60, at Hercules Rd) 727/441-8789 • 10am-6pm, clsd Sun • men's & women's swimwear, gymwear & clubwear

Cocoa

BARS

The Ultra Lounge 407 Brevard Ave, Cocoa Village 321/690-0096 • 6pm-2am, from 4pm wknds • mostly gay men • neighborhood bar

Daytona Beach

ACCOMMODATIONS

The August Seven Inn 1209 S Peninsula Dr (at Silver Beach) 386/248-8420 • gay-friendly • 1 block from ocean • full brkfst • WiFi

Mayan Inn 103 S Ocean Ave 386/252-2378, 800/329-8622 • gay-friendly • pool • kids ok • WiFi • wheelchair access

The Villa B&B 801 N Peninsula Dr 386/248-2020 • gay-friendly • hot tub • pool • nudity • nonsmoking • gay-owned

BARS

Streamline Lounge 140 S Atlantic Ave (at Streamline Hotel) 386/258-6937 • 11am-3am (penthouse lounge) • gay-friendly • dancing/DJ • live entertainment • game room

CAFES

Java Joint & Eatery 2201-E N Oceanshore Blvd, Flagler Beach 386/439-1013 • 7am-4pm

RESTAURANTS

Anna's Trattoria 304 Seabreeze Blvd 386/239-9624 • 5pm-10pm, clsd Sun-Mon • Italian • beer/ wine

The Clubhouse 600 Wilder Blvd (at Daytona Beach Golf & Country Club) 386/257-0727 • 6am-7:30pm

Frappes North 123 W Granada Blvd (at S Yonge St), Ormond Beach **386/615-4888** • lunch Tue-Fri, dinner nightly, clsd Sun • patio • full bar • wheelchair access

Sapporo 501 Seabreeze Ave **386/257-4477** • lunch Mon-Fri, dinner nightly • Japanese steak house & sushi bar • full bar

Publications

Watermark 407/481-2243 • bi-weekly LGBT newspaper for Central FL

Dunedin

see also St Petersburg

Nightclubs

Blur Nighclub 325 Main St 727/736-0206 • 8pm-2am, clsd Sun-Mon • mostly gay men • dancing/DJ • karaoke • drag shows

Fort Lauderdale

Info Lines & Services

Lambda South Inc 1306 E Las Olas Blvd • meeting space for LGBT in recovery • wheelchair access

The Pride Center at Equality Park 2040 N Dixie Hwy, Wilton Manors **954/463-9005** • 10am-10pm, noon-5pm wknds • outreach • wheelchair access

Accommodations

Alhambra Beach Resort 3021 Alhambra St **954/525-7601, 877/309-4014** • gay/ straight • motel • close to gay beach • pool • nonsmoking • WiFi • gay-owned

Blue Lagoon Resort 3801 N Ocean Blvd **954/565-6666, 800/663-2985** • gay-friendly • pool • WiFi • gay-owned

Courtyard Fort Lauderdale 440 Seabreeze Blvd **954/524-8733, 888/821-1366** • gay-friendly • pool • sundeck bar • nonsmoking

The Deauville Hotel 2916 N Ocean Blvd (Oakland Park Blvd & A1A) **954/568-5000** • gay-friendly • pool • non-smoking • wheelchair access

Ed Lugo Resort 2404 NE 8th Ave (Wilton Manors) **954/275-8299** • gay-friendly • pool • WiFi • gay-owned

Island Sands Inn 2409 NE 7th Ave **954/990-6499** • gay/ straight • pool • WiFi • gay-owned

Marriott Harbor Beach Resort 3030 Holiday Dr **954/525-4000, 800/222-6543** • gay-friendly • pool • also restaurant & spa • private beach access

The Royal Palms Resort & Spa 717 Breakers Ave **954/564-6444, 800/237-7256** • mostly gay men • nonsmoking • WiFi • gay-owned

Windamar Beach Club 533 Orton Ave **954/563-7062, 888/243-3454** • lesbians/ gay men • pool • WiFi • pets ok

Bars

Beach Betty's 625 Dania Beach Blvd (at Fronton Blvd), Dania **954/921-9893** • noon-3am • mostly women • neighborhood bar • dancing/DJ • live music • karaoke • lesbian-owned

Bill's 2209 Wilton Dr (off NE 23rd St) **954/567-5978** • 2pm-2am, till 3am Fri-Sat, from noon Sat-Sun • neighborhood bar • drag shows • karaoke • wheelchair access

Cloud 9 Lounge 7126 Stirling Rd, Davie **954/499-3525** • 7am-4am, from noon Sun • mostly women • multiracial clientele • live shows • drag shows • live bands

The Drive 2390 Wilton Dr **954/561-9000** • 11am-2am, till 3am Fri-Sat • mostly gay men • food served

Georgie's Alibi 2266 Wilton Dr (at NE 4th Ave) **954/565-2526** • 11am-2am, till 3am Fri-Sat • lesbians/ gay men • nonsmoking • food served • videos • WiFi • wheelchair access

Infinity Lounge 2184 Wilton Dr **754/223-3619** • 3pm-2am, mostly gay men

J's Bar 2780 Davie Blvd **954/581-8400** • 9am-2am, till 3am Fri-Sat, from noon Sun • lesbians/ gay men • neighborhood bar • dancing/DJ

The Manor Complex 2345 Wilton Dr, Wilton Manors **954/626-0082** • 11am-11pm • lesbians/ gay men • also Epic nightclub • also restaurant & cafe

Mona's 502 E Sunrise Blvd (at 5th Ave) **954/525-6662** • noon-2am, till 3am wknds • mostly gay men • neighborhood bar • karaoke

Monkey Business 2740 N Andrews Ave **954/514-7819** • 9am-2am, till 3am wknds • mostly gay men • neighborhood bar • theme nights • cabaret • drag shows

Naked Grape 2163 Wilton Dr (at NE 20th St), Wilton Manors **954/563-5631** • 4pm-midnight, 2pm-1am Fri-Sat, clsd Sun-Mon • gay-friendly • wine bar

New Moon 2440 Wilton Dr, Wilton Manors **954/563-7660** • 2pm-2am, from noon Fri, from 11am Sat-Sun, from 4pm Mon • mostly women • karaoke Th • dancing/DJ Fri • live music Sat

Noche Latina Saturday 2345 Wilton Dr (at Manor Complex), Wilton Manors **954/626-0082** • 11pm Sat • mostly gay men • dancing/DJ • multiracial

Ramrod 1508 NE 4th Ave (at 16th St) **954/763-8219** • 3pm-2am, till 3am wknds • popular • mostly gay men • leather/ levi cruise bar • patio • also LeatherWerks leather store

Scandals 3073 NE 6th Ave, Wilton Manors **954/567-2432** • noon-2am • mostly men • patio • dancing • country/ western • older crowd • wheelchair access

Sidelines Sports Bar 2031 Wilton Dr, Wilton Manors **954/563-8001** • 3pm-2am, from noon wknds • lesbians/ gay men

Smarty Pants 2400 Oakland Park Blvd **954/561-1724** • 9am-2am, till 3am Sat, noon-2am Sun • popular • mostly gay men • neighborhood bar • food served • karaoke • drag shows • wheelchair access

NIGHTCLUBS

Living Room 300 SW 1st Ave (at Brickell) **888/992-7555** • gay Fri only • mostly men • dancing/DJ

Torpedo 2829 W Broward Blvd (at 28th Ave) **954/587-2500** • 10pm-dawn • mostly men • dancing/DJ • strippers

CAFES

Cafe Emunah 3558 N Ocean Blvd **954/561-6411** • 11am-10pm, clsd Fri, sunset-1am Sat • kosher, kabbalistic cafe & teabar • food served

Java Boys 2230 Wilton Dr, Wilton Manors **954/564-8828** • 7am-11pm • WiFi

Jimmies Chocolates & Cafe 148 N Federal Hwy, Dania Beach **954/921-0688** • bistro w/ fresh fare & wine

Storks 2505 NE 15th Ave (at NE 26th St, Wilton Manors) **954/567-3220** • 6:30am-midnight • ladies night Mon • patio • wheelchair access

---

Fort Lauderdale

LGBT PRIDE:
March. www.pridesouthflorida.org. Also Stonewall Street Festival in June.

ANNUAL EVENTS:
March - AIDS Walk, web: www.floridaaidswalk.org.
April - Miami/Fort Lauderdale Gay & Lesbian Film Festival, web: www.mglff.com.
October-November - Int'l Film Fest 954/760-9898, web: www.fliff.com.

CITY INFO:
Greater Fort Lauderdale Convention & Visitors Bureau 954/765-4466 or 800/227-8669, web: www.sunny.org.

TRANSIT:
Yellow Cab 954/777-7777, web: www.yellowcabbroward.com.
Super Shuttle 954/764-1700, web: www.supershuttle.com.
Broward County Transit 954/357-8400, web: www.broward.org/bct.

ATTRACTIONS:
Broward Center for the Performing Arts 954/462-0222, web: www.browardcenter.org.
Butterfly World 954/977-4400, web: www.butterflyworld.com.
Everglades.
Flamingo Gardens 954/473-2955, web: www.flamingogardens.org.
Museum of Art 954/525-5500, web: www.moafl.com.
Museum of Discovery & Science 954/467-6637, web: www.mods.org.

WEATHER:
The average year-round temperature in this sub-tropical climate is 75-90°.

RESTAURANTS

La Bonne Crêpe 815 E Las Olas Blvd 954/761-1515 • 7am-9:30pm, till 11:30pm Fri-Sat • patio

Canyon 1818 E Sunrise Blvd 954/765-1950 • Southwestern • full bar

Courtyard Cafe 2211 Wilton Dr 954/563-2499 • 7am-11pm, 24hrs Th-Sat • gay-owned

Flip Flops 3051 NE 32nd Ave 954/567-1672 • 11am-9pm, till 10pm Fri-Sat • casual waterfront dining

The Floridian 1410 E Las Olas Blvd 954/463-4041 • 24hr diner • wheelchair access

Fuego Latino Cuban 1417 E Commercial Blvd 954/351-7754 • 11am-10pm, till 11pm Fri-Sat, from noon Sun • beer/wine

Galanga 2389 Wilton Dr, Wilton Manors 954/202-0000 • dinner nightly, lunch weekdays • Thai • also sushi

Hi-Life Cafe 3000 N Federal Hwy (at Oakland Park Blvd, in the Plaza 3000) 954/563-1395 • dinner, clsd Mon • reservations recommended

Humpy's 2244 Wilton Dr, Wilton Manors 954/566-2722 • 11am-10pm, till 2am Th-Sat • pizza & panini

J Marks Restaurant 1245 N Federal Hwy 954/390-0770 • 11am-10pm, till 11pm Fri-Sat • full bar • gay-owned

Kitchenetta 2850 N Federal Hwy 954/567-3333 • dinner nightly, clsd Mon • wheelchair access

La Bamba 4245 N Federal Hwy 954/568-5662 • more gay Mon night

Lester's Diner 250 State Rd 84 954/525-5641 • 24hrs • popular • more gay late nights • wheelchair access

Lips 1421 E Oakland Park Blvd (at Dixie Hwy) 954/567-0987 • 6pm-close, Sun brunch, clsd Mon • "the ultimate in drag dining" • karaoke

Mason Jar Cafe 2980 N Federal Hwy 954/568-4100 • 11:30am-3pm Mon-Fri, dinner nightly • upscale comfort food • gay-owned

Mojo 4140 N Federal Hwy 954/568-4443 • open 4pm, clsd Sun • live shows • full bar

Le Patio 2401 NE 11th Ave 954 /530-4641 • comfort food • lesbian-owned

PL8 Kitchen 210 SW 2nd St 954/524-1818 • lunch & dinner, till 2am wknds • small plates

Rosie's Bar & Grill 2449 Wilton Dr, Wilton Manors 954/563-0123 • 11am-11pm • popular • full bar

SAIA 999 N Fort Lauderdale Beach Blvd 954/302-5252 • authentic Asian cuisine

Sublime 1431 N Federal Hwy 954/539-9000 • 5:30pm-10pm, clsd Mon • vegan/ vegetarian

Tequila Sunrise Mexican Grill 4711 N Dixie Hwy 954/938-4473 • 11:30am-10pm, till 11pm Th-Sat, 1pm-10pm Sun • live shows

Tropics Cabaret & Restaurant 2000 Wilton Dr (at 20th) 954/537-6000 • lunch & dinner, Sun brunch, till 3am Sat • also piano bar • gay-owned • wheelchair access

ENTERTAINMENT & RECREATION

Sebastian Beach • more lesbians on the far north end of the beach

BOOKSTORES

Pride Factory 850 NE 13th St 954/463-6600 • 10am-9pm, 11am-7pm Sun

RETAIL SHOPS

GayMartUSA 2240 Wilton Dr (at NE 6th Ave) 954/630-0360 • 10am-midnight

Out of the Closet 2097 Wilton Dr, Wilton Manors 954/358-5580 • 10am-7pm, till 6pm Sun

To The Moon 2205 Wilton Dr (at 6th Ave), Wilton Manors 954/564-2987 • 10am-11pm • pride gifts, cards & candy candy candy!

GYMS & HEALTH CLUBS

Island City Health & Fitness 2270 Wilton Dr, Wilton Manors 954/318-3900 • 5am-11pm, 8am-8pm wknds

EROTICA

Fetish Factory 855 E Oakland Park Blvd 954/563-5777 • 11am-9pm, noon-6pm Sun

Hustler Hollywood 1500 E Sunrise Blvd (at NE 15th Ave) 954/828-9769

Fort Myers

INFO LINES & SERVICES

Gay AA Lambda Drummers 3049 McGregor Blvd (at St John the Apostle MCC) 239/275-5111 (AA#) • 8pm Tue & Sat in social hall • wheelchair access

ACCOMMODATIONS

The Resort on Carefree Blvd 3000 Carefree Blvd (at Cleveland Ave) 239/731-6366 • mostly women • homes & RV lots • pool • gym • kids/ pets ok • older crowd • nonsmoking • woman-owned

Bars

Boston Ale N Tale 3441 Colonial Blvd (in Sunsports Plaza) **239/274–8253** • 4pm-closing • gay-friendly • food served

The Office Pub 3704 Cleveland Ave (at Grove) **239/936–3212** • noon-2am • mostly gay men • neighborhood bar • bears • theme nights

Tubby's City Hangout 4810 Vincennes St, Cape Coral **239/541–3540** • 2pm-2am • mostly gay men • karaoke • live shows • gay-owned

Nightclubs

The Bottom Line (TBL) 3090 Evans Ave (at Hanson) **239/337–7292** • 2pm-2am • lesbians/ gay men • more women wknds • dancing/DJ • live shows • karaoke • videos • wheelchair access

Restaurants

McGregor Grill 15675 McGregor Blvd, Ste 24 **239/437–3499** • 11:30am-2am, from 4pm Sun • pub fare • some outdoor dining • also full bar • gay-owned

The Oasis 2260 Dr Martin Luther King Blvd **239/334–1566** • breakfast, lunch & dinner • beer/ wine • wheelchair access • women-owned

Gainesville

Info Lines & Services

Free to Be AA 3131 NW 13th St (The Pride Center) **352/372–8091 (AA#)** • 7:30pm Sun, LGBT AA group

Pride Community Center 3131 NW 13th St #62 **352/377–8915** • 3pm-7pm, noon-4pm Sat, clsd Sun

Bars

Spikes 4130 NW 6th St **352/376–3772** • 5pm-2am, till 11pm Sun • popular • lesbians/ gay men • neighborhood bar • wheelchair access

The University Club 18 E University Ave (enter rear) **352/378–6814** • 5pm-2am, from 9pm Sat, till 11pm Sun • lesbians/ gay men • 3 levels • young crowd • dancing/DJ • karaoke • live shows • patio • wheelchair access

Entertainment & Recreation

Ponte Vedra LGBT Beach • Go N from Gainesville on Waldo Rd to N 301, then E on I-10. I-10 becomes 95. Go S on 95, then take a left. Go E onto Butler Blvd, which ends at A1A. Turn right onto A1A & then drive 5 to 7 minutes looking for Guana Boat Landing; park in lot on the right (or get ticketed)

Bookstores

Wild Iris Books 802 W University Ave (at 8th St) **352/375–7477** • 1pm-9pm, till 5pm Sat, clsd Sun-Mon • feminist/ LGBT

Publications

Kindred Sisters Magazine • lesbian/ feminist monthly magazine for N Central FL

Hollywood

Erotica

Pleasure Emporium 1321 S 30th Ave **954/927–8181**

Islamorada

Accommodations

Casa Morada 136 Madeira Rd **305/664–0044, 888/881–3030** • gay-friendly • luxury all-suite hotel w/ private island • pool • pets ok • women-owned

Lookout Lodge Resort 87770 Overseas Hwy (at Plantation Blvd) **305/852–9915, 800/870–1772** • gay-friendly • waterfront resort • kids/ pets ok • nonsmoking • WiFi

Jacksonville

Info Lines & Services

Free to Be LGBT AA 634 Lomax St **904/399–8535 (AA#)** • 6:30pm Mon

Women's Center of Jacksonville 5644 Colcord Ave **904/722–3000**

Accommodations

Comfort Inn Oceanfront 1515 N 1st St, Jacksonville Beach **904/241–2311, 800/654–8776** • gay-friendly • pool • fitness center • restaurant & Tiki bar

Hilton Garden Inn Jacksonville JTB/ Deerwood Park 9745 Gate Pkwy (at Southside Blvd) **904/997–6600, 877/782–9444** • gay-friendly • 15 minutes to beach • pool • jacuzzi • kids ok • WiFi • wheelchair access

Spring Hill Suites Jacksonville 4385 Southside Blvd (at J Turner Butler Blvd) **904/997–6650, 888/287–9400** • gay-friendly • pool • kids ok • nonsmoking • WiFi

Bars

616 Bar 616 Park St (at I-95) **904/358–6969** • 4pm-2am • lesbians/ gay men • neighborhood bar • karaoke • patio

AJ's Bar & Grill 10244 Atlantic Blvd (in Regency Walk Shopping Center) **904/805–9060** • 4pm-2am, from 1pm Sun • mostly women • dancing/DJ • full menu • karaoke • wheelchair access • women-owned

Bo's Coral Reef 201 5th Ave N (at 2nd St), Jacksonville Beach **904/246–9874** • 2pm-2am • lesbians/ gay men • neighborhood bar • dancing/DJ • live shows

Club Sappho 859 Willow Branch Ave (upstairs at Metro) **904/388–8719, 904/388–7192 (INFO LINE)** • 4pm-2am, till 4am Fri-Sat • popular • mostly women • dancing/DJ • multiracial • also Lesbo-a-GoGo 1st Fri

In Cahoots 711 Edison Ave (btwn Riverside & Park) **904/353–6316** • 8pm-2am, from 4pm Sun, clsd Mon-Tue • mostly gay men • dancing/DJ • multiracial • karaoke • drag shows • wheelchair access

The Metro 859 Willow Branch Ave **904/388–8719** • 2pm-2am, till 4am Fri-Sat • popular • lesbians/gay men • dancing/DJ • drag shows • 18+ • wheelchair access

The New Boot Rack Saloon 4751 Lenox Ave (at Cassat Ave) **904/384–7090** • 3pm-2am • mostly gay men • country/ western • WiFi • beer/ wine • patio • wheelchair access

The Norm 2952 Roosevelt Blvd (at College) **904/384–9929** • 4pm-close • mostly women but everyone welcome • dancing/DJ • live shows • wheelchair access

Park Place Lounge 931 King St (at Post) **904/389–6616** • noon-2am • lesbians/ gay men • neighborhood bar • dancing/DJ • wheelchair access

RESTAURANTS

Al's Pizza 1620 Margaret St, Ste 201 **904/388–8384** • 11am-10pm, till 11pm Fri-Sat, noon-9pm Sun • in Riverside/ Little 5 Points area

Biscotti's 3556 Saint Johns Ave (Talbot Ave) **904/387–2060** • 10:30am-10pm, till midnight Fri-Sat, from 8am Sat-Sun • popular • killer desserts • women-owned

Bistro Aix 1440 San Marco Blvd **904/398–1949** • 11am-10pm, till 11pm Fri, 5pm-11pm Sat, 5pm-9pm Sun • upscale French bistro

European Street Cafe 2753 Park St (at King) **904/384–9999** • 10am-10pm • salads • beer/ wine • patio • wheelchair access • gay-owned

Mossfire Grill 1537 Margaret St **904/355–4434** • lunch & dinner • Southwestern • full bar

RETAIL SHOPS

Rainbows & Stars 1046 Park St (in historic 5 Points) **904/356–7702** • 10am-7pm Wed-Fri, noon-7pm Sat, noon-5pm Sun, clsd Mon-Tue

Key West

INFO LINES & SERVICES

Gay & Lesbian Community Center 513 Truman Ave **305/292–3223** • many meetings & groups • WiFi

Keep It Simple (Gay/ Lesbian AA) **305/296–8654 (AA #)** • 8pm Mon-Sat, 5:30pm Sun

➤ **Key West Business Guild** **305/294–4603, 800/535–7797** • see ad in front color section

ACCOMMODATIONS

Alexander Palms Court 715 South St (at Vernon) **305/296–6413, 800/858–1943** • gay-friendly • pool • private patios • wheelchair access • gay-owned

Alexander's Guest House 1118 Fleming St (at Frances) **305/294–9919, 800/654–9919** • lesbians/ gay men • pool • nudity • WiFi • wheelchair access • gay-owned

Ambrosia House Tropical Lodging 615 & 618-622 Fleming St (at Simonton) **305/296–9838** • gay-friendly • pool • hot tub

Andrews Inn Zero Whalton Ln (at Duval) **305/294–7730, 888/263–7393** • gay-friendly • pool • kids ok • nonsmoking • WiFi

The Artist House 534 Eaton St (at Duval) **305/296–3977, 800/582–7882** • gay/ straight • nonsmoking

Avalon B&B 1317 Duval St (at United) **305/294–8233, 800/848–1317** • gay-friendly • swimming • near beach • sundeck • WiFi

Cypress House & Guest Studios 601 Caroline (at Simonton) **305/294–6969, 800/525–2488** • gay-friendly • guesthouse • 1888 Grand Conch mansion • pool • sundeck • WiFi • wheelchair access

The Grand Guesthouse 1116 Grinnell St **305/294–0590, 888/947–2630** • lesbians/ gay men • in converted rooming house built in 1880s for cigar workers • nonsmoking • WiFi • gay-owned

Heartbreak Hotel 716 Duval St (near Petronia) **305/296–5558** • gay/ straight • kitchens • lesbian & gay-owned

Heron House Court 412 Frances St (at Eaton) **800/932–9119** • gay-friendly • full brkfst • swimming • nonsmoking • WiFi • wheelchair access

Key West Harbor Inn B&B 219 Elizabeth St (at Greene) **305/296–2978, 800/608–6569** • lesbians/ gay men • pool • hot tub • nonsmoking • WiFi

Knowles House B&B 1004 Eaton St (at Grinnell) 305/296-8132, 800/352-4414 • gay/ straight • restored 1880s Conch house • pool • nudity • nonsmoking • gay-owned

La Te Da 1125 Duval St (at Catherine) 305/296-6706, 877/528-3320 • popular • lesbians/ gay men • full brkfst • nonsmoking • pool • restaurant & 3 bars • WiFi • gay-owned

Marquesa Hotel 600 Fleming St (at Simonton) 305/292-1919, 800/869-4631 • gay-friendly • 2 pools • also restaurant • full bar • nonsmoking • WiFi • wheelchair access

The Mermaid & the Alligator—A Key West B&B 729 Truman Ave (at Windsor Ln) 305/294-1894, 800/773-1894 • gay/ straight • full brkfst • pool • nonsmoking • WiFi • gay-owned

Pearl's Key West 525 United St (at Duval) 305/292-1450, 800/749-6696 • popular • gay/ straight • 2 hot tubs • pool • sundeck • nonsmoking • WiFi • also bar & restaurant • wheelchair access • lesbian-owned

Pilot House Guest House 414 Simonton St (at Eaton) 305/293-6600, 800/648-3780 • gay/ straight • Victorian mansion in Old Town • pool • nudity • nonsmoking • WiFi • wheelchair access

Seascape Inn 420 Olivia St (at Duval) 305/296-7776, 800/765-6438 • gay-friendly • pool • hot tub • WiFi • nonsmoking

Simonton Court Historic Inn & Cottages 320 Simonton St (at Caroline) 305/294-6386, 800/944-2687 • gay-friendly • built in 1880s • pool • nonsmoking • WiFi

Tropical Inn 812 Duval St (near Petronia) 305/294-9977, 888/611-6510 • gay-friendly • also cottage suites • hot tub • pool • sundeck • WiFi

BARS

The 801 Bourbon Bar 801 Duval St (at Petronia) 305/294-4737 • 10am-4am, from noon Sun • lesbians/ gay men • neighborhood bar • dancing/DJ • drag shows • Sun bingo

Bobby's Monkey Bar 900 Simonton St (at Olivia) 305/294-2655 • noon-4am • mostly gay men • neighborhood bar • WiFi • wheelchair access

Key West

LGBT PRIDE:
June. 305/292-3223, web: www.pridefestkeywest.com.

ANNUAL EVENTS:
February - Kelly McGillis Classic Women's & Girls' Flag Football Tournament 888/464-9332, web: www.iwffa.com.
September - WomenFest, web: www.womenfest.com.
October - Fantasy Fest 305/296-1817, web: www.fantasyfest.net. Weeklong Halloween celebration with parties, masquerade balls & parades.

CITY INFO:
Key West Business Association 800/FLA-KEYS, web: www.fla-keys.com/keywest.

WEATHER:
The average temperature year-round is 78°, and the sun shines nearly every day. Any time is the right time for a visit.

ATTRACTIONS:
Audubon House and Gardens 305/294-2116, web: www.audubonhouse.com.
Dolphin Research Center 305/289-1121, web: www.dolphins.org.
Hemingway House, web: www.hemingwayhome.com.
Red Barn Theatre 305/296-9911, web: www.redbarntheatre.com.
Southernmost Point USA.
Sunset Celebration at Mallory Square.

BEST VIEW:
Old Town Trolley Tour (1/2 hour) 888/910-8687, web: www.historictours.com/keywest.

TRANSIT:
Friendly Cab 305/292-0000.
Key West Express (ferry) 888/539-2628, web: www.seakeywestexpress.com.
Key West Transit Authority, web: www.kwtransit.com.

Bourbon Street Pub 724 Duval St (at Petronia) 305/293–9800 • 11am-4am, from noon Sun • mostly gay men • popular • garden bar w/ pool & hot tub • wheelchair access

Garden of Eden 224 Duval St 305/296–4565 • 10am-4am, from noon Sun • gay/ straight • clothing-optional sun bathing • dancing/DJ • live music

Hog's Breath Saloon 400 Front St 305/296–4222 • gay-friendly • food served • live music

La Te Da 1125 Duval St (at Catherine) 305/296–6706 • lesbians/gay men • 3 bars (piano bar & cabaret) & restaurant • wheelchair access • gay-owned

Virgilio's 524 Duval St (at Fleming in La Trattoria) 305/296–8118 • 7pm-4am • gay/ straight • martini bar • garden • food served • live music • late-night DJ

NIGHTCLUBS

Aqua 711 Duval St 305/294–0555 • 3pm-2am • lesbians/ gay men • dancing/DJ • drag shows • karaoke • wheelchair access • lesbian-owned

Bottle Cap Lounge 305/296–2807 • noon-4am • gay/ straight • dancing/ DJ

CAFES

Croissants de France 816 Duval St 305/294–2624 • bakery 7:30am-6pm, restaurant open till 10pm • beer/ wine • patio

RESTAURANTS

Antonia's Restaurant 615 Duval St (at Southard) 305/294–6565 • lunch & dinner • popular • Italian • full bar

Azur 425 Grinnell St 305/292–2987 • Mediterranean

Blue Heaven 729 Thomas St 305/296–8666 • great brkfst, also lunch & dinner • live entertainment

Bo's Fish Wagon 801 Caroline (at William) 305/294–9272 • lunch & dinner • popular • "seafood & eat it"

Cafe Sole 1029 Southard St (at Frances) 305/294–0230 • dinner nightly, Sun brunch • romantic • candlelit backyard

Camille's 1202 Simonton (at Catherine) 305/296–4811 • brkfst, lunch & dinner • bistro • hearty brkfst

El Meson de Pepe 410 Wall St (in Mallory Sq) 305/295–2620 • lunch & dinner • Cuban • live music

The Flaming Buoy Filet Co 1100 Packer St (at Virginia) 305/295–7970 • lunch & dinner • wheelchair access

Grand Cafe Key West 314 Duval St 305/292–4740 • lunch & dinner

Half Shell Raw Bar 231 Margaret St 305/294–7496 • 11am-10pm • waterfront

Hurricane Hole 305/294–8025, 305/294–0200 • 10am-10pm • dockside bar

Jack Flats 509 Duval St 305/294–7955 • 11am-2am • wheelchair access

Kelly's Caribbean Bar Grill & Brewery 301 Whitehead St (at Caroline) 305/293–8484 • lunch & dinner • full bar • owned by actress Kelly McGillis

La Trattoria Venezia 524 Duval St (at Fleming) 305/296–1075 • 5pm-10:30pm • bar

Lobos Mixed Grill 5 Key Lime Sq (south of Southard St) 305/296–5303 • 11am-6pm • sandwiches • plenty veggie • beer/ wine

Louie's Backyard 700 Waddell Ave (at Vernon) 305/294–1061 • 11:30am-1am • popular • fine cont'l dining

Mangia Mangia 900 Southard St (at Margaret St) 305/294–2469 • dinner only • fresh pasta • beer/ wine • patio

Mangoes 700 Duval St (at Angela) 305/292–4606 • lunch & dinner, bar till 1am • "Floribbean" cuisine • full bar • patio • wheelchair access

Michaels 532 Margaret St 305/295–1300 • dinner only • steakhouse

New York Pasta Garden 1075 Duval St (Duval Square) 305/292–1991 • 11am-10pm

Seven Fish 632 Olivia St (at Elizabeth) 305/296–2777 • 6pm-10pm, clsd Tue • popular

Six Toed Cat 832 Whitehead St 305/294–3318 • brkfst & lunch

Square One 1075 Duval St (at Truman) 305/296–4300 • 4pm-11pm • full bar • wheelchair access

ENTERTAINMENT & RECREATION

Fort Zachary Taylor Beach • more gay to the right

Gay & Lesbian Trolley Tour 305/294–4603 • 10:50am Sat • check out all of the gay hotspots & historical points • look for rainbow-decorated trolley

Island Ceremonies 305/304–0806, 305/745–8886 • commitment ceremonies in the Keys w/ Captain Lynda • woman-owned

Moped Hospital 601 Truman 866/296–1625 • forget the car—mopeds are a must for touring the island

Venus Charters Garrison Bight Marina 305/304–1181 • snorkeling • light-tackle fishing • dolphin-watching • personalized excursions • lesbian-owned

BOOKSTORES

Key West Island Books 513 Fleming St (at Duval) 305/294–2904 • 10am-9pm, till 6pm Sun • new & used rare books • LGBT section

RETAIL SHOPS

In Touch Gay Pride Store 706-A Duval St (at Angela) 305/294–1995 • 9am-9pm • gifts

GYMS & HEALTH CLUBS

Key West Island Gym 1119 White St 305/295–8222 • gay-owned

EROTICA

Fairvilla Megastore 520 Front St 305/292–0448 • 9am-midnight • clean, well-lighted adult store w/ emphasis on couples

Leather Master 418 Appelrouth Ln 305/292–5051 • 11am-10pm, noon-8pm Sun • custom leather, toys & more

Lake Worth

see also West Palm Beach

INFO LINES & SERVICES

Compass LGBT Community Center 201 N Dixie Hwy 561/533–9699 • 9am-9pm, till 7pm Fri, 3pm-7pm Sat, clsd Sun • wheelchair access

BARS

The Bar 2211 N Dixie Hwy 561/370–3954 • 2pm-2am, noon-midnight Sun • lesbians/ gay men • neighborhood bar • dancing/DJ • karaoke • lesbian-owned

The Mad Hatter Bar & Grill 1532 N Dixie Hwy (16th Ave) 561/547–8860 • 1pm-2am, noon-midnight Sun • mostly men • neighborhood bar • older crowd • gay-owned

NIGHTCLUBS

Mara 1132 N Dixie Hwy 561/827–6468 • 7pm-2am Wed, 10pm-2am Th-Fri, till 5am Sat, from 6pm Sun • mostly men • dancing/DJ

CAFES

Mother Earth Sanctuary Cafe & Healing Center 561/460–8647 • 8am-7pm, till 10pm Fri-Sat • fair trade • organic beans • cash only

Largo

BARS

Quench Lounge 13284 66th St N 727/754–5900 • 2pm-2am • mostly gay men • dancing/DJ • karaoke • shows

Marathon

ACCOMMODATIONS

Tropical Cottages 243 61st St Gulf 305/743–6048 • gay-friendly • outdoor hot tub • pets ok • nonsmoking

ENTERTAINMENT & RECREATION

Bahia Honda State Park & Beach 12 miles S of Marathon

Melbourne

ACCOMMODATIONS

Crane Creek Inn B&B 907 E Melbourne Ave 321/768–6416 • gay/ straight • full brkfst • pool • hot tub • dogs ok • WiFi

BARS

Cold Keg 4060 W New Haven Ave (1/2 mile E of I-95) 321/724–1510 • 4pm-2am, clsd Sun • lesbians/ gay men • dancing/DJ • drag shows • 18+ • wheelchair access

MIAMI

Miami is divided into 3 geographical areas:
Miami—Overview
Miami—Greater Miami
Miami—Miami Beach/ South Beach

Miami—Overview

INFO LINES & SERVICES

➤ **Greater Miami CVB** 305/539–3000, 800/933–8448 • plan your Miami vacation! • see ad in front color section

Switchboard of Miami 305/358–1640 • 24hrs • gay-friendly info & referrals for Dade County

ENTERTAINMENT & RECREATION

Sailboat Charters of Miami 3400 Pan American Dr (at S Bayshore Dr) 305/772–4221 • lesbians/ gay men • private sailing charters aboard all-teakwood 46-foot clipper to Bahamas & the Keys

Miami—Greater Miami

BARS

The Dugout 3215 NE 2nd Ave (at NE 32nd St) 305/438–1117 • 5pm-3am, clsd Mon-Tue • mostly gay men

Eros Lounge 8201 Biscayne Blvd 305/754–3444 • 4pm-3am, till midnight Sun-Mon • mostly gay men • neighborhood bar • karaoke • drag shows • monthly ladies night

NIGHTCLUBS

Club Sugar 2301 SW 32nd Ave (at Coral Wy) 305/443–7657 • 10:30pm-5am Th-Sat, 8pm-3am Sun, clsd Mon-Wed

Discotekka 950 NE 2nd Ave (at Metropolis Nightclub) 305/371–3773 • after hours Sat only • mostly gay men • dancing/DJ • 18+

Space Miami 34 NE 11th St (at NE 1st Ave) 305/375–0001 • gay-friendly • dancing/DJ • popular club w/ int'l visiting DJs

CAFES

Gourmet Station 7601 Biscayne Blvd (at NE 71st St) 305/762–7229 • 8am-9pm, till 8pm Fri, clsd Sat-Sun

RESTAURANTS

Area 31 270 Biscayne Blvd Way (at the Epic Hotel) 305/424–5234 • brkfst, lunch & dinner • seafood • amazing view • wheelchair access

Cafeina 297 NW 23rd St (W of Miami Ave) 305/438–0792 • 5pm-3am Th-Fri, from 9pm Sat, clsd Sun-Wed • tapas • also gallery, bands, events

Habibi's Grill 93 SE 2nd St (at NE 1st Ave) 786/425–2699 • 11am-8pm, clsd Sun • Lebanese/ Mediterranean • plenty veggie

Jimmy's East Side Diner 7201 Biscayne Blvd 305/754–3692 • 7am-4pm • wheelchair access

Joey's 2506 NW 2nd Ave 305/438–0488 • lunch & dinner, clsd Sun • Italian • patio

The Magnum Lounge & Restaurant 709 NE 79th St 305/757–3368 • 6pm-midnight, bar open 5pm-2am, clsd Mon • neighborhood bar • piano bar • reservations recommended

Michy's 6927 Biscayne Blvd (at NE 69th) 305/759–2001 • dinner only • "luxurious comfort food"

Ortanique on the Mile 278 Miracle Mile (at Salzedo), Coral Gables 305/446–7710 • lunch Mon-Fri, dinner nightly • Caribbean • full bar

Ristorante Fratelli Milano 213 SE 1st St (at 2nd Ave) 305/373–2300 • 11am-10pm • homemade Italian • wheelchair access

Royal Bavarian Schnitzel Haus 1085 NE 79th St 305/754–8002 • 5pm-11pm • German fare

Soyka 5556 NE 4th Ct 305/759–3117 • lunch & dinner, wknd brunch • full bar

UVA 69 6900 Biscayne Blvd (at NE 69th St) 305/754–9022 • 11am-11pm, 8am-midnight wknds • European bistro & lounge • patio

Wynwood Kitchen & Bar 2550 NW 2nd Ave 305/722–8959 • 5:30pm-midnight • Latin • great art

ENTERTAINMENT & RECREATION

Awarehouse Miami 550 NW 29th St 305/576–4004 • artsy venue w/ live music, art shows & more

Roam Rides 888/760–7626 • Vespa scooter rental • delivered to your hotel • also guided tours of Wynwood neighborhood art murals

BOOKSTORES

Lambda Passages Bookstore 7545 Biscayne Blvd (at NE 76th) 305/754–6900 • 11am-9pm, noon-6pm Sun • LGBT/ feminist

Miami—Miami Beach/ South Beach

ACCOMMODATIONS

The Angler's 660 Washington Ave 305/534–9600, 866/729–8800 • gay/ straight • luxury boutique resort • restaurant & lounge • pool • WiFi

Beachcomber Hotel 1340 Collins Ave (at 13th St) 305/531–3755, 888/305–4683 • gay-friendly • nonsmoking • WiFi

Blue Moon Hotel 944 Collins Ave 305/673–2262 • gay-friendly • pool • also bar

The Cardozo Hotel 1300 Ocean Dr 305/535–6500, 800/782–6500 • gay-friendly • restaurant • Gloria Estefan's plush hotel • kids ok • WiFi • wheelchair access

The Century 140 Ocean Dr 305/674–8855, 877/659–8855 • gay-friendly • nonsmoking • WiFi • wheelchair access

Chesterfield Hotel, Suites & Day Spa 855 Collins Ave 305/531–5831, 877/762–3477 • gay/ straight • super stylish hotel

Circa 39 Hotel 3900 Collins Ave (at 39th St) 305/538–4900, 877/824–7223 • gay-friendly • pool • lounge • WiFi • wheelchair access

The Colony Hotel 736 Ocean Dr (at 7th St) 305/673–0088 • gay-friendly • bistro • oceanfront • WiFi • wheelchair access

Delano Hotel 1685 Collins Ave 305/672–2000, 800/697–1791 • gay-friendly • food served • pool • kids ok • wheelchair access

The European Guesthouse 721 Michigan Ave (btwn 7th & 8th) 305/673–6665 • lesbians/ gay men • B&B • full brkfst • pool • WiFi • gay-owned

The Hotel 801 Collins Ave **305/531–2222, 877/843–4683** • gay-friendly • restaurant & bar • pool • nonsmoking • WiFi • wheelchair access

Hotel Ocean 1230–38 Ocean Dr **305/672–2579** • popular • gay/ straight • great location • pets ok • WiFi • wheelchair access

The King & Grove Tides 1220 Ocean Dr (at 12th St) **305/604–5070, 305/503–3268** • gay/ straight • private beach area • pool • WiFi • also La Marea restaurant

Lords of South Beach 1120 Collins Ave **305/674–7800, 877/448–4754** • mostly men • boutique hotel • spa • pool • kids ok • nonsmoking • wheelchair access

The National Hotel 1677 Collins Ave **305/532–2311, 800/327–8370** • gay/ straight • pool • kids ok • restaurant & lounge • WiFi • wheelchair access

Penguin Hotel 1418 Ocean Dr **305/534–9334** • lesbians/ gay men • full restaurant • kids ok • wheelchair access

The Raleigh, Miami Beach 1775 Collins Ave (at Ocean Front) **305/534–6300, 800/848–1775** • gay-friendly • pool • restaurant & bars • kids/ pets ok • WiFi • wheelchair access

SoBeYou 1018 Jefferson Ave **305/534–5247, 877/599–5247** • gay/ straight • nonsmoking • WiFi • wheelchair access • lesbian-owned

Miami

LGBT Pride:
April, web: www.miamibeach-gaypride.com.

Annual Events:
Feb/March - Winter Party 202/571-1924, web: www.winterparty.com. Beach dance party benefiting the National Gay & Lesbian Task Force.

April/May - Gay & Lesbian Film Festival, web: www.mglff.com.

May - Aqua Girl 305/576.2782, web: www.aquagirl.org. A women's weekend.

November - White Party Vizcaya 305/576–1234, web: www.whiteparty.net. AIDS benefit.

City Info:
Greater Miami Convention & Visitors Bureau 305/539-3000. 701 Brickell Ave, web: www.miamiandbeaches.com.

Transit:
Central Cab 305/532-5555, web: www.centralcab.com.

Swoop is a slightly pimped up electric golf cart for geting around SOBE 305/409-6636, web: www.swoopmiami.com.

Express Shuttle 305/282-4626, web: www.expressshuttlemiami.com

Metro Bus Dial 3-1-1 , web: http://miamidade.gov.

Attractions:
Bayside Marketplace 305/577-3344, web: www.baysidemarket-place.com.

Miami Beach Botanical Garden 305/673-7256, web: www.mbgarden.org.

Miami Design Preservation League 305/672-2014. web: mdpl.org.

Miami Museum of Science & Planetarium 305/646-4200, web: www.miamisci.org.

Monkey Jungle 305/235-1611, web: www.monkeyjungle.com.

Museum of Contempory Art, N Miami 305/893-6211, web: www.mocanomi.com.

Parrot Jungle Island 305/400-7000, web: www.parrotjungle.com.

Jewish Museum of Florida 305/672-5044, web: www.jewishmu-seum.com.

Best View:
If you've got money to burn, a helicopter flight over Miami Beach is a great way to see the city. Otherwise, hit the beach.

Weather:
Warm all year. Temperatures stay in the 90°s during the summer and drop into the mid-60°s in the winter. Be prepared for sunshine!

Something Special, A Lesbian Venture 305/696–8826 • women only • apt, camping & dining

South Seas 1751 Collins Ave 305/538–1411, 800/345–2678 • gay-friendly • clean & basic • beach access • pool • WiFi

The Winterhaven 1400 Ocean Dr 305/531–5571 • gay/ straight • ocean views • also bar • WiFi • wheelchair access

BARS

Buck15 Lounge 437 Lincoln Ln 305/538–3815 • 10pm-5am, clsd Sun-Mon • gay/ straight • more gay Th • gallery

Creme Lounge 725 Lincoln Ln N (upstairs from Score) 305/535–1163 • open Tue & Th-Sat • lesbians/ gay men

Palace Bar & Grill 1200 Ocean Dr (at 12th St) 305/531–7234 • 10am-1am, till 2am Fri-Sat • lesbians/ gay men • also restaurant • drag shows

NIGHTCLUBS

Crush 841 Washington Ave 305/397–8056 • Wed only • mostly women • dancing/DJ

Mova Lounge 1625 Michigan Ave (at Lincoln Rd) 305/534–8181 • 3pm-3am • lesbians/ gay men

Pandora Events 305/975–6933 • monthly women's parties • locations rotate so check website: www.pandoraevents.com

Score 1437 Washington Ave 305/535–1111 • lounge opens 3pm, dance club 10pm-5am Tue & Th-Sat • popular • lesbians/ gay men • drag shows • karaoke • videos

Twist 1057 Washington Ave (at 11th) 305/538–9478 • 1pm-5am • popular • mostly gay men • 7 bars • dancing/DJ • karaoke • drag shows • go-go boys • wheelchair access

CAFES

News Cafe 800 Ocean Dr (at 8th St) 305/538–6397 • 24hrs • also bookstore & bar

RESTAURANTS

11th Street Diner 1065 Washington (at 11th) 305/534–6373 • 24hrs • full bar

B&B: Burger & Beer Joint 1766 Bay Rd (at 18th St) 305/672–3287 • lunch & dinner • the name says it all

Balans 1022 Lincoln Rd (btwn Michigan & Lennox) 305/534–9191 • 8am-midnight

Big Pink 157 Collins (at 2nd St) 305/532–4700 • 8am-midnight, open late wknds • "real food for real people"

David's Cafe II 1654 Meridian Ave 305/672–8707 • 24hrs • Cuban

Juice & Java 1346 Washington Ave (at 14th St) 305/531–6675 • 9am-9pm, 10am-6pm Sun, • healthy fast food • wheelchair access

Larios on the Beach 820 Ocean Dr (at 8th) 305/532–9577 • 11:30am-midnight • Cuban • wheelchair access

Nexxt Cafe 700 Lincoln Rd (at Euclid Ave) 305/532–6643 • 11:30am-11pm, till midnight Fri-Sat

Something Special, a Lesbian Venture 305/696–8826 • women only • 6pm-10pm, clsd Mon-Tue • vegetarian • lesbian-owned

Spiga 1228 Collins Ave (at 12th St) 305/534–0079 • dinner only • tasty homemade pastas

Sushi Rock Cafe 1351 Collins Ave (at 14th) 305/532–2133 • noon-midnight • popular

Tiramesu 721 Lincoln Rd 305/532–4538 • lunch & dinner • Italian

ENTERTAINMENT & RECREATION

Fritz's Skate & Bike 1620 Washington Ave 305/532–1954

The Gay Beach/ 12th St Beach 12th St & Ocean

Haulover Beach Park A1A S of Sunny Isle Blvd, North Miami Beach • popular nude beach

Lincoln Rd Lincoln Rd (btwn Bay Rd & Collins Aves) • pedestrian mall that embodies the rebirth of South Beach

South Beach Bike Tours 305/673–2002 • half-day bike tour of Art Deco district • gay-owned

RETAIL SHOPS

Pink Palm 723 Lincoln Rd (at Meridian Ave) 305/397–8097 • 10am-11pm • unique gifts

GYMS & HEALTH CLUBS

Crunch 1259 Washington Ave 305/674–8222

David Barton Gym 2323 Collins Ave 305/534–1660

EROTICA

Pleasure Boutique 1019 5th St 305/673–3311

Mt Dora

ACCOMMODATIONS

Adora Inn 352/735–3110 • gay/ straight • full brkfst • kids 6+ ok • nonsmoking • WiFi • gay-owned

Naples

see also Fort Myers

BARS

Bambusa Bar & Grill 600 Goodlette Rd N (at 5th Ave N) 239/649-5657 • 4pm-midnight • gay-friendly • neighborhood bar • karaoke Sat • also restaurant • videos • gay-owned

CAFES

Sunburst Cafe 2340 Pine Ridge Rd (at Airport Pulling Rd) 239/263-3123 • 7am-3pm • wheelchair access

RESTAURANTS

Caffe dell'Amore 1400 Gulf Shore Blvd N (at Banyan Blvd) 239/261-1389 • dinner only • clsd Sun-Mon in summer • Italian • beer/wine • reservations required • wheelchair access • gay-owned

The Real Macaw 3275 Bayshore Dr 239/732-1188 • occasionally have gay events

New Port Richey

BARS

Chill Chamber 3501 Universal Plaza (at Moog Rd & US 19) 727/844-3474 • 2pm-2am • lesbians/gay men • dancing/DJ • live music • wheelchair access

Ocala

BARS

Copa/ Tropix 2330 S Pine Ave 352/351-5721 • 2pm-2am • mostly gay men • dancing/DJ • drag shows • food served

The Pub 14 NW 5th St 352/857-7256 • 8pm-2am • mostly gay men • neighborhood bar

Orlando

INFO LINES & SERVICES

GLBT Community Center of Central Florida 946 N Mills Ave 407/228-8272 • 9am-9pm, noon-5pm Sat-Sun

ACCOMMODATIONS

Eo Inn & Spa 227 N Eola Dr (at Robinson) 407/481-8485, 888/481-8488 • gay/ straight • boutique hotel • nonsmoking • sundeck • hot tub • WiFi • cafe on-site

Four Points by Sheraton Studio City 5905 International Dr (at Kirkman) 407/351-2100, 866/716-8105 • gay-friendly • bar & restaurant • pool • WiFi • wheelchair access

Grand Bohemian Hotel Orlando 325 S Orange Ave 407/313-9000, 888/213-9110 • gay-friendly • luxury hotel • pool • kids ok • nonsmoking • WiFi • wheelchair access

Hyatt Residency Grand Cypress I Grand Cypress Blvd 407/239-1234 • gay-friendly • 1,500 acre resort • private lake • horseback riding • golf • pool • WiFi • wheelchair access

The Parliament House Resort 410 N Orange Blossom Tr 407/425-7571 • lesbians/gay men • pool • restaurant • wheelchair access • also 6 bars • multiracial • live shows • dancing/DJ • young crowd • gay-owned

Rick's B&B PO Box 22318, 32830 407/396-7751, 407/414-7751 (CELL) • mostly gay men • full brkfst • pool • nudity • patio • WiFi • gay-owned

Wyndham Orlando Resort 8001 International Dr 407/351-2420 • gay-friendly • villa surrounded by gardens • pools • wheelchair access

BARS

Bear's Den 410 N Orange Blossom Tr (at Parliament House) 407/425-7571 • 6pm-2am, from noon wknds • mostly gay men • country/ western • levi/ leather • strippers • piano • also restaurant

Copper Rocket 106 Lake Ave (at 17-92), Maitland 407/645-0069 • 4pm-2am • gay-friendly • also restaurant • wheelchair access

Hank's 5026 Edgewater Dr (at Lee Rd) 407/291-2399 • noon-2am • mostly gay men • neighborhood bar • beer/ wine • patio • wheelchair access

The New Phoenix 7124 Aloma Ave (at Forsythe), Winter Park 407/678-9070 • 6pm-2am, from 4pm Th-Sat • lesbians/ gay men • neighborhood bar • dancing/DJ • karaoke • live shows • drag shows

The Peacock Room 1321 N Mills Ave (at Montana) 407/228-0048 • 4:30pm-2am, from 8pm wknds • gay-friendly • art shows • live music

Stonewall Bar 741 W Church St (at Glenn Ln) 407/373-0888 • 5pm-2am • mostly gay men • dancing/DJ • karaoke • wheelchair access • gay-owned

NIGHTCLUBS

Club 369 369 N Orange Ave 407/977-2997 • 10:30pm-2:30am Fri only • lesbians/gay men • dancing/DJ • Afrikan-American clientele

Parliament House Resort 410 N Orange Blossom Tr 407/425-7571 • 10:30am-3am • lesbians/ gay men • 6 bars • dancing/DJ • multiracial • live shows • videos • also restaurant • wheelchair access • gay-owned

Pulse Orlando 1912 S Orange Ave (at Kaley St) **407/649–3888** • 9pm-2am, clsd Sun • mostly gay men • dancing/DJ • theme nights • drag shows • 18+

Revolution 375 S Bumby Ave (at South St) **407/228–9900** • 4pm-close, from 10pm Sun • lesbians/ gay men • dancing/DJ • multiracial • Sat women's night • drag shows • 18+ • patio • wheelchair access

CAFES

Pom Pom's 67 N Bumby Ave **407/894–0865** • 11am-5am, 24hrs Fri-Sat • tea & sandwiches

White Wolf Cafe & Antique Shop 1829 N Orange Ave (at Princeton) **407/895–9911** • 7am-9pm, till 10pm Fri-Sat, 8am-3pm Sun • beer/ wine • wheelchair access

RESTAURANTS

Dandelion Communitea Cafe 618 N Thornton Ave (at Colonial) **407/362–1864** • 11am-10pm, till 3pm Mon, till 5pm Sun • vegetarian/ vegan • beer/ wine

Dexter's Thornton Park 808 E Washington St **407/648–2777** • lunch & dinner • also Winter Park & Lake Mary locations

Ethos Vegan Kitchen 601-B New York Ave (at Fairbanks) **407/228–3898** • 11am-10pm, 10am-3pm Sun • WiFi • wheelchair access

Funky Monkey Wine Company **407/427–1447** • 5pm-11pm • sushi • drag shows weekly

Garden Cafe 810 W Colonial Dr (at Westmoreland) **407/999–9799** • 11am-10pm, from noon wknds, clsd Mon • vegetarian Chinese • wheelchair access

Hamburger Mary's Orlando 110 W Church St (at Garland) **321/319–0600** • 11am-midnight, till 1am Th-Sat • full bar • live shows • karaoke • wheelchair access • gay-owned

Houston's 215 South Orlando Ave, Winter Park **407/740–4005** • lunch & dinner • upscale American • wheelchair access

Hue 629 E Central Blvd (at N Summerlin Ave) **407/849–1800** • lunch & dinner • new American • full bar

Loving Hut 2101 E Colonial Dr (at Palm Dr) **407/894–5673** • 11am-9pm, from 3pm Sun, clsd Tue • vegetarian/ vegan • wheelchair access

The Rainbow Cafe at Parliament House **407/425–7571** • 7am-11pm • lesbians/ gay men

BOOKSTORES

Mojo 930 N Mills Ave (at E Marks St) **407/896–0204** • 1pm-8pm, 3pm-6pm Sun • LGBT

RETAIL SHOPS

A Comic Shop 114 South Semoran Blvd, Winter Park **407/332–9636** • 11am-7pm, till 9pm Wed, till midnight Fri-Sat

Fairvilla's Sexy Things 7631 International Blvd **407/826–1627** • gifts • adult toys • clothing

PUBLICATIONS

Hotspots **954/928–1862** • weekly entertainment guide

Watermark PO Box 533655 32853 **407/481–2243** • bi-weekly LGBT newspaper for Central FL

EROTICA

Fairvilla Megastore 1740 N Orange Blossom Tr **407/425–6005** • 9am-2am

Palm Beach

ACCOMMODATIONS

The Chesterfield Hotel 363 Coconut Row **561/659–5800** • gay-friendly • pool • jacuzzi

RESTAURANTS

Ta-boo 221 Worth Ave **561/835–3500** • 11:30am-10pm, till 11pm Fri-Sat • cont'l • wheelchair access

Panama City

ACCOMMODATIONS

Casa de Playa 20304 Front Beach Rd, Panama City Beach **850/236-8436**, **850/381–1351** • lesbians/ gay men • guesthouse • steps from Gulf of Mexico • jacuzzi • pool • nonsmoking • patios • gay-owned

Wisteria Inn 20404 Front Beach Rd, Panama City Beach **850/234-0557** • gay/ straight • tropical inn • hot tub • pool • nonsmoking

BARS

La Royale Lounge & Liquor Store 100 Harrison (at Beach Dr) **850/763–1755** • 3pm-3am, till 4am Fri-Sat, from 7pm Sun • lesbians/ gay men • neighborhood bar • courtyard • wheelchair access

Splash Bar 6520 Thomas Dr, Panama City Beach **850/236-3450** • 6pm-2am, till 4am Th-Sat • mostly gay men • 18+ • drag shows • also pride shop • wheelchair access • gay-owned

NIGHTCLUBS

Fiesta Room 110 Harrison Ave (at Beach Dr) 850/763–1755 • 3pm-3am • popular • lesbians/ gay men • dancing/DJ • drag shows • wheelchair access

Pensacola

INFO LINES & SERVICES

GLBT AA Group 716 9th Ave (at Jackson) 850/433–4191 **(AA#)** • 6pm Sun

BARS

The Cabaret 101 S Jefferson St 850/607–2020 • 3pm-2:30am • lesbians/ gay men • live shows 8 karaoke • wheelchair access

The Round-Up 560 E Heinberg St 850/433–8482 • 2pm-3am • popular • mostly gay men • neighborhood bar • videos • patio • wheelchair access

NIGHTCLUBS

Emerald City 406 E Wright St (at Alcaniz) 850/433–9491 • 3pm-3am, dance club from 9pm, clsd Tue • popular • lesbians/ gay men • dancing/DJ • live shows • 18+ • patio • wheelchair access

CAFES

End of the Line Cafe 610 E Wright St 850/429–0336 • 10am-10pm, 11am-5pm Sun, clsd Mon • vegetarian cafe • live bands • art • WiFi • wheelchair access

Pompano Beach

NIGHTCLUBS

Club Cinema 3251 N Federal Hwy 786/597–4088 • gay/ straight • dancing/DJ

RESTAURANTS

J Marks Restaurant 1490 NE 23th St (at Federal Hwy/ USI) 954/782–7000 • 11am-10pm, till 11pm Fri-Sat • live music wknds • full bar • gay-owned

EROTICA

Exxxit Video 1833 E Sample Rd 954/783–6570

Sarasota

INFO LINES & SERVICES

Gay AA 7225 N Lockwood Ridge Rd (in Pierce Hall, Church of the Trinity MCC) 941/355–0847 **(CHURCH #)** • 7pm Sun & 7pm Th

ACCOMMODATIONS

The Cypress 621 Gulfstream Ave S 941/955–4683 • gay-friendly • B&B inn • full brkfst • nonsmoking • WiFi

Turtle Beach Resort 9049 Midnight Pass Rd 941/349–4554 • gay-friendly • pool • nonsmoking • WiFi • wheelchair access

NIGHTCLUBS

Throb 2201 Industrial Blvd 941/358–6969 • 3pm-2am, till 9pm Mon,Th & Sun • mostly gay men • dancing/DJ • drag shows • gay-owned

RESTAURANTS

Caragiulos 69 S Palm Ave 941/951–0866 • lunch & dinner • Italian-American

South Beach

see **Miami Beach/ South Beach**

St Augustine

see also **Jacksonville**

ACCOMMODATIONS

Alexander Homestead 14 Sevilla St 904/826–4147, 888/292–4147 • gay-friendly • Victorian inn • full brkfst • WiFi

Casa Monica 95 Cordova St 904/827–1888, 888/213–8903 • gay-friendly • restaurant & piano bar • gym • pool • kids ok • wheelchair access

The Inn at Camachee Harbor 201 Yacht Club Dr (at May St) 904/825–0003, 800/688–5379 • gay-friendly • restaurant & bar • WiFi

Our House B&B 7 Cincinnati Ave 904/347–6260 • gay/ straight • full brkfst • WiFi • gay-owned

RESTAURANTS

Collage 60 Hypolita St 904/829–0055 • dinner nightly • "artful global dining" • reservations required

St Petersburg

see also **Tampa**

ACCOMMODATIONS

Bay Palms Waterfront Resort 4237 Gulf Blvd, St Petersburg Beach 727/360–7642, 800/257–8998 • gay-friendly • pool • nonsmoking • WiFi • kids/ pets ok

Boca Ciega B&B 727/381–2755 • women only • B&B in private home • pool • lesbian-owned

Changing Tides Cottages 225 Boca Ciega Dr, Madeira Beach **727/397–7706** • gay/ straight • rental cottages • WiFi • lesbian-owned

Dicken's House B&B 335 8th Ave NE **727/822–8622, 800/381–2022** • gay/ straight • pool • full brkfst • WiFi • gay-owned

Flamingo Resort 4601 34th St South **727/321–5000** • mostly gay men • pool • bars & restaurant • live shows • WiFi • wheelchair access

La Veranda B&B 111 5th Ave N **727/224–1057**
• gay/ straight • 1 block from the beach • women-owned

The Pier Hotel 253 2nd Ave N (at 2nd St) **727/822–7500, 800/735–6607** • gay/ straight • kids ok

Postcard Inn on the Beach 6300 Gulf Blvd **727/367–2711, 800/237–8918** • gay-friendly • pool • restaurant • WiFi

BARS

The Hideaway 8302 4th St N (at 83rd) **727/570–9025** • 2pm-2am, from 4pm Sat, clsd Mon • mostly women • neighborhood bar • live shows • karaoke • wheelchair access

Oar House 4807 22nd Ave S **727/327–1691** • 9am-2am, from 11am Sun • lesbians/ gay men • neighborhood bar • karaoke

A Taste for Wine 241 Central Ave (at 2nd St N) **727/895–1623** • 2pm-9pm, till midnight Fri-Sat, clsd Mon • occasional lesbian events • women-owned

NIGHTCLUBS

Georgie's Alibi 3100 3rd Ave N (at 31st St N) **727/321–2112** • 11am-3am • lesbians/ gay men • neighborhood bar • dancing/DJ • food served • drag shows • videos • WiFi • wheelchair access • patio • gay-owned

RESTAURANTS

Central Avenue Oyster Bar 249 Central Ave **727/897–9728** • 11am-midnight

Sea Porch Cafe 3400 Gulf Blvd (at Don Cesar Beach Resort) **727/360–1884** • beach views

Skyway Jack's 2795 34th St S **727/867–1907** • 5am-3pm • Southern cooking (diner-style)

ENTERTAINMENT & RECREATION

Bedrocks Beach/ Sunset Beach W Gulf Blvd (at S end of Treasure Island, Sunset Beach) • popular park

Dali Museum 1 Dali Blvd **727/823–3767, 800/442–3254**

Fort DeSoto Park Pinellas Bayway S • beautiful gay beach

Tallahassee

INFO LINES & SERVICES

The Family Tree 5126C Woodlane Cir **850/222–8555** • LGBT community center • call for hours

ACCOMMODATIONS

Hampton Inn Quincy 165 Spooner Rd (Pat Thomas Pkwy), Quincy **850/627–7555** • gay-friendly • full brkfst • swimming • WiFi • wheelchair access

Tampa

see also St Petersburg

ACCOMMODATIONS

Don Vicente de Ybor Inn 1915 Republica de Cuba **813/241–4545, 866/206–4545** • gay/ straight • cafe & bar

Gram's Place Hostel 3109 N Ola Ave **813/221–0596** • gay/ straight • nudity • kids ok • nonsmoking • WiFi

Hampton Inn & Suites 1301 East 7th Ave **813/247–6700** • gay/ straight • WiFi • pool • wheelchair access

Hyatt Regency 211 N Tampa St **813/225–1234** • gay/ straight • pool • restaurant & bar • WiFi • wheelchair access

Sawmill Camping Resort 21710 US Hwy 98, Dade City **352/583–0664** • mostly gay men • theme wknds w/ entertainment • RV hookups • cabins • tent spots • dancing • karaoke • pool • nudity • gay-owned

BARS

2606 2606 N Armenia Ave (at St Conrad) **813/875–6993** • 3pm-3am • mostly gay men • also leather shop from 9pm • wheelchair access • gay-owned

Baxter's 1519 S Dale Mabry (at W Neptune) **813/258–8830** • noon-3am • mostly gay men • neighborhood bar • karaoke • wheelchair access

Body Shop Bar 14905 N Nebraska **813/971–3576** • 3pm-3am • mostly gay men • neighborhood bar • karaoke • gay-owned

Bradley's on 7th 1510 E 7th Ave, Ybor City **831/241–2723** • 4pm-3am • mostly gay men • dancing/DJ • drag shows

Chelsea Lounge 1502 N Florida Ave (at Hwy 275) **813/228–0139** • 3pm-3am • lesbians/ gay men • neighborhood bar • dancing/DJ • drag shows • karaoke • hookah • patio

City Side 3703 Henderson Blvd (at Dale Mabry) **813/350-0600** • 11am-3am • lesbians/gay men • dancing/DJ • neighborhood bar • karaoke • WiFi • patio

Hamburger Mary's 1600 E 7th Ave (at N 16th St) **813/241-6279** • 11am-11pm, till 3am wknds • lesbians/gay men • karaoke • drag shows • wheelchair access

NIGHTCLUBS

The Castle 2004 N 16th St **813/247-7547** • 10:30pm-3am, clsd Tue-Wed • mixed gay/straight • dancing/DJ • theme nights

Crowbar 1812 N 17th St **813/241-8600** • 10pm-3am • mixed gay/straight • dancing/DJ • live shows • karaoke

G Bar 1401 E 7th Ave **813/247-1016** • 4pm-3am, clsd Sun-Mon • lesbians/gay men • dancing/DJ • drag shows • 18+ • more women Fri • gay-owned

Liquid 1502 E 7th Ave **813/248-6104** • 4pm-3am, from 7pm Sat, clsd Mon • mostly gay men • dancing/DJ • drag shows

Steam Fridays 1507 E 7th Ave (at the Honey Pot) **813/247-4663** • 10pm Fri only • mostly gay men • dancing/DJ • 18+ • 3 flrs

Tease Saturdays 1507 E 7th Ave (at the Honey Pot) **813/247-4663** • 10pm Sat only • mostly women • dancing/DJ • 18+ • 3 flrs

Valentines Nightclub 7522 N Armenia Ave (btwn Sligh & Waters) **813/936-1999** • 3pm-3am • mostly gay men • dancing/DJ • drag shows • male dancers

CAFES

Joffrey's Coffee 1600 E 8th Ave **813/247-4600** • 7am-10pm, till midnight wknds • WiFi

Sacred Grounds Cafe 4819 E Busch Blvd (at Hyaleah Rd) **813/983-0837** • 6pm-midnight, till 2am Fri-Sat • lesbians/gay men • live music, poetry, performance • WiFi

Tre Amici 1907 19th St N **813/247-6964** • 8am-5pm, till 11pm Th, clsd Sun • cafe & wine bar

RESTAURANTS

Bernini 1702 E 7th Ave **813/248-0099** • lunch Mon-Fri, dinner nightly • Italian

Centro Cantina 1600 E 8th Ave **813/241-8588** • Tex Mex • great balcony

Columbia 2117 E 7th Ave **813/248-4961** • 11am-close, from noon Sun • Cuban & Spanish

Crabby Bill's 401 Gulf Blvd, Indian Rocks Beach **727/595-4825** • inexpensive seafood joint

Gaspar's Grotto 1805 E 7th Ave **813/248-5900** • 11am-3am • live shows • karaoke • WiFi • patio

JJ's Cafe & Bar 1601 E 7th Ave (at N 16th St) **813/247-4125** • 11am-10pm, till 2:30am wknds

The Laughing Cat 1820 N 15th St **813/241-2998** • Italian • wheelchair access

The Metro Restaurant & Lounge 511 N Franklin St **813/225-1111** • 4:30pm-11pm, till 1am Fri-Sat, clsd Mon • drag shows wknds

The Queen's Head 2501 Central Ave, St Petersburg **727/498-8584** • 4:30pm-2am, from noon wknds, clsd Mon • European • full bar

ENTERTAINMENT & RECREATION

Picnic Island Picnic Island Blvd (across from the military base, on E side) • gay beach at end of park

RETAIL SHOPS

King Corona Cigars 1523 E 7th Ave **888/248-3812** • local, handmade cigars • also cafe & bar

The MC Film Festival 1901 N 15th St (at 8th Ave) **813/247-6233** • LGBT pride gift store

PUBLICATIONS

Watermark **813/655-9890, 877/926-8118** • bi-weekly LGBT newspaper for Central FL

Womyn's Words **727/323-5706** • monthly magazine

West Palm Beach

ACCOMMODATIONS

Grandview Gardens B&B 1608 Lake Ave (at Palm) **561/833-9023** • gay-friendly • pool • nonsmoking • WiFi • wheelchair access • gay-owned

Hotel Biba 320 Belvedere Rd **561/832-0094** • mid-century chic motor lodge

Scandia Lodge 625 S Federal Hwy (at 6th Ave), Lake Worth **561/586-3155** • gay/straight • pool • pets ok • nonsmoking

Bars

Fort Dix 6205 Georgia Ave (at Colonial) 561/533–5355 • noon-3am, till 4am Fri-Sat • popular • mostly gay men • neighborhood dive bar • dancing/DJ wknds • patio • wheelchair access

HG Rooster's 823 Belvedere Rd (btwn Parker & Lake) 561/832–9119 • 3pm-3am, till 4am Fri-Sat • popular • mostly gay men • neighborhood bar • drag shows • karaoke • food served • wheelchair access

Nightclubs

Monarchy 221 Clematis St 561/835–6661 • 10pm-3am, till 4am Fri-Sat, clsd Sun, Tue & Th • gay-friendly • dancing/DJ

Respectable Street 518 Clematis St 561/832–9999 • 9pm-3am, till 4am Fri-Sat, clsd Sun-Tue • gay-friendly • dancing/DJ • alternative • retro & new wave nights • live music

Restaurants

Rhythm Cafe 3800-A S Dixie Hwy 561/833–3406 • 6pm-10pm, clsd Sun-Mon • some veggie • beer/ wine

Thai Bay 1900 Okeechobee Blvd (in Palm Beach Market Pl) 561/640–0131 • lunch & dinner, clsd Sun

Entertainment & Recreation

MacArthur Beach Singer Island, N Palm Beach

Bookstores

Changing Times Bookstore 911 Village Blvd #806 (at Palm Beach Lakes) 561/640–0496 • 10am-7pm, till 5pm Sat-Sun • community bulletin board • wheelchair access

Retail Shops

Eurotique 814 Northlake Blvd, North Palm Beach 561/684–2302 • 10am-8pm, till 6pm Sat, noon-5pm Sun • leather • books • videos

Wilton Manors

see Fort Lauderdale

Winter Haven

Bars

Old Man Frank's 1005 S Lake Howard Dr (at Central) 863/294–9179 • 11am-2am, from noon-midnight Sun • gay-friendly • on the lake • food served • smoking allowed • wheelchair access

GEORGIA

Athens

Accommodations

Ashford Manor B&B 5 Harden Hill Rd (at Main St), Watkinsville 706/769–2633 • gay-friendly • pool • nonsmoking • WiFi • gay-owned

Bars

The Globe 199 N Lumpkin St (at Clayton) 706/353–4721 • 11am-2am, till midnight Sun • gay-friendly • 40 single-malt scotches • also restaurant

Nightclubs

Forty Watt Club 285 W Washington St (at Pulaski) 706/549–7871 • call for events• gay-friendly • alternative • live music • wheelchair access

Cafes

Jittery Joe's Coffee 297 E Broad St (at Jackson) 706/613–7449 • 7am-11pm, from 8am wknds • WiFi • gallery • wheelchair access

Restaurants

The Grit 199 Prince Ave 706/543–6592 • 11am-10pm, great wknd brunch 10am-3pm • ethnic vegetarian • wheelchair access

Atlanta

Info Lines & Services

Galano Club 585 Dutch Valley Rd (at Monroe) 404/881–9188 • meetings throughout the day • LGBT recovery club • call for meeting times

Accommodations

The Georgian Terrace Hotel 659 Peachtree St NE (at Ponce de Leon) 404/897–1991, 800/651–2316 • gay-friendly • "Atlanta's only historic luxury hotel" • hosted Gone w/ the Wind world-premier reception in 1939 • pool • kids ok • WiFi • wheelchair access

Glenn Hotel 110 Marietta St NW (at Spring) 404/521–2250, 888/717–8851 • gay/ straight • boutique hotel • also restaurant & rooftop lounge • WiFi

Hotel Indigo 683 Peachtree St NE (at 3rd) 404/874–9200, 800/863–7818 • cozy, stylish no-frills hotel • workout room • also restaurant • WiFi

Stonehurst Place Bed & Breakfast 923 Piedmont Ave NE (at 8th St) **404/881-0722, 877/285-2246** • gay/ straight • in 1896 shingle-style house furnished w/ antiques • full brkfst • nonsmoking • WiFi • lesbian-owned

W Atlanta Midtown 188 14th St NE (at Juniper St NE) **404/892-6000** • gay/ straight • stylish hotel • WiFi • pool • convenient location

Bars

Amsterdam 502 Amsterdam Ave NE **404/892-2227** • 11:30am-close • mostly gay men • dancing/DJ • food served • video & sports bar

Atlanta Eagle 306 Ponce de Leon Ave NE (at Argonne) **404/873-2453** • 7pm-3am, from 5pm Sat, clsd Sun • popular • mostly gay men • dancing/DJ • bears • leather • also leather store • gay-owned

Atlanta

LGBT Pride:
October. 404/382-7588, web: atlantapride.org.

Annual Events:
July - National Black Arts Festival 404/730-7315, web: www.nbaf.org.
Labor Day weekend - Femme-nomen-non (lesbian party), web: www.girlsinthenight.com.
Sept/Oct - Out on Film, lesbian/ gay film festival 404/671-9446, web: www.outonfilm.com.

City Info:
404/521-6600 or 800/285-2682, web: www.atlanta.net.

Best View:
70th floor of the Peachtree Plaza, in the 3-story revolving Sun Dial restaurant (404/589-7506). Also from the top of Stone Mountain (only 20 feet taller).

Weather:
Summers are warm and humid (upper 80°s to low 90°s) with occasional thunderstorms. Winters are icy with occasional snow. Temperatures can drop into the low 30°s. Spring and fall are temperate – spring brings blossoming dogwoods and magnolias, while fall festoons the trees with awesome fall colors.

Attractions:
Atlanta Botanical Garden 404/876-5859, web: www.atlantabotani-calgarden.org.
Centennial Olympic Park.
CNN Center 404/827-2300, web: www.cnn.com/StudioTour.
Coca-Cola Museum 404/676-5151, web: www.woccatlanta.com.
Georgia Aquarium (largest aquarium in the US) 404/581-4000, web: www.georgiaaquarium.org.
High Museum of Art 404/733-5000, web: www.high.org.
Margaret Mitchell House 404/814-4000, web: www.gwtw.org.
Martin Luther King Jr. Memorial Center 404/526-8900, web: www.thekingcenter.org.
Piedmont Park.
Stone Mountain Park 770/498-5690, web: www.stonemountain-park.com.
Underground Atlanta 404/523-2311, web: underground-atlanta.com.

Transit:
Checker Cab 404/351-1111, web: www.atlantacheckercab.com.
Superior Shuttle 770/457-4794, web: www.atlsuperiorshuttle.com.
Marta 404/848-5000, web: www.itsmarta.com.

Blake's on the Park 227 10th St (at Piedmont) 404/892–5786 • 3pm-3am, from 1pm Fri-Sun, till midnight Sun • lesbians/gay men • karaoke • drag shows

Bulldogs 893 Peachtree St NE (btwn 7th & 8th) 404/872–3025 • 4pm-4am Sun-Fri, till 3am Sat, clsd Sun • mostly gay men • African-American clientele

Burkhart's Pub 1492–F Piedmont Ave NE (at Monroe, in Ansley Square) 404/872–4403 • 4pm-3am, from 2pm wknds, till midnight Sun • lesbians/gay men • neighborhood bar • food served • karaoke • live shows • patio • wheelchair access

The Daiquiri Factory 889 W Peachtree St (at 7th) 404/881–8188 • 11am-2:30am • lesbians/gay men • the name says it all

Eddie's Attic 515–B N McDonough St (at Trinity Place), Decatur 404/377–4976 • 5pm-close Mon-Th, till 2am Fri-Sat, open 1 hr before showtime Sun • gay/straight • occasional lesbian hangout • live music • open mic & comedy • restaurant • rooftop deck

Felix's on the Square 1510-G Piedmont Ave NE (Ansley Square) 404/249–7899 • 2pm-2:30am, from noon Sat, 12:30pm-midnight Sun • mostly gay men • food served • karaoke • wheelchair access

Friends on Ponce 736 Ponce de Leon NE (at Ponce de Leon Pl) 404/817–3820 • 2pm-3am, from noon Sat, till midnight Sun • rooftop patio • wheelchair access

Halo Lounge 817 W Peachtree St (6th St, btwn W Peachtree & Peachtree) 404/962–7333 • 9pm-3am, from 6pm Sat, clsd Sun • dinner • gay/straight • DJ

The Hideaway 1544 Piedmont Ave NE #124 (at Monroe, in Ansley Mall) 404/874–8247 • 2pm-2am Mon-Th, till 3am Fri-Sat, 12:30pm-midnight Sun • mostly men • neighborhood bar • wheelchair access

Le Buzz 585 Franklin Rd A-10 (at S Marietta Pkwy, in Longhorn Plaza), Marietta 770/424–1337 • 5pm-3am, clsd Sun • lesbians/gay men • neighborhood bar • dancing/DJ • drag shows • karaoke • also restaurant • patio • wheelchair access

Mary's 1287B Glenwood Ave (at Flat Shoals) 404/624–4411 • 5pm-3am, clsd Sun-Mon • lesbians/gay men • friendly neighborhood • dancing/DJ • karaoke • videos • wheelchair access

Mixx 1492–B Piedmont Ave NE (at Monroe, in Ansley Square) 404/228–4372 • 4pm-2am, till 3am Fri-Sat, clsd Sun • mostly gay men • neighborhood bar • dancing/DJ wknds • karaoke • bears • food served

My Sister's Room 1271 Glenwood Ave 678/705–4585 • 8pm-close, clsd Sun-Tue • popular • mostly women • live music • also restaurant • younger crowd • patio

Opus I 1086 Alco St NE (at Cheshire Bridge) 404/634–6478 • 11am-3am, 12:30pm-midnight Sun • mostly gay men • neighborhood bar • wheelchair access

Oscar's Video Bar 1510-C Piedmont Ave NE (in Ansley Mall) 404/815–8841 • 2pm-2:30am, clsd Sun • mostly gay men • drag shows

Tripps 1931 Piedmont Circle (at Cheshire Bridge) 404/724–0067 • 2pm-3am, 12:30pm-midnight Sun • mostly gay men • neighborhood bar • food served

NIGHTCLUBS

Girls in the Night • women's parties & events around Atlanta • check local listings or girlsinthenight.com

The Heretic 2069 Cheshire Bridge Rd (at Piedmont) 404/325–3061 • 9am-3am, clsd Sun, till 11pm Mon-Tue • mostly gay men • dancing/DJ • wheelchair access

Ladies at Play 79 Poplar St (at Fairlie St) • monthly women's dance party • check ladiesatplay.com for details • mostly women • dancing/DJ • multiracial

Traxx 866/602–5553 • dance parties & events around Atlanta • mostly gay men • dancing/DJ • mostly African American • live shows

Traxx Girls Parties 888/935–8729 • weekly women's dance parties • check traxxgirls.com for info

Wild Mustang/Jungle 2115 Faulkner Rd NE (off Cheshire Bridge Rd NE) 404/844–8800 • 10pm-3am, clsd Sun • lesbians/gay men • dancing/DJ • also Stars of the Century (drag shows) Mon 11pm • cover charge

CAFES

Apache Cafe 64 3rd St NW 404/876–5436 • food served • poetry readings • events • gallery • multiracial

Aurora Coffee 468 Moreland Ave 404/523–6856 • 6:30am-9pm, from 7am wknds

Intermezzo 1845 Peachtree Rd NE 404/355–0411 • noon-11pm • classy cafe • plenty veggie • full bar • great desserts

RESTAURANTS

Amuse 560 Dutch Valley Rd **404/888–1890** • dinner only, wknd brunch, clsd Mon • full bar • int'l bistro

Apres Diem 931 Monroe Dr #C-103 **404/872–3333** • 11:30am-midnight, till 2am Fri-Sat, from 11am wknds, brunch Sat-Sun • French bistro • live jazz Wed • full bar

Aria 490 E Paces Ferry **404/233–7673** • dinner only, clsd Sun

Aurum 915 Peachtree St (at 8th St) **404/815–9426** • 9pm-2am, till 3am wknds • gay/ straight • lounge

Bacchanalia/ Star Provisions/ Quinones 1198 Howell Mill Rd NW **404/365–0410** • dinner only, clsd Sun • upscale • American

Buckhead Diner 3073 Piedmont Rd NE **404/262–3336** • lunch Mon-Sun, dinner nightly, Sun brunch • upscale diner fare

Cafe Sunflower 2140 Peachtree Rd NW (at Bennett St NW) **404/352–8859** • lunch & dinner, clsd Sun • vegetarian

The Colonnade 1879 Cheshire Bridge Rd NE **404/874–5642** • dinner nightly, lunch wknds • traditional Southern

Cowtippers 1600 Piedmont Ave NE (at Monroe) **404/874–3751** • 11am-11pm, till midnight Fri-Sat • steak house • transgender-friendly • wheelchair access

Ecco 40 7th St NE **404/347–9555** • 5:30pm-10pm, till 11pm Fri-Sat, till 10pm Sun • Italian • reservations recommended • wheelchair access

Einstein's 1077 Juniper St (at 12th) **404/876–7925** • 11am-11pm, till midnight Fri-Sat, from 9am Sun, wknd brunch • popular • some veggie • full bar • patio • wheelchair access • reservations accepted

The Flying Biscuit Cafe 1655 McLendon Ave (at Clifton) **404/687–8888** • 7am-10pm • popular • healthy brkfst all day • plenty veggie • beer/ wine • wheelchair access • multiple locations

Fresh To Order 860 Peachtree St NE (at 7th St NE) **404/593–2333** • 11am-10pm, brunch Sun from 10am • healthy fast food • patio

Frogs 931 Monroe Dr NE **404/607–9967** • 11am-10pm, till 11pm wknds • Mexican

Gilbert's Cafe & Bar 219 10th St NE (at Piedmont Ave) **404/872–8012** • dinner Tue-Sat, wknd brunch, food till 2am, bar till 3am, till midnight Sun

Hobnob 1551 Piedmont Ave NE (at Monroe) **404/968–2288** • 11am-11pm, till 3pm Sun • wheelchair access

Joe's On Juniper 1049 Juniper St NE **404/875–6634** • 11am-2am, till midnight Sun • American

Las Margaritas 1842 Chesire Bridge Rd **404/873–4464** • lunch & dinner • Latin fusion • wheelchair access

The Lobby at Twelve 361 17th St **404/961–7370** • brkfst, lunch & dinner • upscale American • reservations recommended

Majestic Diner 1031 Ponce de Leon Ave (at Highland) **404/875–0276** • 24hrs • popular diner right from the '50s w/ cantankerous waitresses included • at your own risk • some veggie • wheelchair access

Mi Barrio Restaurante Mexicano 571 Memorial Dr SE **404/223–9279** • lunch Tue-Sat, dinner nightly, clsd Sun • full bar • wheelchair access

Murphy's 997 Virginia Ave NE (at N Highland Ave) **404/872–0904** • 11am-10pm, till midnight Fri-Sat, from 8am wknds • popular • plenty veggie • wheelchair access

No Más! Cantina 180 Walker St **404/574–5678** • lunch & dinner daily, wknd brunch • Mexican • also huge furniture & gift store • gay-owned

Pastries A Go Go 235 Ponce De Leon Place (at Commerce), Decatur **404/373–3423** • 7:30am-4pm, clsd Tue • delicious baked goods • wheelchair access

R Thomas Deluxe Grill 1812 Peachtree Rd NW (btwn 26th & 27th) **404/872–2942, 404/881–0246** • 24hrs • popular • beer/ wine • healthy Californian/ juice bar • plenty veggie • wheelchair access

Ria's Bluebird Cafe 421 Memorial Dr (at Cherokee) **404/521–3737** • 8am-3pm • very popular • gourmet brunch in quaint old diner in Grant Park • plenty veggie • everything made from scratch • wheelchair access • woman-owned

Roxx Tavern & Diner 1824 Cheshire Bridge Rd NE (at Manchester) **404/892–4541** • lunch & dinner, Sun brunch • patio • wheelchair access

Sawicki's 250 W Ponce De Leon Ave, Decatur **404/377–0992** • 11am-7pm, till 8pm Fri-Sat, noon-5pm Sun • deli • great sandwiches

The Shed at Glenwood 475 Bill Kennedy Way **404/835-4363** • dinner nightly, Sun brunch • also bar

Swan Coach House 3130 Slaton Dr NW **404/261-0636** • 11am-2:30pm, clsd Sun • also gift shop & art gallery

Table 1280 Peachtree St NE (at Woodruff Arts Center) **404/897-1280** • lunch & dinner, wknd brunch, clsd Mon • upscale American & tapas

TWO urban licks 820 Ralph McGill Blvd **404/522-4622** • dinner nightly, brunch Sun • great grill • full bar • live blues • reservations recommended

The Vortex 438 Moreland Ave NE (at Euclid) **404/688-1828** • 11am-midnight, till 3am wknds • biker ambiance • great burgers • 18+

Watershed 1820 Peachtree St **404/809-3561** • 11am-10pm, Sun brunch • wine bar • also gift shop • owned by Emily Saliers of the Indigo Girls • wheelchair access

ENTERTAINMENT & RECREATION

AIDS Memorial Quilt/ NAMES Project 204 14th St **404/688-5500** • visit The Quilt at the foundation offices

Ansley Park Playhouse 1545 Peachtree St **404/941-7453** • some LGBT-themed productions

Atlanta Rollergirls • Atlanta's female roller derby league • visit www.atlantarollergirls.com for events

Joining Hearts, Inc Piedmont Park Pool **678/318-1446** • great dance/ pool party in July • wheelchair access • wheelchair access 100% of every dollar raised donated to our beneficiaries

Little 5 Points, Moreland & Euclid Ave S of Ponce de Leon Ave • hip & funky area w/ too many restaurants & shops to list

Martin Luther King, Jr Center for Non-Violent Social Change 449 Auburn Ave NE **404/526-8900** • 9am-5pm daily • includes King's birth home, the church where he preached in the '60s & his gravesite

BOOKSTORES

Brushstrokes/ Capulets 1510 Piedmont Ave NE (near Monroe) **404/876-6567** • 10am-10pm, till 11pm Fri-Sat • LGBT variety store • gay-owned

Charis Books & More 1189 Euclid Ave NE (at Moreland) **404/524-0304** • 11am-7pm, noon-8pm Sun • feminist • wheelchair access

RETAIL SHOPS

The Boy Next Door 1447 Piedmont Ave NE (btwn 14th & Monroe) **404/873-2664** • 10am-8pm, noon-6pm Sun • clothing

The Junkman's Daughter 464 Moreland Ave NE (at Euclid) **404/577-3188** • 11am-7pm, till 8pm Fri, till 9pm Sat, from noon Sun • hip stuff • wheelchair access

PUBLICATIONS

David Atlanta **404/418-8901** • gay entertainment magazine w/ extensive nightlife calendar, maps & directory

Fenuxe **404/835-2016** • the voice of Atlanta's Gay Community

Georgia Voice **404/815-6941** • bi-weekly LGBT publication

GYMS & HEALTH CLUBS

Gravity Fitness 2201 Faulkner Rd (off Cheshire Bridge Rd) **404/486-0506** • day passes available

Urban Body Fitness 500 Amsterdam Ave **404/885-1499**

EROTICA

Inserection 1739 Cheshire Bridge Rd **404/262-9113**

Southern Nights Videos 2205 Cheshire Br Rd (at Woodland Ave NE) **404/728-0701** • 24hrs

Starship 2275 Cheshire Bridge Rd **404/320-9101, 800/215-1053** • 24hrs • many locations in Atlanta

CRUISY AREAS

Publix on Ponce 1001 Ponce de Leon Ave • supermarket • dyke cruising territory

Augusta

BARS

The Filling Station 1258 Gordon Hwy **706/828-7400** • 8pm-close Th-Sat only, mostly men

Cherry Log

ACCOMMODATIONS

Fox Mountain Camp & Artist Retreat 350 Black Ankle Way **404/502-3538** • women-only • camping • live music

Dewy Rose

Accommodations

The River's Edge 2311 Pulliam Mill Rd
706/213-8081 • mostly gay men • cabins •
camping • RV • live shows • pool • nudity •
nonsmoking • wheelchair access

Lake Lanier

Entertainment & Recreation

Gay Cove btwn Athens Park Rd & Frank
Boyd Rd (Channel Marker 21) • a rainbow
rendezvous for the pleasure-boating crowd—
look for the rainbow flag

Savannah

Info Lines & Services

First City Network 307 E Harris St
912/236-2489 • complete info & events line •
social group • also newsletter

Accommodations

The Azalea Inn & Gardens 217 E
Huntingdon St (at Abercorn St)
912/236-6080, 800/582-3823 • gay-friendly •
19th-c Italianate • vintage gardens • pool • full
Southern brkfst • nonsmoking • WiFi

Catherine Ward House Inn 118 E
Waldburg St (at Abercorn) **912/234-8564,
800/327-4270** • gay/ straight • Victorian
Italianate • full brkfst • WiFi

The Galloway House 107 E 35th St
912/658-4419 • gay/ straight • furnished apts
• cont'l brkfst

Kehoe House 123 Habersham St
912/232-1020, 800/820-1020 • gay-friendly •
full brkfst • WiFi

Mansion on Forsyth Park 700 Drayton St
912/238-5158, 888/213-3671 • gay-friendly •
restored Victorian mansion in historic district •
pool • nonsmoking • WiFi • wheelchair access

Statesboro Inn 106 S Main, Statesboro
912/489-8628, 800/846-9466 • gay-friendly •
full brkfst • WiFi

Thunderbird Inn 611 W Oglethorpe Ave (at
MLK Blvd) **912/232-2661, 866/324-2661** •
gay-friendly • motel • kids ok • nonsmoking •
WiFi • gay-owned

Bars

Chuck's Bar 305 W River St **912/232-1005** •
hrs vary, clsd Sun • gay/ straight •
neighborhood bar • young crowd • student &
artist hangout

Nightclubs

Club One 1 Jefferson St (at Bay)
912/232-0200 • 5pm-3am, till 2am Sun •
lesbians/ gay men • dancing/DJ • food served •
live shows Th-Sun • karaoke • drag shows
• dancers • videos

Cafes

Cafe Gelatohhh 202 W St Julian St
912/234-2344 • artisanal gelato • also coffee,
sandwiches

The Sentient Bean 13 E Park Ave (at Bull
St) **912/232-4447** • 7am-10pm • food served
• vegetarian/ vegan • shows at night

Wright Square Cafe 21 W York St
912/238-1150 • 7:30am-5pm, from 9am Sat,
clsd Sun • large chocolate selection • patio

Restaurants

The 5 Spot 4430 Habersham St
912/777-3021
• 7am-10pm, till 11pm Fri-Sat • modern
American menu with full bar

B Matthews 325 E Bay St **912/233-1319** •
8am-9pm, till 10pm Fri-Sat, till 3pm Sun •
casual bistro • wheelchair access

Bar Food 4523 Habersham St **912/355-5956**
• 4pm-1am, clsd Sun • full bar • wheelchair
access • gay-owned

Casbah 20 E Broughton St **912/234-6168** •
dinner nightly • Moroccan • also
entertainment

Churchill's Pub 13 W Bay St **912/232-8501** •
5pm-1am

Clary's Cafe 404 Abercorn (at Jones)
912/233-0402 • 7am-4pm, from 8am Sat-Sun
• country cookin'

The Distillery 416 W Liberty St
912/236-1772 • 11am-1am, till 3am Fri-Sat,
noon-9pm Sun • wheelchair access

Fannie's on the Beach 1613 Strand Ave (at
Silver Ave), Tybee Island **912/786-6109** •
noon-11pm, till 2am wknds • dancing/DJ • live
shows

Firefly Cafe 321 Habersham St
912/234-1971 • 11am-9pm, till 9:30pm Fri-
Sat, 9am-3pm Sun • wheelchair access

Green Truck Neighborhood Pub 2430
Habersham St **912/234-5885** • 11am-11pm,
clsd Sun-Mon • beer/ wine • wheelchair access
• gay-owned

Local 11 Ten 1110 Bull St **912/790-9000** •
dinner nightly • upscale dining in a restored
1950s bank • also Perch rooftop bar

Mellow Mushroom 11 W Liberty St 912/495-0705 • 11am-10pm • pizza & beer • wheelchair access

Olde Pink House/ Planters Tavern 23 Abercorn St **912/232-4286** • upscale Southern dining upstairs, cozy bar downstairs • live jazz

Rocks on the Roof 102 W Bay St (on the roof of The Bohemian Hotel) **912/721-3900** • 7am-10pm, till 11pm wknds • fantastic views of river & historic district

Soho South Cafe 12 W Liberty St 912/233-1633 • 11am-4pm daily • eclectic

ENTERTAINMENT & RECREATION

Savannah Walks, Inc 912/238-9255, 888/728-9255 • gay-friendly • walking tours of downtown Savannah

Washington

RESTAURANTS

Talk of the Town 10 West Public Sq 706/678-7661 • 11am-2pm • gay-owned

HAWAII

Please note that cities are grouped by islands:
Hawaii (Big Island)
Kauai
Maui
Molokai
Oahu (includes Honolulu)

HAWAII (BIG ISLAND)

Captain Cook

ACCOMMODATIONS

Aloha Guest House 84-4780 Mamalahoa Hwy **808/328-8955, 800/897-3188** • gay/ straight • full organic brkfst • nudity • nonsmoking • WiFi • wheelchair access • gay-owned

Areca Palms Estate B&B 808/323-2276, 800/545-4390 • gay-friendly • full brkfst • nonsmoking

Horizon Guest House 808/938-7822 • gay/ straight • full brkfst • pool • nonsmoking • WiFi • wheelchair access • gay-owned

Ka'awa Loa Plantation 82-5990 Napoopoo Rd 96704 **808/323-2686** • gay/ straight • plantation-style B&B • nonsmoking • WiFi • gay-owned

Kealakekua Bay B&B 808/328-8150, 800/328-8150 • gay/ straight • Mediterranean-style villa • nonsmoking • kids ok • also 2-bdrm guesthouse

South Kona Hideaway 83-5399 Middle Keei Rd (at Mamalahoa Hwy) • gay/ straight • WiFi • two rental suites tucked away in the coffee farms • lesbian -owned

Hilo

ACCOMMODATIONS

Aloha Healing Women 14-4817 Kapoha Kai St **808/936-6067, 877/850-2250** • women only • all-inclusive holistic healing retreats • full brkfst • pool • accupuncture • women-owned

The Butterfly Inn for Women 808/966-7936, 800/546-2442 • women only • kitchens • nonsmoking • WiFi • women-owned

RESTAURANTS

Cafe Pesto 308 Kamehameha Ave **808/969-6640** • lunch & dinner • pizzas, salads, pastas • on the waterfront • also at Kawaihae Shopping Center 808/882-1071

ENTERTAINMENT & RECREATION

Best of Hilo Adventures Tours 1477 Kalanianaole Ave **808/987-3905** • lesbian-owned

Richardson Beach at end of Kalanianaole Ave (Keaukaha)

Sun and Sea Hawaii 224Kamehameha Ave (at Kalakaua Ave) **808/934-0902** • LGBT snorkel rental & tour company • women's party producers • lesbian-owned

Honaunau-Kona

ACCOMMODATIONS

Dragonfly Ranch Healing Arts Center 1 1/2 miles down City of Refuge Rd **808/328-2159** • gay/ straight • hot tub • nonsmoking • eco-spa • luxuriously rustic upscale treehouse

Kailua-Kona

INFO LINES & SERVICES

Gay AA 808/329-1212

ACCOMMODATIONS

1st Class B&B Kona Hawaii 77-6504 Kilohana St **808/329-8778, 888/769-1110** • gay-friendly • ocean views • full brkfst • nonsmoking • WiFi

Holualoa Inn 76-5932 Mamalahoa Hwy **808/324-1121** • gay-friendly • luxury B&B near Kona Beach • WiFi • women owned

KonaLani Hawaiian Inn & Coffee Plantation 76-5917H Mamalahoa Hwy **808/324-0793** • lesbians/ gay men • full brkfst • condo rentals • nonsmoking • gay-owned

Royal Kona Resort 75-5852 Ali'i Dr **808/329-3111, 800/222-5642** • gay-friendly • pool • private beach • bar • live shows • WiFi • wheelchair access

BARS

The Mask-querade 75-5660 Kopiko St **808/329-8558** • noon-2am • lesbians/ gay men • neighborhood bar • dancing/DJ • live shows • karaoke • Mon ladies night • gay-owned

My Bar 74-5606 Luhia St (btwn Kaiwi & Eho St) **808/331-8789** • 11am-2am, from 10am wknds • gay-friendly • karaoke

RESTAURANTS

Agnes' Portuguese Bake Shop 46 Hoolai St **808/262-5367** • 6am-6pm, till 2pm Sun, clsd Mon

Buzz's Original Steak House 413 Kawailoa Rd **808/261-4661** • across from beach, great Mai Tais

Huggo's 75-5828 Kahakai Rd (on Kailua Bay) **808/329-1493** • dinner only • waterfront dining • also bar • live entertainment • patio

Moke's Bread & Breakfast 27 Ho'olai St **808/261-5565** • 6:30am-3pm, clsd Tue, great brkfst

BOOKSTORES

Kona Stories 78-6831 Ali'i Dr #142 (in the Keauhou Shopping Ctr) **808/324-0350** • bookstore that hosts PFLAG meetings & other LGBT groups

RETAIL SHOPS

The Wright Gallery 73-5590 Kauhola St **808/333-6572** • 10am-5pm, clsd Mon • gay-owned

Kamuela

ACCOMMODATIONS

Waimea Views Guest House 65-1546 Kawaihae Rd (at Paki Pl) **808/885-8559** • gay/ straight • peaceful guesthouse on the slopes of Mauna Kea • kids ok • WiFi • wheelchair access • women-owned

Na'alehu

ACCOMMODATIONS

Margo's Corner near South Point **808/929-9614** • gay-friendlyl • cottage & 4 campsites • kids ok • WiFi

Pahoa

ACCOMMODATIONS

Aloha Inn Hawaii **808/965-2211** • mostly women • cooking & massage available • nonsmoking • wheelchair access • lesbian-owned

Coconut Cottage B&B **808/965-0973, 866/204-7444** • gay/ straight • centrally located btwn Hilo & Volcanoes Nat'l Park • gay-owned

Dakini Gardens & Retreat Ala 'Ili Rd, Kehena Beach **808/443-3463** • mostly women • cottage • swimming at beach • hot tub • nonsmoking • women-owned

Green Fire Productions 14-4707 Ewa Ln (Kapoho Beach Estates) **808/965-1733** • women only • artesiian ocean pond • nonsmoking • lesbian-owned

Hawaiian Retreat 14-234 Papaya Farm Rd **808/640-2157** • gay/ straight • kids/ pets ok • organic farm & orchard • WiFi

Kalani **808/965-7828, 800/800-6886** • gay/ straight • coastal wellness retreat & spa • pool • nudity • nonsmoking • WiFi • food served • wheelchair access

Pamalu—Hawaiian Country House **808/965-0830** • gay/ straight • secluded country retreat • pool • kids ok if family rents whole house • nonsmoking • WiFi • gay-owned

Rainbow Retreat Center **808/965-9011** • gay/ straight • large no-chemical pool • kids/ pets ok • nonsmoking • limited wheelchair access • lesbian-owned

ENTERTAINMENT & RECREATION

Kehena Beach off Hwy 137 (trailhead at 19-mile marker phone booth) • lava rock trail to clothing-optional black-sand beach

Volcano Village

ACCOMMODATIONS

The Artist Cottage at Volcano Garden Arts 19-3834 Old Volcano Rd (at Wright Rd) **808/985-8979** • gay-friendly • kids/ pets ok • WiFi

The Chalet Kilauea Collection 19-4178 Wright Rd (at Laukapu) **808/967-7786, 800/937-7786** • gay-friendly • full brkfst • hot tub • nonsmoking • WiFi

Hale Ohia Cottages **808/967-7986, 800/455-3803** • gay/ straight • WiFi • gay-owned

Kulana: The Affordable Artists Sanctuary **808/985-9055** • mostly women • artist retreat • camping, cabins & guest rooms available • no smoking, drugs or alcohol • kids ok • women-owned

CAFES

Ono Cafe 19-3834 Old Volcano Rd (at Wright St, at Volcano Garden Arts) **808/985-8979** • 11am-3pm

KAUAI

Anahola

ACCOMMODATIONS

Mahina Kai Ocean Villa 4933 Aliomanu Rd **808/822-9451, 800/337-1134** • gay/ straight • pool • hot tub • nudity • nonsmoking • WiFi • gay-owned

Hanalei

NIGHTCLUBS

Tahiti Nui 5-5134 Kuhio Hwy (near Hanalei Center) **808/826-6277** • 11am-2am, 4pm-11pm Sun • gay-friendly • dancing/DJ • live music most nights • karaoke • also restaurant • Italian/ local • wheelchair access

Kapaa

ACCOMMODATIONS

17 Palms Kauai **808/822-5659, 888/725-6799** • gay/ straight • 2 secluded cottages 200 steps from beach • kids ok • nonsmoking • WiFi • wheelchair access • gay-owned

Anuenue Plantation B&B **808/823-8335, 888/371-7716** • mostly gay men • plantation house w/ mtn views • full brkfst • nonsmoking • WiFi • gay-owned

Fern Grotto Inn 4561 Kuamoo Rd (at Kuhio Hwy) **808/821-9836, 808/822-4845** • gay/ straight • cottages on the banks of the Wailua River • kids ok • nonsmoking

Plantation Hale Suites 525 Aleka Loop **808/822-4941, 800 /775-4253** • gay-friendly • one bedroom condos • pool • mention DAMRON for a 10% discount off our best available rate • wheelchair access • gay-run

RESTAURANTS

Eggbert's 4-484 Kuhio Hwy (in Coconut Plantation Marketplace) **808/822-3787** • 7am-1pm • light fare until 6pm Mon-Sat • wheelchair access

Mema 4-369 Kuhio Hwy (in shopping center) **808/823-0899** • lunch Mon-Fri, dinner nightly • Thai & Chinese • BYOB • wheelchair access

Lihue

ACCOMMODATIONS

Kauai Beach Resort 4331 Kauai Beach Dr **808/245-1955, 866/971-2782** • gay-friendly • pools• also restaurant/ bar • non-smoking • WiFi

Puunene

RESTAURANTS

Roy's Poipu Bar & Grill 2360 Kiahuna Plantation Dr (in Poipu Shopping Ctr) **808/742-5000** • 5:30pm-10pm

Wailua

RESTAURANTS

Caffe Coco 4-369 Kuhio Hwy **808/822-7990** lunch Tue-Fri, dinner nightly, clsd Mon • live music • BYOB • wheelchair access

Waimea

ACCOMMODATIONS

Aston Waimea Plantation Cottages **808/338-1625, 877/997-6667** • gay-friendly • swimming • kids ok • WiFi

MAUI

INFO LINES & SERVICES

Both Sides Now • all-inclusive LGBT community organization • resources • events

Hana

ACCOMMODATIONS

Hana Accommodations **808/248-7868, 800/228-4262** • gay/ straight • studios & tropical cottages • nonsmoking • kids ok • gay-owned

Kaanapali

ACCOMMODATIONS

The Royal Lahaina Resort 2780 Kekaa Dr **808/661-3611, 800/222-5642** • gay-friendly • full-service resort • pool • wheelchair access

Get a Room!

Receive 10% OFF
when you book online!

Use promo code DAMRON

808.879.1261
MauiSunseeker.com

BOOK ONLINE 24/7

MAUI
LGBT
RESORT

S U N S E E K E R

Kihei

ACCOMMODATIONS

Anfora's Dreams 323/467–2991, 800/788–5046 • gay/ straight • rental condo near ocean • hot tub • pool • gay-owned

Eva Villa 815 Kumulani Dr 808/874–6407, 800/884–1845 • gay-friendly • B&B • near Wailea beaches • hot tub • pool • WiFi • kids over 12 yrs ok • wheelchair access

➤**Maui Sunseeker LGBT Resort** 551 S Kihei Rd (at Wailana Place) 808/879–1261, 800/532–6284 • lesbians/ gay men • ocean views • pool • nudity allowed • nonsmoking • WiFi • gay-owned

Tutu Mermaids on Maui B&B 2840 Umalu Pl 808/874–8687, 800/598–9550 • gay/ straight • jacuzzi • pool • near beach • nonsmoking • WiFi • lesbian-owned

BARS

Diamond's Ice Bar & Grill 1279 S Kihei Rd 808/874–9299 • 11am-2am, from 7am Sun • gay-friendly local bar • food served • live shows

NIGHTCLUBS

Ambrosia Martini Lounge 1913 S Kihei Rd #H (in Kihei Kalama Village) 808/891–1011 • 6pm-2am • gay/straight • dancing/DJ • wheelchair access

CAFES

Cafe at La Plage 2395 S Kihei Rd (at Kam Beach I) 808/875–7668 • 7am-5pm, till 3pm Sun • WiFi • wheelchair access

RESTAURANTS

Jawz Tacos 1279 S Kihei Rd 808/874–8226 • 11am-9pm • fresh fish tacos • wheelchair access

Stella Blues Cafe 1279 S Kihei Rd (in Azeka II Shopping Center) 808/874–3779 • 7:30am-11pm • live music • wheelchair access

EROTICA

The Love Shack 1913 S Kihei Rd (in Kalama Vlg) 808/875–0303 • intimate apparel

Kula

ACCOMMODATIONS

The Upcountry B&B 4925 Lower Kula Rd (at Copp St) 808/878–8083 • gay-friendly • nonsmoking • WiFi • wheelchair access

Lahaina

RESTAURANTS

Betty's Beach Cafe 505 Front St 808/662–0300 • 8am-10pm, fmore gay at bar till midnight

Lahaina Coolers 180 Dickenson St 808/661–7082 • 8am-1am • patio • wheelchair access

RETAIL SHOPS

Skin Deep Tattoo 626 Front St (across from the Banyan Tree) 808/661–8531 • 10am-10pm, till 8pm Sun-Mon

Makawao

ACCOMMODATIONS

Aloha Cottage 808/573–8555, 888/328–3330 • rental cottage • WiFi • designed for comfort, style, charm & seclusion • outdoor soaking tub • lesbian -owned

Hale Ho'okipa Inn B&B 32 Pakani Pl 808/572–6698, 877/572–6698 • gay-friendly • restored Hawaiian plantation home • nonsmoking • WiFi • wheelchair access • woman-owned

RESTAURANTS

Casanova Restaurant & Deli 1188 Makawao Ave 808/572–0220 • lunch & dinner • Italian • full bar till 2am • gay-friendly • ladies night Wed • live music

Makena

ENTERTAINMENT & RECREATION

Little Beach at Makena • lesbians/ gay men • Pilani Hwy S to Wailea, right at Wailea Ike Dr, left on Wailea Alanui Dr to public beach, then take trail up hill at right end of beach

Wailea

ACCOMMODATIONS

Ho'olei at Grand Wailea 146 Ho'olei Cir (at Wailea Alanui Dr) 877/346–6534 • gay-friendly • pool • WiFi • wheelchair access

Wailuku

ACCOMMODATIONS

Maalaea Kai Condo 70 Hauoli St (Maalaea Village) 562/212–3312 • gay-friendly • oceanfront 2-bdrm condo • WiFi

MOLOKAI

Kaunakakai

RESTAURANTS

Kanemitsu Bakery & Coffee Shop 79 Ala Malama St **808/553-5855** • 5:30am-5pm, clsd Tue • great sweet bread

OAHU

PUBLICATIONS

Odyssey Magazine Hawaii 808/955-5959 • everything you need to know about gay Hawaii

Haleiwa

ACCOMMODATIONS

Kelea Surf Spa 949/492-7263 • women only • surf spa & yoga on Oahu's North Shore • open during spring only • 18+

Honolulu

INFO LINES & SERVICES

Gay/ Lesbian AA 310 Pa'okalani Ave, Room 203A **808/946-1438** • 7pm & 8pm Sat

ACCOMMODATIONS

Aqua Palms Waikiki 1850 Ala Moana Blvd (at Kalia & Ena) **808/947-7256, 866/406-2782** • gay-friendly • kids ok • nonsmoking • WiFi • wheelchair access

Aston Waikiki Circle Hotel 2464 Kalakaua Ave (at Uluniu St, Waikiki) **808/923-1571, 877/997-6667** • gay-friendly • kids welcome • nonsmoking • WiFi

Hotel Renew 129 Paoakalani Ave (at Lemon Rd, Waikiki) **808/687-7700, 888/485-7639** • gay-friendly • nonsmoking • WiFi

Waikiki Grand Hotel 134 Kapahulu Ave **808/923-1814, 808/923-1511** • gay/ straight • rentals above Hula's Bar • pool • nonsmoking • women-owned

BARS

Bacchus Waikiki 408 Lewers St **808/926-4167** • noon-2am • lesbians/ gay men • neighborhood bar

In Between 2155 Lau'ula St (off Lewers, across from Planet Hollywood, Waikiki) **808/926-7060** • noon-2am • mostly gay men • neighborhood bar • karaoke

Lo Jax 2256 Kuhio Ave, 2nd flr (at Seaside, Waikiki) **808/922-1422** • noon-2am • lesbians/ gay men • neighborhood/ sports bar • food served • WiFi

Tapa's Restaurant & Lanai Bar 407 Seaside, 2nd flr (at Kuhio Ave) **808/921-2288** • 9am-2am • gay/ straight • lanai bar • karaoke • also restaurant • East-West fusion • gay-owned

Wang Chung's 2410 Koa Ave (at Kaiulani) **808/921-9176** • 5pm-2am • lesbians/ gay men • karaoke • wheelchair access

NIGHTCLUBS

Bar 7 1344 Kona St (at Piikoi Rd) **808/955-2640** • 9pm-4am • gay/ straight • dancing/DJ • mostly Asian American • drag shows Sat • wheelchair access

Downe Towne for Women 35 N Hotel St (at Bar 35) **808/537-3535** • 9pm-2am 1st Sat only • mostly women • dancing/DJ

Fusion Waikiki 2260 Kuhio Ave, 2nd flr (at Seaside) **808/924-2422** • 10pm-4am, from 8pm Fri-Sat • mostly gay men • dancing/DJ • transgender-friendly • live shows • karaoke Mon-Tue • drag shows • videos

Hula's Bar & Lei Stand 134 Kapahulu Ave (2nd flr of Waikiki Grand Hotel) **808/923-0669** • 10am-2am • popular • mostly gay men • dancing/DJ • food served • live shows • videos • young crowd • weekly catamaran cruise • WiFi

CAFES

Leonard's Bakery 933 Kapahulu Ave **808/737-5591** • 5:30am-9pm, till 10pm Fri-Sat • irresistible malasadas & doughnuts

Mocha Java Cafe 1200 Ala Moana Blvd (in Ward Center) **808/591-9023** • 8am-9pm, till 6pm Sun • WiFi • outdoor seating • wheelchair access

Tapa's II 1888 Kalakaua Ave, C106 (in Waikiki Landmark Building) **808/979-2299** • 9am-2am, clsd wknds • full bar • WiFi • patio • gay-owned

RESTAURANTS

Alan Wong's 1857 S King St (at Pumehana St) **808/949-2526** • dinner only • upscale, romantic Hawaiian dining

Arancino di Mare 2552 Kalakaua Ave (in Waikiki Beach Marriott) **808/931-6273** • brkfst, lunch & dinner • Italian

Cafe Che Pasta 1001 Bishop St, Ste 108 (enter off Alakea St) **808/524-0004** • lunch & dinner, clsd Sun • full bar

Cafe Sistina 1314 S King St **808/596-0061** • lunch Mon-Fri, dinner nightly • northern Italian • some veggie • full bar • wheelchair access

Cha Cha Cha 342 Seaside Ave **808/923-7797** • lunch & dinner • Mexican • happy hour

Cheeseburger in Paradise 2500 Kalakaua Blvd **808/923-3731** • 7am-11pm • full bar

Eggs 'n' Things 2464 Kalakaua Ave **808/923-3447** • 6am-2pm, 5pm-10pm • also at 2464 Kalakaua Ave, 808/ 926-3447

House Without A Key 2199 Kalia Rd (at Lewers St, at Halekulani Hotel) **808/923-2311** • 7am-9pm • stunning sunset views • Hawaiian music nightly

Hula Grill 2335 Kalakaua Ave (in Outrigger Hotel) **808/923-4852**

Indigo 1121 Nu'uanu Ave **808/521-2900** • lunch Tue-Fri, dinner Tue-Sat • Eurasian • live music • wheelchair access

Keo's in Waikiki 2028 Kuhio Ave **808/951-9355** • 5pm-10pm • Thai • reservations advised • wheelchair access

La Cucaracha 2446 Koa Ave **808/924-3366** • noon-11pm • Mexican • full bar

Liliha Bakery 515 N Kuakini St (at Liliha St) **808/531-1651** • open 24hrs, till 8m Sun, clsd Mon • diner fare & baked goods • wheelchair access

Lulu's 2586 Kalakaua Ave **808/926-5222** • 7am-2am • full bar • live shows

Rock Island Cafe 131 Kaiulani Ave (off Kalakaua, in King's Village Waikiki) **808/923-8033** • old-fashioned soda fountain

Singha Thai 1910 Ala Moana Blvd **808/941-2898** • 4pm-10pm • Thai dancers

Tiki's Grill & Bar 2570 Kalakaua Ave (in ResortQuest Hotel) **808/923-8454**

Honolulu

LGBT PRIDE:
June, web: www.honolulupff.org.

ANNUAL EVENTS:
April - Merrie Monarch Festival, hula competition in Hilo, web: www.kalena.com/merriemonarch.
April-May - Golden Week, celebration of Japanese culture.
May - Honolulu Rainbow Film Festival 808/675-8428, web: www.hglcf.org.
September - Aloha Festival, web: alohafestivals.com.

CITY INFO:
800/464-2924, web: www.gohawaii.com.
Also www.visit-oahu.com.

ATTRACTIONS:
Bishop Museum 808/847-3511, web: www.bishopmuseum.org.
Foster Botanical Gardens. 808/522-7066, web: www.hawaiimuseums.org/mc/isoahu_foster.htm.
Hanauma Bay.

Honolulu Academy of Arts 808/532-8700, web: www.honoluluacademy.org.
'Iolani Palace 808/522-0822, web: www.iolanipalace.org.
Polynesian Cultural Center 800/367-7060 or 808/293-3333, web: www.polynesia.com.
USS Arizona Memorial, 808/422-3200, web: www.nps.gov/valr.
Waimea Falls Park.

BEST VIEW:
Helicopter tour.

WEATHER:
Usually paradise perfect, but humid. It rarely gets hotter than the upper 80°s.

TRANSIT:
Charley's 808/233-3333, web: charleystaxi.com.
Honolulu Airport Shuttle 800/208-2979 web: www.honoluluairportshuttle.com.
The Bus 808/848-5555, web: www.thebus.org.

ENTERTAINMENT & RECREATION

Diamond Head Beach • gay/ straight • take road from lighthouse to beach • some nude sunbathing

Girls Who Surf 1020 Auahi St, Bldg 4, Ste 4 (Ward Shopping Ctr) **808/772-4583** • surf lessons for all levels • everyone welcome

Hawaii Gay Tours 1947 Alaeloa St 218/234-2310

Honolulu Gay/ Lesbian Cultural Foundation 1670 Makaloa St #204 808/675-8428 • last wknd of May annual Honolulu Rainbow Film Festival • art exhibits • concerts • plays

Rainbow Sailing Charters 808/347-0235 • lesbians/ gay men • day & overnight sailing adventures • whale-watching • sunset cocktail cruises • civil unions • lesbian-owned

PUBLICATIONS

Expression Magazine 808/393-7994 • monthly glossy LGBT magazine

Odyssey Magazine Hawaii 808/955-5959 • everything you need to know about gay Hawaii

EROTICA

Suzie's Secrets 1370 Kapiolani Blvd 808/949-4383 • 24hrs

Windward Coast

ACCOMMODATIONS

Ali'i Bluffs Windward B&B 46-251 Ikiiki St, Kane'ohe 808/235-1124, 800/235-1151 • gay/ straight • pool • nonsmoking • WiFi • gay-owned

IDAHO

Statewide

PUBLICATIONS

Diversity Newsmagazine 208/336-3870 • statewide LGBT newspaper • monthly

http://www.tccidaho.org/DiversityNews2.htm

Boise

INFO LINES & SERVICES

The Community Center 305 E 37th St, Garden City 208/336-3870 • volunteer staff

ACCOMMODATIONS

Hotel 43 981 Grove St 800/243-4622 • gay/ straight • restaurant & bar • WiFi

The Modern Hotel & Bar 1314 W Grove St 208/424-8244, 866/780-6012 • gay-friendly • refurbished 1960's Travelodge & restaurant,• pets ok • WiFi

BARS

The Lucky Dog 2223 W Fairview Ave (at 23rd) 208/333-0074 • 2pm-2am, from noon wknds • mostly gay men • neighborhood bar • patio • WiFi

Neurolux 111 N 11th St (at W Idaho) 208/343-0886 • 1pm-2am • gay-friendly • dancing/DJ • live music

NIGHTCLUBS

The Balcony Club 150 N 8th St #226 (at Idaho) 208/336-1313 • 4pm-2am • lesbians/ gay men • popular • dancing/DJ • karaoke • theme nights • wheelchair access • gay-owned

CAFES

Flying M Coffeehouse 500 W Idaho St (at 5th St) 208/345-4320 • 6:30am-11pm, from 7:30am wknds, till 6pm Sun • WiFi

River City Coffee 5517 W State St 208/853-9161 • 6am-5pm, till 4pm Sun

Tully's 794 Broad St 208/472-1308 • 7am-8pm, till 6pm Sat, 8am-5pm Sun • WiFi

RESTAURANTS

Lucky 13 Pizza 3662 S Eckert Rd 208/344-6967 • 11am-9pm, till 10pm wknds

ENTERTAINMENT & RECREATION

The Flicks 646 Fulton St 208/342-4222 • opens 4pm, from noon Fri-Sun • 4 movie theaters • food served • beer/ wine • patio • wheelchair access

BOOKSTORES

Crone's Cupboard 712 N Orchard 208/333-0831 • 10am-7pm, clsd Sun-Mon • Wiccan • New Age • feminist/ lesbian books & art

RETAIL SHOPS

The Record Exchange 1105 W Idaho St (at 11th) 208/344-8010 • 9am-9pm, till 7pm Sun • gifts • music • also cafe & live music

EROTICA

The O!Zone 1615 Broadway Ave (at Howe) 208/395-1977 • noon-7pm, till 5pm Sun

Pleasure Boutique 5022 Fairview Ave (at Orchard) 208/433-1161 • toys • videos

Vixen Video 5777 W Overland Rd 208/672-1844 • 10am-2am • gay-owned

Coeur d'Alene

see also Spokane, Washington

ACCOMMODATIONS

The Clark House on Hayden Lake 5250 E Hayden Lake Rd, Hayden Lake **208/772–3470, 800/765–4593** • gay-friendly • mansion on a wooded 12-acre estate • full brkfst • also fine dining • hot tub • nonsmoking • WiFi • gay-owned

Lava Hot Springs

see also Pocatello

ACCOMMODATIONS

Aura Soma Lava 196 E Main St **208/776–5800, 800/757–1233** • gay/ straight • pool • also retail store

Moscow

INFO LINES & SERVICES

Inland Oasis LGBTA Center 1320 S Mountain View Rd **208/596–4449** • HIV testing • youth group & more

BOOKSTORES

Bookpeople 521 S Main (btwn 5th & 6th) **208/882–2669** • 9:30am-6:30pm, till 8pm Fri-Sat • general

Nampa

CAFES

Flying M Coffee Garage 1314 2nd St S **208/467–5533** • 7am-11pm, till 6pm wknds • entertainment

Pocatello

NIGHTCLUBS

Club Charleys 331 E Center St **208/232–9606** • 5pm-2am, clsd Sun • lesbians/ gay men • dancing/DJ • live shows • karaoke • drag shows • wheelchair access

CAFES

Main St Coffee & News 234 N Main St (btwn Lander & Clark) **208/234–9834** • 6:30am-4pm, from 8am Sat, from 9am Sun

Twin Falls

CAFES

Annie's Lavender & Coffee Cafe 591 Addison Ave W (at 8th St) **208/736–2003** • 6am-5pm, seasonal wknd hrs • wheelchair access

RESTAURANTS

Pizza Planet 720 Main St (at 8th St), Buhl **208/543–8560** • 11am-8pm, till 9pm Fri-Sat

ILLINOIS

Alton

see also St Louis, Missouri

NIGHTCLUBS

Bubby & Sissy's 602 Belle St (at 6th) **618/465–4773** • 3pm-2am, till 3am Fri-Sat, clsd Mon • lesbians/ gay men • dancing/DJ • karaoke • food served • wheelchair access

Arlington Heights

see Chicago

Bloomington

CAFES

Coffee Hound 407 N Main St **309/827–7575** • 6:30am-6pm, 8am-5pm Sun • WiFi

Kelly's Bakery & Cafe 113 N Center St **309/820–1200** • 7am-6pm, till 2pm Sat, clsd Sun • wheelchair access

Blue Island

see also Chicago

NIGHTCLUBS

Club Krave 13126 S Western Ave (at Grove) **708/597–8379** • 8pm-2am, till 3am Fri-Sat, from 6pm Mon • lesbians/ gay men • neighborhood bar • dancing/DJ • transgender-friendly • karaoke • WiFi • wheelchair access

Bradley

RESTAURANTS

La Villetta 801 W Broadway St **815/939–4960** • 11am-9pm, till 8pm Sun • Italian

EROTICA

Slightly Sinful 101 N Kinzie Ave (at Broadway) **815/937–5744**

Carbondale

INFO LINES & SERVICES

AA Lesbian/ Gay 618/549–4633

NIGHTCLUBS

Two 13 213 E Main St **618/549–4270** • 8pm-2am • gay-friendly • neighborhood bar • dancing/DJ • drag shows

Champaign/ Urbana

ACCOMMODATIONS

Sylvia's Irish Inn 312 W Green St, Urbana **217/384-4800** • gay-friendly • full brkfst • nonsmoking • WiFi

BARS

Emerald City Lounge 118 N First St (at University Ave), Champaign **217/398-8661** • 5pm-2am Th-Sat, from 10am Sun • lesbians/ gay men • food served • live music • wheelchair access • gay-owned

Mike 'N Molly's 105 N Market St (at University), Champaign **217/355-1236** • 4pm-2am • gay-friendly • live music • dancing/DJ • beer garden

NIGHTCLUBS

Chester Street 63 Chester St (at Water St), Champaign **217/356-5607** • 5pm-2am • lesbians/ gay men • dancing/DJ • drag show Sun • gay-owned

CAFES

Aroma Cafe 118 N Neil St, Champaign **217/356-3200** • 7am-10pm, from 8am wknds

Cafe Kopi 109 N Walnut (at University), Champaign **217/359-4266** • 7am-midnight • espresso bar with sandwiches • WiFi

Espresso Royale 602 E Daniel St (at 6th St), Champaign **217/328-1112** • 7am-midnight

Pekara Bakery & Bistro 116 N Neil St, Champaign **217/359-4500** • 7am-8pm, from 8am Sun

RESTAURANTS

Boltini Lounge 211 N Neil St, Champaign **217/378-8001** • 4pm-2am, from 6pm Sat, clsd Sun • also full bar • upscale

The Courier Cafe 111 N Race St, Urbana **217/328-1811** • 7am-11pm

Dos Reales 1407 N Prospect Ave, Champaign **217/351-6879** • 11am-10pm • Mexican • wheelchair access

Farren's Pub & Eatery 308 N Randolph St, Champaign **217/359-6977** • 11am-9pm, till 10pm Fri, from noon wknds • full bar

Fiesta Cafe 216 S 1st St (at E Clark), Champaign **217/352-5902** • 11am-11pm, bar till 1am • Mexican • gay-owned

The Great Impasta 156C Lincoln Sq, Urbana **217/359-7377** • 11am-9pm, till 10pm Fri, 5pm-10pm Sat • live music • wheelchair access

Radio Maria 119 N Walnut St, Champaign **217/398-7729** • 4pm-2am, wknd brunch • eclectic Mexican cuisine

Silvercreek 402 N Race St, Urbana **217/328-3402** • lunch & dinner, brunch Sun • live music

BOOKSTORES

Jane Addams Book Shop 208 N Neil St (S of Main), Champaign **217/356-2555** • 10am-7pm, till 5pm Sat-Sun • LGBT & women's sections

RETAIL SHOPS

Dandelion 9 Taylor St, Champaign **217/355-9333** • 11am-6pm, noon-5pm Sun • vintage & used clothing

GYMS & HEALTH CLUBS

Refinery 2302 W John St, Champaign **217/355-4444** • gay-friendly

CHICAGO

Chicago is divided into 5 geographical areas:
Chicago—Overview
Chicago—North Side
Chicago—Boystown/ Lakeview
Chicago—Near North
Chicago—South Side

Chicago—Overview

includes some listings for Greater Chicagoland; please check individual cities like Oak Park as well

INFO LINES & SERVICES

AA/ New Town Alano Club 909 W Belmont Ave, 2nd flr (btwn Clark & Sheffield) **773/529-0321** • 5pm-11pm, from 8:30am wknds • wheelchair access

Affinity 6400 S Kimbark (at church) **773/324-0377** • nonprofit "serving Chicago's black lesbian & bisexual women's community" through "education, social & community collaborations"

The Center on Halsted 3656 N Halsted St (at Waveland) **773/472-6469, 773/472-1277 (TTY)** • 8am-10pm • LGBT center • organic grocery store • cafe • theater • gym • technology center

ACCOMMODATIONS

Chicago Women's Residence 1957 S Spaulding Ave (at S 21st) 773/542–9126 • women only • furnished rooms in women's residence • WiFi • please call ahead • lesbian-owned

NIGHTCLUBS

Doll House Entertainment 312/927–1144 • women's parties at clubs around the city • www.dollhousechicago.org

ENTERTAINMENT & RECREATION

Artemis Singers 773/764-4465 • lesbian feminist chorus

Chicago Neighborhood Tours 77 E Randolph St (at Michigan Ave, at Chicago Cultural Center) 312/742–1190 • gay-friendly • the best way to make the Windy City your kind of town

Heartland Cafe 7000 N Glenwood Ave (in Rogers Park) 773/465–8005 • cafe w/ full bar, theater, radio show • lots of live music including performers popular on women's music circuit

John Hancock Observatory 875 N Michigan Ave (in John Hancock Center) 312/751–3681, 888/875–8439 • 9am-11pm, also Watch the city lights glimmer in the night sky from "The Signature Lounge at the 96th"

Leather Archives & Museum 6418 N Greenview Ave 773/761–9200 • 11am-7pm Th-Fri, till 5pm Sat-Sun • membership required (purchase at door)

Second City 1616 N Wells St (at North) 312/337–3992, 312/337–3992 • gay-friendly • legendary comedy club • call for reservations

PUBLICATIONS

Nightspots 773/871-7610 • weekly LGBT nightlife magazine

PINK & PINK PAGES 773/765-4712 • LGBT business directory & lifestyle magazine

Windy City Times 773/871-7610 • weekly LGBT newspaper & calendar guide

Chicago—North Side

ACCOMMODATIONS

House 5863 B&B 5863 N Glenwood (at Admore) 773/682–5217 • gay/ straight • nonsmoking • WiFi • gay-owned

Lang House B&B 7421 N Sheridan Rd (at Jarvis) 773/764–9851 • gay/straight • on the Lake Michigan beach block • WiFi • gay-owned

BARS

The Anvil 1137 W Granville (E of Broadway) 773/973–0006 • 9am-2am • mostly gay men • neighborhood bar • videos

Big Chicks 5024 N Sheridan (btwn Foster & Argyle) 773/728–5511 • 4pm-2am, from 3pm wknds • lesbians/ gay men • neighborhood bar • dancing/DJ • videos • patio • Sun BBQ • WiFi • wheelchair access

The Call 1547 W Bryn Mawr (at Clark) 773/334–2525 • 4pm-2am • lesbians/ gay men • dancing/DJ • country/ western • drag shows • videos • wheelchair access

Crew 4804 N Broadway St (at Lawrence) 773/784–2739 • 11:30am-midnight, 11am-2am Fri-Sat • lesbians/ gay men • sports bar & grill • videos • patio

The Glenwood 6962 N Glenwood Ave (at Morse) 773/764–7363 • 3pm-2am, from noon Sun • lesbians/ gay men • neighborhood sports bar • wheelchair access

Green Mill 4802 N Broadway Ave (at Lawrence) 773/878–5552 • noon-4am • gay/ straight • noted jazz venue • hosts the Uptown Poetry Slam

In Fine Spirits 5420 N Clark St (at Rascher Ave) 773/334–9463 • 4pm-midnight, 3pm-2am Fri-Sat • wine bar • patio • food served • also wine store

Joie de Vine 1744 W Balmoral Ave (at Paulina St) 773/989–6846 • 5pm-2am, till 3am Sat • mostly women • wine bar • patio • WiFi • wheelchair access • lesbian-owned

Marty's 1511 W Balmoral Ave (at Clark) 773/321–7481 • 5pm-2am • gay-friendly • upscale wine & martini bar • food served

Parlour on Clark 6341 N Clark St 773/564–9274 • 7pm-2am, from noon Sun, clsd Mon-Tue • lesbian/gay men • girls night Th • dancing/DJ • cabaret/ drag shows

Scot's 1829 W Montrose Ave (at Damen) 773/528–3253 • 3pm-2am, 1pm-3am Sat, from 11am Sun • mostly gay men • neighborhood bar

Sidecar 6920 N Glenwood Ave (at Morse) 773/764–2826 • 5pm-close • gay/ straight • martini lounge

The Sofo Tap 4923 N Clark St (at W Argyle) 773/784–7636 • 5pm-2am, from 3pm Fri, from noon wknds • mostly gay men • video bar • backyard beer garden • wheelchair access

Spyner's Pub 4623 N Western Ave (at W Eastwood) 773/784–8719 • 11am-2am, till 3am Sat • mostly women • neighborhood bar • karaoke

T's 5025 N Clark St (at Winnemac) 773/784-6000 • 5pm-2am, 11am-3am, till 2am Sun • mostly women • neighborhood bar • karaoke • also restaurant

T's Bar & Restaurant 5025 N Clark St 773/784-6000 • 5pm-2am from 11am wknds • gay/ straight • neightborhood bar • nice patio & good burgers

Touché 6412 N Clark St (at Devon) 773/465-7400 • 5pm-4am, 3pm-5am Sat, noon-4am Sun • popular • mostly gay men • leather

Chicago

LGBT Pride:
June. 773/348-8243, web: www.chicagopridecalendar.org.

Annual Events:
www.bearpride.org.

May-June- Chicago Blues Festival 312/744-3315, web: www.chicagofestivals.net/music/blues-2/blues

August - Northalsted Market Days 773/883-0500, web: www.northalsted.com.

November - Chicago Lesbian & Gay Film Festival 773/293-1447, web: www.reelingfilmfestival.org.

City Info:
Chicago Office of Tourism 877/244-2246, web: www.explorechicago.org.

Weather:
"The Windy City" earned its name. Winter temperatures have been known to be as low as -46°. Summers are humid, normally in the 80°s.

Transit:
Yellow Cab 312/ 829-4222, web: www.yellowcabchicago.com

Go Airport Express 888/284-3826. web: www.airportexpress.com.

Chicago Transit Authority 312/836-7000, web: www.transitchicago.com.

Metra Rail 312/322-6777, web: www.metrarail.com.

Attractions:
900 North Michigan Shops.

Jane Addams Hull-House Museum 312/413-5353, www.hullhouse-museum.org.

The Art Institute of Chicago 312/443-3600, web: www.artic.edu.

DuSable Museum of African American History 773/947-0600, web: www.dusablemuseum.org.

Historic Water Tower.

LaSalle Bank Theatre (formerly Schubert Theatre).

Museum of Contemporary Art 312/280-2660, web: www.mcachicago.org.

Museum of Science and Industry 773/684-1414, web: www.msichicago.org.

National Museum of Mexican Art 312/738-1503, web: www.nationalmuseum-ofmexicanart.org.

Steppenwolf Theatre Company, 312/335-1650, web: www.steppenwolf.org.

Terra Foundation for American Art, 312/664-3939, web: www.terraamericanart.org.

Wrigley Field, 773/404-CUBS, web: chicago.cubs.mlb.com.

Best View:
Skydeck of the 110-story Sears Tower, web: www.theskydeck.com, or the open-air observation deck at the John Hancock Observatory, web: www.hancockobservatory.com.

NIGHTCLUBS

Atmosphere 5355 N Clark St (at W Balmoral Ave) **773/784–1100** • 6pm-2am, till 3am Sat, from 3pm Sat-Sun, clsd Mon • lesbians/ gay men • dancing/DJ • male dancers • drag shows • WiFi • gay-owned

CAFES

Charmer's Cafe 1500 W Jarvis (at Greenview) **773/743–2233** • 6am-6pm, from 7am wknds • lesbians/ gay men • WiFi • wheelchair access

Coffee Chicago 5256 N Broadway St (btwn Berwyn & Foster) **773/784–1305** • 7am-9pm, from 8am wknds • WiFi • wheelchair access

KOPI: A Traveler's Cafe 5317 N Clark St **773/989–5674** • 8am-11pm • food served • wheelchair access

Metropolis Coffee 1039 W Granville Ave (at Kenmore) **773/764–0400** • 6:30am-8pm, from 7:30am Sat-Sun • popular • WiFi

RESTAURANTS

A Taste of Heaven 5401 N Clark St **773/989–0151** • brunch, dinner and delicious. savory and sweet items • gay-owned

Andie's 5253 N Clark (btwn Berwyn & Farragut) **773/784–8616** • 11am-11pm • eastern Mediterranean • full bar • wheelchair access

Anteprima 5316 N Clark St (at Summerdale) **773/506–9990** • dinner nightly • Italian • wheelchair access

Deluxe Diner 6349 N Clark St (at Devon) **773/743–8244** • 24hr diner • karaoke

Fat Cat 4840 N Broadway (at Lawrence Ave) **773/506–3100** • 4pm-2am, from 11am wknds • full bar

Fireside 5739 N Ravenswood (at Rosehill) **773/561–7433** • 11am-4am, till 5am Sat, 10am-4am Sun • Cajun & pizza • patio • full bar

Hamburger Mary's/ Rec Room/ Attic 5400 N Clark St (at Balmoral) **773/784–6969** • 11:30am-midnight, till 2am Wed-Sun, from 10:30am wknds • lesbians/ gay men • full bar • karaoke • drag shows • wheelchair access

Hot Woks Cool Sushi 30 S Michigan Ave (at Madison) **312/345–1234** • 11am-9pm • sushi/ Thai

Jin Ju 5203 N Clark (at Summersdale) **773/334–6377** • dinner only, clsd Mon • Korean • also bar • wheelchair access

Pauline's 1754 W Balmoral (at Ravenswood) **773/561–8573** • 7am-3pm • hearty brkfsts • wheelchair access

Reza's Restaurant 5255 N Clark (btwn Berwyn & Farragut) **773/561–1898** • lunch & dinner • Mediterranean/ Persian • full bar • wheelchair access

Svea Restaurant 5236 N Clark (btwn Berwyn & Farragut) **773/275–7738** • 7am-2pm, till 3pm wknds • Swedish/ American comfort food • wheelchair access

Tedino's 5335 N Sheridan Rd (at Broadway) **773/275–8100** • 11am-midnight, from 3pm Mon • popular • pizza • full bar • wheelchair access

Thai Pastry & Restaurant 4925 N Broadway St, Unit E (at Argyle) **773/784–5399** • 11am-10pm, till 11pm Fri-Sat • wheelchair access

Tweet 5020 N Sheridan Rd (at Argyle) **773/728–5576** • 9am-3pm • brkfst & brunch • cash only • WiFi

ENTERTAINMENT & RECREATION

Hollywood /Osterman Beach at Hollywood & Sheridan Sts • popular • "the" gay beach

BOOKSTORES

Women & Children First 5233 N Clark St (at Foster) **773/769–9299** • 11am-7pm, till 9pm Wed-Fri, 10am-7pm Sat, 11am-6pm Sun • wheelchair access • women-owned

RETAIL SHOPS

Enjoy, An Urban General Store 4727 N Lincoln Ave (Lincoln Square) **773/334–8626** • 10am-7pm, till 6pm Sun • cards & gifts • lesbian-owned

Gaymart 3457 N Halsted St (at Cornelius) **773/929–4272** • 11am-8pm, till 6pm Sun

Leather 6410 6410 N Clark St (at Devon, btwn Jackhammer & Touché) **773/508–0900** • noon-midnight, till 4am Th, till 5am Fri, till 6am Sat, from 4pm Sun-Mon • gay-owned

GYMS & HEALTH CLUBS

Cheetah Gym 5248 N Clark St (at Foster) **773/728–7777, 866/961–6840**

EROTICA

Early to Bed 5232 N Sheridan Rd (at Foster) **773/271–1219, 866/585–2233** • clsd Mon • transgender-friendly • 18+ • lesbian-owned

Tulip Sex Toy Gallery 1480 W Berwyn (at Clark) **773/275–6110, 877/708–8547** • noon-10pm, till 7pm Sun • sex toys for women • lesbian-owned

Chicago—Boystown/ Lakeview

Accommodations

Best Western Plus Hawthorne Terrace 3434 N Broadway St (at Hawthorne Pl) 773/244–3434, 888/860–3400 • gay-friendly • in heart of Chicago's gay community • WiFi • wheelchair access

City Suites Hotel 933 W Belmont Ave (btwn Clark & Sheffield) 773/404–3400, 800/248–9108 • gay-friendly • European style • nonsmoking rooms available • WiFi

Majestic Hotel 528 W Brompton Ave (at Addison) 773/404–3499, 800/727–5108 • gay-friendly • romantic 19th-c atmosphere • nonsmoking • WiFi

The Willows 555 W Surf St (at Broadway) 773/528–8400, 800/787–3108 • gay/ straight • nonsmoking • WiFi

Bars

3160 3160 N Clark St (at Belmont) 773/327–5969 • 3pm-2am, noon-3am Sat, 11am-2am Sun • lesbians/ gay men • neighborhood bar • live shows • piano • cabaret • wheelchair access

Beat Kitchen 2100 W Belmont (btwn Hoyne & Damen) 773/281–4444 • 4pm-2am, from 11:30am Sat-Sun, till 3am Sat • gay-friendly • live bands • also grill • some veggie • wheelchair access

Blues 2519 N Halsted St (at Lill Ave) 773/528–1012, / • 8pm-2am, till 3am Sat • gay-friendly • classic Chicago blues spot

Bobby Love's 3729 N Halsted St (at Waveland) 773/525–1200 • 3pm-2am, from noon wknds, till 3am Sat • lesbians/ gay men • neighborhood bar • karaoke • wheelchair access

Buck's Saloon 3439 N Halsted St (btwn Cornelia & Newport) 773/525–1125 • noon-2am, till 3am Sat, from 11am Sun • mostly gay men • neighborhood bar • great beer garden

Cell Block 3702 N Halsted St (at Waveland) 773/665–8064 • 2pm-3am • mostly gay men • leather • also back bar wknds from 10pm • wheelchair access

Charlie's Chicago 3726 N Broadway St (btwn Waveland & Grace) 773/871–8887 • 3pm-4am, till 5am Sat • mostly gay men • dancing/DJ • country/ western • karaoke • club music after 1am

The Closet 3325 N Broadway St (at Buckingham) 773/477–8533 • 4pm-4am, noon-5am Sat, till 4am Sun • popular • lesbians/ gay men • neighborhood video bar • karaoke

D.S. Tequila Company 3352 N Halsted St (at Roscoe) 773/697–9127 • 5pm-2am, noon-3am wknds • gay/ straight • good burgers & tacos

Elixir 3452 N Halsted St (at Cornelia) 773/975–9244 • 6pm-close • mostly gay men • swank cocktails

Little Jim's 3501 N Halsted St (at Cornelia) 773/871–6116 • noon-4am, till 5am Sat • popular • mostly gay men • neighborhood bar

The Lucky Horseshoe Lounge 3169 N Halsted St (at Briar) 773/404–3169 • 3pm-2am, 1pm-3am Sat • mostly gay men • neighborhood bar

Minibar 3341 N Halsted St (at Roscoe) 773/871–6227 • 5pm-2am, from 11am wknds • popular • lesbians/ gay men • food served • wheelchair access

The North End 3733 N Halsted St (at Grace) 773/477–7999 • 2pm-2am, from 11am wknds • mostly gay men • neighborhood sports bar • wheelchair access

Roscoe's 3354–56 N Halsted St (at W Roscoe) 773/281–3355 • 4pm-2am, from 3pm Fri, from 2pm Sat • lesbians/ gay men • food served • neighborhood bar • dancing/DJ • live/drag shows • karaoke • patio •

Scarlet 3320 N Halsted St (at Aldine) 773/348–1053 • 6pm-2am, from 2pm wknds • mostly gay men • upscale piano bar • cabaret

Sidetrack 3349 N Halsted St (at Roscoe) 773/477–9189 • 3pm-2am, till 3am Sat • popular • lesbians/ gay men • upscale video bar • wheelchair access

Nightclubs

Berlin 954 W Belmont (at Sheffield) 773/348–4975 • 5pm-4am, till 5am Sat, from 8pm Sun-Mon • popular • lesbians/ gay men • dancing/DJ • transgender-friendly • live shows • wheelchair access

Circuit/Rehab 3641 N Halsted St (at Addison) 773/325–2233 • 9pm-4am, till 5am Sat, clsd Mon-Wed • mostly gay men • dancing/DJ • multiracial • Latin nights Th & Sun (T-dance)

Hydrate 3458 N Halsted St (at Cornelia) 773/975–9244 • 8pm-4am, till 5am Sat, opens earlier in summer • popular • gay/ straight • dancing/DJ • drag shows

Lipstick & Lace 773/779-2399 • checkwww.madmanprod.com for events • mostly women • dancing/DJ • multiracial

Planet Earth 3534 W Belmont (at Late Bar) 773/267-5283 • 10pm-5am Sat • gay/ straight • dancing/DJ • New Wave

Smart Bar 3730 N Clark St (downstairs at the Metro) 773/549-0203 • 10pm-4am, till 5am Sat, clsd Mon-Tue • gay-friendly • dancing/DJ • popular • theme nights

Spin 800 W Belmont (enter on Halsted) 773/327-7711 • 4pm-2am, till 3am Sat, from 2pm wknds • lesbians/ gay men • dancing/DJ • live shows • karaoke • lounge • young crowd

Stardust Thursdays 954 W Belmont (at Berlin) 773/348-4975 • 10pm-4am Th only • mostly women • dancing/DJ • food served

CAFES

Caribou Coffee 3300 N Broadway St (at Aldine) 773/477-3695 • from 5:30am, from 6:30am Sat, till midnight Fri-Sat • WiFi

The Coffee & Tea Exchange 3311 N Broadway St (at Roscoe) 773/528-2241 • 8am-8pm, 10am-6pm Sun • fair-trade coffee & tea

RESTAURANTS

Angelina Ristorante 3561 N Broadway St (at Addison) 773/935-5933 • 5:30pm-11pm, wknd brunch • Italian • full bar • wheelchair access

Ann Sather's 909 W Belmont Ave (at Sheffield) 773/348-2378 • 7am-3pm, till 4pm Sat-Sun • Swedish diner & Boystown fixture

Cesar's 2924 N Broadway (at Oakdale) 773/296-9097 • 11am-11pm, till midnight Fri-Sat, till 8pm Sun • "home of the killer margaritas"

Chicago Diner 3411 N Halsted St (at Roscoe) 773/935-6696 • 11am-10pm, from 10am wknds, till 11pm Fri-Sat • hip & vegan • beer/ wine & organic booze

Halsted's Bar & Grill 3441 N Halsted St (btwn Newport & Cornelia) 773/348-9696 • dinner nightly, brunch wknds • neighborhood sports bar • gay-owned

Home Bistro 3404 N Halsted St (at Roscoe, btwn Addison & Belmont) 773/661-0299 • dinner only, clsd Mon • upscale American • bring your own bottle • wheelchair access

Horizon Cafe 3805 N Broadway St (corner w/ Halsted & Grace) 773/883-1565 • 7am-9pm, till 10pm Fri-Sat • diner • brkfst anytime

Joy's Noodles & Rice 3257 N Broadway St (at Melrose) 773/327-8330 • 11am-10pm, till 11pm Fri-Sat • Thai • patio • wheelchair access

Kanok 3422 N Broadway St (at W Hawthorne Pl) 773/529-2525 • 4pm-10:30pm • sushi/ Asian • BYOB • wheelchair access

Kit Kat Lounge & Supper Club 3700 N Halsted St (at W Waveland Ave) 773/525-1111 • 5:30pm-1am, brunch Sun (seasonal) • drag cabaret some nights • gay-owned

Kitsch'n On Roscoe 2005 W Roscoe (at Damen) 773/248-7372 • 8:30am-3pm, dinner served in summer • comfort food for hipsters • full bar

Las Mananitas 3523 N Halsted St (at Cornelia) 773/528-2109 • 11am-11pm, till midnight Fri-Sat • strong margaritas • wheelchair access

Melrose Restaurant 3233 N Broadway St 773/327-2060 • 24hrs, great food

Mon Ami Gabi 2300 N Lincoln Park W (at Belden) 773/348-8886 • dinner only • French bistro

Nookie's Tree 3334 N Halsted St (at Roscoe) 773/248-9888 • 7am-midnight, 24hrs wknds • popular • BYOB • wheelchair access

Orange 2413 N Clark St 773/549-7833 • 8am-3pm • popular brunch spot

Panino's Pizzeria 3702 N Broadway (at Waveland) 773/472-6200 • 11:30am-11pm, till 10pm Sun • full bar • wheelchair access

Pick Me Up Cafe 3408 N Clark St (at Roscoe) 773/248-6613 • 11am-3am, 24hrs Fri-Sat • brkfst all day

Pie Hole Pizza 3477 N Broadway 773/525-8888 • 5pm-3am, noon-5am wknds

Pingpong 3322 N Broadway St 773/281-7575 • 5pm-midnight, noon-10pm Sun • Asian fusion • patio • wheelchair access

The Raw Bar & Grill 3720 N Clark St (at Waveland) 773/348-7291, 773/348-7961 • 11am-2am, till 3am Sat • seafood • lounge • live shows • wheelchair access

Stella's Diner 3042 N Broadway St 773/472-9040 • 7am-10pm

Sushisamba Rio 504 N Wells St (at W Illinois) 312/595-2300 • lunch & dinner, popular brunch • glitzy lounge atmosphere • wheelchair access

Tapas Gitana 3445 N Halsted St (btwn Newport & Cornelia) 773/296-6046 • 5pm-11pm, clsd Mon • full bar • patio

Taverna 750 750 W Cornelia Ave (at Halsted) **773/904-7466** • 5:30-late, Sun brunch • some veggie • upscale Italian • full bar • live music nightly • wheelchair access

Yoshi's Cafe 3257 N Halsted St (at Melrose) **773/248-6110** • dinner Tue-Sun, also Sun brunch • Asian-inspired French • wheelchair access

BOOKSTORES

Unabridged Books 3251 N Broadway St (at Aldine) **773/883-9119** • 10am-9pm, till 7pm wknds • popular • LGBT section

RETAIL SHOPS

Brown Elephant 3651 N Halsted St **773/549-5943** • 11am-6pm, all purchases benefit Howard Brown general health center; also in Andersonville and Oak Park

Uncle Fun 1338 W Belmont (at Racine) **773/477-8223** • heaven for kitsch lovers

EROTICA

Batteries Not Included 3420 N Halsted St (at Newport) **773/935-9900** • 11am-midnight, till 1am Fri, 10am-2am Sat

The Pleasure Chest 3436 N Lincoln Ave (btwn Roscoe & Addison) **773/525-7152, 800/525-7152** • clsd Sun

Tulip Sex Toy Gallery 3459 N Halsted St (btwn Newport & Cornelia) **773/975-1515, 877/708-8547** • noon-10pm, till midnight Fri-Sat • lesbian-owned

Chicago—Near North

ACCOMMODATIONS

ACME Hotel Company Chicago 15 E Ohio St (at State St) **312/894-0900** • gay-friendly • gym • kids ok • WiFi • wheelchair access

Allegro Chicago 171 W Randolph St (at LaSalle) **312/236-0123, 866/672-6143** • gay-friendly • Kimpton hotel • upscale lounge & restaurant • live shows • kids/pets ok • WiFi • wheelchair access

Chicago Getaway Hostel 616 W Arlington Pl (at Geneva Terr) **773/929-5380** • gay-friendly • in a trendy university area Lincoln Park • nonsmoking • WiFi

Dana Hotel & Spa 660 N State St (at Erie) **312/202-6000, 888/301-7946** • gay-friendly • rooftop lounge & Asian steakhouse • smoke free rooms • wheelchair access

Flemish House of Chicago 68 E Cedar St (btwn Rush & Lake Shore Dr) **312/664-9981** • gay/ straight • B&B, studios & apts in greystone row house • nonsmoking • WiFi • gay-owned

Gold Coast Guest House B&B 113 W Elm St (btwn Clark & LaSalle) **312/337-0361** • gay-friendly • nonsmoking • WiFi • women-owned

The Hotel Burnham One W Washington St (at State) **312/782-1111, 866/690-1986** • gay-friendly • Chicago landmark • nonsmoking • WiFi • wheelchair access

Hotel Indigo Chicago Gold Coast 1244 N Dearborn Pkwy (btwn Goethe & Division) **312/787-4980, 866/521-6950** • gay-friendly • gym • WiFi • restaurant & lounge • wheelchair access

Hotel Monaco 225 N Wabash (at S Water & Wacker Pl) **312/960-8500, 800/397-7661** • gay-friendly • 4-star luxury hotel • gym • restaurant • WiFi

Millennium Knickerbocker Hotel 163 E Walton Pl (Michigan Ave) **312/751-8100, 800/621-8140** • gay-friendly • restaurant • martini bar • gym • right off Magnificent Mile • wheelchair access

Old Town Chicago Guest House 1442 N North Park Ave (near Wells & North) **312/440-9268** • gay/ straight • whole house or rent by room • nonsmoking • WiFi

Palmer House Hilton 17 E Monroe St (at State St) **312/726-7500** • gay-friendly • pool • fitness center • shopping arcade • business center

W Chicago—Lakeshore 644 N Lake Shore Dr (at Ontario) **312/943-9200, 877/WHOTELS (RESERVATIONS ONLY)** • gay-friendly • overlooking Lake Michigan • pool • nonsmoking • WiFi • also restaurant & bar • wheelchair access

BARS

Club Foot 1824 W Augusta Blvd (at Honore, in Wicker Park) **773/489-0379** • 8pm-2am, till 3am Sat • gay-friendly • neighborhood bar • dancing/DJ • kitschy

Davenport's 1383 N Milwaukee (in Wicker Park) **773/278-1830** • 7pm-midnight, till 2am Fri-Sat, till 11pm Sun, clsd Tue • cabaret • piano bar

Downtown 440 N State (at Illinois) **312/464-1400** • 3pm-2am, till 3am Sat • mostly gay men • live shows • cabaret • professional crowd • videos

Nightclubs

Baton Show Lounge 436 N Clark St (btwn Illinois & Hubbard) 312/644-5269 • showtimes at 8:30pm, 10:30pm, 12:30am, clsd Mon-Tue • lesbians/ gay men • drag shows • reservations recommended • wheelchair access • since 1969!

Chances Dances 2011 W North Ave (at Damen, at Subterranean) • 3rd Mon 10pm-2am • lesbians/ gay men • dancing/DJ • also 2nd Tue at Danny's • 1959 W Dickens Ave • check chancesdances.org for other events

Underground Wonder Bar 710 N Clark St (at Huron) 312/266-7761 • 5pm-close • gay-friendly • live music • multiracial cliente

Cafes

Earwax Cafe & Film 1561 N Milwaukee Ave (in Wicker Park) 773/772-4019 • 11am-5pm, till 8pm wknds • food served • some vegan • wheelchair access

Restaurants

Blackbird 619 W Randolph St (at Des Plaines) 312/715-0708 • lunch Mon-Fri, dinner nightly, clsd Sun

Catch 35 35 W Wacker Dr (at Dearborn) 312/346-3500, 312/346-3535 • lunch Mon-Fri, dinner nightly • steak & seafood

Fireplace Inn 1448 N Wells St (at North Ave) 312/664-5264, 312/664-5264 • lunch & dinner • famous for their ribs • patio • full bar open late

Girl and the Goat 809 W Randolph St 312/492-6262 • 4:30pm-11pm, clsd Mon-Wed • fun foods, craft beers, and making wine in a rustic and bad ass environment • lesbian-owned

Hot Chocolate 1747 N Damen Ave (in Wicker Park) 773/489-1747 • lunch, dinner & dessert, wknd brunch, clsd Mon • full bar • wheelchair access

Ina's 1235 W Randolph St (at Racine) 312/226-8227 • brkfst & lunch • full bar

Kiki's Bistro 900 N Franklin St (at Locust) 312/335-5454 • lunch Mon-Fri, dinner nightly, clsd Sun • French • full bar

Lou Mitchell's 565 W Jackson Blvd (at Jefferson) 312/939-3111 • great brkfst

Manny's 1141 S Jefferson St (at Roosevelt) 312/939-2855 • 6am-8pm, clsd Sun • killer corned beef

Moonshine 1824 W Division St (at Honore, in Wicker Park) 773/862-8686 • dinner nightly, lunch Wed-Fri, wknd brunch • American • also bar

Nacional 27 325 W Huron (at N Orleans) 312/664-2727 • dinner nightly, clsd Sun • Nuevo Latino • also lounge open late

Park Grill 11 N Michigan Ave (in Millennium Park) 312/521-7275 • 11am-10pm • classic American • seasonal outdoor dining

Parthenon Restaurant 314 S Halsted St (near W Jackson) 312/726-2407 • 11am-midnight • full bar • "best gyros in Chicago" • wheelchair access

Shaw's Crab House 21 E Hubbard St (at State St) 312/527-2722 • lunch & dinner • live music • full bar • wheelchair access

Topolobampo/ Frontera Grill 445 N Clark St (btwn Illinois & Hubbard) 312/661-1434 • lunch & dinner, Sat brunch (Frontera only), clsd Sun-Mon • Mexican

Vermilion 10 W Hubbard St (at State) 312/527-4060 • lunch Mon-Fri, dinner nightly • Latin-Indian fusion • full bar • patio • wheelchair access

Bookstores

After-Words New & Used Books 23 E Illinois St (btwn State & Wabash) 312/464-1110 • 10:30am-10pm, till 11pm Fri-Sat, noon-7pm Sun • WiFi • cards • stationery • women-owned

Quimby's Bookstore 1854 W North Ave (at Wolcott, in Wicker Park) 773/342-0910 • noon-9pm, 11am-10pm Sat, noon-6pm Sun • alternative literature & comics • wheelchair access

Retail Shops

Flight 001 1133 N State St (at Elm) 312/944-1001 • 11am-6pm, till 7pm Sat • way cool travel gear

Gyms & Health Clubs

Cheetah Gym 1934 W North Ave (at Damen, in Wicker Park) 773/394-5900

Thousand Waves Spa 1212 W Belmont Ave (at Racine) 773/549-0700 • noon-9pm, till 5:30pm Tue, 10am-7pm Fri-Sun, clsd Mon • women only • women-owned

Chicago—South Side

Bars

Club Escape 1530 E 75th St (at Stoney Island Ave) 773/667-6454 • 4pm-2am, till 3am Sat • lesbians/ gay men • dancing/DJ • drag shows • mostly African American • food served • women's night Th

Inn Exile 5758 W 65th St (at Menard, near Midway Airport; 1 mile W of Midway hotel center at 65th & Cicero) **773/582–3510** • 8pm-2am, till 3am Sat • mostly gay men • dancing/DJ • videos • WiFi • wheelchair access

Jeffery Pub 7041 S Jeffery Blvd (at 71st) **773/363–8555** • noon-4am, till 5am Sat, clsd Mon • popular • lesbians/ gay men • dancing/DJ • mostly African American • drag shows • wheelchair access

BOOKSTORES

57th St Books 1301 E 57th St, Hyde Park (at Kimbark St) **773/684–1300** • 10am-8pm • LGBT section

Powell's Bookstore 1218 S Halsted St (at W Roosevelt) **312/243–9070** • 9am-9pm, 10am-6pm Sun • popular • wheelchair access • other location: 1501 E 57th St, 773/ 955-7780

De Kalb

NIGHTCLUBS

Otto's 118 E Lincoln Hwy **815/758–2715** • 6:30pm-close • gay-friendly • live music venue

Decatur

BARS

The Flashback Lounge 2239 E Wood St (at 22nd) **217/422–3530** • 9am-2am • lesbians/ gay men • neighborhood bar • dancing/DJ

RESTAURANTS

Robbie's Grill 122 N Merchant St **217/423–0448** • 11am-10pm, till 3am Sat, clsd Sun • full bar

EROTICA

Romantix Adult Superstore 2015 N 22nd St **217/362–0105**

Elk Grove Village

see Chicago

Elkhart

CAFES

Bluestem Bake Shop 107 Governor Oglesby St **217/947–2222** • 9am-4pm, clsd Mon, Wed & Sat

Forest Park

NIGHTCLUBS

Hideaway 7301 W Roosevelt Rd (at Marengo) **708/771–4459** • 3pm-2am, till 3am Fri-Sat • mostly gay men • dancing/DJ • karaoke • drag shows • male dancers • videos

Forest View

BARS

Forest View Lounge 4519 S Harlem Ave **208/484–9778** • 11am-midnight, till 2am wknds, clsd Sun • mostly women • neighborhood bar • food served • live shows

Galesburg

EROTICA

Romantix Adult Superstore 595 N Henderson St (at Losey) **309/342–7019**

Joliet

INFO LINES & SERVICES

Community Alliance & Action Network 68 N Chicago St #401 (at Jefferson) **815/726–7906** • by appointment • LGBT community center

NIGHTCLUBS

Maneuvers & Co 118 E Jefferson (at Chicago) **815/727–7069** • 8pm-2am, till 3am Fri-Sat • lesbians/ gay men • more women Tue • dancing/DJ • transgender-friendly • drag shows • frequent events • patio

Monticello

RESTAURANTS

The Brown Bag 212 W Washington St **217/762–9221** • 9am-7pm, till 8pm Tue & Fri, till 4pm Sat, clsd Sun

Normal

CAFES

Coffeehouse & Deli 114 E Beaufort St **309/452–6774** • 7am-10pm • vegetarian/ vegan • WiFi

O'Fallon

RESTAURANTS

Paulo's at the Mansion 1680 Mansion Wy (at Lakepointe Center Dr) **618/624–0629** • 5pm-9pm Tue-Th, till 10pm Fri-Sat • steakhouse • wheelchair access • gay-owned

Oak Park

see Berwyn & Chicago

Ottawa

EROTICA

Brown Bag Video 3042 N State Rte 71 (at I-80, exit 93) **815/313–4125** • 24hrs

Peoria

ACCOMMODATIONS

Hotel Pere Marquette 501 Main St 309/637–6500, 800/447–1676 • gay-friendly • buffet brkfst • WiFi

BARS

Buddies On Adams 807 SW Adams St (at Oak St) 309/676–7438 • 6pm-1am, till 4am Fri-Sat, clsd Mon • lesbians/ gay men • neighborhood bar • karaoke • WiFi

CAFES

One World 1245 W Main St (at University) 309/672–1522 • 7am-11pm, from 8am wknds • WiFi • wheelchair access

RESTAURANTS

Two 25 225 NE Adams St (at Mark Twain Hotel) 309/282–7777 • lunch Mon-Fri, dinner nightly, clsd Sun

EROTICA

Swingers World 335 SW Adams (at Harrison) 309/676–9275

Quincy

NIGHTCLUBS

Irene's Cabaret 124 N 5th St (at Washington Park, enter rear) 217/222–6292 • 9pm-2:30am, from 7pm Fri-Sat, till 3:30am Sat, clsd Sun-Tue • lesbians/ gay men • dancing/DJ • multiracial • karaoke • drag shows • wheelchair access • gay-owned

Rockford

NIGHTCLUBS

The Office Niteclub 513 E State St (btwn 2nd & 3rd) 815/965–0344 • noon-2am • popular • lesbians/ gay men • dancing/DJ • live shows • karaoke • drag shows • male & female strippers • videos

RESTAURANTS

Lucerne's Fondue & Spirits 845 N Church St (at Whitman) 815/968–2665 • 5pm-11pm, clsd Mon • reservations required • full bar • wheelchair access

Maria's 828 Cunningham St (at Corbin) 815/968–6781 • 4:30pm-9pm, clsd Sun-Mon • Italian • full bar

Springfield

INFO LINES & SERVICES

The Phoenix Center 109 E Lawrence Ave 217/528–5253 • 8:30am-4:30pm, clsd wknds

ACCOMMODATIONS

The State House Inn 101 E Adams St (at First St) 217/528–5100 • gay-friendly • kids/ pets ok • WiFi • wheelchair access

BARS

The Station House 304–306 E Washington (btwn 3rd & 4th Sts) 217/525–0438 • 5pm-1am, till 3am Th-Sat • lesbians/ gay men • neighborhood bar • karaoke • dancing/DJ • wheelchair access

RETAIL SHOPS

New Age Tattoos & Body Piercings 2915 S MacArthur Blvd 217/546–5006 • 11am-8pm, till 6pm Sun

INDIANA

Anderson

EROTICA

After Dark 2012 Mounds Rd 765/649–7597 • 10am-11pm, till midnight Fri-Sat, noon-10pm Sun • adult novelties, lingerie, videos, magazines

Bloomington

CAFES

Rachael's Cafe 300 E 3rd St 812/330–1882 • 8am-9pm, till 7pm Sun • live shows

Soma Coffee House 322 E Kirkwood Ave (below Laughing Planet) 812/331–2770 • 7am-11pm, from 8am Sun • WiFi

RESTAURANTS

Laughing Planet Cafe 322 E Kirkwood Ave (enter on Grant) 812/323–2233 • 11am-9pm • outdoor seating

Village Deli 409 E Kirkwood 812/336–2303 • 7am-9pm, 8am-9pm wknds

ENTERTAINMENT & RECREATION

BloomingOut WFHB 91.3 & 98.1 & 100.7 & 106.3FM 812/325–7870 & 323–1200 • 6pm Th, "your midwest queer connection"

RETAIL SHOPS

Athena Gallery 116 N Walnut 812/339–0734 • 10:30am-7pm, till 8:30pm Fri, noon-5pm Sun • clothing, drums, incense, gifts, etc • wheelchair access

Elkhart

see South Bend

Evansville

NIGHTCLUBS

Someplace Else 930 Main St (at Sycamore) **812/424-3202** • 4pm-3am • lesbians/gay men • dancing/DJ • drag shows • karaoke • patio

EROTICA

Exotica 4605 Washington Ave **812/401-7399** • 10am-midnight, noon-8pm Sun

Fort Wayne

INFO LINES & SERVICES

Gay/ Lesbian AA 501 W Berry St (at Plymouth church) **260/423-9424** • 2nd Tue at 6:30pm, 1pm every Sun

NIGHTCLUBS

After Dark 1601 S Harrison St (at Grand St) **260/456-6235** • noon-3am, 6pm-12:30am Sun • mostly gay men • dancing/DJ • karaoke • drag shows • male strippers • wheelchair access • gay-owned

Babylon 112 E Masterson Ave **260/247-5092** • 8pm-3am Fri-Sat only • mostly gay men • dancing/DJ • karaoke • patio

CAFES

Firefly 3523 N Anthony Blvd **260/373-0505** • 6:30am-8pm, from 8am wknds • live entertainment • WiFi

RESTAURANTS

The Loving Cafe 7605 Coldwater Rd **260/489-8686** • 10am-8pm, clsd Sun • vegetarian/ vegan • wheelchair access

RETAIL SHOPS

Boudoir Noir 512 W Superior St **260/420-0557** • 10am-midnight, noon-8pm Sun • gifts • sex toys • leather

Gary

see also Chicago, Illinois

EROTICA

Romantix Adult Superstore 8801 W Melton Rd/ US 20 (at Ripley Rd) **219/938-2194** • 24hrs

Goshen

see also South Bend

CAFES

The Electric Brew 136 S Main St **574/533-5990** • 6am-10pm, noon-7pm Sun • "Goshen's original coffeehouse" • live music

Hammond

BARS

Dick's R U Crazee? 1221 E 150th St **219/852-0222** • 8pm-3am, from 7pm wknds • mostly gay men • neighborhood bar • karaoke • drag shows

Hebron

EROTICA

The Lion's Den Adult Superstore 18010 Colorado St (exit 240, off I-65) **219/696-1276** • 24hrs

Indiana Dunes

ACCOMMODATIONS

The Gray Goose Inn B&B 350 Indian Boundary Rd (at I-95), Chesterton **219/926-5781, 800/521-5127** • gay/ straight • full brkfst • WiFi • nonsmoking rooms available

Indianapolis

INFO LINES & SERVICES

AA Gay/ Lesbian 317/632-7864 • various LGBT meeting • check web (www.indyaa.org) for meeting times & locations

ACCOMMODATIONS

The Alexander 333 S Delaware St **855/200-3002** • gay-friendly • boutique-style art hotel

The Fort Harrison State Park Inn 5830 N Post Rd **317/638-6000** • gay-friendly • luxury inn in historic Fort Harrison in NE Indianapolis • nonsmoking

Stone Soup Inn 1304 N Central Ave (at 13th St) **317/639-9555, 866/639-9550** • gay/ straight • in the heart of the historic Old Northside • WiFi

Sycamore Knoll B&B 10777 Riverwood Ave, Noblesville **317/776-0570** • gay/ straight • 1886 estate near the White River • gardens & apple orchard • full brkfst • nonsmoking • WiFi • lesbian-owned

The Villa 1456 N Delaware St (at 15th) **317/916-8500, 866/626-8500** • gay/ straight • spa and restaurant • WiFi

Wyndham Indianapolis West 2544 Executive Dr (off Airport Expy) **317/248-2481, 800/444-2326** • gay-friendly • seasonal pool • fitness center • WiFi in lobby, restaurant & lounge

Bars

501 Eagle 501 N College (at Michigan St) 317/632–2100 • 5:30pm-3am, from 7:30pm Sat, 4pm-12:30am Sun • popular • mostly gay men • dancing/DJ • bears • leather

Downtown Olly's 822 N Illinois St (at St Clair) 317/636–5597 • open 24hrs • mostly men • sports & video bar • karaoke • brkfst, lunch, dinner

The Metro Nightclub & Restaurant 707 Massachusetts Ave (at College) 317/639–6022 • 3pm-3am, noon-midnight Sun • popular • lesbians/ gay men • neighborhood bar • piano bar • karaoke • patio • also restaurant • giftshop • wheelchair access

Noah Grant's Grill House & Raw Bar 65 S 1st St (at W Oak St), Zionsville 317/732–2233 • 4pm-close, clsd Mon • gay-friendly • wine bar & bistro • serving lunch & dinner, Sun brunch • patio

Varsity Lounge 1517 N Pennsylvania Ave (S of 16th) 317/635–9998 • 10am-3am, till midnight Sun • mostly gay men • neighborhood bar • food served • karaoke • WiFi

Zonie's Closet 1446 E Washington St (at Arsenal) 317/266–0535 • 8am-3am, noon-midnight Sun • gay/ straight • dancing/DJ • karaoke • drag shows

Nightclubs

Greg's 231 E 16th St (at Alabama) 317/638–8138 • 4pm-3am • mostly gay men • drag shows • county/ western • patio • wheelchair access

Talbott Street 2145 N Talbott St (at 22nd St) 317/931–1343 • 9pm-2am Fri-Sat • gay/ straight • dancing/DJ • drag shows • theme nights

The Ten 1218 N Pennsylvania St (at 12th, enter rear) 317/638–5802 • 6pm-3am, till 1am Wed, till midnight Sun, clsd Mon-Tue • very popular w/ lesbians (gay men welcome) • dancing/DJ • live shows • drag shows • wheelchair access

Cafes

Bjava 5510 Lafayette Rd (at 56th St) 317/280–1236 • 6am-5pm, 7am-3pm Sat, clsd Sun

Cornerstone Coffeehouse 651 E 54th St (at N College Ave, Broad Ripple) 317/726–1360 • 6am-10pm, from 7am Sat, till 9pm Sun • food served • full bar • WiFi

Earth House Collective 237 N East St 317/636–4060 • 11am-9pm, clsd Sun • coffeehouse • also art, music & classes • WiFi

Henry's on East Street 627 N East St 317/951–0335 • 7am-7pm, till 9pm Fri, from 8am wknds • popular • gay-owned

Hubbard & Cravens 4930 N Pennsylvania St (in Broad Ripple) 317/251–5161 • 6am-7pm, 7am-3pm Sun • food served • WiFi

Hubbard & Cravens 4930 N Pennsylvania St (in Broad Ripple) 317/251–5161 • 6am-7pm, 7am-3pm Sun • food served • WiFi

Monon Coffee Company 920 E Westfield Blvd (at Guilford) 317/255–0510 • 6:30am-8pm, till 10pm Fri, from 7am Sat, 8am-8pm Sun

Restaurants

14 West 14 W Maryland St 317/636–1414 • lunch & dinner • seafood & steaks • patio

Adobo Grill 110 E Washington 317/822–9990 • lunch Fri-Sun, dinner nightly • Mexican • full bar • wheelchair access

Aesop's Tables 600 E Massachusetts Ave 317/631–0055 • lunch & dinner, clsd Sun • authentic Mediterranean • some veggie • beer/ wine • wheelchair access

BARcelona 201 N Delaware St 317/638–8272 • 11am-11pm • also full bar • tapas

Bazbeaux Pizza 329 Massachusetts Ave 317/636–7662 • lunch & dinner

Cafe Zuppa 320 N Meridian St (at New York St) 317/634–9877 • 7am-2:30pm, Sun brunch buffet

Creation Cafe & Euphoria 337 W 11th St (in Buggs' Temple) 317/955–2389 • 8am-9pm, clsd Sun • outdoor seating

English Ivy's 944 S Alabama (at 10th) 317/822–5070 • 11am-3am from 10am wknds • also full bar • WiFi • wheelchair access

India Garden 830 Broad Ripple Ave (btwn Carrollton & Guilford) 317/253–6060 • lunch & dinner • Indian • wheelchair access • also 207 N Delaware St, 317/634-6060

King David Dogs 15 N Pennsylvania St • great hot dogs

La Piedad 6524 Cornell Ave 317/475–0988 • lunch & dinner • Mexican

Mama Carolla's 1031 E 54th St (at Winthrop) 317/259–9412 • dinner only, clsd Sun-Mon • traditional Italian

Naked Tchopstix 6253 N College Ave (in Broad Ripple) 317/252–5555 • lunch & dinner • popular • Korean, Japanese, Chinese cuisine • also sushi bar

Oakley's Bistro 1464 W 86th St (at Ditch Rd) **317/824–1231** • lunch & dinner, clsd Sun-Mon • popular • gourmet cont'l • reservations suggested • wheelchair access

Pancho's Taqueria 7023 Michigan Rd (at Westlane) **317/202–9015** • 11am-9pm • popular • authentic Mexican • wheelchair access

Sawasdee 1222 W 86th St (at Ditch Rd) **317/844–9451** • lunch Mon-Sat, dinner nightly • Thai • some veggie • wheelchair access

Three Sisters Cafe 6360 N Guilford Ave (at Main St) **317/257–5556** • 8am-9pm, till 3pm Sun • plenty veggie & vegan • popular Sun brunch

Usual Suspects 6319 Guilford Ave (at Broad Ripple) **317/251–3138** • 5pm-10pm, till 11pm Fri-Sat, till 9pm Sun, clsd Mon • eclectic • full bar • patio

Yats 659 Massachusetts Ave (at Walnut) **317/686–6380** • 11am-9pm, till 10pm Fri-Sat, till 7pm Sun • Cajun • also 5363 N College Ave & 8352 E 96th St • wheelchair access

ENTERTAINMENT & RECREATION

Indiana Fever 1 Conseco Ct (in Conseco Fieldhouse) **317/917–2500** • check out the Women's Nat'l Basketball Association while you're in Indianapolis

Indy Indie Artist Colony 26 E 14th St **317/295–9302** • noon-5pm Th-Sat • largest artist community in the city with 72 artist live/work spaces

Theatre on the Square 627 Massachusetts Ave (at East) **317/685–8687** • often presents gay-themed productions

BOOKSTORES

Big Hat Books 6510 Cornell Ave **317/202–0203** • 10am-6pm, noon-5pm Sun • general independent

Bookmamas 9 S Johnson Ave (at E Washington St, in Irvington) **317/375–3715** • open Wed-Sat • call for hours • used bookstore

RETAIL SHOPS

All My Relations 7218 Rockville Rd **317/227–3925** • noon-6pm, till 7pm Wed-Th, 10am-6pm Sat • New Age/ metaphysical store • also classes

Metamorphosis 828 Broad Ripple Ave (at Carrollton) **317/466–1666** • 1pm-9pm, till 5pm Sun • tattoo & piercing parlor

PUBLICATIONS

Nuvo **317/254–2400** • Indy's alternative weekly

The Word **317/632–8840** • LGBT newspaper

Kokomo

BARS

Bar Blue 1400 W Markland Ave (at Park) **765/456–1400** • open Sat only • popular • lesbians/ gay men • dancing/DJ • karaoke • drag shows • patio

Lafayette

INFO LINES & SERVICES

Pride Lafayette, Inc 640 Main St #218 **765/423–7579** • community center 6pm-8pm, 5pm-9pm wknds • support/ social activities

EROTICA

Fantasy East 2315 Concord Rd (at Teal) **765/474–2417** • 10am-1am

Marion

EROTICA

After Dark 1311 W Johnson St **765/662–3688** • 10am-11pm, till midnight Fri-Sat, noon-10pm Sun

Michigan City

ACCOMMODATIONS

Duneland Beach Inn & Restaurant 3311 Pottawattomie Trail (at Duneland Beach Dr) **219/874–7729, 800/423–7729** • gay-friendly • also restaurant/ bar • 1 block away from Lake Michigan & private beach • 60 miles from Chicago

Tryon Farm Guest House 1400 Tryon Rd (at Hwy 212) **219/879–3618** • gay-friendly • full brkfst • hot tub • kids/ pets ok • nonsmoking • WiFi • women-owned

Mishawaka

see also South Bend

ACCOMMODATIONS

The Beiger Mansion 317 Lincolnway E **574/255–6300, 800/437–0131** • gay-friendly • B&B in 4-level neo-classical limestone mansion • pool • nonsmoking • WiFi • gay-owned

New Albany

see Louisville, KY

Noblesville

see Indianapolis

Richmond

EROTICA

Exotic Fantasies 12 S 11th St **765/935-5827** • 9am-midnight, till 2am Fri-Sat

South Bend

ACCOMMODATIONS

Innisfree B&B 702 W Colfax **574/283-0740** • gay-friendly • 1892 Queen Anne minutes from Notre Dame • full brkfst • nonsmoking

BARS

Jeannie's Tavern 621 S Bendix (at Ford St) **574/288-2962** • 2pm-2am • gay-friendly • neighborhood bar • transgender-friendly • gay-owned

Vickies Inc 112 W Monroe St (at S Michigan St) **574/232-4090** • 2pm-2am • gay/ straight • neighborhood bar • transgender-friendly • food served • football party every Sat in season • gay-owned

ENTERTAINMENT & RECREATION

GLBT Resource Center of Michiana **574/254-1411** • 5pm-8pm Mon & 11am-2pm Sat

EROTICA

Romantix Adult Superstore 2715 S Main St (at Eckman St) **574/291-1899**

Terre Haute

NIGHTCLUBS

Zim Marss Nightclub 1500 Locust St (at 15th St) **812/232-3026** • 8pm-3am, 7pm-12:30am Sun, clsd Mon-Tue • lesbians/ gay men • dancing/DJ • transgender-friendly • drag shows • strippers

Valparaiso

ACCOMMODATIONS

Inn at Aberdeen 3158 S State Rd 2 **219/465-3753, 866/761-3753** • gay-friendly • 1880s Queen Anne • full brkfst • nonsmoking • WiFi • wheelchair access

Vevay

CAFES

Java Bean Cafe & Confectionery 117 W Main St **812/427-2888** • 7am-7pm, clsd Sun • gay-owned

IOWA

Statewide

PUBLICATIONS

The ACCESSline 712/560-1807 • the Heartland's LGBT newspaper

Ames

RESTAURANTS

Lucullan's Italian Grill 400 Main St (at Burnett) **515/232-8484** • dinner Tue-Sun • some veggie • full bar

EROTICA

Romantix Adult Superstore 117 Kellogg St (at Lincoln Wy) **515/232-7717** • 9am-4am

Burlington

ACCOMMODATIONS

Arrowhead Motel 2520 Mt Pleasant St **319/752-6353** • gay-friendly • kids ok • WiFi • nonsmoking • wheelchair access • gay-owned •

BARS

Steve's Place 852 Washington St (at Central Ave) **319/754-5868** • 9am-2am, clsd Sun • gay/ straight • full meun • wheelchair access • gay-owned

Cedar Falls

see Waterloo

Cedar Rapids

BARS

The Piano Lounge 208 2nd Ave SE **319/363-0606** • 4pm-2am, clsd Sun • gay/ straight • live entertainment • game room

NIGHTCLUBS

Club Basix 3916 1st Ave NE (btwn 39th & 40th) **319/363-3194** • 5pm-2am, from noon wknds • lesbians/ gay men • transgender-friendly • dancing/DJ • drag shows • gay/ lesbian-owned

CAFES

Blue Strawberry 118 2nd St SE **319/247-2583** • 7am-8pm, 8am-5pm Sun • nonsmoking

ENTERTAINMENT & RECREATION

CSPS Arts Center 1103 3rd St SE **319/364-1580** • galleries • concerts • plays • many LGBT events

Council Bluffs

see also Omaha, Nebraska

RESTAURANTS

Dixie Quick's 157 W Broadway
712/256–4140 • lunch & dinner, brunch from
9am wkds, clsd Mon • Southern • reservations
recommended

Davenport

ACCOMMODATIONS

Hotel Blackhawk 200 East 3rd St **563/322–5000, 888/525–4455** • gay-friendly • newly
renovated • bowling alley on-site

BARS

Mary's on 2nd 832 W 2nd St (btwn Warren &
Brown) **563/884–8014** • 4pm-2am • lesbians/
gay men • neighborhood bar • dancing/DJ •
occasional live shows • videos • patio •
wheelchair access

NIGHTCLUBS

Connections 822 W 2nd St (at Brown)
563/322–1121 • 5pm-2am • lesbians/gay
men • dancing/DJ • drag shows • karaoke

Des Moines

INFO LINES & SERVICES

The Center/ Equality Iowa 515/243–0313

ACCOMMODATIONS

Hotel Fort Des Moines 1000 Walnut St (at
10th St) **515/243–1161, 800/532–1466** • gay-friendly • full brkfst • pool • hot tub • kids ok
• gym • nonsmoking • WiFi • wheelchair
access

The Renaissance Savery Hotel 401 Locust
St (at 4th) **515/244–2151, 800/514** • gay-friendly • pool • kids ok • restaurant • WiFi •
wheelchair access

BARS

The Blazing Saddle 416 E 5th St (btwn
Grand & Locust) **515/246–1299** • 2pm-2am,
from noon wknds • mostly gay men •
dancing/DJ • leather • drag shows • WiFi •
wheelchair access

Buddy's Corral 418 E 5th St (btwn Grand &
Locust) **515/244–7140** • noon-2am, from
10am Sat • gay-friendly • karaoke

NIGHTCLUBS

The Garden 112 SE 4th St **515/243–3965** •
8pm-2am, 5pm-midnight Sun, clsd Mon-Tue •
lesbians/gay men • more women Th •
dancing/DJ • live shows • karaoke • videos •
patio • young crowd • wheelchair access

Le Boi Bar 508 Indianola Ave (at 7th)
515/284–1074 • 8pm-2am, 3pm-midnight
Sun, clsd Mon-Tue • lesbians/gay men •
dancing/DJ • drag shows

CAFES

Drake Diner 1111 25th St (btwn University
& Cottage Grove) **515/277–1111** • 7am-11pm
• try the cake shake • full bar • patio •
wheelchair access

Java Joe's 214 4th St (at Court Ave)
515/288–5282 • 7am-11pm, till midnight Th-Sat, till 10pm Sun • live shows • WiFi •
wheelchair access

Ritual Cafe 1301 E Locust St **515/288–4872**
• 7am-7pm, till 11pm Fri-Sat, clsd Sun • live
music

Zanzibar's Coffee Adventure 2723
Ingersoll Ave (at 28th St) **515/244–7694** •
6:30am-8pm, till 9pm Fri-Sat, 8am-6pm Sun •
wheelchair access

RESTAURANTS

Cafe di Scala 644 18th St (at Woodland)
515/244–1353 • dinner Th-Sat only • Italian •
beer/ wine • wheelchair access

RETAIL SHOPS

Liberty Gifts 333 E Grand Ave, Ste 105
(entrance on E 4th St) **515/508–0825** • 10am-8pm, 11am-7pm Sun• pride store

EROTICA

Gallery Book Store 1000 Cherry St (at 10th)
515/244–2916

Romantix Adult Superstore 2020 E Euclid
Ave (at Delaware) **515/266–7992** • 24hrs

Dubuque

CAFES

Cafe Manna Java 700 Locust St (Roshek
Building) **563/588–3105** • 7am-9pm, 8pm-2am Sun • WiFi • full bar • lesbian-owned

Iowa City

INFO LINES & SERVICES

AA Gay/ Lesbian 500 N Clinton (at church)
319/338–9111 (AA#) • 5pm Sun

Women's Resource & Action Center 130
N Madison St (at Market) **319/335–1486** •
9am-5pm, clsd wknds • community center •
support groups • counseling • wheelchair
access

Bars

Deadwood Tavern 6 S Dubuque St
319/351–9417 • 11am-2am • popular • gay-
friendly • neighborhood bar • college crowd •
wheelchair access

Studio 13 13 S Linn St (in the alley btwn
Linn & Dubuque Sts) **319/338–7185** • 7pm-
2am, clsd Mon lesbians/ gay men • dancing/DJ
• drag shows Fri & Sun • 19+ • gay-owned

Restaurants

The Mill 120 E Burlington St **319/351–9529**
• lunch & dinner, wknd brunch • popular
Americana music venue

Entertainment & Recreation

Old Capitol City Roller Girls • Iowa City's
own female roller derby league •
facebook.com/oldcapitolcityrollergirls

Bookstores

Prairie Lights Bookstore 15 S Dubuque St
(at Washington) **319/337–2681, 800/295–2665**
• 9am-9pm, till 6pm Sun • also cafe & wine
bar • wheelchair access

Retail Shops

New Pioneer Co-op & Bakehouse 22 S
Van Buren (at Washington) **319/338–9441** •
7am-11pm • health food store & deli •
wheelchair access • also Coralville location at
1101 2nd St

Erotica

Romantix Adult Superstore 315 Kirkwood
Ave (at Gilbert) **319/351–9444** • 8am-4am

Marshalltown

Erotica

Adult Odyssey 907 Iowa Ave E **641/752–6550**
• 10am-11pm. till 3am Fri-Sat

Sioux City

Nightclubs

Jones Street Station 412 Jones St (at 5th St)
712/258–6338 • 8pm-2am, clsd Sun-Mon •
gay/ straight • dancing/DJ • karaoke •
wheelchair access • gay-owned

Erotica

Romantix Adult Superstore 511 Pearl St
712/277–8566 • 8am-4am, noon-2am Sun

Waterloo

Accommodations

Stella's Guesthouse & Gardens 324
Summit Ave (at Chicago) **319/232–2122** •
lesbians/ gay men • full brkfst • hot tub •
clothing-optional • shared baths •
nonsmoking • gay-owned

Nightclubs

Kings & Queens Knight Club 304 W 4th St
(at Jefferson) **319/232–3001** • 6:30pm-2am,
clsd Sun-Mon • gay-friendly • dancing/DJ
• transgender-friendly • drag shows • young
crowd • wheelchair access

KANSAS

Statewide

Publications

The Liberty Press **316/652–7737** • Kansas
statewide LGBT newspaper

Junction City

Nightclubs

Xcalibur Club 384 Grant Ave **785/762–2050**
• 6pm-2am, clsd Mon-Tue • lesbians/ gay
men • dancing/DJ • live shows • gay-owned

Kansas City

see also Kansas City, Missouri

Lawrence

Nightclubs

Granada 1020 Massachusetts (at 11th)
785/842–1390 • hours vary • gay/ straight •
dancing/DJ • live bands • wheelchair access

Jazzhaus 926–1/2 Massachusetts St
785/749–3320, 785/749–1387 • 8pm-2am •
gay-friendly • live music • karaoke • WiFi

Wilde's Chateau 2412 Iowa St **785/856–1514**
• 9pm-2am Wed, Fri-Sat only • gay/ straight •
dancing/DJ • theme nights

Cafes

Henry's 11 E 8th St (btwn Massachusetts St
& New Hampshire St) **785/331–3511** • 7am-
2am • cafe downstairs • bar from 5pm upstairs
• WiFi

Java Break 17 E 7th St (at New Hampshire)
785/749–5282 • 24hrs • sandwiches •
desserts • gay-owned

RESTAURANTS

Teller's Restaurant & Bar 746 Massachusetts St (at 8th) **785/843–4111** • 11am-10pm, till 11pm Fri-Sat, from 10am Sun • Italian • some veggie • wheelchair access

BOOKSTORES

The Dusty Bookshelf 708 Massachusetts St **785/749–4643** • 10am-8pm, till 10pm Fri-Sat, noon-6pm Sun • used books • feminist & LGBT section • gay-owned

Manhattan

BOOKSTORES

The Dusty Bookshelf 700 N Manhattan Ave **785/539–2839** • 10am-8pm, till 6pm Sat, noon-5pm Sun • feminist & LGBT section • gay-owned

Overland Park

ACCOMMODATIONS

Hawthorn Suites 11400 College Blvd **913/826–6167** • gay-friendly • pool • jacuzzi • WiFi • wheelchair access

Topeka

INFO LINES & SERVICES

Freedom Group AA 3916 SW 17th St (at Gage, at St David's church) **785/272–9483** • 8pm Fri

BARS

Skivies 921 S Kansas Ave (near 10th St) **785/234–0482** • 3pm-2am • mostly gay men • neighborhood bar • dancing/DJ • drag shows • country/ western • gay-owned

Wichita

INFO LINES & SERVICES

One Day at a Time Gay AA 156 S Kansas Ave (at MCC, enter on English) **316/684–3661** • 8pm Tue & Th

ACCOMMODATIONS

Hawthorn Suites 2405 N Ridge Rd **316/729–5700** • gay-friendly • kids/ small pets ok • brkfst buffet • WiFi • wheelchair access •

BARS

J's Lounge 513 E Central Ave (at N Emporia St) **316/262–1363** • 4pm-2am • lesbians/ gay men • cabaret • live shows • karaoke • patio • wheelchair access • "an upscale dive"

Rain Cafe & Lounge 518 E Douglas Ave **316/261–9000** • 11am-2am • lesbians/ gay men • dancing/DJ Fri-Sat • Karaoke Th • food served till 9pm • gay-owned

The Store 3210 E Osie **316/683–9781** • 2pm-2am • mostly women • men welcome • neighborhood bar

NIGHTCLUBS

Fantasy Complex 3201 S Hillside (at 31st) **316/682–5494** • 8pm-2am Th-Sun • lesbians/ gay men • dancing/DJ • karaoke • drag shows • also South Forty country/ western bar • wheelchair access

CAFES

Riverside Perk 1144 N Bitting Ave (at 11th) **316/264–6464** • 7am-10pm, till midnight Fri-Sat, from 10am Sun • WiFi • also Lava Lounge juice bar next door • wheelchair access

The Vagabond 614 W Douglas Ave **316/303–1110** • 7am-2am • theme nights • art gallery • also bar • WiFi

RESTAURANTS

Moe's Sub Shop 2815 S Hydraulic St (at Wassall) **316/524–5511** • 11am-8pm, clsd Sun

Oh Yeah! China Bistro 3101 N Rock Rd **316/425–7700** • lunch & dinner • wheelchair access

Old Mill Tasty Shop 604 E Douglas Ave (at St Francis) **316/264–6500** • 11am-3pm, from 8am Sat, clsd Sun • old-fashioned soda fountain • some veggie

Rain Cafe & Lounge 518 E Douglas (btwn St Francis & Emporia) **316/261–9000** • 11am-2am, from 1pm Sun • full menu till 9pm • full bar • DJ on wknds

River City Brewing Company 150 N Mosley St **316/263–2739** • 11am-10pm, till 2am wknds • live music

Riverside Cafe 739 W 13th St (at Bitting) **316/262–6703** • 6am-8pm, till 2pm Sun

ENTERTAINMENT & RECREATION

Cabaret Oldtown Theatre 412 1/2 E Douglas Ave (at Topeka) **316/265–4400** • edgy, kitschy productions

Mosley Street Melodrama 234 N Mosley St (btwn 1st & 2nd St) **316/263–0222** • melodrama, homestyle buffet & full bar!

Wichita Arts 334 N Mead **316/462–2787** • promotes visual & performing arts • ArtScene publication has extensive cultural calendar

PUBLICATIONS

The Liberty Press **316/652-7737** • statewide LGBT newspaper

Erotica

Adult Superstore 5858 S Broadway 316/522–9040 • 24hrs

Fetish Lingerie 2150 S Broadway St (btwn E Clark & E Kinkaid Sts) 316/264–7800 • 11:30-7pm, clsd Sun-Mon • all sizes available

Patricia's 6143 W Kellogg (at Dugan) 316/942–1244 • 9am-1am, from noon-10pm Sun

KENTUCKY

Covington

see also Cincinnati, Ohio

Bars

701 Bar & Lounge 701 Bakewell St (at 7th St) 859/431–7011 • 3pm-1am, from 1pm Sun • gay-friendly • neighborhood bar • dancing/DJ • live shows • karaoke • food served

Bar Monet 837 Willard St 859/491-2403 • 4pm-1am • lesbians/ gay men • bar food • dancing/DJ • shows

Rosie's Tavern 643 Bakewell St (at 7th St) 859/291–9707 • 3pm-2:30am • gay/ straight • neighborhood bar • lesbian-owned

Yadda Club 404 Pike St (at Main St) 859/491–5600 • 8pm-2:30am Wed-Sun • lesbians/ gay men • neighborhood bar • dancing/DJ • T-dance Sun • multiracial • live shows • karaoke • food served • patio • wheelchair access • lesbian-owned

Cafes

Pike Street Lounge 266 Pike St 859/916–5430 • 8am-1am, from 11am wknds • coffee & cocktails • karaoke • local art

Lexington

Info Lines & Services

Gay/ Lesbian AA 530 E High St (at Woodland Church) 859/225–1212 (AA#) • 8pm Wed • also 7:30pm Fri at 205 E Short St (church)

GLSO Pride Center of the Bluegrass 389 Waller Ave #100 859/253–3233 • 10am-3pm Mon-Fri

Accommodations

Hyatt Regency Lexington 401 W High St 859/253–1234 • gay-friendly • pool • bar & restaurant • wheelchair access

Ramada Limited 2261 Elkhorn Rd (off I-75) 859/294–7375, 800/272-6232 • gay-friendly • pool • WiFi • nonsmoking • wheelchair access

Bars

The Bar Complex 224 E Main St (at Esplanade) 859/255–1551 • 4pm-midnight, till 2am wknds • popular • lesbians/ gay men • dancing/DJ • drag shows • live shows • WiFi • wheelchair access

Crossings 117 N Limestone St 859/233–7266 • 4pm-2am • mostly gay men • neighborhood bar • live shows • karaoke • wheelchair access

Soundbar 208 S Limestone 859/523–6338 • 4:30pm-close • gay/ straight • dancing/DJ • karaoke

Cafes

Third Street Stuff 257 N Limestone 859/255–5301 • 6:30am-11pm, from 8am Sun, salads & sandwiches • also funky boutique

Restaurants

Alfalfa Restaurant 141 E Main St 859/253–0014 • lunch & dinner, brunch wknds • healthy multi-ethnic • plenty veggie • folk music wknds

Natasha's Bistro & Bar 112 Esplanade (at Main St) 859/259–2754 • lunch & dinner, clsd Sun • eclectic dining • plenty veggie • also live theater & music

Bookstores

Joseph-Beth 161 Lexington Green Circle (at Nicholasville Rd) 859/273–2911, 800/248–6849 • 9am-10pm, till 11pm Fri-Sat, 11am-9pm Sun • also cafe • WiFi • wheelchair access

Sqecial Media 371 S Limestone St (btwn Pine & Winslow) 859/255–4316 • 10am-8pm, noon-6pm Sun • also pride items

Publications

LinQ 859/253–3233 • local news & calendar

Erotica

Romantix Adult Superstore 933 Winchester Rd (at Liberty Rd) 859/252–0357 • 24hrs

Louisville

Info Lines & Services

Gay AA 1432 Highland Ave 502/587–6225 • 4:30pm Sun & 6pm Mon

Accommodations

21c Museum Hotel Louisville 700 W Main St 502/217–6300, 877/217–6400 • gay-friendly • boutique hotel w/ museum • also Proof on Main restaurant

The Brown Hotel 335 W Broadway (at 4th) **502/583–1234, 888/387–0498** • gay-friendly • WiFi • nonsmoking • also restaurant & bar

Columbine B&B 1707 S 3rd St (near Lee St) **502/635–5000, 800/635–5010** • gay-friendly • 1896 Greek Revivial mansion • full brkfst • nonsmoking • WiFi • gay-owned

Galt House Hotel & Suites 140 N 4th St (at W Main) **502/589–5200, 800/843–4258** • gay-friendly • waterfront hotel

Inn at the Park 1332 S 4th St (at Park Ave) **502/638–0045** • gay-friendly • restored mansion • full brkfst • nonsmoking • WiFi

Bars

The Levee 1005 W Market, Jeffersonville, IN • 4pm-3am • gay/ straight • neighborhood bar • dancing/DJ • karaoke • WiFi • 2 minutes from downtown Louisville

Magnolia Bar 1398 S 2nd St (at Magnolia) **502/637–9052** • 2pm-4am • gay-friendly • neighborhood/dive bar

Teddy Bears Bar & Grill 1148 Garvin Pl (at St Catherine) **502/589–2619** • 11am-4am, from 1pm Sun • mostly gay men • neighborhood bar • wheelchair access

Louisville

LGBT Pride:
June. 502/649–4851, web: www.kypride.com.

Annual Events:
May - Kentucky Derby 502/584-6383, web: www.kentuckyderby.com.
June-July - Kentucky Shakespeare Festival 502/574-9900, web: www.kyshakes.org.
October - World's Largest Halloween Party, Louisville Zoo, web: www.louisvillezoo.org.
October - St James Court Art Show 502/ 635-1842, web: www.stjamescourtartshow.com.

City Info:
Louisville Visitor Center 800/626-5646.
Convention & Visitors Bureau, web: www.gotolouisville.com.

Transit:
Yellow Cab 502/636-5511, web: www.yellowcablouisville.com
Louisville's Premier Shuttle 502/897-2835, web: www.louisvilletransport.com.
TARC Bus System 502/585-1234, web: www.ridetarc.org.
Louisville Horse Trams 502/581-0100, web: www.louisvillehorsetrams.com.

Attractions:
Belle of Louisville steamboat 866/832-0011, web: www.belleoflouisville.org.
Churchill Downs 502/636-4400, web: www.churchilldowns.com.
Farmington Historic Home 502/452-9920 web: www.historichomes.org.
Hadley Pottery 502/584-2171, web: www.hadleypottery.com.
Locust Grove Historic Farm 502/897-9845, web: www.locustgrove.org.
Louisville Slugger Tour 877/775-8443, web: www.sluggermuseum.org.

Waterfront Park, web: www.louisvillewaterfront.com.
West Main Street Historic District, web: www.mainstreetassociation.com.

Best View:
Aboard the Belle of Louisville steamboat at Waterfront Park.

Weather:
Mild winters and long, hot summers!

Tryangles 209 S Preston St (at Market) 502/583-6395 • 4pm-4am, from 1pm Sun • mostly gay men • karaoke Tue • wheelchair access

NIGHTCLUBS

The Connection Complex 120 S Floyd St (at Market) 502/585-5752 • 8pm-4am, till 2am Mon-Tue • popular • lesbians/gay men • dancing/DJ • piano bar & cabaret • videos • wheelchair access

Lisa'a Oak Street Lounge 1004 E Oak St 502/637-9315 • 9pm-1am, 7pm-3am Fri-Sat • gay/straight • live shows • karaoke

CAFES

Days Espresso & Coffee 1420 Bardstown Rd (at Edenside) 502/456-1170 • 6:30am-10pm, till 11pm Fri-Sat • WiFi • wheelchair access • lesbian-owned

RESTAURANTS

The Bodega at Felice 829 E Market St 502/569-4100 • 7am-7pm, till 11pm Fri, 9am-4pm Sat, clsd Sun • gourmet market & deli • coffee bar • WiFi • gay-owned

Cafe Mimosa 1543 Bardstown Rd (at Stevens Ave) 502/458-2233 • lunch & dinner • Vietnamese, Chinese & sushi

El Mundo 2345 Frankfort Ave 502/899-9930 • 11:30am-10pm, full bar till 2am Th-Sat, clsd Sun-Mon • popular • Mexican • wheelchair access

Havana Rumba 4115 Oechsli Ave (off State Hwy 1447) 502/897-1959 • lunch & dinner • Cuban

Jack Fry's 1007 Bardstown Rd 502/452-9244 • lunch & dinner • steak/Southern • live jazz • wheelchair access

Mayan Cafe 813 E Market St 502/566-0651 • lunch Mon-Fri, dinner nightly, clsd Sun • Mayan/Mexican

Porcini 2730 Frankfort Ave (at Bayly) 502/894-8686 • dinner nightly, clsd Sun • Italian

Proof on Main 702 W Main St (at 7th, at 21c Hotel) 502/217-6360 • brkfst & lunch Mon-Fri, dinner nightly • upscale • modern American w/Tuscan influence

Ramsi's Cafe on the World 1293 Bardstown Rd 502/451-0700 • 11am-1am, till 2am Fri-Sat, Sun brunch • eclectic menu • wheelchair access

Third Avenue Cafe 1164 S 3rd St (at W Oak) 502/585-2233 • 11am-9pm, till 10pm Fri-Sat, clsd Sun • vegan/vegetarian • patio • wheelchair access

Vietnam Kitchen 5339 Mitscher Ave 502/363-5154 • clsd Wed, Vietnamese • plenty veggie • wheelchair access

Zen Garden 2240 Frankfort Ave 502/895-9114 • lunch & dinner, clsd Sun • Asian • vegetarian • wheelchair access

ENTERTAINMENT & RECREATION

Pandora Productions PO Box 4185 40204 502/216-5502 • LGBT-themed productions

Rudyard Kipling 422 W Oak St (btwn 4th & Garvin) 502/636-1311 • live music & theater, also restaurant, open wknds

BOOKSTORES

Carmichael's 1295 Bardstown Rd (at Longest Ave) 502/456-6950 • 8am-10pm, till 11pm Fri-Sat • LGBT section

PUBLICATIONS

The Community Letter • LGBT newspaper

Midway

CAFES

Tavern 815 131 E Main St (inside Le Marché boutique mall) 859/846-4688 • 11am-3pm, till 4pm Sat • WiFi

Newport

see also Cincinnati, Ohio

BARS

The Crazy Fox Saloon 901 Washington Ave (at 9th) 859/261-2143 • 3pm-2:30am • gay/straight • friendly neighborhood bar • patio

Paducah

EROTICA

Romantix Adult Superstore 243 Brown (at Irvin Cobb Dr) 270/442-5584

LOUISIANA

Statewide

PUBLICATIONS

Ambush Mag 504/522-8049 • oldest LGBT newspaper for the Gulf South (Texas through Florida)

Baton Rouge

INFO LINES & SERVICES

Freedom of Choice/Gay AA 7747 Tom Dr (at MCC) 225/930-0026 (AA#) • 8pm Th & Sat

Bars

George's Place 860 St Louis **225/387–9798**
• 3pm-2am, from 5pm Sat, clsd Sun • popular
• lesbians/gay men • neighborhood bar •
videos • karaoke • male strippers Fri •
wheelchair access

Hound Dogs 668 Main St (at 7th)
225/344–0807 • 2pm-2am, from 4pm Mon-
Tue, from noon Sun • lesbians/gay men •
neighborhood bar • wheelchair access

Nightclubs

Splash 2183 Highland Rd **225/242–9491** •
9pm-2am; clsd Sun-TWed• popular • lesbians/
gay men • dancing/DJ • drag shows • 18+ •
wheelchair access

Restaurants

Drusilla Seafood 3482 Drusilla Ln (at
Jefferson Hwy) **225/923–0896, 800/364–8844**
• 11am-10pm

Mestizo 2323 Acadian Thruway (just off I-10)
225/387–2699 • lunch & dinner • Louisiana-
Mexican fusion

Ralph & Kacoo's 6110 Bluebonnet Blvd (off
I-10 & Perkins) **225/766–2113** • 11am-9:30pm,
till 10:30pm Fri-Sat • Cajun • full bar •
wheelchair access

Publications

Ambush Mag **504/522–8049** • LGBT
newspaper for the Gulf South (TX through FL)

Erotica

Grand Cinema Station 10732 Florida Blvd
225/272–2010

Breaux Bridge

Accommodations

Maison des Amis 111 Washington St (at
Bridge St) **337/507–3399** • gay-friendly •
charming 1870 residence overlooking
legendary Bayou Teche • full brkfst • WiFi

Lafayette

Info Lines & Services

AA Gay/ Lesbian 115 Leonie St
337/991–0830 (AA#) • call for times &
locations

Nightclubs

Bolt 116 E Vermilion St **337/524–1380** •
8pm-2am, 6pm-midnight Sun, clsd Mon-Tue •
lesbians /gay men • dancing/DJ • karaoke

Lake Charles

Accommodations

Aunt Ruby's B&B 504 Pujo St (at Hodges)
337/430–0603 • gay/ straight • full brkfst •
WiFi

Nightclubs

Crystal's 112 E Broad (at Ryan) **337/433–5457**
• 9pm-2am, till 4am Fri • lesbians/gay men •
dancing/DJ • country/ western • drag shows •
wheelchair access

Restaurants

Pujo St Cafe 901 Ryan St (at Pujo)
337/439–2054 • 11am-9pm, till 10pm Fri-Sat,
clsd Sun • full bar • gay-owned

Metairie

see New Orleans

Monroe

Bars

The Corner Bar 512 N 3rd St (at Pine)
318/329–0046 • 8pm-2am, 3pm-midnight
Sun, clsd Mon & Wed, seasonal hrs • lesbians/
gay men • neighborhood bar • multiracial •
live shows • karaoke • drag shows • 18+ • gay-
owned

Nightclubs

Club Pink 1914 Roselawn Ave **318/654–7030**
• 7pm-2am • lesbians/ gay men • dancing/DJ •
karaoke • 18+ • wheelchair access • gay-
owned

Natchitoches

Accommodations

Chez des Amis B&B 910 Washington St
(btwn Texas & Pavie) **318/352–2647** • gay/
straight • full brkfst • nonsmoking • WiFi •
gay-owned

Judge Porter House B&B 321 Second St
318/527–1555, 800/441–8343 • gay/ straight •
full brkfst • nonsmoking • WiFi • gay-owned

New Orleans

Info Lines & Services

AA Lambda Center 1024 Elysian Fields Ave 504/838-3399 (GENERAL AA OFFICE #) • daily meetings • call for schedule

LGBT Community Center of New Orleans 504/945-1103 • noon-8pm, noon-6pm Fri-Sat • call first • wheelchair access

Accommodations

1896 O'Malley House B&B 120 S Pierce St (at Canal St) 504/488-5896, 866/226-1896 • gay/ straight • nonsmoking • WiFi • gay-owned

5 Continents B&B 1731 Esplanade Ave (at Claiborne) 504/324-8594, 800/997-4652 • gay/ straight • B&B • full brkfst • kids/ pets ok • WiFi • gay-owned

Aaron Ingram Haus 1012 Elysian Fields Ave (btwn N Rampart & St Claude) 504/949-3110 • gay/ straight • guesthouse • apts • courtyard • WiFi • gay-owned

Andrew Jackson Hotel 919 Royal St (btwn St Philip & Dumaine) 504/561-5881, 800/654-0224 • gay-friendly • historic inn • WiFi • nonsmoking

Antebellum Guest House 1333 Esplanade Ave (at Marais St) 504/943-1900 • gay/ straight • full brkfst • clothing-optional • nonsmoking • WiFi • gay-owned

Ashton's B&B 2023 Esplanade Ave (at Galvez) 504/942-7048, 800/725-4131 • gay-friendly • quiet location • WiFi

Auld Sweet Olive B&B 2460 N Rampart St (at Spain) 504/947-4332, 877/470-5323 • gay/ straight • popular • kids 13+ ok • nonsmoking • WiFi

B&W Courtyards B&B 2425 Chartres St (btwn Mandeville & Spain) 504/324-3396, 800/585-5731 • gay-friendly • hot tub • nonsmoking • WiFi • gay-owned

Biscuit Palace Guest House 730 Dumaine (btwn Royal & Bourbon) 504/525-9949 • gay-friendly • 1820s Creole mansion • B&B & apts • in the French Quarter • kids ok • WiFi • wheelchair access

Bon Maison Guest House 835 Bourbon St (btwn Lafitte's & Bourbon Pub) 504/561-8498 • gay/ straight • nonsmoking • gay-owned

Bourbon Orleans Hotel 717 Orleans (at Bourbon St) 504/523-2222, 866/513-9744 • gay-friendly • swimming • WiFi • nonsmoking • also restaurant & 2 bars

The Burgundy B&B 2513 Burgundy St (at St Roch) 504/261-9477 • gay/ straight • near French Quarter • clothing-optional hot tub • nonsmoking • WiFi • gay-owned

Bywater B&B 1026 Clouet St 504/944-8438 • gay-friendly • fireplace • nonsmoking • kids/ pets ok • WiFi • lesbian & gay-owned

Canal Street Inn 3620 Canal St (at Telemachus) 504/483-3033 • gay/ straight • nonsmoking • WiFi

Chez Palmiers B&B 1744 N Rampart St (at St Anthony) 504/208-7044, 877/233-9449 • gay/ straight • pool • nonsmoking • kids 13+ ok • WiFi • gay-owned

The Chimes B&B 1146 Constantinople St (in Garden District) 504/899-2621, 504/453-2183 • gay-friendly • 1876 home • nonsmoking • WiFi • kids/ pets ok w/ approval

The Cornstalk Hotel 915 Royal St 504/523-1515, 800/759-6112 • gay-friendly • kids ok • WiFi

Elysian Guest House 1008 Elysian Fields Ave (at Rampart St) 504/324-4311 • gay-friendly • hot tub • nonsmoking • WiFi • gay-owned

The Frenchmen Hotel 417 Frenchmen St (where Esplanade, Decatur & Frenchmen intersect) 504/948-2166, 800/831-1781 • gay/ straight • spa • pool • kids ok • nonsmoking • WiFi • wheelchair access

The Green House Inn 1212 Magazine St (at Erato) 504/525-1333, 800/966-1303 • lesbians/ gay men • 1840s guesthouse • gym • hot tub • pool • nonsmoking • pets ok • WiFi • gay-owned

Harrah's Casino 228 Poydras St 504/533-6000, 800/847-5299 • gay-friendly • restaurants & lounges • wheeelchair access

Hotel Monteleone 214 Royal St (at Iberville) 504/523-3341, 800/535-9595 • gay-friendly • deluxe historic hotel • rumored to be haunted • pool • WiFi

Kerlerec House 928 Kerlerec St (at Dauphine St) 504/944-8544 • gay/ straight • 1 block from the French Quarter • hot tub • gardens • kids ok • nonsmoking • WiFi • gay-owned

La Dauphine, Residence des Artistes 2316 Dauphine St (btwn Elysian Fields & Marigny) 504/948-2217 • gay/ straight • B&B • nonsmoking • WiFi • gay-owned

La Maison Marigny B&B on Bourbon
1421 Bourbon St (at Esplanade)
504/948-3638, 800/570-2014 • gay-friendly •
on the quiet end of Bourbon St • nonsmoking
• WiFi • gay-owned

Lafitte Guest House 1003 Bourbon St (at St Philip) 504/581-2678, 800/331-7971 • gay/straight • elegant French manor house • nonsmoking • kids ok • WiFi

New Orleans

LGBT Pride:

June. New Orleans Gay Pride. web: www.gayprideneworleans.com

Annual Events:

February - Mardi Gras, web: www.mardigras.com. North America's rowdiest block party.

March - Tennessee Williams Festival, web: www.tennesseewilliams.net.

April - Gay Easter Parade 504/522-8049, web: www.gayeasterparade.com.

April/May - New Orleans Jazz & Heritage Festival, web: www.nojazzfest.com.

May - Saints & Sinners, LGBT writers' festival 504/581-1144, web: www.sasfest.org.

August - Southern Decadence 504/522-8047, web: www.southerndecadence.com. Gay mini-Mardi Gras during Labor Day.

City Info:

New Orleans CVB 800/672-6124, web: www.neworleanscvb.com.

Louisiana Office of Tourism 800/994-8620, web: www.louisianatravel.com.

Weather:

Summer temperatures hover in the 90°s with subtropical humidity. And on the heels of all that heat and humidity come hurricanes. Hurricane season stretches from June 1 to November 30. Winters can be rainy and chilly. The average temperature in February (Mardi Gras month) is 58°, while the average precipitation is 5.23".

Attractions:

Bourbon Street in the French Quarter.

Cabildo (to see the Louisiana Purchase) 504/568-6968.

Cafe du Monde for beignets 504/587-0835, web: www.cafedumonde.com.

Garden District.

Haunted History Tour 504/861-2727, web: www.hauntedhistorytours.com.

Moon Walk.

New Orleans Museum of Art 504/488-2631, web: www.noma.org.

Pat O'Brien's for a hurricane 504/525-4823, web: www.patobriens.com.

Preservation Hall 504/522-2841, web: www.preservationhall.com.

Top of the Market.

Transit:

United Cab 504/522-9771, web: www.unitedcabs.com

New Orleans Airport Shuttle 504/522-3500. web: www.airportshuttleneworleans.com.

New Orleans Regional Transit Authority 504/248-3900, web: www.norta.com.

Lamothe House Hotel 621 Esplanade Ave (btwn Royal & Chartres) 504/947-1161, 800/367-5858 • gay/ straight • popular • jacuzzi • pool • kids ok • nonsmoking • WiFi • straight & gay-owned

Maison Dupuy Hotel 1001 Toulouse St 504/586-8000, 800/535-9177 • gay-friendly • luxury boutique hotel • fine dining restaurant • swimming pool • hot tub • WiFi

Mentone B&B 1437 Pauger St (at Kerlerec) 504/943-3019 • gay-friendly • suite in Victorian in the Faubourg Marigny district • nonsmoking • WiFi • women-owned

The Olivier House 828 Toulouse (at Bourbon) 504/525-8456, 866/525-9748 • gay-friendly • pool • kids/ pets ok • WiFi • wheelchair access

Pierre Coulon Guest House 504/943-6692, 877/943-6692 • gay-friendly • quiet apt patio • nonsmoking • WiFi

Royal Street Courtyard 2438 Royal St (at Spain) 504/943-6818, 888/846-4004 • gay/ straight • suites in 1850s guesthouse • hot tub • pets ok • WiFi • gay-owned

W New Orleans—French Quarter 316 Chartres St 504/581-1200, 877/WHOTELS (RESERVATIONS ONLY) • gay-friendly • pool • WiFi • also restaurant • wheelchair access

Bars

700 Club 700 Burgundy (at St Peter) 504/561-1095 • noon-4am • lesbians/ gay men • videos • food served Wed-Sun • wheelchair access

Big Daddy's 2513 Royal St (at Franklin) 504/948-6288 • 24hrs • lesbians/ gay men • neighborhood bar • wheelchair access

Bourbon Pub & Parade 801 Bourbon St (at St Ann) 504/529-2107 • 24hrs • popular • lesbians/ gay men • dancing/DJ • theme nights • Sun T-dance • drag shows/ strippers • videos • 18+ • WiFi

Cafe Lafitte in Exile/ The Balcony Bar 901 Bourbon St (at Dumaine) 504/522-8397 • 24hrs • popular • mostly gay men • dancing/DJ • live shows • videos

Club Tribute 3202 N Arnoult Rd (at 18th St), Metairie 504/455-1311 • 9pm-close Fri-Sat only • mostly women

Country Club 634 Louisa St (at Royal) 504/945-0742 • 11am-1am • popular • gay/ straight • food served • karaoke • swimming • volleyball • nude sunbathing • WiFi • not your father's country club!

Cutter's 706 Franklin Ave (at Royal) 504/948-4200 • 3pm-3am, from 11am wknds• lesbians/ gay men • neighborhood bar • live music • WiFi • wheelchair access

The Double Play 439 Dauphine (at St Louis) 504/523-4517 • 24hrs • mostly gay men • neighborhood bar • transgender-friendly

The Four Seasons 3229 N Causeway Blvd (at 18th), Metairie 504/832-0659 • 3pm-close • mostly gay men • neighborhood bar • live music & shows in summer • patio • also the Out Back Bar summers • gay-owned

The Friendly Bar 2301 Chartres St (at Marigny) 504/943-8929 • 11am-close • popular • mostly gay men • neighborhood bar • wheelchair access • women-owned

Good Friends Bar 740 Dauphine (at St Ann) 504/566-7191 • 1pm-4am, 24hrs wknds • mostly gay men • neighborhood bar • karaoke Tue • wheelchair access • also Queens Head Pub upstairs Fri-Sun, popular piano sing-along 4pm-8pm

Le Roundup 819 St Louis St (at Dauphine) 504/561-8340 • 24hrs • mostly gay men • neighborhood bar • very MTF-friendly crowd

Michael's in the Park 834 N Rampart (at Dumaine) 504/267-3615 • noon-2am * lesbians/ gay men • neighborhood bar • drag shows • patio • wheelchair access

Napoleon's Itch 734 Bourbon (at St Ann) 504/237-4144 • noon-2am, till 4am Fri-Sat • popular • lesbians/ gay men • wine & martini bar

Rawhide 2010 740 Burgundy St (at St Ann) 504/525-8106 • 1pm-5am • mostly gay men • neighborhood bar • dancing/DJ • leather crowd

Rubyfruit Jungle/ 1135 1135 Decatur St (at Governor Nicholls) 504/571-1863 • gay/ straight • dancing/DJ • transgender-friendly • videos • 18+ • goth theme nights & electronica

Spotted Cat 623 Frenchmen St 206/337-3273 • 4pm-2am • gay-friendly • excellent live jazz • dancing • wheelchair access

Tubby's Golden Lantern 1239 Royal St (at Barracks) 504/529-2860 • 8am-2am • mostly gay men • neighborhood bar • drag shows

Nightclubs

Girl Bar New Orleans 801 Bourbon St (above the Bourbon Pub) 504/529-2107 • 10pm-3am Tue only • mostly women • dancing/DJ • video • young crowd

Oz 800 Bourbon St (at St Ann) **504/593–9491, 850/433–7499** • 24hrs • popular • mostly gay men • dancing/DJ • drag shows • live shows • videos • young crowd • wheelchair access

CAFES

Cafe Rose Nicaud 632 Frenchmen St (btwn Royal & Chartres) **504/949–3300** • 7am-7pm • WiFi

CC's Coffee House 941 Royal St **504/581–6996** • 7am-9pm • WiFi

Croissants d'Or 617 Ursulines St **504/524–4663** • 6am-3pm, clsd Tue • delicious pastries • wheelchair access

The Orange Couch 2339 Royal St **504/267–7327** • 7am-10pm • ultra mod cafe • live music • WiFi • wheelchair access

Royal Blend Coffee & Tea House 621 Royal St **504/523–2716** • 6am-8pm, till midnight wknds • on a quiet, hidden courtyard • also salads & sandwiches

Z'otz 8210 Oak St **504/861–2224** • 7am-1am • coffee shop & art space • live entertainment

RESTAURANTS

13 Monaghan's 517 Frenchmen St **504/942–1345** • 11am-4am • brkfst, lunch & dinner all the time • some veggie • full bar • wheelchair access

Acme Oyster House 724 Iberville St (at Royal) **504/522–5973** • 11am-10pm, till 11pm wknds • long line moves quickly, worth the wait!

Angeli on Decatur 1141 Decatur St (at Gov Nicholls) **504/566–0077** • 11am-2am, till 4am Fri-Sat • pizza • WiFi • wheelchair access

Brennan's 417 Royal St (at Conti) **504/525–9711** • brkfst, lunch & dinner • upscale • reservations recommended

Cafe Amelie 912 Royal St (in Princess of Monaco Courtyard) **504/412–8965** • lunch & dinner, Sun brunch, clsd Mon-Tue • Creole

Cafe Negril 606 Frenchman St (at Chartres St) **504/944–4744** • dinner, clsd Sun-Mon, Caribbean • live music • dancing/DJ • woman-owned • wheelchair access

Casamento's 4330 Magazine St (at Napoleon Ave) **504/895–9761** • lunch, dinner Th-Sat, clsd Sun-Mon (also clsd June-Aug) • best oyster loaf in city • wheelchair access

Clover Grill 900 Bourbon St (at Dumaine) **504/598–1010** • 24hrs • popular • diner fare

Commander's Palace 1403 Washington Ave (at Coliseum St, in Garden District) **504/899–8221** • lunch Mon-Fri, dinner nightly, jazz brunch wknds • popular • upscale Creole • dress code • reservations required • wheelchair access

Coquette 2800 Magazine St (at Washington Ave) **504/265–0421** • lunch Wed-Sat, dinner Mon-Sat • wheelchair access

The Court of Two Sisters 613 Royal St **504/522–7261** • daily jazz brunch buffet 9am-3pm, dinner nightly • Creole

Dante's Kitchen 736 Dante St (at River Rd) **504/861–3121** • dinner nightly, wknd brunch, clsd Tue • Cajun • wheelchair access

EAT New Orleans 900 Dumaine St (at Dauphine) **504/522–7222** • lunch & dinner, Sun brunch, clsd Mon • Cajun/ Creole homecooking • some veggie

Elizabeth's 601 Gallier St **504/944–9272** • 7am-10pm, from 8am wknds, clsd Mon • Cajun

Feelings Cafe 2600 Chartres St (at Franklin Ave) **504/945–2222** • dinner Th-Sun, also Sun brunch • Creole • piano bar • courtyard • wheelchair access

Fiorella's Cafe 45 French Market Pl (at Gov Nicholls & Ursulines) **504/553–2155** • noon-midnight, till 2am Fri-Sat • awesome Fried Chicken

Gott Gourmet Cafe 3100 Magazine St (at 8th St) **504/373–6579** • 11am-9pm, 8am-5pm wknds

Gumbo Shop 630 St Peter St (at Chartres) **504/525–1486** • award-winning gumbo

Herbsaint 701 St Charles Ave **504/524–4114** • lunch & dinner, bistro menu afternoons, clsd Sun • French/ Southern

La Peniche 1940 Dauphine St (at Touro St) **504/943–1460** • 24hrs, clsd Tue-Wed • Southern comfort foods • popular for brkfst • some veggie

Marigny Brasserie 640 Frenchmen St **504/945–4472** • lunch Mon-Fri, dinner nightly, wknd brunch • French

Meauxbar Bistro 942 N Rampart St (at St Philip) **504/569–9979** • 6pm-10pm, clsd Sun-Mon

Mike's On The Avenue 628 St Charles Ave (in the Lafayette Hotel) **504/523–7600** • lunch & dinner • great views of St Charles Ave • wheelchair access

Mona Lisa 1212 Royal St (at Barracks) 504/522–6746 • 11am-10pm, from 5pm Mon-Th • Italian • some veggie • beer/ wine • gay-owned • wheelchair access

Mona's 504 Frenchmen St 504/949–4115 • 11am-10pm, till 11pm Fri-Sat, noon-9pm Sun • cheap Middle Eastern eats

Moon Wok 800 Dauphine St 504/523–6910 • 11am-9pm, till 10pm Fri-Sat • Chinese

Napoleon House 500 Chartres St 504/524–9752 • lunch daily, dinner only Mon, clsd Sun • po' boys & muffulettas • wheelchair access

Olivier's 204 Decatur St 504/525–7734 • 5pm-10pm • Creole • wheelchair access

Orleans Grapevine 718-720 Orleans Ave 504/523–1930 • 4pm-10:30pm, till 11:30pm Fri-Sat • wine bar & bistro • wheelchair access

Phillips 733 Cherokee St (at Maple) 504/865–1155 • 4pm-2am • wheelchair access • gay-owned

Praline Connection 542 Frenchmen St (at Chartres) 504/943–3934 • 11am-10pm • soul food

Restaurant August 301 Tchoupitoulas St (at Gravier St) 504/299–9777 • lunch Mon-Fri, dinner nightly • upscale French/ Mediterranean • wheelchair access

Sammy's Seafood 627 Bourbon St (across from Pat O' Brien's) 504/525–8442 • 11am-11pm • Cajun/ Creole

Stanley 547 St Ann St (at Chartres) 504/587–0093 • 7am-10pm • upscale diner fare

Stella 1032 Chartres St (at Ursulines Ave) 504/587–0091 • dinner nightly • upscale global fusion cuisine • wheelchair access

The Upperline Restaurant 1413 Upperline St 504/891–9822 • dinner Wed-Sun • Creole • fine dining • full bar • wheelchair access

Entertainment & Recreation

Big Easy Rollergirls • New Orleans' female roller derby league • visit www.bigeasyrollergirls.com for events

Cafe du Monde 800 Decatur St (at St Ann, corner of Jackson Square) 504/525–4544, 800/772–2927 • till you've had a beignet—fried dough, powdered w/ sugar, that melts in your mouth—you haven't been to New Orleans & this is "the" place to have them 24hrs a day • wheelchair access

Haunted History Tour 504/861–2727, 888/644–6787 • guided 2-1/2-hour tours of New Orleans' most famous haunts, including Anne Rice's former home • other tours available

Mardi Gras World 1380 Port of New Orleans Pl 504/361–7821 • tour this year-round Mardi Gras float workshop

Pat O'Brien's 718 St Peter St (btwn Bourbon & Royal) 504/525–4823, 800/597–4823 • gay-friendly • more than just a bar—come for the Hurricane, stay for the kitsch • wheelchair access

Preservation Hall 726 St Peter St (btwn Bourbon & Royal) 504/522–2841, 888/946–5299 • 8pm-midnight, set begins at 8:30pm • come & hear the music that started jazz: New Orleans-style jazz! • cover charge

St Charles Streetcar St Charles St (at Canal St) 504/248–3900 • it's not named Desire, but you should still ride it, Blanche, if you want to see the Garden District

Bookstores

FAB -Faubourg Marigny Art & Books 600 Frenchmen St (at Chartres) 504/947–3700 • 1pm-11pm • LGBT books & art

Garden District Book Shop 2727 Prytania St (at Washington) 504/895–2266 • 10am-6pm, till 4pm Sun

Kitchen Witch Cook Books 631 Toulouse St (at Royal St) 504/528–8382 • 10am-7pm, clsd Tue • cookbooks from rare to campy

Retail Shops

Angela King Gallery 241 Royal St 504/524–8211 • lesbian-owned

Bourbon Pride 909 Bourbon St (at Dumaine) 504/566–1570 • 10am-8pm, till 11pm wknds • LGBT cards • gifts

Dutch Alley Artist's Co-Op 912 N Peters St 504/412–9220

Hit Parade 741 Bourbon St 504/524–7700 • 3pm-11pm, 11am-2am Fri-Sat, 11am-midnight Sun • gift and clothing store

NOLA Tattoo 1820 Hampson St (Uptown, at Riverbend) 504/524–6147 • tattoos & piercing

Second Skin Leather 521 St Philip St (btwn Decatur & Chartres) 504/561–8167 • noon-8pm, till 10pm wknds

Publications

Ambush Mag 504/522–8049 • LGBT newspaper for the Gulf South (TX through FL)

EROTICA

Mr Binky's 107 Chartres St (off Canal St) **504/302-2095** • 24hrs

Shreveport

ACCOMMODATIONS

Twenty-Four Thirty-Nine Fairfield 2439 Fairfield Ave **318/424-2424, 877/251-2439** • gay-friendly • WiFi • pets ok

BARS

Korner Lounge II 800 Louisiana Ave (near Cotton) **318/222-9796** • 3pm-2am • mostly gay men • neighborhood bar • karaoke

NIGHTCLUBS

Central Station 1025 Marshall St (btwn Fairfield & Creswell) **318/222-2216** • 5pm-close, till 4am Fri-Sat • popular • lesbians/ gay men • dancing/DJ • country/ western wknds • drag shows Fri • transgender-friendly • wheelchair access

EROTICA

Fun Shop Too 9434 Mansfield Rd **318/688-2482** • clsd Sun • adult, novelty & gag gifts • toys

Slidell

BARS

Anything Geauxs 1540 W Lindberg Dr (at Gause Blvd) **504/722-2101** • 6pm-2am, clsd Mon-Wed • lebisan/ gay men • dancing/DJ • drag & live shows • transgender-friendly • karaoke • lesbian owned

Billy's 2600 Hwy 190 W **985/847-1921** • 6pm-1am • lesbians/ gay men • neighborhood bar • drag shows • karaoke • WiFi

MAINE

Aroostook County

ACCOMMODATIONS

Magic Pond Wildlife Sanctuary & Guest House Blaine **215/287-4174** • lesbians/ gay men • nonsmoking • lesbian-owned

Augusta

includes Hallowell

ACCOMMODATIONS

Annabessacook Farm 192 Annabessacook Rd, Winthrop **207/377-3276** • popular • gay/ straight • restored 1810 farmhouse • full brkfst • WiFi

Maple Hill Farm Inn Hallowell **207/622-2708, 800/622-2708** • gay/ straight • Victorian farmhouse on 130 acres • full brkfst • sauna & hot tub • nonsmoking • WiFi • wheelchair access • gay-owned

RESTAURANTS

Slates 167 Water St (Franklin), Hallowell **207/622-9575, 207/622-4104** • lunch Tue-Fri, dinner Mon-Sat, brunch wknds • also bakery • live shows Mon

Bangor

BOOKSTORES

Pro Libris Bookshop 10 3rd St (at Union) **207/942-3019** • 10am-6pm, clsd Sun-Mon • new & used

Bar Harbor

ACCOMMODATIONS

Aysgarth Station 20 Roberts Ave (at Cottage St) **207/288-9655** • gay-friendly • 10-minute drive from Acadia • cats on premises • nonsmoking • WiFi

Manor House Inn 106 West St (near Bridge St) **207/288-3759, 800/437-0088** • open April-Oct • gay-friendly • 1887 Victorian mansion • full brkfst • some rooms w/ whirlpools • nonsmoking • WiFi

RESTAURANTS

Mama DiMatteo's 34 Kennebec Pl (at Firefly Ln) **207/288-3666** • 4:30pm-10pm • upscale casual dining • full bar • gay-owned

ENTERTAINMENT & RECREATION

ImprovAcadia 15 Cottage St (2nd flr) **207/288-2503** • May-Oct • live improvised theater

Bath

ACCOMMODATIONS

The Galen C Moses House 1009 Washington St **207/442-8771, 888/442-8771** • gay/ straight • 1874 Victorian • pets ok • full brkfst • nonsmoking • WiFi • gay-owned

The Inn at Bath 969 Washington St (at North St) **207/443-4294, 800/423-0964** • gay/ straight • 1810 Greek Revival B&B • full brkfst • jacuzzi • nonsmoking • wheelchair access

Boothbay Harbor

ACCOMMODATIONS

Hodgdon Island Inn PO Box 603, Boothbay 04571 207/633-7474, 800/314-5160 • gay/straight • 1810 sea captain's home • full brkfst • pool • nonsmoking • WiFi

Sur La Mer Inn 18 Eames Rd, PO Box 663, 04538 207/633-7400, 207/380-6400 • gay-friendly • seasonal luxury oceanfront B&B • nonsmoking • kids ok • gay-owned

Brunswick

BOOKSTORES

Gulf of Maine Books 134 Maine St (at Pleasant) 207/729-5083 • 9:30am-5:30pm, clsd Sun • alternative

Bucksport

ACCOMMODATIONS

Williams Pond Lodge B&B 207/460-6064 • gay/straight • WiFi • gay-owned

Corea

ACCOMMODATIONS

The Black Duck Inn on Corea Harbor 207/963-2689 • gay/straight • restored farmhouse • also cottages • full brkfst • nonsmoking • WiFi • gay-owned

Deer Isle

RESTAURANTS

Fisherman's Friend 5 Atlantic Ave, Stonington 207/367-2442 • seasonal • 11am-9pm, till 10pm Fri-Sat

Dexter

ACCOMMODATIONS

Brewster Inn 37 Zion's Hill Rd (at Dexter St) 207/924-3130 • gay-friendly • historic mansion • full brkfst • kids ok • nonsmoking • WiFi • wheelchair access

Farmington

BOOKSTORES

Devany, Doak & Garrett Booksellers 193 Broadway (at High St) 207/778-3454 • 10am-5pm, till 5:30pm Th, till 6:30pm Fri, 9am-5pm Sat, noon-3pm Sun • LGBT section

Freeport

ACCOMMODATIONS

The Royalsborough Inn 1290 Royalsborough Rd, Durham 207/353-6372, 800/765-1772 • gay-friendly • full brkfst • spa services • massage • also alpaca farm • nonsmoking • kids ok • conference room for 20 • WiFi

RESTAURANTS

Harraseeket Lunch & Lobster Co 36 Main St (at Harraseeket Rd), S Freeport 207/865-4888, 207/865-3535 • lunch & dinner • open May-Oct

Hancock

RESTAURANTS

Le Domaine Restaurant & Inn 207/422-3395, 800/554-8498 • 6pm-9pm, Sun brunch, clsd Mon • open June-Oct

Kennebec Valley

ACCOMMODATIONS

The Sterling Inn 1041 US Route 201, Caratunk 207/672-3333 • gay-friendly • mention Damron for special rates • WiFi • kids/pets ok • gay-owned

Kennebunkport

ACCOMMODATIONS

Hidden Pond Maine 354 Goose Rocks Rd 207/967-9050, 888/967-9050 • gay-friendly • pool • great restaurant • nonsmoking • WiFi

White Barn Inn & Spa 37 Beach Ave 207/967-2321 • gay-friendly • pool • restaurant • nonsmoking • WiFi

RESTAURANTS

Bartley's Dockside 4 Western Ave 207/967-6244, 207/233-6037 • lunch & dinner • 11:30am-10pm • seafood • some veggie • full bar • WiFi • wheelchair access

Nunan's Lobster Hut 9 Mills Rd 207/967-4362 • seasonal

Kittery

see also Portsmouth, New Hampshire

Lewiston

EROTICA

Paris Adult Book Store 297 Lisbon St (at Chestnut) 207/783-6677, 800/581-6901

Naples

ACCOMMODATIONS

Lambs Mill Inn Lambs Mill Rd (1/2 mile off Rte 302) **207/693-6253** • gay/ straight • 1860s farmhouse • full brkfst • nonsmoking • WiFi • lesbian-owned

Newcastle

ACCOMMODATIONS

The Tipsy Butler B&B 11 High St **207/563-3394** • gay-friendly • on the Damariscotta River • full brkfst • nonsmoking • WiFi

Ogunquit

ACCOMMODATIONS

2 Village Square Inn Ogunquit 14 Village Square Ln (at Main St) **207/646-5779** • open May-Oct • mostly gay men • Victorian w/ ocean views • heated pool • nonsmoking • WiFi • gay-owned

Abalonia Inn 268 Main St (at Shore Rd) **207/646-7001** • gay/ straight • pool & hot tub • WiFi pets ok • women-owned

Beaver Dam Campground 551 School St, Rte 9, Berwick **207/698-2267** • gay-friendly • campground on 20-acre spring-fed pond • pool • kids/ pets ok • women-owned

Belm House Vacation Units **207/641-2637** • lesbians/ gay men • apt rentals • hot tub • kids/ dogs ok • WiFi • gay-owned

Black Boar Inn 277 Main St (at Ogunquit Rd) **207/646-2112** • lesbians/ gay men • kids ok • nonsmoking • weekly rentals only • gay-owned

Leisure Inn 73 School St (at Main St) **207/646-2737** • gay-friendly • nonsmoking • WiFi • seasonal

Meadowmere Resort 74 S Main St (at Rte 1) **207/646-9661, 800/633-8718** • gay-friendly • pool • health club & spa • kids ok • nonsmoking • WiFi • wheelchair access

Moon Over Maine B&B Berwick Rd **207/646-6666** • lesbians/ gay men • hot tub • nonsmoking • WiFi • gay-owned

Ogunquit Beach Inn 67 School St **207/646-1112** • lesbians/ gay men • 5 minutes walk to beach • WiFi • gay-owned

The Ogunquit Inn 17 Glen Ave **207/646-3633, 866/999-3633** • clsd Nov-March • lesbians/ gay men • Victorian B&B • nonsmoking • WiFi • gay-owned

OgunquitCottages.com 25 Mill St, N Reading, MA 01864 **207/646-3840, 978/546-5813** • lesbians/ gay men • weekly rentals • seasonal (June-Sept) • near bars & beach • nonsmoking • pets/ kids ok • gay-owned

Old Village Inn 250 Main St (at Berwick Rd) **207/646-7088** • gay-friendly • 1880s B&B • ocean views • kids/ pets ok • nonsmoking • WiFi • also restaurant • seafood • upscale

Rockmere Lodge B&B 150 Stearns Rd **207/646-2985, 800/646-2985** • gay/ straight • Maine shingle cottage • near beach • nonsmoking • gay-owned

Yellow Monkey Guest Houses & Motel 280 Main St **207/646-9056** • gay/ straight • seasonal • roof deck • ocean view • jacuzzi • fitness room • kids/ pets ok • wheelchair access • gay-owned

BARS

Front Porch Cafe 9 Shore Rd (at Beach St) **207/646-4005** • lunch & dinner (seasonal) • gay/ straight • piano bar upstairs • full menu

NIGHTCLUBS

Maine Street 195 Main St/ US Rte 1 **207/646-5101** • 5pm-1am, T-dance from 3pm wknds • popular • lesbians/ gay men • dancing/DJ • karaoke • cabaret • food served • gay-owned

Women's T Dance 195 Main St/ US Rte 1 (at Maine Street nightclub) **207/646-5101** • monthly, call for dates • popular • mostly women • dancing/DJ

CAFES

Bread & Roses 246 Main St **207/646-4227** • 7am-7pm, seasonal

Fancy That Cafe Main St (at Beach St & Rte 1) **207/646-4118** • 6:30am-11pm • open April-Oct • pastries • sandwiches

RESTAURANTS

Amore Breakfast 309 Shore Rd **207/646-6661, 866/641-6661** • brkfst only • seasonal

Angelina's Ristorante 655 Main St **207/646-0445** • dinner • Italian

Arrows 41 Berwick Rd (2 miles W of Rte 1), Cape Neddick **207/361-1100** • open April-Dec, 6pm-9pm Th-Sun • popular • eclectic • some veggie • gardens • reservations recommended

Beachfire Bar & Grill 658 Main St **207/646-8998** • dinner nightly, wknd brunch • outdoor fire pit

Bessie's 8 Shore Rd (Rte 1) 207/646-0888 • brkfst, lunch & dinner, also bar

Clay Hill Farm 220 Clay Hill Rd (off Logging Rd), Cape Neddick (York) 207/361-2272 • dinner only • seafood • some veggie • also piano bar

Five-0 50 Shore Rd 207/646-5001 • popular • 5pm-midnight • martini bar & restaurant • full bar

Jonathan's 92 Bourne Ln 207/646-4777 • dinner nightly • steak/ seafood • full bar • entertainment • wheelchair access

La Pizzeria 239 Main St 207/646-1143 • lunch & dinner • open April-Dec • some veggie • beer/ wine • gay-owned

Wild Blueberry Cafe & Bistro 82 Shore Rd 207/646-0990 • brkfst, lunch & dinner, jazz brunch 10am-1pm Sun

Entertainment & Recreation

Ogunquit Playhouse 10 Main St 207/646-5511 (BOX OFFICE), 207/646-2402 • summer theater • some LGBT-themed productions

Portland

Accommodations

The Chadwick B&B 140 Chadwick St 207/774-5141, 800/774-2137 • gay/ straight • full brkfst • WiFi • gay-owned

The Inn at St John 939 Congress St 207/773-6481, 800/636-9127 • gay/ straight • kids/ pets ok • nonsmoking • WiFi • gay-owned

The Inn by the Sea 40 Bowery Beach Rd, Cape Elizabeth 207/799-3134, 800/888-4287 • gay-friendly • pool • kids/ pets ok • nonsmoking • wheelchair access • also restaurant

The Percy Inn 15 Pine St (at Longfellow Square) 207/871-7638, 888/417-3729 • gay-friendly • nonsmoking • WiFi

The Pomegranate Inn 49 Neal St (at Carroll St) 207/772-1006, 800/356-0408 • gay-friendly • full brkfst • private garden • nonsmoking • WiFi

Sea View Inn 65 W Grand Ave (at Atlantic Ave), Old Orchard Beach 207/934-4180, 800/541-8439 • gay/ straight • oceanfront motel • pool • patio • kids/ pets ok • gift shop • WiFi • nonsmoking • wheelchair access

West End Inn 146 Pine St (at Neal St) 207/772-1377, 800/338-1377 • gay-friendly • full brkfst • nonsmoking • WiFi

Wild Iris Inn 273 State St (at Grant St) 207/775-0224, 800/600-1557 • gay-friendly • nonsmoking • WiFi • kids ok • women-owned

Bars

Blackstones 6 Pine St (off Longfellow Square) 207/775-2885 • 4pm-1am, from 3pm wknds • mostly gay men • neighborhood bar • leather 3rd Sat • theme nights • wheelchair access

The Wine Bar 38 Wharf St 207/772-6976 • 5pm-close • gay/ straight • food served

Nightclubs

Styxx 3 Spring St (at Center St) 207/828-0822 • 7pm-1am, from 4pm Th-Sat • popular • lesbians/ gay men • more women Th • dancing/DJ • live shows • theme nights • drag shows • gay-owned

Cafes

Coffee by Design 43 Washington Ave (at Oxford St) 207/879-2233 • 8am-5pm, clsd wknds

Restaurants

Becky's 390 Commercial St (at High St) 207/773-7070 • 4am-10pm • great brkfst & chowdah • wheelchair access

Grace 15 Chestnut St 207/828-4422 • fine dining in renovated old church

Katahdin 27 Forest Ave 207/774-1740 • 5pm-11pm, clsd Sun-Mon • American menu • full bar

Portland & Rochester Public House 118 Preble St 207/773-2000 • 3pm-1am, bistro & pub in the Bayside neighborhood

Street & Co 33 Wharf St (btwn Dana & Union) 207/775-0887 • 5:30pm-9:30pm, till 10pm Fri-Sat • popular • seafood • beer/ wine • wheelchair access

Walter's Cafe 2 Portland Sq (at Union) 207/871-9258 • lunch & dinner, dinner nightly • seafood/ pasta • some veggie • wheelchair access

Bookstores

Longfellow Books 1 Monument Way 207/772-4045 • 9am-7pm, till 6pm Sat, 9:30am-5pm Sun • LGBT section

Retail Shops

The Corner General Store 154 Middle St (at Market) 207/253-5280 • 8am-1am • great wine selection

Emerald City 564 Congress St 207/774-8800 • 10am-6pm, First Friday Art Walk • gifts, pride items & more • gay-owned

EROTICA

Condom Sense 424 Fore St (at Union)
207/871–0356, 877/871–0356 • 10am-8pm, till
9pm Th, till 10pm Fri-Sat, till 6pm Sun •
condoms, lube, massage oils, novelties, etc

Richmond

ENTERTAINMENT & RECREATION

Kennebec Tidewater Charters Kennebec
River & Casco Bay 207/737–4695,
866/347–4874 • guided fishing & kayak trips •
scenic coastal tours • women-owned

Rockland

ACCOMMODATIONS

Captain Lindsey House Inn 5 Lindsey St
207/596–7950, 800/523–2145 • gay-friendly •
19th-c Maine sea captain's home •
nonsmoking • WiFi • wheelchair access

The Old Granite Inn 546 Main St
207/594–9036, 800/386–9036 • gay-friendly •
1880s stone guesthouse • full brkfst •
nonsmoking • WiFi

Rockport

RESTAURANTS

Chez Michel 2530 Atlantic Hwy (at Rte 1),
Lincolnville 207/789–5600 • dinner Wed-Sun
• full bar • some veggie

Lobster Pound Rte 1, Lincolnville Beach
207/789–5550 • 11:30am-8pm • May-Oct •
full bar • patio • wheelchair access

Tenants Harbor

ACCOMMODATIONS

Eastwind Inn 207/372–6366, 800/241–8439
• clsd Dec-April • gay-friendly • rooms & apts
• full brkfst • pets ok

Western Mtns

ACCOMMODATIONS

Mountain Village Farm B&B 164 Main St,
Kingfield 04947 207/265–2030 • gay-friendly •
rural & sophisticated B&B • full brkfst •
nonsmoking • WiFi

York Harbor

RESTAURANTS

York Harbor Inn 480 York St 207/363–5119,
800/343–3869 • lunch Mon-Sat, dinner
nightly, Sun brunch • also the Cellar Pub •
also lodging

MARYLAND

Annapolis

INFO LINES & SERVICES

AA Gay/ Lesbian 199 Duke of Gloucester St
(at St Anne's Parish) 410/268–5441 • 8pm
Tue

ACCOMMODATIONS

Two-O-One B&B 201 Prince George St (at
Maryland Ave) 410/268–8053 • gay/ straight •
English country house • full brkfst •
nonsmoking • WiFi • gay-owned

RESTAURANTS

Cafe Sado 205 Tackle Cir (at Castle Marina
Rd), Chester 410/604–1688 • lunch & dinner
• sushi/ Asian fusion

Baltimore

INFO LINES & SERVICES

AA Gay/ Lesbian 410/663–1922 • 6:30pm
Sat • call for other mtg times

**Gay, Lesbian, Bisexual & Transgender
Community Center of Baltimore** 241 W
Chase St (at Read) 410/837–5445 • many
groups & services

ACCOMMODATIONS

**Abacrombie Fine Food &
Accommodations** 58 W Biddle St (at
Cathedral) 410/244–7227, 888/922–3437 •
gay/ straight • 1880s town house •
nonsmoking • also restaurant

Hotel Monaco Baltimore 2 N Charles St
443/692–6170, 888/752–2636 • gay/staight •
also restaurant • wifi • wheelchair access

Pier 5 Hotel 711 Eastern Ave (at President)
410/539–2000, 866/583–4162 • gay/ straight •
full brkfst • restaurant • WiFi • wheelchair
access

Scarborough Fair B&B 801 S Charles St
410/837–0010, 877/954–2747 • gay-friendly •
gay-owned

BARS

Club Bunns 608 W Lexington St (at Greene
St) 410/234–2866 • 5pm-2am, 7pm-1am Sun
• lesbians/ gay men • dancing/DJ • multiracial
• live shows • female strippers Sat

The Gallery Bar & Studio Restaurant
1735 Maryland Ave (at Lafayette)
410/539–6965 • 6pm-1am • lesbians/ gay
men • dinner Mon-Fri • wheelchair access

Grand Central 1001 N Charles St (at Eager) 410/752–7133 • 4pm-close • popular • lesbians/ gay men • Sapphos upstairs for women • dancing/DJ • videos • karaoke • drag shows • 21+

Hippo 1 W Eager St (at Charles) 410/547–0069 • 4pm-2am • popular • lesbians/ gay men • dancing/DJ • transgender-friendly • karaoke • drag shows • piano bar • wheelchair access

Jay's on Read 225 W Read St 410/225–0188 • 4pm-1am • mostly gay men • piano bar

Leon's 870 Park Ave (at Chase) 410/539–4993, 410/539–4850 • 4pm-2am • lesbians/ gay men • neighborhood bar • WiFi • wheelchair access • also Singer's restaurant

Mixers 6037 Belair Rd (at Glenarm Ave) 410/483–6011 • 5pm-2am • lesbians/ gay men • neighborhood bar • dancing/DJ • karaoke • live shows

The Rowan Tree 1633 S Charles St (at E Heath) 410/468–0550 • noon-2am • gay/ straight • karaoke • "where diversity is our name"

Sapphos 1001 N Charles St (upstairs at Central Station) 410/752–7133 • 8pm-2am Fri-Sat only • mostly women • dancing/DJ

Ziascoz 1313 E Pratt St (at Eden) 410/276–5790 • 7pm-2am • gay/ straight • neighborhood bar • karaoke • mostly African American

NIGHTCLUBS

Club 1722 1722 N Charles St (at Lafayette) 410/547–8423 • afterhours club • Fri-Sat only, 2am-close • gay/ straight • dancing/DJ • multiracial • 18+ • BYOB • dress code

Club Orpheus 1003 E Pratt St 410/276–5599 • gay/ straight • Fri-Sat goth/ fetish party

Baltimore

LGBT PRIDE:
June. 410/777-8145, web: www.baltimorepride.org.

CITY INFO:
Maryland Office of Tourism 866/639-3526, web: visitmaryland.org.

ATTRACTIONS:
Baltimore Museum of Art 443/573-1700, web: www.artbma.org.
Fort McHenry 410/962-4290, web: www.nps.gov/fomc.
Harborplace, web: www.harborplace.com.
Lexington Market 410/685-6169, web: www.lexingtonmarket.com.
National Aquarium 410/576-3800, web: www.aqua.org.
Poe House & Museum 410/821-1285, web: eapoe.org.
Walters Art Museum 410/547-9000, web: www.thewalters.org.

BEST VIEW:
Top of the World Trade Center at the Inner Harbor. 401 E Pratt, 410/837-0845, web: www.viewbaltimore.org.

WEATHER:
A temperate and, at times, temperamental climate. Spring brings great temperatures (50°-70°s) and unpredictable rains and heavy winds. In summer, the weather can be hot (90°s) and sticky. Fall cools off with an occasional "Indian Summer" in October. Winter brings cool days and colder nights, along with snow and ice.

TRANSIT:
Yellow Cab 410/685-1212, web: yellowcabofbaltimore.com.
Go The Airport Shuttle 800/776-0323, web: www.theairportshuttle.com
MTA Transit 410/539-5000, web: www.mtamaryland.com.

The Paradox 1310 Russell St (at Ostend) 410/837–9110 • 11pm-5am, midnight-6am Sat • popular • gay/ straight • more gay 3rd Sat • dancing/DJ • multiracial • food served • live shows • videos • wheelchair access

Rehab 1001 N Charles St (at Grand Central) 410/382–7252 • 9pm 2nd Sat only • mostly women • dancing/DJ • multiracial

CAFES

Station North Arts Cafe 1816 N Charles St 410/625–6440 • 8am-3pm, from 10am Sat, clsd Sun • also art gallery • events

RESTAURANTS

Aldos 306 S High St 410/727–0700 • dinner nightly • Italian

Alonso's 415 W Cold Spring Ln (at Keswick Rd) 410/235–3433 • 4pm-10:30pm, from 11:30am Fri-Sat • pizza & burgers • full bar • wheelchair access

Cafe Hon 1002 W 36th St (at Roland) 410/243–1230 • 11am-10pm, from 9am-close wknds • wheelchair access

The Dizz 300 W 30th St 443/869–5864 • 10am-2am • full bar

Golden West Cafe 1105 W 36th St 410/889–8891 • brkfst, lunch & dinner • New Mexican • also bar • live bands

Jerry D's Seafood 7804 Harford Rd, Parkville 410/668–1299

Mari Luna 1225 Cathedral St 410/637–8013 • modern Mexican • also lounge

Mount Vernon Stable & Saloon 909 N Charles St (btwn Eager & Read) 410/685–7427 • 11:30am-midnight, till 1am Fri-Sat, Sun brunch • also bar

Trinidad Gourmet 418 E 31st St 410/243–0072 • 7am-8:30pm, clsd Sun • Caribbean • delicious & inexpensive

Viccino 1317 N Charles St 410/347–0349 • 11am-11pm, till 9pm Sun • New American • full bar

Woodberry Kichen 2010 Clipper Park Rd #126 410/464–8000 • dinner nightly, wknd brunch • organic & sustainable • full bar • wheelchair access

XS Baltimore 1307 N Charles St 410/468–0002 • 7am-midnight, till 2am Fri-Sat • sushi restaurant, cafe & lounge

ENTERTAINMENT & RECREATION

The Charm City Kitty Club 3134 Eastern Ave (at Creative Alliance) 410/276–1651 • performing arts cabaret for lesbian, dyke, bisexual, trans women & allies

Charm City Roller Girls 1301 S Ellwood Ave (DuBurns Arena) 443/475–0088 • Baltimore's own female roller derby league • visit www.charmcityrollergirls.com for events

BOOKSTORES

Read Street Books 229 W Read St 410/669–4103 • 11am-7pm, noon-6pm Sun, clsd Mon • women's bookstore • also cafe

PUBLICATIONS

Baltimore OUTloud 410/244–6780

Gay Life 410/837–7748 • LGBT newspaper

EROTICA

Chained Desires 136 W Read St 410/528–8441 • 11am-8pm, till 9pm Fri-Sat, clsd Mon • custom leather crafts & apparel • adult toys

Sugar 927 W 36th St (at Roland) 410/467–2632 • 11am-close • lesbian-owned sex toy shop • transgender-friendly

Cumberland

RESTAURANTS

Acropolis 45 E Main St, Frostburg 301/689–8277 • 4pm-10pm, clsd Sun-Mon • Greek & American • full bar

Hagerstown

NIGHTCLUBS

The Lodge 21614 National Pike, Boonsboro 301/591–4434 • 9pm-2am, till midnight Sun, clsd Mon-Th • mostly gay men • dancing/DJ • drag shows • gay-owned

Keedysville

ACCOMMODATIONS

Inn at Red Hill 4936 Red Hill Rd (at Rte 67/340) 301/730–2620 • gay/straight • just a morning drive from DC and Baltimore • WiFi • lesbian-owned

Laurel

BARS

PW's Sports Bar & Grill 9855 N Washington Blvd (at Whiskey Bottom Rd) 301/498–4840, 301/498–4841 • 5am-2am • lesbians/ gay men • sports bar • food served • drag shows • karaoke • WiFi • gay-owned

Princess Anne

ACCOMMODATIONS

The Alexander House Booklovers B&B
30535 Linden Ave (at corner of Beckford)
410/651–5195 • gay-friendly • literary-themed
B&B • full brkfst • nonsmoking

Rock Hall

ACCOMMODATIONS

Tallulah's on Main 5750 Main St (at Sharp
St) **410/639–2596** • gay/ straight • small suite
hotel • kids ok • nonsmoking • wheelchair
access • gay-owned

Snow Hill

ACCOMMODATIONS

River House Inn 201 E Market St (at Green
St) **410/632–2722** • gay-friendly • pool • WiFi
• gay-owned

MASSACHUSETTS

Amherst

see also Northampton

BOOKSTORES

Amherst Books 8 Main St **413/256–1547,
800/503–5865** • 6:30am-9pm, till 5pm Sun •
independent • LGBT section

Food For Thought 106 N Pleasant St (at
Main) **413/253–5432** • 10am-6pm •
progressive bookstore • wheelchair access •
collectively run

Barre

ACCOMMODATIONS

Jenkins Inn & Restaurant 978/355–6444,
800/378–7373 • gay-friendly • full brkfst •
restaurant • full bar • nonsmoking • WiFi •
gay-owned

Berkshires

ACCOMMODATIONS

The B&B at Howden Farm 303 Rannapo
Rd, Sheffield **413/229–8481** • gay/ straight •
250-acre working farm • near river • full brkfst •
nonsmoking • some shared baths • gay-
owned

Broken Hill Manor 771 West Rd (at Rte 23),
Sheffield **413/528–6159, 877/535–6159** • gay-
friendly • B&B • full brkfst • hot tub • kids 12+
ok • WiFi • gay-owned

Gateways Inn 51 Walker St (at Church St),
Lenox **413/637–2532, 888/492–9466** • gay-
friendly • full brkfst • also bar & restaurant •
nonsmoking

Guest House at Field Farm 554 Sloan Rd,
Williamstown **413/458-3135** • gay-friendly •
transgender-friendly • nonsmoking • pool •
WiFi

Mount Greylock Inn 6 East St, Adams
413/743–2665 • gay/ straight • views of Mt
Greylock • gay-owned

River Bend Farm B&B 643 Simonds Rd,
Williamstown **413/458–3121** • gay-friendly •
restored 1770s home • shared baths •
seasonal • well-behaved kids ok • nonsmoking

The Rookwood Inn 11 Old Stockbridge Rd
(at Walker St/ Rte 183), Lenox **413/637–9750,
800/223–9750** • gay/ straight • Victorian inn
near Tanglewood & skiing • full brkfst • kids ok
• nonsmoking • WiFi • women-owned

The Thaddeus Clapp House 74 Wendell
Ave, Pittsfield **413/499–6840, 888/499–6840** •
gay-friendly • full brkfst • nonsmoking

Topia Inn 10 Pleasant St (at Rte 8), Adams
413/743–9600, 888/868–6742 • gay-straight •
nonsmoking • WiFi • wheelchair access • eco-
friendly B&B • organic gourmet brkfst • kids ok
• lesbian-owned

Windflower Inn 684 S Egremont Rd, Great
Barrington **413/528–2720, 800/992–1993** •
gay-friendly • gracious country inn • full brkfst
• pool • nonsmoking • WiFi • kids ok

RESTAURANTS

Allium Restaurant + Bar 42 Railroad St (at
Main), Great Barrington **413/528–2118** •
5pm-9pm, till 10pm Fri-Sat • bar open late

Cafe Lucia 80 Church St (at Tucker), Lenox
413/637–2640 • dinner only, clsd Mon,
seasonal

Church Street Cafe 65 Church St (at
Franklin), Lenox **413/637–2745** • lunch &
dinner, seasonal • American bistro • some
veggie

Mezze Bistro + Bar 777 Cold Spring Rd,
Williamstown **413/458–0123** • 5pm-9pm, till
10pm Fri-Sat, seasonal hrs

ENTERTAINMENT & RECREATION

Tanglewood 197 Rte 183, Lenox
888/266–1200 • live music venue • summer
home of the Boston Symphony/ Pops

Williamstown Theatre Festival just E of
Rte 2 & Rte 7 junction, Williamstown
413/597–3400, 413/458–3200 • call for season
calendar

Boston

INFO LINES & SERVICES

Gay AA 12 Channel St #604 **617/426-9444** (AA#)

GLBT Helpline 617/267-9001, 888/340-4528 • 6pm-11pm

ACCOMMODATIONS

463 Beacon St Guest House 463 Beacon St **617/536-1302** • gay-friendly • nonsmoking • WiFi • gay- & straight-owned

Beacon Hill Hotel & Bistro 25 Charles St (at Chestnut St) **617/723-7575** • gay/ straight • bistro onsite • WiFi

Carolyn's B&B 102 Holworthy St (at Huron Ave), Cambridge **617/864-7042** • gay-friendly • near Harvard Square • nonsmoking • women-owned

Chandler Inn 26 Chandler St (at Berkeley) **617/482-3450, 800/842-3450** • gay-friendly • European-style hotel • centrally located • nonsmoking

The Charles Hotel 1 Bennett St (at Eliot), Cambridge **617/864-1200, 800/882-1818** • gay-friendly • in Harvard Square • also restaurants & bar

The Charles Street Inn 94 Charles St (at Mount Vernon, Beacon Hill) **617/314-8900, 877/772-8900** • kids/ pets ok • nonsmoking • wheelchair access • lesbian-owned

Clarendon Square Inn 198 W Brookline St (btwn Tremont & Columbus) **617/536-2229** • gay/ straight • restored Victorian town house • hot tub • kids ok • fireplaces • nonsmoking • WiFi • gay-owned

The College Club 44 Commonwealth Ave (at Berkeley St) **617/536-9510** • gay-friendly • B&B in Back Bay • some shared baths • kids ok • nonsmoking • WiFi

Encore B&B 116 W Newton St (at Tremont) **617/247-3425** • gay-friendly • 19th-c town house in Boston's historic South End • nonsmoking • gay-owned

Boston

LGBT PRIDE:
June. 617/262-9405, web: www.bostonpride.org.

ANNUAL EVENTS:
April - Gay & Lesbian Film/Video Festival, web: bostonlgbtfilm-fest.org

CITY INFO:
Greater Boston Convention & Visitors Bureau 888/733-2678, web: www.bostonusa.com.

WEATHER:
Extreme—from freezing winters to boiling summers with a beautiful spring and fall.

TRANSIT:
Boston Cab 617/536-5010, web: www.bostoncab.us.
Metro Cab 617/782-5500 web: www.boston-cab.com.
MBTA (the "T") 617/222-3200 web: www.mbta.com.

ATTRACTIONS:
Beacon Hill, web: www.beacon-hillonline.com.
Black Heritage Trail, web: www.afroammuseum.org/trail.htm.
Boston Common.
Faneuil Hall, web: www.faneuilhall.com.
Freedom Trail 617/357-8300, web: www.thefreedomtrail.org.
Isabella Stewart Gardner Museum 617/566-1401, web: www.gard-nermuseum.org.
Museum of African American History 617/725-0022, web: www.afroammuseum.org.
Museum of Fine Arts 617/267-9300, web: www.mfa.org.
Museum of Science 617/723-2500, web: www.mos.org.
New England Aquarium 617/973-5200, web: www.neaq.org.
Old North Church 617/523-6676, web: www.oldnorth.org.
Walden Pond.

Fifteen Beacon Hotel 15 Beacon St (at Somerset) 617/670-1500, 877/982-3226 • gay-friendly • in 1903 Beaux Arts bldg • kids/ pets ok

Holiday Inn Express & Suites Boston Garden 280 Friend St (at Causeway) 617/720-5544 • gay-friendly • WiFi • nonsmoking • wheelchair access

Hotel 140 140 Clarendon St (at Stuart St) 617/585-5600, 800/714-0140 • gay/ straight • boutique hotel • near Copley Square • nonsmoking • wheelchair access • women-owned

Hotel Onyx 155 Portland St (at Causeway) 617/557-9955, 866/660-6699 • gay-friendly • kids/ pets ok • WiFi • nonsmoking

The Liberty Hotel 215 Charles St (at Cambridge St) 617/224-4000, 866/507-5245 • gay-friendly • in the former Charles St Jail • full brkfst • nonsmoking • WiFi • wheelchair access

Nine Zero Hotel 90 Tremont St (at Bosworth) 617/772-5800, 866/646-3937 • gay-friendly • luxury hotel • full brkfst • jacuzzi • kids/ pets ok • nonsmoking • wheelchair access

Oasis Guest House 22 Edgerly Rd (at Westland) 617/267-2262, 800/230-0105 • popular • gay/ straight • Back Bay location • some shared baths • nonsmoking • WiFi • wheelchair access • gay-owned

Victorian B&B 617/536-3285 • women only • full brkfst • nonsmoking • kids ok • WiFi • lesbian-owned

Whitman House Inn 17 Worcester St (at Norfolk St), Cambridge 617/945-5350, 617/913-6189 • gay/ straight • nonsmoking • WiFi • gay-owned

Bars

Bella Luna Restaurant & Milky Way Lounge 284 Amory St, Jamaica Plain 617/524-3740 • 6pm-1am • gay/ straight • food served • theme nights • live music

Boston Ramrod 1254 Boylston St (at Ipswich, 1 block from Fenway Park) 617/266-2986 • noon-2am • popular • mostly gay men • bears • leather • dress code Fri-Sat • dancing/DJ • videos • game room • wheelchair access

➤**Club Cafe Restaurant, Nightclub & Cabaret** 209 Columbus Ave (at Berkeley St) 617/536-0966 • 11am-2am, incredible Sunday brunch buffet along with lunch other days • popular • lesbians/ gay men •Th ladies night • dancing/DJ • karaoke • piano bar • live shows • videos • 3 bars • wheelchair access

Dyke Night 284 Amory St (at Milky Way Lounge), Jamaica Plain 617/524-3740 • 9pm 4th Fri • mostly women • dancing/DJ

Encore Lounge 275 Tremont St (at Stuart St, in hotel) 617/728-2162 • 5pm-2am • gay/ straight • lounge & cabaret • live entertainment • wheelchair access

Fritz 26 Chandler St (in the Chandler Inn) 617/482-4428 • noon-2am, Sat-Sun brunch • lesbians/ gay men • neighborhood sports bar • wheelchair access

Jacque's 79 Broadway (at Stuart) 617/426-8902 • 11am-midnight, from noon Sun • mostly gay men • popular • drag cabaret • cover charge

Ryles 212 Hampshire St (at Cambridge St, in Inman Square), Cambridge 617/876-9330 • gay/ straight • live shows • great wknd jazz brunch

Sexy & Sophisticated 284 Amory St (at Milky Way), Jamaica Plain 617/524-3740 • 9pm 2nd Th only • mostly women • dancing/DJ • multiracial

Sister Sorel/ Tremont 647 647 Tremont (at W Brookline) 617/266-4600 • lesbians/ gay men • dinner only, wknd brunch • wheelchair access

Nightclubs

dbar 1236 Dorchester Ave (at Hancock St), Dorchester 617/265-4490 • 5pm-midnight, till 2am wknds • gay/ straight • also restaurant • dinner nightly

Dyke Night Productions • special events in various locations • mostly women • dancing/DJ • live shows • younger crowd • wheelchair access • check www.dykenight.com for info

Epic Saturday 15 Lansdowne St (House of Blues) 888/693-2583 • 10:30pm Sat only • mostly gay men • dancing/DJ

The Estate 1 Boylston Pl (at The Alley) 617/351-7000 • gay Th only for Glam Life • mostly gay men • dancing/DJ

The Glam Life 1 Boylston Pl (at The Estate) 617/819-4297 • Th only • lesbians/ gay men • dancing/DJ • hip-hop • cover charge

Hot Mess Sundays 275 Tremont St (at Underbar) **617/819-4297** • Sun only • mostly gay men • dancing/DJ • cover charge

Machine 1254 Boylston St (at Park, below Boston Ramrod) **617/536-1950** • 10pm-2am • popular • mostly gay men • women's night 2nd Sat • dancing/DJ • go-go boys • wheelchair access

The Middle East & ZuZu 472 Massachusetts Ave (in Central Square), Cambridge **617/864-3278** • 11am-1am, till 2am wknds • gay-friendly • alternative • live music • young crowd • cover charge • also restaurant

Midway Cafe 3496 Washington St (at William), Jamaica Plain **617/524-9038** • gay/straight • mostly women Th • dancing/DJ • theme nights • karaoke • live shows

➤**Napoleon Cabaret** 209 Columbus Ave (at Club Cafe) **617/536-0966** • nightly piano & vocals • also restaurant • wheelchair access

CAFES

1369 Cafe 757 Massachusetts Ave (in Central Square), Cambridge **617/576-4600** • 7am-11pm • also 1369 Cambridge St (Inman Square), 617/576-1369

Berkeley Perk 69 Berkeley St (at Chandler) **617/426-7375** • 6:30am-5pm, from 7:30am Sat, clsd Sun • food served • wheelchair access • gay-owned

Diesel Cafe 257 Elm St (in Davis Square), Somerville **617/629-8717** • 6am-11pm, from 7am wknds • pool tables • lesbian-owned • wheelchair access

Fiore's Bakery 55 South St (at Bardwell), Jamaica Plain **617/524-9200** • 7am-7pm, from 8am wknds • some vegan • gay-owned

Francesca's 564 Tremont St (at Clarendon) **617/482-9026** • 8am-11pm • wheelchair access

South End Buttery 314 Shawmut Ave (at Union Park St) **617/482-1015** • cupcakes! also brkfst, lunch & dinner • full bar • wheelchair access

True Grounds 717 Broadway (at Boston Ave), Somerville **617/591-9559** • 7am-9pm, 8am-7pm wknds • live shows • WiFi • wheelchair access

RESTAURANTS

BarLola 160 Commonwealth Ave (at Dartmouth) **617/266-1122** • 4pm-midnight • tapas lounge • flamenco performed Sun • gay-owned

Boston Pita Pit 479 Harvard St (at Commonwealth), Brookline **617/738-7482** • 10am-midnight, till 2am wknds • wheelchair access

Casa Romero 30 Gloucester St (at Commonwealth) **617/536-4341** • dinner • Mexican • also bar

Charlie's Sandwich Shoppe 429 Columbus Ave (at Pembroke St) **617/536-7669** • great brkfst, clsd Sun • wheelchair access

City Girl Cafe 204 Hampshire St (at Inman), Cambridge **617/864-2809** • noon-10pm, from 10am Sat-Sun, clsd Mon • Italian • great sandwiches • lesbian-owned

➤**Club Cafe** 209 Columbus Ave (adjacent to Club Cafe) **617/536-0966** • dinner & Sun brunch • popular • some veggie • also 3 bars • piano • videos • wheelchair access

Ecco 107 Porter St **617/561-1112** • 4pm-midnight, from noon Sun, Sun gay event night 8pm

Johnny D's Restaurant & Music Club 17 Holland St (in Davis Square), Somerville **617/776-2004** • dinner nightly, lunch Th-Sun • live music • wheelchair access

My Thai Cafe 3 Beach St, 2nd flr (at Washington) **617/451-2395** • 11am-10pm, till 11pm Fri-Sat • Asian • vegetarian/ vegan

Rabia's 73 Salem St (at Cross St) **617/227-6637** • 11am-10:30pm • fine Italian • wheelchair access

Ristorante Lucia 415 Hanover St (at Harris) **617/367-2353** • lunch & dinner • great North End pasta • wheelchair access

Stella 1525 Washington St (at W Brookline) **617/247-7747** • dinner & Sun brunch, full bar till 2am • also cafe 7am-3pm • WiFi • wheelchair access

Sweet Cheeks Q 1381 Boylston St **617/266-1300** • 11:30am-11pm • American south north of the Mason Dixon • lesbian owned

Trattoria Pulcinella 147 Huron Ave (at Concord), Cambridge **617/491-6336** • 5pm-10pm • fine Italian

Veggie Planet 47 Palmer St (at Club Passim), Cambridge **617/661-1513** • 11:30am-10:30pm • live music venue nights

ENTERTAINMENT & RECREATION

Boston Derby Dames • Boston's first & only women's flat-track roller derby league • visit www.bostonderbydames.com for events

Freedom Trail **617/357-8300** • start at the Visitor Information Center in Boston Common (at Tremont & West Sts), the most famous cow pasture & oldest public park in the US, then follow the red line to some of Boston's most famous sites

Jamaica Pond • great girl-watching

New Repertory Theatre 321 Arsenal St, Watertown **617/923-8487** (BOX OFFICE), **617/923-7060**

Urban AdvenTours 103 Atlantic Ave (at Richmond St) **617/670-0637, 800/979-3370** • guided bike tours of Boston & bike rentals

BOOKSTORES

Calamus Bookstore 92-B South St **617/338-1931, 888/800-7300** • 9am-7pm, noon-6pm • complete GLBT bookstore

Trident Booksellers & Cafe 338 Newbury St (off Mass Ave) **617/267-8688** • 8am-midnight • good magazine browsing • also restaurant • beer/ wine • WiFi • wheelchair access

PUBLICATIONS

Bay Windows **617/464-7280** • LGBT newspaper

The Rainbow Times **413/282-8881, 617/444-9618** • bi-weekly LGBT news magazine for MA, northern CT & southern VT

EROTICA

Good Vibrations 308 Harvard St, Brookline **617/264-4400** • 10am-9pm, till 10pm Th-Sat • clean, well-lighted sex toy store • workshops & events • wheelchair access

Hubba Hubba 534 Massachusetts Ave (at Brookline, in Central Square), Cambridge **617/492-9082** • fetish gear

Brookline

see Boston

Cambridge

see Boston

Cape Cod

see also Provincetown listings

INFO LINES & SERVICES

Gay/ Lesbian AA 508/775-7060 • call for info

ACCOMMODATIONS

The Colonial House Inn & Restaurant 277 Main St, Rte 6A (at Strawberry Ln), Yarmouthport **508/362-4348, 800/999-3416** • gay-friendly • dinner & light brkfst included • pool • jacuzzi • also restaurant & lounge • nonsmoking • WiFi • wheelchair access

Lamb & Lion Inn 2504 Main St (Rte 6A), Barnstable **508/362-6823, 800/909-6923** • gay-friendly • pool • pets ok • WiFi

White Swan B&B 146 Manomet Point Rd, Plymouth **508/224-3759** • gay-friendly • in 200-year-old farmhouse • open year-round • at mouth of Cape Cod • nonsmoking • WiFi

Woods Hole Passage 186 Woods Hole Rd, Falmouth **508/548-9575, 800/790-8976** • gay-friendly • full brkfst • non-smoking • WiFi

Chelsea

see Boston

Greenfield

ACCOMMODATIONS

Brandt House 29 Highland Ave **413/774-3329, 800/235-3329** • gay-friendly • 16-rm estate on hill • full brkfst • kids ok • nonsmoking • WiFi

RESTAURANTS

Hope & Olive 44 Hope St **413/774-3150** • lunch & dinner, clsd Mon

BOOKSTORES

World Eye Bookshop 156 Main St (at Miles St) **413/772-2186** • 9:30am-6:30pm, 9am-5pm Sat, 11am-4pm Sun • general • LGBT section • community bulletin board • women-owned

Haverhill

CAFES

Wicked Big Cafe 19 Essex St (at Wingate) **978/556-5656** • 7am-4pm, 8am-1pm Sat, clsd Sun • coffee house w/ excellent food • WiFi • wheelchair access • lesbian-owned

Lenox

see Berkshires

Lynn

BARS

The Cirque 47 Central Ave **781/586-0551** • 11am-1am • lesbians/ gay men • neighborhood bar • dancing/DJ wknds • leather • karaoke • drag shows • videos • gay-owned

Fran's Place 776 Washington St (at Sagamore) **781/598-5618** • 3pm-1am • lesbians/ gay men • dancing/DJ • also sports bar • wheelchair access

Martha's Vineyard

ACCOMMODATIONS

Arbor Inn 222 Upper Main St, Edgartown **508/627-8137, 888/748-4383** • gay-friendly • B&B • some shared baths • nonsmoking

Martha's Vineyard Surfside Motel 7 Oak Bluffs Ave, Oak Bluffs **508/693-2500, 800/537-3007** • gay-friendly • non-smoking • jacuzzis some rooms • pets ok • WiFi • wheelchair access

The Shiverick Inn 5 Pease's Pt Wy, Edgartown (at Pent Ln) **508/627-3797, 800/723-4292** • gay/ straight • full brkfst • nonsmoking • WiFi • gay-owned

RESTAURANTS

The Black Dog Tavern Beach St Extension #21 (at Water St) **508/693-9223** • brkfst, lunch & dinner, seasonal • wheelchair access

Le Grenier 96 Main St (at Drummer Ln), Vineyard Haven **508/693-4906** • dinner • French • beer/ wine

BOOKSTORES

Bunch of Grapes 44 Main St (at Center St), Vineyard Haven **508/693-2291, 800/693-0221** • 9am-6pm, 11am-5pm Sun • some LGBT titles & magazines

New Bedford

BARS

Le Place 20 Kenyon St (at Belleville Ave) **508/990-1248** • 2pm-2am • popular • lesbians/ gay men • karaoke • dancing/DJ • women-owned

Newton

see Boston

North Adams

see Berkshires

Northampton

see also Amherst

ACCOMMODATIONS

Clarion Hotel & Conference Center 1 Atwood Dr 413/586–1211, 800/582–2929 • gay-friendly • pool • kids ok • nonsmoking • WiFi • also restaurants & bar • wheelchair access

Corner Porches 82 Baptist Corner Rd (at Main), Ashfield 413/628–4592 • gay/ straight • 1880s farmhouse • 30 minutes from Northampton • shared bath • pets on premises • full brkfst • kids ok • nonsmoking • woman-owned

The Hotel Northampton 36 King St (near Bridge St) 413/584–3100, 800/547–3529 • gay-friendly • gym • cafe & historic tavern • nonsmoking • WiFi • wheelchair access

NIGHTCLUBS

Diva's 492 Pleasant St (at Conz St) 413/586–8161 • 9pm-2am, clsd Sun-Mon • lesbians/ gay men • dancing/DJ • live music • theme nights • 18+ Tue-Fri

Pearl Street 10 Pearl St (at Main) 413/586–8686 • 7pm-1am • gay/ straight • dancing/DJ • live music • young crowd

CAFES

Haymarket Cafe 185 Main St 413/586–9969 • 7am-10pm, till 11pm Fri-Sat, from 8am Sun • popular • also restaurant • wheelchair access

RESTAURANTS

Bela 68 Masonic St 413/586–8011 • noon-8:30pm, clsd Sun-Mon • vegetarian • wheelchair access • lesbian-owned

Blue Heron Restaurant 112 N Main St, Sunderland 413/665–2102 • 4pm-9pm, till 10pm Fri-Sat, clsd Sun- Mon • fine dining • 10 minutes out of town • lesbian-owned

Bueno Y Sano 134 Main St (at Center St) 413/586–7311 • 11am-10pm, till 9pm Sun • Mexican

The Old Creamery Co-op 445 Berkshire Tr, Cummington 413/634–5560 • 7am-7:30pm • delicious, quality, homemade deli and bakery foods; abundant fresh produce, try the Spicy Maddow (hint hint) • lesbian-owned

Paul & Elizabeth's 150 Main St (in Thorne's Marketplace) 413/584–4832 • lunch & dinner, Sun brunch • seafood • plenty veggie • beer/ wine • wheelchair access

ENTERTAINMENT & RECREATION

The Iron Horse 20 Center St (at Main) 413/586–8686 • 5:30pm-close • restaurant & bar • live music all ages • nonsmoking

RETAIL SHOPS

Oh My A Sensuality Shop 122 Main St (at Center) 413/584–9669 • noon-7pm, till 8pm Fri-Sat, noon-5pm Sun • informative, helpful & intimate sex toy store

Provincetown

see also Cape Cod listings

INFO LINES & SERVICES

Provincetown Business Guild 508/487–2313

ACCOMMODATIONS

A Secret Garden Inn 300–A Commercial St 508/487–9027 • lesbians/ gay men • kids ok • nonsmoking

Admiral's Landing 158 Bradford St (btwn Conwell & Pearl) 508/487–9665, 800/934–0925 • lesbians/gay men • WiFi • nonsmoking • lesbian-owned

Aerie House & Beach Club 184 Bradford St (at Miller Hill) 508/487–1197, 800/487–1197 • lesbians/ gay men • hot tub • sundeck • WiFi • gay-owned

Anchor Inn Beach House 175 Commercial St (at Winthrop) 508/487–0432, 800/858–2657 • gay/ straight • nonsmoking • private beach • wheelchair access • lesbian & straight-owned/ run

Bayberry Accommodations 16 Winthrop St (at Commercial) 508/487–4605, 800/422–4605 • lesbians/ gay men • hot tub • nonsmoking • WiFi • gay-owned

Bayshore 493 Commercial St (at Howland) 508/487–9133 • gay/ straight • apts • private beach • kitchens • pets ok • WiFi • nonsmoking • lesbian-owned

Beaconlight Guest House 12 Winthrop St (at Bradford) 508/487–9603, 800/696–9603 • mostly gay men • WiFi • nonsmoking • parking • gay-owned

Benchmark Inn 6–8 Dyer St 508/487–7440, 888/487–7440 • lesbians/ gay men • nonsmoking • WiFi • wheelchair access • gay-owned

The Black Pearl Inn 11 Pearl St (at Bradford) 508/487–0302, 800/761–1016 • lesbians/ gay men • hot tub • nonsmoking • WiFi • "friends of Bill welcome"

Boatslip Resort 161 Commercial St
508/487-1669, 877/786-9662 • popular •
mostly gay men • resort • pool • seasonal •
also several bars • popular T-dance • gay-
owned

The Bradford Carver House 70 Bradford
St **508/487-0728, 800/826-9083** • lesbians/
gay men • restored mid-19th-c home •
centrally located • nonsmoking • WiFi • gay-
owned

Bradford House & Motel 41 Bradford St
(at Conant) **508/487-0173** • gay-friendly •
near town center • 1 block from the beach •
wheelchair access • women-owned

Brass Key Guesthouse 67 Bradford St (at
Carver) **508/487-9005, 800/842-9858** •
popular • mostly gay men • hot tub • pool •
nonsmoking • pets ok • WiFi • wheelchair
access • gay-owned

Carpe Diem Guesthouse & Spa 12
Johnson St **508/487-4242, 800/487-0132** •
lesbians/gay men • also cottage • full German
brkfst • hot tub • nonsmoking • WiFi • gay-
owned

The Carriage House Guesthouse 7
Central St (at Commercial) **508/487-8855,
800/309-0248** • gay/straight • hot tub • gay-
owned

Chicago House 6 Winslow St (at Bradford)
508/487-0537, 800/733-7869 • lesbians/gay
men • rooms & apts • hot tub • some shared
baths • nonsmoking • WiFi • gay-owned

Christopher's by the Bay 8 Johnson St (at
Commercial) **508/487-9263** • lesbians/gay
men • Victorian guesthouse • some shared
baths • patio • nonsmoking • gay-owned

Crown & Anchor 247 Commercial St
508/487-1430 • lesbians/gay men • pool •
nonsmoking • WiFi • also bars • cabaret • gay-
owned

Crowne Pointe Historic Inn & Shui Spa
82 Bradford St **508/487-6767, 877/276-9631** •
lesbians/gay men • full brkfst • heated pool•
nonsmoking • WiFi • wheelchair access • gay-
owned

Designer's Dock 349 Commercial St
508/776-5746, 800/724-9888 • gay/straight •
weekly condos in town & on beach • June-Sept
• kitchens • WiFi • gay-owned

Enzo 186 Commercial St (at Court)
508/487-7555, 888/873-5001 • gay/straight •
WiFi • Italian restaurant & piano bar on
premises

Fairbanks Inn 90 Bradford St **508/487-0386,
800/324-7265** • popular • lesbians/gay men
• nonsmoking • WiFi • parking • fireplaces •
lesbian-owned • see ad

Gabriel's at The Ashbrooke Inn 102
Bradford St **508/487-3232** • popular •
lesbians/gay men • full brkfst • nonsmoking •
sundecks • kids/pets ok • WiFi • lesbian &
gay-owned

Gifford House Inn 11 Carver St
508/487-0688, 800/434-0130 • lesbians/gay
men • seasonal • WiFi • also several bars &
restaurant • gay-owned

Grand View Inn 4 Conant St (at
Commercial) **508/487-9193** • lesbians/gay
men • nonsmoking • kids/pets ok • gay-
owned

Heritage House 7 Center St **508/487-3692**
• lesbians/gay men • shared baths • WiFi •
lesbian-owned

The Inn at Cook Street 7 Cook St (at
Bradford) **508/487-3894, 888/266-5655** • gay-
friendly • nonsmoking • women-owned

►**Inn at the Moors** 59 Provincelands Rd
508/487-1342, 800/842-6379 • gay-friendly •
motel • across from Nat'l Seashore Province
Lands • seasonal • nonsmoking • WiFi • pool
• lesbian-owned

John Randall House 140 Bradford St (at
Center) **508/487-3533, 800/573-6700** •
lesbians/gay men • kids ok • nonsmoking •
WiFi • gay-owned

Land's End Inn 22 Commercial St
508/487-0706, 800/276-7088 • gay/straight •
nonsmoking • WiFi

Lotus Guest House 296 Commercial St (at
Standish) **508/487-4644, 888/508-4644** •
lesbians/gay men • seasonal • decks • garden
• teens ok • WiFi • lesbian & gay-owned

Moffett House 296-A Commercial St (at
Ryder) **508/487-6615, 800/990-8865** •
lesbians/gay men • gay-owned

Prince Albert Guest House 164-166
Commercial St (at Central) **508/487-1850** •
mostly gay men • Victorian • nonsmoking •
WiFi • gay-owned

Ravenwood Guest House 462 Commercial
St (at Cook) **508/487-3203** • lesbians/gay
men • also apts & cottage • nonsmoking •
private beach • wheelchair accessible cottage
• lesbian-owned

The Red Inn 15 Commercial St (at Point)
508/487-7334, 866/473-3466 • gay-friendly •
historic B&B • nonsmoking • wheelchair
access • gay-owned

Revere Guesthouse 14 Court St (btwn Commercial & Bradford) 508/487-2292, 800/487-2292 • lesbians/gay men • nonsmoking • gay-owned

Rose Acre 5 Center St (at Commercial) 508/487-2347 • women only • suites • also apts & cottage • nonsmoking • decks • gardens • parking • always open • WiFi • women-owned

Rose & Crown Guest House 158 Commercial St (at Central) 508/487-3332 • gay/straight • lesbian-owned

Sage Inn & Lounge 336 Commercial St 508/487-6424 • gay/straight • WiFi • wheelchair access

Salt House Inn 6 Conwell St (at Railroad) 508/487-1911 • lesbians/gay men • B&B • nonsmoking • WiFi • sundeck • gay-owned

Sandcastle Resort and Club 929 Commercial St 508/487-9300 • gay/straight • beachfront resort w/ kitchen facilities & private bath in every room pool • WiFi

Seasons, An Inn for All 160 Bradford St (at Pearl) 508/487-2283, 800/563-0113 • lesbians/gay men • Victorian B&B • full brkfst • nonsmoking • WiFi • gay-owned

Snug Cottage 178 Bradford St 508/487-1616, 800/432-2334 • gay/straight • nonsmoking • WiFi • gay-owned

Somerset House 378 Commercial St (at Pearl) 508/487-0383, 800/575-1850 • lesbians/gay men • Victorian mansion • nonsmoking • WiFi • gay-owned

Sunset Inn 142 Bradford St (at Center) 508/487-9810, 800/965-1801 • lesbians/gay men • some shared baths • seasonal • clothing-optional sundeck • nonsmoking • WiFi • gay-owned

Provincetown

LGBT Pride:
August - Provincetown Carnival, web: ptown.org.

Annual Events:
August - Provincetown Carnival, web: www.ptown.org.
October - Fantasia Fair - for trannies & their admirers, web: www.fantasiafair.org.
October - Women's Week, web: www.womeninnkeepers.com. It's very popular, so make your reservations early!
December - Holly Folly, web: www.ptown.org. Gay & Lesbian Holiday Festival.

City Info:
Provincetown Tourism Office 508/487-7000, web: www.provincetowntourism-office.org.

Weather:
New England weather is unpredictable. Be prepared for rain, snow, or extreme heat! Otherwise, the weather during the season consists of warm days and cooler nights.

Attractions:
The beach.
Galleries.
Herring Cove Beach.
Pilgrim Monument.
Provincetown Museum 508/487-1310, web: www.pilgrim-monument.org.
Whale-watching.

Best View:
People-watching from an outdoor cafe or on the beach.

Transit:
Cape Cab 508/487-2222, web: capecabtaxi.com.
Ferry: Bay State Cruise Company (from Commonwealth/World Trade Center Pier in Boston, during summer) 877/783-3779, web: www.baystatecruisecompany.com.
Air: Cape Air 508/771-6944, 866/227-3247, web: www.flycapeair.com.

Surfside Hotel & Suites 543 Commercial (at Kendall Ln) 508/487-1726, 800/421-1726 • gay/ straight • waterfront hotel • lots of amenities • private beach • pool • nonsmoking • WiFi • kids/ pets ok • gay-owned

The Tucker Inn 12 Center St (at Bradford) 508/487-0381, 800/477-1867 • lesbians/ gay men • full brkfst • WiFi • also cottage • nonsmoking • gay-owned

Victoria House 5 Standish St 508/487-4455, 877/867-8696 • lesbians/ gay men • WiFi • nonsmoking • gay-owned

The Waterford 386 Commercial St (at Pearl) 508/487-6400, 800/487-0784 • gay/ straight • deck w/ full bar • also restaurant • WiFi

Watermark Inn 603 Commercial St 508/487-0165 • gay/ straight • kids ok • nonsmoking • WiFi

Watership Inn 7 Winthrop St (at Commercial St) 508/487-0094, 800/330-9413 • mostly gay men • sundeck • WiFi • gay-owned

White Wind Inn 174 Commercial St (at Winthrop) 508/487-1526, 888/449-9463 • lesbians/ gay men • WiFi • gay-owned

Women Innkeepers of Provincetown PO Box 573, 02657 • women-owned accommodations in Provincetown • see ad in front color section

Bars

The Boatslip Resort 161 Commercial St 508/487-1669, 877/786-9662 • seasonal • popular • lesbians/ gay men • T-dance 4pm daily during season • young crowd • swimming • outdoor/ waterfront grill

Governor Bradford 312 Commercial St (at Standish) 508/487-2781 • 11am-1am, from noon Sun • gay-friendly • "drag karaoke" Sat (nightly in season) • also restaurant in summer

PiedBar 193–A Commercial St (at Court St) 508/487-1527 • seasonal May-Oct, noon-1am • popular • lesbians/ gay men • dancing/DJ • more women Fri-Sat • wheelchair access

Porchside Lounge 11 Carver St (in the Gifford House) 508/487-0688 • 5pm-1am • mostly gay men • neighborhood bar • also restaurant

Shipwreck Lounge 10 Carver St (at Bradford) 508/487-1472 • lesbians/ gay men • upscale lounge • outdoor seating w/ fire pit

Wave Video Bar 247 Commercial St (in the Crown & Anchor) 508/487-1430 • 6pm-1am, from noon in season • lesbians/ gay men • neighborhood bar • karaoke • T-dance Sun

Nightclubs

Atlantic House (The "A-House") 6 Masonic Pl 508/487-3169 • 10pm-1am • popular • mostly gay men • neighborhood bar • 3 bars • dancing/DJ • theme parties

Club Purgatory 9-11 Carver St (at Bradford St, in the Gifford House) 508/487-8442 • opens 7pm, from 9pm Sun (in season) • lesbians/ gay men • dancing/DJ

Girl Power 193–A Commercial St (at The PiedBar) • Provincetown events for women • check www.provincetownforwomen.com for events • see ad in front color section

Paramount in the Crown & Anchor 508/487-1430 • 10:30pm-1am (seasonal) • popular • lesbians/ gay men • dancing/DJ • live shows • drag shows • cabaret

Cafes

Post Office Cafe Cabaret 303 Commercial St (upstairs) 508/487-3892 • 8am-11pm, seasonal hours • some veggie

Restaurants

Bayside Betsy's 177 Commercial St 508/487-6566 • brkfst , lunch & dinner, bar till 10pm • on waterfront • wheelchair access

Big Daddy's Burritos 205 Commercial St 508/487-4432 • 11am-10pm (May-Oct) • Tex-Mex, burritos, veggie wraps, salads & nachos

Bubala's by the Bay 183–185 Commercial 508/487-0773 • lunch & dinner • popular • seasonal • patio

Ciro & Sal's 4 Kiley Ct (btwn Bangs St & Lovett's Ct) 508/487-6444 • dinner from 5:30pm • Northern Italian • reservations recommended

Fanizzi's 539 Commercial St (at Kendall Lane) 508/487-1964 • popular • lunch & dinner • some veggie • full bar • on the water • wheelchair access

Front Street Restaurant 230 Commercial St 508/487-9715 • 6pm-10:30pm, bar till 1am • bistro beer/ wine • seasonal

Lobster Pot harborside (at 321 Commercial St) 508/487-0842 • 11:30am-10pm (April-Nov) • "a Provincetown tradition" • wheelchair access

The Mews Restaurant & Cafe 429 Commercial St (at Bangs St) 508/487-1500 • dinner • seasonal Sun brunch • popular • off-season live shows • wheelchair access • waterfront dining

Napi's Restaurant 7 Freeman St 508/487-1145, 800/571-6274 • dinner • lunch Oct-April • int'l/ seafood • plenty veggie • wheelchair access

The Red Inn 15 Commercial St (at Point) 508/487-7334, 866/473-3466 • dinner nightly, brunch Th-Sun, clsd Jan-April • reservations a must • full bar

Relish 93 Commercial St 508/487-8077 • yummy baked goods • pick up a sandwich on the way to the beach!

Spiritus Pizza 190 Commercial St 508/487-2808 • noon-2am • popular • great espresso shakes & late-night hangout for a slice

ENTERTAINMENT & RECREATION

Art House Theatre & Cafe 214 Commercial St 508/487-9222

Art's Dune Tours 4 Standish St 508/487-1950, 800/894-1951 • day trips, sunset tours & charters through historic sand dunes & Nat'l Seashore Park • kids ok • gay-owned

Dolphin Fleet Whale Watch 305 Commercial St 508/240-3636, 800/826-9300 • gay-friendly • 3-hr day & evening cruises • full galley & bar on board • wheelchair access

Herring Cove Beach

Ptown Bikes 42 Bradford 508/487-8735 • 9am-6pm • rentals • gay-owned

Spaghetti Strip • nude beach • 1.5 miles south of Race Point Beach

RETAIL SHOPS

HRC Action Center & Store 209-211 Commercial St 508/487-7736 • Human Rights Campaign merchandise & info

Recovering Hearts 4 Standish St 508/487-4875 • 10am-11pm (in summer), call for off-season hours • recovery • LGBT & New Age books • wheelchair access

➤**Womencrafts** 376 Commercial St (at Pearl St) 508/487-2501 • 11am-10pm (in summer), call for off-season hours • women-crafted jewelry, porcelain, pottery, glass, sculpture, mosaics, photographs, books, CDs, & DVDs, opened since 1976, currently representing over 100 women in their art

PUBLICATIONS

Provincetown Banner 167 Commercial St **508/487-7400** • newspaper

Provincetown Magazine 508/487-1000 • seasonal • Provincetown's oldest weekly magazine

GYMS & HEALTH CLUBS

Mussel Beach Health Club 35 Bradford St (btwn Montello & Conant) **508/487-0001** • 6am-9pm, till 8pm in winter

Provincetown Gym 82 Shank Painter Rd (at Winthrop) **508/487-2776**

Quincy

see also Boston

NIGHTCLUBS

My House 609 Washington St (at Cleverly Ct) **617/302-4285** • 6pm-1am, clsd Mon • lesbians/ gay men • dancing/DJ • food served • karaoke

Randolph

BARS

Randolph Country Club/ RCC 44 Mazzeo Dr **781/961-2414** • 2pm-2am, from 10am summer • popular • lesbians/ gay men • dancing/DJ • food served • live shows • karaoke • male dancers • videos • volleyball court • pool • wheelchair access

Somerville

see Boston

Springfield

BARS

Pure 234 Chestnut St (E of Main) **413/205-1483** • noon-2am • mostly gay men • neighborhood bar • food served • wheelchair access

NIGHTCLUBS

The X Room 395 Dwight St **413/732-4562** • 7pm-2am, from 2pmTh-Sun • mostly gay men • dancing/DJ • strippers/ nude dancers

Taunton

BARS

Bobby's Place 62 Weir St (at Route 44, 138 & 140, at Taunton Green) **508/824-9997** • 5pm-1am, till 2am Fri-Sat, from 2pm Sun • lesbians/ gay men • dancing/DJ • food served • karaoke • drag shows

Williamstown

see Berkshires

Worcester

BARS

MB Lounge 40 Grafton St (at Franklin) **508/799-4521** • 5pm-2am, from 3pm wknds • lesbians/ gay men • neighborhood bar • WiFi • wheelchair access • gay-owned

Mixers Cocktail Lounge 105 Water St **508/756-2227** • 6pm-2am, clsd Mon • lesbians/ gay men • dancing/DJ

NIGHTCLUBS

Club Remix 105 Water St (at Harrison) **508/756-2227** • 9pm-2am, from 8pm Wed, clsd Mon-Tue • mostly men • dancing/DJ • karaoke

RETAIL SHOPS

Glamour Boutique 850 Southbridge St, Auburn **508/721-7800** • large-size dresses, wigs, etc

PUBLICATIONS

Central Mass Pride Magazine • centralmasspridemag.com

MICHIGAN

Statewide

PUBLICATIONS

Out Post 313/702-0272 • bi-weekly nightlife guide for SE Michigan

What Helen Heard PO Box 811, East Lansing 48826 **517/371-5257** • what's happening for MI lesbians

Ann Arbor

INFO LINES & SERVICES

The Jim Toy Community Center 319 Braun Ct **734/995-9867** • LGBT resource center, HIV testing 5pm-7pm Sun

Lesbian/ Gay AA 734/482-5700

BARS

\'aut\ Bar 315 Braun Ct (at Catherine) **734/994-3677** • 4pm-2am, from 11am Sat, 10 am Sun • popular • lesbians/ gay men • also restaurant (dinner & wknd brunch) • American/ Mexican • patio • wheelchair access

NIGHTCLUBS

The Necto 516 E Liberty (at Maynard) **734/994–5436** • 9pm-2am • gay/ straight • dancing/DJ • videos • young crowd • 18+ • theme nights • gay night Fri

CAFES

Cafe Verde 214 N Fourth Ave (at Catherine St) **734/994–9174** • 7am-9:30pm, 9am-8pm Sun • fair trade & organic coffee & tea • also soups, sandwiches & salads

RESTAURANTS

Dominick's 812 Monroe St (at Tappan Ave) **734/662–5414** • 10am-10pm, clsd Sun • Italian • beer/ wine • wheelchair access

The Earle 121 W Washington (at Ashley) **734/994–0211** • 5:30pm-9pm, till 11pm Fri-Sat, 5pm-8pm Sun • cont'l • some veggie • beer/ wine • wheelchair access

Mani Osteria & Bar 341B E Liberty **734/769-6700** • 11:30am-10pm, from 4pm wknds, clsd Mon • great pizza

Seva 314 E Liberty (at 5th Ave) **734/662–1111** • 11am-9pm, from 10am wknds • vegetarian • also cafe & wine bar

Zingerman's Delicatessen 422 Detroit St (at Kingsley) **734/663–3354, 888/636–8162** • 7am-10pm • also ship food worldwide

ENTERTAINMENT & RECREATION

The Ark 316 S Main St (btwn William & Liberty) **734/761–1818, 734/761–1800** • gay-friendly • concert house • women's music shows

BOOKSTORES

Common Language 317 Braun Ct (at 4th) **734/663–0036** • 11am-10pm, till midnight Fri-Sat, till 7pm Sun • LGBT • wheelchair access

Crazy Wisdom Books & Tea Room 114 S Main St (btwn Huron & Washington) **734/665-2757** • 11am-9pm, till 11pm Fri-Sat, 11am-8pm Sun • holistic & metaphysical • live music

Battle Creek

NIGHTCLUBS

Partners 910 North Ave (at Morgan) **269/964-7276** • 7pm-2am, clsd Mon • lesbians/ gay men • dancing/DJ • karaoke • wheelchair access

EROTICA

Romantix Adult Superstore 690 W Michigan Ave (at Grand) **269/964-3070**

Bay City

BARS

Malickey's Pub 501 S Madison **989/414-6667** • 11:30am-1:30am • gay/ straight • theme nights

Bellaire

ACCOMMODATIONS

Applesauce Inn B&B 7296 S M-88 **231/533-6448** • gay-friendly • B&B in 100-year-old farmhouse • dog-friendly • WiFi • nonsmoking

Bellaire B&B 212 Park St (at Antrim) **231/533-6077, 800/545-0780** • gay/ straight • stately 1879 home • full brkfst • nonsmoking • WiFi • gay-owned

Detroit

INFO LINES & SERVICES

Affirmations Community Center 290 W 9 Mile Rd (at Planavon), Ferndale **800/398-4297** • 9am-9pm, clsd Sun • helpline line 4pm-9pm

Helpline 800/398-4297 • 4pm-9pm Tue-Sat • support & resources line

ACCOMMODATIONS

The Atheneum Suite Hotel 1000 Brush Ave (at Lafayette) **313/962-2323, 800/772-2323** • gay-friendly • restaurant & lounge • gym • WiFi • wheelchair access

Detroit Marriott at the Renaissance Center 400 Renaissance Center Dr **313/568-8000, 800/228-9290** • gay-friendly • wheelchair access

Honor & Folly 2138 Michigan Ave (above Slows BBQ) • gay/ straight • WiFi • design-focused B&B with cooking classes, bike rentals and goods made by local designers and artisantisan

Milner Hotel 1538 Centre St (at Grand River Ave) **313/963-3950, 877/645-6377** • gay-friendly • downtown

BARS

Centaur Bar 2233 Park Ave (at W Montcalm St) **313/963-4040** • 4pm-2am • gay/ straight • sports bar • food served

Club Gold Coast 2971 E 7 Mile Rd (at Conant) **313/366-6135** • 7pm-2am • popular • mostly gay men • dancing/DJ • male dancers nightly • WiFi • wheelchair access

Gigi's 16920 W Warren (at Clayburn, enter rear) 313/584–6525 • noon-2am, from 2pm wknds • mostly gay men • dancing/DJ • transgender-friendly • drag shows • gay-owned

Menjo's 928 W McNichols Rd (at Hamilton) 313/863–3934 • 1pm-2am, popular happy hour • mostly gay men • dancing/DJ • karaoke • live shows • videos • young crowd

Pronto 608 S Washington (at 6th St), Royal Oak 248/544–7900 • 11am-2am • popular • lesbians/gay men • patio • also restaurant

Soho 205 W 9 Mile (at Woodward), Ferndale 248/542–7646 • 4pm-close, from 6pm wknds • lesbians/gay men • karaoke • swank cocktail lounge

The Woodward Video Bar & Grill 6426 Woodward Ave (at Milwaukee, rear entrance) 313/872–0166 • 2pm-2am • mostly gay men • DJ Th-Sun • karaoke • videos

NIGHTCLUBS

Birdcage 6640 E 8 Mile Rd (at Sherwood) 313/891–1020 • 4pm-2am Fri-Sun • lesbians/gay men • drag shows

Detroit

LGBT PRIDE:
June. 313/537-7000, web: www.pridefest.net.
July. Hotter Than July 888/755-9165, web: www.hotterthanjuly.com. "The Midwest's oldest black lesbian, gay, bi-affectional and transgender pride celebration."

ANNUAL EVENTS:
End of April/early May - London Lesbian Film Festival, web: www.llff.ca. Held in London, Ontario.
August - Detroit International Jazz Festival, web: www.detroitjazzfest.com.
August -Michigan Womyn's Music Festival 231/757-4766, web: www.michfest.com. One of the biggest annual gatherings of lesbians on the continent, in Walhalla, in Western Michigan.

CITY INFO:
313/202-1800 or 800/338-7648, web: www.visitdetroit.com.

TRANSIT:
Checker Cab 313/963-7000, web: www.checkercab-det.com.
Detroit Cab 313/841–6000.
AA Airport Service 800/720–0797, web: www.metroairportservice.com.
DDOT bus service 313/933-1300, web: www.detroittransit.org.
Detroit People Mover 313/224-2160, web: www.thepeoplemover.com.
SMART, web: www.smartbus.org.

ATTRACTIONS:
Belle Isle Park.
Detroit Institute of Arts 313/833-7900, web: www.dia.org.
Greektown.
Motown Historical Museum 313/875-2264, web: www.motownmuseum.com.
Museum of African American History 313/494-5800, web: www.maah-detroit.org.
North American Black Historical Museum in Windsor, Ontario, 800/713–6336, web: www.black-historicalmuseum.com.
Renaissance Center 313/568–5600, web: www.gmrencen.com.

BEST VIEW:
From the top of the 73-story Marriott Hotel at the Renaissance Center.

WEATHER:
Be prepared for hot, humid summers and cold, dry winters.

Escape 19404 Sherwood (at 7 Mile) **313/892–1765** • 10pm-5am • lesbians/ gay men • neighborhood bar • drag shows • grill menu • gay-owned

Leland City Club 400 Bagley St (at Leland Hotel) **313/962–2300** • 10pm-4:30am Fri-Sat • gay-friendly • dancing/DJ • goth/ alternative • 18+

Luna 1815 N Main St (at 12 Mile), Royal Oak **248/589–3344** • from 9pm, clsd Sun-Tue • gay-friendly • dancing/DJ • theme nights

Stiletto's 1641 Middlebelt Rd (btwn Michigan Ave & Cherry Hill Rd), Inkster **734/729–8980** • 8pm-2am Th-Sun • lesbians/ gay men • dancing/DJ • drag shows • karaoke

Temple 2906 Cass Ave (btwn Charlotte & Temple) **313/832–2822** • 1pm-2am • mostly gay men • dancing/DJ • transgender-friendly • mostly African American • popular wknds • wheelchair access

CAFES

Avalon International Breads 422 W Willis (at Cass) **313/832–0008** • 6am-6pm, clsd Sun-Mon • lesbian-owned

Coffee Beanery Cafe 28557 S Woodward Ave (S of 12 Mile), Berkley **248/336–9930** • 7am-11pm • WiFi

Five 15 515 S Washington St, Royal Oak **248/515–2551** • 11am-5pm, till 5pm Sun, clsd Mon • Drag Bingo Fri-Sat • performances • art shows • WiFi • gay-owned

RESTAURANTS

Amici's 3249 12 Mile Rd (at Gardner Ave), Berkley **248/544–4100** • gourmet pizza & martinis

Atlas Global Bistro 3111 Woodward Ave (at Charlotte) **313/831–2241** • lunch & dinner • Sun brunch • American/ int'l • upscale

Cacao Tree Cafe 204 W 4th St, Royal Oak **248/336–9043** • 9am-9pm • gourmet raw food/ vegan

Cass Cafe 4620 Cass Ave (at Forest) **313/831–1400** • 11am-2am, 5pm-1am Sun • plenty veggie • full bar • WiFi

Coach Insignia 200 Renaissance Ctr, 71st Fl **313/567–2622** • dinner, clsd Sun • steakhouse

Como's 22812 Woodward (at 9 Mile), Ferndale **248/548–5005** • 11am-2am, till 4am Fri-Sat • Italian • full bar • patio • wheelchair access

Elwood Bar & Grill 300 Adams (at Brush, by Comerica Park) **313/962–2337** • 11am-8pm, till 2pm Mon, clsd Sun (unless there's a Tiger's game) • Art Deco diner

Inn Season 500 E 4th St (at Knowles), Royal Oak **248/547–7916** • lunch & dinner • Sun brunch • clsd Mon • organic vegetarian/ vegan

La Dolce Vita 17546 Woodward Ave (at McNichols) **313/865–0331** • lunch & dinner, Sun brunch • clsd Mon • lesbians/ gay men • Italian • plenty veggie • full bar • patio • wheelchair access

Mercury Burger & Bar 2163 Michigan Ave **313/964–5000** • 11am-11pm

One-Eyed Betty's 175 W Troy, Ferndale **248/808–6633** • 4pm-2am, from 9am wknds • many beers on tap • gay-owned

Red Star 13944 Michigan Ave, Dearborn **313/581–1451** • Chinese • plenty veggie/ vegan

Roast 1128 Washington Ave (at State St) **313/961–2500** • dinner nightly • steakhouse

Seva 66 E Forest **313/974–6661** • 11am-9pm, till 11pm Fri-Sat • vegetarian

Sweet Lorraine's Cafe & Bar 29101 Greenfield Rd (at 12 Mile), Southfield **248/559–5985** • 11am-10pm, till midnight Fri-Sat • popular • modern American • wheelchair access

Traffic Jam & Snug 511 W Canfield St (at SE corner of 2nd Ave) **313/831–9470** • 11am-10:30pm, till midnight Fri-Sat, till 9pm Sun • eclectic • plenty veggie • also full bar, bakery, dairy & brewery • wheelchair access

Vivio's 2460 Market St (at Napoleon St) **313/393–1711** • lunch & dinner, clsd Sun • Italian, famous bloody marys & steamed pot o' mussels• full bar • wheelchair access

Wolfgang Puck Grille 1777 3rd St (at the MGM Grand Hotel) **313/465–1648** • 5pm-10pm, 9am-2pm Sat-Sun, clsd Mon-Tue

ENTERTAINMENT & RECREATION

Charles H Wright Museum of African American History 315 E Warren Ave (at Cass) **313/494–5800**

Detroit Derby Girls 37637 Five Mile Rd #311, Livonia • visit www.detroitrollerderby.com for events

Motown Historical Museum 2648 W Grand Blvd **313/875–2264** • come see where the Motown Sound began • guided tours & gift shop

BOOKSTORES

Just 4 Us 211 W 9 Mile Rd (at Woodward), Ferndale **248/547–5878** • 11am-8pm, till 10pm Th-Fri, till 5pm Sun • also cafe • gay-owned

RETAIL SHOPS

Royal Oak Tattoo 820 S Washington Ave (at Lincoln), Royal Oak 248/398-0052 • tattoo & piercing studio

PUBLICATIONS

Between the Lines 734/293-7200 • statewide LGBT weekly

Metra Magazine PO Box 71844, Madison Heights 48071 248/543-3500 • covers IN, IL, MI, OH, PA, WI & Ontario, Canada

EROTICA

Noir Leather 124 W 4th St (at S Center St), Royal Oak 248/541-3979 • 11am-9pm, till 10pm Fri-Sat, noon-7pm Sun • wheelchair access

Douglas

see Saugatuck

Escanaba

EROTICA

Sensual Arts Adult Bookstore 615 N Lincoln Rd (at 6th Ave N) 906/786-9020 • 10am-midnight, till 1am Sat, 1pm-11pm Sun • gay-owned

Flint

BARS

MI 2406 N Franklin Ave (at Belle Ave) 810/234-9481 • 5pm-2am • popular • lesbians/ gay men • dancing/DJ • multiracial • WiFi

Pachyderm Pub G–1408 E Hemphill Rd (btwn I-475 & Saginaw St), Burton 810/744-4960 • 3pm-2am, from 5pm wknds • lesbians/ gay men • also restaurant • dancing/DJ • karaoke • male dancers • multiracial • transgender-friendly • patio • WiFi • gay-owned

State Bar 2512 S Dort Hwy (at Lippincott) 810/767-7050 • 2pm-2am • popular • lesbians/ gay men • dancing/DJ • karaoke • wheelchair access

NIGHTCLUBS

Club Triangle 2101 S Dort (at Lippincott) 810/767-7550 • 9pm-close Wed-Sun • popular • lesbians/ gay men • dancing/DJ • male dancers • 18+

CAFES

The Good Beans Cafe 328 N Grand Traverse (at 1st Ave) 810/237-4663 • 7:30am-4pm, till 9pm Th-Fri, open some wknds • espresso & pastries • live shows • WiFi • gay-owned • wheelchair access

Frankfort

ACCOMMODATIONS

Wayfarer Lodgings 1912 S Scenic Hwy (M-22) 231/352-9264, 800/735-8564 • gay-friendly • cottages • near Frankfort, Lake Michigan & Betsie River • kids/ pets ok • nonsmoking • WiFi

Glen Arbor

ACCOMMODATIONS

Duneswood at Sleeping Bear Dunes Nat'l Lakeshore 231/668-6789 • women only • located in northern MI • nonsmoking • lesbian-owned

Grand Rapids

INFO LINES & SERVICES

Lesbian/ Gay Network of W Michigan 343 Atlas Ave SE (behind Spirit Dreams in Eastown) 616/458-3511 • 11am-5:30pm, clsd wknds • lounge • library • evening social groups

ACCOMMODATIONS

Radisson Riverfront Hotel 270 Ann St NW (at Turner Ave) 616/363-9001, 800/395-7046 • gay-friendly • nonsmoking • pool • wheelchair access • WiFi

BARS

Apartment Lounge 33 Sheldon NE (at Library) 616/451-0815 • 1pm-2am, from noon wknds • mostly gay men • neighborhood bar • sandwiches served • wheelchair access

Diversions 10 Fountain St NW (at Division) 616/451-3800 • 8pm-2am • popular • lesbians/ gay men • dancing/DJ • karaoke • 18+ • videos • wheelchair access

Pub 43 43 S Division St (at Weston) 616/458-2205 • 3pm-2am • lesbians/ gay men • neighborhood bar • food served

NIGHTCLUBS

Rumors Nightclub 69 S Division Ave (at Oakes St) 616/454-8720 • 4pm-2am • mostly gay men • women's night Fri • dancing/DJ • karaoke • male strippers • wheelchair access

RESTAURANTS

Brandywine 1345 Lake Dr SE (in East Town) **616/774-8641** • 7am-8pm, from 7:30am Sat, 8am-2:30pm Sun

Cherie Inn 969 Cherry St SE (at Lake Dr) **616/458-0588** • 7am-3pm, from8am wknds, clsd Mon • some veggie • wheelchair access

Gaia Cafe 209 Diamond Ave SE (at Cherry St) **616/454-6233** • 8am-8pm, till 3pm wknds, clsd Mon • vegetarian

ENTERTAINMENT & RECREATION

Grand Raggidy Roller Girls **616/752-8475** • Grand Rapids' female roller derby league

Honor

ACCOMMODATIONS

Labrys Wilderness Resort 231/882-5994 • women only • cabins in Sleeping Bear Dunes Nat'l Lakeshore • lesbian-owned

Kalamazoo

INFO LINES & SERVICES

Kalamazoo Gay/ Lesbian Resource Center 629 Pioneer St **269/349-4234** • 9am,-5pm, clsd wknds • educational/ support groups • youth group • hotline

Lansing

BARS

Esquire 1250 Turner St (at Clinton) **517/487-5338** • 3pm-2am • lesbians/ gay men • neighborhood bar • karaoke

NIGHTCLUBS

Spiral 1247 Center St (at Clinton) **517/371-3221** • 8pm-2am, clsd Mon-Tue • mostly gay men • dancing/DJ • theme nights • shows • videos • 18+ • wheelchair access

BOOKSTORES

Everybody Reads 2019 E Michigan Ave **517/346-9900** • 11am-7pm, 10am-4pm Sun • cool general bookstore • also coffeehouse

Marquette

ACCOMMODATIONS

The Landmark Inn 230 N Front St (at Ridge St) **906/228-2580, 888/752-6362** • gay-friendly • historic boutique hotel overlooking Lake Superior • restaurant & bar • gym • nonsmoking • WiFi • kids ok

Owendale

ACCOMMODATIONS

Windover Resort 3596 Blakely Rd **989/375-2586** • women only • seasonal private resort • campsites & RV hookups • pool

Petoskey

ACCOMMODATIONS

Coach House Inn 1011 N US 31 (at Mitchell) **231/347-8281, 877/347-8088** • gay-friendly • basic amenities • WiFi • nonsmoking • gay-owned

Pontiac

BARS

Liberty Bar 85 N Saginaw **248/758-0771** • 11:30am-2am, from 2pm wknds • lesbians/ gay men • dancing/DJ • food served

EROTICA

Fantasies Unlimited 974 Joslyn Ave **248/338-2442** • 10am-9pm, till10pm Fri-Sat, clsd Sun

Port Huron

NIGHTCLUBS

Seekers 3301 24th St (btwn Oak & Little) **810/985-9349** • 7pm-2am • lesbians/ gay men • dancing/DJ • drag shows

Saginaw

NIGHTCLUBS

The Mixx Nightclub 115 N Hamilton St (at Court St) **989/498-4022** • 5pm-close Th-Sun • lesbians/ gay men • dancing/DJ • food served • karaoke • videos • 18+ • wheelchair access

Saugatuck

ACCOMMODATIONS

Beechwood Manor Inn & Cottage 736 Pleasant St (at Allegan) **269/857-1587, 877/857-1587** • gay/ straight • full brkfst • nonsmoking • WiFi • gay-owned

Bella Vita Spa & Suites 119 Butler St **269/857-8482** • gay-friendly • upscale, modern suites overlooking downtown Saugatuck • also day spa • WiFi

The Belvedere Inn & Restaurant 3656 63rd St **269/857-5777, 877/858-5777** • gay-friendly • full brkfrst •

Bird Center Resort 584-586 Lake St 269/857-1750 • gay-friendly • cottages across from Saugatuck Harbor • WiFi

The Bunkhouse B&B at Campit 269/543-4335, 877/226-7481 • lesbians/gay men • cabins • private baths • access to Campit Resort amenities (see listing below) • pool • nonsmoking • WiFi

Campit Outdoor Resort 6635 118th Ave, Fennville 269/543-4335, 877/226-7481 • lesbians/gay men • campsites • RV hookups • separate women's area • pool • seasonal • pets ok • WiFi • membership required • lesbian & gay-owned

Deerpath Lodge 269/857-3337 • women only • large king suites on 35 waterfront acres • heated pool • hot tub • swimming free use of kayaks and canoe • lesbian-owned

Douglas House B&B 41 Spring St (at Wall St), Douglas 269/857-1119 • gay/straight • near gay beach • gay-owned • open April-Oct

The Dunes Resort 333 Blue Star Hwy, Douglas 269/857-1401 • lesbians/gay men • motel & cottages • transgender-friendly • pool • food served • women's wknds in April, June & Oct • dancing/DJ • live shows • pets ok • wheelchair access • gay-owned

Hidden Garden Cottages & Suites 247 Butler St 269/857-8109, 888/857-8109 • gay-friendly • cottages & suites • nonsmoking • WiFi

Hillby Thatch Cottages 1438-1440 71st St, Glenn 847/864-3553 • gay/straight • kitchens • fireplaces • kids ok • nonsmoking • woman-owned

The Hunter's Lodge 2790 68th St (at US 31), Fennville 269/857-5402 • gay/straight • vintage rustic log cabin • seasonal • kids ok • nonsmoking • WiFi • gay-owned

J Paules Fenn Inn 2254 S 58th St, Fennville 269/561-2836, 877/561-2836 • gay-friendly • full brkfst • kids/pets ok • nonsmoking

The Kingsley House B&B 626 West Main St, Fennville 269/561-6425, 866/561-6425 • gay-friendly • full brkfst • nonsmoking • WiFi • gay-owned

Saugatuck

ANNUAL EVENTS:

May - Tulip Time Festival, Holland 800/822-2770, web: www.tuliptime.com.

June - Waterfront Film Festival 269/857-8351, web: www.waterfrontfilm.org.

August - Michigan Womyn's Music Festival 231/757-4766, web: www.michfest.com. One of the biggest annual gatherings of lesbians on the continent, in Walhalla.

CITY INFO:

Saugatuck-Douglas Convention & Visitors Bureau 269/857-1701, web: www.saugatuck.com.

City of the Village of Douglas, web: www.douglasmichigan.com.

Holland Chamber of Commerce 616/392-2389, web: www.westcoastchamber.org.

ATTRACTIONS:

Fenn Valley Wineries 269/561-2396, web: www.fennvalley.com.

Galleries.

Historical Holland (home of the Wooden Shoe Factory), web: www.dutchvillage.com.

Mason Street Warehouse (theatre) 269/857-4898, web: www.masonstreetwarehouse.org.

Saugatuck Center for the Arts 269/857-2399, web: www.sc4a.org.

Saugatuck-Douglas Historical Society Museum 269/857-7900, web: sdhistoricalsociety.org.

Saugatuck Dunes State Park.

TRANSIT:

Saugatuck Douglas Taxi Service 269/543-3355.

Interurban Transit Authority 269/857-1418.

Kirby House 294 Center St (at Blue Star Hwy) 269/857–2904, 800/521–6473 • gay/ straight • full brkfst • pool • nonsmoking • WiFi • gay-owned

Maple Ridge Cottages 713-719 Maple 269/857–5211 (**Pines #**) • gay/ straight • quaint cottages • hot tub • nonsmoking • gay-owned

The Newnham SunCatcher Inn 131 Griffith (at Mason) 269/857–4249, 800/587–4249 • gay-friendly • full brkfst • hot tub • pool • nonsmoking • WiFi

The Park House Inn B&B 888 Holland St 269/857–4535, 866/321–4535 • gay-friendly • B&B in one of Saugatuck's oldest residences • full brkfst • nonsmoking • WiFi • also cottage

The Pines Motor Lodge & Cottages 56 Blue Star Hwy (at Center St), Douglas 269/857–5211 • gay/ straight • newly renovated boutique retro motel • nonsmoking • also retro gift gallery • WiFi • gay-owned

The Spruce Cutter's Cottage 6670 126th Ave (at Blue Star Hwy & M–89), Fennville 269/543–4285, 800/493–5888 • gay/ straight • full brkfst • gay-owned

Bars

Dunes Disco 333 Blue Star Hwy (at the Dunes Resort) 269/857–1401 • 9am-2am • lesbians/ gay men • dancing/DJ • transgender-friendly • cabaret • patio • gay-owned

Cafes

Uncommon Grounds 127 Hoffman (at Water) 269/857–3333 • 6:30am-10pm • coffee & juice bar • WiFi

Restaurants

Back Alley Pizza Joint 22 Main St (at Center), Douglas 269/857–7277 • 11am-10pm, till 11pm Fri-Sat • fresh grinder bread daily

Chequers 220 Culver St 269/857–1868 • 11:30am-9pm • seasonal • great fish & chips

Everyday People Cafe 11 Center St (at Main), Douglas 269/857–4240 • call for hours • wheelchair access

Kalico Kitchen 312 Ferry St, Douglas 269/857–2678 • 7am-9pm winter, till 10pm summer • wheelchair access

Marro's Italian 147 Water St (at Mason St) 269/857–4248 • dinner only, clsd Mon-Tue, nightclub till 2am Fri-Sat

Monroe's Cafe-Grille 302 Culver St (at Griffith) 269/857–1242 • 8am-9pm, clsd Nov-March • great brkfst

Phil's Bar & Grille 215 Butler St (at Mason) 269/857–1555 • 11:30am-10pm, till 11pm Fri-Sat • patio

Pumpernickel's 202 Butler St (at Mason) 269/857–1196 • 8am-4pm • WiFi

Restaurant Toulouse 248 Culver 269/857–1561 • dinner nightly, lunch wknds (seasonal) • full bar • reservations required • entertainment • wheelchair access

Scooters 322 Culver St (at Griffith) 269/857–1041 • noon-9pm, till 10pm wknds, clsd Tue • great pizza

The White House Bistro 149 Griffith (at Mason) 269/857–3240 • 4pm-10pm, 9am-midnight Sat, 9am-9pm Sun • live music

Wicks Park 449 Water St 269/857–2888 • dinner nightly • live music wknds • wheelchair access

Wild Dog Grill 24 W Center St (at Spring), Douglas 269/857–2519 • dinner nightly, from noon wknds, clsd Mon-Tue

Entertainment & Recreation

Earl's Farm Market 1630 Blue Star Hwy, Fennville 269/227–2074 • 8am-9pm May-Oct only • pick your own berries! • gay-owned

Oval Beach consult local map for driving directions, Douglas • popular beach on Lake Michigan

Tulip Time Festival Holland 800/822–2770

Retail Shops

Amaru Leather 322 Griffith St (at Hoffman St) 269/857–3745 • "original & custom creations in leather by two resident designers"

Groovy! Groovy! Retro Gift Gallery 56 Blue Star Hwy (at Center St), Douglas 269/857–5211 • seasonal hours • antiques, funky gifts & goods • gay-owned

Hoopdee Scootee 133 Mason (at Butler) 269/857–4141 • seasonal • clothing • gifts

Saugatuck Drug Store 201 Butler St (at Mason) 269/857–2300 • seasonal • old-fashioned corner drug store, including actual soda fountain!

Gyms & Health Clubs

Pump House Gym 6492 Blue Star Hwy (at 135th) 269/857–7867 • day passes

South Haven

Accommodations

Yelton Manor B&B 140 North Shore Dr (at Dyckman) 269/637–5220 • gay/ straight • full brkfst • nonsmoking • WiFi • wheelchair access

St Ignace

Accommodations

Budget Host Inn & Suites 700 N State St 906/643–9666, 800/872–7057 • gay-friendly • pool • facing harbor of Lake Huron & across from ferries to Mackinac Island • WiFi • kids/ pets ok • wheelchair access

Traverse City

Accommodations

Neahtawanta Inn 1308 Neahtawanta Rd (at Peninsula Dr) 231/223–7315, 800/220–1415 • gay-friendly • swimming • sauna • nonsmoking • WiFi • wheelchair access

Nightclubs

Side Traxx 520 Franklin St (at E 8th) 231/935–1666 • 5pm-2am • lesbians/ gay men • dancing/DJ • videos • gay-owned

Bookstores

The Bookie Joint 124 S Union St (btwn State & Front) 231/946–8862 • noon-6pm, clsd Sun • pride gifts • used books

Union Pier

Accommodations

Blue Fish Guest House & Cottage 10234 Community Hall Rd 269/469–0468 x112 • gay/ straight • cottages & guesthouses available • some shared baths • nonsmoking • kids/ pets ok • gay-owned

Fire Fly Resort 15657 Lakeshore Rd 269/469–0245 • gay/ straight • 1- & 2–bdrm units • kitchens • nonsmoking • gay-owned

Ypsilanti

see also Ann Arbor

MINNESOTA

Duluth

see also Superior, Wisconsin

Accommodations

The Olcott House B&B Inn 2316 E 1st St (at 23rd Ave) 218/728–1339, 800/715–1339 • gay-friendly • nonsmoking • WiFi • gay-owned

Bars

Duluth Flame 28 N 1st Ave W 218/727–2344 • 3pm-2:30am • lesbians/ gay men • dancing/DJ • live entertainment • karaoke • drag shows

Cafes

Amazing Grace Bakery & Cafe 394 Lake Ave S 218/723–0075 • 7am-10pm, till 11pm Fri-Sat • live shows • more women 2nd Sun for Chick Jam • WiFi

Jitters 102 W Superior St 218/720–6015 • 7am-7pm, 8am-5pm Sat, 9am-1pm Sun • WiFi

Restaurants

At Sara's Table Chester Creek Cafe 1902 E 8th St (at 19th) 218/724–6811 • 7am-8pm • live music • WiFi • wheelchair access • women-owned

Lanesboro

Accommodations

Stone Mill Hotel & Suites 100 E Beacon St (at Parkway Ave) 507/467–8663, 866/897–8663 • gay/ straight • WiFi • non-smoking • wheelchair access • gay-owned

Mankato

Cafes

The Coffee Hag 329 N Riverfront Dr 507/387–5533 • 7am-10pm, till 11pm Fri-Sat • veggie menu • live shows • wheelchair access • women-owned

Minneapolis/ St Paul

Info Lines & Services

AA Intergroup 952/922–0880

OutFront Minnesota 310 E 38th St #204, Minneapolis 612/822–0127, 800/800–0350 • info line w/ 24hr pre-recorded visitor info

Quatrefoil Library 1619 Dayton Ave #105, St Paul 651/641–0969 • 7pm-9pm, 10am-5pm Sat, 1pm-5pm Sun • LGBT library & resource center

Accommodations

The Depot Renaissance Minneapolis 225 3rd Ave S, Minneapolis 612/375–1700, 866/211–4611 • gay-friendly • bar & restaurant • ice rink and water park

Graves 601 Hotel 601 1st Ave N (at 6th St N), Minneapolis 612/677–1100, 866/523–1100 • gay-friendly • WiFi • gym • restaurant & bar

Hotel 340 340 Cedar St 651/280–4120 • gay-friendly • boutique hotel on the upper 3 floors of the Saint Paul Athletic Club • pool, • WiFi

Le Meridien Chambers 901 Hennepin Ave, Minneapolis 612/767–6900, 800/543–4300 • gay-friendly • art-filled hotel •restaurant & bar • WiFi • kids/ pets ok • wheelchair access

Namaste Cafe 2512 Hennepin Ave S, Minneapolis 612/827-2496 • 11am-10pm, full bar, great Indian & Napali food

Water Street Inn 101 S Water St, Stillwater 651/439-6000 • gay-friendly • full brkfst • WiFi • wheelchair access • also restaurant & pub

BARS

19 Bar 19 W 15th St (at Nicollet Ave), Minneapolis 612/871-5553 • 3pm-2am, from 1pm wknds • mostly gay men • neighborhood bar • wheelchair access

Bev's Wine Bar 250 3rd Ave N #100 (at Washington Ave), Minneapolis 612/337-0102 • 4:30pm-1am • gay-friendly • food served • patio • wheelchair access

Brass Rail 422 Hennepin Ave (at 4th), Minneapolis 612/332-7245 • noon-2am • popular • mostly gay men • karaoke • videos • wheelchair access

Bryant Lake Bowl 810 W Lake St (near Bryant), Minneapolis 612/825-3737 • 8am-2am • gay-friendly • bowling alley • also theater • restaurant • plenty veggie/ vegan • wheelchair access

Camp Bar 490 N Robert St (at 9th St), St Paul 651/292-1844 • 4pm-2am • mostly gay men • dancing/DJ • karaoke • male dancers • videos • also restaurant • wheelchair access

Jetset 115 N First St (at 1st Ave N), Minneapolis 612/339-3933 • 5pm-close, from 6pm Sat, clsd Sun-Mon • lesbians/ gay men • dancing/DJ • karaoke • nonsmoking

Lush Food Bar 990 Central Ave (at Spring St), Minneapolis • 8am-2am, clsd Mon • lesbians/ gay men • dancing/DJ • cabaret • drag shows • food served, brunch everyday till 2pm

The Town House 1415 University Ave W (at Elbert), St Paul 651/646-7087 • 2pm-2am, from noon wknds • popular • lesbians/ gay men • dancing/DJ • food served • karaoke • drag shows • piano bar • women-owned

NIGHTCLUBS

Gay 90s 408 Hennepin Ave (at 4th St S), Minneapolis 612/333-7755 • 8am-2am (dinner Wed-Sun) • popular • mostly gay men • dancing/DJ • multiracial • karaoke • drag shows Wed-Sun • 18+ • wheelchair access

Ground Zero 15 NE 4th St (at Hennepin), Minneapolis 612/378-5115 • 10pm-2am Th-Sat only • gay/ straight • more gay Sat for Bondage-A-Go-Go • dancing/DJ • live shows • wheelchair access

Kitty Cat Klub 315 14th Ave SE (at SE University Ave) 612/331-9800 • gay-friendly • lounge w/ eclectic decor • food served • live bands

The Saloon 830 Hennepin Ave (at 9th), Minneapolis 612/332-0835 • noon-2am, from 11am Sun • lesbians/ gay men • dancing/DJ • food served • young crowd • wheelchair access • gay-owned

CAFES

Anodyne at 43rd 4301 Nicollet Ave S (at 43rd), Minneapolis 612/824-4300 • 7am-10pm, till 8pm Fri-Sun • food served • open mic/ live music • wheelchair access

Black Dog Coffee & Wine Bar 308 Prince St (at Broadway), St Paul 651/228-9274 • 7am-10pm, till 11pm Fri-Sat, 8am-8pm Sun • food served • beer & wine

Blue Moon 3822 E Lake St, Minneapolis 612/721-9230 • 7am-10pm, from 8am wknds • WiFi • lesbian-owned

Cahoots 1562 Selby Ave (at Snelling), St Paul 651/644-6778 • 6:30am-10:30pm, from 7am wknds • coffee bar • WiFi • wheelchair access

Moose & Sadie's 212 3rd Ave N (at 2nd St), Minneapolis 612/371-0464 • 7am-8pm, 9am-2pm wknds • WiFi • wheelchair access

Uncommon Grounds 2809 Hennepin Ave (at W 28th St), Minneapolis 612/872-4811 • noon-midnight, till 1am Fri-Sat • outdoor seating

The Urban Bean 3255 Bryant Ave S (at 33rd), Minneapolis 612/824-6611 • 6:30am-11pm, from 7:30am Sun • patio • WiFi • wheelchair access

Wilde Roast Cafe 65 Main St SE (at Hennepin Ave), Minneapolis 612/331-4544 • 7am-10pm • beer/ wine • wheelchair access • gay-owned

RESTAURANTS

Al's Breakfast 413 14th Ave SE (at 4th), Minneapolis 612/331-9991 • 6am-1pm, from 9am Sun • popular • great hash

Barbette 1600 W Lake St (at Irving), Minneapolis 612/827-5710 • 8am-1am, till 2am Fri-Sat • French/ American • women-owned

Birchwood Cafe 3311 E 25th St, Minneapolis 612/722-4474 • 7am-9pm, from 8am Sat, 9am-8pm Sun • veggie/ vegan • WiFi • wheelchair access

Brasa Premium Rotisserie 600 E Hennepin, Minneapolis **612/379-3030** • 11am-9pm, till 10pm Fri-Sat • beer/ wine • wheelchair access

French Meadow 2610 Lyndale Ave S, Minneapolis **612/870-7855** • 6:30am-9pm, till 10pm Fri-Sat• organic & local • plenty veggie/ vegan • beer/ wine

Hard Times Cafe 1821 Riverside Ave, Minneapolis **612/341-9261** • 6am-4am • vegan/ vegetarian • punk rock ambiance • WiFi

Hell's Kitchen 80 9th St S, Minneapolis **612/332-4700** • 7:30am-10pm, till 2am Fri-Sat• great brkfst & free music wknds 11am-2pm

Loring Kitchen & Bar 1359 Willow St, Minneapolis **612/843-0400** • 11am-11pm, till 1am Fri-Sat, from 9am Sat-Sun • delicious food w/ an enticing bar • gay-owned

Lucia's Restaurant & Wine Bar 1432 W 31st St, Minneapolis **612/825-1572** • lunch & dinner, clsd Mon • wheelchair access

Monte Carlo 219 3rd Ave N, Minneapolis **612/333-5900** • lunch & dinner, bar till 1am • wheelchair access

Murray's 26 S 6th St (at Hennepin), Minneapolis **612/339-0909** • lunch Mon-Fri, dinner nightly • steak & seafood

Minneapolis/St Paul

LGBT PRIDE:
June. 612/836-4830, web: www.tcpride.com.

ANNUAL EVENTS:
May - Minnesota AIDS Walk 612/341-2060, web: www.mnaidsproject.org.
August - Minnesota Fringe Festival 612/872-1212, web: www.fringefestival.org.

CITY INFO:
612/767-8000, web: www.minneapolis.org.

BEST VIEW:
Observation deck of the 32nd story of Foshay Tower, 821 Marquette Ave (closed in winter).

WEATHER:
Winters are harsh. If driving, carry extra blankets and supplies. The average temperature is 19°, and it can easily drop well below 0°, and then there's the wind chill! Summer temperatures are usually in the upper-80°s to mid-90°s and HUMID.

TRANSIT:
Yellow Cab (Minn) 612/788-8888, web: www.yellowcabmn.com.
Super Shuttle 612/827-7777.
MTC 612/373-3333, web: www.metrotransit.org.

ATTRACTIONS:
American Swedish Institute 612/871-4907, web: www.asimn.org.
Collection of Questionable Medical Devices at The Science Museum of Minnesota 651/221-9444, web: www.smm.org.
Frederick R Weisman Art Museum 612/625-9494, web: www.weisman.umn.edu.
Mall of America (the largest mall in the US w/indoor theme park) 952/883-8800, web: www.mallofamerica.com.
Minneapolis American Indian Center 612/879-1700, web: www.maicnet.org.
Minneapolis Institute of Arts 888/642-2787, web: www.artsmia.org.
Walker Art Center/Minneapolis Sculpture Garden 612/375-7600, web: www.walkerart.org.

Nye's Polonaise 112 E Hennepin Ave, Minneapolis **612/379–2021** • 4pm-2am, from 11am Fri-Sat • piano bar • live polka & bands • full bar

Psycho Suzi's Motor Lounge 2519 Marshall St NE, Minneapolis **612/788–9069** • 11am-2am • pu-pu's & pizza • live music • wheelchair access

Punch Neapolitan Pizza 704 Cleveland Ave S, St Paul **651/696–1066** • 11am-9:30pm • wheelchair access • also at 210 E Hennepin Ave

Red Stag Supperclub 509 1st Ave NE (at 5th St), Minneapolis **612/767–7766** • 11am-2am, from 9am Sat-Sun • live music • wheelchair access

Restaurant Alma 528 University Ave SE, Minneapolis **612/379–4909** • dinner nightly, organic New American

Seward Cafe 2129 E Franklin Ave, Minneapolis **612/332–1011** • 7am-3pm, 8am-4pm wknds • vegetarian/ vegan • wheelchair access

Toast Wine Bar & Cafe 415 N 1st St (in the Heritage Landing Bldg) **612/333–4305** • 5pm-11pm, till midnight Fri-Sat

Trattoria da Vinci 400 Sibley St, St Paul **651/222–4050** • 11am-9pm, 5pm-10pm Sat, clsd Sun-Mon • live music • wheelchair access

ENTERTAINMENT & RECREATION

Calhoun 32nd Beach 3300 E Calhoun Pkwy (33rd & Calhoun Blvd), Minneapolis **612/230–6400**

Minnesota RollerGirls • MN's female roller derby league • visit www.mnrollergirls.com for events

RETAIL SHOPS

The Rainbow Road 109 W Grant St (at LaSalle), Minneapolis **612/872–8448** • 10am-10pm • LGBT • wheelchair access

PUBLICATIONS

Lavender Magazine **612/436–4660, 877/515–9969** • LGBT newsmagazine for IA, MN, ND, SD, WI

Minnesota Women's Press 970 Raymond Ave #201, St Paul **651/646–3968** • newspaper

Scene **612/886–3151** • LGBTQA Twin Cities publication

EROTICA

Fantasy Gifts 1437 University Ave, St Paul **651/256–7484** • noon-8pm, clsd Sun-Tue

The Smitten Kitten 3010 Lyndale Ave S, Minneapolis **612/721–6088, 888/751–0523** • 11am-9pm, noon-7pm Sun • transgender-friendly • lesbian-owned

Moorhead

see also Fargo, North Dakota

INFO LINES & SERVICES

Pride Collective & Community Center 810 4th Ave S #220 **218/287–8034** • 6pm-7:30pm Tue & 1pm-3pm Sat

CAFES

Atomic Coffee 16 4th St S (at Main) **218/299–6161** • 6:30am-9pm, from 8am Sun • also gallery • live shows • gay-owned

MISSISSIPPI

Biloxi

BARS

Club Veaux 834 Howard Ave **228/207–3271** • 11am-5am, from 8am Fri-5am Mon • mostly gay men, more women Wed • dancing/DJ • food served

Just Us Lounge 906 Division St (at Caillavet) **228/374–1007** • 24hrs • lesbians/ gay men • neighborhood bar • live shows • dancing/DJ • drag shows • go-go boys • karaoke

Gulfport

BARS

Knuckle Heads 1105 Broad Ave (at Railroad) **228/864–0463** • 10am-2am • gay-friendly • neighborhood bar • dancing/DJ • karaoke

The Other Bar 2218 25th Ave **228/284–1674** • 4pm-close • lesbians/ gay men • dancing/DJ • drag shows • wheelchair access

Jackson

INFO LINES & SERVICES

Lambda AA 4866 N State St (at Unitarian Church) **601/856–5337** • 6:30pm Mon

BARS

Bottoms Up 3911 Northview Dr **601/981–2188** • 9pm Fri-Sat only • lesbians/ gay men • dancing/DJ

Jack's Construction Site (JC's) 425 N Mart Plaza **601/362–3108** • 5pm-2am, from 7pm Th-Sat, clsd Mon • mostly gay men • more women Wed & Fri • neighborhood bar • BYOB • WiFi

Natchez

ACCOMMODATIONS

Historic Oak Hill Inn B&B 409 S Rankin St
(at Orleans St) 601/446-2500, 601/446-8641
• antebellum mansion near the Mississippi •
nonsmoking • WiFi • gay-owned

Mark Twain Guesthouse 25 Silver St
601/446-8023 • above Under the Hill Saloon

BARS

Under the Hill Saloon 25 Silver St
601/446-8023 • 10am-close • gay-friendly •
neighborhood bar • live music • WiFi

MISSOURI

Branson

see also **Springfield & Eureka Springs,
Arkansas**

ACCOMMODATIONS

Branson Stagecoach RV Park 5751 State
Hwy 165 417/335-8185, 800/446-7110 • gay-
friendly • pull-thru & back-in RV sites • cabins
• pool • WiFi

Cape Girardeau

NIGHTCLUBS

Independence Place 5 S Henderson St (at
Independence, at Holiday Happenings)
573/334-2939 • 8:30pm-1:30am, from 7pm
Fri-Sat, clsd Sun • lesbians/ gay men •
dancing/DJ • transgender-friendly • drag shows

Columbia

BARS

SoCo Club 119 S 7th St 573/499-9483 •
3:30pm-1:30am, till midnight Sun, clsd Mon •
lesbians/ gay men • dancing/DJ • food served •
karaoke Tue & Fri • drag shows • patio •
wheelchair access

CAFES

Ernie's Cafe 1005 E Walnut St (at 10th)
573/874-7804 • 6:30am-3pm

Uprise Baker/ RagTag Cinema 10 Hitt St
(Broadway) 573/443-4359, 573/441-8504 •
5pm-close, from 2pm wknds • independent &
alternative cinema • also theater, music &
dance • food served • beer & wine

RESTAURANTS

Main Squeeze 28 S 9th St (at Cherry St)
573/817-5616 • 10am-8pm, till 5pm Sun •
local organic ingredients • vegetarian • WiFi •
wheelchair access

BOOKSTORES

The Peace Nook 804 C East Broadway
(btwn 8th & 9th) 573/875-0539 • 10am-9pm,
noon-6pm Sun • LGBT section • books • pride
products

EROTICA

Bocomo Bay 1122–A Wilkes Blvd
573/443-0873 • smoke shop too

Hannibal

ACCOMMODATIONS

Garden House B&B 301 N 5th St (at Bird)
573/221-7800, 866/423-7800 • gay-friendly •
WiFi • nonsmoking • gay-owned

Rockcliffe Mansion 1000 Bird St (at 10th
St) 573/221-4140, 877/423-4140 • gay-
friendly • guilded-age Mansion built in 1898
on a limestone bluff • nonsmoking • WiFi •
gay-owned

RESTAURANTS

LaBinnah Bistro 207 N 5th St (at Center)
573/221-7800 • dinner only, clsd Mon • in a
Victorian home • beer/ wine • gay-owned

Joplin

INFO LINES & SERVICES

Gay Lesbian Family & Corporate Center
417/434-1149 • a community center &
clearinghouse for gay & lesbian events in the
greater Joplin, MO area

Kansas City

see also **Kansas City & Overland Park,
Kansas**

INFO LINES & SERVICES

**Lesbian & Gay Community Center of
Greater Kansas City** 4008 Oak St #10
816/931-4420 • call for events

Live & Let Live AA 3901 Main St #211 (at
39th) 816/531-9668 • 6pm daily, noon Sun

ACCOMMODATIONS

Hotel Phillips 816/221-7000, 800/433-1426
• gay-friendly • art deco landmark in
downtown KC

Q Hotel & Spa 560 Westport Rd (at Mill St)
816/931-0001, 800/942-4233 • gay-friendly •
in Westport district • WiFi • wheelchair access

The Raphael 325 Ward Pkwy (at Wornall Rd)
816/756-3800, 800/821-5343 • gay-friendly •
WiFi • also restaurant

Southmoreland on the Plaza 116 E 46th St (at Main St) **816/531–7979** • gay-friendly • 1913 B&B • full brkfst • veranda • nonsmoking

Su Casa B&B 9004 E 92nd St (off James A Reed Rd) **816/965–5647, 816/916–3444 (CELL)** • gay-friendly • Southwest-style home • full brkfst wknds • kids/ dogs/ horses ok • jacuzzi • pool • nonsmoking • WiFi • woman-owned

BARS

Buddies 3715 Main St (at 37th) **816/561–2600** • 6am-3am, clsd Sun, mostly gay men, neighborhood bar

Hamburger Mary's KC 101 Southwest Blvd (at Baltimore Ave) **816/842–1919** • 11am-1:30am • lesbians/ gay men • theme nights • karaoke • live entertainment • food served • juicy burgers w/ a side of camp

Missie B's/ Bootleggers 805 W 39th St (at SW Trafficway) **816/561–0625** • noon-3am • lesbians/ gay men • neighborhood bar • dancing/DJ • transgender-friendly • live shows • karaoke • drag shows

Sidekicks 3707 Main St (at 37th) **816/931–1430** • 2pm-3am, from 4pm Sun, clsd Mon • lesbians/ gay men • dancing/DJ • country/ western • drag shows • wheelchair access

Social 1118 McGee **816/472–4900** • 3pm-3am, from 5pm Sat, clsd Sun-Mon • lesbians/ gay men • dancing/DJ • food served 8 karaoke • wheelchair access • gay-owned

The View 204 Orchard St (at Tenny Ave), KS **913/281–0833** • 4pm-2am, from noon Sun, clsd Mon • mostly men • neighborhood bar • gay-owned

CAFES

Broadway Cafe 4106 Broadway (at Westport) **816/531–2432** • 7am-9pm • food served • nonsmoking • also 412 Washington

RESTAURANTS

Beer Kitchen 435 Westport Rd (at Pennsylvania) **816/389–4180** • 11am-3am, from 10am wknds • gastro pub • live music

Bistro 303 303 Westport Rd **816/753–2303** • open 3pm, from 11am Sat-Sun • patio • wheelchair access • gay-owned

Blue Bird Bistro 1700 Summit St (at W 17th St) **816/221–7559** • 7am-10pm, 10am-2pm Sun • organic fare • wheelchair access

Cafe Trio/ Starlet Lounge 4558 Main St **816/756–3227** • 5pm-11pm, clsd Sun • piano • gay-owned

Chubby's 3756 Broadway St (at 38th) **816/931–2482** • open 24hrs • popular late nights • diner fare • wheelchair access

Classic Cup Cafe 301 W 47th St (at Central) **816/753–1840** • brkfst, lunch, dinner, Sun brunch • great appetizers • wheelchair access

Grand Street Cafe 4740 Grand St (at 47th St) **816/561–8000** • lunch & dinner, Sun brunch • patio seating • nonsmoking • wheelchair access

Le Fou Frog 400 E 5th St (at Oak St) **816/474–6060** • dinner only • French bistro

McCoy's Public House 4057 Pennsylvania Ave **816/960–0866** • 11am-3am, till midnight Sun • huge patio

The Mixx 4855 Main St (at W 48th) **816/756–2300** • lunch & dinner • fast & healthy • huge selection of salads • wheelchair access

Tannin Wine Bar **816/842–2660** • 11:30am-1:30am, from 4pm wknds • wine & cheese flights • full dinner menu • patio seating

YJ's Snack Bar 128 W 18th St (at W Baltimore Ave) **816/472–5533** • 8am-10pm, 24hrs Th-Sat • inexpensive • wheelchair access

ENTERTAINMENT & RECREATION

First Fridays Art Walk Crossroads District (Baltimore & 20th) **816/994–9325** • 5pm-10pm 1st Fri • art gallery walk • also live music & vendors

Kansas City Roller Warriors **816/809–8496** • KC's female roller derby league • visit kcrollerwarriors.com for events

Nelson-Atkins Museum 4525 Oak St **816/751–1278** • American Indian galleries

EROTICA

Erotic City 8401 E Truman Rd (off I–435, at Alice Ave) **816/252–3370**

Hollywood at Home 9063 Metcalf Ave (at 91st), Overland Park, KS **913/649–9666** • 10am-11pm

Osage Beach

ACCOMMODATIONS

Utopian Inn 1962 Alcorn Hollow Rd, Roach **573/347–3605** • lesbians/ gay men • 3 bdrm rental on a lake • kids/ small pets ok • nonsmoking • gay-owned

Overland

EROTICA

Patricia's 10210 Page Ave (E of Ashby) **314/423–8422**

Springfield

INFO LINES & SERVICES

AA Gay/ Lesbian 518 E Commercial St
417/823-7125 (AA #) • 6pm Sat • nonsmoking

Gay & Lesbian Community Center of the Ozarks 518 E Commercial St **417/869-3978** • many groups • newsletter • wheelchair access

BARS

Martha's Vineyard 219 W Olive St (at S Patton) **417/864-4572** • 5pm-1:30am, from 2pm Sun, clsd Mon • lesbians/ gay men • neighborhood bar • dancing/DJ • drag shows • Th women's night • patio • wheelchair access • cover charge wknds

Mud Lounge 321 E Walnut **417/865-6964** • 4pm-1:30am, clsd Sun • food served

CAFES

Mudhouse 323 South Ave **417/832-1720** • 7am-midnight, 9am-8pm Sun • food served

BOOKSTORES

Renaissance Books & Gifts 1337 E Montclair St **417/883-5161** • 10am-6:30pm, noon-5pm Sun • women's/ alternative • wheelchair access

EROTICA

Patricia's 1918 S Glenstone (at E Cherokee) **417/881-8444**

St Louis

ACCOMMODATIONS

A St Louis Guesthouse 1032 Allen Ave (at Menard) **314/773-1016** • mostly gay men • located in historic Soulard district • hot tub (nudity ok) • nonsmoking • WiFi • gay-owned

Brewers House B&B 1829 Lami St (at Lemp) **314/771-1542, 888/767-4665** • lesbians/ gay men • 1860s home • jacuzzi • pets ok • nonsmoking • WiFi • gay-owned

The Cheshire 6300 Clayton Rd **314/647-7300** • gay/ straight • pool • WiFi

Dwell 912 B&B 912 Hickory St (at S 9th St) **314/599-3100** • gay-friendly • nonsmoking • WiFi • gay-owned

Grand Center Inn 3716 Grandel Sq (at N Grand Blvd) **314/533-0771** • gay/ straight • WiFi • nonsmoking • gay-owned

BARS

Absolutli Goosed Martini Bar, Etc 3196 S Grand (at Wyoming) **314/771-9300** • 4pm-midnight, till 1am Fri-Sat, clsd Sun • lesbians/ gay men • neighborhood bar • also desserts • appetizers • patio • wheelchair access • lesbian-owned

Bad Dog Bar & Grill 3960 Chouteau Ave (at S Vandeventer Ave) **314/652-0011** • 4pm-1:30am, 2pm-midnight Sun • mostly men • neighborhood bar • bears • leather • food served • gay-owned

Cicero's 6691 Delmar Blvd (at Kingsland Ave), University City **314/862-0009** • 11am-12:30am, till 11pm Sun • gay/ straight • Italian restaurant • live music venue

Clementine's 2001 Menard St (at Allen) **314/664-7869** • 10am-midnight, from 11am Sun • popular • mostly gay men • neighborhood bar • leather • food served • patio • wheelchair access

Club Escapades 133 W Main St (at 2nd), Belleville, IL **618/222-9597** • 6pm-2am, clsd Sun-Mon • lesbians/ gay men • dancing/DJ • drag shows • food served • karaoke • live shows • WiFi

Erney's 32 Degree 4200 Manchester Ave (at Boyle) **314/652-7195** • 8pm-3am, clsd Mon • mostly gay men • dancing/DJ

Grey Fox Pub 3503 S Spring (at Potomac) **314/772-2150** • 2pm-1:30am, noon-midnight Sun • lesbians/ gay men • neighborhood bar • drag shows • transgender-friendly • patio

Hummel's Pub 7101 S Broadway (at Blow St) **314/353-5080** • 11am-1am, from 2pm Mon • lesbians/ gay men • neighborhood bar • full menu • karaoke • lesbian-owned

Just John 4112 Manchester Ave **314/371-1333** • 3pm-3am, from noon-1am Sun • lesbians/ gay men • neighborhood bar • dancing/DJ Fri-Sat • drag shows • karaoke • videos

Keypers Piano Bar 2280 S Jefferson (at Shenandoah) **314/664-6496** • 1pm-1:30am, 2pm-midnight Sun, patio • lesbians/ gay men • piano bar • food served • patio

Korners Bar 7109 S Broadway (at Blow St) **314/352-3088** • 4pm-1:30am, clsd Sun-Mon • lesbians/ gay men • dancing/DJ • drag shows

Meyer's Grove 4510 Manchester Ave **314/932-7003** • 4pm-1:30pm, clsd Sun • lesbians/ gay men • drag shows

Premium Lounge 4199 Manchester Rd (at Boyle) **314/652-8585** • opens 4pm, clsd Sun • gay/ straight • food served

Rehab Lounge 4052 Chouteau Ave (at Boyle) **314/652–3700** • 11:30am-1:30am • gay/ straight • neighborhood bar • also restaurant

Rosie's Place 4573 Laclede Ave **314/361–6423** • 11am-1:30am • gay/ straight • neighborhood bar

Soulard Bastille 1027 Russell Blvd (at Menard) **314/664–4408** • 11am-1:30am • mostly gay men • neighborhood bar

Sub Zero Vodka Bar 308 N Euclid Ave **314/367–1200** • 11:30am-1:30am • gay/ straight • full menu includes sushi and burgers

NIGHTCLUBS

Atomic Cowboy 4140 Manchester Ave (btwn Kentucky & Talmadge) **314/775–0775** • 11am-3am, from 5pm Sat-Sun • gay/ straight • dancing/DJ • live shows • burlesque • also Fresh-Mex Mayan grill • art lounge • WiFi • patio

Attitudes 4100 Manchester Ave (at S Sarah) **314/534–0044** • 7pm-3am, clsd Mon • popular • lesbians/ gay men • dancing/DJ • drag shows • karaoke

Bubby & Sissy's 602 Belle St (at 6th St), Alton, IL **618/465–4773** • 3pm-2am, till 3am Fri-Sat • lesbians/ gay men • dancing/DJ • live shows • karaoke • drag shows • food served • wheelchair access

St Louis

LGBT PRIDE:
June. PrideFest 314/772-8888, web: www.pridestl.org.

ANNUAL EVENTS:
February - Soulard Mardi Gras 314/771-5110, web: www.mardigrasinc.com.
July - Fair St Louis & LIVE on the Levee 314/434-3434, web: www.fairstlouis.org.
September - The Great Forest Park Balloon Race, web: www.great-forestparkballoonrace.com

CITY INFO:
800/325-7962, web: www.explorestlouis.com.

WEATHER:
100% midwestern. Cold winters— little snow and the temperatures can drop below 0°. Hot, muggy summers raise temperatures back up into the 100°s. Spring and fall bring out the best in Mother Nature.

TRANSIT:
County Cab 314/993-8294, web: www.countycab.com.
GO BEST Express 877/785-4682, web: www.gobestexpress.com.
MetroBus 314/231-2345, web: www.metrostlouis.org.

ATTRACTIONS:
Anheuser-Busch Brewery 800/342-5283 web: www.budweisertours.com.
Cathedral Basilica of St Louis (world's largest collection of mosaic art) 314/373-8242, web: www.cathedralstl.org.
Gateway Arch 877/982-1410, web: www.gatewayarch.com.
Grant's Farm 314/843-1700, web: www.grantsfarm.com.
Soulard, the "French Quarter of St Louis."
St Louis Art Museum 314/721-0072, web: www.slam.org.
Stone Hill Winery (in Hermann) 800/909-9463, web: www.stone-hillwinery.com.
The extremely quaint town of St Charles.

BEST VIEW:
Where else? Top of the Gateway Arch in the Observation Room, web: www.gatewayarch.com.

Magnolia's 5 S Vandeventer Ave (at Laclede) **314/652-6500** • lesbians/ gay men • dancing/DJ • mostly African American • hip hop/ R&B club

CAFES

Coffee Cartel 2 Maryland Plaza (at Euclid) **314/454-0000** • 24hrs • popular • food served • WiFi • wheelchair access

MoKaBe's 3606 Arsenal (at S Grand) **314/865-2009** • 8am-midnight, from 9am Sun • popular • plenty veggie • occasional shows • wheelchair access

Soulard Coffee Garden Cafe 910 Geyer Ave (btwn 9th & 10th) **314/241-1464** • 6:30am-4pm, from 8am wknds • food served • WiFi • wheelchair access

RESTAURANTS

Billie's Diner 1802 S Broadway **314/621-0848** • 5am-2:30pm, midnight-1:30pm wknds • wheelchair access

Cafe Osage 4605 Olive St **314/454-6868** • 7am-2pm, till 5pm Th-Sat, from 9am Sun

City Diner 3139 S Grand Blvd **314/772-6100** • 7am-11pm, 24hrs Fri-Sat, till 10pm Sun • wheelchair access

Dressel's 419 N Euclid Ave (at McPherson) **314/361-1060** • 11am-1am, till midnight Sun • great Welsh pub food • full bar • live shows • wheelchair access

Eleven Eleven Mississippi 1111 Mississippi **314/241-9999** • lunch Mon-Fri, dinner nightly, clsd Sun • wine country bistro

Hamburger Mary's 3037 Olive St **314/533-6279** • 11am-midnight, till 1am Th-Sat • live shows • karaoke

Joanie's Pizza 2101 Menard St **314/865-1994** • 11am-11pm, till midnight wknds

Majestic Cafe 4900 Laclede Ave (at Euclid) **314/361-2011** • 6am-10pm, bar till 1:30am • Greek-American diner fare • wheelchair access

Mango 1101 Lucas Ave **314/621-9993** • 11am-10pm, bar till 1:30am Fri-Sat, 4pm-9pm Sun • Latin American/ Peruvian

Meskerem 3210 S Grand Blvd **314/772-4442** • lunch & dinner • Ethiopian • plenty veggie

Mojo Tapas 3117 S Grand Blvd (at Arsenal St) **314/865-0500** • 4pm-11pm, full bar till 1:30am

Molly's in Soulard 816 Geyer Ave **314/241-6200** • 11am-9pm, full bar till 1:30am • old-world New Orleans charm • live music • huge patio

Pappy's Smokehouse 3106 Olive St **314/535-4340** • 11am-8pm, till 4pm Sun • excellent BBQ

Rue 13 1311 Washington **314/588-7070** • 5pm-3am, clsd Sun-Mon • sushi • full bar • dancing/DJ • burlesque

Ted Drewes Frozen Custard 6726 Chippewa (at Jameson) **314/481-2652, 314/481-2124** • 11am-10pm • seasonal • a St Louis landmark • also 4224 S Grand Blvd, 314/352-7376 • wheelchair access

Three Monkey's 153 Morgan Ford Rd **314/772-9800** • 11am-1:30am

Tony's 410 Market St (at Broadway) **314/231-7007** • dinner only, clsd Sun-Mon • Italian fine dining • reservations advised • wheelchair access

Van Goghz 3200 Shenandoah (at Compton) **314/865-3345** • 11am-11pm, till 1:30am Fri-Sat, 9:30am-3pm Sun • also bar • WiFi • wheelchair access

Vin de Set 2017 Chouteau Ave (at S 21st St) **314/241-8989** • lunch & dinner, dinner only wknds, clsd Mon • rooftop bar & bistro • wheelchair access

The Wild Flower Restaurant & Bar 4590 Laclede Ave (at Euclid) **314/367-9888** • lunch & dinner, bar till 1:30am, clsd Tue, Sun brunch • wheelchair access

BOOKSTORES

Left Bank Books 399 N Euclid Ave (at McPherson) **314/367-6731** • 10am-10pm, 11am-6pm Sun • popular • feminist & LGBT titles • also at 321 N 10th St

Not Just A Bookstore 4507 Manchester Ave **314/531-5900** • 10am-6pm • also herbal loose teas and all natural soaps and oils • WiFi

RETAIL SHOPS

CheapTRX 3211 S Grand Blvd (at Wyoming St) **314/664-4011** • alternative shopping • body piercing • tattoos • wheelchair access

PUBLICATIONS

Vital Voice **314/256-1196** • bi-weekly news & features publication

EROTICA

Patricia's 3552 Gravois Ave (at Grand) **314/664-4040** • 10am-10pm, till midnight Fri-Sat • fetish clothes • toys • videos

MONTANA

Billings

BARS

The Loft 1123 1st Ave N (at 12th)
406/259-9074 • 10am-2am • lesbians/gay
men • dancing/DJ • karaoke • shows •
wheelchair access

EROTICA

Big Sky Books 1203 1st Ave N (at 12th St)
406/259-0051

The Victorian 2019 Minnesota Ave (at 21st)
406/245-4293 • noon-midnight, clsd Sun-
Mon • fireplace & piano • HIV testing

Bozeman

ACCOMMODATIONS

Lehrkind Mansion Inn 719 N Wallace Ave
406/585-6932 • gay/ straight • full brkfst • hot
tub • nonsmoking • WiFi • gay-owned

CAFES

The Leaf & Bean 35 W Main St
406/587-1580 • 6am-9pm, till 10pm Fri-Sat •
live shows • wheelchair access • women-
owned • also 1500 N 19th Ave, 406/587-2132

The Nova Cafe 312 E Main St (at Rouse
Ave) **406/587-3973** • 7am-2pm

EROTICA

Erotique 12 N Willson Ave (at Main)
406/586-7825

Butte

RESTAURANTS

Four Seasons 3030 Elm St **406/723-3888** •
11am-9:30pm, from noon wknds

Matt's Place 2339 Placer St (btwn Montana
& Rowe) **406/782-8049** • 11:30am-7pm, clsd
Sun-Mon • classic soda-fountain diner

Pork Chop John's 2400 Harrison Ave
406/782-1783 • 10:30am-10:30pm, clsd Sun •
also 8 W Mercury, 406/782-0812

Uptown Cafe 47 E Broadway **406/723-4735**
• lunch weekdays & dinner nightly • bistro •
full bar • wheelchair access

Kalispell

INFO LINES & SERVICES

Flathead Valley Alliance 406/758-6707 •
LGBT referral service

Missoula

INFO LINES & SERVICES

KISMIF Gay/ Lesbian AA 405 University
Ave (at church) **406/543-0011** • 7pm Mon

**Western Montana Gay/ Lesbian
Community Center** 127 N Higgins Ave #202
406/543-2224 • LGBT resource center • call
for hours

BARS

The Oxford 337 N Higgins Ave (at Pine)
406/549-0117 • popular • gay-friendly • 8am-
2am • 24hr cafe & casino

CAFES

The Catalyst 111 N Higgins **406/542-1337** •
7am-3pm

RESTAURANTS

Montana Club 2620 Brooks **406/543-3200** •
6am-10pm, till 11pm Fri-Sat, casino open till
2am • full bar • wheelchair access

BOOKSTORES

Fact & Fiction 220 N Higgins **406/721-2881**
• 9am-6pm, 10am-5pm Sat, noon-4pm Sun •
many LGBT titles • wheelchair access

RETAIL SHOPS

Jeannette Rankin Peace Center 519 S
Higgins Ave **406/543-3955** • 10am-6pm,
noon-4pm Sun • fair trade gift store • peace
resource center • events

PUBLICATIONS

Out Words 127 N Higgins Ave #202
406/543-2224 • Montana's LGBT publication

Swan Valley

ACCOMMODATIONS

Holland Lake Lodge 1947 Holland Lake Rd
(at Hwy 83) **406/754-2282, 877/925-6343** •
gay-friendly • resort w/ lakefront cabins • full
brkfst • hot tub • kids ok • WiFi • restaurant &
bar • wheelchair access • gay-owned

NEBRASKA

Lincoln

INFO LINES & SERVICES

Rainbow Group Gay/ Lesbian AA 2325 S 24 St (at Sewell, at St Matthew's) **402/438-5214** • 7:30pm Mon & Fri

BARS

Panic 200 S 18th St (at N St) **402/435-8764** • 4pm-1am, from 1pm wknds • lesbians/ gay men • live shows • WiFi • patio • wheelchair access • gay-owned

NIGHTCLUBS

The Q 226 S 9th St (btwn M & N Sts) **402/475-2269** • 8pm-1am, clsd Mon • lesbians/ gay men • dancing/DJ • live shows • drag shows •

ENTERTAINMENT & RECREATION

No Coast Derby Girls • Lincoln's female roller derby league • visit www.nocoastderbygirls.com for events

Omaha

INFO LINES & SERVICES

AA Gay/ Lesbian 851 N 74th St (at Presbyterian Church) **402/556-1880** • 8:15pm Fri

Rainbow Outreach Center 1719 Leavenworth St **402/341-0330** • call for hrs

ACCOMMODATIONS

Castle Unicorn 57034 Deacon Rd (at Hwy 34 & I-29), Pacific Jct, IA **712/527-5930** • gay/ straight • medieval-style B&B • full brkfst • hot tub • WiFi • nonsmoking • patio • gay-owned

The Cornerstone Mansion Inn 140 N 39th St (at Dodge) **402/558-7600, 888/883-7745** • gay-friendly • fireplaces • brkfst served • nonsmoking • WiFi

NIGHTCLUBS

Flixx Lounge 1019 S 10th St **402/408-1020** • 5pm-1am • mostly men • dancing/DJ • cabaret • drag shows

The Max 1417 Jackson St (at 15th St) **402/346-4110** • 4pm-1am, till 2am Th-Sat • popular • mostly gay men • dancing/DJ Wed-Sun • drag shows • strippers patio • wheelchair access • cover charge Fri-Sat

RESTAURANTS

The Boiler Room 1110 Jones St **402/916-9274** • dinner only, clsd Sun • full bar • wheelchair access

California Tacos & More 3235 California St **402/342-0212** • 11am-9pm, clsd Sun • beer/ wine • wheelchair access

The Flatiron Cafe 1722 St Marys Ave **402/345-7477** • dinner only, clsd Sun • full bar • wheelchair access

M's Pub 422 S 11th St **402/342-2550** • 11am-1am, from 5pm Sun • full bar • wheelchair access

McFoster's Natural Kind Cafe 302 S 38th St **402/345-7477** • lunch & dinner • vegetarian • full bar • wheelchair access

ENTERTAINMENT & RECREATION

Omaha Rollergirls • Omaha's female roller derby league • visit www.omaharollergirls.org

NEVADA

Carson City

ACCOMMODATIONS

West Walker Motel 106833 Hwy 395, Walker, CA **530/495-2263** • gay-friendly • WiFi • kids/ pets ok • in Toiyabe Nat'l Forest near West Walker River • women-owned

Lake Tahoe

see also Lake Tahoe, California

Las Vegas

INFO LINES & SERVICES

Alcoholics Together 900 E Karen, 2nd flr #A-202 (at Sahara, in Commercial Center) **702/598-1888** • 12:15pm & 8pm daily • call for other meeting times

The Gay/ Lesbian Community Center of Southern Nevada 953 E Sahara Ave #B-31 **702/733-9800** • 11am-7pm, clsd wknds

ACCOMMODATIONS

El Cortez Cabana 651 E Ogden Ave (at 7th St) **702/385-5200, 800/634-6703** • gay-friendly • recently renovated, bringing Miami-style glamour to Fremont St

Paris, Las Vegas Resort & Casino 3655 Las Vegas Blvd S **702/946-7000, 800/630-7933** • gay-friendly • also restaurants, bars, spas • LGBT honeymoon packages • see ad in front color section

Vdara Hotel & Spa 2600 W Harmon Ave **702/590-2767, 866/745-7767** • gay-friendly • pool • non-smoking

Bars

Badlands Saloon 953 E Sahara #22 (in Commercial Center) **702/792-9262** • 24hrs • mostly gay men • neighborhood bar • dancing/DJ • country/ western • wheelchair access • gay-owned

Charlie's Las Vegas 5012 S Arville St (at Tropicana) **702/876-1844** • popular • mostly gay men • dancing/DJ • country/ western • dance lessons 7pm-9pm Mon, Th-Sat • drag shows • wheelchair access

Club Metro 1000 E Sahara Ave **702/629-2368** • 4pm-5am • mostly gay men, 3rd Sat women's party • ultra-lounge and dance club •

Flex 4347 W Charleston (at Arville) **702/385-3539, 702/878-3355** • 24hrs • lesbians/ gay men • dancing/DJ • drag shows • strippers • wheelchair access

Freezone 610 E Naples **702/794-2300** • 24hrs • lesbians/ gay men • women's night Tue • neighborhood bar • dancing/DJ • transgender-friendly • drag shows Fri-Sat • karaoke • young crowd • also restaurant • gay-owned

Goodtimes 1775 E Tropicana Ave (at Spencer, in Liberace Plaza) **702/736-9494** • 24hrs • mostly gay men • neighborhood bar • dancing/DJ karaoke Wed • wheelchair access

Krazy Bar 4503 Paradise Rd (across from the Hard Rock) **702/998-9994** • 5pm-1am Th-Sat • mostly gay men • non-smoking lounge

Las Vegas

LGBT Pride:
Sept. 866/930-3336, web: www.lasvegaspride.org.

Annual Events:
April - Dinah Vegas, web: www.dinahshoreweekend.com.
May - NGRA (Nevada Gay Rodeo Assn) Bighorn Rodeo, web: www.ngra.com.

City Info:
Convention & Visitors Authority 877/847-4858, web: www.lasvegas.com/planning-tools/lgbt-travel/out-and-about.

Weather:
It's in the desert! Hotter by day, cooler by night.

Transit:
Lucky Cab 702/732-4400, web: www.luckycablv.com.
Various resorts have their own shuttle service.
Las Vegas Monorail 866/466–6672, web: www.lvmonorail.com.

Best View:
Top of the Stratosphere, Top of the Eiffel Tower Experience, or hurtling through the loops of the rollercoaster atop the New York New York Hotel or the Ling. (Note: Do not ride immediately after the buffet.)

Attractions:
Neon Museum and Boneyard, web: www.vegas.com/attractions/off-the-strip/neon-museum.
The Linq, web: www.vegas.com/attractions/on-the-strip/linq.
Mob Museum 702/ 229-2734, web: www.vegas.com/attractions/off-the-strip/mob-museum.
Bellagio Art Gallery 702/693-7871, web: www.bellagio.com.
Divas Las Vegas, web: www.frankmarinosdivas.com.
Fremont Street Experience, web: www.vegasexperience.com.
Hoover Dam & Museum, 866/730-9097,
web: www.usbr.gov/lc/hooverdam.
Auto Collection 702/794-3174, web: hautocollections.com.
Las Vegas Art Museum 702/360-8000, web: www.lasvegasartmuseum.com.
Las Vegas Arts District, web: www.18b.org.
Natural History Museum 702/384-3466, web: www.lvnhm.org.

The Las Vegas Eagle 3430 E Tropicana (at Pecos) **702/458-8662** • 24hrs • mostly gay men • leather • DJ Wed & Fri

Las Vegas Lounge 900 E Karen Ave (at Maryland Pkwy) **702/737-9350** • 24hrs • gay-friendly • neighborhood bar • mostly transgender

Phoenix Bar & Lounge 4213 W Sahara Ave **702/826-2422** • noon-4am • lesbians/gay men • karaoke • wheelchair access • gay-owned

The Spotlight Lounge 975 E Sahara (at Commercial Center's entrance) **702/431-9775** • 24hrs • mostly gay men • neighborhood bar • Wifi

NIGHTCLUBS

Don't Tell Mama 517 Fremont St #A (downtown) **702/207-0788** • 8pm-3am, clsd Mon • mostly gay men • great piano bar • wheelchair access

Drink & Drag 450 Fremont St #250 (at Neonopolis) **702/489-3724** • 4pm-4am • gay/straight • drag shows

The Light Las Vegas 3950 Las Vegas Blvd S (Mandalay Bay Las Vegas) **702/693-8300** • open Wed, Fri-Sat • gay/straight • dancing/DJ • nightclub by Cirque du Soleil

Mix 3950 Las Vegas Blvd S (at Mandalay Bay) **702/632-9500** • gay-friendly • stylish lounge • DJ • cover charge wknds

Piranha 4633 Paradise Rd (at Naples) **702/791-0100** • opens 10pm nightly • lesbians/gay men • dancing/DJ • wheelchair access

QueerKat • check www.LesbiansInVegas.com for events • popular • mostly women • dancing/DJ • multiracial

Revolution Lounge 3400 Las Vegas Blvd S (at the Mirage) **702/791-7111** • 10pm-4am, clsd Tue • gay-friendly • psychedelic Beatles-influenced decor • gay night Sun

Share Nighclub and Ultra Lounge 4636 Wynn Rd **702/258-2681** • 6pm-2am, till 4am Mon, Th-Sat • mostly gay men • dancing/DJ

RESTAURANTS

Bootlegger Bistro 7700 S Las Vegas Blvd (btwn Windmill & Robindale) **702/736-4939** • 24hrs • a Vegas classic • Italian • musical entertainment nightly

Border Grill 3950 Las Vegas Blvd S (at the Mandalay Bay Resort & Casino) **702/632-7403** • 11:30am-close • Mexican • full bar • patio

Chicago Joe's 820 S 4th St (at Gass Ave) **702/382-5637** • 11am-10pm, from 5pm Sat, clsd Sun-Mon • old-school Italian • in downtown arts district

Cupcakery 7175 W Lake Mead **702/835-0060**

The Egg & I 4533 W Sahara Ave (near Arville) **702/364-9686** • popular • 6am-3pm • wheelchair access

Firefly 3900 Paradise Rd #A **702/369-3971** • 11am-2am • tapas • also bar • wheelchair access

Go Raw 2381 E Windmill Ln **702/450-9007** • 8am-8pm, till 5pm Sun • organic vegan • also juice bar • also at 2910 Lake East Dr, 702/254-5382

Grand Lux Cafe 3355 Las Vegas Blvd S (at the Venetian) **702/414-3888** • open 24hrs • generous portions

Lindo Michoacan 2655 E Desert Inn Rd (near Eastern) **702/735-6828** • 11am-11pm, till midnight wknds • popular • Mexican

Lotus of Siam 953 E Sahara Ave #A-5 (in Commercial Center) **702/735-3033** • lunch Mon-Fri, dinner nightly • Thai • wheelchair access

Mingo Kitchen & Lounge 1017 S First St #180 (in the heart of the Arts District) **702/685-0328** • 11am-10pm, from 5pm Mon & Sat, till midnight Tue-Sat, from 11am-6pm Sun • gay owned

Mon Ami Gabi 3655 Las Vegas Blvd S (at Paris Las Vegas) **702/944-4224** • 7am-11pm • outdoor seating • wheelchair access

Paymon's Mediterranean Cafe & Lounge 4147 S Maryland Pkwy (at E Flamingo Rd) **702/731-6030** • 11am-1am • plenty veggie • wheelchair access • also at 8380 W Sahara Ave, 702/731-6030

Society Cafe Encore 3121 Las Vegas Blvd S (at Encore) **702/248-3463** • 7am-11pm, till 1am wknds • upscale American

Stir Krazy Mongolian Gril 4503 Paradise Rd (across from the Hard Rock) **702/998-9994** • 11:30am-9pm, till 10pm Fri-Sat • Asian Cuisine Stir-Fry • gay-owned

ENTERTAINMENT & RECREATION

18b Arts District bounded by Commerce St, Hoover Ave, Fourth St and Las Vegs Blvd (at Charleston and Colorado Ave) • mix of galleries, one-of-a-kind stores, and restaurants just a short walk or bus ride from Fremont St, aslo sponsor 1st Fridat festival

Cupid's Wedding Chapel 827 Las Vegas Blvd S (1 block N of Charleston) 702/598-4444, 800/543-2933 • commitment ceremonies • "Have the Vegas wedding you've always dreamed of!"

Erotic Heritage Museum 3275 Industrial Rd 702/369-6442 • 6pm-10pm Wed-Th, 3pm-midnight Fri, from noon wknds, clsd Mon-Tue

Frank Marino's Divas Las Vegas 3535 Las Vegas Blvd S (at the Imperial Palace) 702/794-3261, 888/777-7664 • show at 7:30pm • the biggest drag show in town: Frank Marino & friends impersonate the divas, from Joan Rivers to Tina Turner

Onyx Theatre 953 E Sahara Ave # 16A (at Maryland Pkwy) 702/732-7225 • alternative films & performances

Sin City Rollergirls • Vegas' female roller derby league • visit www.sincityrollergirls.com for events

Thanks Babs, the Day Tripper 702/370-6961 • tours, shows, attractions & getaways • full service concierge for Las Vegas, state of NV, & the Southwest • it's like having a lesbian aunt in Las Vegas!

Viva Las Vegas Wedding Chapel 1205 Las Vegas Blvd 800/574-4450 • gay-owned

BOOKSTORES

Get Booked 4640 S Paradise Rd #15 (at Naples) 702/737-7780 • 10am-midnight, till 2am Fri-Sat • LGBT

RETAIL SHOPS

Glamour Boutique II 714 E Sahara Ave #104 (at S 6th St) 702/697-1800, 866/692-1800 • clsd Sun • large-size dresses, wigs, etc

The Rack 953 E Sahara Ave, Ste 101, Bldg 16 (in Commercial Center) 702/732-7225 • leather • fetish • wheelchair access

PUBLICATIONS

Las Vegas Night Beat 702/369-8441 • monthly news & entertainment magazine

QVegas 702/650-0636 • monthly LGBT news & entertainment magazine

GYMS & HEALTH CLUBS

The Las Vegas Athletic Club 2655 S Maryland Pkwy 702/734-5822 • day passes

SEX CLUBS

Power Exchange 3610 S Highland Dr 702/255-4739 • play space open to hetero, gay, bi, trans, men & women • free for women & trans people

EROTICA

Bare Essentials Fantasy Fashions 4029 W Sahara Ave (near Valley View Blvd) 702/247-4711 • exotic/ intimate apparel • toys • gay-owned

Rancho Adult Entertainment Center 4820 N Rancho Dr (at Lone Mtn) 702/645-6104 • 24hrs

Wild J's 2923 S Industrial Rd (behind Circus Circus) 702/892-0699 • 24hrs

Laughlin

see Bullhead City, Arizona

Reno

ACCOMMODATIONS

Silver Legacy Resort & Casino 407 N Virginia St 775/325-7401, 800/687-8733 • gay-friendly • pool • restaurant & bar

BARS

Cadillac Lounge 1114 E 4th St (at Sutro) 775/324-7827 • noon-2am • lesbians/ gay men • neighborhood bar

Chapel Tavern 1099 S Virginia St (at Vassar) 775/324-2244 • 2pm-4am, from 10am wknds • gay/straight • patio

Five Star Saloon 132 West St (at 1st) 775/329-2878 • 24hrs • gay/ straight • neighborhood bar • dancing/DJ • wheelchair access

The Patio 600 W 5th St (btwn Washington & Ralston) 775/323-6565 • 11am-2am • lesbians/ gay men • neighborhood bar • live shows • karaoke

NIGHTCLUBS

Tronix 340 Kietzke Ln (btwn Glendale & Mill) 775/786-2121 • 2pm-close, clsd Sun-Tue • popular • gay/ straight • dancing/DJ • Latina/o cliente • drag shows • patio

RESTAURANTS

4th Street Bistro 3065 W 4th St 775/323-3200 • dinner nightly, clsd Sun-Mon • upscale • extensive wine list

Brasserie Saint James 901 S Center St 775/348-8888 • 11am-11pm, till 1am Fri-Sat, full bar • great roof deck

The Daily Bagel 495 Morill Ave # 102 775/786-1611 • 6:30am-2pm, till 3pm Wed-Fri, 8am-2pm, Sat, clsd Sun

Old Granite Street Eatery 243 S Sierra St 775/622-3222 • 11am-11pm, from 10am wknds, full bar

Pneumatic Diner 501 W 1st St (in Truckee River Apts, 2nd flr) 775/786-8888 x106 • 11am-10pm, from 8am Sun • vegetarian

ENTERTAINMENT & RECREATION

Brüka Theatre 99 N Virginia St 775/323-3221 • alternative theater & performance space

BOOKSTORES

Sundance Books 1155 W 4th St #106 (at Keystone) 775/786-1188 • 9am-9pm, 9am-5pm wknds • independent

PUBLICATIONS

Reno Gay Page 775/453-4058 • monthly • bar & resource listings • community events • arts & entertainment

EROTICA

Suzie's 195 Kietzke Ln (at E 2nd St) 775/786-8557 • 24hrs

Winnemuca

BARS

Cheers 320 S Bridge St 775/623-2660 • 9am-close • gay-friendly • neighborhood bar

NEW HAMPSHIRE

Concord

ACCOMMODATIONS

Idleday Guest Rooms 180 W Parish Rd 603/520-6886, 603/753-6113 • women only • secluded setting on river • nonsmoking

Keene

ACCOMMODATIONS

The Lane Hotel 30 Main St 603/357-7070, 888/300-5056 • gay/ straight • WiFi • also restaurant • nonsmoking • wheelchair access

Manchester

ACCOMMODATIONS

Radisson Hotel Manchester 700 Elm St 603/625-1000, 800/395-7046 • gay-friendly • food served • pool • kids/ pets ok • WiFi • wheelchair access

BARS

The Breezeway 14 Pearl St 603/621-9111 • 4pm-1am • lesbians/ gay men • neighborhood bar • dancing/DJ • theme nights • cabaret • drag shows • gay-owned

Club 313 93 S Maple St (at S Willow) 603/628-6813 • 7pm-1am, clsd Sun-Mon & Wed • lesbians/ gay men • dancing/DJ • live entertainment • karaoke • drag shows • WiFi • wheelchair access

Doogie's Bar & Grill 37 Manchester St 603/232-0732 • 4pm-1am • mostly gay men • neighborhood bar • food served • dancing/DJ • patio • wheelchair access

Element Lounge 1055 Elm St 603/627-2922 • 3pm-1:30am, clsd Mon • lesbians/ gay men • dancing/DJ • food served • karaoke • drag shows

Nashua

ACCOMMODATIONS

Radisson Hotel 11 Tara Blvd 603/888-9970 • gay-friendly • pool • WiFi • wheelchair access

Newfound Lake

ACCOMMODATIONS

The Inn on Newfound Lake 1030 Mayhew Tpke Rte 3-A, Bridgewater 603/744-9111, 800/745-7990 • gay/ straight • private beach on cleanest lake in NH • also renowned restaurant • full bar • nonsmoking • WiFi • gay-owned

Portsmouth

ACCOMMODATIONS

Ale House Inn 121 Bow St (at Market St) 603/431-7760 • gay-friendly • WiFi • gay-owned

The Hotel Portsmouth 40 Court St 603/433-1200

CAFES

Breaking New Grounds 14 Market Square 603/436-9555 • 6:30am-11pm • espresso shakes • WiFi

RESTAURANTS

The Mombo 66 Marcy St (at State St) 603/433-2340 • dinner only, clsd Sun-Mon • wheelchair access

White Mtns

ACCOMMODATIONS

Beal House 2 W Main St, Littleton 603/444-2661 • gay-friendly • WiFi • restaurant

Highlands Inn 240 Valley View Lane, Bethlehem **603/869–3978, 877/LES–B–INN (537–2466)** • Women only • 100 acres • full brkfst • outdoor & indoor spas • pool • 100 mtn acres • special events • concerts • kids/pets ok • non-smoking • WiFi • wheelchair access • ignore No Vacancy sign • lesbian-owned

The Horse & Hound Inn 205 Wells Rd, Franconia **603/823–5501, 800/450–5501** • gay-friendly • 1840s fully restored lodge stye • full brkfst • nonsmoking • WiFi • also restaurant • gay-owned

The Inn at Bowman 1174 Rte 2 (Presidential Hwy), Randolph **603/466–5006** • gay/ straight • swimming • hot tub • nonsmoking • wheelchair access • gay-owned

Inn at Crystal Lake 2356 Eaton Rd (at Rte 16), Eaton **603/447–2120, 800/343–7336** • gay/ straight • full brkfst • also restaurant • kids age 12+ ok • dogs ok • WiFi • gay-owned

The Notchland Inn 2 Morey Rd, Hart's Location **603/374–6131, 800/866–6131** • gay/ straight • full brkfst • other meals available • nonsmoking • also cottages • gay-owned

Riverbend Inn B&B 273 Chocorua Mtn Hwy (at Rte 113), Chocorua **603/323–7440, 800/628–6944** • gay/ straight • full brkfst • located on the Chocorua River • WiFi • nonsmoking • gay-owned

The Sunny Grange B&B 1354 Rte 175 (Mad River Rd), Campton **603/726–5555, 877/726–5553** • gay-friendly • full brkfst • kids ok • nonsmoking • WiFi

Wildcat Inn & Tavern Rte 16A, Jackson Village **603/383–4245, 855/532–7727** • gay-friendly • full brkfst • also tavern & dining room • nonsmoking

Wyatt House Country Inn 3046 White Mountain Hwy, N Conway **603/356–7977 , 800/527–7978** • gay/ straight • full brkfst • WiFi • lesbian-owned

RESTAURANTS

Polly's Pancake Parlor 672 Rte Sugar Hill Rd (exit 38 off 93 N), Sugar Hill **603/823–5575** • 7am-2pm, till 3pm wknds, clsd winters

The Red Parka Steakhouse & Pub Rte 302, Glen **603/383–4344** • open from 3pm, also bar

ENTERTAINMENT & RECREATION

Reel North Fly Fishing **603/858–4103** • casting lessons • half & full day river trips • lesbian-owned/run

NEW JERSEY

Statewide

PUBLICATIONS

Out in Jersey 743 Hamilton Ave, Trenton 08629 **609/213–9310** • bimonthly glossy magazine for all of New Jersey's LGBT community

Asbury Park

ACCOMMODATIONS

Empress Hotel 101 Asbury Ave **732/774–0100** • gay-friendly • swimming • WiFi • also Empress Lobby Lounge on wknds

BARS

Georgie's 812 5th Ave (at Main) **732/988–1220** • 2pm-2am • lesbians/ gay men • neighborhood bar • food served • karaoke • drag shows

NIGHTCLUBS

Ladies 2000 **856/869–0193** • seasonal parties • call hotline for details

Paradise 101 Asbury Ave (at Ocean Ave) **732/988–6663** • 4pm-2am, from 2pm Sat, from noon Sun • lesbians/ gay men • dancing/DJ • 2 dance flrs • live shows • piano bar • tiki/ pool bar in summer

RESTAURANTS

Bistro Olé 230 Main St **732/897–0048** • dinner nightly, clsd Mon-Tue • Spanish-Portuguese • BYOB • gay-owned

Moonstruck 517 Lake Ave (at Grand) **732/988–0123** • dinner only, clsd Mon-Tue • also bar • live music wknds

Atlantic City

ACCOMMODATIONS

The Carisbrooke Inn 105 S Little Rock Ave, Ventnor **609/822–6392** • gay-friendly • on a beach block • nonsmoking • WiFi

Tropicana Casino & Resort 2831 Boardwalk (at Brighton) **609/340–4000, 800/345–8767** • gay-friendly • pool • oceanview rooms

BARS

Rainbow Room 55 S Bellevue Ave **609/317–4593** • 6pm-2am • lesbians/gay men • neighborhood bar

NIGHTCLUBS

Pro Bar 1133 Boardwalk (at Resorts Casino) 800/334-6378 • 8pm-3am, clsd Mon-Wed • lesbians/ gay men • dancing/DJ • drag shows

RESTAURANTS

Dock's Oyster House 2405 Atlantic Ave 609/345-0092 • 5pm-10pm, till 11pm Fri-Sat • wheelchair access

White House Sub Shop 2301 Arctic Ave (at Mississippi) 609/345-1564 • 10am-8pm, till 9pm Fri-Sat

Boonton

NIGHTCLUBS

Switch 202 Myrtle Ave (off Washington) 973/263-4000 • 3pm-2am • lesbians/gay men • dancing/DJ • country/western • food served • drag shows

Camden

ENTERTAINMENT & RECREATION

The Walt Whitman House 30 Mickle Blvd (btwn S 3rd & S 4th Sts) 856/964-5383 • the last home of America's great & controversial poet

Cape May

ACCOMMODATIONS

Congress Hall 251 Beach Ave 609/884-8421, 888/944-1816 • gay-friendly • pool • WiFi

Cottage Beside the Point 609/204-0549, 609/898-0658 • gay/ straight • studio • kids ok • nonsmoking • lesbian-owned

Highland House 131 N Broadway (at York) 609/898-1198 • gay-friendly • B&B • kids/ pets ok • gazebo • nonsmoking • gay & straight-owned

The Virginia Hotel 25 Jackson St (btwn Beach Dr & Carpenter's Ln) 609/884-5700, 800/732-4236 • gay-friendly • WiFi • also The Ebbitt Room restaurant • seafood/ cont'l

BARS

The King Edward Room 301 Howard St (at The Chalfonte Hotel) 609/884-8409 • 3pm-1am summer only • mostly gay men

CAFES

Higher Grounds 479B W Perry St 609/884-1131 • 8:30am-4:30pm, clsd Sun • events • music • food served • WiFi

Hammonton

NIGHTCLUBS

Club In Or Out 19 N Egg Harbor Rd (at Orchard Ave) 609/561-2525 • 6pm-3am Fri-Sat, 5pm-1am Sun • lesbians/ gay men • dancing/DJ • shows • karaoke • lesbian-owned

Highland Park

INFO LINES & SERVICES

Pride Center of New Jersey 85 Raritan Ave (at S 1st Ave) 732/846-2232 • info line • meeting space for various groups

Hoboken

NIGHTCLUBS

Maxwell's 1039 Washington St 201/653-1703 • popular • gay-friendly • alternative • live music venue • food served

Jamesburg

RESTAURANTS

Fiddleheads 27 E Railroad Ave 732/521-0878 • lunch & dinner, Sun brunch, clsd Mon-Tue • upscale bistro • BYOB

Jersey City

INFO LINES & SERVICES

Hudson Pride Connections 32 Jones St 201/963-4779 • "serving the LGBT communities & all people living w/ HIV, since 1993"

ACCOMMODATIONS

Hyatt Regency Jersey City 2 Exchange Pl (on the Hudson) 201/645-4712, 201/469-1234 • gay-friendly • luxury waterfront hotel • short ride to NYC • pool • nonsmoking • WiFi

BARS

Lamp Post 382 2nd St 201/222-1331 • 11:30am-2am, till 3am Fri-Sat • gay/ straight • food served • live bands

LITM 140 Newark Ave (at Grove) 201/536-5557 • 5pm-1am, till 2am Fri-Sat, 11am-midnight Sun • gay/ straight • also restaurant & gallery

RESTAURANTS

Baja 117 Montgomery St 201/915-0062 • lunch & dinner • Mexican

Linden

BARS

Duval Bar & Lounge 9 Cedar Ave
908/290-3535 • 6pm-2am, till 3am Th-Sat,
clsd Sun-Mon • lesbians/gay men, more
women Th • dancing/DJ • food served •
karaoke

Lodi

RESTAURANTS

Penang Malaysian & Thai Cuisine 334 N
Main St (at Garibaldi Ave) **973/779-1128** •
11am-11pm • full bar • gay-owned

Morristown

INFO LINES & SERVICES

**GAAMC (Gay Activist Alliance in Morris
County)** 21 Normandy Hts Rd (at Columbia
Rd, Unitarian Fellowship) **973/285-1595** •
info line 7:30pm-9pm, also recorded info •
also women's network

New Brunswick

BARS

The Den 700 Hamilton St (at Douglas),
Somerset **732/545-7354** • 8pm-2am Wed-Sat
only • popular • mostly gay men • dancing/DJ
wknds • multiracial • live shows • wheelchair
access

RESTAURANTS

The Frog & the Peach 29 Dennis St (at
Hiram Square) **732/846-3216** • lunch Mon-
Fri, dinner nightly • full bar • upscale •
wheelchair access

Sofie's Bistro 700 Hamilton St (at Douglas),
Somerset **732/545-7778** • dinner only, clsd
Mon • patio

Stage Left 5 Livingston Ave (at George)
732/828-4444 • popular • expensive • full bar
• patio • wheelchair access • gay-owned

River Edge

NIGHTCLUBS

Feathers 77 Kinderkamack Rd (at Grand)
201/342-6410 • 9pm-2am, till 3am Sat, clsd
Mon-Tue • mostly gay men • dancing/DJ •
karaoke • live shows • videos • young crowd •
wheelchair access

NEW MEXICO

Alamogordo

ACCOMMODATIONS

Best Western Desert Aire Motor Inn 1021
S White Sands Blvd **505/437-2110,
800/637-5956** • gay-friendly • pool • WiFi •
wheelchair access

Albuquerque

includes Bernalillo, Corrales, Placitas &
Rio Rancho

INFO LINES & SERVICES

AA Gay/ Lesbian 505/266-1900 (AA#) •
7pm Mon & Th

Common Bond Info Line 505/891-3647 •
24hrs • covers LGBT community

ACCOMMODATIONS

Adobe Nido 1124 Major Ave NW (at 12th St
& Candilaria NW) **505/344-1310,
866/435-6436** • gay-friendly • B&B • also
aviary • nonsmoking • WiFi

Bottger Mansion of Old Town 110 San
Felipe (at Central Ave) **505/243-3639,
800/758-3639** • gay-friendly • transgender-
friendly • B&B • WiFi

Brittania & W E Mauger Estate B&B 701
Roma Ave NW (at 7th) **505/242-8755,
800/719-9189** • gay-friendly • full brkfst •
nonsmoking • WiFi

Casa Manzano B&B 103 Forest Rd 321 (at
State Rte 55), Tajique **505/384-9767** • gay/
straight • full brkfst • nonsmoking • kids/ pets
ok • wheelchair access

Casas de Suenos 310 Rio Grande Blvd SW
(btwn York & Alhambra) **505/247-4560,
800/665-7002** • gay/ straight • spacious
casitas • full brkfst • kids ok • nonsmoking •
WiFi

La Casita B&B 317 16th St NW (at Lomas
Blvd) **505/242-0173** • gay-friendly • adobe
guesthouse • nonsmoking • WiFi

Golden Guesthouses 2645 Decker NW (at
Glenwood) **505/344-9205, 888/513-GOLD** •
lesbians/ gay men • individual & shared units
• nonsmoking • lesbian-owned

The Nativo Lodge 6000 Pan American Fwy
NE **505/798-4300, 888/628-4861**

Sheraton Albuquerque Airport Hotel
2910 Yale Blvd SE (at Gibson) **505/843-7000,
800/325-3535** • gay-friendly • 4-star hotel •
pool • also restaurant

BARS

Albuquerque Social Club 4021 Central Ave NE (at Morningside, enter rear) 505/262-1088 • 3pm-2am, noon-midnight Sun • popular • lesbians/ gay men • dancing/DJ • private club

Sidewinders Ranch 8900 Central SE (at Wyoming) 505/554-2078 • 4pm-2am, till midnight Sun, clsd Mon • mostly gay men • dancing/DJ • country/ western • karaoke • wheelchair access

NIGHTCLUBS

Effex 420 Central SW (at 5th) 505/842-8870 • 9pm-2am Th-Sat • lesbians/ gay men • dancing/DJ

Fire • monthly dance party • women only • check local listings for location

CAFES

Java Joe's 906 Park Ave SW 505/765-1514 • 6:30am-3:30pm • coffee & pastries • monthly art shows

RESTAURANTS

Artichoke Cafe 424 Central Ave SE (at Arno St) 505/243-0200 • lunch Mon-Fri, dinner nightly • bistro • plenty veggie • wheelchair access

Cafe Cubano at Laru Ni Hati 3413 Central Ave NE (btwn Tulane & Amherst) 505/255-1575 • 10am-9pm, till 8pm Sat, noon-5pm Sun, clsd Mon • cigars • cheap Cuban food • also unisex hair salon • gay-owned

Copper Lounge 1504 Central Ave SE (at Maple) 505/242-7490 • 11am-2am, clsd Sun • pizza, burgers • full bar • wheelchair access

Desert Fish 4214 Central Ave SE 505/266-5544 • dinner nightly, wknd brunch, clsd Mon • seafood

El Patio 142 Harvard St SE (at Central) 505/268-4245 • 11am-9pm • popular • young crowd • beer/ wine • plenty veggie • wheelchair access

El Pinto 10500 4th St NW (at Roy Ave) 505/898-1771 • lunch & dinner, Sun brunch • Mexican

Albuquerque

LGBT PRIDE:
June. 505/873-8084, web: www.abqpride.com.

ANNUAL EVENTS:
October - Closet Cinema, LGBT film festival 505/243-1870, web: www.closetcinema.org.
October - Albuquerque Int'l Balloon Fiesta 505/821-1000 or 888/422-7277, web: www.balloonfiesta.com.

CITY INFO:
800/284-2282, web: www.itsatrip.org.

BEST VIEW:
Sandia Peak Tramway (505/856-7325) at sunset.

WEATHER:
Sunny and temperate. Warm days and cool nights in summer, with average temperatures from 65° to 95°. Winter is cooler, from 28° to 57°.

ATTRACTIONS:
Albuquerque Museum 505/842-0111, web: www.albuquerquemuseum.com.
Indian Pueblo Cultural Center 505/843-7270 or 866/855-7902, web: www.indianpueblo.org.
New Mexico Museum of Natural History & Science 505/841-2800, web: www.nmnaturalhistory.org.
Old Town.
Petroglyph National Monument 505/899-0205 x331, web: www.nps.gov/petr.
Rattlesnake Museum 505/242-6569, web: www.rattlesnakes.com.
Sandia Peak Tramway 505/856-7325, web: www.sandiapeak.com.
Wildlife West Nature Park 505/281-7655, web: www.wildlifewest.org.

Flying Star Cafe 3416 Central Ave SE (2 blocks W of Carlisle) **505/255-6633** • 6am-10pm, till 11pm Fri-Sat • plenty veggie • WiFi • wheelchair access

Frontier 2400 Central Ave SE (at Cornell) **505/266-0550** • 5am-1am • good brkfst burritos

The Original Garcia's Kitchen 1113 4th St NW (at Mountain) **505/247-9149** • 7am-9pm • awesome little down home place • wheelchair access

The Range Cafe 2200 Menaul NE (at University Blvd) **505/888-1660** • 7:30am-9pm • Southwestern

Romano's Macaroni Grill 2100 Louisiana NE (at Winrock Mall) **505/881-3400** • 11am-10pm • Italian • wheelchair access

Sadie's Cocinita 6230 4th St NW (near Osuna) **505/345-5339** • 11am-10pm, 10am-9pm Sun • popular • New Mexican • wheelchair access

Zinc Wine Bar & Bistro 3009 Central Ave NE (at Dartmouth) **505/254-9462** • lunch & dinner, brunch wknds • live music • reservations recommended

ENTERTAINMENT & RECREATION

Bio Park Botanic Garden 2601 Central Ave NW (at New York Ave) **505/768-2000** • an oasis in the desert: native & exotic plants, butterflies

Duke City Derby • Albuquerque's female roller derby league • visit www.dukecityderby.com for events

BOOKSTORES

Page One 11018 Montgomery NE (at Juan Tabo Blvd) **505/294-2026, 800/521-4122** • 9am-9pm, till 6pm Sun • "New Mexico's largest independent bookstore"

EROTICA

Castle Megastore 5110 Central Ave SE (at San Mateo) **505/262-2266**

Self Serve 3904-B Central Ave SE (at Morningside) **505/265-5815** • noon-7pm, till 8pm Fri, till 6pm Sun • erotica store & sexuality resource center • lesbian-owned

Chimayo

ACCOMMODATIONS

Casa Escondida B&B **505/351-4805, 800/643-7201** • gay-friendly • full brkfst • hot tub • kids/pets ok w/ approval • nonsmoking • WiFi

Cloudcroft

RETAIL SHOPS

Off The Beaten Path 100 Glorietta Ave (at 1st) **575/682-7284** • eclectic gifts • original artwork • wheelchair access • lesbian-owned

Farmington

ACCOMMODATIONS

Quality Inn 1901 E Broadway **505/325-3700, 877/424-6423** • gay-friendly • kids/pets ok • WiFi • wheelchair access

Las Cruces

ACCOMMODATIONS

Hotel Encanto de Las Cruces 705 S Telshor Blvd **575/522-4300, 866/383-0443**

RETAIL SHOPS

Spirit Winds Gifts & Cafe 2260 S Locust St (at Thomas Dr) **575/521-0222** • 7:30am-7pm, 8am-6pm Sun • live music some wknds • food served • patio • WiFi • wheelchair access

Madrid

BARS

Mineshaft Tavern 2846 State Hwy 14 **505/473-0743** • 11:30am-close • gay-friendly • live shows • also restaurant • some veggie

CAFES

Java Junction 2855 State Hwy 14 **505/438-2772** • 7am-4pm, till 5pm wknds • WiFi • also giftshop & B&B

Ojo Caliente

RESTAURANTS

Mesa Vista Cafe 35323 Hwy 285 **505/583-2245** • 8am-9pm • wheelchair access

Ramah

ACCOMMODATIONS

El Morro RV Park, Cabins & Cafe 4018 Hwy 53 **505/783-4612** • gay/ straight • in Zuni Mtns • full brkfst • nonsmoking • WiFi • also cafe • lesbian-owned

Ruidoso

ENTERTAINMENT & RECREATION

Mountain Annie's Center for the Arts 2710 Sudderth Dr (at Grindstone Canyon Rd) **575/257-7982** • wheelchair access

Santa Fe

INFO LINES & SERVICES

AA Gay/ Lesbian 1601 S St Francis Dr 505/982–8932 • 6pm Mon • also 6pm Tue at Friendship Club, 1915 Rosina St

ACCOMMODATIONS

Bishop's Lodge Resort & Spa 1297 Bishops Lodge Rd 505/983–6377, 800/419–0492 • gay-friendly • on 450 acres • kids/pets ok • pool • hot tub • nonsmoking • wheelchair access • WiFi

Dragonfly Canyon Retreat Glorieta 505/757–2991 • gay/ straight • 3-bdrm casita • near Pecos Wilderness • nonsmoking • also women's retreats • lesbian-owned

El Farolito B&B 514 Galisteo St (at Paseo de Peralta) 505/988–1631, 888/634–8782 • gay/ straight • adobe compound w/ romantic, private casitas • kids ok • nonsmoking • WiFi • gay-owned

Four Kachinas Inn 512 Webber St 505/982–2550, 800/397–2564 • gay/ straight • courtyard • kids ok • nonsmoking • WiFi • wheelchair access • gay-owned

Hacienda Nicholas 320 E Marcy St 505/986–1431, 888/284–3170 • gay/ straight • adobe home • full brkfst • teens/ pets ok • nonsmoking • WiFi • wheelchair access

Inn at Vanessie 427 W Water St 505/984–1193, 800/646–6752 • gay-friendly • historic adobe inn • nonsmoking • kids/pets ok • WiFi • wheelchair access • also restaurant & live music club

The Inn of the Five Graces 150 E DeVargas St 505/992–0957 , 866/992–0957 • gay-friendly • guest rooms and suites are each individual, mysterious & deeply luxurious

➤ **Inn of the Turquoise Bear B&B** 342 E Buena Vista St (at Old Santa Fe Tr) 505/983–0798, 800/396–4104 • lesbians/ gay men • B&B in historic Witter Bynner estate • nonsmoking • WiFi • gay-owned

Inn on the Alameda 303 E Alameda (at Canyon Rd) 505/984–2121, 888/984–2121 • gay-friendly • afternoon wine reception • hot tubs • WiFi • wheelchair access

Las Palomas 460 W San Francisco St 505/982–5560, 877/982–5560 • gay-friendly • luxury hotel 3 blocks from Plaza • kids ok • nonsmoking • WiFi • wheelchair access

The Madeleine Inn 106 Faithway St
505/982-3465, 888/877-7622 • gay/ straight
• Queen Anne Victorian • full brkfst • hot tub •
kids ok • nonsmoking • WiFi • also spa

**New Mexico Women's Guesthouse,
Retreat & Healing Center** PO Box 130,
Serafina 87569 **575/421-2533** • women only •
guesthouses on 1,000-acre wildlife refuge •
healing workshops • hot tub • nonsmoking •
lesbian-owned

Rosewood Inn of the Anasazi 113
Washington Ave **505/988-3030, 888/767-3966**
• gay-friendly • luxury hotel 1/2 block from
Plaza • kids ok • WiFi • nonsmoking •
wheelchair access • also restaurant

The Triangle Inn—Santa Fe 14 Arroyo
Cuyamungue (12 miles N of Santa Fe)
505/455-3375, 877/733-7689 • lesbians/ gay
men • secluded rustic adobe compound • hot
tub • nonsmoking casitas available • WiFi •
kids/ pets ok • wheelchair access • lesbian-
owned

BARS

The Matador 116 W San Francisco St (at
Galisteo) **505/984-5050** • gay-friendly
neighborhood dive bar

Starlight Lounge 500 Rodeo Rd
505/428-7777 • 5pm-midnight Wed-Sun •
lesbians/ gay men • cabaret & lounge

RESTAURANTS

Anasazi Restaurant 113 Washington Ave (at
Inn of the Anasazi) **505/988-3030** • brkfst,
lunch, dinner & wknd brunch • wheelchair
access

Cafe Pasqual's 121 Don Gaspar Ave (at
Water St) **505/983-9340, 800/722-7672** •
brkfst, lunch, dinner & Sun brunch • popular •
Southwestern • some veggie • beer/ wine
• wheelchair access

The Compound Restaurant 653 Canyon
Rd (at Delgado) **505/982-4353** • lunch Mon-
Sat, dinner nightly • upscale • Southwestern •
nonsmoking • patio • reservations
recommended • wheelchair access

Cowgirl BBQ 319 S Guadalupe St (at Aztec)
505/982-2565 • 11am-11pm, till midnight Fri-
Sat • great margaritas • plenty veggie

El Farol 808 Canyon Rd **505/983-9912** •
Spanish/ tapas • live music

Geronimo 724 Canyon Rd (at Camino del
Monte Sol) **505/982-1500** • dinner nightly •
eclectic gourmet • full bar 11am-11pm •
wheelchair access

Harry's Roadhouse 96 Old Las Vegas Hwy
505/989-4629 • 7am-9:30pm • outdoor
seating • popular brunch

Pink Adobe 406 Old Santa Fe Trl
505/983-7712 • steak & seafood • also
Dragon Room bar

Santacafe 231 Washington Ave
505/984-1788 • lunch & dinner • New
American • some veggie • full bar • wheelchair
access

Tune Up Cafe 1115 Hickox St (at Cortez)
505/983-7060 • 7am-10pm, from 8am wknds
• New Mexican • some veggie • beer/ wine •
wheelchair access

ENTERTAINMENT & RECREATION

Ten Thousand Waves 3451 Hyde Park Rd (4
miles out of town) **505/982-9304** • Japanese
health spa & lodging • clothing-optional • kids
ok

Wise Fool New Mexico 2778 Agua Fria Unit
D (at Siler Rd) **505/992-2588** • women & kids
circus art classes, workshops & performances •
social justice theatre & puppetry • check local
listings for upcoming events & info

BOOKSTORES

Downtown Subscription 376 Garcia St (at
Acequia Madre) **505/983-3085** • 7am-6pm •
newsstand • coffee shop • wheelchair access

RETAIL SHOPS

The Ark 133 Romero St (at Agua Fria)
505/988-3709 • 10am-6pm, 11am-5pm Sun •
spiritual

Silver City

ACCOMMODATIONS

Gila House Hotel & Gallery 400 N Arizona
575/313-7015 • gay-friendly • also Gallery 400

West Street Inn **575/534-2302** •
guesthouse • kids/ pets ok (call for details)

CAFES

Shevek & Co 602 N Bullard St (at 6th St)
575/534-9168 • dinner nightly, clsd Wed •
Mediterranean cuisine • espresso • "the best
service in town" • beer/ wine • patio • gay-
owned

RESTAURANTS

Diane's Restaurant & Bakery 510 N
Bullard **575/538-8722** • 7am-6pm, 8am-3pm
Sun • beer/ wine

Taos

ACCOMMODATIONS

Adobe & Stars B&B 584 State Hwy 150 (at Valdez Rim Rd) 575/776-2776, 800/211-7076 • gay/ straight • full brkfst • nonsmoking • WiFi • wheelchair access • woman-owned

Casa Benavides B&B 137 Kit Carson Rd (at Paseo del Pueblo Sur) 575/758-1772, 800/552-1772 • gay-friendly • fireplaces • hot tubs • gardens • full brkfst • nonsmoking • kids ok • WiFi • wheelchair access

Casa Europa Inn & Gallery 840 Upper Ranchitos Rd (at Ranchitos Rd) 575/758-9798, 888/518-9798 • gay/ straight • full brkfst • hot tub • sauna • nonsmoking • WiFi

Casa Gallina 575/758-2306 • gay/ straight • charming guesthouse in pastoral setting • nonsmoking • wheelchair access • gay-owned

Dobson House 484 Tune Dr 575/776-5738 • gay-friendly • luxury suites • N of Taos • full brkfst • solar-powered eco-resort • nonsmoking

Dreamcatcher B&B 416 La Lomita Rd (at Valverde) 575/758-0613, 888/758-0613 • gay-friendly • near Taos Plaza • full brkfst • hot tub • nonsmoking • WiFi • wheelchair access

The Historic Taos Inn 125 Paseo del Pueblo Norte (at Bent St) 575/758-2233, 888/518-8267 • gay-friendly • several adobe houses date from the 1800s • pueblo-style fireplaces • also restaurant & bar

San Geronimo Lodge 1101 Witt Rd (off Kit Carson) 575/751-3776, 800/894-4119 • popular • gay/ straight • full brkfst • pool • hot tub • massage available • kids/ pets ok • nonsmoking • WiFi • wheelchair access

RESTAURANTS

Sabroso 470 State Hwy 150, Arroyo Seco 575/776-3333 • 5pm-10pm • American & Mediterranean • also full bar • patio • wheelchair access

ENTERTAINMENT & RECREATION

Llama Trekking Adventures 800/758-5262 • day hikes & multiday llama treks in Sangre de Cristo Mtns & Rio Grande Gorge

Truth or Consequences

ACCOMMODATIONS

The Belair Inn 705 N Date St (at 7th Ave) 575/894-8977 • gay/ straight • "retro 1950s motel w/ 21st-century amenities" • nonsmoking • WiFi

NEW YORK

Adirondack Mtns

ACCOMMODATIONS

The Cornerstone Victorian 3921 Main St (Rte 9), Warrensburg 518/623-3308 • gay-friendly • gourmet brkfst

The Doctor's Inn 304 Trudeau Rd (at Bloomingdale Ave), Saranac Lake 607/316-6455 • gay-friendly • Adirondack guesthouse • nonsmoking

Falls Brook Yurts in Adirondacks John Brannon Rd, Minerva 518/761-6187 • gay-friendly • access to hiking, fishing & boating • kids/ pets ok

King Hendrick Motel 1602 State Rte 9, Lake George 518/792-0418, 866/521-6883 • gay-friendly • swimming • WiFi • nonsmoking • small pets ok • wheelchair access

Secluded Retreat Cabin Lake Luzerne 518/361-2375 • lesbians/ gay men • nonsmoking • secluded, rustic cabin • women-owned

Tea Island Resort 3020 Lake Shore Dr, Lake George 518/668-2776 • gay-friendly • chalets, cottages & suites

Albany

see **Capital District**

Binghamton

INFO LINES & SERVICES

AA Gay/ Lesbian 607/722-5983

BARS

Merlin's 73 Court St 607/722-1022 • 4pm-1am , till 3am Fri-Sat • lesbians/ gay men • neighborhood bar • dancing/DJ • live shows • karaoke • patio

Squiggy's 34 Chenango St (at Court) 607/722-2299 • 6pm-midnight, till 2am Fri-Sat, from 8pm Sat, clsd Sun • lesbians/ gay men • neighborhood bar • dancing/DJ Fri-Sat • karaoke

CAFES

Lost Dog Cafe 222 Water St (at Henry) 607/771-6063 • 11:30am-10pm, till 11pm Fri-Sat, clsd Sun • popular • some veggie • beer/ wine • live shows • wheelchair access

RESTAURANTS

The Whole in the Wall 43 S Washington St 607/722-5138 • 11:30am-9pm, clsd Sun-Mon • plenty veggie/ vegan

Buffalo

INFO LINES & SERVICES

Lesbian/ Gay AA 18 Trinity Pl (at AIDS Comm Svc) **716/852–7743** • 8pm Mon & Wed

Pride Center of Western NY 206 S Elmwood Ave **716/852–7743** • meetings, resources & more

ACCOMMODATIONS

Beau Fleuve B&B 242 Linwood Ave **716/882–6116, 800/278–0245** • gay-friendly

The Mansion on Delaware 414 Delaware Ave **716/886–3300** • gay/ straight • WiFi • wheelchair access

BARS

Cathode Ray 26 Allen St (at N Pearl) **716/884–3615** • 1pm-4am • mostly gay men • neighborhood bar • wheelchair access

Fugazi 503 Franklin St (near Allen St) **716/881–3588** • 5pm-2am • gay/ straight • intimate cocktail lounge • videos

K Gallagher's 73 Allen St **716/886–6676** • lunch & dinner, till 3pm Sun • gay-friendly • neighborhood bar • multiracial clientele • comfort food served • wheelchair access

Q 44 Allen St **716/332–2223** • 3pm-4am, from noon wknds • lesbians/ gay men • neighborhood bar

Roxy 884 Main St (at Carlton) **716/882–9293** • 8pm-4am Wed-Sat • mostly women • dancing/DJ • alternative • live shows • karaoke

The Underground 274 Delaware Ave (at Johnson) **716/853–0092** • noon-4am • mostly gay men • neighborhood bar • dancing/DJ • karaoke

NIGHTCLUBS

Club Marcella 622 Main St **716/847–6850** • 10pm-4am, clsd Mon-Wed • lesbians/ gay men • dancing/DJ • drag shows • wheelchair access

CAFES

Cafe 59 59 Allen St (at Franklin) **716/883–1880** • 7am-4pm, 10am-4pm Sat, clsd Sun • WiFi • gay-owned

RESTAURANTS

Allen Street Hardware Cafe 245 Allen St (at College) **716/882–8843** • from 5pm daily • full bar • live music • art

Anchor Bar 1047 Main St **716/886–8920, 716/884–4083** • 11am-10pm, till midnight Fri-Sat

Atmosphere 62 62 Allen St (at Franklin) **716/881–0062** • from 4pm Wed-Sat • full bar

Mothers 33 Virginia Pl (at Virginia St) **716/882–2989** • 4pm-11pm, till 2am Sat

Rue Franklin 341 Franklin St (at W Tupper) **716/852–4416** • 5:30pm-10pm, clsd Sun-Mon • upscale, contemporary French

Tempo 581 Delaware Ave (at Allen St) **716/885–1594** • dinner only, clsd Sun • upscale Italian/ American

Towne Restaurant 186 Allen St **716/884–5128** • 7am-5am, clsd Sun • Greek

ENTERTAINMENT & RECREATION

Babeville 341 Delaware Ave (at W Tupper) **716/852–3835** • Ani Di Franco's rehabbed church performance space • also Hallwalls Arts Center

Buffalo United Artists 119 Chippewa (btwn Delaware & Elmwood) **716/886–9239** • gay-themed theater company

BOOKSTORES

Talking Leaves 3158 Main St (btwn Winspear & Hertel Aves) **716/837–8554** • 10am-6pm, till 8pm Wed-Th, clsd Sun • also 951 Elmwood Ave

PUBLICATIONS

Outcome Buffalo 495 Linwood Ave **716/228–8828** • monthly

EROTICA

Elmwood Books Adult Mart 3102 Delaware Ave (at Sheridan), Kenmore **716/874–1045** • 24hrs • women receive 20% off Wed

Video Liquidators 1770 Elmwood Ave **716/874–7223** • 24hrs

Canton

RESTAURANTS

Spicy Iguana 21 Miner St **315/714–2155** • 4pm-9pm, till 2am Fri-Sat, clsd Sun-Mon • Mexican

Capital District

includes Albany, Cohoes, Salem, Schenectady & Troy

INFO LINES & SERVICES

Capital District Lesbian/ Gay Community Center 332 Hudson Ave, Albany **518/462–6138** • social & human service programs • also Rainbow Cafe 6pm-9pm, clsd Sat

Gay AA 332 Hudson Ave (at L/G Community Center), Albany **518/462–6138** • 7pm Sun

Women's Building 373 Central Ave, Albany 518/462-2871 • community center • call for hours

ACCOMMODATIONS

The Morgan State House 393 State St, Albany 518/427-6063, 888/427-6063 • gay-friendly • 1800s town house • nonsmoking • WiFi

BARS

Clinton Street Pub 159 Clinton St, Schenectady 518/377-8555 • 11am-close, from 8am Sat, from noon Sun • lesbians/gay men • neighborhood bar • dancing/DJ • live shows • karaoke

Oh Bar 304 Lark St (at Madison), Albany 518/463-9004 • 2pm-4am • lesbians/gay men • neighborhood bar • multiracial • karaoke • videos • wheelchair access

Waterworks Pub 76 Central Ave (btwn Lexington & Northern), Albany 518/465-9079 • 1pm-4am • popular • mostly gay men • neighborhood bar • dancing/DJ wknds • garden bar • food served • karaoke • 18+ • wheelchair access

NIGHTCLUBS

Fuze Box 12 Central Ave, Albany 518/703-8937 • 8pm-4am Th-Sat • gay/straight • dancing/DJ • live shows • swing dancing • gay-owned

RESTAURANTS

Bomber's Burrito Bar 258 Lark St, Albany 518/463-9636 • 11am-2am, till 3am wknds • plenty veggie • gay-owned

Bomber's Burrito Bar 447 State St, Schenectady 518/374-3548 • 11am-2am, till 3am wknds • plenty veggie • gay-owned

Debbie's Kitchen 456 Madison Ave (btwn Lark St & Washington Park), Albany 518/463-3829 • 10am-7pm, 11am-6pm Sat, clsd Sun

El Loco Mexican Cafe 465 Madison Ave (btwn Lark & Willett), Albany 518/436-1855 • lunch Wed-Sat, dinner nightly, clsd Mon • healthy Tex-Mex • full bar

Midtown Tap & Tea Room 289 New Scotland Ave, Albany 518/435-0202 • 11am-10pm, from 4pm Sat, clsd Mon • wheelchair access lesbian-owned

Yono's 25 Chapel St (at Sheridan), Albany 518/436-7747 • 5:30pm-10pm, clsd Sun-Mon • full bar • live music • wheelchair access

ENTERTAINMENT & RECREATION

Albany All Stars Albany • Albany's female roller derby league

RETAIL SHOPS

Romeo's Gifts 299 Lark St (at Madison), Albany 518/434-4014 • noon-9pm, till 5pm Sun

Catskill Mtns

INFO LINES & SERVICES

Wise Woman Center 845/246-8081 • women only • workshops • correspondence courses • newsletter

ACCOMMODATIONS

Beds on Clouds 5320 Main St/ Rte 23 (at CR21), Windham 518/734-4692 • gay/straight • 1854 mansion features suites & famous artwork • woman-owned

Bradstan Country Hotel 1561 Rte 17-B, White Lake 845/583-4114 • gay-friendly • also cottages • piano bar & cabaret from 9pm-1am Fri-Sat

Country Suite Rte 23, Windham 518/734-4079 • B&B • Victorian-style farmhouse • full brkfst • nonsmoking • kids ok • lesbian-owned

Cuomo's Cove 33 Cumo's Cove Rd (at South St), Windham 518/734-5903, 800/734-5903 • gay-friendly • nonsmoking • women-owned

ECCE B&B 19 Silverfish Rd, Barryville 845/557-8562, 888/557-8562 • gay/straight • above Upper Delaware River • full brkfst • WiFi • nonsmoking • gay-owned

Fairlawn Inn 7872 Main St, Hunter 518/263-5025 • gay-friendly • kids/pets ok • WiFi • gay-owned

Kate's Lazy Meadow Motel 5191 Rte 28, Mt Tremper 845/688-7200 • gay-friendly • love shack owned by Kate Pierson of the B-52s • WiFi • nonsmoking

The Roxbury, Contemporary Catskill Lodging 2258 County Hwy 41 (at Bridge St), Roxbury 607/326-7200 • gay/straight • hip country motel • kids ok • nonsmoking • WiFi • wheelchair access • gay-owned

Village Green 845/679-0313 • B&B • gay-owned

BARS

Public Restaurant & Lounge 2318 City Hwy 41 (Bridge St), Roxbury 607/326-4026 • 5pm-9pm, till midnight Fri-Sat, clsd Mon-Tue • gay-friendly

RESTAURANTS

Catskill Rose 5355 Rte 212, Mt Tremper 845/688-7100 • 5pm-close Th-Sun • some veggie • full bar • patio • also lodging

BOOKSTORES

Golden Notebook 29 Tinker St, Woodstock **845/679-8000** • 11am-6pm, till 7pm Fri-Sat • LGBT section • wheelchair access

Cherry Creek

ACCOMMODATIONS

The Cherry Creek Inn 1022 West Rd (CR68) (at Center Rd) **716/296-5105** • gay-friendly • B&B • full brkfst • in wine & Amish country • kids ok

Cooperstown

ACCOMMODATIONS

Cobblescote on the Lake 6515 State Hwy 80 **607/437-1146** • gay-friendly • spectacular views at refurbished waterfront resort • food served • gay-owned

Corning

ACCOMMODATIONS

Black Sheep Inn 8329 Pleasant Valley Rd (Rte 54), Hammondsport **607/569-3767, 877/274-6286** • gay/ straight • full brkfst • nonsmoking • WiFi

Hillcrest Manor B&B 227 Cedar St (at Fourth St) **607/936-4548, 607/654-9136** • gay-friendly • 1890 neo-classical mansion • nonsmoking • WiFi • gay-owned

Rufus Tanner House B&B 60 Sagetown Rd, Pine City **607/732-0213, 800/360-9259** • gay/ straight • full brkfst • hot tub • nonsmoking • WiFi • wheelchair access

Croton-on-Hudson

ACCOMMODATIONS

Alexander Hamilton House 49 Van Wyck St **914/271-6737** • gay/ straight • full brkfst • pool • nonsmoking • kids/ pets ok • WiFi

Elmira

BARS

Chill 200 W 5th **607/738-9343** • 6pm-1am, clsd Sun-Tue • lesbians/ gay men • neighborhood bar • dancing/DJ • karaoke • drag shows • gay-owned

Findley Lake

ACCOMMODATIONS

Blue Heron Inn 10412 Main St (at Shadyside Rd) **716/769-7852** • gay-friendly • B&B • full brkfst • kids ok • nonsmoking

Fire Island

see also Long Island

INFO LINES & SERVICES

AA **631/654-1150** • call for meeting times

ACCOMMODATIONS

Dune Point Guesthouse **631/597-6261, 631/560-2200 (CELL)** • lesbians/ gay men • hot tub • kids/ pets ok • nonsmoking • wheelchair access • lesbian & gay & straight-owned/ run

Grove Hotel Dock Walk, Cherry Grove **631/597-6600** • mostly gay men • pool • nudity • nonsmoking room available • wheelchair access • gay-owned

Hotel Ciel Harbor Walk **631/597-6500** • mostly gay men • swimming • also restaurant • wheelchair access

The Madison Fire Island Pines 22 Atlantic Walk **631/597-6061** • mostly gay men • guesthouse w/ full amenities • pool • nonsmoking • WiFi • gay-owned

BARS

Blue Whale Harbor Walk, The Pines **631/597-6500** • seasonal • lesbians/ gay men • popular • dancing/DJ • popular Low Tea dance • also restaurant • wheelchair access

Cherry's On the Bay 158 Bayview Walk, Cherry Grove **631/597-7859** • seasonal • noon-4am • popular • lesbians/ gay men • dancing/DJ • piano bar • live shows • drag shows • also restaurant • patio

Pines Bistro & Martini Bar 36 Fire Island Blvd, The Pines **631/597-6862** • seasonal, opens 6pm

Sip • n • Twirl 36 Fire Island Blvd, The Pines **631/597-3599** • seasonal • noon-4am • mostly gay men • dancing/DJ

NIGHTCLUBS

Ice Palace Bayview Walk, Cherry Grove **631/597-6600** • hours vary • popular • lesbians/ gay men • dancing/DJ • drag shows • wheelchair access

CAFES

Canteen Harbor Walk, The Pines **631/597-6500** • coffee, smoothies, cocktails & food

RESTAURANTS

Cherry Grove Pizza Dock Walk (under the GroveHotel), Cherry Grove **631/597-6766** • seasonal • 11am-10pm

Marina Meat Market Harbor Walk, The Pines **631/597-6588** • great sandwiches

Pines Pizza 36 Fire Island Blvd, The Pines **631/597–3597** • seasonal, 11am-11pm

Sand Castle 140 Lewis Walk, Cherry Grove **631/597–4174** • seasonal • lunch & dinner • also bar

ENTERTAINMENT & RECREATION

Cherry Grove Beach • lesbians/ gay men • nude beach

Invasion of the Pines The Pines dock (July 4th wknd) • come & enjoy the annual fun as boatloads of drag queens from Cherry Grove arrive to terrorize the posh Pines

GYMS & HEALTH CLUBS

Deck Pool & Gym Harbor Walk, The Pines • 7am-6pm • day passes available

Geneva

ACCOMMODATIONS

Belhurst 4069 Rte 14 S (near Snell Rd) **315/781–0201** • gay-friendly • in historic castle overlooking Seneca Lake • fireplaces • also restaurant

Glens Falls

ACCOMMODATIONS

Glens Falls Inn 25 Sherman Ave **646/743–9365** • gay-friendly • B&B in Victorian • full brkfst • WiFi • woman-owned

Hamptons

see Long Island—Suffolk/ Hamptons

Hudson Valley

Hudson Valley includes Catskill, High Falls, Highland, Hudson, Hyde Park, Kinderhook, Kingston, New Paltz, Poughkeepsie, Rhinebeck & Saugerties

ACCOMMODATIONS

Barclay Heights B&B 158 Burt St (at Trinity Place), Saugerties **845/246–3788** • gay-friendly • full brkfst • cozy Victorian cottage • nonsmoking

The Country Squire B&B 251 Allen St (at 3rd), Hudson **518/822–9229** • gay/ straight • restored Queen Anne • kids ok • nonsmoking • WiFi

Harmony House B& B 1659 Route 212, Saugertie **845/679–1277** • gay/ straight • full brkfst • WiFi • gay-owned

Van Schaack House 20 Broad St (at Albany Rd), Kinderhook **518/758–6118** • gay-friendly • B&B • full brkfst • nonsmoking • gay-owned

RESTAURANTS

Armadillo Bar & Grill 97 Abeel St, Kingston **845/339–1550** • lunch wknds, dinner nightly, clsd Mon • full bar • patio

Northern Spy Cafe Rte 213, High Falls **845/687–7298** • dinner only, clsd Mon • plenty veggie • full bar • wheelchair access

Rock & Rye 215 Hugenot St (behind conference center), New Paltz **845/255–7888** • 5pm-close, Sun brunch 11am-3pm, clsd Mon-Tue

Terrapin 6426 Montgomery St, Rhinebeck **845/876–3330** • lunch & dinner • bistro & bar • patio

The Would Restaurant 120 North Rd (off Rte 9 W), Highland **845/691–9883** • dinner nightly, clsd Sun • some veggie • full bar • patio • gay-owned

ENTERTAINMENT & RECREATION

Dia:Beacon Riggio Galleries 3 Beekman St (at Rte 9D), Beacon **845/440–0100** • modern art museum

Ithaca

INFO LINES & SERVICES

AA Gay/ Lesbian 607/273–1541

ACCOMMODATIONS

Juniper Hill B&B 16 Elm St (at Main St), Trumansburg **607/387–3044, 888/809–1367** • gay-friendly • full brkfst • nonsmoking • WiFi • gay-owned

Noble House Farm 215 Connecticut Hill Rd, Newfield **607/277–4798** • gay-friendly • near gorges & wine tours • kids/ pets ok • nonsmoking • wheelchair access • lesbian-owned

William Henry Miller Inn 303 N Aurora St (at E Buffalo St) **607/256–4553, 877/256–4553** • gay-friendly • full brkfst • pets ok • kids over 12 ok • WiFi • nonsmoking

BARS

Felicia's Atomic Lounge 508 W State St (Meadow St) **607/273–2219** • 4pm-1am • clsd Mon • gay-friendly • food served • live entertainment • piano bar • lesbian-owned

Oasis 1230 Danby Rd/ Rte 96-B (at Comfort) **607/273–1505** • 4pm-1am, clsd Mon • popular • lesbians/ gay men • dancing/DJ • multiracial • live music Fri • also restaurant • wheelchair access

CAFES

Sarah's Patisserie 200 Pleasant Grove Rd (at Hanshaw Rd) **607/257-4257** • 10am-6pm, clsd Sun-Mon • lesbian-owned

ENTERTAINMENT & RECREATION

Out Loud Chorus 607/280-0374

Jamestown

ACCOMMODATIONS

Fairmount Motel 138 W Fairmount (Rte 394) **716/763-9550** • gay-friendly • near Chautauqua Institution • kids ok • WiFi • gay-owned

BARS

Sneakers 100 Harrison (at Institute) **716/484-8816** • 2pm-2am, clsd Mon • lesbians/ gay men • wheelchair access

ENTERTAINMENT & RECREATION

The Lucille Ball/ Desi Arnaz Center 2 W 3rd St (at Main) **716/484-0800, 877/582-9326** • for those who love Lucy

Little Falls

CAFES

Piccolo Cafe 365 Canal Pl **315/823-9856** • lunch Tue-Fri, dinner Wed-Sun, clsd Mon

LONG ISLAND

Long Island is divided into 2 geographical areas:
Long Island—Nassau
Long Island—Suffolk/ Hamptons
see also Fire Island

Long Island—Nassau

INFO LINES & SERVICES

Long Island GLBT Center 400 Garden City Plaza #110, Garden City **516/323-0011** • Long Island GLBT services network

NIGHTCLUBS

Pure Silk Westbury **516/474-1707** • 4pm-9pm Sun only • monthly party • check puresilkproductions.com • mostly women • dancing/DJ

RESTAURANTS

RS Jones 153 Merrick Ave (off Sunrise), Merrick **516/378-7177** • dinner, clsd Mon • Tex-Mex • women-owned

ENTERTAINMENT & RECREATION

Pride for Youth Coffeehouse 2050 Bellmore Ave, Bellmore **516/679-9000** • 7:30pm-11:30pm Fri • ages 13-20 • live music

Long Island—Suffolk/ Hamptons

INFO LINES & SERVICES

The Center at Bay Shore 34 Park Ave, Bay Shore **631/665-2300** • drop-in lounge w/ cybercenter • events

The Hamptons GLBT Center 44 Union St, Sag Harbor **831/899-4950** • Long Island GLBT services network

ACCOMMODATIONS

The Atlantic 1655 Country Rd 39, Southampton **631/283-6100** • gay-friendly • pool • jacuzzi • kids/pets ok • wheelchair access

East Hampton Village B&B 172 Newtown Ln (at McGuirk St), East Hampton **631/324-1858** • gay/ straight • lovely turn-of-the-century home • nonsmoking • WiFi

Mill House Inn 31 N Main St (at Newtown Lane), East Hampton **631/324-9766** • gay-friendly • full brkfst • nonsmoking • kids/ dogs ok • WiFi • wheelchair access

Stirling House B&B 104 Bay Ave, Greenport **631/477-0654, 800/551-0654** • gay-friendly • full brkfst • jacuzzi • nonsmoking • WiFi • gay-owned

Sunset Beach 35 Shore Rd, Shelter Island **631/749-2001** • gay-friendly • seasonal • food served

NIGHTCLUBS

Bunkhouse 620 Waverly Ave, Patchouge • 8pm-4am • mostly gay men • dancing/DJ • karaoke • live shows • wheelchair access • gay-owned

Wall Street Saturdays 575 Nesconset Hwy/ Rte 347, Hauppauge **516/909-4779** • Sat only • lesbians/ gay men • dancing/DJ

RESTAURANTS

Babette's 66 Newtown Ln, East Hampton **631/329-5377** • seasonal • brkfst, lunch & dinner • healthy • plenty veggie • woman-owned

ENTERTAINMENT & RECREATION

Fowler Beach Southampton

Middletown

ACCOMMODATIONS

Best Western Inn at Hunt's Landing 120 Rtes 6 & 209, Matamoras, PA 570/491-2400, 800/528-1234 • gay-friendly • pool • gym • restaurant & bar • WiFi

Montgomery

ACCOMMODATIONS

The Borland House B&B 130 Clinton St 845/457-1513 • gay-friendly • full brkfst • nonsmoking • WiFi

NEW YORK CITY

New York City is divided into 9 geographical areas:
NYC—Overview
NYC—Soho, Greenwich & Chelsea
NYC—Downtown
NYC—Midtown
NYC—Uptown
NYC—Brooklyn
NYC—Queens
NYC—Bronx
NYC—Staten Island

BARS

The Dalloway 525 Broome St 212/966-9620 • 5pm-2am, clsd Mon • two-level restaurant and cocktail lounge • lesbian-owned

The Rust Knot 425 West St (at 11th St) 212/645-5668 • 4pm-2am, from 2pm wknds • gay/ straight • LGBT Sunday Tea dance called Scissor Sundays • bar food served • wheelchair access

NYC—Overview

INFO LINES & SERVICES

AA Gay/ Lesbian Intergroup at Lesbian/ Gay Community Center 212/647-1680

Lesbian Herstory Archives 718/768-3953 • exists to gather & preserve records of lesbian lives & activities • located in Park Slope, Brooklyn • wheelchair access

LGBT Community Center 208 W 13th (at 7th Ave) 212/620-7310 • 9am-11pm • many group meetings & resources • museum • wheelchair access

ENTERTAINMENT & RECREATION

Before Stonewall: A Lesbian & Gay History Tour meet: Washington Square Arch (at Big Onion Walking Tours) 212/439-1090

Gotham Girls Roller Derby 888/830-2253 • NYC's female roller derby league

New York Liberty Madison Square Garden, New York 212/465-6766 • check out the Women's Nat'l Basketball Association while you're in New York

PUBLICATIONS

Gay City News 646/229-1890 • LGBT newspaper • weekly

Get Out Magazine 646/761-3325 • content from the hottest gay and gay-friendly spots in New York

GO Magazine 888/466-9244 • the nation's most widely distributed, free, lesbian publication • "cultural road map for the city girl" • listings, features, entertainment, style, fitness & more

MetroSource 212/691-5127 • LGBT lifestyle magazine & resource directory

Next Magazine • entertainment & nightlife paper

Odyssey Magazine 323/874-8788 • dish on NYC's club scene

Velvetpark Magazine 347/881-1025, 888/616-1989 • quarterly lesbian/ feminist glossy w/ focus on the arts

SEX CLUBS

Submit 718/789-4053 • monthly • women & trans play party • takes place in Park Slope, Brooklyn, call for exact location

NYC—Soho, Greenwich & Chelsea

INFO LINES & SERVICES

Audre Lorde Project 147 W 24th St 212/463-0342 • 1pm-7pm Tue-Th only • LGBT center for people of color • transgender welcoming

ACCOMMODATIONS

Ace Hotel 20 W 29th St (at Broadway) 212/679-2222 • gay-friendly • hip hotel near Flatiron District

Chelsea Pines Inn 317 W 14th St (btwn 8th & 9th Aves) 212/929-1023, 888/546-2700 • gay/ straight • WiFi • gay-owned

The Chelsea Savoy Hotel 204 W 23rd St (at 7th Ave) 212/929-9353, 866/929-9353 • gay/ straight • kids ok • WiFi • wheelchair access

Chelsea Star Hotel 300 W 30th St (at 8th Ave) 212/ 244-7827, 877/ 827-6969 • gay/ straight • WiFi

New York City

LGBT Pride:
Last Sunday in June. 212/807-7433, web: www.nycpride.org.
Brooklyn Pride - June. 718/928-3320, web: www.brooklynpride.org.

Annual Events:
May - AIDS Walk 212/807-9255, web: www.aidswalk.net/newyork.
May/June - NewFest: NY LGBT Film Festival 212/571–2170, web: www.newfestival.org.
July - HOT Festival of queer performance, web: hotfestival.org.
July - Siren Music Festival, web: www.villagevoice.com/siren.
September - Howl Festival 212/466–6666, web: www.howlfestival.com. Poetry & cabaret in Tompkins Square Park in the East Village.
November - New York Lesbian/Gay Experimental Film/Video Fest 212/742–8880, web: www.mixnyc.org. Film, videos, installations & media performances.

City Info:
212/484-1200 web, nycgo.com

Best View:
Coming over any of the bridges into New York or from the Empire State Building.

Weather:
A spectrum of extremes with pleasant moments thrown in. Spring and fall are the best times to visit.

Transit:
Wave an arm on any streetcorner for a taxi.
Public transit MTA 718/330-1234, web: www.mta.info.

Attractions:
American Museum of Natural History 212/769-5100, web: www.amnh.org.
Broadway.
Brooklyn Botanic Garden 718/623-7200, web: www.bbg.org.
Carnegie Hall 212/247-7800, web: www.carnegiehall.org.
Central Park.
Ellis Island, web: www.ellisisland.org.
Elizabeth A. Sackler Center for Feminist Art 718/638-5000, web: www.brooklynmuseum.org/eascfa.
Empire State Building 212/736-3100, web: www.esbnyc.com.
Greenwich Village.
9/11 Memorial Museum , web: www.911memorial.org.
Guggenheim Museum 212/423-3500, web: www.guggenheim.org.
International Center of Photography 212/857-0000, web: www.icp.org.
Lincoln Center 212/875-5000, web: www.lincolncenter.org.
Metropolitan Museum of Art 212/535-7710, web: www.metmuseum.org.
Museum of Modern Art 212/708-9400, web: www.moma.org.
Radio City Music Hall 212/307-7171, web: www.radiocity.com.
Rockefeller Center.
Statue of Liberty 866/782-8834.
Times Square.
United Nations 212/963-8687, web: www.un.org.
Wall Street.
World Trade Center Memorial.

Crosby Street Hotel 79 Crosby St (at Spring) 212/226-6400 • gay-friendly • chic boutique hotel in Soho • WiFi

Eventi 851 6th Ave (at 30th St) 212/564-4567, 866/996-8396 • gay-friendly • pets ok

The GEM Hotel Chelsea 300 W 22nd St (at 8th Ave) 212/675-1911 • gay/ straight • WiFi • wheelchair access • see ad in front color section

The GEM Hotel SoHo 135 E Houston St (btwn 1st & 2nd Aves) 212/358-8844 • gay/ straight • WiFi • wheelchair access • see ad in front color section

Gershwin Hotel 7 E 27th St (at 5th Ave) 212/545-8000 • gay-friendly • artsy hotel w/ model's floor dorms & rooms • art gallery • WiFi

Hotel 17 225 E 17th St 212/475-2845 • gay-friendly • "East Village chic" budget hotel • shared baths

Incentra Village House 32 8th Ave (at W 12th St) 212/206-0007 • gay/straight • nonsmoking • WiFi • gay-owned

The Jade Hotel 52 W 13th St (at 6th Ave) 212/375-1300 • gay-friendly

The Jane 113 Jane St (at Hudson River Pk) 212/924-6700 • gay/ straight • inspired by luxury train cabins • some shared baths • WiFi

Soho Grand Hotel 310 W Broadway (at Canal St) 212/965-3000, 800/965-3000 • gay-friendly • big, glossy, over-the-top hotel • WiFi • wheelchair access

The Standard Hotel 848 Washington St (at W 13th) 212/645-4646, 877/550-4646 • gay-friendly • ultra-modern, luxe hotel straddling the High Line • pool • WiFi

Tribeca Grand 2 Ave of the Americas 212/519-6600 • gay/ straight • WiFi • pets ok

Washington Square Hotel 103 Waverly Pl (at MacDougal St) 212/777-9515, 800/222-0418 • gay-friendly • on historic Washington Square Park • also North Square restaurant & lounge • WiFi

Wyndham Garden Hotel Chelsea 37 W 24th St 212/243-0800 • gay-friendly • WiFi • wheelchair access

BARS

Arrow Bar 85 Ave A (btwn 5th & 6th) 212/673-1775 • 4pm-close • gay/ straight • dancing/DJ • theme nights

Barracuda 275 W 22nd St (at 8th Ave) 212/645-8613 • 4pm-4am • popular • mostly gay men • live DJs • drag shows

Beauty Bar 231 E 14th St (at 3rd Ave) 212/539-1389 • 5pm-4am, from 7pm wknds • gay/ straight • dancing/DJ

The Boiler Room 86 E 4th St (at 2nd Ave) 212/254-7536 • 4pm-4am • mostly gay men • neighborhood bar • WiFi

Boots & Saddle 76 Christopher St (at 7th Ave S) 212/633-1986 • noon-4am • mostly gay men • neighborhood bar • bears & leather crowd • multiracial clientele

Cake Shop 152 Ludlow St (btwn Stanton & Rivington) 212/253-0036 • 9am-2am, till 4am wknds • gay-friendly • cafe/ bakery by day, punk bands at night

Cubbyhole 281 W 12th St (at 4th St) 212/243-9041 • 4pm-4am, from 2pm wknds • lesbians/ gay men • neighborhood bar

Eastern Bloc 505 E 6th St (at Ave A) 212/777-2555 • 7pm-4am • popular • lesbians/gay men • trendy lounge w/ DJ • go-go boys Th-Sat • wheelchair access

G Lounge 225 W 19th St (at 7th Ave) 212/929-1085 • 4pm-4am • mostly gay men • lounge • live DJs • gay-owned

Gym Sports Bar 167 8th Ave (btwn 18th & 19th) 212/337-2439 • 4pm-close, from 1pm wknds • mostly gay men • neighborhood sports bar

Henrietta Hudson 438 Hudson (at Morton) 212/924-3347 • 4pm-4am, from 2pm wknds • mostly women • neighborhood bar • dancing/DJ • wheelchair access

Julius' 159 W 10th St 212/243-1928 • 11am-2am, till 4am wknds • mostly gay men • neighborhood bar • food served

Marie's Crisis 59 Grove St (at 7th Ave) • 4pm-4am • lesbians/ gay men • piano bar from 9:30pm

The Monster 80 Grove St (at W 4th St, Sheridan Square) 212/924-3558 • 4pm-4am, from 2pm wknds • popular • mostly gay men • dancing/DJ • piano bar & cabaret • T-dance Sun • wheelchair access

Nowhere 322 E 14th St (btwn 1st & 2nd) 212/477-4744 • 3pm-4am • lesbians/ gay men • transgender-friendly • neighborhood bar

Phoenix 447 E 13th St (at Ave A) 212/477-9979 • 4pm-4am • lesbians/ gay men • neighborhood bar • patio

Stonewall Inn 53 Christopher St (at 7th Ave) 212/488-2705 • 2pm-4am • mostly gay men • neighborhood bar • dancing/DJ • drag shows

NIGHTCLUBS

Bar 13 35 E 13th St (btwn Broadway & 5th Ave) **212/979–6677** • 5pm-4am, till midnight Mon • gay/ straight • check local listings for gay events

Big Apple Ranch 39 W 19th St, 5th flr (btwn 5th & 6th, at Dance Manhattan) • 8pm-1am Sat only • lesbians/ gay men • dancing/DJ • country/ western • two-step lessons • beer & wine only • cover charge

Boys Night Out 369 W 46th St (at the Ritz) • Th only, mostly gay men, younger crowd

Happy Ending 302 Broome St (at Forsyth) **212/334–9676** • 7pm-4am, from 10pm Tues, clsd Sun-Mon • gay/ straight • theme nights

Hot Rabbit 80 Grove St (at W 4th, at the Monster) • 10pm Fri only • queer dance party • lots of girls

LipStik Productions 24 Murray St (at Broadway, at Club Remix) **917/363–6907** • 10pm Sat only, dress to impress • mostly women • dancing/DJ • multiracial • dress to impress

Penthaus Fridays 760 8th Ave (btwn 46th & 47th, at the Copa) • 11pm Fri • mostly men • rooftop dancing & cocktails • younger crowd

Pyramid 101 Ave A (at 7th St) **212/228–4888** • gay/ straight • dancing/DJ • theme nights

Sea Tea leaves from Pier 40 (West Side Hwy at Houston St) **212/675–2971** • 6pm-10pm Sun (June-Sept) • mostly gay men • dancing/DJ • professional • multiracial • buffet • live shows • gay-owned • cover

Stiletto 363 W 16th St (enter on W 17th St & 9th Ave, at the Cabanas at Maritime Hotel) • 7pm-2am Sun only (seasonal) • mostly women • dancing/DJ • upscale party

Sweet Fox 92 2nd Ave (at Lit Lounge) • 10pm Th only • lesbians/ gay men • dancing/DJ

CAFES

Brown Cup Cafe 334 8th Ave (at 27th St) **212/675–7765** • 7am-8pm, 8am-6pm Sat, clsd Sun

RESTAURANTS

7A 109 Ave A (at 7th St) **212/475–9001** • 24hrs • great fake meat & tasty mimosas!

Agave 140 Seventh Ave (btwn 10th St & Charles) **212/989–2100** • noon-close • popular brunch • Southwestern

Angelica Kitchen 300 E 12th St (at 1st Ave) **212/228–2909** • 11:30am-10:30pm • vegetarian/ vegan

Awash 338 E 6th (btwn 1st & 2nd Aves) **212/982–9589** • 11am-11pm • Ethiopian

Benny's Burritos 113 Greenwich (at Jane) **212/633–9210** • 11am-11pm, till midnight Fri-Sat • cheap & huge

Big Gay Ice Cream Shop 125 E 7th St (at 1st Ave) **212/533–9333** • 1pm-midnight • also Big Gay Ice Cream Truck from May-Oct

Blossom 187 9th Ave (at 21st) **212/627–1144** • lunch Fri-Sun, dinner nightly • gourmet vegan

Blue Ribbon 97 Sullivan St (at Spring St) **212/274–0404** • 4pm-4am • chef hangout • wheelchair access

Bone Lick Park 75 Greenwich Ave (at 7th Ave) **212/647–9600** • 11:30am-11pm • real pit BBQ • full bar • wheelchair access

Budhu Lounge 531 Hudson St (at Charles St) **917/262–0836** • 5:30pm-2am, till 4am Fri-Sat, 11am-midnight Sun

Cola's 148 8th Ave (at 17th St) **212/633–8020** • lunch & dinner • popular • Italian • some veggie

Cowgirl Hall of Fame 519 Hudson St (at W 10th) **212/633–1133** • lunch, dinner, wknd brunch

Crispo 240 W14th St (at 7th) **212/229–1818** • dinner only, great caramelized cauliflower & carbonara

East of Eighth 254 W 23rd St (at 8th) **212/352–0075** • lunch & dinner, bar open late

Elmo 156 7th Ave (at 20th St) **212/337–8000** • lunch & dinner, also lounge

Les Enfants Terribles 37 Canal St (at Ludlow) **212/777–7518** • 8am-4am • African/Moroccan, Brazilian, French • full bar & DJ

Gobo 401 Ave of the Americas (at W 8th) **212/255–3242** • 11:30am-11pm • vegetarian/ vegan

Intermezzo 202 8th Ave (at 21st St) **212/929–3433** • noon-midnight • Italian • great wknd brunch

LaVagna 545 E 5th St (btwn Aves A & B) **212/979–1005** • dinner only • Italian • some veggie

The Meatball Shop 200 9th St **212/257–4363** • 6pm-midnight, till 1am Fri-Sat, also on 84 Stanton, 64 Greenwich & 170 Bedford

The Noho Star 330 Lafayette St (at Bleecker) **212/925–0070** • 8am-midnight, from 10:30am wknds • eclectic European & Chinese

Omai 158 9th Ave (at 19th St) 212/633–0550 • dinner nightly • Vietnamese

Philip Marie 569 Hudson St (at 11th St) 212/242–6200 • noon-11pm, clsd Mon • New American dining • outside seating

Red Bamboo 140 W 4th St (at MacDougal) 212/260–1212 • noon-midnight • vegetarian/vegan

Sacred Chow 227 Sullivan St (btwn W 3rd St & Bleecker) 212/337–0863 • 11am-10pm, till 11pm Fri-Sat • gourmet vegan • juice & smoothie bar • baked goods • kosher • wheelchair access

Sigiri 91 1st Ave (btwn 5th & 6th Sts) 212/614–9333 • lunch & dinner • Sri Lankan

Trattoria Pesce Pasta 262 Bleecker St (at 6th Ave) 212/645–2993 • noon-midnight

Veselka 144 2nd Ave (at 9th St) 212/228–9682 • 24hrs • Ukrainian • great pierogi

ENTERTAINMENT & RECREATION

Chelsea Classics 260 W 23rd St (btwn 7th & 8th, at Clearview Cinema) 212/691–5519 • Th night only • drag diva Hedda Lettuce hosts camp movies

Dixon Place 161 Chrystie St (at Delancey) 212/219–0736 • many gay-themed productions • also HOT Festival of queer performance in July

High Line Gansevoort & W 30th St (btwn 9th & 11th Ave) 212/500–6035 • elevated train track converted to beautiful urban park

La Mama 74 E 4th St 212/475–7710 • experimental theater

Leslie/ Lohman Gay Art Foundation & Gallery 26 Wooster St (btwn Grand & Canal) 212/431–2609 • noon-6pm, clsd Sun-Mon

PS 122 150 1st Ave (at E 9th St) 212/477–5829, 212/352–3101 (TICKETS) • it's rough, it's raw, it's real New York performance art

WOW Cafe Theatre 59-61 E 4th St, 4th flr (btwn 2nd Ave & Bowery) • open Th-Sat • women & trans theater

BOOKSTORES

Bluestockings Women's Bookstore 172 Allen St (btwn Stanton & Rivington) 212/777–6028 • 11am-11pm • also cafe • nightly readings • performances • live music

The Bureau of General Services—Queer Division 27 Orchard St (nr Canal St) 646/457–0859 • 11am-7pm, noon-6pm Sun, clsd Mon • queer bookstore and event space hosted by Strange Loop Gallery

RETAIL SHOPS

Flight 001 96 Greenwich Ave (btwn Jane & 12th) 212/989–0001, 877/354–4481 • 11am-8pm, noon-6pm Sun • way cool travel gear

Rainbows & Triangles 192 8th Ave (at 19th St) 212/627–2166 • 11am-10pm, noon-9pm Sun • LGBT cards, books, gifts & more

EROTICA

Babeland 43 Mercer St (btwn Broome & Grande) 212/966–2120 • 11am-10pm, till 7pm Sun

Babeland 94 Rivington (btwn Orchard & Ludlow) 212/375–1701 • noon-10pm • owned by women

Pleasure Chest 156 7th Ave S (at Charles) 212/242–2158

NYC—Downtown

ACCOMMODATIONS

Gild Hall Wall Street 15 Gold St (at Platt) 212/232–7700, 212/232–7800 (RESERVATIONS) • gay/ straight • high-tech boutique hotel • also restaurant & lounge • wheelchair access

Millenium Hilton 55 Church St 212/693–2001, 877/692–4458 • pool • nonsmoking • wheelchair access

RESTAURANTS

La Flaca 384 Grand St 646/692–9259 • noon-4am • Mexican • full bar

NYC—Midtown

ACCOMMODATIONS

Chambers Hotel 15 W 56th St (at 5th Ave) 212/974–5656, 866/204–5656 • gay-friendly • upscale boutique hotel • fabulous art collection

Comfort Inn - Midtown West 442 W 36th St (btwn 9th & 10th) 212/714–6699 • gay-friendly • WiFi • wheelhair access

Distrikt Hotel 342 W 40th St (at 9th Ave) 646/831–6780, 888/444–5610 • gay-friendly • WiFi • upscale boutique hotel

The GEM Hotel Midtown West 449 W 36th St (at 10th Ave) 212/967–7206 • gay/ straight • WiFi • wheelchair access • see ad in front color section

Hotel 57 130 E 57th St (at Lexington) 212/753–8841, 800/497–6028 • gay-friendly • nonsmoking • WiFi • wheelchair access

The Hotel Metro 45 W 35th St (at 5th Ave) 212/947–2500, 800/356–3870 • gay-friendly • WiFi • wheelchair access

Hudson Hotel 356 W 58th St (at 9th) 512/554-6000, 800/697-1791 • magical hotel w/ trendy bars

Ink48 653 11th Ave (at 48th St) 212/757-0088, 877/843-8869 • gay-friendly • WiFi • luxe hotel in former printing house

Ivy Terrace 230 E 58th St 516/662-6862 • private studio rental • terrace • nonsmoking • women-owned

The MAve 61 Madison Ave (at 27th St) 212/532-7373 • gay-friendly • WiFi • pets ok

The Out NYC 510 W 42nd S 212/947-2999, 855/568-8692 • lesbians/ gay men • NYC's first straight-friendly urban resort • restaurant & club on-site

The Pod Hotel 230 E 51st Street (near 2nd Ave) 212/355-0300, 800/742-5945 • gay-friendly • nonsmoking • WiFi • compact rooms • rooftop lounge • wheelchair access

Room Mate Grace 125 W 45th St (near Sixth Ave) 212/354-2323 • gay-friendly • swimming pool nonsmoking • WiFi • wheelchair access

The Strand 33 W 37th St 212/448-1024 • gay-friendly • WiFi • cont'l brkfst

Travel Inn 515 W 42nd St (at 10th Ave) 212/695-7171, 800/869-4630 • gay-friendly • outdoor pool • fitness center • wheelchair access

The Tuscany 120 E 39th St (at Park Ave) 212/686-1600, 877/WHOTELS (RESERVATIONS ONLY) • gay/ straight • WiFi • also Parisian-style cafe-bar • wheelchair access

Bars

9th Avenue Saloon 656 9th Ave (at 46th St) 212/307-1503 • noon-4am • mostly gay men • neighborhood bar • karaoke

Atlas Social Club 753 9th Ave (btw 59th & 51) 212/262-8527 • 4pm-4am, decorated like an old school boxing gym

Bar Centrale 324 W 46th St (at 8th Ave) 212/581-3130 • 5pm-close • gay/ straight • neighborhood bar • celebs a-plenty

Bar Tini Ultra Lounge 642 10th Ave (at 45th) 917/388-2897 • 4pm-4am • mostly gay men • theme nights

Don't Tell Mama 343 W 46th St (at 9th Ave) 212/757-0788 • 4pm-4am • popular • gay-friendly • young crowd • piano bar & cabaret • cover + 2-drink minimum for cabaret • call for shows

Evolve 221 E 58th St (at 2nd Ave) 212/355-3395 • 4pm-4am • mostly gay men • theme nights

Flaming Saddle's Saloon 793 9th Ave 212/713-0481 • 4pm-2am, from 2pm Sat-Sun • lesbians/ gay men • dancing/DJ • country western

HK Hell's Kitchen 523 9th Ave (at 39th St) 212/913-9092 • swank lounge • also restaurant • theme nights

Industry 355 W 52nd St (at 9th Ave) 646/476-2747 • 4pm-4am • mostly gay men

The Ritz 369 W 46th St (btwn 8th & 9th Aves) 212/333-2554 • 4pm-4am • mostly gay men • dancing/DJ • great place for a drink pre- or post- theater • frag shows

Therapy 348 W 52nd St (at 9th) 212/397-1700 • 5pm-4am • lesbians/ gay men • live shows • cabaret • food served

Uncle Charlie's 139 E 45th St (btwn 3rd & Lexington) 212/661-9097 • 4pm-4am • mostly gay men • mostly Asian • open mic Fri-Sun • karaoke • piano bar

Vlada 331 W 51st St (btwn 8th & 9th) 212/974-8030 • 4pm-4am • mostly gay men • slick gay lounge & restaurant

Nightclubs

Escuelita 301 W 39th St (at 8th Ave) 212/631-0588 • 10pm-5am, more women Fri , clsd Mon & Wed • mostly gay men • dancing/DJ • drag shows • Latino/a • cover • 18+

Girlnation 531 Hudson St (at Charles St, at Budhu Lounge) 212/391-8053 • check facebook.com/girlnationnyc1 for events • mostly women • popular lounge party • dancing/DJ

LoverGirl NYC 60 E 2nd Ave (btwn 3rd & 4th at Bonafide) 212/252-3397 • 10:30pm-4am Sat • mostly women • dancing/DJ • multiracial • live shows • cover charge

The XL 512 W 42nd St 917/239-2999 • 4pm-4am • mostly gay men • dancing/DJ • live shows • cabaret • drag shows

Restaurants

44 1/2 626 10th Ave (btwn 44 & 45) 212/399-4450 • 5:30pm-close, brunch wknds • wheelchair access • gay-owned

44 & X Hell's Kitchen 622 10th Ave (at 44th St) 212/977-1170 • lunch & dinner • American comfort food • wheelchair access • gay-owned

A Voce 41 Madison Ave (at 26th) 212/545-8555 • lunch Mon-Fri, dinner nightly • Italian • reservations recommended

Arriba Arriba 762 9th Ave (at 51st) 212/489–0810 • noon-midnight, till 1am wknds • Mexican • great margaritas

Bamboo 52 344 W 52nd St (btwn 8th & 9th Aves) 212/315–2777 • noon-4am, from 4pm Sun • sushi • also sake bar • garden

Bann 350 W 50th St (btwn 8th & 9th Aves) 212/582–4446 • lunch Mon-Fri, dinner nightly • Korean

Lips 227 E 56th St (at 3rd Ave) 212/675–7710 • 6pm-midnight, till 1:30am Fri-Sat, gospel brunch Sun, clsd Mon • Italian/ American • served by queens

Lucky Cheng's 240 W 52nd St (btw B'way & 8th) 212/995–5500 • 5:30pm-midnight • popular • Asian/ fusion • full bar • drag shows • karaoke

Market Cafe 496 9th Ave (at 38th St) 212/967–3892 • lunch & dinner, wknd brunch • great food • gay-owned

Vynl 754 9th Ave (at 51st St) 212/974–2003 • 11am-11pm • also bar • also at 102 8th Ave

ENTERTAINMENT & RECREATION

Ars Nova 511 W 54th St (at 10th Ave) 212/489–9800 • many gay-themed productions

Empire State Building 350 5th Ave (btwn 33rd & 34th) • spectacular views of the city • visit day or night

Sex & the City Hotspots Tour 5th Ave, in front of the Pulitzer Fountain (at 58th St) 212/209–3370 • 3 hours • reservations a must!

EROTICA

Eve's Garden 119 W 57th St #1201 (btwn 6th & 7th) 212/757–8651 • 11am-7pm, clsd Sun • women's sexuality boutique

NYC—Uptown

ACCOMMODATIONS

710 Guest Suites 710 St Nicholas Ave (at 145th) 212/491–5622 • gay-friendly • modern, chic apt suites

BB Lodges 1598 Lexington Ave (btwn 101st & 102nd) 917/345–7914 • gay/ straight • private rooms w/ private kitchens • nonsmoking • WiFi • gay-owned

Harlem Renaissance House 212/226–1590 • gay/ straight • in heart of Harlem's Striver Row District • kids ok • nonsmoking • WiFi • gay-owned

Hotel Newton 2528 Broadway (btwn 94th & 95th) 212/678–6500, 800/643–5553 • gay/ straight • hotel on Upper West Side • nearest to Columbia University • wheelchair access

Mount Morris House B&B 12 Mount Morris Park W (at 121st St) 917/478–6214 • gay/ straight • private suites & apartments in 1888 historic Manhattan Mansion • WiFi • gay-owned

BARS

Brandy's Piano Bar 235 E 84th St (at 2nd Ave) 212/650–1944 • 4pm-4am • lesbians/ gay men • piano bar from 9:30pm

Cava Wine Bar 185 W 80th St (at Amsterdam) 212/724–2282 • 5:30pm-2am, from 3:30pm Sun • gay-friendly • also tapas

Suite 992 Amsterdam (at 109th St) 212/222–4600 • 5pm-4am • mostly gay men • friendly neighborhood bar • karaoke • drag shows

RESTAURANTS

Billie's Black 271 W 119th St (at St Nicholas Ave) 212/280–2248 • noon-midnight, till 4am Fri-Sat • soul food • also full bar • live music Th-Fri • karaoke • gay-owned

Joanne Trattoria 70 W 68th St (btw Columbus & Central Park W), New York 212/721–0068

NYC—Brooklyn

INFO LINES & SERVICES

Audre Lorde Project 85 S Oxford St 718/596–0342 • 1pm-7pm Tue-Th only • LGBT center for people of color • transgender welcoming • events, resources, HIV services

ACCOMMODATIONS

Hotel Le Bleu 370 4th Ave 718/625–1500, 866/427–6073 • gay-friendly • WiFi • cont'l bkfst

Hotel Le Jolie 235 Meeker Ave 718/625–2100, 866/526–4097 • gay-friendly • WiFi • cont'l bkfst •

The Loralei B&B 667 Argyle Rd (at Foster Ave) 646/228–4656 • gay/ straight • 1904 Victorian • nonsmoking • WiFi • gay-owned

South Slope Green B&B 452A 17th St (at 8th Ave) 347/721–6575 • gay/ straight • nonsmoking • WiFi • lesbian-owned

BARS

The Abbey 536 Driggs Ave (btwn N 7th & 8th), Williamsburg 718/599–4400 • 3pm-4am • gay/ straight • neighborhood bar

Alligator Lounge 600 Metropolitan Ave (at Lorimer) **718/599–4440** • 3pm-4am, from 1pm wknds • gay/straight • free pizza from 6pm • karaoke Th

Bar 4 444 7th Ave (at 15th St, in Park Slope) **718/832–9800** • 6pm-4am • gay/straight • neighborhood bar • DJ Fri-Sat • live music & performances

Branded Saloon 603 Vanderbilt Ave (at Bergen) **718/484–8704** • gay/straight • neighborhood bar • live shows • karaoke • gay-owned

Excelsior 390 5th Ave (btwn 6th & 7th) **718/832–1599** • 6pm-4am, from 2pm wknds • lesbians/gay men • patio

Ginger's Bar 363 5th Ave (btwn 5th & 6th Sts, in Park Slope) **718/788–0924** • 5pm-4am, from 2pm wknds • lesbians/gay men • neighborhood bar • patio • occasional live shows

Metropolitan 559 Lorimer St (at Metropolitan, in Williamsburg) **718/599–4444** • 3pm-4am • lesbians/gay men • comfy neighborhood bar w/ 2 fireplaces & patio • more women Wed • WiFi

Sugarland 221 N 9th St (at Driggs Ave) **718/599–4044** • 9pm-4am • gay/lesbian • dancing/DJ • live shows • karaoke

This N That 108 N 6th St (at Berry), Williamsburg **718/599–5959** • 4pm-4am • lesbians/gay men • neighborhood bar

NIGHTCLUBS

Club Langston 1073 Atlantic Ave (btwn Franklin & Classon) **718/622–5183** • 11pm-4am Th-Sun • mostly gay men • mostly African American • theme nights

Glasslands Gallery 289 Kent Ave, Williamsburg (btwn S 1st & S 2nd) **718/599–1450** • performance, art & dance space

Public Assembly 70 N 6th St **718/384–4586** • 7pm-2am • gay-friendly • performance venue • events & live bands, dance parties • check calendar for upcoming shows

CAFES

Outpost 1014 Fulton St (at Downing) **718/636–1260** • 7:30am-midnight, 9am-11pm wknds • lesbians/gay men • art gallery • young, artsy crowd • also beer/wine • gay-owned

RESTAURANTS

Alma 187 Columbia St (at Degraw) **718/643–5400** • dinner nightly, wknd brunch • upscale Mexican • outdoor rooftop seating w/ view of Manhattan • also B61 Bar downstairs

Beast 638 Bergen St (at Vanderbilt Ave) **718/399–6855** • dinner nightly, wknd brunch, also bar from 5pm

Bogota Latin Bistro 141 5th Ave (at St John's Pl) **718/230–3805** • dinner nightly, wknd brunch, clsd Tue • live music • gay-owned

ChipShop 383 5th Ave (at 6th St) **718/244–7746** • noon-10pm, till 11pm Th-Sat, from 11am wknds • home of the famous fried Twinkie!

home made 293 Van Brunt St (btwn Pioneer & King) **347/223–4135** • dinner & wknd brunch • lesbian-owned

Johnny Mack's 1114 8th Ave (btwn 11th & 12th) **718/832–7961** • 4pm-2am, from noon wknds

Krescendo 364 Atlantic Ave • famed chef Elizabeth Falkner makes pizza

Melt 440 Bergen St (btwn 5th & Flatbush) **718/230–5925** • dinner nightly, brunch wknds, clsd Mon

Nita Nita 146 Wythe Ave (at N 8th) **718/388–5328** • 4pm-2am, brunch wknds • also full bar • tapas

Santa Fe Grill 62 7th Ave (at Lincoln) **718/636–0279** • 5pm-close, from noon wknds • also bar

Superfine 126 Front St (at Pearl St) **718/243–9005** • 11:30am-3am, 2pm-11pm Sat, 11am-10pm Sun, clsd Mon • relaxed atmosphere • live shows • also bar • lesbian-owned

Tandem 236 Troutman St (btwn Wilson & Knickerbocker, in Bushwick) **718/386–2369** • 6pm-4am • also full bar • occasional gay parties

ENTERTAINMENT & RECREATION

The Elizabeth A Sackler Center for Feminist Art 200 Eastern Pkwy (at the Brooklyn Museum, at Washington Ave) **718/638–5000**

Galapagos Art Space 16 Main St (at Water St) **718/222–8500** • performance & art space • occasional gay parties

Ova the Rainbow 59 Montrose Ave (at The Spectrum) • monthly queer dance party • transgender-friendly

The Spectrum 59 Montrose Ave • queer performance space

EROTICA

Babeland 462 Bergen St (at 5th Ave) **718/638-3820** • noon-9pm, till 7pm Sun

NYC—Queens

BARS

Albatross 36-19 24th Ave (at 37th), Astoria **718/204-9045** • 6pm-4am • gay/ straight • neighborhood bar • more gay wknds • gay-owned

Elixir Lounge 43-03 Broadway, Astoria **347/642-5804** • 4pm-2am, till 4am Fri-Sat, mostly gay men • dancing/DJ • karaoke • drag shows

Hell Gate Social 12-21 Astoria Blvd (at 14th St) **718/204-8313** • 7pm-4am • gay/ straight • dancing/DJ

True Colors 79-15 Roosevelt Ave (btwn 79th & 80th Sts, Jackson Hts) **718/672-7505** • 4pm-4am • mostly gay men • neighborhood bar • dancing/DJ • multiracial

NIGHTCLUBS

Bum Bum Bar 6314 Roosevelt Ave **718/651-4145** • 10pm-4am Fri only • mostly women • dancing/DJ • mostly Latina

Evolution 76-19 Roosevelt Ave (at 77th St), Jackson Hts **718/457-3939** • 4pm-4am • lesbians/ gay men • dancing/DJ • mostly Latino/a • drag shows

RESTAURANTS

Monika's Cafe Bar 3290 36th St, Astoria **718/204-5273** • 10am-2am, till 4am Fri-Sat, Th gay night • Th gay night & great brunch menu

NYC—Bronx

BARS

No Parking 4168 Broadway (at 177th St) **212/923-8700** • 6pm-3am • mostly gay men • ¡Latina/o clientele • dancing/DJ • karaoke

Nyack

NIGHTCLUBS

Barz 327 Rte 9 W **845/353-4444** • 8pm-4am, from 3pm Sun, clsd Sun-Mon • lesbians/ gay men • dancing/DJ • alternative • karaoke

Orange County

EROTICA

Exotic Gifts & Videos 658 Rte 211 E (exit 120, off Rte 17), Middletown **845/692-6664**

Rochester

INFO LINES & SERVICES

Gay Alliance of the Genesee Valley (GAGV) 875 E Main St, 5th flr **585/244-8640** • events • education • SAGE & youth services

ACCOMMODATIONS

Silver Waters Bed & Breakfast 8420 Bay St (at Lummis), Sodus Point **315/483-8098** • gay/ straight • full brkfst • gay-owned

BARS

140 Alex Bar & Grill 140 Alexander St (at Broadway) **585/256-1000** • 4pm-2am, from 2pm Sun • lesbians/ gay men • neighborhood bar • also restaurant • dancing/DJ • live shows • karaoke • drag shows • gay-owned

Avenue Pub 522 Monroe Ave (at Goodman) **585/244-4960** • 4pm-2am • popular • mostly gay men • neighborhood bar • dancing/DJ • patio

NIGHTCLUBS

Tilt Nightclub 444 Central Ave **585/232-8440** • 10pm-2:30am Th-Sat • gay/ straight • dancing/DJ • drag shows

Vertex 169 N Chestnut St **585/232-5498** • 10pm-2am Wed-Sat • gay/ straight • dancing/DJ • goth club

CAFES

Little Theatre Cafe 240 East Ave **585/258-0400** • 5pm-10pm, till 11pm Fri-Sat, till 8pm Sun • popular • beer/ wine • soups • salads • live jazz • wheelchair access • art gallery

RETAIL SHOPS

Equal Grounds 750 South Ave (at Caroline) **585/256-2362** • 7am-midnight, from 10am wknds • LGBT gifts & books • also coffeehouse

Outlandish 274 N Goodman St (in the Village Gate) **585/760-8383** • 11am-9pm, noon-5pm Sun • videos • pride items • books • toys • gay-owned

PUBLICATIONS

Empty Closet **585/244-8640** • LGBT newspaper • resource listings

Saratoga Springs

ACCOMMODATIONS

The Inn at Round Lake 14 Covel Ave (at Burlington), Round Lake 518/899-4914 • gay-friendly • Victorian B&B • pool • nonsmoking • WiFi • gay-owned

The Mansion 801 Rte 29, Rock City Falls 518/885-1607, 888/996-9977 • gay-friendly • 1860 Victorian mansion • full brkfst • fireplaces • nonsmoking • wheelchair access • gay-owned

BARS

Desperate Annie's 12 Caroline St (off Broadway) 518/587-2455 • 4pm-close • gay-friendly • neighborhood bar

RESTAURANTS

Esperanto 6 1/2 Caroline St (off Broadway) 518/587-4236 • 11:30am-close • doughboys!

Little India 60 Court St 518/583-4151 • lunch & dinner • tasty & authentic Indian food • beer/ wine only

Seneca Falls

RETAIL SHOPS

WomanMade Products 91 Fall St 315/568-9364 • 10am-6pm, till 4pm wknds • lesbian & feminist T-shirts • crafts

Sharon Springs

ACCOMMODATIONS

American Hotel 192 Main St 518/284-2105 • gay/ straight • 1847 Nat'l Register hotel • kids ok • also restaurant & bar • WiFi • wheelchair access • gay-owned

Edgefield 153 Washington St 518/284-3339 • gay/ straight • full brkfst • nonsmoking • gay-owned

The TurnAround Spa Lodge 105 Washington St 518/284-9708 • lesbians/ gay men • small hotel & health spa • full brkfst • hot tub • food served • nonsmoking • kids ok • clsd Nov-April • lesbian- & gay-owned

Syracuse

INFO LINES & SERVICES

AA Gay/ Lesbian 315/463-5011 (AA#) • call for meeting schedule

BARS

Rain Lounge 103 N Geddes St 315/218-5951 • 4pm-2:30am • mostly men • neighborhood bar • multiracial • transgender-friendly • videos • gay-owned

Wolf's Den 617-619 Wolf St 315/560-5637 • 4pm -2am, till midnight Sun-Tue, from noon Sun for brunch • lesbians/gay men • neighborhood bar • karaoke

NIGHTCLUBS

Trexx 319 N Clinton St (exit 18, off Rte 81) 315/474-6408 • 8pm-2am, till 4am Fri-Sat, clsd Sun-Wed • mostly gay men • dancing/DJ • drag shows • videos • 18+ • wheelchair access

RESTAURANTS

Cafe Mira 14 Main St, Adams 315/232-4470 • open 5pm Wed-Sat only • wheelchair access • lesbian-owned

Utica

NIGHTCLUBS

That Place 216 Bleecker St (at Genesee) • 9pm-2am Th & Sat • popular • mostly gay men • dancing/DJ • young crowd • wheelchair access

RESTAURANTS

The Hadley 2008 Genesee St (at Arnold Ave) 315/507-4264 • 5pm-10pm, clsd Sun • also bar • pianist Fri-Sat • wheelchair access • gay-owned

Westchester

BARS

B Lounge 4 Broadway , Valhalla 914/437-5093 • 5pm-1am, till 4am Wed-Fri, 8pm-4am Sat, 6pm-1am Sun • lesbians/ gay men • dancing/DJ • karaoke

White Plains

INFO LINES & SERVICES

The LOFT 252 Bryant Ave 914/948-2932, 914/948-4922 (HELPLINE) • LGBT community center • call for hours • also newsletter

North Carolina

Asheville

Info Lines & Services

Lambda AA 9 Swan St (at Cathedral of All Souls Episcopal Church) **828/254–8539 (AA#), 800/524–0465** • 7pm Mon & Wed, 8pm Fri

Accommodations

1889 WhiteGate Inn & Cottage 173 E Chestnut St **828/253–2553, 800/485–3045** • gay/ straight • 3-course brkfst • nonsmoking • WiFi • gay-owned

The 1900 Inn on Montford 296 Montford Ave **828/254–9569, 800/254–9569** • gay-friendly • full brkfst • kids/ pets ok • nonsmoking • WiFi

27 Blake Street 27 Blake St **828/252–7390** • gay/ straight • private entrance in Victorian home • gardens • nonsmoking • WiFi • woman-owned

Biltmore Village Inn 119 Dodge St (at Irwin) **828/274–8707, 866/274–8779** • gay-friendly • nonsmoking • WiFi • gay-owned

Cedar Crest Inn 674 Biltmore Ave **828/252–1389 , 877/251–1389** • gay/ straight • full brkfst • gay-owned

Compassionate Expressions Mtn Inn & Healing Sanctuary **828/683–6633** • mostly women • cabins & rooms w/ a view of Blue Ridge Mtns • spa services • commitment ceremonies • nonsmoking • wheelchair access • women-owned

Mountain Laurel B&B 139 Lee Dotson Rd, Fairview **828/628–9903, 828/712–6289 (CELL)** • lesbians/ gay men • full brkfst • nonsmoking • kids ok • WiFi • lesbian-owned

North Lodge on Oakland B& B 84 Oakland Rd (at Victoria Rd) **828/252–6433, 800/252–3602** • gay-friendly • nonsmoking • WiFi • gay-owned

Rainbows End 23 Deaver St (at Reynolds) **253/732–0458** • mostly women • guest room in private home • shared baths • lesbian-owned

The Tree House 190 Tessie Ln, Black Mountain **828/669–3889** • mostly women • transgender-friendly • nonsmoking • lesbian/ trans-owned

Bars

O Henry's/ The Underground 237 Haywood St **828/254–1891** • 4pm-2am • mostly gay men • Underground from 10pm Fri-Sat only • dancing/DJ

Tressa's 28 Broadway **828/254–7072** • 4pm-2:30am, from 6pm Sat, clsd Sun • gay/ straight • jazz/ cigar bar • dancing/DJ • live shows

Nightclubs

Club Hairspray 38 N French Broad Ave (at Patton Ave) **828/258–2027** • 8pm-2am • lesbians/ gay men • neighborhood bar • drag shows • game room • patio

Scandals 11 Grove St (at Patton) **828/252–2838** • 10pm-3am Th-Sun • lesbians/ gay men • dancing/DJ • drag shows • videos • 18+ • private club • wheelchair access

Cafes

Edna's of Asheville 870 Merrimon Ave **828/255–3881** • 6am-10pm • beer/wine • WiFi • private club • wheelchair access • gay-owned

Laurey's 67 Biltmore Ave **828/252–1500** • 9am-6pm, till 4pm Sat, clsd Sun • popular • lesbian-owned • wheelchair access

Restaurants

Avenue M 791 Merrimon Ave **828/350–8181** • 5pm-late, 10am-2:30pm Sun, clsd Mon • full bar

Barley's Taproom & Pizzeria 42 Biltmore **828/255–0504** • 11:30am-2am, till midnight Sun

Charlotte Street Grill & Pub 157 Charlotte St **828/252–2948** • noon-2am • WiFi • lesbian-owned

Early Girl Eatery 8 Wall St **828/259–9292** • brkfst & lunch daily, dinner Tue-Sun, wknd brunch • Southern • local ingredients

Firestorm Cafe & Books 48 Commerce St **828/255–8115** • 10am-11pm, clsd Sun • vegetarian • WiFi • worker-owned

Laughing Seed Cafe 40 Wall St (at Haywood) **828/252–3445** • 11:30am-9pm, till 10pm Fri-Sat, Sun brunch from 10am, clsd Tue • vegetarian/ vegan • beer/ wine • patio • wheelchair access

Table 48 College St **828/254–8980** • 11am-2:30pm & 5:30pm-11pm, Sun brunch, clsd Tue • moderately priced New American

Tupelo Honey Cafe 12 College St **828/255–4404** • 9am-10pm • "Southern homecookin' w/ an uptown twist" • woman-owned

Entertainment & Recreation

LaZoom Tours 90 Biltmore Ave **828/225–6932** • city-wide comedy tours of Asheville, afternoons & evenings • BYOB

BOOKSTORES

Malaprop's Bookstore/ Cafe 55 Haywood St (at Walnut) 828/254–6734, 800/441–9829 • 9am-9pm, till 7pm Sun

RETAIL SHOPS

Jewels That Dance: Jewelry Design 63 Haywood St 828/254–5088 • 10:30am-6pm, clsd Sun • gay-owned

EROTICA

BedTyme Stories 2334 Hendersonville Rd, Arden 828/684–8250

Va Va Voom 36 Battery Park Ave 828/254–6329 • women's lingerie, toys, etc

Blowing Rock

ACCOMMODATIONS

Blowing Rock Victorian Inn 242 Ransom St (at US 321) 828/295–0034 • gay-friendly • full brkfst • pets ok • nonsmoking • WiFi • gay-owned

Brevard

ACCOMMODATIONS

Ash Grove Mountain Cabins & Camping 749 E Fork Rd 828/885–7216 • gay/ straight • camping & cabins • nonsmoking • WiFi • gay-owned

Charlotte

INFO LINES & SERVICES

Acceptance Group Gay/ Lesbian AA 2830 Dorcester Pl (at St. Paul United Methodist Church) 704/377–0244, 877/233–6853 • 8pm Fri

The Lesbian/ Gay Community Center 2508 N Davidson St 704/333–0144 • 5pm-8pm Tue-Th, 10am-1pm Fri-Sat, clsd Sun-Mon

ACCOMMODATIONS

VanLandingham Estate 2010 The Plaza (at Belvedere) 704/334–8909, 888/524–2020 • gay-friendly • full brkfst • nonsmoking • WiFi • gay-owned

BARS

The Bar At 316 316 Rensselaer Ave (at South Blvd) 704/910–1478 • 5pm-2am, from 3pm Sun • popular • lesbians/ gay men • neighborhood bar • private club

Hartigan's Irish Pub 601 S Cedar St (at W Hill St) 704/347–1841 • 11am-10pm, till 2am wknds, clsd Sun • gay/ straight • neighborhood bar • dancing/DJ Fri-Sat • live shows • karaoke • food served • popular lesbian hangout • gay-owned

Petra's Piano Bar 1917 Commonwealth Ave (at Thomas) 704/332–6608 • 5pm-2am, clsd Mon • gay/ straight • live shows • karaoke • WiFi

Sidelines Sports Bar & Billiards 704/525–2608 • 4pm-2am, from noon wknds • gay-friendly • neighborhood bar • food served • WiFi • private club • wheelchair access • gay-owned

NIGHTCLUBS

Cathode Azure Club 1820 South Blvd (near East Blvd) 704/823–6066 • 7pm-2am, from noon Sun • mostly gay men • dancing/DJ • drag shows

Marigny Dance Club 1440 S Tryon St #110 704/910–4444 • 10pm-2am, clsd Sun-Wed • gay/straight • dancing/DJ

The Nickel Bar 704/916–9389 • 9pm-2am, from 5pm Sun, clsd Mon-Wed • lesbians/ gay men • dancing/DJ • mostly African American

Scorpio's 2301 Freedom Dr (at Berryhill Rd) 704/373–9124 • 9pm-3am Wed & Fri-Sun • lesbians/ gay men • dancing/DJ • multiracial • 18+ • private club • wheelchair access

UpStage 3306 N Davidson St (at E 36th St) 704/430–4821 • gay/ straight • performing arts and creative events

CAFES

Amelie's French Bakery 2424 N Davidson St 704/376–1781 • open 24hrs • soup & sandwiches, & of course pastries!

Smelly Cat Coffee 514 E 36th St 704/374–9656 • 7am-10pm, till 1am Fri-Sat

RESTAURANTS

300 East 300 East Blvd (at Cleveland) 704/332–6507 • 11am-10pm, till 11pm Fri-Sat, Sun brunch • full bar • wheelchair access

Alexander Michael's 401 W 9th St (at Pine) 704/332–6789 • lunch & dinner, clsd Sun • pub fare • full bar

Cosmos Cafe 300 N College (at 6th) 704/372–3553 • 11am-2am, clsd Sun • also martini lounge

Dish 1220 Thomas Ave (at Central) 704/344–0343 • 11am-10pm, till 11pm Fri-Sat, clsd Sun • comfort food • patio

Lupie's Cafe 2718 Monroe Rd (near 5th St) 704/374-1232 • 11am-10pm, from noon Sat, clsd Sun • homestyle cookin' • some veggie

Penguin Drive-In 1921 Commonwealth Ave (at Thomas) 704/375-1925 • 11am-1am, till 2am wknds • diner extraordinaire • full bar

ENTERTAINMENT & RECREATION

One Voice Chorus PO Box 9241 28299 • LGBT chorus

BOOKSTORES

Paper Skyscraper 330 East Blvd (at Euclid Ave) 704/333-7130 • 10am-7pm, till 6pm Sat, noon-5pm Sun • books • funky gifts • wheelchair access

White Rabbit Books 920 Central Ave (at E 10th) 704/377-4067 • 10am-9pm, noon-6pm Sun • LGBT • books • magazines • T-shirts • DVDs • novelties

RETAIL SHOPS

The Bag Lady 1710 Kenilworth Ave (at East Blvd) 704/338-9778 • books & gifts • events

PUBLICATIONS

Q Notes 704/531-9988 • bi-weekly LGBT newspaper for the Carolinas

Fayetteville

NIGHTCLUBS

Alias 984 Old McPherson Church Rd (at Raeford Rd) 910/484-7994 • 9pm-2:30am Fri-Sat only • lesbians/ gay men • dancing/DJ • multiracial • transgender-friendly • 18+ • private club • gay-owned

EROTICA

Cupid's Boutique 137 N Reilly Rd (at Morganton) 910/860-7716

Fort Video & News 4431 Bragg Blvd (near 401 overpass) 910/868-9905 • 24hrs

Priscilla McCall's 3800 Sycamore Dairy Rd (at Bragg Blvd) 910/860-1776

Greensboro

INFO LINES & SERVICES

Live & Let Live AA 617 N Elm St (at Presbyterian Church) 336/854-4278 (AA#) • 8pm Tue • also Free Spirit, 8pm Sat, 2105 W Market St (at Episcopal Church)

ACCOMMODATIONS

Biltmore Greensboro Hotel 111 W Washington St (at Elm St) 336/272-3474, 800/332-0303 • gay/ straight • fully restored historic hotel • gym • WiFi • kids/ pets ok • wine & cheese tastings • nonsmoking • gay-owned

O Henry Hotel 624 Green Valley Rd (at Benjamin Pkwy) 336/854-2000, 800/965-8259 • gay-friendly • pool • full brkfst • afternoon tea • bar/ restaurant popular w/ local gay community • wheelchair access

BARS

The Q 708 W Market St 336/272-2587 • 4pm-close, from 9pm Sat, from 7pm Sun • lesbians/ gay men • more women Sun • neighborhood bar • DJ • karaoke • 18+ • WiFi • patio

Time Out Saloon 330 Bellemeade St 336/272-8108 • 8:30pm-2:30am, clsd Sun-Mon • mostly women • neighborhood bar • dancing/DJ • karaoke • private club • lesbian-owned

NIGHTCLUBS

Chemistry 2901 Spring Garden St 336/617-8571 • 8pm-2:30am, from 5pm Fri & Sun • mostly gay men • dancing/DJ • drag shows • karaoke

Warehouse 29 1011 Arnold St 336/333-9333 • 9:30pm-2:30am Th-Sun, add'l summer hours • mostly gay men • dancing/DJ • live shows • T-dance Sun (summers) • patio bar • volleyball • 18+ • private club

Havelock

NIGHTCLUBS

Club Above & Beyond 114 Crocker Rd 252/266-0114 • open 8pm, from 10pm Sat, clsd Wed • lesbians/ gay men • dancing/DJ • drag shows • private club

Hickory

NIGHTCLUBS

Club Cabaret 101 N Center St (at 1st Ave) 828/322-8103 • 8pm-2am, from 9pm Fri-Sat, clsd Mon-Wed • lesbians/ gay men • dancing/DJ • live shows • WiFi • private club • wheelchair access

CAFES

Taste Full Beans 29 2nd St NW 828/325-0108 • 7am-5:30pm, till 2:30 Sat, clsd Sun • art exhibits • gay-owned

Jacksonville

EROTICA

Priscilla McCall's 113–A Western Blvd
910/355-0765

Little Switzerland

ACCOMMODATIONS

La Petite Chalet 38 Orchard Ln (at Hwy
226A) **888/828-1654** • gay/ straight • located
on the Blue Ridge Parkway of North Carolina
midway between Asheville & Blowing Rock •
gay-owned

Madison

ACCOMMODATIONS

Hunter House B&B 216 W Hunter St
336/445-4730 • gay/ straight • patio •
gardens • pool • pets on premises •
nonsmoking • WiFi • gay-owned

Mooresville

RESTAURANTS

Pomodoro's Italian American Cafe 168
Norman Station Blvd **704/663-6686** • 11am-
10pm, till 11pm Fri-Sat • beer/ wine •
wheelchair access • gay-owned

Raleigh/Durham/Chapel Hill

INFO LINES & SERVICES

Common Solutions Gay/ Lesbian AA
Crownwell Bldg, East Campus (at Duke
University), Durham **919/286-9499** (AA#) •
6:30pm Mon

LGBT Center of Raleigh 411 Hillsborough
St, Raleigh **919/832-4484** • social &
educational activities, services & groups

ACCOMMODATIONS

Heartfriends Inn B&B 4389 Siler City/Snow
Camp Rd (at Ed Clapp Rd), Siler City
919/663-1707, 877/679-0980 • gay/ straight •
WiFi • women-owned • wheelchair access

The King's Daughters Inn 204 N Buchanan
Blvd, Durham **919/354-7000, 877/534-8534** •
gay-friendly • complimentary bikes

BARS

Flex 2 S West St (at Hillsborough), Raleigh
919/832-8855 • 5pm-close, from 2pm Sun •
popular • mostly gay men • karaoke • drag
shows • private club

Hibernian Restaurant & Pub 311
Glenwood Ave (at W Lane St), Raleigh
919/833-2258 • 11am-2am • gay-friendly •
live music

NIGHTCLUBS

313 313 W Hargett St (at Harrington),
Raleigh **919/755-9599** • 8pm-close • mostly
gay men • dancing/DJ • live/ drag shows •
piano bar • private club • wheelchair access

The Bar 711 Rigsbee Ave, Durham
919/956-2929 • 4pm-2am • lesbians/ gay
men • dancing/DJ • deck • karaoke • private
club • wheelchair access • lesbian-owned

Icon Nightclub 320 E Durham Rd, Cary
919/460-4343 • 8pm-2am Tue & 9pm-3:30am
Fri-Sat • lesbians/ gay men • dancing/DJ •
drag shows • karaoke • mostly African
American

Legends/ View 330 W Hargett St (at S
Harrington St), Raleigh **919/831-8888** • 5pm-
2:30am • lesbians/ gay men • dancing/DJ •
strippers • drag shows • young crowd • private
club • wheelchair access

The Pinhook 117 W Main St, Durham
991/667-1100 • 5pm-2am, 6pm-midnight
Sun • gay/ straight • live music • patio

Stir 157 E Rosemary (at The Thrill), Chapel
Hill **919/929-0024** • 9pm Sun only • mostly
gay men • dancing/DJ

The T 423 W Franklin St (at the Lantern),
Chapel Hill **919/969-8846** • 10pm Tue only •
lesbians/ gay men • chic, eclectic crowd

CAFES

Bean Traders 105-249 W NC Hwy 54,
Durham **919/484-2499** • 6am-8pm, from 8am
wknds

Cafe Helios 413 Glenwood Ave (at North St),
Raleigh **919/838-5177** • 7am-10pm, 8am-
6pm Sun • also beer & wine • patio

Caffe Driade 1215 E Franklin St #A (at
Elizabeth St), Chapel Hill **919/942-2333** •
7am-11pm • live music • also beer & wine
served

Third Place 1811 Glenwood Ave (at W
Whitaker Mill Rd), Raleigh **919/834-6566** •
6am-7pm • also sandwiches & salads

RESTAURANTS

Blu Seafood & Bar 2002 Hillsborough Rd
(at 9th St), Durham **919/286-9777** • lunch &
dinner, clsd Sun

The Borough 317 W Morgan St, Raleigh
919/832-8433 • 4pm-2am • also bar • WiFi

Crooks Corner 610 Franklin St (at Merritt Mill Rd), Chapel Hill **919/929–7643** • dinner nightly, Sun brunch, clsd Mon • Southern • full bar • patio • wheelchair access

Dain's Place 754 9th St (at Markham), Durham • 11am-2am, from 5pm Mon, 9am Sat • great burgers & pub food • also bar • WiFi

Elmo's Diner 776 9th St (in the Carr Mill Mall), Durham **919/416–3823** • 6:30am-10pm

Five Star 511 W Hargett St (at West St), Raleigh **919/833–3311** • 5:30pm-2am • Asian-fusion • sexy ambiance for cocktails & nibbles

Humble Pie 317 S Harrington St (at Martin), Raleigh **919/829–9222** • 5pm-11pm, bar open late, brunch only Sun • small plates

Irregardless Cafe 901 W Morgan St (at Hillsborough), Raleigh **919/833–8898** • lunch Tue-Fri, dinner Tue-Sat, Sun brunch, clsd Mon • plenty veggie • live music • dancing Sat

Lantern 423 W Franklin St, Chapel Hill **919/969–8846** • dinner nightly, clsd Sun • Asian • also cocktail lounge till 2am

The Mad Hatter's Bakeshop & Cafe 1802 W Main St (at Broad), Durham **919/286–1987** • 7am-9pm, 8am-3pm Sun • awesome cakes & baked goods • WiFi

The Pit 328 W Davie St (at S Dawson), Raleigh **919/890–4500** • 11am-10pm, till 11pm wknds • upscale BBQ

Rue Cler 401 E Chapel Hill St (at Mangum St), Durham **919/682–8844** • lunch & dinner, wknd brunch • French

Raleigh/Durham/Chapel Hill

LGBT PRIDE:
September, Durham. web: www.ncpride.org.

ANNUAL EVENTS:
August - North Carolina Gay and Lesbian Film Festival, web: www.carolinatheatre.org/ncglff.

CITY INFO:
919/834-5900 or 800/849-8499, web: www.visitraleigh.com. Chapel Hill/Orange County Visitors Bureau 888/968-2060, web: www.chocvb.org.

TRANSIT:
Regional Transit Information 919/485-7433, web: www.gotriangle.org.

ATTRACTIONS:
Ackland Art Museum, Chapel Hill 919/966-5736, web: www.ackland.org.
African-American Dance Ensemble, Durham 919/560-2729, web: www.africanamerican-danceensemble.org.
City Market, Raleigh, web: citymarketraleigh.com.
Duke University, Durham.

Exploris (interactive global learning center), Raleigh 919/834-4040, web: www.marbleskidsmuseum.org.
Morehead Planetarium & Science Center 919/962-1236, web: www.moreheadplanetarium.org.
NC Botanical Garden, Chapel Hill 919/962-0522, web: www.ncbg.unc.edu.
NC Museum of Art, Raleigh 919/839-6262, web: www.ncartmuseum.org.
NC Museum of Life & Science, Durham 919/220-5429, web: www.ncmls.org.
Oakwood Historic District, Raleigh.
University of North Carolina, Chapel Hill.
W. Franklin St. in Chapel Hill, south of UNC and into Carrboro— charming and hip shopping area.

Solas 919/755-0755 • dinner, Sun brunch • upscale dining • dress code • also rooftop lounge & nightclub

Spotted Dog 111 E Main St (at N Greensboro St), Carrboro 919/933-1117 • 11:30am-midnight, clsd Mon • full bar • plenty veggie

Sunrise Biscuit Kitchen 1305 E Franklin St, Chapel Hill 919/933-1324 • great brkfst • drive-thru only

Vivace 4209 Lassiter Mill Rd #115 (at Pamlico Dr), Raleigh 919/787-7747 • lunch & dinner, Sun brunch • Italian • patio seating • full bar

ENTERTAINMENT & RECREATION

Carolina Rollergirls • NC's female roller derby league • visit carolinarollergirls.com for events

BOOKSTORES

Internationalist Books & Community Center 405 W Franklin St (at Kenan St), Chapel Hill 919/942-1740 • 11am-8pm, noon-6pm Sun • progressive/ alternative • cooperatively run • nonprofit • readings & events

Quail Ridge Books 3522 Wade Ave (at Ridgewood Center), Raleigh 919/828-1588, 800/672-6789 • 9am-9pm • LGBT section

The Regulator Bookshop 720 9th St (btwn Hillsborough & Perry), Durham 919/286-2700 • 10am-9pm, noon-6pm Sun

EROTICA

Castle Video & News 1210 Capitol Blvd, Raleigh 919/836-9189 • 24hrs

Cherry Pie 1819 Fordham Blvd, Chapel Hill 919/928-0499 • 10am-midnight • adult toys

Frisky Business Boutique 1720 New Raleigh Hwy, Durham 919/957-4441 • adult toys • also classes

Rocky Mount

NIGHTCLUBS

Liquid Nightclub 313 Falls Rd 252/266-6464 • 8pm-3am Sat only • mostly gay men • dancing/DJ • go-go dancers • mostly African American

Washington

CAFES

Back Water Jack's Tiki Bar 1052 E Main St (at Havens St) 252/975-1090 • lunch & dinner, clsd Mon • also bar • wheelchair access

Wilmington

ACCOMMODATIONS

Best Western Coastline Inn 503 Nutt St 910/763-2800 • gay/ straight • kids ok • nonsmoking • wheelchair access • WiFi • gay-owned

Rosehill Inn B&B 114 S 3rd St (at Dock St) 910/815-0250, 800/815-0250 • gay-friendly • WiFi

The Taylor House Inn 14 N 7th St 910/763-7581, 800/382-9982 • gay/ straight • romantic 1905 house • full brkfst • nonsmoking • kids ok

BARS

Costello's 211 Princess St (btwn 2nd & 3rd) 910/470-9666 • 7pm-2am, from 5pm Fri • mostly gay men, more women Mon • piano bar • videos • private club • wheelchair access • gay-owned

Tool Box 2325 Burnett Blvd 910/343-6988 • 7pm-1am, till 2am Th-Sat • mostly gay men • neighborhood bar • dancing/DJ • karaoke • WiFi • gay-owned

NIGHTCLUBS

Ibiza 118 Market St (rear) 910/251-1301 • 8pm-3am Wed-Sun only • mostly gay men • dancing/DJ • more women Th • karaoke • drag shows • strippers • young crowd • private club • wheelchair access • gay-owned

RESTAURANTS

Caffe Phoenix 9 S Front St 910/343-1395 • 11:30am-10pm, Sun brunch • Mediterranean • some veggie • gay-owned

ENTERTAINMENT & RECREATION

Cinematique 310 Chestnut St (at Thalian Hall) 910/343-1640 • classic, foreign & notable films

NORTH DAKOTA

Fargo

INFO LINES & SERVICES

Pride Collective & Community Center 116 12th St S (at Main Ave), Moorhead, MN 218/287-8034 • 6pm-7:30pm Tue • referrals • support • social groups • check www.pridecollective.com for events

ACCOMMODATIONS

The Hotel Donaldson 101 Broadway 701/478-1000, 888/478-8768 • gay/ straight • restaurant & bar • WiFi

CAFES

Atomic Coffee 701/478-6160 • 7am-11pm, 8pm-10pm Sun • food served • plenty veggie/vegan • WiFi

RESTAURANTS

Fargo's Fryn' Pan 300 Main St (at 4th) 701/293-9952 • 24hrs • popular • wheelchair access

Mom's Kitchen 1322 Main St 701/235-4460 • 6am-10pm • full bar

RETAIL SHOPS

Zandbroz Variety 420 N Broadway 701/239-4729 • 9am-8pm, noon-5pm Sun • books & gifts

EROTICA

Romantix Adult Superstore 417 N Pacific Ave 701/235-2640 • 9am-3am

Grand Forks

EROTICA

Romantix Adult Superstore 102 S 3rd St (at Kittson) 701/772-9021

Minot

EROTICA

Risque's 1514 S Broadway 701/838-2837

OHIO

Statewide

PUBLICATIONS

Gay People's Chronicle 216/916-9338 • Ohio's largest bi-weekly LGBT newspaper w/ extensive listings

Outlook 614/268-8525 • statewide LGBT newsweekly • good resource pages

Akron

INFO LINES & SERVICES

AA Intergroup 330/253-8181 (AA#)

Akron Pride Center 895 N Main St 330/252-1559 • call for meeting schedule

BARS

Adams Street Bar 77 N Adams St (at Upson) 330/434-9794 • 4pm-2am, from 9pm Sun • popular • mostly gay men • piano bar Wed • dancing/DJ Fri-Sat • food served • strippers • WiFi

Cocktails 1009 S Main St (at Crosier) 330/376-2625 • 11am-2:30am • mostly gay men • videos • drag king show Mon • Daddy's leather bar upstairs wknds

The Office Bistro & Lounge 778 N Main St (at Cuyahoga Falls Ave) 330/376-9550 • 11am-2:30am • gay-friendly • bi-sexual friendly • neighborhood bistro & lounge • multiracial • WiFi • wheelchair access

Roseto Club 627 S Arlington St (at Bittaker) 330/724-4228 • 6pm-2:30am, clsd Sun • mostly women • dancing/DJ • karaoke • wheelchair access

Tear-Ez 360 S Main St (near Exchange St) 330/376-0011 • 11am-2:30am, from noon Sun • lesbians/gay men • neighborhood bar • drag shows Th & Sun • WiFi • wheelchair access

NIGHTCLUBS

Interbelt 70 N Howard St (near Perkins & Main) 330/253-5700 • 9pm-2:30am • lesbians/gay men • dancing/DJ • live shows • videos • patio

Square 820 W Market St (near Portage Path) 330/374-9661 • 5pm-2:30am, from 8pm Sat, from 7pm Sun • mostly gay men • dancing/DJ • karaoke • wheelchair access • gay-owned

CAFES

Angel Falls Coffee Company 792 W Market St (btwn S Highland & Grand) 330/376-5282 • 7am-10pm • lunch & desserts • patio • WiFi • wheelchair access • gay-owned

RESTAURANTS

Aladdin's Eatery 782 W Market St (at Grand) 330/535-0110 • 11am-10pm • Middle Eastern

Bricco 1 W Exchange St (at S Main St) 330/475-1600 • 11am-midnight, till 1am Fri-Sat, 4pm-9pm Sun • Italian • also bar • gay-owned

Bruegger's Bagels 1821 Merriman Rd 330/867-8394 • 6am-4pm

Athens

ACCOMMODATIONS

SuBAMUH (Susan B Anthony Memorial UnRest Home) Womyn's Land Trust PO Box 5853, 45701 740/448-6424 • women only • cabins & camping • summer workshops • swimming • hot tub • nonsmoking • lesbian-owned

Brunswick

see also Akron & Cleveland

RESTAURANTS

Pizza Marcello 67–A Pearl Rd (near Boston Rd) 330/225-1211 • 3pm-close, from noon wknds • Italian

Canton

NIGHTCLUBS

Crew 304 Cherry Ave NE (at 3rd) 330/452-2739 • 6pm-2:30am, from 9pm Sat-Sun • lesbians/ gay men • dancing/DJ • karaoke • cabaret

Cincinnati

INFO LINES & SERVICES

AA Gay/ Lesbian 328 W McMillan St (enter at 445 Herman St), Corryville 513/351-0422 (AA#) • 8pm Wed • call for locations of wknd meetings

Gay/ Lesbian Community Center of Greater Cincinnati 4119 Hamilton Ave (near Blue Rock) 513/591-0200 • 6pm-9pm, noon-4pm Sat, clsd Sun

ACCOMMODATIONS

Cincinnatian Hotel 601 Vine St (at 6th St) 513/381-3000, 800/942-9000 • gay-friendly • restaurant & lounge • kids ok • nonsmoking • WiFi • wheelchair access

Crowne Plaza 5901 Pfeiffer Rd (at I-71) 513/793-4500, 800/468-3597 • gay-friendly • pool • kids ok • WiFi • wheelchair access

First Farm Inn 2510 Stevens Rd, Petersburg, KY 859/586-0199 • gay-friendly • 20 minutes from Cincinnati • full brkfst • WiFi • nonsmoking

Millennium Hotel Cincinnati 150 W 5th St 513/352-2100, 800/876-2100 • gay-friendly • outdoor rooftop pool & sundeck • WiFi • wheelchair access

Weller Haus B&B 319 Poplar St, Bellevue, KY 859/391-8315, 800/431-4287 • gay-friendly • jacuzzis • nonsmoking • WiFi

BARS

Below Zero Lounge 1120 Walnut St (at E Central Pkwy) 513/421-9376 • 4pm-2:30am, clsd Mon-Tue • dancing/DJ • live music • karaoke • dancing/DJ • food served • WiFi

Junkers Tavern 4158 Langland St (at Chase) 513/541-5470 • 9am-1am • gay-friendly • neighborhood bar • karaoke • live bands

Cincinnati

LGBT PRIDE:
May/June. web: www.cincinnatipride.org.

CITY INFO:
513/621-2142 or 800/543-2613, web: www.cincyusa.com.

BEST VIEW:
Mt Adams & Eden Park.

TRANSIT:
Yellow Cab 513/821-8294, web: aaataxi.net.
SORTA 513/621-4455, web: www.sorta.com.

ATTRACTIONS:
The Beach waterpark (in Mason) 513/398-7946, web: www.thebeachwaterpark.com.
Carew Tower 513/241-3888.
Cincinnati Art Museum 513/639-2995, web: www.cincinnatiartmuseum.org.
Fountain Square.
Krohn Conservatory 513/421-4086.
Museum Center at Union Terminal 513/287-7000, web: www.cincymuseum.org.
Paramount King's Island (24 miles N of Cincinnati) 513/754-5700, web: www.visitkingsisland.com.

The Main Event 835 Main St (at 9th) 513/421–1294 • 6am-2:30am, from 11am Sun • gay/ straight • neighborhood bar

Milton's 301 Milton St (at Sycamore) 513/784–9938 • 4pm-2:30am • gay-friendly • neighborhood bar

Shooters 927 Race St (at Court) 513/381–9900 • 4pm-2:30am • mostly gay men • dancing/DJ • country/ western • more women Th • karaoke Wed

Simon Says 428 Walnut St (at 5th) 513/381–7577 • 11am-2:30am, from 1pm Sun • popular • mostly gay men • professional • neighborhood bar • wheelchair access

NIGHTCLUBS

Adonis 4601 Kellogg Ave (at Stites Rd) 513/871–1542 • 9pm-3am Sat only • lesbians/ gay men • dancing/DJ • transgender-friendly • drag shows

The Cabaret 1122 Walnut St (at E Central Pkwy) 513/284–2050 • 10pm-2am Th-Sun • mostly gay men • drag shows

The Dock 603 W Pete Rose Wy (near Central) 513/241–5623 • 10pm-3am, till 4am Fri-Sat, clsd Mon-Wed • popular • lesbians/ gay men • multiracial • dancing/DJ • drag shows • live shows • 19+ • volleyball court • wheelchair access

Girlicious 4601 Kellogg Ave (at Stites Rd, at Adonis) 513/871–1542 • 9pm-3am 4th Fri only • mostly women • dancing/DJ • transgender-friendly

CAFES

College Hill Coffee Co 6128 Hamilton Ave (at North Bend Rd) 513/542–2739 • 6:30am-6:30pm, till 10pm Fri, 8:30am-10pm Sat, till 4pm Sun, clsd Mon • live music Sat • WiFi • wheelchair access

Zen & Now 4453 Bridgetown Rd 513/598–8999 • 7am-7pm, till 10pm Fri-Sat, clsd Sun • WiFi

RESTAURANTS

Boca 3200 Madison Rd (at Brazee St), Oakley 513/542–2022 • dinner Tue-Sat, clsd Sun • full bar • patio • wheelchair access

Honey 4034 Hamilton Ave (at Blue Rock) 513/541–4300 • dinner & Sun brunch, clsd Mon, casual fine dining • wheelchair access

The Loving Hut 6227 Montgomery Rd (at Woodmont) 513/731–2233 • 11am-7pm, clsd Sun-Mon • vegetarian/ vegan

Melt Eclectic Deli 4165 Hamilton Ave (at Lingo St) 513/681–6358 • 11am-9pm, 10am-3pm Sun

Myra's Dionysus 121 Calhoun St (at Dennis St) 513/961–1578 • 11am-10pm, till 11pm Fri-Sat, from 5pm Sun • diverse menu • plenty veggie

Tucker's 1637 Vine St (at Green) 513/721–7123 • great brkfst hole-in-wall • vegan too • wheelchair access

ENTERTAINMENT & RECREATION

Ensemble Theatre of Cincinnati 1127 Vine St (at 12th) 513/421–3555

Know Theatre 1120 Jackson St (at Central Pkwy) 513/300–5669 • contemporary multicultural theater

Ohio Lesbian Archives 3416 Clifton Ave (at Clifton United Methodist Church) 513/256–7695 • call first for appt

RETAIL SHOPS

Park & Vine 1202 Main St 513/721–7275 • eco-friendly merchandise

Pink Pyramid 907 Race St (btwn 9th & Court) 513/621–7465 • noon-9pm, till 11pm Fri-Sat, 1pm-7pm Sun • pride items • also leather

PUBLICATIONS

CNKY Scene 513/309–9729 • LGBT publication

Gay People's Chronicle 440/986–0051 • Ohio's largest bi-weekly LGBT newspaper

Cleveland

INFO LINES & SERVICES

AA Gay/ Lesbian 6600 Detroit Ave (at LGBT Center) 216/241–7387, 800/835–1935

LGBT Community Center 6600 Detroit Ave 216/651–5428 • 1pm-8pm, clsd wknds • wheelchair access

ACCOMMODATIONS

Clifford House 1810 W 28th St (at Jay) 216/589–0121 • gay/ straight • 1868 historic brick home • near downtown • fireplaces • nonsmoking • WiFi • gay-owned

Radisson Hotel Cleveland—Gateway 651 Huron Rd (at Prospect) 216/377–9000, 800/967–9033 • gay-friendly • also restaurant • kids ok • WiFi • wheelchair access

Stone Gables B&B 3806 Franklin Blvd (at W 38th) 216/961–4654, 877/215–4326 • gay/ straight • full brkfst • jacuzzi • kids/ pets ok • WiFi • wheelchair access • gay-owned

Bars

ABC The Tavern 1872 W 25th St
216/861–3857 • 4pm-2:30am, from noon
wknds • gay-friendly dive bar w/ great food

Bounce 2814 Detroit Ave (at W 28th)
216/357–2997 • 5pm-2:30am • popular •
lesbians/ gay men, more women Sat night •
dancing/DJ • drag shows • videos • also
restaurant • gay-owned

The Hawk 11217 Detroit Ave (at 112th St) •
noon-2:30am, from 1pm Sun • lesbians/ gay
men • neighborhood bar • wheelchair access

Now That's Class 11213 Detroit Ave (at
112th St) **216/221–8576** • 4pm-close • gay-
friendly • punk & metal bands • food served
• plenty veggie/ vegan • wheelchair access

Paradise Inn 4488 State Rd (Rte 94, at Rte
480) **216/741–9819** • 11am-2:30am •
lesbians/ gay men • neighborhood bar •
lesbian-owned

Twist 11633 Clifton (at 117th St)
216/221–2333 • 11:30am-2:30am, from noon
Sun • popular • lesbians/ gay men •
neighborhood bar • dancing/DJ • professional
crowd

Cafes

Grumpy's Cafe 2621 W 14th St
216/241–5025 • 7am-9pm, till 3pm Sun-Mon

Gypsy Beans & Baking Co 6425 Detroit
Ave (at W 65th St, next to Cleveland Public
Theatre) **216/939–9009** • 7am-9pm, till 11pm
Fri-Sat • popular • fresh-baked gourmet
pastries, soups, sandwiches • WiFi •
wheelchair access

Lucky's Cafe 777 Starkweather Ave (at
Professor Ave) **216/622–7773** • 7am-5pm,
8am-3pm wknds, popular wknd brunch • cafe
& bakery • outdoor seating • WiFi • woman-
owned • wheelchair access

Phoenix Coffee 2287 Lee Rd (at Essex),
Cleveland Heights **216/932–8227** • 6am-
10pm, till 11pm Fri, from 7am Sat, 7am-7pm
Sun • great sandwiches • WiFi • patio •
wheelchair access

Restaurants

Ali Baba 12021 Lorain Ave (at W 120th St)
216/251–2040 • 5pm-10pm Th-Sat • popular
• the best Middle Eastern food you'll have
outside the Middle East • vegan/veggie •
BYOB • woman-owned

Cleveland

LGBT Pride:
June. 216/226-0004, web:
www.clevelandpride.org.

Annual Events:
March - Cleveland International Film
Festival 216/623-3456, web:
www.clevelandfilm.org.
June - Tri-C JazzFest 216/987-4444,
web: www.tri-cjazzfest.com.
June - Avon Heritage Duct Tape
Festival 866/818-1116, web:
www.ducttapefestival.com.

Transit:
Ace 216/361-4700, web:
www.acetaxi.com.
Regional Transit Authority (RTA)
216/566-5100, web:
www.gcrta.org.
Lolly the Trolley 216/771-4484, web:
www.lollytrolley.com.

Attractions:
Cleveland Metroparks Zoo 216/661-
6500, web: www.clemetzoo.com.
Cleveland Museum of Art 216/421-
7340, web: www.clemusart.com.
Coventry Road district.
Cuyahoga Valley National
Recreation Area 216/524–1497,
web: www.nps.gov/cuva.
The Flats.
Rock and Roll Hall of Fame 216/781-
7625, web: www.rockhall.com.

City Info:
800/321–1001, web:
www.positivelycleveland.com.

Bar Cento 1948 W 25th St (at Lorain Ave) 216/274–1010 • 4:30pm-2am, from noon Sat • great pizza • beer/ wine • patio • wheelchair access

Battiste & Dupree Cajun Grill & Bar 1992 Warrensville Ctr Rd (at Wyncote) 216/381–3341 • lunch & dinner, clsd Sun-Mon • wheelchair access

Cafe Tandoor 2096 S Taylor Rd (at Cedar), Cleveland Heights 216/371–8500 • lunch & dinner, 3pm-9pm Sun • Indian • plenty veggie • wheelchair access

The Coffee Pot 12415 Madison Ave (at Robin), Lakewood 216/226–6443 • 6am-4pm, till 3pm Sat, till 2pm Sun, clsd Mon • diner • woman-owned

Crop Bistro 2537 Lorain Ave (at 25th) 216/696–2767 • lunch Tue-Fri, dinner nightly, clsd Mon • innovative American

Diner on Clifton 11637 Clifton Blvd (at W 117th St) 216/521–5003 • 7am-11pm

Flying Fig 2523 Market Ave (at W 25th St) 216/241–4243 • lunch & dinner, wknd brunch

The Greenhouse Tavern 2038 E 4th St 216/241–5025 • 11am-11pm, till 1am Fri-Sat • organic and environmentally friendly

Hecks 2927 Bridge Ave (at W 30th) 216/861–5464, 800/677–8592 • lunch & dinner, brunch Sun • popular • gourmet burgers • wheelchair access

Hodge's 668 Euclid Ave 216/771–4000 • 11am-10pm, from 4pm wknds • global comfort food

The Inn on Coventry 2785 Euclid Heights Blvd (at Coventry), Cleveland Heights 216/371–1811 • 7am-8:30pm, from 8:30am-3pm wknds • homestyle • popular Bloody Marys • some veggie • full bar • wheelchair access • women-owned

Johnny Mango World Cafe & Bar 3120 Bridge Ave (btwn Fulton & W 32nd, in Ohio City) 216/575–1919 • 11am-10pm, till 11pm Fri-Sat • healthy world food • juice bar • also full bar till 1am

Latitude 41N 5712 Detroit Ave (at W 58th St, Detroit Shoreway) 216/961–0000 • 8am-9pm, till 10pm Fri, till 3pm Sun • restaurant & cafe • WiFi • wheelchair access • lesbian-owned

Lolita 900 Literary Rd (at Professor Ave, in Tremont) 216/771–5652 • 5pm-11pm, till 1am Fri-Sat, 4pm-9pm Sun, clsd Mon • popular • upscale cont'l • full bar

Luchita's 3456 W 117th St (at Governor) 216/252–1169 • lunch & dinner, clsd Mon • popular • Mexican • full bar

Luxe 6605 Detroit Ave (at W 65th St) 216/920–0600 • 5pm-midnight, lounge till 2am • gourmet comfort food • also lounge • live music • wheelchair access

Momocho 1835 Fulton Rd (at Woodbine Ave) 216/694–2122 • 5pm-close, from 4pm Sun • modern Mexican • also bar • wheelchair access

My Friend's Deli & Restaurant 11616 Detroit Ave (at W 117th) 216/221–2575 • 24hrs • beer/ wine • WiFi

Pearl of the Orient 19300 Detroit Rd (in Beachcliff Market Sq), Rocky River 440/333–9902 • lunch & dinner • pan-Asian • some veggie • also restaurant on East Side • wheelchair access

Tommy's 216/321–7757 • 9am-9pm, till 10pm Fri, 7:30am-10pm Sat • plenty veggie • great milkshakes • WiFi • wheelchair access

ENTERTAINMENT & RECREATION

Rock & Roll Hall of Fame 1100 Rock & Roll Blvd (at E 9th & Lake Erie) 216/781–ROCK • even if you don't like rock, stop by & check out IM Pei's architectural gift to Cleveland

BOOKSTORES

Loganberry Books 13015 Larchmere Blvd, Shaker Heights 216/795–9800 • 10am-6pm, till 8pm Th, clsd Sun • used & rare books • woman-owned

Mac's Backs 1820 Coventry Rd (next to Tommy's), Cleveland Heights 216/321–2665 • 10am-10pm, till 10pm Fri-Sat, 11am-8pm Sun • great new & used • 3 floors • reading series • some LGBT titles

RETAIL SHOPS

The Dean Rufus House of Fun 1422 W 29th St (at Detroit) 216/348–1386 • 1pm-midnight, till 2:30am Fri-Sat, clsd Mon • clothing • DVDs

Torso 11520 Clifton Blvd (at Warren), Lakewood 216/862–3987 • 11am-9pm, till 5pm Sun, clsd Mon • clothing • gay-owned

PUBLICATIONS

Gay People's Chronicle 216/916–9338 • Ohio's largest bi-weekly LGBT newspaper w/ extensive listings

EROTICA

Adult Mart 16700 Brookpark Rd (at W 150th) 216/267–9019

Rocky's Entertainment & Emporium 13330 Brookpark Rd (at W 130th) 216/267–4659

Columbus

INFO LINES & SERVICES

AA Gay/ Lesbian 614/253-8501, 800/870-3795 (IN OH)

Stonewall Columbus Community Center/ Hotline 1160 N High St (at E 4th Ave) 614/299-7764 • 9am-5pm, clsd wknds • wheelchair access

ACCOMMODATIONS

The Blackwell 2110 Tuttle Park Pl (at Lane Ave) 614/247-4000, 866/247-4000 • gay-friendly • on OSU campus • also restaurant

Harrison House B&B 313 W 5th Ave (at Neil Ave) 614/421-2202, 800/827-4203 • gay-friendly • nonsmoking • WiFi • kids/pets ok • woman-owned

The Lofts 55 E Nationwide Blvd (at High St) 614/461-2663, 800/735-6387 • gay-friendly • boutique hotel

The Westin Columbus 310 S High St (at Main) 614/223-3800, 800/937-8461 • gay-friendly • beautiful old 100+ year old hotel, great location • also restaurant

BARS

Arch City Tavern 862 N High (at 1st Ave) 614/421-9697 • 6pm-2am, clsd Mon • popular • lesbians/ gay men • neighborhood bar • dancing/DJ • karaoke • live bands

Cavan Irish Pub 1409 S High St (at Jenkins) 614/725-5502 • 2pm-2:30am, from noon wknds • gay-friendly • shows • karaoke

Club Diversity 863 S High St (at Whittier) 614/224-4050 • 4pm-midnight, till 2:30am Fri, noon-2:30am Sat • lesbians/ gay men • piano bar Fri-Sat

Inn Rehab 627 Greenlawn Ave (at Harmon) 614/754-7326 • 11am-2:30am • mostly gay men • food served • dancing/DJ • drag shows

Columbus

LGBT PRIDE:
June. 614/299-7764 (Stonewall #), web: www.columbuspride.org.

ANNUAL EVENTS:
June - Columbus Arts Festival 614/224-2606, web: www.gcac.org.
July/August - Ohio State Fair 888/646-3976, web: www.ohioexpocenter.com.
September - Ohio Lesbian Festival, web: www.ohiolba.org.

CITY INFO:
800/282-5393, web: www.ohiotourism.com.

WEATHER:
Truly midwestern. Winters are cold, summers are hot.

TRANSIT:
Yellow Cab 614/221-3800, web: yellowcabofcolumbus.com.
Acme Taxi 614/777-7777, web: www.acmetaxi.com.
Central Ohio Transit Authority (COTA) 614/228-1776, web: www.cota.com.

ATTRACTIONS:
Brewery District.
Columbus Jazz Orchestra 614/294-5200, web: www.jazzartsgroup.com.
Columbus Museum of Modern Art 614/221-6801, web: www.columbusmuseum.org.
Columbus Zoo 800/666-5397 web: www.columbuszoo.org.
Franklin Park Conservatory 614/645-8733, web: www.fpconservatory.org.
German Village district.
The Short North neighborhood (popular "Gallery Hop" 1st Sat), 614/299-8050 web: www.shortnorth.org.
Wexner Center for the Arts 614/292-0330, web: www.wexarts.org.

Level Dining Lounge 614/754-7111 • 11am-2:30am • gay/ straight • restaurant w/ great bar • dancing/DJ • karaoke • wheelchair access

Slammers 202 E Long St (at N 5th St) 614/221-8880 • 11am-12:30am, till 2:30am Fri-Sat, from 4pm wknds, clsd Mon-Tue • mostly women • dancing/DJ • food served • WiFi • wheelchair access

The South Bend Tavern 126 E Moler St (at 4th St) 614/444-3386 • noon-2:30am • lesbians/ gay men • neighborhood bar • drag shows Sat • wheelchair access

Union Cafe 782 N High St (at Hubbard) 614/421-2233 • 11am-2:30am • popular • lesbians/ gay men • video bar • also restaurant • plenty veggie • WiFi • wheelchair access

NIGHTCLUBS

Axis 775 N High St (at Hubbard) 614/291-4008 • 10pm-2:30am Fri-Sat only • popular • mostly gay men • dancing/DJ • also Pump cabaret lounge • drag shows • 18+ • wheelchair access • gay-owned

Wall Street 144 N Wall St (at Spring St) 614/464-2800 • 9pm-2:30am, from 10pm Wed, 8pm-midnight Th, clsd Mon-Tue • popular • lesbians/ gay men • more women Fri-Sat • dancing/DJ • country/ western Th • wheelchair access

CAFES

Cup O Joe Cafe 627 S 3rd St (at Sycamore) 614/221-1563 • 6am-10pm, till 11pm Fri-Sat, from 7am wknds, till 10pm Sun • food served • WiFi • wheelchair access

RESTAURANTS

Alana's Food & Wine 2333 N High St (at Patterson) 614/294-6783 • from 5pm, clsd Sun-Tue

Banana Leaf 816 Bethel Rd (at Olentangy River Rd) 614/459-4101 • 11:30am-9:30pm • vegetarian/ vegan Indian • wheelchair access

Betty's 680 N High St 614/228-6191 • 11am-2am • plenty veggie • also bar

Blue Nile 2361 N High St (at W Patterson) 614/421-2323 • lunch & dinner, clsd Mon • Ethopian

Cap City Diner 1299 Olentangy River Rd (at W 5th) 614/291-3663 • 11am-10pm, till 11pm Fri-Sat, till 9pm Sun

L'Antibes 772 N High St #106 (at Warren) 614/291-1666 • dinner from 5pm, clsd Sun-Mon • full bar • wheelchair access • gay-owned

Lemongrass 641 N High (at Russell) 614/224-1414 • lunch & dinner, clsd Sun-Mon • popular • Asian cuisine • reservations advised

Northstar Cafe 951 N High St (at W 2nd Ave) 614/298-9999 • 9am-10pm • popular • plenty veggie

Surly Girl Saloon 1126 N High St (at W 4th Ave) 614/294-4900 • 11am-2am • plenty veggie • also bar • open mic comedy Wed & punk rock aerobics 6:30 Tue

Till 247 King Ave 614/298-9986 • lunch & dinner, wknd brunch • patio

Tip Top Kitchen & Cocktails 73 E Gay St (at 3rd St) 614/221-8300 • 11am-2am

Whole World Bakery & Restaurant 3269 N High St (at W Como Ave) 614/268-5751 • 11am-8pm, Sun brunch, clsd Mon • vegetarian/vegan • wheelchair access

ENTERTAINMENT & RECREATION

Ohio Roller Girls • Columbus' female roller derby league • visit www.ohiorollergirls.com for events

BOOKSTORES

The Book Loft of German Village 631 S 3rd St (at Sycamore) 614/464-1774 • 10am-11pm, till midnight Fri-Sat • LGBT section

RETAIL SHOPS

Hausfrau Haven 769 S 3rd St (at Columbus) 614/443-3680 • 10am-7pm, noon-5pm Sun • greeting cards • wine • gifts

Piercology 190 N 2nd Ave (at Hunter Ave) 614/297-4743 • noon-8pm, 1pm-7pm Sun • body-piercing studio • gay-owned • wheelchair access

Schmidt's Fudge Haus 220 E Kossuth St (in Historic German Village) 614/444-2222 • noon-close • old fashioned fudge & candy • gifts

Torso 772 N High St (at Warren) 614/421-7663 • 11am-10pm, till 5pm Sun-Mon • clothing • gay-owned

PUBLICATIONS

Gay People's Chronicle 440/986-0051

Outlook Weekly 614/268-8525 • statewide LGBT weekly • good resource pages

EROTICA

The Garden 1174 N High St (btwn 4th & 5th Ave) 614/294-2869 • 11am-3am, noon-midnight Sun • adult toys

Dayton

INFO LINES & SERVICES

AA Gay/ Lesbian 20 W 1st St (off Main, at Christ Episcopal Church) **937/222-2211** • 8pm Sat

Greater Dayton Lesbian/ Gay Center 117 E 3rd St **937/274-1776**

ACCOMMODATIONS

Dayton Marriott 1414 S Patterson Blvd **937/223-1000, 800/450-8625**

BARS

MJ's Cafe 119 E 3rd St (at S Jefferson) **937/223-3259** • 3pm-2:30am • mostly gay men • dancing/DJ • food served • karaoke • male strippers • deck

Stage Door 44 N Jefferson St (at 2nd) **937/223-7418** • 3pm-2:30am • mostly gay men • leather • wheelchair access

NIGHTCLUBS

Masque 34 N Jefferson St (btwn 2nd & 3rd) **937/228-2582** • 8pm-2:30am, till 5am wknds • popular • mostly gay men • dancing/DJ • drag shows • strippers • 18+

CAFES

Expressions Coffee House **937/308-8345** • 7am-9pm, 9am-2pm Sat, clsd Sun • live music • gay-owned

RESTAURANTS

Cold Beer & Cheeseburgers 33 S Jefferson St (at 4th St) **937/222-2337** • 11am-close • grill • full bar • wheelchair access

The Spaghetti Warehouse 36 W 5th St (at Ludlow) **937/461-3913** • 11am-10pm, till 11pm wknds • more gay Tue w/ Friends of the Italian Opera

BOOKSTORES

Books & Co 4453 Walnut St (in Greene Shopping Ctr) **937/429-2169** • 9am-11pm, till 8pm Sun

PUBLICATIONS

Gay Dayton **937/623-1590** • monthly LGBT publication

Findlay

EROTICA

Findlay Adult Books & Video 623 Trenton Ave (at I-75, exit 159) **419/422-1301**

Kent

BARS

The Zephyr Pub 106 W Main St (at Water St) **330/678-4848** • 3pm-close • gay-friendly • live shows • wheelchair access

Lima

NIGHTCLUBS

Somewhere in Time 804 W North St (at Baxter) **419/227-7288** • 5pm-2:30am, from 8pm wknds • lesbians/ gay men • dancing/DJ • drag shows • male & female strippers

Logan

ACCOMMODATIONS

Glenlaurel—A Scottish Country Inn 14940 Mt Olive Rd (off State Rte I-80), Rockbridge **740/385-4070, 800/809-7378** • gay/ straight • full brkfst & dinner • hot tub • nonsmoking • wheelchair access

Inn & Spa at Cedar Falls 21190 State Rte 374 **740/385-7489, 800/653-2557** • gay/ straight • rooms, log cabins & cottages • fine dining on-site • nonsmoking • WiFi • wheelchair access

Lazy Lane Cabins **740/385-3475, 877/225-6572** • gay-friendly • secluded cabins sleep 2-8 • hot tubs • fireplaces • nonsmoking • kids/ pets ok

Lorain

BARS

Tim's Place 2223 Broadway (btwn 22nd & 23rd) **440/218-2223** • 8pm-2:30am, clsd Mon • lesbians/ gay men • neighborhood bar • dancing/DJ • drag shows • patio • wheelchair access

Monroe

BARS

Old Street Saloon 13 Old St (at Elm St) **513/539-9183** • 8pm-2am Th-Sat, till 1am Wed, clsd Sun-Tue • lesbians/ gay men • neighborhood bar • dancing/DJ • drag shows • karaoke

Niles

EROTICA

Niles Books 5970 Youngstown Warren Rd (off Rte 46) **330/544-3755**

Oberlin

ACCOMMODATIONS

Hallauer House B&B 14945 Hallauer Rd 440/774-3400, 877/774-3406 • gay-friendly • eco-friendly historic inn 3 miles S of Oberlin • pool • nonsmoking • WiFi

RESTAURANTS

The Feve 30 S Main St (at College St) 440/774-1978 • 11am-midnight • popular wknd brunch • plenty veggie • full bar from 5pm

Weia Teia 9 S Main St (at College St) 440/774-8880 • lunch & dinner • Thai/Asian fusion • upscale • full bar • some veggie

BOOKSTORES

MindFair Books 13 W College St (shares storefront w/ Ben Franklin) 440/774-6463 • 10am-6pm, till 8pm Fri, noon-5pm Sun

Sandusky

NIGHTCLUBS

Crowbar 206 W Market St (at Jackson St) 419/624-0109 • 6pm-2:30am, clsd Tue • lesbians/gay men • dancing/DJ • karaoke • gay-owned

RESTAURANTS

Mona Pizza Gourmet 135 Columbus Ave (at Market St) 419/626-8166 • 11am-10pm, till 3am wknds • multiracial • transgender-friendly • gay-owned

Springfield

NIGHTCLUBS

Diesel 1912-14 Edwards Ave (at N Belmont Ave) 937/324-0383 • 8:30pm-2:30am, clsd Mon-Tue • gay-friendly • dancing/DJ • live shows • karaoke • patio

Toledo

INFO LINES & SERVICES

AA Gay/ Lesbian 3535 Executive Pkwy (at Unity) 419/380-9862 • 8pm Wed

ACCOMMODATIONS

Mansion View Inn 2035 Collingwood Blvd (at Irving) 419/244-5676 • gay-friendly • 1887 Victorian near downtown • nonsmoking • WiFi

BARS

Blush 119 N Erie St 419/255-4010 • 9pm-2:30am Fri-Sat only • mostly gay men • drag shows

Outskirts 5038 Lewis Ave 419/476-1577 • 5pm-2:30am, till midnight Sun & Wed, clsd Mon, Tue & Th • mostly women • dancing/DJ • karaoke • 18+

R House 5534 Secor Rd (btwn Laskey & Alexis) 419/474-2929 • 4pm-2:30am • mostly gay men • dancing/DJ • patio

Rip Cord 115 N Erie St (btwn Jefferson & Monroe) 419/243-3412 • 9am-2:30am • mostly gay men • more women Mon • neighborhood bar • Sun brunch • karaoke • strippers • food served

NIGHTCLUBS

Bretz 2012 Adams St 419/243-1900 • 9pm-2:30am, till 4:30am Fri-Sat, clsd Mon-Tue • lesbians/gay men • dancing/DJ • karaoke • drag shows • strippers • 18+ • wheelchair access

BOOKSTORES

People Called Women 6060 Reinaissance Pl #F 419/469-8983 • 11am-7pm, clsd Sun-Mon • multicultural • feminist

Warren

NIGHTCLUBS

Club 441 441 E Market St (at Vine, enter rear) 330/394-9483 • 4pm-2:30am, from 2pm wknds • lesbians/gay men • dancing/DJ • live shows • wheelchair access

The Funky Skunk 143 E Market St (at Park Ave) • 9pm-close • mostly gay men • ladies night Sun • dancing/DJ • drag shows • karaoke

West Lafayette

RESTAURANTS

Lava Rock Grill at Unusual Junction 56310 US Hwy 36 740/545-9772 • '50s-style diner in restored railroad station • wheelchair access • gay-owned

Yellow Springs

RESTAURANTS

Winds Cafe & Bakery 215 Xenia Ave (at Cory St) 937/767-1144 • lunch & dinner, Sun brunch, clsd Mon • plenty veggie • full bar • wheelchair access • women-owned

Youngstown

NIGHTCLUBS

Liquid Niteclub 1281 Salt Springs Rd 234/855-0351 • 4pm-2:30am, from 8pm Sat-Sun • lesbians/gay men • dancing/DJ • karaoke

Split Level/ Pulse 169 S Four Mile Run Rd (at S Mahoning Ave) 330/318–9830 • lesbians/ gay men • dancing/DJ • drag shows • karaoke

Utopia Video Nightclub 876 E Midlothian Blvd (at Zedaker St) 330/781–9000 • 5pm-close, clsd Mon • lesbians/ gay men • dancing/DJ • drag shows

CAFES

The Lemon Grove Cafe 122 W Federal Plaza W (at Hazel St) 330/744–7683 • 7am-2am, from 11am wknds • food served • also bar • events, movies, art & more

OKLAHOMA

Grand Lake

ACCOMMODATIONS

Southern Oaks Resort & Spa 2 miles S of Hwy 28/ 82 Junction, Langley 918/782–9346, 866/452–5307 • gay-friendly • 19 cabins on 30 acres • pool • hot tub • nonsmoking • gay-owned

RESTAURANTS

The Artichoke Restaurant & Bar 35896 S Hwy 82, Langley 918/782–9855 • 5pm-10pm, clsd Sun-Mon

Frosty & Edna's Cafe Highway 28, Langley 918/782–9123 • 6am-9:30pm

Lighthouse Supper Club Highway 85 & Main, Ketchum 918/782–3316 • 5pm-9pm, clsd Sun-Tue

Oklahoma City

INFO LINES & SERVICES

AA Live & Let Live 3405 N Villa 405/947–3834 • 8pm Mon

Herland Sister Resources 2312 NW 39th St 405/521–9696 • 1pm-5pm Sat • women's resource center w/ books, crafts & lending library • also sponsors monthly events • wheelchair access

ACCOMMODATIONS

Habana Inn 2200 NW 39th St (at Youngs) 405/528–2221, 800/988–2221 (RESERVATIONS ONLY) • popular • lesbians/ gay men • resort • pool • nonsmoking • also 3 bars • restaurant • gift shop • wheelchair access

Hawthorn Suites 1600 NW Expy (Richmond Square) 405/840–1440, 800/527–1133 • gay-friendly • full brkfst • pool • WiFi

Waterford Marriott 6300 Waterford Blvd (at Pennsylvania) 405/848–4782 • gay-friendly • pool • fitness center • also bar & restaurant • nonsmoking • WiFi

BARS

Alibi's 1200 N Pennsylvania (at NW 11th) 405/605–3795 • noon -2am • gay/ straight • neighborhood bar • transgender-friendly • gay-owned

The Boom 2218 NW 39th St (at Pennsylvania) 405/601–7200 • 4pm-2am, from 11am Sun, clsd Mon • lesbians/ gay men • neighborhood bar • food served • karaoke • drag shows • WiFi • patio • wheelchair access

Edna's 5137 N Classen Blvd (at NW 51st) 405/840–3339 • 2pm-2am, from noon wknds • gay-friendly • neighborhood dive bar • food served

➤ **The Finishline** at Habana Inn 405/525–2900 • noon-2am • lesbians/ gay men • neighborhood bar • dancing/DJ • country/ western • poolside bar • wheelchair access

Hi-Lo Club 1221 NW 50th St (btwn Western & Classen) 405/843–1722 • noon-2am • lesbians/ gay men • neighborhood bar • live bands • drag shows

KA's 2024 NW 11th (at Pennsylvania) 405/525–3734 • 3pm-close, from 5pm Mon, clsd Tue • 2nd oldest lesbian bar in the US • neighborhood bar • karaoke • beer bar • patio • WiFi • wheelchair access

➤ **The Ledo** at Habana Inn 405/525–0730 • 4pm-10:30pm, till 2am Fri-Sat • lesbians/ gay men • martini lounge • food served • karaoke • nonsmoking • wheelchair access

Partners 4 Club 2805 NW 36th St (at May Ave) 405/602–2030 • 5pm-close, from 7pm Fri-Sat, clsd Mon • popular • mostly women • neighborhood bar • dancing/DJ • karaoke • live shows • patio • wheelchair access

Partners Too 2807 NW 36th St (at May Ave) 405/942–2199 • open Wed-Sat • lesbians/gay men • dancing/DJ • patio • wheelchair access

Tramps 2201 NW 39th St (at Barnes) 405/521–9888 • noon-2am, from 10am wknds • mostly gay men • drag shows • WiFi • wheelchair access

NIGHTCLUBS

➤ **The Copa** at Habana Inn 405/525–0730 • 9pm-2am, clsd Mon • popular • lesbians/ gay men • dancing/DJ • drag shows • karaoke • wheelchair access

Oklahoma City

LGBT PRIDE:
June, web: www.okcpride.com.

ANNUAL EVENTS:
May & November - Herland Spring & Fall Retreats 405/521-9696. Music, workshops, web: www.herlandsisters.org.
May - Paseo Arts Festival 405/525-2688, web: www.thepaseo.com.

CITY INFO:
800/225-5652, web: www.okccvb.org.

BEST VIEW:
From a water taxi on the Bricktown Canal (www.bricktownwatertaxi.com). Or anywhere in Myriad Gardens.

WEATHER:
Spring brings out the best of Oklahoma—blue skies for miles and the dogwood, redbud, and azaleas in bloom. (It's also the start of tornado season.) Summer gets mighty hot (90°s-100°s), with thunderstorms thrown in for relief. Fall is the time to head east to the hills of "Green Country" and watch the leaves change. Winters bring cold temps (20°s-30°s), gray skies, a brown landscape, and the occasional dusting of snow and the even rarer but more serious ice storm.

ATTRACTIONS:
Bricktown—renovated nightlife district with canal, web: bricktownokc.com.
Historic Paseo Arts District, web: www.thepaseo.com.
Myriad Gardens' Crystal Bridge 405/297-3995, web: www.myriadgardens.com.
National Cowboy and Western Heritage Museum 405/478-2250, web: www.nationalcowboymuseum.org.
National Softball Hall of Fame 405/424-5266, web: www.softball.org.
Oklahoma City Museum of Art 405/236-3100, web: www.okcmoa.com.
Oklahoma City National Memorial 405/235-3313, web: www.oklahomacitynationalmemorial.org.
Oklahoma City Zoo 405/424-3344, web: www.okczoo.com.
Science Museum Oklahoma 405/602-6664, web: www.sciencemuseumok.org.
State Capitol: only one in country with its own oil well before running dry in 1986.
Sylvan Goldman monument (inventor of the shopping cart).
Will Rogers Park.

TRANSIT:
Thunder Cab 405/600-6161, web: www.thundercab.net.
Yellow Cab 405/232-6161.
Airport Express 877/688-3311, web: www.airportexpressokc.com.
Metro Transit 405/235-7433, web: www.gometro.org.

The Park 2125 NW 39th St (at Pennsylvania) **405/528-4690** • 5pm-2am, from 3pm Sun (free buffet) • mostly gay men • dancing/DJ • patio • wheelchair access

Wreck Room 2127 NW 39th St (at Pennsylvania) **405/525-7610** • 10pm-close Fri-Sat only • lesbians/ gay men • dancing/DJ • live shows • drag shows • young crowd • 18+ after 1am

CAFES

The Red Cup 3122 N Classen Blvd (at NW 30th St) **405/525-3430** • 7am-5pm, till 8pm Th-Fri, from 9am wknds • vegetarian • nonsmoking • WiFi • live music

RESTAURANTS

Bricktown Brewery Restaurant 1 N Oklahoma Ave (at Sheridan) 405/232–2739 • 11am-10pm, till midnight Sat, from noon Sun • full bar

Cheever's Cafe 2409 N Hudson Ave (at NW 23rd) 405/525–7007 • 11am-9:30pm, 5pm-10:30pm Sat, brunch Sun • reservations recommended

Earl's Rib Palace 216 Johnny Bench Dr, Ste BBQ (in Bricktown) 405/272–9898 • 11am-9pm, till 10pm Fri-Sat, noon-8pm Sun

➤ **Gusher's** at Habana Inn 405/525–0730 • 11am-10:30pm, from 9am wknds, till 3:30am Fri-Sat for after-hours brkfst • wheelchair access

Iguana Bar & Grill 9 NW 9th St (at N Santa Fe Ave) 405/606–7172 • lunch & dinner • Mexican

Ingrid's Kitchen 3701 N Youngs (btwn Penn & May, on NW 36th) 405/946–8444 • 7am-8pm, 10am-2pm Sun • German/ American bakery & deli

Pops 660 W Hwy 66, Arcadia 405/928–7677 • brkfst, lunch & dinner • diner fare • look for the 66-foot tall soda bottle

Rococo Restaurant & Fine Wine 2824 N Pennsylvania (at NW 27th St) 405/528–2824 • lunch Mon-Fri, dinner nightly, Sun jazz brunch • full bar

Someplace Else Deli & Bakery 2310 N Western Ave 405/524–0887 • 7am-6:30pm, 9:30am-4pm Sat, clsd Sun • popular

Sushi Neko 4318 N Western (btwn 42nd & 43rd) 405/528–8862 • 11am-11pm, clsd Sun

Ted's Cafe Escondido 8324 S Western Ave (at 84th St) 405/635–8337 • lunch & dinner • popular • Tex-Mex

ENTERTAINMENT & RECREATION

First Friday Gallery Walk from 28th at N Walker to 30th at N Dewey 405/525–2688 • open tour of Paseo Arts District galleries • first Fri-Sat

BOOKSTORES

Full Circle Bookstore 50 Penn Pl, 1900 NW Expwy (in NE corner of 1st level) 405/842–2900, 800/683–7323 • 10am-9pm, noon-5pm Sun • also cafe & coffee bar

RETAIL SHOPS

➤ **Jungle Red** at Habana Inn 405/524–5733 • 1pm-close • novelties • leather • gifts • wheelchair access

PUBLICATIONS

The Herland Voice 405/521–9696 • monthly newsletter for OKC women's community

Oklahoma Gazette 405/528–6000 • "Metro OKC's independent weekly"

EROTICA

Christie's Toy Box 7914 N MacArthur 405/720–2453 • multiple locations in OKC

Naughty & Nice 3121 SW 29th St (at I-44) 405/681–5044 • 24hrs

Tulsa

INFO LINES & SERVICES

Dennis R Neill Equality Center 621 E 4th St (at Kenosha) 918/743–4297 • 3pm-9pm, clsd Sun • many activities & Pride store • wheelchair access

Gay/ Lesbian AA 2545 S Yale Ave (at Community of Hope) 918/627–2224 • 5:30pm Sat

ACCOMMODATIONS

The Mayo Hotel 115 W 5th St 918/582–6296 • gay-friendly • luxury hotel • restaurant • WiFi • wheelchair access

Tulsa Hyatt 100 E Second St (at 2nd St) 918/582–9000, 800/980–6429 • gay-friendly • restaurant • pool • kids/ pets ok • wheelchair access

BARS

Bamboo Lounge 7204 E Pine 918/836–8700 • noon-2am • mostly gay men • neighborhood bar • dancing/DJ • live shows • karaoke • patio • wheelchair access

Club 209 209 N Boulder Ave (at Brady) 918/584–9944 • 7pm-2am, clsd Mon-Wed • gay/ straight • live shows/ music • karaoke

New Age Renegade 1649 S Main St (at 17th) 918/585–3405 • 4pm-2am • lesbians/ gay men • neighborhood bar • live shows • karaoke • patio

TNT's 2114 S Memorial Dr 918/660–0856 • 8pm-2am, clsd Sun-Tue • popular • mostly women • neighborhood bar • dancing/DJ • karaoke

The Yellow Brick Road 2630 E 15th St (at Harvard) 918/293–0304 • 1pm-2am • lesbians/ gay men • neighborhood bar • wheelchair access

NIGHTCLUBS

Club Majestic 124 N Boston (at Brady) **918/584–9494** • 9pm-2am Th-Sun • dancing/DJ • drag/live shows • transgender-friendly • WiFi • wheechair access • gay-owned

CAFES

Gypsy's Coffee House 303 N Cincinnati Ave **918/295–2181** • 7am-10pm, till 2am Fri-Sat, from 10am Sat-Sun • live shows • WiFi

RESTAURANTS

Cancun International 705 S Lewis Ave (at 11th) **918/583–8089** • 11am-9pm, from 10am Sat-Sun, clsd Wed

Eloté 514 S Boston Ave **918/582–1403** • 11am-10pm, till 2pm Mon, clsd Sun, fresh Mexican • full bar

James E McNellie's Public House 409 E 1st St **918/382–7468** • 11am-2am • great burgers • full bar • wheelchair access

White Lion Pub 6927 S Canton Ave (off 71st) **918/491–6533** • 4pm-10pm, clsd Sun-Mon • British-style pub

Wild Fork 1820 Utica Square **918/742–0712** • 7am-10pm, clsd Sun • full bar • wheelchair access • women-owned

ENTERTAINMENT & RECREATION

Gilcrease Museum 1400 N Gilcrease Museum Rd **918/596–2700, 888/655–2278** • one of the best collections of Native American & cowboy art in the US

Green Country Roller Girls **918/269–7228** • Oklahoma's female roller derby league • visit greencountryrollergirls.com for events

Philbrook Museum of Art 2727 S Rockford Rd (1 block E of Peoria, at end of 27th St) **918/324–7941** • clsd Mon • Italian villa built in the '20s oil boom complete w/ kitschy lighted dance flr • the gardens are a must in spring & summer

PUBLICATIONS

Urban Tulsa Weekly **918/592–5550** • "Tulsa Metro's only independent newsweekly"

OREGON

Ashland

INFO LINES & SERVICES

Gay/ Lesbian AA 541/732–1850

ACCOMMODATIONS

The Arden Forest Inn 261 W Hersey St (at N Main) **541/488–1496, 800/460–3912** • gay/ straight • full brkfst • nonsmoking • pool • kids 10+ ok • wheelchair access • WiFi • gay-owned

Ashland Creek Inn 70 Water St **541/482–3315** • gay-friendly • secluded forest location • kitchens • gourmet brkfst • nonsmoking • gay-owned

Country Willows B&B Inn 1313 Clay St (at Siskiyou Blvd) **541/488–1590, 800/945–5697** • gay-friendly • full brkfst • pool • jacuzzi • nonsmoking • WiFi • wheelchair access • gay-owned

Lithia Springs Resort 2165 W Jackson Rd (at N Main) **541/482–7128, 800/482–7128** • gay/ straight • full brkfst • natural hot-springs-fed whirlpools in rooms • nonsmoking • WiFi

Romeo Inn B&B 295 Idaho St **800/915–8899** • gay-friendly • full brkfst • jacuzzi • pool • nonsmoking • WiFi

RESTAURANTS

The Black Sheep Pub & Restaurant 51 N Main St (on the Plaza) **541/482–6414** • 11:30am-1am • WiFi • woman-owned

Greenleaf Restaurant 49 N Main St (on The Plaza) **541/482–2808** • 8am-8pm • creekside dining • beer/ wine

BOOKSTORES

Bloomsbury Books 290 E Main St (btwn 1st & 2nd) **541/488–0029** • 8:30am-9pm, 10am-6pm Sun

RETAIL SHOPS

Travel Essentials 252 E Main St **541/482–7383, 800/258–0758** • 10am-5:30pm, 11am-5pm Sun • luggage • books • accessories

Bend

ACCOMMODATIONS

Dawson House Lodge 109455 Hwy 97 N, Chemult **541/365–2232, 888/281–8375** • gay-friendly • rustic inn w/ modern amenities • near Crater Lake • nonsmoking • kids/ pets ok • WiFi

Eugene

INFO LINES & SERVICES

Gay/ Lesbian AA 1166 Oak St (at First Christian Church) 541/342-4113 • 7pm Th, Fri & Sat & 5pm Sun

ACCOMMODATIONS

C'est La Vie Inn 1006 Taylor St (at W 10th) 541/302-3014, 866/302-3014 • gay-friendly • full brkfst • nonsmoking • WiFi

Valley River Inn 1000 Valley River Wy 541/743-1000, 800/543-8266 • gay-friendly • pool • also restaurant • nonsmoking • WiFi • wheelchair access

NIGHTCLUBS

Diablo's Downtown Lounge 959 Pearl St 541/343-2346 • 1pm-2:30am, from 3pm wknds • gay-friendly • dancing/DJ • karaoke

CAFES

Eugene Coffee Company 240 E 17th St 541/344-0002 • 7am-6pm • lesbian-owned

RESTAURANTS

Glenwood Restaurant 1340 Alder St (at 13th Ave) 541/687-0355 • 7am-9pm

Keystone Cafe 395 W 5th Ave (at Lawrence) 541/342-2075 • 7am-3pm • popular brkfst • plenty veggie

ENTERTAINMENT & RECREATION

Glassbar Island Nude Beach/ Willamette River Beach on the Coast Fork (Franklin Blvd and I-5) • gay/ straight • nude beach, also hiking & biking • www.glassbarisland.org for details

EROTICA

Exclusively Adult 1166 South A St (at 10th St), Springfield 541/726-6969 • 8pm-midnight, 24hrs Th-Sun

Grants Pass

ACCOMMODATIONS

Rainbows on the Fly 541/324-0485 • women's land on 40 acres • cabin, campsites, RV hookups • also guided flyfishing • nonsmoking • WiFi • lesbian-owned

WomanShare 541/862-2807 • women only • cabins • shared kitchen • bathhouse • hot tub • girls/ pets ok • nonsmoking • lesbian-owned

CAFES

Sunshine Natural Foods Cafe 128 SW H St (btwn 5th & 6th Sts) 541/474-5044 • 9am-6pm, 9:30am-5pm Sat, clsd Sun • vegetarian • also market • WiFi • wheelchair access

Idleyld Park

ACCOMMODATIONS

Umpqua's Last Resort Wilderness RV Park & Campground 115 Elk Ridge Ln 541/498-2500 • gay/ straight • WiFi • gay-owned

Jacksonville

ACCOMMODATIONS

The TouVelle House 455 N Oregon St (at E St) 541/899-8938, 800/846-8422 • gay-friendly • 1916 Craftsman • full brkfst • pool • WiFi • nonsmoking

Klamath Falls

ACCOMMODATIONS

Crystal Wood Lodge 38625 Westside Road (at Hwy 140) 541/381-2322, 866/381-2322 • gay-friendly • non-smoking • pets ok • WiFi • lesbian-owned

Portland

INFO LINES & SERVICES

Live & Let Live Club 1210 SE 7th Ave 503/238-6091 • 12-step meetings

Q Center 4115 N Mississippi Ave (at N Mason St) 503/234-7837 • LGBTQ community center • WiFi

ACCOMMODATIONS

The Ace Hotel 1022 SW Stark St (at 11th) 503/228-2277 • gay/ straight • hip hotel for "cultural influencers on a budget" • nonsmoking • WiFi • kids/ pets ok • wheelchair access

Hotel deLuxe 729 SW 15th Ave (at SW Morrison) 503/219-2094, 866/895-2094 • gay-friendly • 1940s Hollywood decor • nonsmoking • WiFi

Hotel Monaco Portland 506 SW Washington (at 5th Ave) 503/222-0001, 866/861-9514 • gay-friendly • restaurant • gym • kids/ pets ok • WiFi

Hotel Vintage Plaza 422 SW Broadway (at SW Washington) 503/228-1212, 800/263-2305 • popular • gay-friendly • upscale hotel • restaurant & lounge • WiFi • wheelchair access •

Inn at Northrup Station 2025 NW Northrup St (at NW 21st) 503/224-0543, 800/224-1180 • gay-friendly • cute, colorful boutique hotel

Jupiter Hotel 800 E Burnside 503/230-9200, 877/800-0004 • gay-friendly • boutique hotel • nonsmoking • restaurant & lounge • kids/pets ok • WiFi • wheelchair access

The Lion & the Rose 1810 NE 15th Ave (at NE Schuyler) 503/287-9245, 800/955-1647 • gay/straight • in 1906 Queen Anne mansion • nonsmoking • WiFi • gay-owned

The Mark Spencer Hotel 409 SW Eleventh Ave (near Stark) 503/224-3293, 800/548-3934 • gay-friendly • nonsmoking • kids/pets ok • WiFi

McMenamins Crystal Hotel 303 SW 12th Ave (at Stark) 503/972-2670, 855/205-3930 • gay/straight • pool • WiFi • also restaurant & bar

The Nines 525 SW Morrison St 877/229-9995 • gay-friendly • great art, rooftop deck & bar with vew of the west side

Portland's White House B&B 1914 NE 22nd Ave (at NE Hancock St) 503/287-7131, 800/272-7131 • gay/straight • in 1911 Greek Revival mansion • nonsmoking • WiFi • gay-owned

Riverplace Hotel 1510 SW Harbor Way 503/228-3233 • gay-friendly • restaurant & bar • WiFi • pets ok

Portland

LGBT Pride:
June. 503/295-9788, web: www.pridenw.org.

Annual Events:
May - QDoc Portland Queer Documentary Film Festival, web: www.queerdocfest.org.

May/June - Rose Festival, web: www.rosefestival.org.

September - La Femme Magnifique International Pageant, web: www.darcellexv.com.

September- AIDS Walk 503/223-9255, web: www.aidswalkportland.org.

October - Portland LGBT Film Festival, web: www.plgff.org.

City Info:
503/275-9750, web: www.travelportland.com.
800/547-7842, web: www.traveloregon.com.

Transit:
Radio Cab 503/227-1212, web: www.radiocab.net.
USA Shuttle 800/997-4599, web: www.portlandride.com.
Tri-Met System 503/238-7433, web: www.trimet.org.

Attractions:
The Grotto 503/254-7371, web: www.thegrotto.org.
Microbreweries.
Old Town.
Pioneer Courthouse Square 503/223-1613, web: www.thesquarepdx.org.
Portland Art Museum 503/226-2811, web: www.portlandartmuseum.org.
Washington Park.
World Forestry Center & Discovery Museum 503/228-1367, web: www.worldforestry.org.

Best View:
International Rose Test Gardens at Washington Park.

Weather:
The wet and sometimes chilly winter rains give Portland a lush landscape that bursts into beautiful colors in the spring and fall. Summer brings sunnier days. (Temperatures can be in the 50°s one day and the 90°s the next.)

Bars

Boxxes 1035 SW 11th Ave (at SW 11th) **503/226-4171** • 5pm-close • popular • mostly gay men • karaoke • videos • WiFi • wheelchair access • also Brig • lesbians/ gay men • dancing/DJ • also Red Cap Garage

CC Slaughter's 219 NW Davis St (at 3rd) **503/248-9135, 888/348-9135** • 3pm-2am • popular • mostly gay men • dancing/DJ • karaoke • videos • also martini lounge • WiFi • wheelchair access

Chopsticks Express II 2651 E Burnside St (at NE 26th Ave) **503/234-6171** • noon-2am • gay/ straight • karaoke • young crowd • food served • wheelchair access

Crush 1400 SE Morrison (at SE 14th) **503/235-8150** • 4pm-2am, clsd Mon • gay/ straight • wine & martini bar • food served • WiFi • wheelchair access

Darcelle XV 208 NW 3rd Ave (at NW Davis St) **503/222-5338** • 6pm-11pm, till 2am Fri-Sat, clsd Sun-Tue • gay/ straight • cabaret • strippers • drag shows • food served • wheelchair access

Fox & Hounds 217 NW 2nd Ave (btwn Everett & Davis) **503/243-5530** • 11am-2am • popular • mostly gay men • also restaurant • brunch wknds • wheelchair access

Hot Flash Portland 9 NW 2nd Ave (at Barracuda) **503/252-9333** • 6pm-10pm 4th Sat only • "for seasoned lesbians 36+ (& the women who love us!)" • dancing/DJ • cover charge

JOQ's Tavern 2512 NE Broadway (at NE 25th Ave) **503/287-4210** • 1pm-2am • mostly gay men • neighborhood bar • food served, wheelchair access

Moonstar 7410 NE Martin Luther King Jr Blvd (at NE Lombard St) **503/285-1230** • 11am-1:30am • gay/ straight

Rotture 315 SE 3rd Ave (at SE Pine) **503/234-5683** • 9pm-2:30am • gay-friendly • live music venue

Scandals 1125 SW Stark St (at SW 12th) **503/227-5887** • noon-2am • mostly gay men • friendly neighborhood bar • karaoke • bands • food served • wheelchair access • gay-owned

Shaker and Vine 2929 SE Powell Blvd (at SE 29th) **503/231-8466** • 1pm-9pm, till 11pm Th, till midnight Fri-Sat • gay/ straight • "Portland's first rock 'n' roll wine shop" • retail & lounge • nonsmoking

Silverado 318 SW 3rd Ave (at SW Oak St) **503/224-4493** • 9am-2:30am • mostly gay men • dancing/DJ • strippers • karaoke More • food served • wheelchair access • gay-owned

Starky's 2913 SE Stark St (at SE 29th Ave) **503/230-7980** • 11am-2am • popular • lesbians/ gay men • neighborhood bar • also restaurant • Sun brunch • some veggie • patio • wheelchair access

Vault Martini Bar 226 NW 12th Ave (btwn 12th & Davis Sts) **503/224-4909** • 4pm-1am, till 2am Th-Sat, 1pm-10pm Sun • gay/ straight • full menu • wheelchair access

Nightclubs

Casey's 610 NW Couch St (at 6th) **503/505-9468** • 11am-2:30am • lesbians/ gay men • dancing/DJ • karaoke

Embers 110 NW Broadway (at NW Couch St) **503/222-3082** • 11am-2am • popular • mostly gay men • dancing/DJ • drag shows • also restaurant • wheelchair access

Holocene 1001 SE Morrison (at SE 10th) **503/239-7639** • gay/ straight • popular dance club • many LGBT theme nights • live music • check local listings

Under Wonder Lounge 128 NE Russell **503/284-8686** • 5pm-midnight, open show nights only • transgender-friendly • nonsmoking • gay-owned

Cafes

Blend 2710 N Killingsworth (at Greeley) **503/473-8616** • 7am-6pm, 8am-5pm Sun • WiFi • wheelchair access

Cup & Saucer Cafe 3566 SE Hawthorne Blvd (at SE 36th) **503/236-6001** • 7am-9pm • popular w/ lesbians • full menu • vegan-friendly • beer/ wine • nonsmoking • wheelchair access

Elephant's Delicatessen 115 NW 22nd Ave (at NW Davis) **503/299-6304** • 7am-7:30pm, 9:30am-6:30pm Sun • wheelchair access

Marco's Cafe & Espresso Bar 7910 SW 35th (at Multnomah Blvd), Multnomah **503/245-0199** • 7am-9pm, from 8am Sat, 8am-2pm Sun • food served • plenty veggie • beer/ wine • wheelchair access

Pix Pâtisserie 3402 SE Division St (at SE 34th) **503/232-4407** • 2pm-midnight, noon-2am Fri-Sat • dessert • beer/ wine • wheelchair access

Three Friends Coffeehouse 201 SE 12th Ave (at Ash) **503/236-6411** • 7am-10pm, from 9am Sun • WiFi • wheelchair access

Voodoo Doughnut 22 SW 3rd Ave
503/241–4704 • 24hrs

RESTAURANTS

Andina 1314 NW Glisan St (at 13th Ave)
503/228–9535 • lunch, dinner & tapas •
Peruvian • full bar

Aura Restaurant & Lounge 1022 W
Burnside St (btwn SW 10th & 11th)
503/597–2872 • 5pm-midnight, till 2:30am Fri-
Sat, clsd Sun-Tue • also bar • wheelchair
access

Bastas Trattoria 410 NW 21st (at Flanders)
503/274–1572 • dinner nightly • northern
Italian • some veggie • full bar till late •
wheelchair access

Berbati's Pan 19 SW 2nd Ave (btwn
Burnside & Ankeny) **503/226–2122** • 11am-
2am, from 3pm Sun-Mon • Greek • full bar •
wheelchair access

Besaw's 2301 NW Savier (at NW 23rd)
503/228–2619 • 7am-10pm Tue-Fri, from 8am
Sat, 8am-3pm Sun-Mon • American •
wheelchair access

Bijou Cafe 132 SW 3rd Ave (at Pine St)
503/222–3187 • 7am-2pm, from 8am wknds •
popular • plenty veggie • "farm-fresh brkfst" •
WiFi • wheelchair access

Bluehour 250 NW 13th Ave (at NW Everett
St) **503/226–3394** • lunch Sun-Fri, dinner
nightly, Sun brunch • extensive wine list •
upscale • wheelchair access

Bread & Ink Cafe 3610 SE Hawthorne Blvd
(at 36th) **503/239–4756** • brkfst, lunch &
dinner, packed for brunch on Sun • popular
• full bar • WiFi • wheelchair access

Dingo's Mexican Grill 4612 SE Hawthorne
Blvd (at SE 46th) **503/233–3996** • noon-
10pm, till 11pm Th, till 9pm Sun • wheelchair
access • lesbian-owned

Dot's Cafe 2521 SE Clinton (at 26th)
503/235–0203 • noon-2am • popular • full
bar • eclectic American • plenty veggie •
wheelchair access

Equinox 830 N Shaver St (at Mississippi)
503/460–3333 • dinner, brunch wknds, clsd
Mon • int'l • patio • wheelchair access

Esparza's Tex-Mex Cafe 2725 SE Ankeny
St (at 28th) **503/234–7909** • 11:30am-10pm •
popular • funky • wheelchair access

Farm Cafe 503/736–3276 • 5pm-11pm •
Northwest cuisine • wheelchair access

Fish Grotto 1035 SW Stark (at SW 11th Ave,
at Boxxes) **503/226–4171** • 5pm-10pm, till
9pm Sun-Mon • popular • some veggie • full
bar • wheelchair access

Genie's Cafe 1101 SE Division St (at 12th)
503/445–9777 • 8am-3pm • brunch • house-
infused vodkas • wheelchair access

Gypsy Restaurant & Lounge 625 NW 21st
(btwn Hoyt & Irving) **503/796–1859** • 4pm-
2:30am, clsd Sun-Mon • some veggie • full bar
• inexpensive • karaoke

Hobo's 120 NW 3rd Ave (btwn Davis &
Couch) **503/224–3285** • 4pm-2:30am • piano
bar • some veggie • wheelchair access

Masu 406 SW 13th Ave (at Burnside)
503/221–6278 • lunch Mon-Th, dinner nightly
• sushi • WiFi • wheelchair access

Melt Bistro & Bar 716 NW 21st Ave (at
Johnson) **503/295–4944** • 11am-10pm, clsd
Sun • sandwiches & more

Mint 816 N Russell St **503/284–5518** • 5pm-
10pm, till 11pm Fri-Sat, clsd Sun-Mon • fusion
food • also 820 Lounge • wheelchair access

Montage 301 SE Morrison (at 3rd)
503/234–1324 • lunch Tue-Fri, dinner till 2am,
till 4am Fri-Sat • popular • Louisiana-style
cookin' • full bar • wheelchair access

Nicholas' 318 SE Grand (btwn Oak & Pine)
503/235–5123 • 11am-9pm, from noon Sun •
Middle Eastern • wheelchair access

Nostrana 1401 SE Morrison **503/234–2427** •
lunch Mon-Fri, dinner nightly • fresh, local,
wood-fired Italian • wheelchair access

Old Town Pizza 226 NW Davis (at NW 3rd)
503/222–9999 • 11:30am-11pm, till midnight
Fri-Sat • above Shanghai Tunnels •
supposedly home to 100-year-old ghost •
wheelchair access

Old Wives Tales 1300 E Burnside St (at
13th) **503/238–0470** • 8am-9pm, till 10pm Fri-
Sat • popular • multi-ethnic & vegetarian •
beer/ wine • live music • wheelchair access

Oven & Shaker 1134 NW Everett St
503/241–1600
• 11:30am-midnight

Paley's Place 1204 NW 21st Ave (at NW
Northrup St) **503/243–2403** • dinner nightly •
Northwest cuisine

Paradox Cafe 3439 SE Belmont St (at SE
35th) **503/232–7508** • brkfst, lunch & dinner •
popular • vegetarian diner • killer Reuben •
wheelchair access

Pour 2755 NE Broadway (at NE 28th) 503/288-7687 • 4:30pm-11pm, till close Fri-Sat, clsd Sun • wine bar & bistro • wheelchair access

The Roxy 1121 SW Stark St (btwn 11th & 12th) 503/223-9160 • 24hrs, clsd Mon • popular • retro American diner • WiFi • wheelchair access

Santa Fe Taqueria 831 NW 23rd (at Kearney) 503/220-0406 • 11am-midnight • live entertainment • wheelchair access

Saucebox 214 SW Broadway (at Burnside) 503/241-3393 • 5pm-close • pan-Asian • plenty veggie • full bar • DJ • wheelchair access • gay-owned

Tasty n Sons 3808 N Williams 503/241-1600 • 9am-10pm, till 11pm Fri-Sat • full bar

Vita Cafe 3023 NE Alberta St (btwn 30th & 31st) 503/335-8233 • brkfst, lunch & dinner • mostly vegetarian/vegan • some free-range meat • wheelchair access

West Cafe 1201 SW Jefferson St (12th Ave) 503/227-8189 • lunch Mon-Fri, dinner nightly, Sun brunch • "comfort food w/ a twist" • live entertainment • WiFi • wheelchair access

Yakuza Lounge 5411 NE 30th Ave (at Killingsworth) 503/450-0893 • 5pm-close, clsd Mon-Tue • Japanese • full bar • wheelchair access

ENTERTAINMENT & RECREATION

Gay Skate 1 SE Spokane St (at Oaks Park Way, at Oaks Rink) 503/233-5777 • 7pm-9pm 3rd Mon only

Out Dancing 975 SE Sandy Blvd (at SE Ankeny St & SE 9th Ave) 503/236-5129 • LGBT dance lessons

Rose City Rollers • Portland's female roller derby league • visit www.rosecityrollers.com for events

Sauvie's Island Beach 25 miles NW (off US 30) • follow Reeder Rd to the Collins beach area, park at the farthest end of the road, then follow path to beach

BOOKSTORES

CounterMedia 927 SW Oak (btwn 9th & 10th) 503/226-8141 • 11am-7pm, noon-6pm Sun • alternative comics • vintage gay books/ periodicals/ erotica

In Other Words 14 NE Killingsworth St (at Williams) 503/232-6003 • noon-7pm, clsd Sun-Mon • feminist lit • music • resource center • wheelchair access

Laughing Horse Bookstore 12 NE 10th Ave (near Burnside) 503/236-2893 • 11am-7pm, clsd Sun • alternative/ progressive • wheelchair access

Powell's Books 1005 W Burnside St (at 10th) 503/228-4651, 800/878-7323 • 9am-11pm • popular • largest new & used bookstore in the world • cafe • readings • wheelchair access

RETAIL SHOPS

Fat Fancy 1013 SW Morrison (btwn 10th & 11th) 503/445-4353 • plus-size clothing boutique • wheelchair access

Hip Chicks Do Wine 4510 SE 23rd Ave (SE Holgate & 26th) 503/234-3790 • 11am-6pm

GYMS & HEALTH CLUBS

Common Ground Wellness Center 5010 NE 33rd Ave (at Alberta St) 503/238-1065 • 10am-11pm • gay-friendly • wellness center • call for women's & trans nights • reservations required

EROTICA

Fantasy for Adults 1512 W Burnside (near 15th) 503/295-6969 • 24hrs

Spartacus Leathers 300 SW 12th Ave (at Burnside) 503/224-2604

Salem

NIGHTCLUBS

Southside Speakeasy 3529 Fairview Industrial Dr SE (at Madrona) 503/362-1139 • 11am-2am, from 3:30pm wknds • gay/ straight • neighborhood bar • dancing/DJ • food served • karaoke • drag shows • WiFi • gay-owned

RESTAURANTS

Davinci's 180 High St SE 504/399-1413 • dinner only, clsd Sun • full bar

Word Of Mouth 503/930-4285 • 7am-3pm

Sauvie Island

ENTERTAINMENT & RECREATION

Collins Beach take Hwy 30 N from Portland, turn onto "Sauvie Island Bridge" (then take Gillihan Rd to Reeder Rd) • gay/ straight • nude beach • get a parking permit before you go (available at general store at base of Sauvie Island Bridge)

Silverton

ACCOMMODATIONS

The Oregon Garden Resort 895 W Main St 800/966-6490 • gay-friendly • restaurant & lounge • pool • WiFi

PENNSYLVANIA

Abington

BARS

Kitchen Bar 1482 Old York Rd **215/576-9766**
• noon-2am, from 8am wknds • gay-friendly •
dancing/DJ • food served • live entertainment

RESTAURANTS

Vintage Bar & Restaurant 1116 Old York
Rd **215/887-8500** • 11am-2am • wheelchair
access

Allentown

see also Bethlehem

ACCOMMODATIONS

Grim's Manor B&B 10 Kern Rd, Kutztown
610/683-7089 • lesbians/gay men • 200-yr-old
stone farmhouse on 5 acres • full brkfst •
nonsmoking • gay-owned

BARS

Candida's 247 N 12th St (at Chew)
610/434-3071 • 4pm-2am, from 2pm Fri-Sun
• lesbians/gay men • dancing/DJ •
neighborhood bar • food served • karaoke

Stonewall, Moose Lounge Bar & Grille
28 N 10th St (at Hamilton) **610/432-0215** •
7pm-2am, clsd Sun- Mon • popular • mostly
gay men • dancing/DJ • food served • live
shows • karaoke • drag shows • male dancers
• videos

Altoona

NIGHTCLUBS

Escapade 2523 Union Ave, Rte 36
814/946-8195 • 8pm-2am • lesbians/gay
men • dancing/DJ • gay-owned

Bethlehem

NIGHTCLUBS

Diamonz 1913 W Broad St (at Pennsylvania
Ave) **610/865-1028** • 7pm-2am, from 5pm Fri-
Sat • mostly women • dancing/DJ • live shows
• karaoke • also restaurant • some veggie •
wheelchair access

Bristol

EROTICA

Bristol News World 576 Bristol Pike/ Rte 13
N **215/785-4770**

Bryn Mawr

RETAIL SHOPS

TLA Video 761 Lancaster Ave **610/520-1222**
• 10am-11pm • extensive LGBT titles

Butler

NIGHTCLUBS

M&J's Lounge 124 Mercer St **724/496-8955**
• 9pm-midnight Th, 9:30pm-3am Fri-Sat •
lesbians/gay men • neighborhood bar • 18+ •

Erie

NIGHTCLUBS

Craze Nightclub 1607 Raspberry St (at 16th)
814/456-3027 • 9pm-2am, from 5pm Wed,
clsd Tue & Th • gay/ straight • dancing/DJ •
karaoke • drag shows • 18+ Mon • patio

The Zone 133 W 18th St (at Peach)
814/452-0125 • 8pm-2am, from 4pm Wed •
lesbians/gay men • dancing/DJ • food served

RESTAURANTS

La Bella 802 W 18th St **814/456-2244** •
5pm-9pm, clsd Sun-Tue • BYOB • gay-owned

Pie in the Sky Cafe 463 W 8th St (at
Walnut) **814/459-8638** • lunch & dinner, clsd
Sun-Mon • BYOB • reservations
recommended • wheelchair access

RETAIL SHOPS

Ink Assassins Tattoos & Piercings 2601
Peach St **814/455-6752** • noon-10pm, till
6pm Sun

PUBLICATIONS

Erie Gay News **814/456-9833** • covers
news & events in the Erie, Cleveland,
Pittsburgh, Buffalo & Chautauqua County (NY)
region

Gay People's Chronicle **216/916-9338** •
Ohio's largest bi-weekly LGBT newspaper w/
extensive listings

Gettysburg

ACCOMMODATIONS

Battlefield B&B 2264 Emmitsburg Rd (at
Ridge Rd) **717/334-8804, 888/766-3897** •
gay/ straight • full brkfst • Civil War home •
kids ok • WiFi • lesbian-owned • wheelchair
access

The Beechmont Inn B&B 315 Broadway,
Hanover **717/632-3013, 800/553-7009** • gay-
friendly • WiFi • wheelchair access

Sheppard Mansion B&B 117 Frederick St (at High St), Hanover **717/633-8075, 877/762-6746** • gay/ straight • full brkfst • kids 12 years & up ok • nonsmoking • WiFi • also restaurant & bar

Greensburg

NIGHTCLUBS

Longbada Lounge 108 W Pittsburgh St (at Pennsylvania Ave) **724/837-6614** • 9pm-2am, clsd Sun-Mon • lesbians/ gay men • dancing/DJ • karaoke • drag shows • patio • wheelchair access

Harrisburg

INFO LINES & SERVICES

LGBT Community Center Coalition of Central PA 1306 N 3rd St **717/920-9534**

BARS

Bar 704 704 N 3rd St **717/234-4226** • 4pm-2am • mostly gay men • neighborhood bar • older crowd • wheelchair access

The Brownstone Lounge 412 Forster St (btwn 3rd & 6th) **717/234-7009** • 11am-2am, from 5pm wknds • lesbians/ gay men • neighborhood bar • wheelchair access

NIGHTCLUBS

Stallions 706 N 3rd St (enter rear) **717/232-3060** • 7pm-2am • popular • mostly gay men • dancing/DJ • live shows • karaoke • drag shows • strippers • wheelchair access

Johnstown

NIGHTCLUBS

Lucille's 520 Washington St (near Central Park) **814/539-4448** • 6pm-2am, clsd Sun-Mon • lesbians/ gay men • dancing/DJ • drag shows • strippers • karaoke

Lancaster

ACCOMMODATIONS

Cameron Estate Inn 1855 Mansion Ln, Mount Joy **717/492-0111, 888/422-6376** • gay/ straight • full brkfst • nonsmoking • restaurant • wheelchair access • gay-owned

Lancaster Arts Hotel 300 Harrisburg Ave **717/299-3000, 866/720-2787** • gay-friendly • great restaurant • wheelchair access

BARS

Dad's Bar & Grill 168 S Main St, Manheim **717/665-1960** • 4pm-2am • gay/ straight • food served • karaoke

Tally Ho 201 W Orange St (at Water) **717/299-0661** • 8pm-2am • lesbians/ gay men • dancing/DJ • karaoke • drag shows • young crowd

RESTAURANTS

The Loft above Tally Ho bar **717/299-0661** • lunch Mon-Fri, dinner Mon-Sat • contemporary American/ French

Milford

ACCOMMODATIONS

Hotel Fauchere 401 Broad St (at Catharine St) **570/409-1212** • gay-friendly • historic boutique hotel • full brkfst • also restaurant & bar • nonsmoking • kids/ pets ok • wheelchair access

New Hope

see also Lambertville & Sergeantsville, New Jersey

ACCOMMODATIONS

Ash Mill Farm B&B 5358 York Rd (at Rte 202), Holicong **215/794-5373** • gay-friendly • full brkfst • nonsmoking • WiFi • gay-owned

The Lexington House 6171 Upper York Rd **215/794-0811** • gay/ straight • 1749 country home • pool • nonsmoking • gay-owned

The Wishing Well Guesthouse 144 Old York Rd **215/862-8819** • gay/ straight • nonsmoking • kids ok • gay-owned

BARS

Bob Eagans 6426 Lower York Rd (at the Nevermore Hotel) **215/862-5225** • gay/ straight • cabaret • dinner served • also hotel

Havana 105 S Main St **215/862-9897** • noon-2am • gay/ straight • concert venue & restaurant • karaoke

RESTAURANTS

Eagle Diner 6522 Lower York Rd **215/862-5575** • 24hrs • wheelchair access

Karla's 5 W Mechanic St (at Main) **215/862-2612** • noon-10pm, till midnight Fri-Sat, from 11am Sun • some veggie • full bar till 2am

Wildflowers 8 W Mechanic St **215/862-2241** • seasonal, noon-9pm • full bar • outdoor dining

EROTICA

Grownups 2 E Mechanic St (at Main) **215/862-9304** • toys etc • gay-owned

Le Chateau Exotique 27 W Mechanic St **215/862-3810** • fetishwear

Norristown

BARS

Beagle Tavern 1003 E Main St
610/272–3133 • 11am-2am • gay/ straight •
more gay Wed & Fri • dancing/DJ • food served
• karaoke

Philadelphia

INFO LINES & SERVICES

William Way LGBT Community Center
1315 Spruce St (at Juniper) 215/732–2220 •
11am-10pm, noon-5pm wknds

ACCOMMODATIONS

Alexander Inn Spruce (at 12th St)
215/923–3535, 877/253–9466 • gay/ straight •
gym • nonsmoking • WiFi • gay-owned

The Gables B&B 4520 Chester Ave
215/662–1918 • gay/ straight • nonsmoking •
WiFi • gay-owned

The Independent Hotel 1234 Locust St (at
13th) 215/772–1440 • gay/ straight • boutique
hotel • WiFi • wheelchair access

Latham Hotel 135 S 17th St (at Walnut)
215/563–7474, 877/528–4261 • gay-friendly •
WiFi • wheelchair access

Morris House Hotel 225 S 8th St
215/922–2446 • gay-friendly • nonsmoking •
WiFi • also M Restaurant

Palomar Philadelphia 117 S 17th St
215/563–5006, 888/725–1778 • gay-friendly •
WiFi • wheelchair access

BARS

Bike Stop 204-206 S Quince St (btwn 11th &
12th) 215/627–1662 • 4pm-2am, from 2pm
wknds • mostly gay men • DJ • leather (very
leather-women-friendly) • karaoke

ICandy 254 S 12th St (btwn Locust & Spruce)
267/324–3500 • 4pm-2am • mostly gay men •
dancing/DJ • multi-level entertainment
complex

Khyber Pass Pub 56 S 2nd St (btwn Market
& Chestnut) 215/238–5888 • 11am-2am •
gay-friendly • food served • live bands •
wheelchair access

L'Etage 624 S 6th St (at Bainbridge)
215/592–0656 • 7:30pm-1am, till 2am Fri-Sat,
clsd Mon • gay/ straight • dancing/DJ • cabaret
• also crepe restaurant downstairs

North Third 801 N 3rd St (at Brown)
215/413–3666 • 4pm-2am, from 10am wknd
brunch • gay/ straight • also restaurant

Stir Lounge 1705 Chancellor St (at
Rittenhouse Sq btwn Walnut & Spruce)
215/732–2700 • 4pm-2am • lesbians/ gay
men • neighborhood bar • dancing/DJ • girl
party 1st Sat

Tabu Lounge & Sports Bar 200 S 12th St
215/964–9675 • noon-2am • gay/ straight •
food served • karaoke

Tavern on Camac 243 S Camac St (at
Spruce) 215/545–0900 • 4pm-2am • lesbians/
gay men • dancing/DJ • piano bar • food
served

Venture Inn 255 S Camac (at Spruce)
215/545–8731 • 11am-2am • lesbians/ gay
men • neighborhood bar • food served

The Westbury 261 S 13th (at Spruce)
215/546–5170 • 4pm-2am. from 11am wknds
• lesbians/ gay men • neighborhood bar •
food seved • wheelchair access • gay-owned

Woody's 202 S 13th St (at Walnut)
215/545–1893 • 4pm-2am • mostly gay men •
dancing/DJ • country/ western • karaoke •
Latin Th • strippers • WiFi • wheelchair access

NIGHTCLUBS

Bob & Barbara's Lounge 1509 South St
215/545–4511 • 3pm-2am, from 5pm Sun •
gay/ straight • drag shows Th • live jazz Fri-Sat

Groove Philly • mostly women • dancing/DJ
• occasional events by Denise Cohen and the
former staff of Sisters , check
www.groovephilly.com for events

Ladies 2000 856/869–0193 • seasonal
parties • call hotline for details

Shampoo 417 N 8th St (at Willow)
215/922–7500 • 9pm-2am, clsd Mon-Tue & Th
• gay/ straight • more gay Fri • dancing/DJ

Voyeur 1221 St James St (off 13th & Locust)
215/735–5772 • 11am-3am, from 9pm wknds •
mostly gay men • dancing/DJ • live bands •
karaoke • cabaret • private club

CAFES

10th Street Pour House 262 S 10th St (at
Spruce) 215/922–5626 • 6am-2pm, popular
brunch wknds • wheelchair access

B2 Cafe 1500 E Passyunk Ave 215/271–5520
• great vegan soft serve ice cream • WiFi

Capriccio 110 N 16th St (at Benjamin
Franklin Pkwy) 215/735–9797 • 6:30am-7pm,
8am-8pm wknds

Cosi 1128 Walnut St 215/413–1608 • 7am-
11pm

Green Line Cafe 4239 Baltimore Ave (at
43rd) 215/222–3431 • 7am-11pm, 8am-8pm
Sun • live shows

RESTAURANTS

13th Street Pizza 209 S 13th St (at Chancellor St) 215/546-4453 • 11am-4am • popular late night

Alfa 1709 Walnut St (at 17th) 215/751-0201 • 5pm-2am • also bar

Bar Ferdinand 1030 N 2nd St • great tapas & wine

Cantina Feliz 424 S Bethlehem Pike, Fort Washington 215/646-1320 • 11am-9pm, from 4pm Sat-Sun, till 10pm Fri- Sat

The Continental 138 Market St (at 2nd) 215/923-6069 • lunch, dinner, wknd brunch • also bar until 2am

Geno's Steaks 1219 S 9th St 215/389-0659 • 24hrs • great cheesesteak • gay-owned

Honey's 800 N 4th St 215/925-1150 • 7am-4pm, till 5pm wknds • BYOB

Knock 226 S 12th St 215/925-1166 • lunch & dinner, Sun brunch • American • also bar

Liberties 705 N 2nd St (at Fairmount) 215/238-0660 • lunch & dinner • full bar till 2am

Lolita 106 S 13th St (at Sansom) 215/546-7100 • 5pm-10pm • upscale Mexican • BYOB

Mercato 1216 Spruce St 215/985-2962 • dinner • Italian • BYOB

Philadelphia

LGBT PRIDE:

June. 215/875-9288, web: www.phillypride.org.

ANNUAL EVENTS:

April/May - Equality Forum 215/732-3378, web: www.equalityforum.com. Weekend of LGBT film, performances, literature, sports, seminars, parties & more.

June - Womongathering, web: wherewomyngather.com. Women's spirituality fest.

July - QFest Int'l Gay & Lesbian Film Festival 267/765-9800 x701, web: www.qfest.com.

October - OutFest 215/875-9288, web: www.phillypride.org.

CITY INFO:

Philadelphia Convention & Visitors Bureau 215/636-3300, web: www.pcvb.org.

TRANSIT:

Quaker City Cab 215/726-6000, web: www.quakercitycab.com.
Lady Liberty Shuttle 215/724-8888, web: www.ladylibertyshuttle.com.
Transit Authority (SEPTA) 215/580-7800, web: www.septa.org.

ATTRACTIONS:

Academy of Natural Sciences 215/299-1000, web: www.acnatsci.org.
African American Museum 215/574-0380, web: www.aampmuseum.org.
Betsy Ross House 215/629-4026, web: www.betsyrosshouse.org.
Independence Hall 215/965-2305, web: www.nps.gov/inde.
Liberty Bell Pavilion.
National Museum Of American Jewish History 215/923-3811, web: www.nmajh.org.
Philadelphia Museum of Art 215/763-8100, web: www.philamuseum.org.
Reading Terminal Market 215/922-2317, web: www.readingterminalmarket.org.
Rodin Museum 215/568-6026, web: www.rodinmuseum.org.

BEST VIEW:

Top of Center Square, 16th & Market.

WEATHER:

Winter temperatures hover in the 20's. Summers are humid with temperatures in the 80's and 90's.

Midtown II 122 S 11th St 215/627–6452 • 24hrs • diner • popular late night • transgender-friendly

Mixto 1141 Pine St 215/592–0363 • lunch & dinner, brkfst wknds • Latin American

My Thai 2200 South St (at 22nd) 215/985–1878 • 5pm-10pm, till 11pm Fri-Sat • full bar

New Harmony 135 N 9th St (at Cherry) 215/627–4520 • 11am-11pm • vegan/ Chinese

Paesano's 1017 S 9th St 215/440–0371 • 11am-7pm • great sandwiches

Sabrina's 910 Christian St 215/574–1599 • 8am-10pm, till 8pm Tue-Th, till 4pm Sun-Mon

El Vez 121 S 13th St (at Sansom) 215/928–9800 • lunch Mon-Sat, dinner nightly, Sun brunch • Latin American/ Mexican • full bar

White Dog Cafe 3420 Sansom St (at Walnut) 215/386–9224 • lunch & dinner, brunch Sun • full bar

ENTERTAINMENT & RECREATION

Philly Roller Girls • Philly's female roller derby league • visit www.phillyrollergirls.com for events

The Walt Whitman House 328 Mickle Blvd, Camden, NJ 856/964–5383 • the last home of America's great & controversial poet, just across the Delaware River

BOOKSTORES

Giovanni's Room 345 S 12th St (at Pine) 215/923–2960 • 11:30am-7pm, from 1pm Sun • popular • legendary LGBT bookstore

RETAIL SHOPS

Philadelphia AIDS Thrift 710 S 5th St 215/922–3186 • 11am-8pm, till 9pm Fri-Sat, till 7pm Sun

PUBLICATIONS

PGN (Philadelphia Gay News) 215/625–8501 • LGBT newspaper w/ extensive listings

GYMS & HEALTH CLUBS

12th St Gym 204 S 12th St (btwn Locust & Walnut) 215/985–4092 • pool • day passes

EROTICA

The Mood 531 South St 215/413–1930

Passional Boutique 317 South St 215/829–4986, 877/826–7738 • noon-10pm • corsets • fetishwear • toys • woman-owned

Sexploratorium 317 South St (across from TLA theater) 215/923–1398 • noon-10pm • workshops • gallery

Pittsburgh

INFO LINES & SERVICES

AA Gay/ Lesbian 412/471–7472 • call for times & location

Gay/ Lesbian Community Center 210 Grant St 412/422–0114 • 9am-9pm, noon-6pm Sun

ACCOMMODATIONS

Camp Davis 311 Red Brush Rd, Boyers 724/637–2402 • April-Oct • lesbians/ gay men • cabins, trailer, & campsites • pool • adults 21+ only • 1 hour from Pittsburgh

The Inn on Negley 703 S Negley Ave (at Elmer St) 412/661–0631 • gay-friendly • full brkfst • nonsmoking • WiFi • wheelchair access • women-owned

The Inn on the Mexican War Streets 604 W North Ave 412/231–6544 • lesbians/ gay men • nonsmoking • WiFi • gay-owned

Morning Glory Inn B&B 2119 Sarah St 412/431–1707 • gay-friendly • WiFi • woman-owned

The Parador Inn 939 Western Ave 412/231–4800, 877/540–1443 • gay-friendly • WiFi • gay-owned

The Priory 614 Pressley St (near Cedar Ave) 412/231–3338, 866/377–4679 • gay-friendly • nonsmoking • kids ok • WiFi • wheelchair access

BARS

5801 5801 Ellsworth Ave (at Maryland) 412/661–5600 • 4pm-2am, from 2pm Sun • lesbians/ gay men • deck • also restaurant • wheelchair access

The Backdraft Bar & Grill 3049 Churchview Ave 412/885–1239 • 11am-2am, till midnight Sun • gay/ straight • live bands • karaoke

Blue Moon Bar & Lounge 5115 Butler St (in Lawrenceville) 412/781–1119 • 5pm-2am, 4pm-1am Mon • mostly gay men • neighborhood bar • transgender-friendly • go-go dancers

Cattivo 146 44th St 412/687–2157 • 4pm-2am Wed-Sun, clsd Mon-Tue • mostly women • dancing/DJ • karaoke • drag shows • food served

Cruze Bar 1600 Smallman St (at 16th St) 412/471–1400 • 4pm-2am, clsd Mon • lesbians/ gay men • dancing/DJ • live entertainment • gay-owned

Images 965 Liberty Ave (at 10th St) 412/391–9990 • 2pm-2am • mostly gay men • karaoke • videos

PTown 4740 Baum Blvd 412/621-0111 • 6pm-2am • lesbians/ gay men • dancing/DJ • strippers • WiFi

Real Luck Cafe 1519 Penn Ave (at 16th) 412/471–7832 • 4pm-2am • lesbians/ gay men • neighborhood bar • go-go dancers • food served • wheelchair access • gay-owned

Remedy 5121 Butler St, Lawrenceville 412/781–6771 • 4pm-2am, from 12:30pm Sun • gay/ straight • multiracial • neighborhood bar • dancing/DJ • also restaurant upstairs

Spin Bartini/ Ultra Lounge 5744 Ellsworth Ave, Shadyside 412/362–7746 • 4pm-2am • gay/ straight • live jazz • wheelchair access

There Ultra Lounge 931 Liberty Ave (at Smithfield) 412/642-4435 • 3:30pm-2am, from 7:30pm Sat-Sun • lesbians/ gay men • karaoke • wheelchair access

NIGHTCLUBS

1226 on Herron 1226 Herron Ave (at Liberty) 412/682–6839 • 6pm-2am, clsd Mon-Wed • mostly men

941 Saloon 941 Liberty Ave (at Smithfield St, 2nd flr) 412/281–5222 • 2pm-2am • lesbians/ gay men • dancing/DJ • karaoke

The Link 91 Wendel Rd, Herminie 724/446–7717 • 7pm-2am, clsd Mon • lesbians/ gay men • dancing/DJ • live shows • drag shows • male dancers • food served • patio

CAFES

Square Cafe 1137 S Braddock Ave 412/244–8002 • 7am-3pm, from 8am Sun • live shows monthly • lesbian-owned

Zeke's Coffee 6012 Penn Ave 724/201–1671 • 9am-5pm, till 2pm Mon, till 8pm Th, clsd Sun

RESTAURANTS

Abay 130 S Highland Ave (at Baum Blvd) 412/661–9736 • lunch & dinner, clsd Mon • Ethiopian • plenty veggie

Capri 6001 Penn Ave (at Highland Ave) 412/363–1250 • 11am-midnight, 6pm-2am Th-Sat • pizza

Dinette 5996 Penn Cir S 412/362–0202 • dinner only, clsd Sun-Mon • plates to share, starters & thin-crust pizzas • women-owned

Pittsburgh

LGBT PRIDE:
June. 412/246- 4451, web: www.pittsburghpride.org.

ANNUAL EVENTS:
June - Three Rivers Arts Festival, web: www.artsfestival.net.
October - Pittsburgh International Lesbian & Gay Film Festival 412/422-6776, web: www.plgfs.org.

CITY INFO:
800/359-0758, web: www.visitpittsburgh.com.

TRANSIT:
Yellow Cab 412/665-8100, web: www.pghyellowcab.com. 888/258-3826.
Port Authority Transit (PAT) 412/442-2000, web: www.portauthority.org.

ATTRACTIONS:
Andy Warhol Museum 412/237-8300, web: www.warhol.org.
Carnegie Museums of Pittsburgh 412/622-3131, web: www.carnegiemuseums.org.
Fallingwater (in Mill Run) 724/329-8501, web: www.paconserve.org.
Frick Art & Historical Center 412/371-0600, web: www.frickart.org.
Golden Triangle District.
Shopping & dining in the Strip District.
National Aviary 412/323-7235, web: www.aviary.org.
Phipps Conservatory 412/622-6914, web: www.phipps.conservatory.org.
Rachel Carson Homestead (in Springdale) 724/274-5459, web: www.rachelcarsonhomestead.org.
Station Square.

Dish 128 S 17th St (at Sarah) **412/390–2012** • 5pm-2am, clsd Sun • Italian • also bar

Double Wide Grill 2339 E Carson St (at S 24th St) **412/390–1111** • lunch & dinner, wknd brunch • BBQ • plenty veggie/ vegan

Eleven 1150 Smallman St (at 11th) **412/201–5656** • lunch & dinner, Sun brunch

Harris Grill 5747 Ellsworth Ave **412/362–5273** • dinner nightly, wknd brunch • full bar

Kaya 2000 Smallman St (at 20th) **412/261–6565** • lunch & dinner • Latin/ Caribbean • plenty veggie

NOLA On the Square 24 Market Sq **412/471–9100** • 11am-11pm, clsd Sun • live music

OTB Bicycle Cafe 2518 East Carson St (at S 26th) **412/381-3698** • 11am-10pm • burgers • plenty veggie • also bar • occasional events

Pamela's Diner 60 21st St **412/281–6366** • 7am-3pm, from 8am Sun • also 5 other locations in Pittsburgh • lesbian-owned

Point Brugge Cafe 401 Hastings (at Reynolds) **412/441–3334** • lunch & dinner, Sun brunch, clsd Mon • Belgian/ European

Primanti Brothers 46 18th St **412/263–2142** • Pittsburgh's iconic sandwich shop • many locations

Quiet Storm 5430 Penn Ave (at Graham St) **412/661–9355** • 9am-9pm, 10am-4pm Sat, clsd Sun & Tue • vegetarian/ vegan • WiFi • wheelchair access

Red Oak Cafe 3610 Forbes Ave (at Lothrop) **412/621–2221** • 7am-7pm, till 5pm Fri, clsd wknds • salads & sandwiches • plenty veggie/ vegan

Spoon 134 S Highland Ave **412/362–6001** • fresh "farm to table" menu • also lounge

Zenith 86 S 26th St **412/481–4833** • 11am-9pm, Sun brunch, clsd Mon-Wed • vegetarian/ vegan • also antiques store • wheelchair access

ENTERTAINMENT & RECREATION

Andy Warhol Museum 117 Sandusky St (at General Robinson) **412/237–8300** • 10am-5pm, till 10pm Fri, clsd Mon • is it soup or is it art? see for yourself

Burgh Bits & Bites Food Tour **412/209–3370, 800/979–3370** • explore the vivid history & culinary delights of the Steel City

Pittsburgh Public Market 2100 Smallman St **412/281–4505** • the goodness of locally grown produce, fresh-baked goods, handmade crafts

RETAIL SHOPS

Slacker 1321 E Carson St (btwn 13th & 14th) **412/381–3911** • noon-9pm, 11am-6pm Sun • magazines • clothing • leather • wheelchair access

Who New? 5156 Butler St **412/781–0588** • noon-6pm, clsd Mon-Tue, open Sun by chance • vintage modern design • gay-owned

EROTICA

Adult Mart 346 Blvd of the Allies **412/261-9119** • 24hrs

Poconos

ACCOMMODATIONS

Frog Hollow 3535 High Crest Rd, Canadensis **570/595–2032** • lesbians/ gay men • secluded 1920s cottage • kids/ pets ok • lesbian-owned

Rainbow Mountain Resort **570/223–8484** • lesbians/ gay men • transgender-friendly • swimming • hot tub • WiFi • gay-owned • also restaurant & bar • dancing/DJ Fri-Sat • piano bar • karaoke

The Woods Campground 845 Vaughn Acres Ln, Lehighton **610/377–9577** • lesbians/ gay men • 84 campsites • RV spots • also cabins • swimming • 18+ • WiFi

Reading

BARS

The Peanut Bar & Restaurant 332 Penn St **610/376-8500, 800/515-8500** • 11am-11pm, till midnight Fri-Sat, clsd Sun • a Reading landmark! • non-smoking • WiFi

The Red Star 11 S 10th St (at Penn St) **610/375-4116** • 9pm-2am, clsd Sun-Tue • mostly gay men • neighborhood bar • dancing/DJ • leather • multiracial • transgender-friendly • older crowd • gay-owned

RESTAURANTS

Judy's On Cherry 332 Cherry St **610/374-8511** • lunch Tue-Fri, dinner Tue-Sat, clsd Sun-Mon • Mediterranean

The Ugly Oyster 21 S 5th St (at Cherry) **610/373-6791** • 11:30am-10pm, from noon Sat, clsd Sun • traditional Irish pub (bar open till 2am) • live shows

Scranton

BARS

Twelve Penny Saloon 3501 Birney Ave, Moosic **570/941-0444** • 6pm-2am, from 3pm wknds • lesbians/ gay men • neighborhood bar • dancing/DJ • leather • transgender-friendly • food served • karaoke • drag shows • wheelchair access • gay-owned

State College

ACCOMMODATIONS

The Atherton Hotel 125 S Atherton St (at College Ave) **814/231-2100, 800/832-0132** • gay-friendly • nonsmoking • WiFi • also restaurant & bar • wheelchair access

BARS

Chumley's 100 W College **814/238-4446** • 5pm-2am, from 6pm Sun • popular • lesbians/ gay men • neighborhood bar • wheelchair access

NIGHTCLUBS

Indigo 112 W College Ave **814/234-1031** • 9pm-2am, clsd Mon-Wed • gay/ straight • "Alternative" night Sun • dancing/DJ • young crowd

Sunbury

BARS

CC's 555 Klinger Rd **570/286-6022** • 7pm-2am Th-Sat, clsd Sun-Wed • lesbians/ gay men • karaoke • drag shows

Uniontown

BARS

Eddie's Tavern 200 Francis St **724/438-9563** • 11am-midnight • gay-friendly • karaoke • try the wings

NIGHTCLUBS

Club 231 231 Pittsburgh St/ Rte 51 (at Fulton) **724/430-1477** • 9pm-close • mostly men • dancing/DJ • karaoke • drag shows • gay-owned

Wilkes-Barre

INFO LINES & SERVICES

NEPA Rainbow Alliance Resource Center 67 Public Square, 5th flr, Edwardsville **570/763-9877** • coalition of NE PA's LGBT organizations & businesses • WiFi

NIGHTCLUBS

Twist 1170 Hwy 315 (in Fox Ridge Plaza) **570/970-7503** • 8pm-2am, from 6pm Sun • mostly gay men • dancing/DJ • karaoke • drag shows • patio • wheelchair access

York

ACCOMMODATIONS

Yorktowne Hotel 48 E Market St **717/848-1111** • gay-friendly • restaurant • WiFi • wheelchair access

NIGHTCLUBS

Altland's Ranch 8505 Orchard Rd, Spring Grove **717/225-4479** • 8pm-2am Fri-Sat only • lesbians/ gay men • dancing/DJ • country western 3rd Fri • karaoke

EROTICA

Cupid's Connection Adult Boutique 244 N George St (at North) **717/846-5029**

RHODE ISLAND

Coventry

RESTAURANTS

Indigo Lounge & Pizzeria 599 Tiogue Ave **401/615-9600** • 4pm-10pm, till 1am wknds • live music

Newport

INFO LINES & SERVICES

Sobriety First 135 Pelham St (at Channing Memorial Church) **401/438-8860** • 8pm Fri

ACCOMMODATIONS

Architect's Inn 2 Sunnyside Pl **401/845-2547, 877/466-2547** • gay-friendly • WiFi • gay-owned

Francis Malbone House Inn 392 Thames St (at Memorial Blvd) **401/846-0392, 800/846-0392** • gay-friendly • nonsmoking • WiFi • wheelchair access

Hilltop Inn 2 Kay St **800/846-0392** • gay-friendly • craftsman-style inn • full brkfst • WiFi • gay-owned

Hydrangea House Inn 16 Bellevue Ave **401/846-4435, 800/945-4667** • popular • gay/ straight • full brkfst • near beach • nonsmoking • WiFi • gay-owned

The Spring Seasons Inn 86 Spring St (btwn Mary St & Touro) **401/849-0004, 877/294-0004** • gay-friendly • full brkfst • jacuzzi baths • nonsmoking

RESTAURANTS

Donick's Restaurant & Ice Cream Spa 16 Broadway 401/835–5183 • 6am-2am • BYOB • gay-owned

Whitehorse Tavern 26 Marlborough St (at Farewell) 401/849-3600 • lunch & dinner, Sun brunch • upscale dining • nonsmoking • patio

Pawtucket

INFO LINES & SERVICES

Gay & Lesbian AA 71 Park Place (at Park Place Congregational Church) 401/438–8860 • 7:30pm Tue

RESTAURANTS

Garden Grill 727 East Ave (and of Blackstone Blvd) 401/454-8951 • 11am-10pm • vegetarian, vegan & wheat- and gluten-free

Providence

ACCOMMODATIONS

Edgewood Manor 232 Norwood Ave (at Broad) 401/781-0099 • gay-friendly • 1905 Greek Revival mansion • nonsmoking • WiFi

Hotel Dolce Villa 63 De Pasquale Square (at Atwells) 401/383-7031 • gay/ straight • boutique hotel • nonsmoking

The Hotel Providence 139 Mathewson 401/861-8000, 800/861-8990 • gay/ straight • Aspire restaurant onsite • WiFi • nonsmoking

NYLO Hotel 400 Knight St, Warwick 401/734-4460 • gay/ straight • restaurant & bar • WiFi • whelchair access

Renaissance Providence Hotel 5 Avenue of the Arts (at Francis) 401/919-5000, 800/468-3571 • gay/ straight • restaurant & bar • WiFi • nonsmoking

BARS

Alleycat 17 Snow St (at Washington) 401/272-6369 • 3pm-1am, till 2am Fri-Sat • lesbians/ gay men • neighborhood bar • videos • gay-owned

Deville's Cafe 345 S Water St 401/383-8883 • 4pm-midnight, till 1am Fri-Sat, clsd Mon • lesbians/ gay men • food served • lesbian-owned

The Stable 125 Washington (at Mathewson) 401/272-6950 • 2pm-1am, till 2am Fri-Sat, from noon Sat-Sun • lesbians/ gay men • neighborhood bar • videos • wheelchair access

NIGHTCLUBS

Girl Spot 65 Poe St (at Platforms) 401/781-3121 • Sat only • mostly women • dancing/DJ • live music • 18+ • cover charge

Luna's Ladies Night 276 Westminster St (at Roots Cultural Center) 401/499-9753 • 9pm-1am Fri only • mostly women • dancing/DJ • live shows • food served

Mirabar 15 Elbow St 401/331-6761 • 3pm-1am, till 2am Fri-Sat • mostly gay men • dancing/DJ • live shows • male dancers • wheelchair access

Platforms Dance Club 165 Poe St 401/781-3121 • gay/ straight • dancing/DJ • gay night Sat • Salsa Sun • 18+

CAFES

Coffee Exchange 207 Wickenden St 401/273-1198 • 6:30am-11pm • deck

Nicks on Broadway 500 Broadway 401/421-0286 • lunch & dinner Wed-Sat, Sun brunch, clsd Mon-Tue

Pastiche Fine Desserts 92 Spruce St 401/861-5190 • 8:30am-11pm, 10am-10pm Sun

White Electric Coffee 711 Westminster 401/453-3007 • 7am-6:30pm

RESTAURANTS

Al Forno 577 S Main St 401/273-9760 • dinner only, clsd Sun-Mon

Blaze Restaurant 776 Hope St 401/277-2529 • lunch & dinner, clsd Mon • lesbian-owned

Bravo Brasserie 123 Empire St 401/490-5112 • lunch Tue-Sat, dinner nightly, Sun brunch

Cafe' Paragon / Viva 234 Thayer St 401/331-6200 • 11am-1am • European Bistro/Café style atmosphere with a full bar

Caffe Dolce Vita 59 DePasquale Plaza (at Spruce St) 401/331-8240 • 8am-1am, till 2am wknds, wknd brunch • authentic Italian cafe • patio

Camille's 71 Bradford St (at Atwell's Ave) 401/751-4812 • lunch & dinner, clsd Sun • full bar

CAV 14 Imperial Pl 401/751-9164 • 11am-10pm, till 1am Fri, wknd brunch • eclectic menu & decor

Don José Tequilas Mexican 351 Atwells Ave 401/454-8951 • 11:30-11pm, from 3pm-10pm Mon-Wed, till 1am Fri-Sat

Fellini Pizzeria 166 Wickenden St
401/751–6737 • open late • free delivery •
lesbian-owned

Julian's 318 Broadway (at Vinton)
401/861–1770 • lunch & dinner • beer/ wine
only

Kartabar
284 Thayer St **401/331–8111** • 11:30am-1am
• mixed-Mediterranean, with some American
classic

Local 121 121 Washington St (at
Matthewson St) **401/274–2121** • lunch Tue-
Sat, dinner nightly,Sun brunch

Mill's Tavern 101 N Main St **401/272–3331**
• Mon-Fri happy hour oysters , dinner nightly

ENTERTAINMENT & RECREATION

Cable Car Cinema & Cafe 204 S Main St
401/272–3970 • art-house flicks & free
popcorn refills

Providence Roller Derby • Providence's
female roller derby league • visit
www.providencerollerderby.com for events

WaterFire Waterplace Park **401/272–3111** •
May-Oct only • bonfire installations along the
Providence River at sunset

BOOKSTORES

Books on the Square 471 Angell St (at
Wayland) **401/331–9097, 888/669–9660** •
9am-9pm, 10am-6pm Sun • some LGBT

PUBLICATIONS

Get RI Magazine **401/226–9033** • GLBT
magazine

Metroline 860/231-8845, 800/233-8334 •
regional newspaper & entertainment guide •
covers CT, RI & MA

Options 401/724–5428 • LGBT community
magazine

EROTICA

Mister Sister 268 Wickenden St
401/421–6969 • women-oriented • fetishwear
• sex toys • classes

SOUTH CAROLINA

Aiken

NIGHTCLUBS

Marlboro Station 141 Marlboro St NE
803/644–6485 • 10pm-close Fri-Sun •
lesbians/ gay men • dancing /DJ • live shows

Blacksburg

EROTICA

BedTyme Stories 145 Simper Rd (I-85, exit
100) **864/839–0007** • 9am-midnight • videos,
sex toys, lingerie and more

Charleston

INFO LINES & SERVICES

Acceptance Group (Gay AA) 45 Moultrie
St (at St Barnabus Lutheran Church)
843/723–9633 (AA#) • 7pm Mon, Th & Sat

ACCOMMODATIONS

A B&B @ 4 Unity Alley 4 Unity Alley
843/577–6660 • gay/ straight • 18th-c
warehouse • full brkfst • nonsmoking

**Aloft Charleston Airport & Convention
Center** 4875 Tanger Outlet Blvd (at
International Blvd), N Charleston
843/566–7300, 877/462–5638 • gay-friendly •
gym • pool • WiFi • wheelchair access

Charleston Place 205 Meeting St
843/722–4900, 888/635–2350 • gay-friendly •
restaurant

BARS

Dudley's on Ann 42 Ann St (at King St)
843/577–6779 • 4pm-2am • mostly gay men •
neighborhood bar • karaoke • gay-owed/ run

NIGHTCLUBS

Club Pantheon 28 Ann St (at King)
843/577–2582 • 10pm-2am Fri-Sun only •
mostly gay men • dancing • multiracial • live
shows • drag shows • cabaret • 18+ • gay-
owned

Deja Vu II 4628 Spruill Ave **843/554–5959** •
5pm-close Th, from 10pm Fri-Sat • mostly
women • dancing/DJ • live shows • food
served • karaoke • private club • wheelchair
access • lesbian-owned

CAFES

Bear E Patch 1980-A Ashley River Rd
843/766–6490 • 7am-9pm, 8am-8pm Sat, clsd
Sun • wheelchair access

RESTAURANTS

82 Queen 82 Queen St **843/723–7591,
800/849–0082** • lunch & dinner, Sun brunch •
Lowcountry cuisine

The Beach Bar 1124 Sam Rittenhouse Bkvd
843/212–3100 • 11am-2am, call about
monthly drag brunch

Fat Hen 3140 Maybank Hwy, St Johns Island
843/559–9090 • dinner nightly, Sun brunch •
French bistro • seafood

Fig 232 Meeting St (near Hasell)
843/805–5900 • 5:30pm-10:30pm, till 11pm
Fri-Sat, clsd Sun • local ingredients • full bar •
wheelchair access

High Cotton 199 E Bay St **843/724–3815** •
dinner nightly, lunch Sat, Sun brunch •
Southern cuisine • full bar

Hominy Grill **843/937–0930** • brkfst, lunch &
dinner, wknd brunch

Joe Pasta 428 King St (at John)
843/965–5252 • 11:30am-11pm, till midnight
Fri-Sat • also full bar

Melvin's Legendary Bar-B-Que 538 Folly
Rd **843/762–0511** • 10:30am-9pm, clsd Sun•
"the #1 cheeseburger in America"

ENTERTAINMENT & RECREATION

Historic Charleston Foundation 40 E Bay
St **843/723–1623** • call for info on city walking
tours (March-April only)

Columbia

INFO LINES & SERVICES

**The Harriet Hancock GLBT Community
Center** 1108 Woodrow St (at Millwood)
803/771–7713 • community info • resources
& more

Primary Purpose Gay/ Lesbian AA 5220
Clemson (in the house behind St Martin's
Church) **803/254–5301(AA#)** • 6:30 Tue, 7pm
Fri & Sun

ACCOMMODATIONS

Holiday Inn Express 1011 Clemson
Frontage Rd **803/419–3558**

BARS

Art Bar 1211 Park St **803/929–0198** • 8pm-
2am • gay/ straight • dancing/DJ • karaoke •
live music

Capital Club 1002 Gervais St **803/256–6464**
• 5pm-2am • mostly gay men • neighborhood
bar • professional crowd • private club •
wheelchair access

NIGHTCLUBS

The "L" Word 625 Frink St (at State St),
Cayce **803/794–2111** • 5pm-close • mostly
women • dancing/DJ • live shows • karaoke •
wheelchair access

PTS 1109 1109 Assembly St (at Gervais St)
803/253–8900 • 5pm-2am, till 6am Fri, till
3am Sat-Sun • lesbians/ gay men • dancing/DJ
• live shows • WiFi • multiracial • transgender-
friendly • private club • gay-owned

RESTAURANTS

Garibaldi's of Columbia 2013 Greene St
803/771–8888 • dinner nightly • full bar

Greenville

ACCOMMODATIONS

Walnut Lane Inn 110 Ridge Rd (at Groce
Rd), Lyman **864/949–7230** • gay-friendly •
B&B • full brkfst • kids ok • WiFi • mention
Damron at booking for discount

BOOKSTORES

Out of Bounds 21 S Pleasanburg Dr
864/239–0106 • 2pm- 8pm, till 6pm Sun, from
11am Fri-Sat • community pride store

Hilton Head

ACCOMMODATIONS

Sonesta Resort Hilton Head Island 130
Shipyard Dr **843/842–2400, 800/334–1881**

BARS

Club Vibe 32 Palmetto Bay Rd #D-2 (at Sea
Pines Cir) **843/341–6933** • 5pm-3am, from
8pm Sat, clsd Sun • lesbians/ gay men •
neighborhood bar • transgender-friendly •
food served

Lake Wylie

NIGHTCLUBS

The Rainbow In 4376 Charlotte Hwy
803/831–0093 • 9pm-3am, clsd Sun •
lesbians/ gay men • dancing/ DJ • karaoke •
drag shows • private club

Myrtle Beach

BARS

Club Pulse 803 Main St **843/315–0019** •
5pm-4am • lesbians/ gay men • dancing/DJ •
food served • karaoke • drag shows •
wheelchair access • gay-owned

RESTAURANTS

Carolina Roadhouse 4617 N Kings Hwy
843/497–9911 • 11am-10pm

Mr Fish 3401 N Kings Hwy **843/839–3474** •
11am-9:30pm • full bar

Sticky Fingers Smokehouse 2461 Coastal
Grand Cir **843/839–7427** • a chain, but a good
one

RETAIL SHOPS

Kilgor Trouts Music & More 512 8th Ave N
843/445–2800

Rock Hill

Bars

Hideaway 405 Baskins Rd **803/328–6630** • 9pm-2am Th-Sat • lesbians/ gay men • neighborhood bar • drag shows • karaoke • private club

Spartanburg

Nightclubs

Club Chameleon 995 Asheville Hwy **864/699–9160** • 8pm-midnight, till 3am Fri-Sat, clsd Sun-Tue • mostly gay men • dancing/DJ • drag shows

Club South 29 9112 Greenville Hwy (off I-85 exit 66 or I-26 exit 21a) **864/574–6087** • 9pm-4am Fri-Sat only • mostly gay men • dancing/DJ

SOUTH DAKOTA

Murdo

Accommodations

Iversen Inn 108 E 5th St (on I-90 Business Loop) **605/669–2452** • gay-friendly • kids/ pets ok • WiFi • gay-owned

Rapid City

Info Lines & Services

The Black Hills Center for Equality 1102 West Rapid St (at Omaha St) **605/348–3244** • call for hours, clsd Sun • LGBT resource center

Salem

Accommodations

Camp America 25495 US 81 **605/425–9085** • gay-friendly • 35 miles west of Sioux Falls • camping • RV hookups • pool • kids/ pets ok • nonsmoking • WiFi • lesbian-owned

Sioux Falls

Info Lines & Services

The Center for Equality 406 S 2nd Ave #102 **605/331–1153** • support groups • counseling • library & more

Bars

Toppers 1213 N Cliff Ave **605/339–7686** • 4pm-close, clsd Sun • lesbians/ gay men • more women Wed • karaoke

Nightclubs

Club David 214 W 10th St (btwn Main & Dakota) **605/274–0700** • 4:30pm-2am • gay/ straight • dancing/DJ • karaoke • drag shows • live music • also restaurant

Erotica

Romantix Adult Superstore 311 N Dakota Ave (btwn 6th & 7th) **605/332–9316** • 9am-2am, from noon Sun

Spearfish

Cafes

The Bay Leaf Cafe 126 W Hudson St **605/642–5462** • lunch & dinner • plenty veggie • espresso bar

TENNESSEE

Bucksnort

Erotica

Miranda's 4970 Hwy 230 **931/729–2006**

Chattanooga

Bars

Chuck's II 27–1/2 W Main St (at Market) **423/265–5405** • 6pm-1am, till 3am Fri-Sat • lesbians/ gay men • neighborhood bar • dancing/DJ • patio

Nightclubs

Alan Gold's 1100 McCallie Ave (at National) **423/629–8080** • 4:30pm-3am • popular • lesbians/ gay men • dancing/DJ • drag shows • food served • young crowd • wheelchair access

Images 6005 Lee Hwy **423/855–8210** • 5pm-3am Th-Sun • lesbians/ gay men • dancing/DJ • drag shows • also restaurant • wheelchair access

Publications

Out & About Newspaper 615/596–6210 • LGBT newspaper for Nashville, Knoxville, Chattanooga & Atlanta area • monthly

Erotica

Miranda's 2025 Broadway **423/266–5956** • 8am-3am, from noon Sun, largest selection of LGBT products in TN

Clifton

Accommodations

Bear Inn Resort 2250 Billy Nance Hwy **931/676–5552** • gay/ straight • WiFi • also bar & restaurant • gay-owned

Gatlinburg

ACCOMMODATIONS

Big Creek Outdoors 5019 Rag Mtn Rd, Hartford 423/487–5742, 423/487–3490 • gay/ straight • cabins • camping • horseback riding • kids ok • wheelchair access

Christopher Place, An Intimate Resort 1500 Pinnacles Wy, Newport 423/623–6555, 800/595–9441 • gay/ straight • full brkfst • pool • nonsmoking • wheelchair access

Mountain Vista Cabins 1805 Shady Grove Rd (at Old Birds Creek Rd), Sevierville 865/712–9897 • lesbians/ gay men • hot tub • well-behaved kids/ pets welcome • nonsmoking • WiFi • woman-owned

Stonecreek Cabins 865/429–0400 • gay/ straight • private Smoky Mtn cabins • hot tub • nonsmoking • lesbian-owned

Johnson City

ACCOMMODATIONS

Safe Haven Farm 336 Stanley Hollow Rd, Roan Mountain 423/725–4262 • gay-friendly • cabins • creekside privacy • fireplace & legally ordained minister • kids/ pets ok

NIGHTCLUBS

Fuzzy Holes 1410 E Main St (at S Broadway St) 423/929–9800 • 8pm-close • gay/ straight • transgender-friendly • sex-positive strip club • food served • BYOB • 18+ • wheelchair access • lesbian-owned • cover charge

New Beginnings 2910 N Bristol Hwy 423/282–4446 • 9pm-2am, from 8pm Fri-Sat, clsd Sun-Mon • popular • mostly gay men • dancing/DJ • restaurant • wheelchair access

RETAIL SHOPS

My Secret Closet 2910 N Bristol Hwy (inside New Beginnings) 423/282–4446 • 10pm-3am Fri-Sat only • pride gifts

Knoxville

INFO LINES & SERVICES

AA Gay/ Lesbian 2931 Kingston Pike (at Unitarian Church) 865/522–9667 (AA#) • 7pm Th

Lesbian Social Group 865/531–7788 • meet 7pm Wed • call for info

BARS

Club Exile 4928 Homberg Dr (at Kingston Pike) 865/919–7490 • 5pm-3am, from 11am Sun • mostly gay men • dancing/DJ • restaurant • WiFi • patio, wheelchair access • gay-owned

NIGHTCLUBS

Club XYZ 1215 N Central 865/637–4999 • 5:30pm-3am, from 9pm Sat, from 7pm Sun • lesbians/ gay men • dancing/DJ • drag shows • karaoke

The Edge Knox 7211 Kingston Pike SW (at Cheshire Dr) 865/602–2094 • 5pm-3am • lesbians/ gay men • dancing/DJ • food served • karaoke • drag shows • wheelchair access

GyrlGroove 865/356–7671 • bi-monthly womens dance parties • check gyrlgroove.com for location

Memphis

INFO LINES & SERVICES

AA Intergroup 1835 Union Ave #302 (at McLean) 901/726–6750 • call for times & locations

Memphis Gay/ Lesbian Community Center 892 S Cooper (at Nelson) 901/278–6422 • 2pm-9pm Mon-Fri

ACCOMMODATIONS

Madison Hotel 79 Madison Ave (at Center Ln) 901/333–1200 • gay-friendly • swimming

Talbot Heirs Guesthouse 99 S 2nd St (btwn Union & Peabody Pl) 901/527–9772, 800/955–3956 • gay-friendly • suites w/ kitchens • funky decor • nonsmoking • kids ok

BARS

Dru's Place 1474 Madison (at McNeil) 901/275–8082 • 11am-midnight, till 3am Fri-Sat, from noon Sun • mostly women • neighborhood bar • dancing/DJ • karaoke • drag shows • beer & set-ups only

Mollie Fontaine Lounge 679 Adams Ave (at Orleans) 901/524–1886 • 5pm-2am, clsd Sun-Tue • gay/ straight • food served

P&H Cafe 1532 Madison (at Adeline) 901/726–0906 • 3pm-3am, from 5pm Sat, clsd Sun gay/ straight • dive bar • beer/ wine • food served • live shows • karaoke • wheelchair access

NIGHTCLUBS

901 Complex 136 Webster Ave (at S 2nd St) 901/522–8455 • from 10pm Fri-Sat only • lesbians/ gay men • ladies night Fri • mostly African American • dancing/DJ • drag shows • BYOB

CAFES

Java Cabana 2170 Young Ave (at Cooper) 901/272–7210 • 6:30am-10pm, 9am-midnight Fri-Sat, noon-10pm Sun, clsd Mon • poetry readings & live shows • also art gallery • WiFi • wheelchair access

Otherlands Coffee Bar 641 S Cooper (at Central) 901/278-4994 • 7am-8pm • live music till 11pm Fri-Sat • plenty veggie • WiFi • also gift shop • wheelchair access

RESTAURANTS

Automatic Slim's Tonga Club 83 S 2nd St (at Union) 901/525-7948 • lunch & dinner, Sun brunch • Caribbean & Southwestern • plenty veggie • full bar • wheelchair access

Cafe Eclectic 603 N McLean Blvd (at Faxon Ave) 901/725-1718 • 6am-10pm, 9am-3pm Sun; also Harbortown location

Cafe Society 212 N Evergreen St (at Poplar) 901/722-2177 • lunch Mon-Fri, dinner nightly • full bar • wheelchair access

India Palace 1720 Poplar Ave (at Lemaster St) 901/278-1199 • lunch & dinner

Leonard's Pit Barbecue 5465 Fox Plaza Dr (at Mt Moriah Rd) 901/360-1963 • 11am-9pm, till 2:30pm Sun-Wed• Elvis ordered the pork sandwich at the original Leonard's (now closed), but the food is just as good here!

Molly's La Casita 2006 Madison Ave (at N Morrison St) 901/726-1873 • lunch & dinner • Mexican

Restaurant Iris 2146 Monroe Ave (at Cooper) 901/590-2828 • dinner Mon-Sat • French/ Creole • upscale • wheelchair access

RP Tracks 3547 Walker Ave (at Brister) 901/327-1471 • lunch & dinner, open till 3am • burgers • some veggie

Saigon Le 51 N Cleveland (at Jefferson) 901/276-5326 • 11am-9pm, clsd Sun • Chinese/ Vietnamese/ Thai

Tsunami 928 S Cooper (at Young) 901/274-2556 • dinner only • Pacific rim cuisine • wheelchair access

ENTERTAINMENT & RECREATION

Center for Southern Folklore 119 S Main St (at Peabody Pl) 901/525-3655 • 11am-5pm, clsd Sun, open later for shows • live music • gallery • cybercafe • food served

Graceland 3734 Elvis Presley Blvd 901/332-3322, 800/238-2000 • no visit to Memphis would be complete w/out a trip to see The King

Memphis Rock 'N Roll Tours 901/359-3102 • historical tour of Memphis music scene

RETAIL SHOPS

Inz & Outz 553 S Cooper (at Peabody) 901/728-6535 • 10am-8pm, noon-6pm Sun • pride items • books • gifts • wheelchair access

EROTICA

Paris Theater 2432 Summer Ave (at Hollywood) 901/323-2665

Romantix Adult Superstore 2220 E Brooks Rd 901/396-9050

Nashville

INFO LINES & SERVICES

AA Gay/ Lesbian 615/831-1050 • call for info

ACCOMMODATIONS

The Big Bungalow B&B 618 Fatherland St (at 7th) 615/256-8375 • gay-friendly • full brkfst • live music • massage available • nonsmoking • WiFi • woman-owned

Hutton Hotel 1808 West End Ave (at 19th Ave) 615/340-9333 • gay-friendly • also restaurant • WiFi • fitness center

Top O' Woodland Historic B&B Inn 1603 Woodland St (at 16th) 615/228-3868, 888/228-3868 • gay-friendly • also wedding chapel • nonsmoking • WiFi • woman-owned

BARS

Canvas Lounge 1707 Church St 615/320-8656 • 4pm-3am • mostly gay men • dancing/DJ • karaoke

The Patterson House 1711 Division St 615/636-7724 • 5pm-3am • gay/straight • food served • great speakeasy vibe

Purple Heys 1401 4th Ave S (at Rains) 615/244-4433 • 11am-3am • lesbians/ gay men • neighborhood bar • food served • wheelchair access

Stirrup Nashville 1529 4th Ave S (at Mallory) 615/782-0043 • noon-3am • mostly gay men • multiracial • transgender-friendly • neighborhood bar • food served • patio • wheelchair access

The Stone Fox 712 51st Ave N 615/953-1811 • 5pm-3am, from 11am wknds • gay/straight • food served • live music & cheap beer

Trax 1501 2nd Ave S (at Carney) 615/742-8856 • noon-3am • mostly gay men • neighborhood bar • karaoke • WiFi

Tribe/ Suzy Wong's House of Yum 1517 Church St (at 15th Ave S) 615/329-2912 • 4pm-midnight, till 2am wknds • lesbians/ gay men •popular • live entertainment • upscale • full restaurant • wheelchair access • gay-owned

NIGHTCLUBS

Bluebird Cafe 4104 Hillsboro Pike (nr Warfield Dr) **615/383-1461** • live country music venue

Lipstick Lounge 1400 Woodland St (at 14th) **615/226-6343** • 6:30pm-3am, 11am-close Sun, clsd Mon • mostly women • dancing/DJ • karaoke • live music

Play Dance Bar 1519 Church St (at 16th Ave) **615/322-9627** • 9pm-3am Wed-Sun • mostly gay men • dancing/DJ • multiracial • transgender-friendly • drag shows • 18+ • wheelchair access

Vibe 1713 Church St (at 17th & 18th) **615/329-3838** • afterhours bar • mostly gay men • dancing/DJ • Latina/o clientele • BYOB • patio

CAFES

Bongo Java 2007 Belmont Blvd **615/385-5282** • 7am-11pm, from 8am wknds • coffeehouse • deck • also serves brkfst, lunch & dinner

Fido 1812 21st Ave S **615/777-3436** • 7am-11pm, till midnight Fri-Sat, from 8am wknds • also full menu

Grins Vegetarian Cafe 2421 Vanderbilt Pl (at 25th Ave) **615/322-8571** • 7am-9pm, till 3pm Fri, clsd wknds

RESTAURANTS

Battered & Fried 1008 Woodland St (at S 10th) **615/226-9283** • lunch & dinner • seafood • full bar • also Wave sushi bar • patio • wheelchair access

Beyond the Edge 112 S 11th St **615/226-3343** • 11am-2am • pizza & sandwiches • full bar

Cafe Coco 210 Louise Ave (at State) **615/321-2626** • 24hrs • live music • beer/ wine • patio

Couva Calypso Cafe 2424 Elliston Pl **615/321-3878** • 11am-9pm, 11:30am-8:30pm wknds • Caribbean

Mad Donna's 1313 Woodland St (at 14th) **615/226-1617** • 11am-10pm, till 11pm Sat, clsd Mon • also lounge • drag bingo Tue

Nashville

LGBT PRIDE:
June. 615/844-4159, web: www.nashvillepride.org.
October. Black Pride 800/845-4866 x 269, web: www.brothersunited.com.

ANNUAL EVENTS:
April - Nashville Film Festival (some gay films), web: nashvillefilmfestival.org.
September - AIDS Walk 615/259-4866, web: www.nashvillecares.org.

CITY INFO:
800/657-6910, web: www.visitmusiccity.com.

TRANSIT:
Yellow Cab 615/256-0101, web: www.yellowcab-nashville.com.
Gray Line Airport Shuttle 615/ 883-5555, web: www.graylinenashville.com.
MTA 615/862-5950, web: www.nashvillemta.org.

ATTRACTIONS:
Country Music Hall of Fame 615/416-2001, web: www.countrymusichalloffame.com.
Grand Ole Opry & Opryland USA 615/871-OPRY, web: www.opry.com.
Jack Daniel's Distillery 615/279-4100, web: www.jackdaniels.com.
The Parthenon 615/862-8431, web: www.parthenon.org.
Ryman Auditorium 615/889-3060, web: www.ryman.com.
Tennessee Antebellum Trail 888/852-1860

BEST VIEW:
Try a walking tour of the city.

WEATHER:
See Memphis.

The Mad Platter 1239 6th Ave N (at Monroe) **615/242–2563** • lunch Mon-Fri, dinner Wed-Sun • eclectic, local & fresh • wheelchair access

Pancake Pantry 1796 21st Ave S (at Wedgewood Ave) **615/383–9333** • 6am-3pm, till 4pm wknds • popular for brkfst

Rumours Wine & Art Bar 2304 12th Ave S (at Linden) **615/292–9400** • 5pm-midnight, till 9pm Sun• wheelchair access

Sky Blue Coffeehouse & Bistro 700 Fatherland St (at S 7th St) **615/770–7097** • brkfst & lunch

Sole Mio 311 3rd Ave S **615/256–4013** • 11am-10pm, till 11pm Fri-Sat, clsd Mon • Italian • wheelchair access

The Standard at the Smith House 167 Rosa Parks Ave (at Charlotte) **615/254–1277** • dinner Tue-Sat, clsd Sun-Mon • wheelchair access

Watermark 507 12th Ave S (at Division) **615/254–2000** • dinner nightly, clsd Sun • seafood & more • great wine list • wheelchair access

Yellow Porch 734 Thompson Ln (at Bransford Ave) **615/386–0260** • lunch & dinner, clsd Sun • fresh Southern cuisine • wheelchair access

ENTERTAINMENT & RECREATION

NashTrash Tours tours leave from the Farmers Market (900 8th Ave N) **615/226–7300, 800/342–2132** • campy tours of Nashville w/ the Jugg Sisters • ages 13+ • reservations required

PUBLICATIONS

Inside Out Nashville **615/831–1806** • LGBT newspaper & bar guide

Out & About Newspaper **615/596–6210** • LGBT newspaper for Nashville, Knoxville, Chattanooga & Atlanta area • monthly

EROTICA

Miranda's 822 5th Ave S **615/256–1310** • 8am-3am, from noon Sun • largest selection of LGBT products in TN

TEXAS

Amarillo

BARS

212 Club 212 SW 6th Ave (at Harrison) **806/372–7997** • 3pm-2am • lesbians/ gay men • neighborhood bar • dancing/DJ • drag shows • wheelchair access

Kicked Back 521 SE 10th Ave (at Buchanan St) **806/371–3535** • 3pm-2am, clsd Sun • lesbians/ gay men • neighborhood bar • karaoke • lesbian-owned

R&R 701 S Georgia St **806/342–9000** • 4pm-2am • gay-friendly • neighborhood bar • wheelchair access • gay-owned

RESTAURANTS

Furrbie's 210 W 6th Ave **806/220–0841** • 11am-7pm, till 3pm Sat & Mon • gay-owned

EROTICA

Fantasy Gifts & Video 440 N Lakeside Dr **806/372–6500**

Arlington

see also Dallas & Fort Worth

INFO LINES & SERVICES

Tarrant County Lesbian/ Gay Alliance **817/877–5544** • info line • meetings

NIGHTCLUBS

The 1851 Club 931 W Division **682/323–5315** • 3pm-2am • lesbians/ gay men • dancing/DJ • drag shows • karaoke • videos • wheelchair access

Austin

INFO LINES & SERVICES

Lambda AA (Live & Let Live) 6809 Guadalupe St (at Galano Club) **512/444–0071, 512/832–6767 (EN ESPAÑOL)** • 6:30pm & 8pm daily, 10am Sat, 11am Sun

ACCOMMODATIONS

Austin Folk House 506 W 22nd St (at Nueces) **512/472–6700, 866/472–6700** • gay/ straight • kids ok • nonsmoking • WiFi • wheelchair access

Brava House 1108 Blanco St (at W 12th) **512/478–5034, 866/892–5726** • gay-friendly • close to downtown & 6th Street • nonsmoking • WiFi • lesbian-owned

Crowne Plaza Hotel Austin 6121 North IH 35 **512/323–5466**

Hilton Garden Inn Austin Downtown 500 North IH 35 **512/480-8181**

Hotel Saint Cecilia 112 Academy Dr **512/852-2400** • gay-friendly • pool • wheelchair access

Hotel San Jose 1316 S Congress Ave **512/852-2350, 800/574-8897** • gay/ straight • pool • nonsmoking • kids/ pets ok • wheelchair access

Kimber Modern 110 The Circle **512/912-1046** • gay/ straight • WiFi • women-owned

Mt Gainor Inn B&B 2390 Prochnow Rd (at Mt Gainor Rd), Dripping Springs **512/858-0982, 888/644-0982** • gay/ straight • nonsmoking • hot tub • WiFi

Park Lane Guest House 221 Park Ln (at Drake) **512/447-7460, 800/492-8827** • gay/ straight • full brkfst • pool • also cottage • wheelchair access • lesbian-owned

riverbarnsuites 30 minutes from Austin airport, Kingsbury **512/488-2175** • women only • river resort w/ lots of outdoor activities • swimming • lesbian-owned

Robin's Nest 1007 Stewart Cove **512/266-3413** • gay-friendly • on Lake Travis • WiFi

BARS

'Bout Time II 6607 I-35 N **512/419-9192** • 2pm-3am • lesbians/ gay men • neighborhood bar • DJ/dancing • transgender-friendly • karaoke • WiFi • wheelchair access

Casino El Camino 517 E 6th St (at Red River) **512/469-9330** • 4pm-2am • gay-friendly • neighborhood bar • psychedelic punk jazz lounge • great burgers • WiFi • wheelchair access

Cheer Up Charlie's 900 Red River • 5pm-2am • lesbians/ gay men • live bands/ shows • also vegan restaurant

Austin

LGBT PRIDE:
September.
web:www.austinpride.org.

ANNUAL EVENTS:
March - South by Southwest Music Festival, web: www.sxsw.com.
September - Splash Days, web: splashdays.com.
October - Austin G/L Int'l Film Festival, web: www.agliff.org

CITY INFO:
Austin Convention & Visitors Bureau 800/926-2282, web: www.austintexas.org.er-metro-politan-park.

BEST VIEW:
Texas State Capitol or the University of Texas Tower, web: www.utexas.edu/tower.

TRANSIT:
Yellow Cab 512/452-9999, web: www.yellowcabaustin.com.
Various hotels have their own shuttles.
Capital Metro 512/474-1200, web: www.capmetro.org.

ATTRACTIONS:
Aqua Festival.
Austin Museum of Art at Laguna Gloria 512/458-8191, web: www.amoa.org.
Elisabet Ney Museum 512/458-2255, web: austintexas.gov/department/elisabet-ney-museum.
George Washington Carver Museum 512/974-6700, web: www.nps.gov/gwca.
Hamilton Pool 512/264-2740, web: www.texasoutside.com/hamiltonpool.htm.
LBJ Library & Museum 512/721-0200, web: www.lbjlibrary.org.
McKinney Falls State Park 512/243-1643, web: www.tpwd.state.tx.us.
Mount Bonnell.
Zilker Park/Barton Springs, web: austintexas.gov/department/zilk.

WEATHER:
Summers are real scorchers (high 90°s-low 100°s) and last forever. Spring, fall, and winter are welcome reliefs.

NIGHTCLUBS

404 404 Colorado 512/522-4044 • 9pm-close Wed-Sat, from 5pm Sun • lesbians/ gay men • dancing/DJ • wheelchair access

The Basement 422 Congress (at 5th) • 9pm-2am, till 3am wknds • mostly gay men • dancing/DJ • drag shows

The Belmont 305 W 6th St 512/457-0300 • gay-friendly • live music venue

Elysium 705 Red River (7th St) 512/478-2979 • 9:30pm-2am • gay/ straight • dancing/DJ • '80s Sun • '90s Tue • rest of the week goth, industrial & electronica club

Rain 217-B W 4th St (at Colorado St) 512/494-1150 • 4pm-close, from 3pm Fri-Sun • mostly gay men • dancing/DJ • go-go dancers • wheelchair access

CAFES

Austin Java Cafe 1608 Barton Springs Rd (at Kinney Ave) 512/482-9450 • 7am-11pm, from 8am Sat-Sun • also 1206 Parkway, 512/476-1829 & 300 W 2nd St, 512/481-9400

Bouldin Creek Coffeehouse 1900 S 1st St 512/416-1601 • 7am-midnight, from 8am wknds • completely vegetarian menu (brkfst all day) • occasional live music

Joe's Bakery & Coffee Shop 2305 E 7th St (at Morelos & Northwestern) 512/472-0017 • 6am-3pm, clsd Mon • Tex-Mex • wheelchair access

Spider House Patio Bar & Cafe 2908 Fruth St (at West Dr) 512/480-9562 • 10am-2am • full bar • art & performance • patio

RESTAURANTS

Changos 3023 Guadalupe 512/480-8226 • taqueria, open all day

Chez Nous 510 Neches St 512/473-2413 • lunch Tue-Fri, dinner nightly, clsd Mon • wheelchair access

Chuy's 1728 Barton Springs Rd 512/474-4452 • 11am-10pm, till 11pm Fri-Sat • Tex-Mex • full bar • wheelchair access

Corazon at Castle Hill 1101 W 5th St (at Baylor) 512/476-0728 • lunch weekdays & dinner nightly, clsd Sun • inspired cuisine • some veggie • wheelchair access

Eastside Cafe 2113 Manor Rd (at Breeze Terrace) 512/476-5858 • 11:30am-9:30pm, 10am-10pm wknds • some veggie • beer/ wine • wheelchair access

El Sol y La Luna 600 E 6th St (at Red River) 512/444-7770 • 11am-10pm, 9am-1pm Fri-Sat, 9am-4pm Sun • great brkfst • live music • wheelchair access • lesbian-owned

Fonda San Miguel 2330 W North Loop (at Hancock Rd) 512/459-4121 • dinner only, popular Sun brunch • Mexican • full bar

Galaxy 1000 W Lynn 512/478-3434 • 7am-10pm • quick, stylish & tasty

Guero's 1412 S Congress (at Elizabeth) 512/447-7688 • 11am-11pm, from 8am wknds • great Mexican & people-watching • outdoor seating • live music outdoors on wknds

Imperia 310 Colorado St 512/472-6770 • dinner only • upscale Asian • full bar • wheelchair access

Jo's Hot Coffee & Good Food 1300 S Congress Ave (at James) 512/444-3800 • 7am-9pm, till 10pm Sat • "best lazy day outdoor dining scene" • wheelchair access • also 242 W 2nd St, 512/469-9003 • lesbian-owned

Kenichi 419 Colorado St 512/320-8883 • dinner nightly • Asian/ sushi • wheelchair access

Mother's Cafe & Garden 4215 Duval St (at 43rd) 512/451-3994 • 11:15am-10pm, from 10am wknds • vegetarian • beer/ wine • wheelchair access

Mr Natural 1901 E Cesar Chavez St 512/477-5228 • 8am-8pm • vegetarian/ vegan

Polvos 2004 S 1st St (at Johanna) 512/441-5446 • 7am-11pm • Mexican • outdoor seating

Santa Rita Cantina 1206 W 38th St 512/419-7482 • lunch & dinner, wknd brunch

Threadgill's 6416 N Lamar 512/451-5440 • 10am-10pm, till 9pm Sun • great chicken-fried steak • live music Wed • also 301 W Riverside Dr, 512/472-9304 • beer garden • live music

Wink 1014 N Lamar Blvd 512/482-8868 • dinner nightly, clsd Sun • upscale • also wine bar • wheelchair access

ENTERTAINMENT & RECREATION

Barton Springs Barton Springs Rd (in Zilker Park) 512/867-3080 • natural swimming hole

Bat Colony Congress Ave Bridge (at Barton Springs Dr) • everything's bigger in Texas—including the colony of bats that flies out from under this bridge every evening March-Oct

BOOKSTORES

Bookpeople 603 N Lamar Blvd (at 6th) 512/472-5050, 800/853-9757 • 9am-11pm • independent

BookWoman 5501 N Lamar Blvd (at Nelray) **512/472–2785** • 10am-8pm, noon-6pm Sun • books • cards • jewelry • music • DVDs • wheelchair access • woman-owned

MonkeyWrench Books 110 E North Loop **512/407–6925** • 11am-8pm, from noon wknds • independent, radical bookstore

Retail Shops

Tapelenders 1114 W 5th St #501 (at Baylor) **512/472–0844** • 10am-10pm, till midnight Fri-Sat • LGBT videos • novelties • gay-owned

Publications

Austin Chronicle **512/454–5766** • Austin's alternative paper • weekly • has extensive online gay guide (check out www.austinchronicle.com)

Gyms & Health Clubs

Hyde Park Gym 4125 Guadalupe (at 41st St) **512/459–9174** • 5am-10pm, 7am-7pm Sat, 8am-7pm Sun

Milk + Honey Spa 204 Colorado St (at 2nd) **512/236–1115** • 9am-9pm

Erotica

Forbidden Fruit 108 E North Loop **512/453–8090** • woman-owned & operated

Beaumont

Bars

Orleans Street Pub & Patio 650 Orleans St (at Forsythe) **409/835–4243** • 7pm-2am, clsd Mon-Tue • lesbians/ gay men • neighborhood bar • dancing/DJ • karaoke • drag shows

Bryan

Bars

Revolution Cafe & Bar 211 B S Main St (at 27th) **979/823–4044** • 6pm-2am, from 8pm Sun-Mon, from 4pm Fri • gay-friendly • neighborhood bar • food served • live music • WiFi • wheelchair access

Nightclubs

Halo Bar 121 N Main St (at William J Bryan Pkwy) **979/823–6174** • 9:30pm-2am Th-Sat • lesbians/ gay men • dancing/DJ • drag shows • karaoke • wheelchair access

Corpus Christi

Info Lines & Services

Clean & Serene AA 3026 S Staples (at MCC church) **361/992–8911, 866/672–7029** • 8pm Fri

Accommodations

Anthony's By The Sea 732 S Pearl St, Rockport **361/729–6100, 800/460–2557** • gay/ straight • quiet retreat 4 blocks from water • full brkfst • pool • nonsmoking • wheelchair access • lesbian-owned

Port Aransas Inn 1500 S 11th St (at Ave G), Port Aransas **361/749–5937** • gay/ straight • pool • hot tub • WiFi • wheelchair access

Bars

The Hidden Door 802 S Staples St (at Coleman) **361/882–5002** • noon-2am • lesbians/ gay men • neighborhood bar • dancing/DJ • patio • wheelchair access • also the Loft piano bar Fri-Sun

Nightclubs

Triangle Niteclub **361/903–0977** • 5pm-2am, clsd Mon • lesbians/ gay men • dancing/DJ • drag shows

Dallas

see also Arlington, Fort Worth

Info Lines & Services

John Thomas Gay/ Lesbian Community Center 2701 Reagan St (at Brown) **214/528–0144, 214/528–0022** • 9am-9pm, till 5pm Sat, noon-5pm Sun • wheelchair access

Lambda AA 2438 Butler #106 **214/267–0222**

Accommodations

Bailey's Uptown Inn 2505 Worthington St (at Hibernia) **214/720–2258** • gay-friendly • nonsmoking • WiFi

Hotel ZaZa 2332 Leonard St (at State) **214/468–8399, 888/880–3244** • gay-friendly • full spa & restaurant

Lumen 6101 Hillcrest Ave **214/219–2400, 800/908–1140** • gay–friendly • WiFi • wheelchair access

MCM Elegante' Hotel and Suites 2330 W Northwest Hwy **214/358–7846, 877/351–4477** • gay-friendly • pool • WiFi • wheelchair access

Palomar Dallas 5300 E Mockingbird Ln **214/520–7969, 888/253–9030** • gay-friendly • pool • WiFi

BARS

Alexandre's 4026 Cedar Springs Rd (at Knight St) 214/559-0720 • 9am-2pm, from 2pm Sun • gay/ straight • live music • karaoke • wheelchair access

Barbara's Pavillion 325 Centre St 214/941-2145 • 4pm-2am, from 2pm Sun • mostly gay men • neighborhood bar • karaoke • patio • wheelchair access

Grapevine 3902 Maple Ave (at Shelby) 214/522-8466 • 3pm-2am, from 1pm Sun • gay/ straight • classic dive bar • WiFi • wheelchair access

The Hidden Door 5025 Bowser Ave (at Mahanna) 214/526-0620 • 7am-2am, from noon Sun • mostly gay men • neighborhood bar • leather • patio • wheelchair access

JR's Bar & Grill 3923 Cedar Springs Rd (at Throckmorton) 214/528-1004 • 11am-2am, from noon Sun-Mon • popular • lesbians/ gay men • grill till 4pm • live shows bar • videos • young crowd • WiFi • wheelchair access

Pekers 2615 Oak Lawn Ave, Ste 101 (btwn Fairmount & Brown) 214/528-3333 • 10am-2am • lesbians/ gay men • neighborhood bar • live music • karaoke • drag shows • wheelchair access

Sue Ellen's 3014 Throckmorton (at Cedar Springs) 214/559-0707 • 5pm-2am, 2pm-close wknds • popular • mostly women • dancing/DJ • live shows/ bands • Sun BBQ (summers) • patio • wheelchair access

Tin Room 2514 Hudnall St (at Maple Ave) 214/526-6365 • 10am-2am, from noon Sun • mostly gay men • neighborhood bar • wheelchair access

Woody's 4011 Cedar Springs Rd (btwn Douglas & Throckmorton) 214/520-6629 • 2pm-2am • lesbians/ gay men • live shows • sports bar • videos • nonsmoking upstairs • karaoke • patio • wheelchair access

NIGHTCLUBS

The Brick/Joe's Dallas 2525 Wycliff Ave (btwn Maple & Tollway) 214/521-3154 • 4pm-2am, till 4am Fri-Sat, from noon Sat-Sun • lesbians/ gay men • dancing/DJ • multiracial • drag shows

Exklusive 4207 Maple Ave (at Knight St) 469/556-1395 • 9pm-close Th-Sun • lesbians/ gay men • dancing/DJ • drag shows • mostly Latino/a

Havana Bar & Grill 4006 Cedar Springs Rd (at Throckmorton) 214/526-9494 • grill 5pm-10pm, lounge from 10pm, clsd Mon • gay/ straight • dancing/DJ

Kaliente 4350 Maple Ave (at Hondo) 214/520-6676 • 9pm-2am, clsd Tue • mostly gay men • mostly Latino • dancing/DJ • salsa & Tejano • karaoke • drag shows • wheelchair access

Panoptikon 3025 Main St (at Excuses) 214/741-1111 • monthly gothic/electro dance party • gay/ straight

Round-Up Saloon 3912 Cedar Springs Rd (at Throckmorton) 214/522-9611 • 3pm-2am, from noon wknds • popular • mostly gay men • dancing/DJ • country/ western • karaoke • dance lessons • patio • wheelchair access

Station 4 3911 Cedar Springs Rd (at Throckmorton) 214/526-7171 • 9pm-4am Wed-Sun • popular • lesbians/ gay men • dancing/DJ • drag shows • videos • also Rose Room cabaret • 18+

CAFES

Buli 3908 Cedar Springs Rd 214/528-5410 • 7am-close • WiFi • wheelchair access

Opening Bell Coffee 1409 S Lamar St, Ste 012 214/565-0383 • 7am-10pm, from 9am wknds, till midnight wknds • beer/ wine • live music • WiFi

RESTAURANTS

3025 Main/ Excuses Cafe 3025 Main St (in Deep Ellum) 214/741-1111 • 11am-2am • WiFi

Ali Baba Cafe 1901 Abrams Rd (near La Vista Dr) 214/823-8235 • lunch & dinner • Middle Eastern

Bangkok Orchid 331 W Airport Fwy (at N Beltline), Irving 972/252-7770 • lunch & dinner, clsd Mon • ask for Danny • BYOB • wheelchair access • gay-owned

Black-Eyed Pea 3857 Cedar Springs Rd (at Reagan) 214/521-4580 • 11am-10pm • wheelchair access

Blue Mesa Grill 5100 Belt Line Rd (at Tollway), Addison 972/934-0165 • 11am-10pm • great fajitas • full bar

Bread Winners 3301 McKinney Ave 214/754-4940 • 4pm-2am, from 10am wknds • full bar • wheelchair access

Cafe Brazil 3847 Cedar Springs Rd 214/461-8762 • open 24hrs

Cosmic Cafe 2912 Oak Lawn Ave 214/521-6157 • 11am-10:30pm, till 11pm Fri-Sat, noon-10pm Sun • vegetarian • also yoga & meditation • live events • WiFi

Cremona Bistro 2704 Worthington St (at Howell) **214/871–1115** • lunch weekdays & dinner nightly • Italian • full bar • patio • live music

Dish 4123 Cedar Springs Rd #110 **214/522–3474** • dinner & Sun brunch • full bar • patio • live shows • wheelchair access

Dream Cafe 2800 Routh St (in the Quadrangle) **214/954–0486** • 7am-9pm, till 10pm Fri-Sat • plenty veggie • beer/ wine • WiFi • wheelchair access

Hattie's 418 N Bishop Ave **214/942–7400** • lunch daily, dinner Tue-Sun • Southern • wheelchair access

Hibiscus 2927 N Henderson Ave **214/827–2927** • dinner only, clsd Sun • steak & seafood • wheelchair access

Hunky's 3940 Cedar Springs Rd (at Reagan) **214/522–1212** • 11am-10pm, till 11pm Sat, from noon Sun • popular • burgers & salads • beer/ wine • patio • wheelchair access • gay-owned

Dallas

LGBT Pride:
September. Web: www.dallastavern-guild.org.

Annual Events:
March-April - Dallas Blooms at Dallas Arboretum & Botanical Garden with over 400,000 spring-blooming bulbs.

April - AFI Dallas Int'l Film Festival, web: dallasfilm.org.

April – Deep Ellum Arts Festival, web: www.deepellumartsfesti-val.com.

September-October - Texas State Fair, web: www.bigtex.com. Largest in the country.

October - Out Takes Dallas 972/988-6333, web: www.outtakesdallas.org. LGBT film festival.

City Info:
800/232-5527, web: www.visitdallas.com.

Best View:
Hyatt Regency Tower.

Weather:
Can be unpredictable. Hot summers (90°s — 100°s) with possible severe rain storms. Winter temperatures hover in the 20°s through 40°s range.

Transit:
Yellow Cab 214/426-6262, web: www.dallasyellowcab.com.
Dallas Area Rapid Transit (DART) 214/979-1111, web: www.dart.org.

Attractions:
African American Museum 214/565-9026, web: www.aamdallas.org.

Crow Collection of Asian Art 214/979-6430, web: www.crowcollection.com.

Dallas Arboretum & Botanical Garden 214/515–6500, web www.dallasarboretum.org.

Dallas Museum of Art 214/922-1200, web: www.dallasmuseumofart.org.

Dallas Theater Center/ Frank Lloyd Wright 214/522–8499, web: www.dallastheatercenter.org.

Dallas World Aquarium 214/720-2224, web: www.dwazoo.com.

Deep Ellum district.

Meadows Museum at SMU 214/768-2516, web: smu.edu/meadows/museum/index.htm.

Modern Art Museum, Fort Worth 817/738-9215, web: www.themodern.org.

Nasher Sculpture Center 214/242-5100, web: www.nashersculpturecenter.org.

Sixth Floor Museum 214/747-6660, web: www.jfk.org.

Texas State Fair & State Fair Park 214/565-9931, web: www.bigtex.com.

The Women's Museum 214/915–0860, web: www.thewomensmuseum.org.

Lucky's Cafe 3531 Oak Lawn **214/522-3500**
• 7am-10pm • classic comfort food • great
brkfst • wheelchair access

Mario's 5404 Lemmon Ave **214/599-9744** •
11am-11pm, Mexican & Salvadorian

Monica Aca y Alla 2914 Main St (at
Malcolm X) **214/748-7140** • lunch Mon-Fri,
dinner Tue-Sun, brunch wknds • popular •
contemporary Mexican • full bar • live music
wknds • Latin jazz/ salsa • transgender-friendly
• wheelchair access

Naga Kitchen & Bar 665 High Market St
(Victory Park) **214/953-0023** • lunch Mon-Sat,
dinner nightly • authentic Thai

Stephan Pyles 1807 Ross Ave, Ste 200
214/580-7000 • lunch Mon-Fri, dinner Mon-
Sat, clsd Sun • Southwestern cuisine

Taco Joint 911 N Peak St **214/826-8226** •
6:30am-2pm, from 8am Sat, clsd Sun •
wheelchair access

Thai Soon 101 S Coit, Ste 401 (at Belt Line)
972/234-6111 • lunch & dinner • wheelchair
access

Ziziki's 4514 Travis St, #122 (in Travis Walk)
214/521-2233 • 11am-10pm, Sun brunch •
Greek & Italian • full bar • wheelchair access

ENTERTAINMENT & RECREATION

Assassination City Derby 1438 Coliseum Dr
• Dallas' female roller derby league • visit
www.acderby.com for events

RETAIL SHOPS

Obscurities 4008 Cedar Springs
214/559-3706 • 11am-9pm, 2pm-8pm Sun,
clsd Mon • tattoo & piercing

Tapelenders 3926 Cedar Springs Rd (at
Throckmorton) **214/528-6344** • 9am-
midnight • LGBT gifts • gay-owned

PUBLICATIONS

Dallas Voice **214/754-8710** • LGBT
newspaper

EROTICA

Alternatives 1720 W Mockingbird Ln (at
Hawes) **214/630-7071** • 24hrs

Leather Masters 3000 Main St
214/528-3865 • noon-10pm, clsd Sun-Mon •
handmade leather clothes • rubber/ fetishwear

Denison

BARS

Good Time Lounge 2520 Hwy 91 N
903/463-6086 • 7pm-2am Wed-Sun •
lesbians/ gay men • karaoke Th & Sun • drag
shows • private club

Denton

NIGHTCLUBS

**Mable Peabody's Beauty Parlor &
Chainsaw Repair** 1125 E University Dr
940/566-9910 • 4pm-2am • lesbians/ gay
men • dancing/DJ • live shows • karaoke •
drag shows • wheelchair access • lesbian-
owned

El Paso

see also Ciudad Juárez, Mexico

BARS

Briar Patch 508 N Stanton St (at Missouri)
915/577-9555 • 2pm-2am, from noon wknds
• lesbians/ gay men • neighborhood bar •
karaoke • patio

Chiquita's Bar 310 E Missouri Ave (at
Stanton) **915/351-0095** • 2pm-2am •
lesbians/ gay men • neighborhood bar •
mostly Latino/a • wheelchair access

Epic 510 N Stanton St (at Missouri)
915/566-0378 • mostly women • live bands

The Whatever Lounge 701 E Paisano Dr (at
Ochoa) • 2pm-2am • lesbians/ gay men •
dancing/DJ • karaoke • mostly Latino/a • drag
shows • wheelchair access

RESTAURANTS

The Little Diner 7209 7th St, Canutillo
915/877-2176 • 11am-8pm, clsd Wed • true
Texas fare • beer/ wine • wheelchair access

Eustace

ACCOMMODATIONS

Captain's Quarters PO Box 577 75124
903/802-2771 • gay/ straight • cabin rentals

Fort Worth

see also Arlington & Dallas

INFO LINES & SERVICES

Tarrant County Lesbian/ Gay Alliance
817/877-5544 • info line • newsletter

ACCOMMODATIONS

Hotel Trinity InnSuites Hotel 2000 Beach
St **817/534-4801, 800/989-3556** • gay-friendly
• pool • nonsmoking • kids/ pets ok • WiFi •
wheelchair access

BARS

Best Friends Club 2620 E Lancaster Ave
817/420-9220 • 4pm-2am, from 3pm wknds,
clsd Mon • lesbians/ gay men • neighborhood
bar • dancing/DJ • food served • karaoke

Crossroads 515 S Jennings Ave (at Pennsylvania) **817/332–0071** • 11am-2am, from noon Sun • mostly gay men • neighborhood bar

NIGHTCLUBS

Rainbow Lounge 651 S Jennings Ave (at Pennsylvania) **817/744–7723** • 9am-2am • mostly gay men • dancing/DJ • drag shows • theme nights • wheelchair access

ENTERTAINMENT & RECREATION

National Cowgirl Museum 1720 Gendy St **817/336–4475, 800/476–3263**

Galveston

ACCOMMODATIONS

Hotel Galvez 2024 Seawall Blvd **409/765–7721, 877/999–3223** • gay-friendly • nonsmoking • WiFi • kids ok • wheelchair access

Lost Bayou Guesthouse B&B 1607 Ave L (at 16th) **409/770–0688** • gay-griendly • 1890 Victorian home survived hurricane of 1900 • nonsmoking • kids 10 or over ok • WiFi

BARS

3rd Coast Beach Bar 2416 Post Office St **409/765–6911** • 4pm-2am, from 2pm wknds • mostly gay men • drag shows • male dancers • deck

Pink Dolphin 1706 23rd St (at O Ave) **409/621–1808** • 10am-midnight • mostly gay men • karaoke • BYOB

Robert's Lafitte 2501 Q Ave (at 25th St) **409/765–9092** • 7am-2am, from 10am Sun • mostly gay men • drag shows wknds • patio • wheelchair access

Stars Beach Club 3102 Seawall Blvd **409/497–4113** • noon-2am • lesbians/ gay men • more women Th • dancing/DJ • karaoke • drag shows • theme nights

CAFES

Mod Coffee & Tea House 2126 Post Office St (at 22nd) **409/765–5659** • 7am-10pm • live shows• also art gallery • beer/ wine • WiFi

RESTAURANTS

Eat Cetera 408 25th St **409/762–0803** • 11am-7pm, clsd Sun • beer/ wine • wheelchair acccess

Luigi's 2328 The Strand (at Tremont) **409/763–6500** • dinner only, clsd Sun

Mosquito Cafe 628 14th St (at Winnie) **409/763–1010** • 8am-9pm, 8am-9pm Sat, till 3pm Sun, clsd Mon • some veggie • wheelchair access

The Spot 3204 Seawall Blvd (at 32nd St) **409/621–5237** • good burgers, great view • also Tiki Bar • wheelchair access

Star Drug Store 510 23rd St **409/766–7719** • 9am-3pm • old-fashioned drug store & soda fountain • wheelchair access

Groesbeck

ACCOMMODATIONS

Rainbow Ranch Campground 1662 LCR 800 **254/729–8484, 888/875–7596** • lesbians/ gay men • on Lake Limestone • pool • campsites • cabins • nonsmoking • gay-owned

Gun Barrel City

BARS

Garlow's 308 E. Main St **903/887–0853** • 4pm-close • lesbians/ gay men • dancing/DJ • drag shows

Houston

INFO LINES & SERVICES

Gay & Lesbian Switchboard Houston 713/529–3211, 888/843–4564 • 24hr crisis hotline and resource directory

Lambda AA Center 1201 W Clay (btwn Montrose & Waugh) 713/521–1243 • wheelchair access

ACCOMMODATIONS

Hotel Derek 2525 W Loop S (at Westheimer) **713/961–3000, 866/292–4100** • gay-friendly • modern, chic hotel

Hotel Sorella 800 W Sam Houston Pkwy N **713/973–1600, 866/842–0100** • gay-friendly

The Houstonian 111 N Post Oak Ln (near Woodway Dr) **713/680–2626, 800/231–2759** • gay-friendly • urban resort

Robin's Nest B&B Inn 4104 Greeley St **713/528–5821, 800/622–8343** • gay-friendly • Montrose Museum District • WiFi

The Sam Houston 1117 Prairie St (at Fannin) **832/200–8800** • gay-friendly • boutique hotel • dogs ok • also restaurant & bar • WiFi

Sycamore Heights B&B 245 W 18th St **713/861–4117** • gay-friendly • circa 1905 • garden • nonsmoking • WiFi • gay-owned

BARS

Bayou City Bar & Grill 2409 Grant St (at Hyde Park Blvd) **713/522–2867** • 4pm-2am, clsd Mon • lesbians/ gay men * food served • more women Wed

Blur 710 Pacific St (at Crocker) **713/529–3447**
• 10pm-2am, closed Mon-Tue • lesbians/ gay
men • dancing/DJ • 18+

Boom Boom Room 2518 Yale St
713/868–3740 • 5pm-2am, closed Sun-Tue• gay-
friendly • wine & panini bar

Club 2020 2020 Leeland **713/227–9667** •
10pm-4am Sat • lesbians/ gay men • women's
night Fri • dancing/DJ • mostly African
American • hip hop • 18+

Cockpit Bar & Grill 101 Airport Blvd
713/640–7139 • 4pm-2am. from 5pm Sat, closed
Sun • gay/ straight • lil ol' dive bar by Hobby
Airport • WiFi • gay-owned

Crocker 2312 Crocker St **713/529–3355** •
11am-2am • mostly gay men • neighborhood
bar • karaoke • WiFi

EJ's 2517 Ralph (at Westheimer)
713/527–9071 • 10am-2am • mostly gay men
(women's bar upstairs) • dancing/DJ • live
shows

Guava Lamp 570 Waugh Dr **713/524–3359** •
4pm-2am, from 2pm Sun • lesbians/ gay men
• karaoke • WiFi • wheelchair access

JR's 808 Pacific (at Grant) **713/521–2519** •
noon-2am • popular • mostly gay men •
karaoke • drag shows • videos • patio •
wheelchair access

Meteor 2306 Genesee St (at Fairview)
713/521–0123 • 4pm-2am • mostly gay men •
drag shows • wheelchair access • gay-owned

Michael's Outpost 1419 Richmond (at
Mandell) **713/520–8446** • 3pm-2am, from
noon wknds • mostly gay men •
neighborhood bar • piano • live entertainment
• older crowd

Neon Boots 11410 Hempstead Hwy (in the
Historic Esquire Ballroom) **713/677–0828** •
4pm-2am, from noon wknds, till midnight Sun •
popular • lesbians/gay men • country
western dancing • gay-owned

TC's Show Bar 817 Fairview (at Converse)
713/526–2625 • 10am-2am • lesbians/gay
men • neighborhood bar • karaoke • drag
shows • transgender-friendly

Tony's Corner Pocket 817 W Dallas (btwn
Arthur & Crosby) **713/571–7870** • noon-2am
• lesbians/ gay men • neighborhood bar •
karaoke • male dancers • large deck • WiFi

The Usual Pub 5519 Allen St **281/501–1478**
• 4pm-2am, from 3pm Sat, noon Sun • gay/
straight • neighborhood bar • karaoke • live
music • lesbian-owned

Nightclubs

F Bar Houston 202 Tuam St **713/522–3227** •
5pm-2am, from 9pm Sat, 3pm Sun, clsd Mon
• lesbians/ gay men • dancing/DJ • karaoke •
live shows

Numbers 300 Westheimer (at Taft)
713/526–6551 • gay-friendly • dancing/DJ •
80's Fri • also live music venue • video • young
crowd

Ranch Hill Saloon 24704 I-45 N, Spring
281/298–9035 • 1pm-2am • lesbians/ gay
men • neighborhood bar • dancing/DJ •
country/ western • drag shows • karaoke •
wheelchair access • lesbian-owned

South Beach Nightclub 810 Pacific
713/521–0107, 713/529–7623 • 9pm-4am Fri-
Sat • mostly gay men • dancing/DJ • live
shows

Venus 2901 Fannin St **713/751–3185** •
lesbians/gay men • dancing/DJ • open mic
nights • karaoke

Cafes

Dirk's Coffee 4005 Montrose (btwn
Richmond & W Alabama) **713/526–1319** •
6am-6pm, 7am-5pm Sun

Empire Cafe 1732 Westheimer Rd
713/528–5282 • 7:30am-10pm, till 11pm Fri-
Sat • WiFi • wheelchair access

Java Java Cafe 911 W 11th (at Shepherd)
713/880–5282 • 7:30am-3pm, from 8:30am
wknds • wheelchair access

The Path of Tea 2340 W Alabama St
713/252–4473 • 10am-9pm, till 11pm Fri-Sat,
1pm-6pm Sun • tea house • wheelchair access

Restaurants

Aka Sushi House 2390 W Alabama St
713/807–7875 • noon-11pm

Argentina Cafe 3055 Sage Rd (at Hidalgo
St) **713/622–8877** • 9am-9pm, from 10am
wknds • wheelchair access

Baba Yega's 2607 Grant (at Pacific)
713/522–0042 • 11am-10pm, till 11pm Fri-Sat,
from 10am Sun • plenty veggie• full bar •
patio • wheelchair access

Barnaby's Cafe 604 Fairview (btwn Stanford
& Hopkins St) **713/522–0106** • 11am-10pm,
till 11pm Fri-Sat • beer/ wine • wheelchair
access • multiple locations

Beaver's 2310 Decatur (at Sawyer)
713/864–2328 • 11am-10pm, till midnight Sat,
clsd Mon • BBQ

Brasil 2604 Dunlavy (at Westheimer)
713/528–1993 • 7:30am-midnight • plenty
veggie • beer/ wine • wheelchair access

Chapultepec 813 Richmond (btwn Montrose & Main) 713/522–2365 • 24hrs • Mexican • full bar • wheelchair access

El Tiempo Cantina 1308 Montrose Blvd 713/807–8996 • 11am-9pm, till 10pm Wed-Th, till 11pm Fri-Sat • Mexican seafood • wheelchair access

House of Pies 3112 Kirby Dr (btwn Richmond & Alabama) 713/528–3816 • 24hrs • popular • wheelchair access

Hugo's 1600 Westheimer Rd (at Mandell) 713/524–7744 • lunch & dinner • Mexican • popular brunch • wheelchair access

Julia's Bistro 3722 Main St (at W Alabama) 713/807–0090 • lunch Mon-Fri, dinner Mon-Sat, clsd Sun • Mexican • wheelchair access

Kelley's Country Cookin' 8015 Park Pl (at Gulf Fwy) 713/645–6428 • 6am-10pm • great brkfst • wheelchair access

Mark's American Cuisine 1658 Westheimer Rd 713/523–3800 • lunch Mon-Fri, dinner nightly • located in renovated 1920s church • wheelchair access

Mo Mong 1201 Westheimer #B (at Montrose) 713/524–5664 • 11am-10pm, clsd Sun • Vietnamese • full bar

Ninfa's 2704 Navigation Blvd (at N Delano St) 713/228–1175 • 11am-11pm • popular • Mexican • some veggie • full bar

Ruggles Green 2311 W Alabama 713/533–0777 • 11am-10pm • organic & all-natural American

Sparrow Bar + Cookshop 3701 Travis St 713/524–6922 • lunch & dinner Tue-Sat • also bar • patio • wheelchair access • lesbian-owned

ENTERTAINMENT & RECREATION

After Hours - Queer Radio With Attitude KPFT 90.1 FM (also 89.5 Galveston) 713/526–4000, 713/526–5738 (REQUEST LINE) • midnight-3am Sat/Sun • LGBT radio

Beer Can House 222 Malone St 713/926–6368 • seasonal; 10am-2pm Wed-Fri • 50,000+ beer cans cover the building!

Houston

LGBT PRIDE:
June. 713/529-6979, web: www.pridehouston.org.

ANNUAL EVENTS:
March - AIDS Walk 713/403-9255, web: www.aidswalkhouston.org.
May- Splash, web: www.houston-splash.com. Dance party benefiting HIV/AIDS education, research & care.
July - Q Fest LGBT Film Festival, web: www.q-fest.org.

CITY INFO:
713/437-5200, web: www.visithoustontexas.com.

WEATHER:
Humid all year round—you're not that far from the Gulf. Mild winters, although there are a few days when the temperatures drop into the 30°s. Winter also brings occasional rainy days. Summers are very hot.

ATTRACTIONS:
Contemporary Arts Museum 713/284-8250, web: www.camh.org.
The Galleria, 713/622–0663, web: www.galleriahouston.com.
The Menil Collection 713/525-9400, web: www.menil.org.
Museum of Fine Arts 713/639-7300, web: www.mfah.org.
Rothko Chapel 713/524-9839, web: www.rothkochapel.org.
San Jacinto Monument 281/479–2421, web: www.sanjac-into-museum.org.
SplashTown 281/355–3300, web: www.splashtownpark.com.

BEST VIEW:
JP Morgan Chase Tower, web: www.chasetower.com.

TRANSIT:
Yellow Cab 713/236-1111, web: www.yellowcabhouston.com.
Metropolitan Transit Authority 713/635-4000, web: www.ridemetro.org.

DiverseWorks Art Space 1117 East Fwy (I-10 at N Main) **713/223–8346, 713/335–3443** • seasonal • some LGBT-themed art & performance

Houston Roller Derby • Houston's female roller derby league • visit ww.houstonrollerderby.com for events

RETAIL SHOPS

The Chocolate Bar 1835 W Alabama St **713/520-8599** • chocolate gifts & yummy desserts

Hollywood Super Center 2409 Grant St (at Crocker St) **713/527–8510** • 10am-1am, till 3am Fri-Sat • gifts • T-shirts • novelties

PUBLICATIONS

abOUT Magazine PO Box 130948, **713/396–2688**

OutSmart **713/520–7237** • monthly LGBT newsmagazine

GYMS & HEALTH CLUBS

Houston Gym 1501 Durham Rd (at Washington & Eigel) **713/880–9191** • 5am-10pm, 8am-8pm wknds • gay-owned

EROTICA

Eros 1207 1207 Spencer Hwy (at Allen Genoa) **713/910–0220** • gay-owned

Loveworks 25170 I-45 N, Spring **281/292–0070**

Lockhart

ACCOMMODATIONS

Lazy J Paradise Campground & Park 270 Hidden Path (CR 303 and FM 2001) **210/863–9314** • campground w/ RV area catering to the LGBT community • pool • WiFi

Longview

NIGHTCLUBS

Rainbow Members Club (RMC) 203 S High (at Cotton) **903/753–9393** • 5pm-2am Wed-Sat, from 3pm Sun • lesbians/ gay men • dancing/DJ • private club • wheelchair access

Lubbock

INFO LINES & SERVICES

AA Lambda 4501 University Ave (at MCC) **806/792–5562** • 8pm Fri

ACCOMMODATIONS

LaQuinta Inns & Suites North 5006 Auburn St (at Winston) **806/749–1600** • gay-friendly • pool • pets ok • gym • nonsmoking • WiFi • wheelchair access • gay-owned

NIGHTCLUBS

Club Luxor 2211 4th St **806/744–3744** • 9pm-2am Fri-Sun • gay/ straight • more gay Fri & Sun • dancing/DJ • karaoke • drag shows • wheelchair access

Heaven Nightclub 1928 Buddy Holly Ave (at I-27) **806/762–4466** • 9pm-3am Th-Sun • gay-friendly • dancing/DJ • multiracial • drag shows • 18+ • young crowd

Marfa

ACCOMMODATIONS

El Cosmico 802 S. Highland Ave **432/729–1950, 877/822–1950** • gay/ straight • vintage trailer, yurt & teepee hotel & campground • WiFi • lesbian-owned

McAllen

see Rio Grande Valley

Rio Grande Valley

BARS

PBD's 2908 N Ware Rd (at Daffodil), McAllen **956/682–8019** • 8pm-2am, clsd Mon • mostly gay men • dancing/DJ Th-Sat • drag shows • wheelchair access

San Antonio

INFO LINES & SERVICES

Lambda AA 319 Camden Rm #4 (Madison Square Presbyterian Church) **210/979–5939** • 8:15pm daily

ACCOMMODATIONS

1908 Ayres Inn 124 W Woodlawn Ave (at N Main) **210/736–4232** • gay/ straight • nonsmoking • WiFi • wheelchair access • gay-owned

Arbor House Suites B&B 109 Arciniega (btwn S Alamo & S St Mary's) **210/472–2005, 888/272–6700** • gay/ straight • kids/ pets ok • hot tub • nonsmoking • wheelchair access • gay-owned

Brackenridge House 230 Madison (at Beauregard) **210/271–3442, 877/271–3442** • gay-friendly • B&B in historic King William district • pool • hot tub • WiFi

Emily Morgan Hotel 705 E Houston St (at Ave E) **210/225–5100, 800/824–6674** • gay-friendly • gym • pets ok • retaurant & bar • WiFi

Hotel Havana 1015 Navarro St **210/222–2008** • gay/ straight • also restaurant & lounge • gay-owned

Bars

2015 Place 2015 San Pedro (at Woodlawn) 210/733-3365 • 4pm-2am • mostly gay men • neighborhood bar • patio • karaoke Wed

The Annex 330 San Pedro Ave (at Euclid) 210/223-6957 • 2pm-2am • mostly gay men • neighborhood bar • WiFi • wheelchair access

The Boss 1006 VFW Blvd (Jeffersonville) 210/550-2322, 210/449-8506 • 8pm-2am • mostly gay men • neighborhood dive bar

Electric Company 820 San Pedro Ave (at W Laurel) 210/212-6635 • 9pm-3am, clsd Mon • lesbians/ gay men, more women Wed & Sun • dancing/DJ • live shows • 18+

Essence 1010 N Main Ave (at E Euclid) 210/223-5418 • 2pm-2am • mostly gay men • neighborhood bar • karaoke

The Flying Saucer 11255 Huebner Rd #212 (at I-10) 210/696-5080 • 11am-1am, till 2am Th-Sat, noon-midnight Sun • gay-friendly • large beer selection

Mix 2423 N St Marys St 210/735-1313 • 5pm-2am, from 7:30pm Sat-Sun, dive bar • gay-friendly dive bar • live music

One-Oh-Six Off Broadway 106 Pershing St (at Broadway) 210/820-0906 • noon-2am • lesbians/ gay men • neighborhood bar

Silver Dollar Saloon 1818 N Main Ave (at Dewey) 210/227-2623 • 4pm-2am, clsd Mon • lesbians/ gay men • dancing/DJ • country/ western • karaoke

Sparky's Pub 1416 N Main Ave (at Evergreen) 210/320-5111 • 3pm-2am • pub atmosphere

Nightclubs

The Bonham Exchange 411 Bonham St (at 3rd/ Houston) 210/271-3811 • 4pm-2am, from 8pm Sat • popular • in 120-year-old mansion • lesbians/ gay men • dancing/DJ • videos • 18+ • gay-owned

The Industry 8021 Pinebrook Dr (at Callaghan) 210/366-3229 • 10pm-2am Th, from 8pm Fri-Sat • gay/ straight • dancing/DJ

The Saint 800 Lexington Ave 210/225-7330 • 4pm-3am • mostly gay men • dancing/DJ • drag shows • 18+

Cafes

Candlelight Coffeehouse & Wine Bar 3011 N St Mary's (at Rte 281) 210/738-0099 • 2pm-midnight, wknd brunch 10am-2pm, clsd Mon • live music • WiFi • wheelchair access

Restaurants

Chacho's 7870 Callaghan Rd (at I-10) 210/366-2023 • 24hrs • Mexican • live bands • karaoke • wheelchair access

Cool Cafe 12651 Vance Jackson 210/8775/5/20115001 • brkfst, lunch & dinner • Mediterranean

Giovanni's Pizza & Italian Restaurant 913 S Brazos (at Guadalupe) 210/212-6626 • 11am-7pm • some veggie

Guenther House 129 E Guenther (at S Alamo St) 210/227-1061, 800/235-8186 • 7am-3pm • located in restored Pioneer Flour Mills founding family home

Lulu's Bakery & Cafe 918 N Main (at W Elmira) 210/222-9422 • 24hrs • Tex-Mex • wheelchair access

Luther's Cafe 1425 N Main Ave (at Evergreen) 210/223-7727 • 11am-3am • great burgers • karaoke • live music • wheelchair access • gay-owned

Madhatter's Tea House 320 Beauregard 210/212-4832 • 8am-9pm, till 3pm Sun • BYOB • patio • WiFi • wheelchair access

El Mirador 722 S St Mary's St (at Durango Blvd) 210/225-9444 • 6:30am-9pm, till 2pm Sun • Tex-Mex • plenty veggie • beer/ wine • patio • wheelchair access

Taco Taco Cafe 145 E Hildebrand 210/822-9533 • 7am-2pm

WD Deli 3123 Broadway St 210/828-2322 • 10:30am-5pm, till 4pm Sat, clsd Sun

Entertainment & Recreation

Alamo City Rollergirls 223 Recoleta Rd (at the Rollercade) • San Antonio's female flat track roller derby league • visit www.alamocityrollergirls.com for events

Retail Shops

On Main/ Off Main 120 W Mistletoe Ave 210/737-2323 • 10am-6pm, till 5pm Sat, clsd Sun • gifts • cards • T-shirts

ZEBRAZ.com 1608 N Main Ave (at E Park Ave) 210/472-2800, 800/788-4729 • 9am-midnight, till 10pm Sun-Tue • LGBT dept store

Erotica

Dreamers 2376 Austin Hwy (at Walzem) 210/653-3538 • 24hrs

Tyler

Info Lines & Services

Tyler Area Gays/ TAG 5701 Old Bullard Road #96 • social events & LGBT resources

ACCOMMODATIONS

Cross Timber Ranch B&B 6271 FM 858 (at Hwy 64), Ben Wheeler 903/833-9000, 877/833-9002 • gay/ straight • full brkfst • nonsmoking • WiFi • gay-owned

Waco

NIGHTCLUBS

Club Trix 110 S 6th St 254/714-0767 • 10pm-2am Th, 9pm-2am Fri-Sat • lesbians/ gay men • transgender-friendly • dancing/DJ • videos

Webster

BARS

Club Pride 229 E NASA Pkwy 281/557-4800 • 9pm-2am Th-Sat • lesbians/ gay men • dancing/DJ

Wichita Falls

BARS

Krank It Karaoke Kafe 1400 N Scott Ave (at Old Iowa Park Rd) 940/761-9099 • 8:30pm-2am, from 7pm Fri-Sat, clsd Mon-Tue • gay-friendly • dancing/DJ • 18+ • wheelchair access

Odds 1205 Lamar St (at 12th) 940/322-2996 • 4pm-2am, from 3pm Sun • lesbians/ gay men • more women Th • neighborhood bar • dancing/DJ • karaoke • drag shows • 18+ • beer/ wine

Wimberley

ACCOMMODATIONS

Bella Vista 2121 Hilltop 512/847-6425 • gay/ straight • pool • nonsmoking • gay-owned

UTAH

Bryce Canyon

ACCOMMODATIONS

Hatch Station 177 S Main, Hatch 435/735-4015 • gay-friendly • also restaurant, laundry & convenience store • safe oasis for LGBT travelers in S UT • WiFi • wheelchair access

The Red Brick Inn of Panguitch B&B 161 N 100 West (at 200 North), Panguitch 435/676-2141, 866/733-2745 • gay-friendly • full brkfst • kids ok

CAFES

Scoops from the Past 105 N Main St, Panguitch 435/676-8885 • noon-10pm, till 11pm Fri-Sat, till 6pm Sun • retro ice cream parlor • WiFi

Moab

ACCOMMODATIONS

Mayor's House B&B 505 Rose Tree Ln (at 400 E) 435/259-6015, 888/791-2345 • gay-friendly • full brkfst • pool • hot tub • kids ok • nonsmoking • WiFi • gay-owned

Mt Peale Resort Inn, Lodge & Cabins 1415 E Hwy 46 (at mile marker 14), Old La Sal 435/686-2284, 888/687-3253 • gay/ straight • B&B & cabins • hot tub • hiking • nonsmoking • WiFi • kids/ pets ok • lesbian-owned

Red Cliffs Lodge Hwy 128 (at mile marker 14) 435/259-2002, 866/812-2002 • gay-friendly • resort • on Colorado River • pool • hot tub • kids ok • nonsmoking • wheelchair access

Park City

RESTAURANTS

Loco Lizard Cantina 1612 Ute Blvd (in Kimball Jct Shopping Ctr) 435/645-7000 • 11am-10pm, till 11pm Fri-Sat, brunch wknds • Mexican • full bar • transgender-friendly • wheelchair access

Salt Lake City

INFO LINES & SERVICES

Utah Pride Center 361 N 300 W, 1st flr 801/539-8800, 888/874-2743 • info • resource center • meetings • coffee shop • programs • youth activity center • much more

ACCOMMODATIONS

Anniversary Inn 460 S 1000 E (at 400) 435/879-5839, 800/324-4152 • gay-friendly • elaborate, kitschy theme rms • WiFi • women owned

Hotel Monaco Salt Lake City 15 W 200 S (at S Main) 801/595-0000, 877/294-9710 • gay-friendly • restaurant & bar • WiFi • gym • kids/ pets ok • wheelchair access

Parrish Place 720 E Ashton Ave (at 700 E) 801/832-0970, 855/832-0970 • gay/ straight • Victorian mansion • hot tub • nonsmoking • WiFi

Peery Hotel 110 W 300 S 801/521-4300, 800/331-0073 • gay-friendly • kids/pets ok • also 2 restaurants • full bar • nonsmoking • WiFi • wheelchair access

Under the Lindens 128 S 1000 E (downtown) **801/355-9808** • mostly gay men • studios • hot tub • nonsmoking • WiFi • commitment ceremonies • mention Damron for discount • gay-owned

BARS

Jam 751 North 300 West (at Reed Ave) **801/891-1162** • 5pm-2am, clsd Sun • lesbians/ gay men • neighborhood bar • dancing/DJ • karaoke • WiFi

Paper Moon 3737 S State St (at E 3750 S) **801/713-0678** • 3pm-1am, from 6pm Mon • mostly women • dancing/DJ • karaoke • live music • private club • food served • wheelchair access

The Tavernacle Social Club 201 E 300 South (at 200 E) **801/519-8900** • 5pm-close, from 8pm Sun-Mon • gay-friendly • food • karaoke • "Duelin' Pianos" • nonsmoking • private club

The Trapp 102 S 600 W (at 100 S) **801/531-8727** • 11am-2am • lesbians/ gay men • dancing/DJ • country/ western • karaoke • WiFi • wheelchair access

NIGHTCLUBS

Area 51 451 South 400 West (at 400 S) **801/534-0819** • gay/ straight • dancing/DJ • 80s & goth theme nights Th-Sat only

Fusion 540 W 200 South (at Metro Bar) • 9pm-2am Sat only• mostly gay men • dancing/DJ

Hydrate SLC 579 W 200 S (at 600 W, at Club Sound) **801/328-0255** • 9:30pm-2am Fri only • mostly gay men • dancing/DJ

Mixx 615 W 100 South **801/575-6499** • 9pm-2am Fri-Sat • mostly gay men • dancing/DJ • karaoke

Pachanga at Karamba 1051 East 2100 South **801/696-0639** • 9pm Sun only • mostly gay men • gay Latin night • dancing/DJ

CAFES

Coffee Garden 878 E 900 S **801/355-3425** • 6am-11pm • light fare • wheelchair access

RESTAURANTS

Bambara 202 S Main St **801/363-5454** • lunch Mon-Fri, brkfst & dinner daily • upscale American

Salt Lake City

LGBT PRIDE:
June. 801/539-8800, web: utah-pridefestival.org.

ANNUAL EVENTS:
Jan - Gay/ Lesbian Ski Week
  877/429-6368, web:
  gayskiing.org/SKIING/indexu.htm

CITY INFO:
801/534-4900, web: www.visitsalt-lake.com.

WEATHER:
Home of "The Greatest Snow on Earth," the Wasatch Mtns get an average of 535 inches of powder, while the valley averages 59 inches. Spring is mild with an average of 62°, while summer temps average 88°, topping out at an average of 92° in July.

ATTRACTIONS:
Family History Library, one of the largest genealogical research databases in the country 801/240-2584, web: www.familysearch.org.
Great Salt Lake.
Mormon Tabernacle Choir 801/240-4150, web: www.mormontabernaclechoir.org.
Skiing!
Temple Square.
Trolley Square.

TRANSIT:
Yellow Cab 801/521-2100, web: www.yellowcabutah.com.
Utah Transit Authority (UTA) 801/743-3882, web: www.utabus.com.

Blue Plate Diner 2041 S 2100 E
801/463-1151 • 7am-9pm, till 10pm Fri-Sat

Cafe Trio Downtown 680 S 900 E
801/533-8746 • 11am-10pm, Italian

Cedars of Lebanon 152 E 200 South (at State St) 801/364-4096 • lunch & dinner • Lebanese • veggie/ vegan-friendly • belly dancers wknds • WiFi

Citris Grill 2991 E 3300 South 801/466-1202 • 8am-10pm

Finn's 1624 S 1100 East (at Logan) 801/467-4000 • 7:30am-2:30pm

Fresco Italian Cafe 1513 S 1500 East 801/486-1300 • dinner nightly • patio

Himalayan Kitchen 360 S State St (at 400 S) 801/328-2077 • lunch & dinner, dinner only Sun • Indian/Himalayan • plenty veggie

Market St Grill 48 W Market St 801/322-4668 • 11:30-9pm, from 9am Sun • fresh seafood, • full bar • wheelchair access

The Med 420 E 3300 South 801/493-0100 • lunch & dinner • Mediterranean

The Metropolitan 173 W Broadway 801/364-3472 • lunch Mon-Fri, dinner nightly, clsd Sun • New American

The New Yorker 60 W Market St 801/363-0166 • lunch Mon-Fri, dinner nightly, clsd Sun • fine dining • steak

Off Trax 259 W 900 S 801/364-4307 • 7am-7pm, till 3pm Fri, brunch Sun, also from 1am-3am Fri-Sat nights • lesbians/ gay men • WiFi • gay-owned

Omar's Rawtopia 2148 Highland Dr 801/486-0332 • noon-8pm, till 9pm Fri-Sat, clsd Sun • raw food

Red Iguana 736 W North Temple 801/322-1489 • popular • lunch & dinner • Mexican

Sage's Cafe 234 W 900 S 801/322-3790 • lunch & dinner, brkfst wknds • vegan/ vegetarian

Stoneground 249 E 400 South 801/364-1368 • 11am-11pm, 5pm-9pm Sun • pizza & more

Vertical Diner 2280 S West Temple 801/484-8378 • 10am-9pm • vegetarian diner • wheelchair access

Zest Kitchen & Bar 275 S 200 W 801/433-0589 • 4pm-1am, till 11pm Tues, clsd Sun-Mon

ENTERTAINMENT & RECREATION

Lambda Hiking Club • hiking & other activities

Plan B Theatre Company 138 West 300 South (at Rose Wagner Performing Arts Center, btwn W Temple & 200 West) 801/355-2787 • at least one LGBT-themed production each season

Pygmalion Productions Theatre Company 138 W Broadway (at Rose Wagner Performing Arts Center) 801/355-2787, 888/451-2787 • a "feminine perspective" on theatre

Tower Theatre 876 E 900 South 801/321-0310 • alternative films • many LGBT movies

BOOKSTORES

Golden Braid Books 151 S 500 E 801/322-1162 • 10am-9pm, till 6pm Sun • also Oasis Cafe, 8am-9pm, till 10pm wknds • WiFi

Weller Book Works 607 Trolley Sq 801/328-2586 • 10am-9pm, noon-5pm Sun

RETAIL SHOPS

Cahoots 878 E 900 S (at 900 E) 801/538-0606 • 10am-9pm • unique gift shop • wheelchair access • gay-owned

PUBLICATIONS

Q Salt Lake 801/649-6663, 800/806-7357 • bi-weekly LGBT newspaper

EROTICA

All For Love 3072 S Main St (at 33rd St S) 801/487-8358 • clsd Sun • lingerie & S/M boutique • transgender-friendly • wheelchair access

Blue Boutique 1383 E 2100 South 801/485-2072 • also piercing

Mischievous 559 S 300 W (at 6th St S) 801/530-3100 • clsd Sun

Zion Nat'l Park

ACCOMMODATIONS

Canyon Vista Lodge B&B 2175 Zion Park Blvd (at Hwy 9), Springdale 435/772-3801 • gay-friendly • nonsmoking

Red Rock Inn 998 Zion Park Blvd, Springdale 435/772-3139 • gay/ straight • cottages w/ canyon views • full brkfst • hot tub • nonsmoking • wheelchair access • lesbian-owned

CAFES

Cafe Soleil 205 Zion Nat'l Park Blvd 435/772-0505 • 6am-8pm seasonal • lesbian-owned

VERMONT

Statewide

INFO LINES & SERVICES

Vermont Gay Tourism Association • Vermont's official organization to promote gay & lesbian travel throughout the state • see www.vermontgaytourism.com

Brattleboro

ACCOMMODATIONS

Nutmeg Inn 153 Rte 9 W, Wilmington **802/464-3907, 855/868-8634** • gay/ straight • WiFi • wheelchair access • gay-owned

RESTAURANTS

Peter Havens 32 Elliot St (at Main) **802/257-3333** • 6pm-10pm, clsd Sun-Tue • cont'l • gay-owned

BOOKSTORES

Everyone's Books 25 Elliot St **802/254-8160** • 9:30am-6pm, till 8pm Fri, till 7pm Sat, 11am-5pm Sun • wheelchair access

Burlington

INFO LINES & SERVICES

R.U.1.2? Community Center 55 S Champlain St #12 **802/860-RU12 (7812)** • drop-in & cybercenter • advocacy & support • events

ACCOMMODATIONS

The Black Bear Inn 4010 Bolton Access Rd, Bolton Valley **802/434-2126, 800/395-6335** • gay/ straight • mtn-top inn • full brkfst • hot tub • pool • kids/ pets ok • nonsmoking • WiFi

Hartwell House B&B Gallery 170 Ferguson Ave **802/658-9242, 888/658-9242** • gay-friendly • pool • shared bath • nonsmoking • woman-owned

The Inn at Essex 70 Essex Way, Essex **802/878-1100, 800/727-4295** • gay-friendly • culinary resort • pool • kids/ pets ok • WiFi • wheelchair access

One of a Kind B&B 53 Lakeview Terrace **802/862-5576** • nonsmoking • 2-rm suite & cottage • WiFi • woman-owned

NIGHTCLUBS

Metronome/ Nectar's 188 Main St **802/658-4771, 802/865-4563** • gay-friendly • popular 80s night Sat • live bands • also restaurant

CAFES

Muddy Waters 184 Main St **802/658-0466** • 9am-11pm • coffeehouse, try the white hot chocolate

Radio Bean Coffeehouse 8 N Winooski Ave (at Pearl) **802/660-9346** • 8am-midnight, till 2am Th-Sat, 10am-11pm Sun • cool bohemian coffeehouse • live bands & open mic nights

RESTAURANTS

Bluebird Tavern 86 St Paul St **802/540-1786** • 4pm-10pm Th-Sat, 5pm-9pm Tue-Wed, clsd Sun-Mon • locally grown • beer/ wine • lesbian-owned

Daily Planet 15 Center St (at College) **802/862-9647** • 4pm-close, also bar till 2am • plenty veggie

Leunig's Bistro & Cafe 115 Church St **802/863-3759** • lunch & dinner, gulten free options • lesbian-owned

Loretta's 44 Park St (near 5 Corners), Essex Junction **802/879-7777** • lunch weekdays, dinner nightly, clsd Sun-Mon • Italian • plenty veggie • lesbian-owned

Shanty on the Shore 181 Battery St **802/864-0238** • 11am-9pm • seafood • views of Lake Champlain

Silver Palace 1216 Williston Rd **802/864-0125** • 11:30am-9pm, 5pm-9pm Sun• Chinese • full bar

RETAIL SHOPS

Peace & Justice Store 60 Lake St (at College St) **802/863-2345** • 10am-6pm, limited hrs in winter • fair trade retail store

Chester

ACCOMMODATIONS

Chester House Inn 266 Main St **888/875-2205** • gay/ straight • full brkfst • nonsmoking • kids ok • WiFi • wheelchair access • gay-owned

Jay Peak

ACCOMMODATIONS

Phineas Swann B&B **802/326-4306** • gay/ straight • restored Victorian on Trout River • full brkfst • nonsmoking • WiFi • gay-owned

Killington

ACCOMMODATIONS

Huntington House Inn 19 Huntington Pl, Rochester **802/767–9140** • gay-friendly • located on the park w/ a restaurant & lounge • WiFi • wheelchair access • gay-owned

The Inn of the Six Mountains 2617 Killington Rd **802/422–4302, 800/228–4676** • gay-friendly • pool • jacuzzi • WiFi • kids ok • wheelchair access

Salt Ash Inn 4758 Rte 100A (at Rte 100), Plymouth **802/672–3224** • gay/ straight • 1830s country inn • full brkfst • hot tub • kids/ small pets ok • pool • WiFi • wheelchair access

Manchester

ACCOMMODATIONS

Hill Farm Inn 458 Hill Farm Rd (at Historic Rte 7-A), Arlington **802/375–2269, 800/882–2545** • gay-friendly • full brkfst • nonsmoking • WiFi

CAFES

Little Rooster Cafe Rte 7-A (at Hillvale Dr), Manchester Center **802/362–3496** • 7am-2:30pm, clsd Wed (winters)

RESTAURANTS

Bistro Henry 1942 Depot St (.5 mile E of Rte 7), Manchester Center **802/362–4982** • dinner only, clsd Mon • Mediterranean • also bar • reservations advised

Chanteleer Rte 7-A N, E Dorset **802/362–1616** • call for hours • seasonal

BOOKSTORES

Northshire Bookstore 4869 Main St, Manchester Center **802/362–2200, 800/437–3700** • 10am-7pm, till 9pm Fri-Sat

Marshfield

ACCOMMODATIONS

Marshfield Inn & Motel 5630 US Rte 2 **802/426–3383** • gay-friendly • full brkfst • WiFi • lesbian-owned

Montpelier

RESTAURANTS

Julio's 54 State **802/229–9348** • 11:30am-10pm, till 11pm Fri-Sat• Mexican • WiFi

Sarducci's 3 Main St **802/223–0229** • 11:30am-9:30pm, from 4:30pm Sun • Italian • some veggie • full bar • wheelchair access

Wayside Restaurant 1873 Rte 302 **802/223–6611** • 6:30am-9:30pm • wheelchair access

Plainfield

ACCOMMODATIONS

Comstock House 1620 Middle Rd **802/272–2693** • gay-friendly • overlooks Winooski River Valley • full brkfst • WiFi • gay-owned

Richmond

RESTAURANTS

The Kitchen Table Bistro 1840 W Main St **802/434–8686** • 5pm-9pm, clsd Sun-Mon • seasonal menu • local food

Rutland

ACCOMMODATIONS

Lilac Inn 53 Park St, Brandon **802/247–5463, 800/221–0720** • full brkfst • teens/ pets ok • wheelchair access

Saxtons River

ACCOMMODATIONS

The Saxtons River Inn 27 Main St (at Academy Ave) **802/869–2110** • gay-friendly • historic Victorian inn • pub & restaurant • nonsmoking • WiFi • pets ok

St Johnsbury

ACCOMMODATIONS

Comfort Inn & Suites 703 US Rte 5 S (at I-91) **802/748–1500, 800/424–6423** • gay-friendly • pool • hot tub • kids ok • WiFi • wheelchair access

Fairbanks Inn 401 Western Ave **802/748–5666** • gay-friendly • motel • pool • kids & pets ok • WiFi • wheelchair access

RESTAURANTS

Elements 98 Mill St **802/748–8400** • dinner, clsd Sun-Mon • local food

Stowe

ACCOMMODATIONS

Arbor Inn 3214 Mountain Rd **802/253–4772, 800/543–1293** • gay/ straight • full brkfst • hot tub • pool • nonsmoking • WiFi

Fitch Hill Inn 258 Fitch Hill Rd (at Rte 15/100), Hyde Park **802/888–3834, 800/639–2903** • gay/ straight • full brkfst • older kids ok • WiFi • nonsmoking

The Green Mountain Inn 18 Main St
802/253-7301, 800/253-7302 • gay-friendly •
kids ok • heated pool • hot tub • nonsmoking
• WiFi • wheelchair access • 2 restaurants

Northern Lights Lodge 4441 Mountain Rd
802/253-8541, 800/448-4554 • gay-friendly •
full brkfst • hot tub • pool • sauna • kids/pets
ok • WiFi • gay-owned

The Old Stagecoach Inn 18 N Main St (at
Stowe St), Waterbury 802/244-5056,
800/262-2206 • gay-friendly • historic village
inn • full brkfst • kids/pets ok • also full bar

Timberholm Inn 452 Cottage Club Rd
802/253-7603, 800/753-7603 • gay/straight •
B&B • full brkfst • hot tub • nonsmoking

Waterbury

ACCOMMODATIONS

Grünberg Haus B&B & Cabins 94 Pine St,
Rte 100 S 802/244-7726, 800/800-7760 • gay/
straight • Austrian chalet • also cabins May-
Oct • full brkfst • fireplace • nonsmoking •
WiFi

Moose Meadow Lodge 607 Crossett Hill
802/244-5378 • gay/straight • full brkfst •
nonsmoking • WiFi • gay-owned

RESTAURANTS

Cider House BBQ & Pub 1675 US Rte 2
802/244-8400 • noon-9pm, clsd Mon-Wed •
full bar • patio • gay-owned

West Dover

ACCOMMODATIONS

Deerhill Inn 14 Valley View Rd
802/464-3100, 800/993-3379 • gay/straight •
inn • pool • teenagers ok • nonsmoking • WiFi
• also restaurant

Inn at Mount Snow 401 Rte 100
802/464-8388 • gay-friendly • at foot of Mt
Snow • • kids ok • nonsmoking • WiFi • gay-
owned

The Inn at Sawmill Farm 7 Crosstown Rd
(at Rte 100) 802/464-8131, 800/493-1133 •
gay-friendly • kids/pets ok • nonsmoking •
WiFi • wheelchair access

Windham

ACCOMMODATIONS

A Stone Wall Inn 578 Hitchcock Hill Rd
802/875-4238 • gay/straight • hot tub • WiFi
• nonsmoking • gay-owned

Woodstock

ACCOMMODATIONS

The Ardmore Inn 23 Pleasant St
802/457-3887 • gay-friendly • 1867 Greek
Revival • full brkfst • nonsmoking • WiFi

Deer Brook Inn 4548 W Woodstock Rd
802/672-3713 • gay-friendly • full brkfst • kids
ok • WiFi • gay-owned

The Woodstocker Inn B&B 61 River St
802/457-3896 • gay/straight • WiFi

VIRGINIA

Alexandria

see also Washington, District of
Columbia

ACCOMMODATIONS

Crowne Plaza Old Town Alexandria 901
N Fairfax St 703/683-6000

Lorien Hotel & Spa 1600 King St
703/894-3434, 877/956-7436 • gay-friendly •
restaurant on-site • kids/pets ok • wheelchair
access

Morrison House 116 S Alfred St
703/838-8000, 866/834-6628

Arlington

see also Washington, District of
Columbia

INFO LINES & SERVICES

Arlington Gay/Lesbian Alliance •
monthly meetings • outreach events • check
website for schedule: www.agla.org

BARS

Freddie's Beach Bar & Restaurant 555 S
23rd St (at Fern St) 703/685-0555 • 4pm-
2am, from 11am Fri, fron 10an wknds for
brunch • lesbians/gay men • karaoke • drag
show • patio • live bands • food served •
wheelchair access

CAFES

Java Shack 2507 N Franklin Rd (at Wilson
Blvd & N Barton) 703/527-9556 • 7am-8pm,
8am-6pm Sun

Cape Charles

ACCOMMODATIONS

Cape Charles House B&B 645 Tazewell Ave
(at Fig) 757/331-4920 • gay-friendly • 1912
colonial revival home filled w/ antiques •
nonsmoking

Sea Gate B&B 9 Tazewell Ave **757/331–2206** • gay-friendly • full brkfst • near beach on quiet, tree-lined street • WiFi • gay-owned

Charlottesville

ACCOMMODATIONS

CampOut **804/301–3553** • women only • 100-acre rustic campground • nonsmoking • pets ok • wheelchair access • women-owned

The Inn at Court Square 410 E Jefferson St **434/295–2800, 866/466–2877** • gay-friendly • restored house w/ period antiques • lunch served Mon-Fri, dinner Fri-Sat • kids ok • nonsmoking • women-owned

RESTAURANTS

Escafe 215 W Water St **434/295–8668** • lunch & dinner • full bar • live music • gay-owned

EROTICA

Sneak Reviews Video 2244 Ivy Rd **434/979–4420**

Hampton

CAFES

The Java Junkies 768 Settlers Landing Rd **757/722–6300** • 8am-5pm, till 3pm Sat-Sun • food served

Harrisonburg

CAFES

Artful Dodger Coffeehouse 47 W Court Square **540/432–1179** • 8:30am-2am, from 9:30am wknds • DJ • entertainment • also bar • wheelchair access

Norfolk

ACCOMMODATIONS

B&B at Historic Page House Inn 323 Fairfax Ave **757/625–5033, 800/599–7659** • gay-friendly • 1899 mansion • nonsmoking • WiFi

Tazewell Hotel & Suites 245 Granby St (at Tazewell St) **757/623–6200** • gay-friendly • kids ok • WiFi • wheelchair access

BARS

The Garage 731 Granby St (at Brambleton) **757/623–0303** • 4pm-2am • popular • mostly gay men • neighborhood bar • food served • karaoke • wheelchair access

Hershee Lounge & He Bar 6117 Sewells Pt Rd (at Norview) **757/853–9842** • 4pm-2am • mostly women • dancing/DJ • live shows • food served • wheelchair access • woman-owned

NIGHTCLUBS

The Wave 4107 Colley Ave (at 41st St) **757/440–5911** • 10pm-2am, clsd Sun, Mon & Wed • lesbians/ gay men • dancing/DJ • live shows • wheelchair access

RESTAURANTS

Charlie's Cafe 1800 Granby St (at 18th) **757/625–0824** • 7am-2pm • some veggie • beer/ wine

Tortilla West 508 Oropax St **757/440–3777** • dinner only, Sun brunch, open till 1am • Mexican • plenty veggie/ vegan

EROTICA

Leather & Lace 745 Battlefield Blvd N #104, Chesapeake **757/436–2525** • 11am-8pm, noon-6pm

Richmond

ACCOMMODATIONS

Omni Richmond Hotel 100 S 12th St (at Cary St) **804/344–7000, 800/843–6664** • gay-friendly • pool • views of city & James River • WiFi • wheelchair access

BARS

Babes of Carytown 3166 W Cary St (at Auburn) **804/355–9330** • 11am-2am, from noon Sat, from 9am Sun • lesbians/ gay men • dancing/DJ • country/ western • karaoke • drag shows • live music • food served • wheelchair access • women-owned

Barcode 6 E Grace St (btwn 1st & Foushee Sts) **804/648–2040** • 4pm-2am, from 3pm wknds • mostly gay men • neighborhood bar • karaoke • food served • WiFi • wheelchair access

Godfrey's 308 E Grace St (btwn 3rd & 4th) **804/648–3957** • 10pm-close, clsd Mon-Tue, brunch Sun • lesbians/ gay men • dancing/DJ • karaoke • drag shows

NIGHTCLUBS

Club Colours 536 N Harrison St (at Broad) **804/353–9776** • 9pm-3am Sat • lesbians/ gay men • dancing/DJ • multiracial • food served • live shows • wheelchair access

RESTAURANTS

Galaxy Diner 3109 W Cary St **804/213–0510** • 11am-midnight, till 2am wknds • some veggie • full bar

The Village 1001 W Grace **804/353–8204** • 8am-2am • American • plenty veggie

ENTERTAINMENT & RECREATION

Richmond Triangle Players 1300 Altamont Ave (at W Marshall St) **804/346–8113** • LGBT-themed plays, films & cabaret

Venture Richmond **804/788–6466** • tour the James River • lots of shops, restaurants, etc

BOOKSTORES

Phoenix Rising 19 N Belmont Ave **804/355–7939** • 11am-7pm, clsd Tue • LGBT • wheelchair access

Roanoke

BARS

Backstreet Cafe 356 Salem Ave (off Jefferson) **540/345–1542** • 7pm-2am, clsd Sun-Mon • lesbians/gay men • neighborhood bar • food served

Cuba Pete's 120 Church Ave SW (at First St SW, inside Macado's) **540/342–7231** • 11am-2am • gay-friendly • more gay wknds • also Macado's restaurant • karaoke • wheelchair access

RESTAURANTS

Metro Restaurant & Nighclub 14 Campbell Ave SE • 11:30am-midnight, till 2:30am Fri-Sat • dancing/DJ

Shenandoah Valley

ACCOMMODATIONS

Frog Hollow B&B 492 Greenhouse Rd (at Rte 11), Lexington **540/463–5444** • gay/straight • full brkfst • hot tub • also cottage • gay-owned

The Olde Staunton Inn 260 N Lewis St, Staunton **540/886–0193, 866/653–3786** • gay/straight • B&B • hot tub • WiFi • nonsmoking

Piney Hill B&B 1048 Piney Hill Rd (at Mill Creek Crossroads), Luray **540/778–5261, 800/644–5261** • gay/straight • country B&B • full brkfst • hot tub • gay-owned

Virginia Beach

ACCOMMODATIONS

Capes Ocean Resort Hotel 2001 Atlantic Ave (at 20th St) **757/428–5421, 877/956–5421** • gay-friendly • oceanfront rooms • private balconies • pool • nonsmoking • WiFi • kids ok • wheelchair access

Ocean Beach Club 3401 Atlantic Ave (at 34th St) **800/245–1003** • gay-friendly • also cafe & tiki bar • wheelchair access

BARS

Klub Ambush 475 S Lynnhaven Rd (at Lynnhaven Pkwy) **757/498–4301** • 5pm-2am • lesbians/gay men • neighborhood bar • dancing/DJ • food served • shows • karaoke • gay-owned

Rainbow Cactus 3472 Holland Rd (at Diana Lee) **757/368–0441** • 7pm-2am, clsd Mon-Tue • mostly gay men • dancing/DJ • country/western • drag shows • food served • wheelchair access

EROTICA

Nancy's Nook 1301 Oceana Blvd **757/428–1498** • 24hrs

Washington

ACCOMMODATIONS

Gay Street Inn 160 Gay St **540/316–9220** • gay-friendly • nonsmoking • WiFi • gay-owned

WASHINGTON

Bainbridge Island

BOOKSTORES

Eagle Harbor Book Co 157 Winslow Wy E **206/842–5332** • 9am-7pm, till 9pm Th, till 6pm Sat, 10am-6pm Sun

Bellevue

see also Seattle

Bellingham

BARS

Rumors 1119 Railroad Ave (at Chestnut) **360/671–1846** • 4pm-2am • lesbians/gay men • dancing/DJ • multiracial • wheelchair access

CAFES

Tony's Coffee House 1101 Harris Ave (at 11th), Fairhaven **360/738–4710** • 7am-6pm • plenty veggie • patio • wheelchair access

RESTAURANTS

Bobby Lee's Pub & Eatery 108 W Main St (Washington Ave), Everson **360/966–8838** • 11am-2am, clsd Mon • gay-owned • wheelchair access

Skylark's Hidden Cafe 1308 11th St (at McKenzie) 360/715–3642 • 7am-midnight • great soups • full bar • outdoor seating • live jazz wknds

BOOKSTORES

Village Books 1200 11th St (at Harris) 360/671–2626 • 10am-7:30pm, till 7pm Sun • new & used

EROTICA

Great Northern Bookstore 1308 Railroad Ave (at Holly) 360/733–1650

Bender Creek

ACCOMMODATIONS

Triangle Recreation Camp PO Box 1226, Granite Falls 98252 • lesbians/ gay men • members-only camping on 80-acre nature conservancy • www.camptrc.org

Bremerton

INFO LINES & SERVICES

AA Gay/ Lesbian 700 Callahan Dr (at St Paul's Episcopal) 360/475–0775, 800/562–7455 • 7:30pm Tue

Everett

INFO LINES & SERVICES

AA Gay/ Lesbian 2624 Rockefeller 425/252–2525 • 7pm Sun

Glacier

ACCOMMODATIONS

Mt Baker B&B & Cabins 9434 Cornell Creek Rd 360/599–2299 • gay/ straight • modern chalet • hot tub • kids ok • some shared baths • nonsmoking • WiFi

Kent

EROTICA

The Voyeur 604 Central Ave S 253/850–8428 • videos • toys • clothing

La Conner

ACCOMMODATIONS

The Wild Iris 121 Maple Ave 360/466–1400, 800/477–1400 • gay-friendly • inn • nonsmoking • full brkfst • kids ok • WiFi • wheelchair access • gay-owned

Long Beach Peninsula

ACCOMMODATIONS

Anthony's Home Court 1310 Pacific Hwy N, Long Beach 360/642–2802, 888/787–2754 • gay/ straight • cabins & RV hookups • nonsmoking • WiFi • gay-owned

The Historic Sou'wester Lodge, Cabins & RV Park Beach Access Rd (38th Pl), Seaview 360/642–2542 • gay-friendly • inexpensive suites • cabins w/ kitchens • vintage trailers • RV hookups • pets ok in cabins & trailers • nonsmoking

Shakti Cove Cottages 360/665–4000 • lesbians/ gay men • cabins on the peninsula • pets ok • nonsmoking • lesbian-owned

Mt Vernon

RESTAURANTS

Deli Next Door 202 S 1st St (at Memorial Hwy) 360/336–3886 • 8am-9pm, 9pm-8pm Sun • healthy American • plenty veggie • WiFi • wheelchair access

Olympia

INFO LINES & SERVICES

Free at Last AA 360/352–7344 • call for info

ACCOMMODATIONS

Swantown Inn B&B 1431 11th Ave SE (at Central St) 360/753–9123, 877/753–9123 • gay-friendly • nonsmoking • full brkfst • WiFi

BARS

Hannah's 123 5th Ave SW (at Columbia) 360/357–9890 • 11am-2am, till midnight Sun-Mon • gay/ straight • neighborhood bar • food served

NIGHTCLUBS

Jakes on 4th 311 E 4th 360/956–3247 • 10am-2am • lesbians/ gay men • dancing/DJ • karaoke

CAFES

Darby's Cafe 211 SE 5th Ave (at Washington) 360/357–6229 • 7am-2pm, 8am-2pm wknds, clsd Mon-Tue • gay/ straight • gay-owned

RESTAURANTS

Saigon Rendez-Vous 117 5th Ave SW (btwn Columbia & Capitol Wy) 360/352–1989 • lunch & dinner • Vietnamese • plenty veggie

Urban Onion 116 Legion Wy SE (at Capitol) 360/943–9242 • 11am-9pm, 9am-2am wknds • plenty veggie • lounge • wheelchair access

RETAIL SHOPS

Dumpster Values 302 4th (at Franklin)
360/705-3772 • 10am-8pm, noon-6pm Sun •
new & used clothing • zines • records • toys •
women-owned

Pasco

NIGHTCLUBS

Out & About Restaurant & Lounge 327 W
Lewis **509/543-3796, 877/388-3796** • 6pm-
2am, clsd Sun-Mon • lesbians/ gay men •
dancing/DJ wknds • karaoke • drag shows •
cabaret • 18+ Fri • also restaurant •
wheelchair access

San Juan Islands

ACCOMMODATIONS

Inn on Orcas Island 360/376-5227,
888/886-1661 • gay-friendly • luxury • full
brkfst • nonsmoking • wheelchair access •
gay-owned

Lopez Farm Cottages & Tent Camping
555 Fisherman Bay Rd, Lopez Island
360/468-3555, 800/440-3556 • gay/ straight •
on 30-acre farm • hot tub • nonsmoking

ENTERTAINMENT & RECREATION

Western Prince Whale & Wildlife Tours 2
Spring St (at Front), Friday Harbor
360/378-5315, 800/757-6722 • whale-
watching & wildlife tours April-Oct

Seattle

ACCOMMODATIONS

The Ace Hotel 2423 1st Ave (at Wall St)
206/448-4721 • gay/ straight • kids/ pets ok •
nonsmoking • WiFi • restaurant & bar

Alexis Hotel 1007 1st Ave (at Madison)
206/624-4844, 866/356-8894 • gay-friendly •
luxury hotel w/ Aveda spa • kids/ pets ok • WiFi
• wheelchair access

Artist's Studio Loft B&B 16529 91st Ave
SW, Vashon Island **206/463-2583** • gay-
friendly • on 5 acres • garden • hot tub •
nonsmoking

Bacon Mansion 959 Broadway E (at E
Prospect) **206/329-1864, 800/240-1864** • gay/
straight • Edwardian-style Tudor •
nonsmoking • WiFi • wheelchair access

Bed & Breakfast on Broadway 722
Broadway Ave E (at Aloha) **206/329-8933** •
gay/ straight • nonsmoking • WiFi

Gaslight Inn 1727 15th Ave (at E Howell St)
206/325-3654 • popular • gay/ straight • B&B
in Arts & Crafts home • pool • WiFi •
nonsmoking • gay-owned

Hotel 1000 1000 First Ave **206/957-1000,
877/315-1088** • gay-friendly • WiFi •
wheelchair access

Inn at the Market 86 Pine St **206/443-3600,
800/446-4484** • gay/friendly • in Pike Place
Market

MarQueen Hotel 600 Queen Anne Ave N
(btwn Roy & Mercer) **206/282-7407,
888/445-3076** • gay/ straight • in Theater
District • kitchenettes

Seahurst Garden Studio 13713 16th Ave
SW (at Ambaum Ave), Burien **206/551-7721**
• women only • nonsmoking • WiFi •
wheelchair access • lesbian-owned

Sleeping Bulldog Bed & Breakfast 816
19th Ave S (at S Dearborn St) **206/325-0202**
• gay/ straight • nonsmoking • WiFi • gay-
owned

The Sorrento Hotel 900 Madison St
206/622-6400, 800/426-1265 • gay-friendly •
restaurant • WiFi

BARS

The Baltic Room 1207 Pine St (at Melrose)
206/625-4444 • 9pm-2am, LGBT night Th •
gay/ straight • live music

The Bottleneck Lounge 2328 Madison St
(at John St) **206/323-1098** • 4pm-2am • gay/
straight • bar snacks • lesbian-owned

CC Attle's 1701 E Olive Way **206/323-4017** •
noon-2am • popular • mostly gay men •
neighborhood bar • videos • also restaurant •
wheelchair access

Cha Cha Lounge & Bimbo's Cantina 1013
E Pike St (at 11th Ave) **206/322-0703** • 4pm-
2am • gay-friendly • hipster lounge • big
burritos • gay-owned

Changes In Wallingford 2103 N 45th St (at
Meridian) **206/545-8363** • noon-2am •
mostly gay men • neighborhood bar • food
served • karaoke • videos • wheelchair access

The Crescent Lounge 1413 E Olive Wy (at
Bellevue) • noon-2am • gay/ straight •
neighborhood bar • karaoke nightly •
wheelchair access

The Cuff 1533 13th Ave (at Pine)
206/323-1525 • 2pm-2am, after-hours wknds,
T-dance Sun • popular • mostly gay men •
dancing/DJ • country/ western Fri • WiFi •
patio • wheelchair access

Double Header 407 2nd Ave S Extension (at Washington) **206/464–9918** • 10am-11pm, till 1am Fri-Sat • gay/ straight • neighborhood bar

Hot Flash Seattle 1509 Broadway (at Neighbours) **206/252–9333** • T-dance 5pm-9pm 1st & 3rd Sat only • "for seasoned lesbians 36+ (& the women who love us!)" • cover charge

Hula Hula 106 1st Ave N (at Denny) **206/284–5003** • 4pm-close • gay-friendly • tiki bar • karaoke

The Lobby Bar 916 E Pike St (at Broadway) **206/328–6703** • 3pm-midnight, till 2am Th-Sat • mostly gay men • bar food • live shows

OutWest 5401 California Ave SW **206/937–1540** • 4pm-midnight, til 2am Th-Sat • lebians /gay men • neighborhood bar • live Jazz • karaoke

Poco Wine Room 1408 E Pine St (at 14th Ave) **206/322–9463** • 4pm-2am • gay/ straight • neighborhood bistropub

R Place 619 E Pine St (at Boylston Ave) **206/322–8828** • 4pm-2am, from 2pm wknds • mostly gay men • neighborhood bar • dancing/DJ • food served • karaoke • videos • WiFi • wheelchair access

Rendezvous 2322 2nd Ave (at Battery) **206/441–5823** • 4pm-2am • gay/ straight • live bands • cabaret • theater • also restaurant

The Seattle Eagle 314 E Pike St (at Bellevue) **206/621–7591** • 2pm-2am • mostly gay men • leather • rock 'n' roll • theme nights • patio • wheelchair access

Temple Billiards 126 S Jackson **206/682–3242** • 11am-2am, from 3pm wknds • gay-friendly • more women Wed • food served

Wildrose Bar & Restaurant 1021 E Pike St (at 11th) **206/324–9210** • 3pm-2am, 5pm-midnight Mon • mostly women • neighborhood bar • dancing/DJ • karaoke • live shows • food served • wheelchair access

NIGHTCLUBS

The Can Can 93 Pike St #307 (in the Pike Place Market) **206/652–0832** • 6pm-2am • gay/ straight • food served • cabaret

Contour 807 1st Ave (at Columbia) **206/447–7704** • 3pm-2am, till 6am Fri-Sat • gay-friendly • fire performances • dancing/DJ • also bar & restaurant

Dimitriou's Jazz Alley 2033 6th Ave (at Lenora) **206/441–9729** • gay-friendly • call for events & reservations • live music • nonsmoking • cover charge • also restaurant

Neighbours Dance Club 1509 Broadway (btwn Pike & Pine) **206/324–5358** • 9pm-2am, till 3am Th, till 4am Fri-Sat • popular • lesbians/ gay men • dancing/DJ • 2 flrs • also 18+ room Th-Sat • young crowd • wheelchair access

Purr 1518 11th Ave (at Pike St) **206/325–3112** • 4pm-2am, from noon wknds • mostly gay men • karaoke * Mexican-inspired food

Re-bar 1114 Howell (at Boren Ave) **206/233–9873** • 10pm-2am, clsd Mon • popular • gay/ straight • more women Sat • dancing/DJ Wed-Sun • cabaret/ theater

Showbox 1426 1st Ave (at Pike) **206/628–3151** • gay-friendly • live music venue

CAFES

The Allegro 4214 University Wy NE (at NE 42nd St) **206/633–3030** • 7am-10:30pm • WiFi

Cafe Besalu 5909 24th Ave NW **206/789–1463** • 7am-3pm, clsd Mon-Tue • great pastries

Espresso Vivace 532 Broadway Ave **206/860–5869** • 6am-11pm • popular • WiFi

Fuel Coffee 610 19th Ave E **206/329–4700** • 6am-9pm • WiFi

Kaladi Brothers Coffee 511 E Pike St (at Summit) **206/388–1700** • 6am-9pm, from 8am wknds • WiFi

Louisa's 2379 Eastlake Ave E **206/325–0081** • 7am-9pm, till 10pm Fri-Sat, 8am-3pm Sun

RESTAURANTS

Al Boccalino 1 Yesler Wy (at Alaskan) **206/622–7688** • lunch Tue-Fri, dinner nightly • classy southern Italian

Bamboo Garden 364 Roy St (at Mercer St) **206/282–6616** • 11am-10pm • Chinese vegetarian & kosher

Cafe Flora 2901 E Madison St **206/325–9100** • lunch, dinner, wknd brunch • vegetarian • beer/ wine • wheelchair accessible

Canlis 2576 Aurora Ave N **206/283–3313** • dinner only • fancy seafood

Dahlia Lounge 2001 4th Ave (at Virginia) **206/682–4142** • lunch Mon-Fri, dinner nightly, wknd brunch • some veggie • full bar

Dick's Drive In 115 Broadway E (at Denny) **206/323–1300** • 10:30am-2am • excellent fries & shakes

Flying Fish 300 Westlake Ave N **206/728–8595** • lunch Mon-Fri, dinner nightly, bar till 2am • lesbian chef

Fresh Bistro 4725 42nd Ave SW (btwn Alaska St & Edmunds) **206/935-3733** • dinner Mon-Sat, lunch Wed-Fri, wknd brunch

Glo's 1621 E Olive Wy (at Summit Ave E) **206/324-2577** • 7am-3pm, midnight -4pm wknds • brkfst only • popular

The Grill on Broadway 314 Broadway E (at E Harrison) **206/328-7000** • 11am-11pm, from 8am wknds • popular • full bar

Grim's Provisions & Spirits 1512 11th Ave **206/324-7467** • 3pm-2am, from 10am wkknds, Capitol Hill's most unique three level Restaurant

Julia's 300 Broadway E (at Thomas) **206/860-1818** • 8am-11pm, till midnight Fri-Sat • full bar • drag shows Sat

Kabul 2301 N 45th St **206/545-9000** • 5pm-9:30pm, till 10pm Fri-Sat • Afghan • some veggie

Lola 2000 4th Ave (at Virginia) **206/441-1430** • 6am-midnight, till 2am wknds • popular brunch

Mama's Mexican Kitchen 2234 2nd Ave (in Belltown) **206/728-6262** • lunch & dinner • cheap & funky

Seattle

LGBT PRIDE:
Last Sunday in June. 206/322-9561, web: www.seattlepride.org.

ANNUAL EVENTS:
September - Bumbershoot music & arts festival 206/673-5060, web: www.bumbershoot.org.

September - AIDS Walk 206/329-6923.

October - Seattle Gay & Lesbian Film Festival 206/323-4274, web: www.threedollarbillcinema.org.

CITY INFO:
206/461-5800, web: www.seattle.com.

WEATHER:
Winter's average temperature is 50° while summer temperatures can climb up into the 90°s. Be prepared for rain at any time during the year.

TRANSIT:
Farwest 206/622-1717, web: www.farwesttaxi.net.

Yellow 206/622-6500, web: www.yellowtaxi.net.

Airport Shuttle Express 206/622-1424.

Metropolitan Transit 206/553-3000, web: metro.kingcounty.gov.

ATTRACTIONS:
Experience Music Project 206/367-5483, web: www.empsfm.org.

Fremont, web: www.fremontseattle.com.

International District.

Museum of Flight 206/764-5720, web: www.museumofflight.org.

Pike Place Market, web: www.pikeplacemarket.org.

Pioneer Square, web: www.pioneersquare.org.

Seattle Art Museum 206/654-3100, web: www.seattleartmuseum.org.

Seattle Aquarium 206/386-4300, web: www.seattleaquarium.org.

Seattle Center Monorail 206/905-2620, web: www.seattlemonorail.com

Seattle Underground 206/682-4646, web: www.undergroundtour.com.

Space Needle 206/905-2100, web: www.spaceneedle.com.

Woodland Park Zoo 206/684-4800, web: www.zoo.org.

BEST VIEW:
Top of the Space Needle, or from Admiral Way Park in West Seattle.

Paseo 4225 Fremont Ave N (at N 43rd St) 206/545-7440 • 11am-9pm, clsd Sun-Mon • Cuban

Queen City Grill 2201 1st Ave (at Blanchard) 206/443-0975 • dinner only • popular • fresh seafood • some veggie • full bar • wheelchair access

Restaurant Zoe 2137 2nd Ave (at Blanchard) 206/256-2060 • dinner only

Saint John's Bar & Eatery 719 E Pike St (at Harvard Ave) 206/245-1390 • 2pm-2am, from 10am wknds

Snappy Dragon 8917 Roosevelt Wy NE 206/528-5575 • 11am-9:30pm, 4pm-9pm Sun • Chinese

Spinasse 1531 14th Ave E 206/251-7673 • clsd Tue, traditional cuisine of the Piedmont region of Northern Italy

Sunlight Cafe 6403 Roosevelt Wy NE (at 64th) 206/522-9060 • 8am-9pm • vegetarian • beer/ wine • wheelchair access

Szmania's 3321 W McGraw St (in Magnolia Bluff) 206/284-7305 • dinner nightly • full bar

Tamarind Tree 1036 S Jackson St 206/860-1404 • 10am-10pm, till midnight Fri-Sat • Vietnamese

Teapot Vegetarian House 345 15th Ave E 206/325-1010 • 11am-10pm • vegan

Thaiger Room 206/632-9299 • 11am-10pm, from noon wknds • Thai

Wild Ginger Asian Restaurant & Triple Bar 1401 3rd Ave (at Union) 206/623-4450 • lunch Mon-Sat, dinner nightly • popular • bar till 1am

Wild Mountain 1408 NW 85th St 206/297-9453 • 8:30am-9pm, clsd Tue • woman-owned

ENTERTAINMENT & RECREATION

Alki Beach Park 1702 Alki Ave SW, West Seattle • popular on warm days

Garage 1130 Broadway 206/322-2296 • 3pm-2am • popular • way-cool pool hall • food served • full bar • ladies 1/2 price Sun • also bowling alley • 21+

Northwest Lesbian & Gay History Museum Project 206/903-9517 • exhibits & publication

Rat City Roller Girls 206/599-9613 • Seattle's female roller derby league • visit www.ratcityrollergirls.com for events

Richard Hugo House 1634 11th Ave 206/322-7030 • noon-6pm, till 5pm Sat, clsd Sun • houses the Zine Archive & Publishing Project • open later for events • also cafe & cabaret

The Vera Project corner of Warren Ave N & Republican St (in Seattle Center) 206/956-8372 • queer-friendly • all-ages music arts center

BOOKSTORES

Elliott Bay Book Company 1521 10th Ave 206/624-6600, 800/962-5311 • 10am-10pm, till 11pm Fri-Sat, till 9pm Sun

Left Bank Books 92 Pike St (at 1st Ave) 206/622-0195 • 10am-7pm, 11am-6pm Sun • worker-owned collective

RETAIL SHOPS

Broadway Market 401 Broadway E (at Harrison & Republican) • popular mall full of funky, hip stores

Lifelong Thrift 1002 E Seneca 206/328-8979 • all sales from donated items fund Lifelong AIDS

Metropolis 7321 Greenwood Ave N 206/782-7002 • 10am-6pm, 11am-4pm Sun, clsd Mon cards & gifts

Two Big Blondes 2501 S Jackson St (at 25th Ave) 206/762-8620 • 11am-6pm, clsd Sun-Mon • gay/ straight • transgender-friendly • consignment women's clothing for plus sizes • lesbian-owned

PUBLICATIONS

The Seattle Lesbian 206/714-2277 • LGBT online magazine

SGN (Seattle Gay News) 206/324-4297 • weekly LGBT newspaper

The Stranger 206/323-7101 • queer-positive alternative weekly

GYMS & HEALTH CLUBS

Hothouse Spa & Sauna 1019 E Pike St (at 11th, 2 blocks E of Broadway) 206/568-3240 • noon-midnight, clsd Tue • women only • baths • hot tub • massage

EROTICA

Babeland 707 E Pike (btwn Harvard & Boylston) 206/328-2914 • 11am-10pm, noon-7pm Sun • wheelchair access • lesbian-owned

Castle Megastore 206 Broadway Ave E 206/204-0126

The Crypt Off Broadway 1516 11th Ave (at E Pine) 206/325-3882

Sequim

ACCOMMODATIONS

Sunset Marine Resort 40 Buzzard Ridge Rd 360/591-4303 • gay-friendly • waterfront cabins • nonsmoking • kids ok • lesbian-owned

Spokane

INFO LINES & SERVICES

AA Gay/ Lesbian 1614 W Riverside 509/624-1442 • call for meeting times

Inland Northwest LGBT Center 9414A E 1st Ave, Spokane Valley 509/489-1914 • support groups • events • also art gallery

ACCOMMODATIONS

The Davenport 10 S Post St 509/455-8888, 800/899-1482 • gay-friendly • pool • WiFi

RESTAURANTS

Mizuna 214 N Howard 509/747-2004 • lunch Mon-Fri, dinner nightly • seasonal menu • plenty veggie • full bar

BOOKSTORES

Auntie's Bookstore 402 W Main Ave (at Washington) 509/838-0206 • 9am-9pm, 11am-6pm Sun-Mon • wheelchair access

Suquamish

INFO LINES & SERVICES

Kitsap Lesbian/ Gay AA 18732 Division Ave NE (at Congregational Church of Christ) 360/475-0775, 800/562-7455 • 7pm Sun

Tacoma

INFO LINES & SERVICES

AA Gay/ Lesbian 759 S 45th St (at MCC) 253/474-8897 • 7:30pm Fri

Rainbow Center 741 St Helens Ave 253/383-2318 • 1pm-5pm Mon-Fri, till 4pm Sat • community & resource center

Tacoma Lesbian Concern 253/777-3357 • social events • resource list • newsletter

ACCOMMODATIONS

Chinaberry Hill 302 Tacoma Ave N 253/272-1282 • gay-friendly • 1889 Victorian inn • also cottage • full brkfst • fireplaces • kids ok • nonsmoking • WiFi

Hotel Murano 1320 Broadway Plaza (at S 15th) 253/238-8000, 866/986-8083 • gay-friendly • restaurants & bars • WiFi • wheelchair access

BARS

Airport Bar & Grill 5406 S Tacoma Wy (at 54th) 253/475-9730 • 2pm-2am • lesbians/ gay men • neighborhood bar

NIGHTCLUBS

Club Silverstone 739 1/2 St Helens Ave (at 9th) 253/404-0273 • 11am-2am • lesbians/ gay men • neighboorhood bar • dancing/DJ • karaoke

CAFES

Shakabrah Java Cafe 253/572-2787 • 7am-4pm, clsd Sun • wheelchair access

EROTICA

Castle Megastore 6015 Tacoma Mall Blvd 253/471-0391

Vancouver

see also Portland, Oregon

BARS

Tiger Lily 1109 Washington St (at W 12th St) 360/828-1245 • 10am-2am • lesbians/ gay men • also restaurant • karaoke • entertainment

Wenatchee

CAFES

The Cellar Cafe 249 N Mission St (at 5th) 509/662-1722 • 9am-3pm Mon-Fri • some veggie • beer/ wine • patio • lesbian-owned

Whidbey Island

ACCOMMODATIONS

Whidwood Inn 360/720-6228 • gay/ straight • near historic Coupeville • nonsmoking • hot tub • gay-owned

Winthrop

ACCOMMODATIONS

Chewuch Inn 223 White Ave 509/996-3107, 800/747-3107 • gay-friendly • inn & cabins • E of N Cascades Mtns • hot tub • kids ok • nonsmoking • WiFi • wheelchair access

WEST VIRGINIA

Statewide

PUBLICATIONS

Out 724/733-0828 • Pittsburgh's only LGBTQ newspaper since 1973! news, local events, classifieds & more for Western & Central PA, OH & WV

Charleston

BARS

Broadway 210 Leon Sullivan Wy (at Lee) 304/343-2162 • 12:30pm-3am • mostly gay men • dancing/DJ • live shows

ENTERTAINMENT & RECREATION

Living AIDS Memorial Garden corner of Washington St E (at Sidney Ave) 304/346-0246

BOOKSTORES

Taylor Books 226 Capitol St 304/342-1461 • 7:30am-8pm, till 10pm Fri, 9am-10pm Sat, till 3pm Sun • WiFi • also cafe, art gallery & boutique

Follansbee

BARS

Wild Coyote Saloon 869 Main St 304/527-7191 • 6pm-close • lesbians/ gay men • dancing/ DJ Fri-Sat • drag shows

Harpers Ferry

ACCOMMODATIONS

Laurel Lodge 844 Ridge St 304/535-2886 • gay-friendly • bungalow overlooking Potomac River gorge • full brkfst • nonsmoking • WiFi • gay-owned

Huntington

ACCOMMODATIONS

Pullman Plaza Hotel 1001 3rd Ave (at 10th St) 304/525-1001, 866/613-3611 • gay-friendly • full brkfst • pool • nonsmoking • WiFi • wheelchair access

BARS

Club Deception 1037 7th Ave (at 11th St) 304/522-3146 • 5pm-2am • mostly gay men • dancing/DJ • live shows • karaoke • private club • wheelchair access

The Stonewall 820 7th Ave (enter in alley) 304/523-2242 • 8pm-3am, clsd Mon-Tue • popular • lesbians/ gay men • dancing/DJ • karaoke • live shows • wheelchair access • gay-owned

RESTAURANTS

Sharkey's 410 10th St 304/523-3200 • 4pm-2:30am, clsd Sun • full bar • karaoke

Lost River

ACCOMMODATIONS

Guest House at Lost River 288 Settlers Valley Wy (at Mill Gap Rd) 304/897-5707 • lesbians/ gay men • full brkfst • also fine-dining restaurant • full bar • pool • hot tub • gym • nonsmoking • WiFi • gay-owned

RESTAURANTS

Lost River Grill & Motel St Rd 259 304/897-6482 • 11:45am-9pm, 8am-10pm Sat, 4pm-9pm Mon • full bar • also motel & cabins

Lost River Trading Post 295 E. Main St, Wardensville 304/874-3300 • 12pm-7pm Fri, 10am-6pm Sat-Sun • antiques and cafe

Martinsburg

BARS

The Club 5268 Williamsport Pike (Rte 11) 304/274-6080 • 6pm-1am, till 3am Fri-Sat, clsd Sun-Tue • mostly gay men • dancing/DJ • bar snacks • karaoke

Martinsburg

EROTICA

Variety Books & Video 255 N Queen St (at Race) 304/263-4334 • 24hrs

Morgantown

NIGHTCLUBS

Vice Versa 335 High St (enter rear) 304/292-2010 • 8pm-3am Th-Sun • lesbians/ gay men • dancing/DJ • karaoke • live shows • private club • 18+ • wheelchair access

Parkersburg

NIGHTCLUBS

The Otherside of the Nip n Cue 1300 19th St 304/485-7752 • 9pm Fri-Sat only • lesbians/ gay men • dancing/DJ • karaoke • drag shows

Wheeling

EROTICA

Market St News 1437 Market St (at 14th St) **304/232–2414** • 24hrs, till midnight Sun-Mon

WISCONSIN

Algoma

RETAIL SHOPS

The Flying Pig N6975 Hwy 42 (at Tenth) **920/487–9902** • 9am-6pm May-Oct, call for hrs off season • art gallery & coffee bar • lesbian-owned

Appleton

BARS

Rascals Bar & Grill 702 E Wisconsin Ave (at Lawe) **920/954–9262** • 5pm-2am, from noon Sun • lesbians/ gay men, ladies night Wed • fish-fry Fri • patio

Ravens 215 E College Ave **920/364–9599** • 8pm-2am, clsd Sun-Mon • mostly gay men, Th ladies night • dancing/DJ • karaoke • drag shows

CAFES

Harmony Cafe 233 E College Ave **920/734–2233** • 7am-9pm, till 10pm Th-Sat, 8am-6pm Sun • live entertainment • also educational & support groups

EROTICA

Eldorado's 2545 S Memorial Dr (at Hwys 47 & 441) **920/830–0042**

Beloit

BARS

Club Impulse 132 W Grand Ave **608/361–0000** • 4pm-2am, till 2:30am Fri-Sat, from 7pm Sat • lesbians/ gay men • dancing/DJ • karaoke • drag shows

Eau Claire

INFO LINES & SERVICES

LGBT Community Center of the Chippewa Valley 1305 Woodland Ave **715/552–5428** • drop-in 7pm-10pm Fri, call for other hours • library & variety of events

NIGHTCLUBS

Scooters 411 Galloway (at Farwell) **715/835–9959** • 3pm-2am • lesbians/ gay men • dancing/DJ • karaoke • drag shows • wheelchair access

Green Bay

INFO LINES & SERVICES

Gay AA **920/432–2600** • call for times & locations

BARS

Napalese Lounge 1351 Cedar St **920/432–9646** • 11am-close • mostly gay men • neighborhood bar • DJ Fri-Sat • food served • drag shows • wheelchair access

Roundabout 1264 Main St **920/544–9544** • 2pm-2am • lesbians/ gay men

NIGHTCLUBS

Club XS 1106 Main St • 7pm-2am • lesbians/ gay men • dancing/DJ

The Shelter 730 N Quincy St (at 54302) **920/432–2662** • lesbians/ gay men • dancing/DJ • country/ western • transgender-friendly • food served • karaoke • drag shows • gay-owned

CAFES

Harmony Cafe 1660 W Mason St **920/569–1593** • 7am-9pm, 10am-6pm Sun • live entertainment • support groups

PUBLICATIONS

Outbound/ Quest **920/655–0611, 800/578–3785** • news & arts reviews for WI's LGBT community

EROTICA

Lion's Den Adult Superstore 836 S Broadway (at 5th) **920/433–9640**

Hayward

ACCOMMODATIONS

The Lake House 5793 Division, Stone Lake **715/865–6803** • lesbians/ gay men • full brkfst • swimming • nonsmoking • kids ok by arrangement • WiFi • wheelchair access • lesbian-owned

Kenosha

see also Racine

BARS

Club Icon 6305 120th Ave (on E Frontage road of I-94) **262/857–3240** • 7pm-2am, from 3pm Sun, clsd Mon • lesbians/ gay men • dancing/DJ • drag shows

La Crosse

ACCOMMODATIONS

Rainbow Ridge Farms B&B N 5732 Hauser Rd (at County S), Onalaska **608/783-8181, 888/347-2594** • gay-friendly • working hobby farm on 35 acres • WiFi • nonsmoking

BARS

Chances R 417 Jay St (at 4th) **608/782-5105** • 3pm-close • lesbians/ gay men • neighborhood bar

My Place 3201 South Ave (at East Ave) **608/788-9073** • 3pm-close, from noon wknds • lesbians/ gay men • friendly neighborhood bar • games • gay-owned

Players 300 S 4th St (at Jay St) **608/784-4200** • 5pm-2am, from 3pm Fri-Sun, till 2:30am Fri-Sat • popular • lesbians/ gay men • dancing/DJ • transgender-friendly • wheelchair access • gay-owned

EROTICA

Pleasures 405 S 3rd **608/784-6350** • DVDs • toys • magazines • lingerie

Madison

INFO LINES & SERVICES

OutReach, Inc 600 Williamson St #P-1 **608/255-8582** • 10am-7pm, noon-4pm Sat, clsd Sun

BARS

Five Nightclub 5 Applegate Ct (btwn Fish Hatchery Rd & W Beltline Hwy) **608/277-9700, 877/648-9700** • 4pm-2am, from 2pm Sun • popular • lesbians/ gay men • dancing/DJ • karaoke • live shows

Green Bush 914 Regent St (at Park) **608/257-2874** • 4pm-midnight, clsd Sun • gay-friendly • also Sicilian restaurant

Woof's 114 King St (on Capitol Sq) **608/204-6222** • 4pm-2am, from noon Sun • lesbians/ gay men • neighborhood bar • leather/ levi • dancing/DJ • food served

NIGHTCLUBS

Cardinal 418 E Wilson St (at S Franklin) **608/257-2473** • 7pm-2am, from 4pm Fri • gay/ straight • dancing/DJ • live music

IQ/ IndieQueer • weekly & monthly queer parties in Madison • check local listings for dates & info

Plan B 924 Williamson St **608/257-5262** • 4pm-2am, from 9pm Sun, clsd Mon • lesbians/ gay men • dancing/DJ • karaoke • 1st & 3rd Fri women's night • Th 18+

Sotto 303 N Henry St **920/251-2753** • 9pm-2am, clsd Sun-Mon • lesbians/ gay men • dancing/DJ

CAFES

Java Cat 3918 Monona Dr (at Cottage Grove Rd) **608/223-5553** • 6am-8pm, 7am-8pm Sat-Sun • light food served • WiFi

RESTAURANTS

Fromagination 12 S Carroll (on Capital Sq) **608/255-2430** • 9:30am-6pm, 9am-5pm Sat, clsd Sun

La Hacienda 515 S Park St **608/255-8227** • 9am-3am • popular • Mexican • post–Club 5 spot

Monty's Blue Plate Diner 2089 Atwood Ave (at Winnebago) **608/244-8505** • 7am-9pm, till 10pm wknds • some veggie • beer/ wine • wheelchair access

BOOKSTORES

A Room of One's Own Feminist Books & Gifts 315 W Gorham St **608/257-7888** • 10am-8pm, till 8pm Sat, noon-5pm Sun • wheelchair access

PUBLICATIONS

Our Lives • LGBT publication • www.ourlivesmadison.com

EROTICA

A Woman's Touch 600 Williamson (at Gateway Mall) **608/250-1928, 888/621-8880** • 11am-6pm, till 8pm Tue-Th, till 7pm Fri-Sat, noon-5pm Sun • wheelchair access

Red Letter News 2528 E Washington (btwn North & Milwaukee) **608/241-9958**

Milwaukee

INFO LINES & SERVICES

AA Galano Club 315 W Court #201 (in LGBT Community Center) **414/276-6936**

Milwaukee LGBT Community Center 1110 N Market St, 2nd Fl **414/271-2656** • 10am-10pm, from 6pm Sat, till 5pm Mon, clsd Sun

ACCOMMODATIONS

Ambassador Hotel 2308 W Wisconsin Ave (at N 24th) **414/345-5000, 888/322-3326** • gay/ straight • nonsmoking • WiFi • wheelchair access

The Brumder Mansion 3046 W Wisconsin Ave (at N 31st) **414/342-9767, 866/793-3676** • gay-friendly • full brkfst • nonsmoking • WiFi

Hotel of the Arts/ Days Inn 1840 N 6th St (at Reservoir Ave) 414/265-5629 • gay-friendly • nonsmoking • WiFi

The Iron Horse Hotel 500 W Florida St (at S 5th St) 888/543-4766 • gay-friendly hotel geared toward motorcycle enthusiasts

The Milwaukee Hilton 509 W Wisconsin Ave (at 5th St) 414/271-7250, 800/445-8667 • gay-friendly • also restaurant & pub • pool • WiFi • wheelchair access

BARS

Art Bar 722 E. Burleigh St (at Fratney) 414/372-7880 • 3pm-2am, from 10am wknds • live entertainment • WiFi • gay-owned

Boom/ The Room 625 S 2nd (at W Bruce) 414/277-5040 • 5pm-2am, from 2pm wknds • lesbians/ gay men • neighborhood bar • food served • videos • patio • also martini bar

D.I.X. 739 S 1st St (at National) 414/231-9085 • 4pm-2am, from noon Sun • mostly gay men • videos

Fluid 819 S 2nd St (at W National) 414/643-5843 • 5pm-close, from 3pm Fri, from 2pm wknds • mostly gay men • neighborhood bar

Hamburger Mary's Milwaukee 2130 Kinnickinnic 414/988-9324 • 11am-10pm, 10am-midnight wknds • food served • drag shows • karaoke

Hybrid Lounge 707 E Brady (at Van Buren) 414/810-1809 • 4pm-close, from 10am Sat-Sun • mostly gay men

The Nomad 1401 E Brady St (at Warren) 414/224-8111 • 2pm-2am, from noon wknds • gay-friendly • soccer pub

Nut Hut 1500 W Scott (at 15th St) 414/647-2673 • 2pm-2am, from noon Fri-Sun • mostly women • neighborhood bar

Taylor's 795 N Jefferson St (at Wells) 414/271-2855 • 4pm-close • gay/ straight • neighborhood bar • patio • wheelchair access • gay-owned

Two 718 E Burleigh St (at Fratney) / • 7pm-close Wed-Sat • gay/ straight

Milwaukee

LGBT PRIDE:
June. 414/272-3378, web: www.pridefest.com.

ANNUAL EVENTS:
June-July - Summerfest, web: www.summerfest.com.
August - Wisconsin State Fair 414/266-7000, 800/884-3247 web: wistatefair.com
October - AIDS Walk 800/348-WALK, web: www.aidswalkwis.org.
October - LGBT Film Festival, web: www4.uwm.edu/psoa/film/ lgbtfilmfestival.

TRANSIT:
Yellow Cab 414/271-1800, web: www.yellowcabmilwaukee.com.
Milwaukee Transit 414/344-6711, web: www.ridemcts.com.

CITY INFO:
414/273-7222 or 800/554-1448, web: www.visitmilwaukee.org.

ATTRACTIONS:
Annunciation Greek Orthodox Church 414/461-9400, web: www.annunciationwi.com.
Breweries.
Grand Avenue.
Harley-Davidson Museum, web: www.hdmuseum.com.
Milwaukee Art Museum, web: www.mam.org.
Mitchell Park Horticultural Conservatory, 414/649-9830.
Pabst Theatre 414/286-3663, web: www.pabsttheater.org.

WEATHER:
Summer temperatures can get up into 90°s. Spring and fall are pleasantly moderate but too short. Winter brings snow, cold temperatures, and even colder wind chills.

Walker's Pint 818 S 2nd St (at National Ave) **414/643–7468** • 4:30pm-2am, from noon Sun • mostly women • neighborhood bar • dancing/DJ • live shows • karaoke • patio • WiFi • lesbian-owned

Woody's 1579 S 2nd St (at Lapham St) **414/672–0806** • 4pm-close, from 2pm wknds • mostly men • neighborhood sports bar • WiFi

NIGHTCLUBS

La Cage/ ETC/Montage Lounge 801 S 2nd St (at National) **414/278–9192** • 6pm-close, from 10pm Fri-Sat • mostly gay men • dancing/DJ • live shows • videos • wheelchair access

CAFES

Alterra Coffee Roasters 2211 N Prospect Ave (at North) **414/273–3753** • 7am-6pm

Bella Caffe 189 N Milwaukee St **414/273–5620** • 6am-9pm, till 11pm Fri-Sat, 8am-6pm Sun

Fuel Cafe 818 E Center St **414/374–3835** • 7am-10pm, from 8am wknds• WiFi • wheelchair access

RESTAURANTS

Beans & Barley 1901 E North Ave (at Oakland Ave) **414/278–7878** • 8am-9pm • vegetarian cafe & deli

Coquette Cafe 316 N Milwaukee St (btwn Buffalo & St Paul) **414/291–2655** • 11am-10pm, till 11pm Fri, 5pm-11pm Sat, 11am-5pm Sun • bistro fare

Crisp Pizza Bar & Lounge 1323 E Brady St **414/727–4217** • 4pm-2am, from 11:30am wknds • also full bar

Harvey's 1340 W Towne Sq Rd, Mequon **262/241–9589** • dinner nightly • cont'l

Honeypie Cafe 2643 S Kinnickinnic Ave (at Potter) **414/489–7437** • 10am-10pm, from 9am wknds, till 9pm Sun • homemade midwestern classics

The Knick 1030 E Juneau Ave (at Waverly) **414/272–0011** • 11am-midnight, from 9am wknds • popular • some veggie • full bar • wheelchair access

La Perla 734 S 5th St (at National) **414/645–9888** • 11am-10pm, till 11:30pm Fri-Sat • Mexican • also bar

Lulu 2261 & 2265 S Howell Ave **414/294–5858** • 11am-2am • also bar till late • live music wknds

Meritage 5921 W Vliet St **414/479–0620** • 5pm-10pm, till 11pm Fri-Sat, till 9pm Mon, clsd Sun • American

Range Line Inn 2635 W Mequon Rd, Mequon **262/242–0530** • 4:30pm-10pm, clsd Sun-Mon • reservations recommended

Sanford Restaurant 1547 N Jackson St **414/276–9608** • dinner only, clsd Sun • Milwaukee fine dining Euro-style

ENTERTAINMENT & RECREATION

Boerner Botanical Gardens 9400 Boerner Dr (in Whitnall Park), Hales Corners **414/525–5600, 414/525–5601** • 8am-dusk • 40-acre garden & arboretum, garden clsd in winter

Harley-Davidson Museum 400 Canal St (at N 6th St) **877/287–2789**

Mitchell Park Domes 524 S Layton Blvd (27th St, at Pierce) **414/257–5611** • 9am-5pm, till 4pm wknd • botanical gardens

Off the Wall Theatre 127 E Wells St **414/327–3552** • alternative theatre group

BOOKSTORES

OutWords Books, Gifts & Coffee 2710 N Murray Ave (at Park Pl) **414/963–9089** • 11am-7pm, till 8pm Fri-Sat, noon-6pm Sun • pride items • wheelchair access

Peoples' Books 804 E Center **414/962–0575** • 10am-6pm, clsd Sun

Woodland Pattern 720 E Locust St **414/263–5001** • 11am-8pm, noon-5pm wknds, clsd Mon

PUBLICATIONS

Quest/Outbound 920/655–0611, 800/578–3785 • news & arts reviews for WI's LGBT community

EROTICA

Booked Solid 7035 W Greenfield Ave (at 70th), West Allis **414/774–7210**

Norwalk

ACCOMMODATIONS

Daughters of the Earth 18134 Index Ave **608/269–5301** • women only • women's land • camping • retreat space • lesbian-owned

Oshkosh

BARS

Deb's Spare Time 1303 Harrison St (btwn Main & New York) **920/235–6577** • 11am-2am, from 9am wknds • lesbians/ gay men• neighborhood bar • food served • live shows • 18+ • gay-owned

PJ's 1601 Oregon St **920/385–0442** • 5pm-close Tue-Sat, clsd Sun-Mon • lesbians/gay men • neighborhood bar • dancing/DJ wknds

EROTICA

Pure Pleasure 1212 Oshkosh Ave (off Hwy 21) **920/235–9727**

Racine

NIGHTCLUBS

JoDee's International 2139 Racine St/ S Hwy 32 (at 22nd) **262/880-0058** • 9pm Fri-Sun only • lesbians/gay men • dancing/DJ • live shows • karaoke • drag shows • park in rear

Sheboygan

BARS

The Blue Lite 1029 N 8th St (off Rte 143) **920/457–1636** • 7pm-close, from 3pm Sun • lesbians/gay men • neighborhood bar • dancing/DJ Fri-Sat

Filibusters 434 Pennsylvania Ave **920/287–3300** • 4pm-2am, from 1pm wknds • clsd Mon • lesbians/gay men • dancng/DJ

Sturgeon Bay

ACCOMMODATIONS

The Chadwick Inn 25 N 8th Ave **920/743–2771** • gay-friendly • 1890 Queen Anne • nonsmoking • lesbian-owned

The Chanticleer Guest House 4072 Cherry Rd **920/746–0334, 866/682–0384** • popular • gay-friendly • on 70 acres • pool • WiFi • nonsmoking • wheelchair access • gay-owned

Superior

BARS

The Flame 1612 Tower Ave **715/395–0101** • 3pm-2:30am • lesbians/gay men • dancing/DJ • live entertainment • karaoke • drag shows • WiFi

The Main Club 1217 Tower Ave (at 12th) **715/392–1756** • 3pm-2am • mostly gay men • dancing/DJ • live shows • WiFi • wheelchair access

Wausau

NIGHTCLUBS

Oz 320 Washington **715/842–3225** • 7pm-close • mostly gay men • dancing/DJ • karaoke • drag shows • videos

Wisconsin Dells

BARS

Captain Dix 4124 River Rd (at Rainbow Valley Resort) **608/253–1818** • 6pm-close, from 11am wknds • lesbians/gay men • karaoke • also accommodations

WYOMING

Cheyenne

see also Fort Collins, Colorado

INFO LINES & SERVICES

Wyoming Equality/ United Gays & Lesbians of Wyoming **307/778–7645** • 10am-2pm Mon-Fri • info • referrals • newsletter • social activities • also youth services

BARS

Choice City Shots 124 LaPorte Ave (at College), Fort Collins, CO **970/221–4333** • open 6:30pm • lesbians/gay men • neighborhood bar • dancing/DJ • karaoke • live shows • wheelchair access • lesbian/gay-owned

Etna

RETAIL SHOPS

Blue Fox Studio & Gallery 107452 N US Hwy 89 **307/883–3310** • open 7 days • hours vary • pottery, jewelry & mask studio • local travel info • gay-owned

Evanston

EROTICA

Romantix Adult Superstore 1939 Harrison Dr **307/789–0800** • 7am-2am

Laramie

ACCOMMODATIONS

Cowgirl Horse Hotel 32 Black Elk Trail **307/745–8794 OR 399–2502** • specializing in women travelers & their horses • men welcome

BOOKSTORES

The Second Story 105 Ivinson Ave **307/745–4423** • 10am-6pm, clsd Sun • independent

ALBERTA

Calgary

INFO LINES & SERVICES

Calgary Outlink: Centre for Gender & Sexual Diversity 223 12th Ave SW (at the Old Y Centre) **403/234-8973** • 11am-2pm Tues, 4pm-7pm Wed, 3pm-6pm Th, Community Cafe is the 2nd Fri of the month at 7pm

Front Runners AA 1227 Kensington Close NW (at Hillhurst United Church) **403/777-1212** • 8:30pm Wed & Sat

ACCOMMODATIONS

11th Street Lodging 403/209-1800 • gay/ straight • kids 10+ ok • "no shoe" policy inside • nonsmoking • gay-owned

Calgary Westways Guest House 216 25th Ave SW **403/229-1758, 866/846-7038** • gay/ straight • full brkfst • hot tub • nonsmoking • pets ok • WiFi • gay-owned

BARS

The Back Lot 209 10th Ave SW (at 1st St SW) **403/265-5211** • 2pm-2am • mostly gay men • martini lounge • patio • wheelchair access

Ming 520 17th Ave SW **403/229-1986** • 4pm-2am • gay-friendly • martini lounge • food served

NIGHTCLUBS

GirlsGroove • women's dance parties • check local listings for upcoming events • www.girlsgroove.ca

Lolita's 1413 9th Ave SE **403/265-5739** • cabaret/ performance club • also restaurant

Twisted Element 1006 11th Ave SW **403/802-0230** • 9pm-close, clsd Mon • mostly men • dancing/DJ • karaoke • drag shows • strippers • WiFi

CAFES

Caffe Beano 1613 9th St SW (at 17th Ave) **403/229-1232** • 6am-midnight, from 7am wknds • some veggie • wheelchair access

RESTAURANTS

Halo 13226 Macleod Trail SE **403/271-4111** • lunch & dinner • steak, seafood & wine bar

Melrose Cafe & Bar 730 17th Ave SW (at 7th St) **403/228-3566** • 11am-2am, from 10am wknds • full bar till 2am • patio

Thai Sa-On 351 10th Ave SW (at 4th) **403/264-3526** • lunch & dinner, clsd Sun

BOOKSTORES

Daily Globe News Shop 1004 17th Ave SW (at 10th St) **403/244-2060** • 9am-10pm • periodicals

PUBLICATIONS

Gay Calgary & Edmonton Magazine 888/543-6960 • monthly LGBT publication

Edmonton

INFO LINES & SERVICES

AA Gay/ Lesbian 11355 Jasper Ave (at church) **780/424-5900** • 7:30pm Mon • also 8pm Fri at 10804 119th St

Pride Centre of Edmonton 10608 105 Ave **780/488-3234** • noon-9pm, 2pm-6:30pm Sat, clsd Sun-Mon

Womonspace 9540 111 Ave (Pride Centre of Edmonton) **780/482-1794** • social & recreational society • dances & other events • monthly newsletter

ACCOMMODATIONS

Labyrinth Lake Lodge 780/878-3301 • gay/ straight • lodge on private lake • hot tubs • kids/ pets ok • nonsmoking • WiFi

Northern Lights B&B 780/483-1572 • lesbians/ gay men • full brkfst • pool • nonsmoking • gay-owned

BARS

The Junction 10242 106th St **780/756-5667** • 4pm-close • lesbians/ gay men • dancing/DJ • live music • drag shows • private club

Woody's Pub & Cafe 11723 A Jasper (above Buddy's) **780/488-6557** • 3pm-midnight, till 3am wknds • lesbians/ gay men • neighborhood bar • food served • karaoke

NIGHTCLUBS

Buddy's Nite Club 11725-B Jasper **780/488-6636** • 8pm-3am • lesbians/ gay men • dancing/DJ • drag shows

Flash 10018 105th St **780/969-9965** • 9pm-3am Fri-Sat only • lesbians/ gay men • dancing/DJ

RESTAURANTS

Cafe de Ville 10137 124th St **780/488-9188** • 11:30am-10pm, till midnight Fri-Sat, 10am-2pm & 5pm-10pm Sun • reservations recommended

RETAIL SHOPS

Divine Decadence 10441 82nd Ave (at 105th) **780/439-2977** • hip fashions • accessories

PUBLICATIONS

Gay Calgary & Edmonton Magazine
Calgary **888/543-6960** • monthly LGBT
publication

Westerose

ACCOMMODATIONS

Pine Trails Getaway RR1 **780/586-0002** •
gay campground • pets ok

BRITISH COLUMBIA

Birken

ACCOMMODATIONS

Birken Lakeside Resort 9179 Portage Rd
604/452-3255 • gay-friendly • cabins •
campsites • hot tub • swimming • pets ok •
lesbian-owned

Chilliwack

RESTAURANTS

Bravo Restaurant & Lounge 46224 Yale Rd
(at Nowell St) **604/792-7721** • 5pm-close,
clsd Sun-Tue • martinis • wheelchair access •
gay-owned

Gulf Islands

INFO LINES & SERVICES

**Gays & Lesbians of Salt Spring Island
(GLOSSI)** PO Box 644,, Salt Spring Island
V8K 2W2 **250/537-7773** • social events • info
line

ACCOMMODATIONS

Bellhouse Inn 29 Farmhouse Rd, Galiano
Island **250/539-5667, 800/970-7464** • gay/
straight • historic waterfront inn • full brkfst •
nonsmoking • WiFi

Birdsong B&B 153 Rourke Rd, Salt Spring
Island **250/537-4608** • gay/ straight • ocean &
harbor views • WiFi

Fulford Dunderry Guest House 2900
Fulford-Ganges Rd, Salt Spring Island
250/653-4860 • gay-friendly • oceanfront
guesthouse • nonsmoking • WiFi • gay-owned

Hummingbird Lodge B&B 1597 Starbuck
Ln (at Whalebone Dr), Gabriola
250/247-9300, 877/551-9383 • gay-friendly •
nonsmoking

Island Farmhouse B&B 185 Horel Rd W,
Salt Spring Island **250/653-9898,
877/537-5912** • gay/ straight • kids/ pets ok •
nonsmoking • lesbian-owned

Okanagan County

INFO LINES & SERVICES

Okanagan Rainbow Coalition 1476 Water
St, Kelowna **250/860-8555** • 24-hr recorded
info • support groups • social events • dances

ACCOMMODATIONS

Creek View B&B 1520 Pasadena Rd,
Kelowna **250/862-3653** • gay/ straight •
swimming • lesbian-owned • nonsmoking
• WiFi

Eagles Nest B&B 15620 Commonage Rd
(at Carrs Landing Rd), Kelowna
250/766-9350, 866/766-9350 • mostly men •
overlooking Lake Okanagan • full brkfst • hot
tub • nonsmoking • WiFi • gay-owned

Grapeseed Guesthouse & Gardens 607
Munson Mountain Rd, Penticton
250/809-9998 • lesbians/ gay men • WiFi •
lesbian-owned

CAFES

Bean Scene 274 Bernard Ave, Kelowna
250/763-1814 • 6am-9pm, till 11pm Wed-Sat
• patio • wheelchair access

RESTAURANTS

Greek House 3159 Woodsdale Rd, Kelowna
250/766-0090 • 4pm-9pm • cont'l

Prince George

INFO LINES & SERVICES

GALA North **250/562-7124** • 24-hr recorded
info • social group • call for drop-in hours &
location

EROTICA

Doctor Love 1412 Patricia Blvd
250/614-1411

Tofino

ACCOMMODATIONS

Beachwood 1368 Chesterman Beach Rd
250/725-4250 • gay-friendly • private apt •
steps to the beach • nonsmoking • gay-owned

BriMar B&B 1375 Thornberg Crescent
250/725-3410, 800/714-9373 • gay/ straight •
on the beach • full brkfst • teens ok

Eagle Nook Wilderness Resort & Spa
Ucluelet **800/760-2777** • gay-friendly • private
log cabins • gourmet meals • health spa

RESTAURANTS

Blue Heron 634 Campbell St **250/725-2043**
• 7am-10pm • full bar • wheelchair access

Vancouver

INFO LINES & SERVICES

AA Gay/ Lesbian 604/434–3933

The Greater Vancouver Pride Line
604/684–6869 x290, 800/566–1170 • 7pm-
10pm • info & support

QMUNITY: BC's Resource Centre 1170
Bute St (btwn Davie & Pendrell Sts)
604/684–5307, 800/566–1170 • also Out on
the Shelves LGBT lending library

ACCOMMODATIONS

Arbutus Guest House 1904 Arbutus St (at
W Third Ave) 604/325–3013 • gay-friendly •
lesbian-owned

Barclay House B&B 1351 Barclay St (at
Jervis) 604/605–1351, 800/971–1351 • gay/
straight • full brkfst • nonsmoking • WiFi •
gay-owned

Granville B&B 5050 Granville St (at 34th
Ave) 604/739–9002, 866/739–9002 • gay-
friendly • nonsmoking • WiFi

L' Hermitage Hotel 788 Richards St (at
Robson) 778/327–4100 • gay/ straight • pool
• nonsmoking • WiFi • wheelchair access

The Listel Hotel 1300 Robson Street (at
Jervis) 604/684–8461, 800/663–5491 • gay-
friendly • boutique hotel • restaurant & bar •
swimming • hot tub • gym • nonsmoking •
WiFi

Moda Hotel 900 Seymour St (at Smithe)
604/683–4251, 877/683–5522 • gay/ straight •
restaurant • kids ok • WiFi • also 3 bars

Nelson House B&B 977 Broughton St
(btwn Nelson & Barclay) 604/684–9793,
866/684–9793 • lesbians/ gay men • full brkfst
• jacuzzi in suite • sundeck • WiFi • lesbian- &
gay-owned

"O Canada" House B&B 1114 Barclay St
(at Thurlow) 604/688–0555, 877/688–1114 •
gay/ straight • restored 1897 Victorian home •
full brkfst • WiFi • gay-owned

Opus Hotel 322 Davie St (at Hamilton,
Yaletown) 604/642–6787, 866/642–6787 •
gay-friendly • hip luxury boutique hotel • also
bar & restaurant wheelchair access

The West End Guest House 1362 Haro St
(at Broughton) 604/681–2889, 888/546–3327
• gay/ straight • full brkfst • nonsmoking • gay-
owned

BARS

1181 1181 Davie St (at Bute) 604/687–3991 •
4pm-close • mostly gay men • upscale cocktail
lounge

Avanti's Pub 1601 Commercial Dr (at 1st
Ave) 604/254–5466 • 11am-midnight, till 1am
Fri-Sat • gay-friendly • sports bar • popular w/
local lesbian ball teams

The Fountainhead Pub 1025 Davie St (at
Burrard) 604/687–2222 • 11am-midnight, till
2am Fri-Sat • wknd brunch • lesbians/ gay
men • neighborhood bar • transgender-
friendly • patio

Guilt and Company 1 Alexander St
(downstairs) 604/288–1704 • 7pm-1am •
gay/straight • live shows 8 infused drinks and
homemade beef jerky

The Oasis 1240 Thurlow (at Davie)
604/685–1724 • 5pm-close • lesbians/ gay
men • martini bar • dancing/DJ • theme nights

NIGHTCLUBS

816 Granville/ The World 816 Granville St
• midnight-6am Fri-Sun • mostly gay men •
dancing/DJ

Club 23 West 23 W Cordova (at Carrall)
604/200–2923 • 10pm-4am Fri-Sat • gay/
straight • dancing/DJ

Crema 604/875–9907 • women's dance party
• www.cremaproductions.com

Five Sixty 560 Seymour St (at Pender)
604/678–6322 • gay/ straight • dancing/DJ •
live bands • art gallery

Flygirl Productions 604/839–9819 •
women's parties • check
www.flygirlproductions.com for details

Hershe Bar 604/839–9819 • long wknds
only • mega lesbian dance party • check local
listings for info

Junction Pub 1138 Davie St 604/669–2013 •
1pm-3am Fri-Sat , from noon wknds • mostly
gay men • dancing/DJ • patio

Shine 364 Water St (at Richards)
604/408–4321 • gay-friendly • dancing/DJ

CAFES

Coming Home 753 6th St (at 8th Ave), New
Westminster 604/544–5018 • 9am–3pm, clsd
Mon • gay-owned

Delaney's 1105 Denman St 604/662–3344 •
6am-9pm, from 6:30am wknds • coffee shop

JJ Bean 2206 Commercial Dr 604/254–3723
• 6am-10pm

Rhizome Cafe 317 E Broadway **604/872-3166** • 11am-10pm, till midnight Fri-Sat, till 3pm Sun, clsd Mon • plenty veggie/vegan • local artists • workshops

Sweet Revenge 4160 Main St (at 26th) **604/879-7933** • 7pm-midnight, till 1am Fri-Sat • patisserie • gay-owned

Turk's Coffee Exchange 1276 Commercial Dr **604/255-5805** • 6:30am-11pm • WI

RESTAURANTS

Bin 941 941 Davie St **604/683-1246** • 5pm-2am, till midnight Sun • tiny tapas parlor • popular

Brioche 401 W Cordova (at Homer, in Gastown) **604/682-4037** • 7am-8:30pm, 8am-7:30pm wknds • Italian restaurant & bakery

Cafe Deux Soleils 2096 Commercial Dr **604/254-1195** • 8am-midnight, till 5pm Sun • lesbians/gay men • vegetarian • live shows

Vancouver

LGBT PRIDE:
August. 604/687-0955, web: www.vancouverpride.ca.

ANNUAL EVENTS:
January/February - Gay & Lesbian Ski Week, web: www.gaywhistler.com.

May - Vancouver International Marathon 604/872-2928, web: www.bmovanmarathon.ca.

June - Dragon Boat Festival 604/688-2382, web: www.dragonboatbc.ca.

June-July - Vancouver Int'l Jazz Festival 604/872-5200, web: www.coastaljazz.ca.

July - Folk Music Festival 604/602-9798, web: www.thefestival.bc.ca.

August - Queer Film & Video Festival 604/844-1615, web: www.outonscreen.com.

September - BOLD Fest (Bold, Older Lesbians & Dykes), web: www.soundsandfuries.com/BOLD.html.

September/October - International Film Festival 604/685-0260, web: www.viff.org.

CITY INFO:
604/683-2000, web: www.tourismvancouver.com.

TRANSIT:
Yellow Cab 604/681-1111, web: www.yellowcabonline.com.
TransLink 604/953-3333, web: www.translink.bc.ca.
A Visitors' Map of all bus lines is available through the tourist office.hrough the tourist office.

ATTRACTIONS:
Capilano Suspension Bridge, web: www.capbridge.com.
Chinatown.
Dr Sun Yat-Sen Chinese Garden 604/662-3207, web: vancouverchinesegarden.com
Gastown.
Granville Island, web: www.granvilleisland.com.
Grouse Mountain, web: www.grousemountain.com.
Museum of Anthropology 604/822-5087, web: www.moa.ubc.ca.
Science World 604/443-7443, web: www.scienceworld.ca.
Stanley Park.
Vancouver Aquarium 604/659-3474, web: www.vanaqua.org.
Vancouver Lookout 604/689-0421, web: www.vancouverlookout.com.
Vancouver Museum 604/736-4431 web: www.museumofvancouver.ca.
Van Dusen Botanical Gardens 604/878-9274, web: www.vandusengarden.org.

BEST VIEW:
Biking in Stanley Park, or on a ferry between peninsulas and islands. Atop one of the surrounding mountains.

WEATHER:
It's cold and wet in the winter (32-45°F), but it's absolutely gorgeous in the summer (52-75°F)!

Cascade Room 2616 Main St (at 10th) 604/709-8650 • 5pm-1am, from noon-2am wknds

Chill Winston 3 Alexander St 604/288-9575 • 11am-1am • in Gastown

The Dish 1068 Davie St 604/689-0208 • 7am-10pm, 9am-9pm Sun • veggie fast food • gay-owned

Elbow Room Cafe 560 Davie St (at Seymour) 604/685-3628 • 8am-4pm • great brkfst

Foundation Lounge 2301 Main St 604/708-0881 • noon-1am, till 2am wknds • vegetarian

Glowbal Grill & Satay Bar 1079 Mainland St (Yaletown) 604/602-0835 • lunch, dinner, brunch wknds • also Afterglow Lounge

Hamburger Mary's 1202 Davie St (at Bute) 604/687-1293 • 8am-3am, till 4am Fri-Sat, till 2am Sun • some veggie • full bar

Havana 1212 Commercial Dr 604/253-9119 • 11am-11pm, from 10am wknds • popular • Cuban fusion • full bar • patio • also gallery & theater

Lickerish 903 Davie St (at Hornby) 604/696-0725 • 5:30pm-midnight, till 1am Th-Sun • global cuisine • cocktail lounge

Lift Bar & Grill 333 Menchions Mews 604/689-5438 • 11:30am-midnight

Lolita's 1326 Davie St (at Jervis) 604/696-9996 • 4:30pm till late, wknd brunch • innovative Mexican • tiny space but worth the wait

Maenam 1938 W 4th Ave 604/730-5579 • lunch Tue-Sat, dinner 5pm-midnight • Thai

Martini's Whole Wheat Pizza 151 W Broadway (btwn Cambie & Main) 604/873-0021 • 11am-2am, from 2pm Sat, till 1am Sun • great pizza • full bar

Miura Waffle Milk Bar 829 Davie St 604/687-2909 • 9am-7pm, from 10am Sat, clsd Sun

Naam 2724 W 4th St (at MacDonald) 604/738-7151 • 24hrs • vegetarian • live music • wheelchair access

Score 1262 Davie St (at Jervis St) 604/632-1646 • 11am-late • lesbians/gay men • sports bar

Seasons in the Park Cambie St & W 33rd Ave 604/874-8008 • from 11:30am, 10:30am Sun

Tanpopo Sushi 1122 Denman (at Pendrell) 604/681-7777 • lunch & dinner • excellent, affordable sushi

ENTERTAINMENT & RECREATION

Capilano Suspension Bridge 3735 Capilano Rd, N Vancouver 604/985-7474

Cruisey T leaves from N foot of Denman St (at Harbor Cruises) 604/551-2628 • Sun (seasonal) • 4-hour party cruise around Vancouver Harbour • lesbians/ gay men • dancing/DJ • live shows • food served

Girl Gig Productions 604/516-9696 • women's performance promoters • popular "Chicks With Picks" series • check girlgigs.com for info

Rockwood Adventures 6578 Acorn Rd, Sechelt 604/741-0802, 888/236-6606 • rain forest walks & city tours for all levels w/ free hotel pickup

Sunset Beach Beach Ave, right in the West End (near Burrard St Bridge) • home of Vancouver AIDS memorial

Vancouver Nature Adventures 1251 Cardero St #2005 604/684-4922, 800/528-3531 • orca-watching safari • guided kayaking day trip & beach BBQ • no experience required • free hotel pickup

Wreck Beach below UBC

BOOKSTORES

Little Sister's 1238 Davie St (btwn Bute & Jervis) 604/669-1753, 800/567-1662 (IN CANADA ONLY) • 10am-11pm • popular • LGBT • wheelchair access

People's Co-op Bookstore 1391 Commercial Dr (btwn Kitchener & Charles) 604/253-6442, 888/511-5556 • LGBT section

RETAIL SHOPS

Cupcakes 1116 Denman St (at Pendrell) 604/974-1300 • 10am-9pm, till 10pm Fri-Sat • women-owned cupcake shop • also at 2887 W Broadway

Mintage 1714 Commercial Dr 604/646-8243 • vintage & future fashions • woman-owned

Next Body Piercing 1068 Granville St (at Nelson) 604/684-6398 • noon-6pm, 11am-7pm Fri-Sat • also tattooing

PUBLICATIONS

Xtra! West 604/684-9696 • LGBT newspaper

GYMS & HEALTH CLUBS

Fitness World 1214 Howe St (at Davie) 604/681-3232 • day passes

Spartacus Gym 1522 Commercial Dr 604/254-6267

EROTICA

Love's Touch 1069 Davie St 604/681-7024

Victoria

ACCOMMODATIONS

Albion Manor B&B 224 Superior St 250/389-0012, 877/389-0012 • gay/ straight • full brkfst • nonsmoking • WiFi • wheelchair access • gay-owned

Ambrosia Historic B&B 522 Quadra (at Humboldt) 250/380-7705, 877/262-7672 • gay/ straight • 5-star B&B 3 blocks from Victoria's inner harbor • full brkfst • nonsmoking

Dashwood Manor Seaside B&B 1 Cook St 250/385-5517, 800/667-5517 • gay/straight • heritage designated 1912 British Arts and Crafts Tudor Revival home with great views of the ocean • WiFi • gay-owned

Inn at Laurel Point 680 Montreal St (at Quebec St) 250/386-8721, 800/663-7667 • gay-friendly • restaurant • pool • WiFi • nonsmoking • kids/ pets OK • wheelchair access

Oak Bay Guest House 1052 Newport Ave 250/598-3812 • gay-friendly • 1912 Tudor-style house • full brkfst • near beaches • kids 10+ ok • nonsmoking

BARS

Paparazzi 642 Johnson St (enter on Broad St) 250/388-0505 • 1pm-2am, till midnight Sun • lesbians/ gay men • dancing/DJ • karaoke • drag shows • videos • wheelchair access

NIGHTCLUBS

Hush 1325 Government St (in basement) 250/385-0566 • 9pm-2am, clsd Sun-Tue • gay/ straight • dancing/DJ

RESTAURANTS

Green Cuisine 560 Johnson St #5 (in Market Square) 250/385-1809 • 10am-8pm • vegan • also juice bar & bakery

Rosie's Diner 253 Cook St 250/384-6090 • 8am-9pm • '50s & '60s music & videos • wheelchair access • gay-owned

Santiago's Cafe 660 Oswego St 250/388-7376 • 11am-9pm • tapas bar • patio • gay-owned

ENTERTAINMENT & RECREATION

Butchart Gardens 800 Benvenuto Ave, Brentwood Bay 250/652-5256, 866/652-4422

BOOKSTORES

Bolen Books 1644 Hillside Ave #111 (in shopping center) 250/595-4232 • 8:30am-10pm • LGBT section

RETAIL SHOPS

Oceanside Gifts 812 Wharf St, Ste 102 (across from Empress Hotel on the lower causeway) 250/380-1777 • 10am-10pm • gifts from across Canada • wheelchair access

Whistler

ACCOMMODATIONS

Best Western Listel Whistler Hotel 4121 Village Green (at Whistler Way) 604/932-1133, 800/663-5472 • gay-friendly • pool • hot tub • nonsmoking • WiFi • wheelchair access

Coast Blackcomb Suites at Whistler 4899 Painted Cliff Rd 604/905-3400, 800/716-6199 • gay-friendly • full bar & restaurant • hot tub • pool • nonsmoking • wheelchair access

Four Seasons Resort Whistler 4591 Blackcomb Wy 604/935-3400, 800/268-6282 • gay-friendly • luxury resort & spa • pool • nonsmoking • wheelchair access

Westin Whistler 4090 Whistler Wy 604/905-5000, 800/937-8461 • gay-friendly • full-service resort • full bar & restaurant • spa • hot tub • pool • nonsmoking • WiFi • wheelchair access

RESTAURANTS

Araxi 4222 Village Square 604/932-4540 • lunch & dinner • local ingredients • also seafood bar & lounge

The Bearfoot Bistro 4121 Village Green 604/932-3433 • 6pm-midnight • excellent wine cellar • reservations recommended

La Rua 4557 Blackcomb Blvd 604/932-5011 • 6pm-close, clsd Tue

Quattro 4319 Main St 604/905-4844 • dinner nightly • Italian

Sachi Sushi 106-4359 Main St 604/935-5649 • lunch & dinner

Southside Diner 2102 Lake Placid Rd (off Hwy 99) 604/966-0668 • 7am-midnight • hosts occasional Gay Social

Trattoria di Umberto 4417 Sundial Pl 604/932-5858 • lunch & dinner • reservations recommended

ENTERTAINMENT & RECREATION

Ziptrek Ecotours PO Box 734 V0N 1B0 604/935-0001, 866/935-0001 • ziplines crisscross the Fitzsimmons Creek btwn Whistler & Blackcomb

EROTICA

The Love Nest #102-4338 Main St 604/932-6906

MANITOBA

Winnipeg

INFO LINES & SERVICES

Rainbow Resource Centre 170 Scott St (at Wardlaw) 204/474–0212, 204/284–5208 • call for hrs, clsd wknds • also info line • many social/ support groups

BARS

Club 200 190 Garry St (at St Mary Ave) 204/943–6045 • 4pm-2am, 6pm-midnight Sun • lesbians/ gay men • dancing/DJ • karaoke • drag shows • go-go dancers • wheelchair access

Fame 279 Garry St 204/414–9433 • 9pm-2am Fri-Sat only • lesbians/ gay men • dancing/DJ • drag shows • transgender-friendly

RESTAURANTS

Buccacino's Cucina Italiana 155 Osborne St 204/452–8251 • 11am-10pm, till 11pm Fri-Sat, from 10am Sun • live music • full bar • patio

Step'N Out 157 Provencher Blvd 204/956–7837 • 5pm-9pm, clsd Sun-Mon • wheelchair access

BOOKSTORES

McNally Robinson 1120 Grant Ave #4000 (in the mall) 204/475–0483, 800/561–1833 • 9am-10pm, till 11pm Fri-Sat, noon-6pm Sun • wheelchair access

PUBLICATIONS

Outwords 204/942–4599 • LGBT newspaper

EROTICA

Love Nest 172 St Anne's Rd 204/254–0422 • also 1341 Main St, 204/589–4141 • also Portage & Westwood, 204/ 837–6475

NEW BRUNSWICK

Fredericton

NIGHTCLUBS

boom! 474 Queen St 506/463–2666 • 8pm-2am, 4pm-7pm Sun, clsd Mon-Wed • lesbians/ gay men • dancing/DJ

RESTAURANTS

Molly's Cafe 554 Queen St 506/457–9305 • 9am-10pm, noon-midnight Fri-Sun • full bar • garden patio • some veggie

EROTICA

Pleasures N' Treasures 558 Queen St 506/458–2048 • 11am-10pm, till 11pm Th-Sat

Moncton

ACCOMMODATIONS

Auberge Au Bois Dormant Inn 67 rue John (at Birch) 506/855–6767 • gay-friendly • affordable luxury inn • full brkfst • nonsmoking • WiFi • gay-owned

NIGHTCLUBS

Triangles 234 St George St (at Archibald) 506/857–8779 • 8pm-2am • lesbians/ gay men • neighborhood bar • dancing/DJ • karaoke Th

RESTAURANTS

Calactus Cafe 125 Church St (at St George) 506/388–4833 • 11am-10pm • vegetarian

St John

ACCOMMODATIONS

Mahogany Manor 220 Germain St 506/636–8000, 800/796–7755 • gay/ straight • full brkfst • nonsmoking • kids ok • wheelchair access • gay-owned

NIGHTCLUBS

Happinez Wine Bar 42 Princess St 506/634–7340 • 4pm-midnight, till 2am Fri-Sat • gay-friendly

RESTAURANTS

Opera Bistro 60 Prince William St 506/642–2822 • lunch & dinner

NOVA SCOTIA

Annapolis

ACCOMMODATIONS

By the Dock of the Bay Cottages 28 Haddock Alley (at Lower Road), Margaretsville 416/588–1500, 800/407–2856 • gay-friendly • lesbian-owned

Annapolis Royal

ACCOMMODATIONS

Bailey House B&B 150 St George St (at Drury Ln) 902/532–1285, 877/532–1285 • gay/ straight • circa 1770 historic waterfront home • full brkfst • nonsmoking • WiFi

King George Inn 902/532–5286, 888/799–5464 • lesbians/ gay men • full brkfst • jacuzzi • nonsmoking • WiFi • gay-owned

Antigonish

INFO LINES & SERVICES

Antigonish Women's Resource Centre 219 Main St, Ste 204 (Kirk Place) **902/863–6221** • 9am-4:30pm Mon-Fri • info • support services & programs

Digby

ACCOMMODATIONS

Harbourview Inn 25 Harbourview Rd (at Hwy 1), Smith's Cove **902/245–5686, 877/449–0705** • gay-friendly • century-old country inn • full brkfst • pool • kids/pets ok • nonsmoking • WiFi • wheelchair access • gay-owned

Seawinds Motel 90 Montague Row **902/245–2573** • gay-friendly • kids/ pets ok • nonsmoking

Halifax

ACCOMMODATIONS

Fresh Start B&B 2720 Gottingen St (at Black) **902/453–6616, 888/453–6616** • gay-friendly • Victorian mansion • nonsmoking • WiFi • women-owned

BARS

Menz & Mollyz Bar 2182 Gottingen St, Level 2 (btw Cunard & Agricola) **902/446–6969** • 4pm-2:30am • lesbians/ gay men • neighborhood bar • dancing/DJ • drag shows • karaoke • piano bar

Reflections Cabaret 5184 Sackville St (at Barrington) **902/422–2957** • 10pm-4am, clsd Tue• lesbians/ gay men • dancing/DJ • live shows • cabaret • drag shows • wheelchair access

CAFES

Coburg Coffee House 6085 Coburg Rd **902/429–2326** • 7am-9pm • WiFi

The Daily Grind 5686 Spring Garden Rd (near South Park) **902/429–6397** • 8am-6pm, noon-5pm Sun • also newsstand

The Second Cup 5425 Spring Garden Rd **902/429–0883** • 7am-11pm, till midnight Th-Sat • WiFi

Uncommon Grounds 1030 S Park St **902/404–3124** • 7am-10pm •WiFi

RESTAURANTS

Chives Canadian Bistro 1537 Barrington St **902/420–9626** • 5pm-9:30pm

Heartwood 6250 Quinpool Rd **902/425–2808** • 11am-9pm, 10am-3pm Sun • vegetarian

Tess 5687 Charles St **902/406–3133** • lunch & dinner, wknd brunch, clsd Mon • gay-owned

ENTERTAINMENT & RECREATION

The Khyber 1588 Barrington St **902/422–9668** • visual & performing arts center

BOOKSTORES

Atlantic News 5560 Morris St (at Queen) **902/429–5468** • 8am-9pm, from 9am Sun

Trident Booksellers & Cafe 1256 Hollis St (at Morris St) **902/423–7100** • 8am-5:30pm, 10am-5pm Sun • used • popular cafe • WiFi

RETAIL SHOPS

Venus Envy 1598 Barrington St **902/422–0004, 877/370–9288** • 10am-6pm, till 7pm Th-Fri, noon-5pm Sun • "a store for women & the people who love them" • books • sex toys • alternative health products

PUBLICATIONS

Wayves PO Box 34090 Scotia Square B3J 3S1 **902/889–2229** • monthly magazine "for the rainbow community of Atlantic Canada"

EROTICA

Night Magic Fashions 5268 Sackville St **902/420–9309** • clsd Sun

X-Citement 6260 Quinpool Rd **902/492–0026**

Scotsburn

ACCOMMODATIONS

The Mermaid & the Cow West Branch **902/351–2714** • lesbians/ gay men • cabin & 20 campsites • dogs ok on leash • pool • lesbian-owned

Tangier

ACCOMMODATIONS

Spry Bay Campground & Cabins 19867 Highway #7 **902/772–2554, 866/229–8014** • gay/ straight • also restaurant & convenience store • lesbian-owned

ONTARIO

Grand Valley

ACCOMMODATIONS

Rainbow Ridge Resort Country Rd 109 (at Hwy 25 S) **519/928–3262** • lesbians/ gay men • trailers & tents • located on 72 acres on Grand River • pool • restaurant • dance hall • day visitors welcome • seasonal • pets ok • gay-owned

Hamilton

ACCOMMODATIONS

BurrBrookHaven 336 8th Concession Rd E (Centre Rd), Carlisle **905/689-7550** • women only • country home, single or groups 8-10 • lesbian-owned

Cedars Campground 1039 5th Concession W Rd, Millgrove **905/659-3655, 905/659-7342** • lesbians/ gay men • private campground,seasonal • pool • also bar • dancing/DJ • restaurant wknds • gay-owned

BARS

The Embassy Club 54 King St E (at Houston) **905/522-1100** • noon-3am, nightclub from 10pm wknds • lesbians/ gay men • dancing/DJ • transgender-friendly • karaoke • drag shows • videos

EROTICA

Stag Shop 58 Centennial Pkwy N **905/573-4242** • also 980 Upper James St, 905/385-3300

Kingston

NIGHTCLUBS

Girls' Night Out 105 Clergy St East (at Bens Pub) **613/546-7600** • 2nd Sat of the month • mostly women • dancing/DJ

Kitchener

NIGHTCLUBS

Club Renaissance 24 Charles St W **519/570-2406, 877/635-2352** • 9pm-3am, clsd Sun-Tue • lesbians/ gay men • dancing/DJ • food served • drag shows • also billiards lounge

EROTICA

Stag Shop 10 Manitou Dr **519/895-1228**

Londonr

ACCOMMODATIONS

Hilton Hotel 300 King St **800/210-9336** • gay-friendly • pool • WiFi • wheelchair access

NIGHTCLUBS

Club Lavish 238 Dundas St **519/667-1222** • 9pm-2am, clsd Sun-Wed • gay/ straight • dancing/DJ • karaoke

RESTAURANTS

Blackfriars Bistro 46 Blackfriars (2 blocks S of Oxford) **519/667-4930** • lunch & dinner, Sun brunch • popular • plenty veggie • full bar

EROTICA

Stag Shop 1548 Dundas St E **519/453-7676** • also 371 Wellington Rd S, 519/668-3334

Niagara Falls

ACCOMMODATIONS

Absolute Elegance B&B 6023 Culp St (at Main & Ferry) **905/353-8522, 877/353-8522** • gay/ straight • full brkfst • nonsmoking • gay-owned

Angels Hideaway 4360 Simcoe St (at River Rd) **905/354-1119** • gay-friendly • full brkfst • nonsmoking

Britaly B&B 57 The Promenade (at Charlotte & John), Niagara-on-the-Lake **905/468-8778** • gay-friendly • full brkfst • gay-owned

Oshawa

NIGHTCLUBS

Club 717 717 Wilson Rd S #7 **905/434-4297** • 7pm-midnight, 9pm-2am Fri-Sat, clsd Mon-Wed • lesbians/ gay men • dancing • drag shows

EROTICA

Forbidden Pleasures 1268 Simcoe St N **905/728-0834**

Ottawa

INFO LINES & SERVICES

Pink Triangle Services 251 Bank St #301 **613/563-4818** • many groups & services • library • call for times

ACCOMMODATIONS

Ambiance B&B 330 Nepean St **613/563-0421, 888/366-8772** • gay/ straight • full brkfst • some shared baths • kids ok • nonsmoking • WiFi • lesbian-owned

Brookstreet 525 Legget Dr **613/271-1800, 888/826-2220** • gay-friendly • pool • golf • also restaurant

Lord Elgin Hotel 100 Elgin St **613/235-3333, 800/267-4298** • gay-friendly • pool • also restaurant & bar

Rideau Inn 177 Frank St **613/688-2753, 877/580-5015** • gay-friendly • some shared baths • nonsmoking • gay-owned

BARS

Centretown Pub 340 Somerset St W (at Bank) **613/594-0233** • 2pm-2am • lesbians/ gay men • dancing/DJ • leather bar upstairs • Silhouette Lounge piano bar Fri-Sat

The Lookout 41 York, 2nd flr (in Byward Market) **613/789–1624** • 2pm-2am, from noon wknds • lesbians/ gay men • more women Fri • food served • wheelchair access • lesbian-owned

Swizzles 246 Queen St **613/232–4200** • 11am-2am, from 7pm wknds, noon-10pm Tue, clsd Mon • lesbians/ gay men • karaoke • WiFi

NIGHTCLUBS

Lotus Lounge 129 Bank St **613/216–9661** • 10pm-2am Fri, till 7am Sat

Mercury Lounge 56 Byward Market Sq (side door upstairs) **613/789–5324** • 8pm-3am, clsd Sun-Tue • popular Wed Hump night party • gay/ straight • dancing/DJ • WiFi

Zaphod Beeblebrox 27 York **613/562–1010** • 4pm-2am • gay/ straight • neighborhood bar • dancing/DJ • live music

CAFES

Bridgehead Coffee 366 Bank St (at Gilmour) **613/569–5600** • 7am-9pm • WiFi • gay-owned

Raw Sugar Cafe 692 Somerset W **613/216–2850** • vegan & gluten-free options • aslo occasional Femme Tea parties • live music

RESTAURANTS

Ahora Mexican Cuisine 307 Dalhousie St (below Sweet Art) **613/562–2081** • noon-10pm • gay-owned

The Buzz 374 Bank St **613/565–9595** • dinner nightly, Sun brunch • also bar

Johnny Farina 216 Elgin St **613/565–5155** • Italian • wheelchair access

Kinki 41 York St **613/789–7559** • lunch & dinner • Asian fusion • full bar • DJ • live entertainment • patio

La Dolce Vita 180 Preston Street **613/233–6239** • lunch & dinner, except Mon-Wed dinner only • gluten-free menu available

Shanghai Restaurant 651 Somerset St W (at Bronson Ave) **613/233–4001** • lunch Tue-Fri, dinner nightly, clsd Mon • also bar • DJ • karaoke

BOOKSTORES

Mags & Fags 254 Elgin St (btwn Somerset & Cooper) **613/233–9651** • till 10pm • gay magazines

RETAIL SHOPS

Venus Envy 320 Lisgar St (at Bank St) **613/789–4646** • 11am-6pm, till 8pm Fri, noon-5pm Sun • award-winning sex shop & bookstore

PUBLICATIONS

Capital Xtra! 416/925–6665 • LGBT newspaper

EROTICA

Wicked Wanda's 382 Bank St 613/820–6032

Wilde's 367 Bank St (at Gilmour) **613/234–5512** • 11am-7:30pm, till 9pm Fri, noon-5pm Sun • pride items • wheelchair access

St Catharines

BARS

Envy 127 Queenston St **905/682–7774** • lesbians/ gay men • dancing/DJ • theme nights • gay-owned

Stratford

RESTAURANTS

Down the Street 30 Ontario St **519/273–5886** • 11am-midnight, clsd Mon • popular • bar till 1am

Rundles 9 Cobourg St **519/271–6442** • dinner Tue-Sun, lunch wknds • wheelchair access • gay-owned

Toronto

INFO LINES & SERVICES

519 Church St Community Centre 519 Church St (on Cawthra Park) **416/392–6874** • 9am-10pm, till 5pm wknds • LGBT info center & cafe • wheelchair access

AA Gay/ Lesbian 416/487–5591

Canadian Lesbian/ Gay Archives 34 Isabella **416/777–2755** • 7:30pm-10pm Tue-Th & by appt

ACCOMMODATIONS

213 Carlton—Toronto Townhouse B&B **416/323–8898, 877/500–0466** • gay/ straight • some shared baths • nonsmoking • WiFi • gay-owned

Bonnevue Manor B&B 33 Beaty Ave (at Queen St & Roncesvalles) **416/536–1455** • gay/ straight • full brkfst • kids ok • nonsmoking • WiFi

Drake Hotel 1150 Queen St W (at Beaconsfield) **416/531–5042, 866/372–5386** • gay-friendly • boutique hotel • nonsmoking

Dundonald House 35 Dundonald St (at Church) **416/961–9888, 800/260–7227** • mostly gay men • full brkfst • hot tub • sauna • gym • bicycles • nonsmoking • gay-owned

The Gladstone Hotel 1214 Queen St W (at Gladstone Ave) **416/531-4635** • gay/ straight • artistic • nonsmoking • WiFi • also Melody bar & cafe

Hazelton Hotel 118 Yorkville Ave (at Avenue Rd) **416/963-6300, 866/473-6301** • gay-friendly • luxury property • nonsmoking

Hotel Le Germain 30 Mercer St (at Peter St) **416/345-9500, 866/345-9501** • gay-friendly • kids/ pets ok • also restaurant & bar • wheelchair access

BARS

Andy Poolhall 489 College St (at Markham) **416/923-5300** • 7pm-2am • clsd Sun-Mon • gay/ straight • dancing/DJ • also Cherry Bomb party for queer women second-to-last Saturday month

Beaver Cafe 1192 Queen St W (at Northcote Ave) **416/537-2768** • 11am-2am • lesbians/ gay men • DJs • food served • patio • gay-owned

Bistro 422 422 College St (at Bathurst St) **416/963-9416** • 5pm-2am • gay/straight • food served

Boutique Bar 506 Church St (at Maitland) **647/705-0006** • 2:30pm-2am • lesbians/ gay men • patio

The Cameron House 408 Queen St W (at Cameron St) **416/703-0811** • 4pm-close • gay/ straight • live music • also theater

Church 504 Church St (at Alexander) **647/352-5223**
• 5pm-2:30am, clsd Sun-Tue • gay/straight • dancing/DJ

The Churchmouse & Firkin 475 Church St (at Maitland) **416/927-1735** • 11am-2am • lesbians/ gay men • English pub • neighborhood bar • leather brunch 3rd Sun

Dakota Tavern 249 Ossington Ave (at Dundas) **416/850-4579** • 6pm-2am • gay-friendly • live country music • bluegrass brunch Sun

The Hair of the Dog 425 Church St (at Wood) **416/964-2708** • 11am-2am • gay/ straight • neighborhood pub & restaurant • patio

The House on Parliament Pub 456 Parliament St (at Carlton) **416/925-4074** • 11:30am-2am • gay/ straight • neighborhood bar • food served • patio

LeVack Block 88 Ossington Ave (at Humbert) **416/916-0571** • 5pm-close, from 11am wknds, clsd Mon • gay/ straight • dancing/DJ • also restaurant

Melody Bar 1214 Queen St W (at Gladstone Hotel) **416/531-4635** • clsd Mon, more gay Wed • gay/ straight • karaoke • live music

O'Grady's 518 Church St (at Maitland) **416/323-2822** • 11am-2am, till 3am Fri-Sat • gay/ straight • casual dining • huge patio • also lounge upstairs

Pegasus 489-B Church St (at Wellesley, upstairs) **416/927-8832** • 11am-2am • lesbians/ gay men • neighborhood bar

Pic Nic 747 Queen St E **647/435-5298** • 5pm-11pm, till midnight Fri-Sat, 4pm-10pm Sun • gay-friendly • wine bar • food served

The Raq 739 Queen St W, 2nd flr (at Palmerston) **416/504-9120** • 5pm-1am, from 4pm Th-Sun, clsd Mon • gay/ straight • DJs • upscale pool hall

Smiling Buddha 961 College St (at Dovercourt) **416/516-2531** • 7:30pm-2am • gay/ straight • cabaret • younger crowd

Sneaky Dee's 431 College St (at Bathurst) **416/603-3090** • 11am-3am, from 9am Sun • gay-friendly • live bands • kitchen open late • Tex/Mex

WAYLA (What Are You Looking At)Lounge 996 Queen St E **406/901-5570** • 5pm-2am • gay/straight • karaoke

Woody's/ Sailor 465-467 Church (at Maitland) **416/972-0887** • 1pm-2am • popular • mostly gay men • neighborhood bar • live shows • drag shows • 18+ • wheelchair access

NIGHTCLUBS

The Annex Wreck Room 794 Bathurst St (at Bloor) **416/536-0346** • 10pm-close • gay/ straight • dancing/DJ • bands

Big Primpin' 1279 Queen St W (at Wrongbar) • 10pm 1st Fri • lesbians/ gay men • monthly hip-hop, dancehall, R&B club • check local listings

Cherry Bomb 489 College St (at Andy Poolhall) **416/923-5300 (CLUB#)** • 9pm 2nd to last Sat • inclusive party for queer women & all of our friends • transgender-friendly • dancing/DJ

The Comfort Zone 480 Spadina Ave (N of College) **416/763-9139** • after-hours wknds only • gay/ straight • dancing/DJ

El Convento Rico 750 College St (at Crawford) **416/588-7800** • 9pm-4am, clsd Mon-Th • gay/ straight • dancing/DJ • Latin/ salsa music • mostly Latino • transgender-friendly • drag shows

Fly Toronto 8 Gloucester St (2 streets N of Yonge & Wellesley) **416/410–5426, 416/925–6222** • open Fri-Sat only • popular • mostly gay men • dancing/DJ • cover charge

Guvernment 132 Queens Quay E (at Lower Jarvis) **416/869–0045** • gay-friendly • dancing/DJ • visiting big-name DJs

Henhouse 1532 Dundas St W (at Dufferin) **416/534–5939** • 8pm-2am, clsd Sun-Mon • gay/ straight • karaoke • lesbian-owned

Lee's Palace/ Dance Cave 529 Bloor St (at Albany) **416/532–1598** • gay/ straight • live bands • dance cave Mon, Th-Sat

The Mod Club 722 College (at Crawford) **416/588–4663** • 10pm Fri-Sat • gay/ straight • dancing/DJ

Pink Mafia • alternative queer & straight events in hip locations • check www.pinkmafia.ca

Toronto

LGBT Pride:
June. 416/927-7433, web: www.pridetoronto.com.

Annual Events:
May - International Gay & Lesbian Comedy & Music Festival 416/907-9099, web: www.qcomedy.com/fests.htm.

May - Inside Out: Lesbian & Gay Film & Video Festival 416/977–6847, web: www.insideout.ca.

June - Downtown Jazz Festival 416/928-2033, web: www.torontojazz.com.

June - International Dragon Boat Race Festival 416/595-1739, web: www.dragonboats.com.

August - Queer West Arts Festival 416/879-7954, web: www.queerwest.org.

September - International Film Festival 416/968-3456, web: www.tiff.net.

City Info:
800/499–2514, web: www.seetorontonow.com.

Best View:
The top of one of the world's tallest buildings, of course: the CN Tower. Or try a sight-seeing air tour or a three-masted sailing ship tour.

Transit:
Co-op Taxi 416/504-2667, web: co-opcabs.com.
TTC 416/393-4636, web: www.ttc.ca.

Attractions:
Art Gallery of Ontario 416/979-6648, web: www.ago.net.
Bata Shoe Museum 416/979-7799, web: www.batashoemuseum.ca.
CN Tower 416/868-6937, web: www.cntower.ca.
Dr Flea's International Flea Market 416/745-3532, web: www.drfleas.com.
Gardiner Museum of Ceramic Art, 416/586-8080, web: www.gardinermuseum.on.ca.
Harbourfront Centre 416/973-4000, web: www.harbourfrontcentre.com.
Hockey Hall of Fame 416/360-7765, web: www.hhof.com.
Kensington Market, web: www.kensington-market.ca.
Ontario Place 416/314-9900, web: www.ontarioplace.com.
Rogers Centre 416/341-1707, web: www.rogerscentre.com.
Royal Ontario Museum 416/586-8000, web: www.rom.on.ca.
St Lawrence Market, web: www.stlawrencemarket.com.
Underground City.

Weather:
Summers are hot (upper 80°s—90°s) and humid. Spring is gorgeous. Fall brings cool, crisp days. Winters are cold and snowy, just as you'd imagined they would be in Canada!

Swagger Productions • parties & events for women of color • weaponoftherevolution.com for details

Tattoo Rock Parlour 567 Queen St W (at Denison) 416/703-5488 • 10am-3am Fri-Sun • gay/ straight • dancing/DJ • live shows

Wrongbar 1279 Queen St W (at Brock) 415/516-8677 • gay/ straight • dancing/DJ • Big Primpin 1st Fri • check listing for other queer events

CAFES

Alternative Grounds 333 Roncesvalles Ave 416/534-5543 • 7am-7pm

Fuel Plus 471Church St 647/352-8807 • 7:30am-10pm, 8:30am-11pm Sat • gay-owned

JetFuel 519 Parliament St 416/968-9982 • 7am-8pm • WiFi

Timothy's 500 Church St (at Alexander) 416/925-8550 • 7am-midnight, till 3:30am wknds • WiFi

RESTAURANTS

Black Hoof 938 Dundas St W 416/551-8854 • 6pm-midnight, clsd Tue-Wed • charcuterie & cheese • not for vegetarians!

Byzantium 499 Church St (S of Wellesley) 416/922-3859 • 5pm-11pm • patio • gay-owned

Cafe 668 885 Dundas St W 416/703-0668 • lunch & dinner • vegetarian

Cafe Diplomatico 594 College (at Clinton, in Little Italy) 416/534-4637 • 8am-2am, clsd Mon • Italian

Corner Cafe 1150 Queen St W (at Drake Hotel) 416/531-5042 • 8am-6pm, till 9pm Wed-Th,till 11pm Fri-Sat • popular brkfst spot

Easy Restaurant 1645 Queen St W 416/537-4893 • 9am-5pm

Fire on the East Side 6 Gloucester St (at Yonge) 416/960-3473 • noon-1am, 10am-midnight wknds • Southern comfort food • patio

Flo's Diner 70 Yorkville Ave (near Bay St) 416/961-4333 • 7:30am-4pm Mon till 9pm Tu-Fri, from 8am -9pm wknds• gay-owned

Joy Bistro 884 Queen St E 416/465-8855 • noon-1am

Kalendar 546 College 416/923-4138 • 10:30am-1am, patio

La Hacienda 640 Queen St W (near Bathurst) 416/703-3377 • noon-1am, from 11am wknds

Lee Restaurant 603 King S W 416/504-7867 • lunch & dinner, Asian fusion, also Madeline's next door

Mitzi's Cafe 100 Sorauren Ave (at Pearson) 416/588-1234 • 7:30am-4pm, popular wknd brunch from 9am • gay-owned

Nota Bene 180 Queen St W 416/977-6400 • lunch Mon-Fri, dinner nightly, clsd Sun • Mediterranean

The Sister 1554 Queen St W 416/532-2570 • 4pm-2am, till midnight Sun-Wed, popular wknd brunch from 10am • upscale pub eats • full bar • live music

Smith 553 Church St (at Dundonald) 416/926-2501 • dinner & drinks

Supermarket 268 Augusta St (at College) 416/840-0501 • call for hours • Thai • also bar w/ DJs

Urban Herbivore 64 Oxford St (at Augusta) 416/927-1231 • 9am-7pm • vegetarian/vegan

Wine Bar 9 Church St 416/504-9463 • noon-11pm • tapas-style dishes

ENTERTAINMENT & RECREATION

AIDS Memorial in Cawthra Square Park

The Bata Shoe Museum 327 Bloor St W 416/979-7799 • 10,000 shoes from over 4,500 years—including the platforms of Elton John & the pumps of Marilyn Monroe

Buddies in Bad Times Theatre 12 Alexander St (at Yonge) 416/975-8555 • LGBT theater; also Tallulah's cabaret

Hanlan's Pt Beach Toronto Islands • nude beach • 10 minutes from downtown

BOOKSTORES

Glad Day Bookshop 598-A Yonge St (at Wellesley) 416/961-4161 • 10am-7pm, till 9pm Th-Sat, noon-6pm Sun • LGBT books, mags & videos

RETAIL SHOPS

Out on the Street 551 Church St 416/967-2759, 800/263-5747 • 10am-8pm, till 9pm Th-Sat, 11am-7pm Sun • LGBT

Secrets From Your Sister 560 Bloor St W 416/538-1234, 888/868-8007 • 11am-7pm • "beautiful lingerie in realistic sizes for the modern woman" • wheelchair access

Take a Walk on the Wild Side 161 Gerrard St E (at Jarvis) 416/921-6112, 800/260-0102 • "hotel, boutique & club for crossdressers, transvestites, transexuals & other persons of gender"

PUBLICATIONS

Odyssey Magazine 323/874-8788 • dish on Toronto's club scene

Xtra! 416/925-6665, 800/268-9872 • LGBT newspaper

SEX CLUBS

Pleasure Palace Toronto 231 Mutual St (at Oasis Aqualounge) • occasional women- & trans-only sex club • check out www.pussypalacetoronto.com for events

EROTICA

Come As You Are 701 Queen St W (at Bathurst) 416/504-7934 • 11am-7pm, till 9pm Th-Fri, noon-5pm Sun • co-op-owned sex store

Good For Her 175 Harbord St (near Bathurst) 416/588-0900, 877/588-0900 • 11am-7pm • women & trans-only hours: noon-5pm Sun • women's sexuality products • wheelchair access

North Bound Leather 586 Yonge (W of Wellesley St) 416/972-1037 • toys & clothing • wheelchair access

Seduction 577 Yonge St 416/966-6969

Waterloo

ACCOMMODATIONS

Colonial Creekside 485 Bridge St W (at Lexington) 519/886-2726 • gay/ straight• pool • WiFi • • gay-owned

RESTAURANTS

Ethel's Lounge 114 King St N (at Spring) 519/725-2361 • 11:30am-2am • full bar • patio

EROTICA

Stag Shop 7 King St N 519/886-4500

Windsor

ACCOMMODATIONS

Windsor Inn on the River 3857 Riverside Dr E (at George Ave) 519/945-2110, 866/635-0055 • gay-friendly • full brkfst • kids ok • nonsmoking

BARS

Phog 157 University Ave W (at Church St) 519/253-1605 • 5pm-2am, from 8pm Sun-Mon • gay-friendly • food served • art & events

Vermouth 333 Ouellette 519/977-6102 • 5pm-2am, from 6pm Sat, clsd Sun-Mon • gay-friendly • popular martini lounge

NIGHTCLUBS

Club 2012 1056 Wyandotte St E (at Langlois Ave) 519/791-0816 • 7pm-2am, till 4am Sat, clsd Sun-Mon • lesbians/ gay men • dancing/DJ

The Loop 156 Chatham St W (at Ferry St) 519/253-3474 • 10pm-2am, clsd Mon & Wed • gay-friendly • dancing/DJ • live shows • theme nights • young crowd

CAFES

The Coffee Exchange 266 Ouellette 519/971-7424 • 7am-11pm, 8am-midnight wknds • WiFi

EROTICA

Stag Shop 2950 Dougall Ave 519/967-8798

PRINCE EDWARD ISLAND

Charlottetown

INFO LINES & SERVICES

Abegweit Rainbow Collective 375 University Avenue #2 (at Eden St, in AIDS PEI office) 902/894-5776, 877/380-5776 • 24-hour info line • monthly dances & other social activities

ACCOMMODATIONS

Evening Primrose 114 Lord's Pond Rd, Albany 902/437-3134 • gay-friendly • full brkfst • nonsmoking • kids/ pets ok • cottage wheelchair access • seasonal • WiFi • lesbian-owned

The Great George 58 Great George 902/892-0606, 800/361-1118 • gay-friendly • kids ok • nonsmoking • WiFi • wheelchair access • gay-owned

The Hotel on Pownal 146 Pownal St 902/892-1217, 800/268-6261 • gay-friendly • WiFi

Rodd Charlottetown Hotel 75 Kent St (at Pownall) 902/894-7371, 800/565-7633 • gay-friendly • pool • kids/ pets ok • WiFi • also restaurant & lounge

Shipwright Inn Heritage B&B 51 Fitzroy St 902/368-1905, 888/306-9966 • gay-friendly • full brkfst • nonsmoking

BARS

Baba's Lounge 81 University Ave 902/892-7377 • 11am-11pm, till midnight Fri-Sat from 5pm Sun • gay-friendly • live bands • also Cedars Lebanese restaurant

ENTERTAINMENT & RECREATION

Blooming Point Blooming Point • nude beach

BOOKSTORES

Book Mark 172 Queen St (in mall) **902/566-4888** • 9am-8pm, till 9pm Th-Fri, till 5:30pm Sat, clsd Sun

Hermanville

ACCOMMODATIONS

Johnson Shore Inn 9984 Rte 16 **902/687-1340, 877/510-9669** • gay/ straight • full brkfst • kids 10+ ok • wheelchair access • lesbian-owned

York

ACCOMMODATIONS

Little York B&B 775 Rte 25 **902/569-0271, 800/953-6755** • gay-friendly • full brkfst • WiFi • gay-owned

Stanhope Beach Resort 3445 Bayshore Rd **902/672-2701, 866/672-2701** • gay-friendly • restaurant & bar • pool • WiFi • wheelchair access • gay-owned

PROVINCE OF QUÉBEC

Hull

RESTAURANTS

Le Twist 88 Montcalm St, Gatineau **819/777-8886** • opens 11am daily, full bar

Laurentides (Laurentian Mtns)

ACCOMMODATIONS

Havre du Parc Auberge 2788 Rte 125 N, St-Donat **819/424-7686** • gay/ straight • quiet lakeside inn for nature lovers • full brkfst • gay-owned

Le Septentrion B&B 901 chemin St-Adolphe, Morin-Heights/ St-Sauveur **450/226-2665** • lesbians/ gay men • full brkfst • pool • hot tub • sauna • nonsmoking • gay-owned

Magog

ACCOMMODATIONS

Au Gîte du Cerf Argenté B&B 2984 chemin Georgeville Rd (off Hwy 10) **819/847-4264** • gay/ straight • renovated century-old farmhouse • 4 beaches nearby • kids ok • nonsmoking • gay-owned

Auberge aux Deux Pères 680 chemin des Pères **819/769-3115, 514/616-3114** • gay-friendly • pool • WiFi • gay-owned

Montréal

Note: M°=Metro station

INFO LINES & SERVICES

AA Gay/ Lesbian 514/376-9230

Gay/ Lesbian Community Centre of Montréal 2075 rue Plessis #110 (at Ontario) **514/528-8424** • 10am-5:30pm, 1pm-8pm Wed & Fri, clsd wknds • library

Gay Line/ Gai Ecoute 514/866-5090 (ENGLISH) • 7pm-11pm

The Village Tourism Information Center/ Gay Chamber of Commerce 1307 rue Ste-Catherine Est **514/522-1885, 888/595-8110** • 10am-6pm, clsd wknds

ACCOMMODATIONS

Alexandre Logan 1631 rue Alexandre DeSève (at Logan) **514/598-0555, 866/895-0555** • gay-friendly • WiFi

Alexandrie Hostel 1750 Amherst (at Robin) **514/525-9420** • gay-friendly • also bistro • kids/ pets ok • nonsmoking • WiFi • gay-owned

Auberge le Pomerol 819 boul de Maisonneuve E (at St-Christophe) **800/361-6896** • gay-friendly • also restaurant • nonsmoking • WiFi

B&B Le Cartier 1219 rue Cartier (at Ste-Catherine Est) **514/917-1829, 877/524-0495** • gay/ straight • private studio • WiFi • gay-owned

B&B Le Terra Nostra 277 rue Beatty (at Lasalle) **514/762-1223, 866/550-5235** • gay-friendly • full brkfst • nonsmoking • WiFi • woman-owned

Les Bons Matins 1401 Argyle Ave **514/931-9167, 800/588-5280** • lesbians/ gay men • apt rental • nonsmoking • WiFi

Le Chasseur B&B 1567 rue St-André (at Maisonneuve) **514/521-2238, 800/451-2238** • gay/ straight • Victorian row house • summer terrace • gay-owned

Hôtel Dorion 1477 rue Dorion (at Maisonneuve) **514/523-2427, 877/523-5908** • gay/ straight • in the Gay Village • WiFi

Hotel du Fort 1390 rue du Fort (at Ste-Catherine) **514/938-8333, 800/565-6333** • gay/ straight • wheelchair access

Hôtel Gouverneur Montréal Place Dupuis 1415 rue St-Hubert (at Maisonneuve) **888/910-1111** • gay-friendly • pool • also restaurant & bar • WiFi

Hotel Lord Berri 1199 rue Berri (at Ste-Catherine) **514/845-9236, 888/363-0363** • gay-friendly • also Italian resto-bar • WiFi • wheelchair access

Jade Blue B&B 1225 de Bullion St (at Ste-Catherine) **514/878-9843, 800/878-5048** • gay/ straight • theme rooms • full brkfst • nonsmoking • WiFi

L Hotel Montreal 262 rue St-Jacques W (at St Nicolas) **514/985-0019, 877/553-0019** • gay-friendly • also bar & lounge • WiFi

Loews Hotel Vogue 1425 rue de la Montagne (near Ste-Catherine) **514/285-5555, 800/465-6654** • gay-friendly • kids/ pets ok • wheelchair access

La Loggia Art & Breakfast 1637 rue Amherst (at Maisonneuve) **514/524-2493, 866/524-2493** • gay/ straight • nonsmoking • in Gay Village • WiFi • gay-owned

Turquoise B&B 1576 rue Alexandre DeSève (at Maisonneuve) **514/523-9943, 877/707-1576** • mostly gay men • shared baths • gay-owned

Montréal

LGBT Pride:

July/August. 514/285-4011, web: www.diverscite.org.

Annual Events:

February/March - Festival Montréal en Lumière (Montréal High Lights Festival) 514/288-9955, web: www.montrealenlumiere.com.

June/July - L'International des Feux Loto-Québec (fireworks competition) 514/397-2000, web: www.internationaldesfeux.com.

Festival International de Jazz de Montréal 514/871-1881, 888/515-0515, www.montrealjazzfest.com.

Festival International Montréal en Arts 514/522-4646, web: www.festivaldesarts.org.

July - Just For Laughs Comedy Festival 888/244-3155, web: www.hahaha.com.

August/September - Montréal World Film Festival 514/848-3883, web: www.ffm-montreal.org.

October - Black & Blue Party 514/875-7026, web: www.bbcm.org. AIDS benefit dance & circuit party.

November - International Gay/ Lesbian Film Festival, web: www.image-nation.org.

City Info:

514/844-5400, web: www.tourism-montreal.org.

Attractions:

Bonsecours Market 514/872-7730, web: www.marchebonsecours.qc.ca.

Latin Quarter.

Montréal Biodome 514/868-3000, web: www2.ville.montreal.qc.ca/ biodome.

Montréal Botanical Garden & Insectarium 514/872-1400, web: www2.ville.montreal.qc.ca/jardin.

Montréal Museum of Fine Arts 514/285-2000, web: www.mmfa.qc.ca.

Old Montréal & Old Port.

Olympic Park.

Underground City.

Best View:

From a caleche ride (horse-drawn carriage) or from the top of the Montréal Tower or from the patio of the old hunting lodge atop Mont Royal.

Weather:

It's north of New England so winters are for real. Beautiful spring and fall colors. Summers get hot and humid.

Transit:

Diamond Cab 514/273-6331, web: www.taxidiamond.com.

Montréal Urban Transit, web: www.stm.info.

BARS

Bar Le Cocktail 1669 Ste-Catherine Est (at Champlain) **514/597-0814** • 11am-3am • lesbians/ gay men • neighborhood bar • karaoke

Bar Rocky 1673 rue Ste-Catherine Est (at Papineau) **514/521-7865** • 8am-close • mostly gay men • drag shows • older crowd

Cabaret Mado 1115 rue Ste-Catherine Est (at Amherst, below Le Campus) **514/525-7566** • 11am-3am • popular • lesbians/ gay men • theme nights • dancing/DJ • karaoke • cabaret • drag shows • owned by the fabulous Mado! • wheelchair access

Citibar 1603 Ontario Est (at Champlain) **514/525-4251** • 11am-3am • gay/ straight • neighborhood bar • live shows

Club Bolo 2093 rue de la Visitation (at Association Sportive) **514/849-4777** • 9:30pm-12:30am Fri, special events Sat, T-dance from 3:30pm Sun • lesbians/ gay men • dancing/DJ • country/ western • also lessons • cover charge

Club Date Piano Bar 1218 rue Ste-Catherine Est (at Beaudry) **514/521-1242** • 8am-3am • lesbians/ gay men • neighborhood bar • karaoke nightly • piano

Le Drugstore 1366 rue Ste-Catherine Est (at Panêt) **514/524-1960** • 10am-3am • mostly women • 8-bar complex • food served

Foufounes Electriques 87 Ste-Catherine Est (at St-Laurent) **514/844-5539** • 4pm-3am • gay-friendly • dancing/DJ • live bands • patio

Fun Spot 1151 rue Ontario Est (at Wolfe) **514/522-0416** • 11am-3am • lesbians/ gay men • neighborhood bar • dancing/DJ • transgender-friendly • food served • drag shows • karaoke • WiFi

La Relaxe 1309 rue Ste-Catherine Est, 2nd flr (at Visitation) **514/523-0578** • noon-3am • mostly gay men • neighborhood bar • open to the street • as the name implies, a good place to relax & people-watch

Royal Phoenix 5788 St Laurent Blvd (at Bernard) **514/658-1622** • 5pm-3am • lesbians/ gay men • dancing/DJ • food served • terrace

St-Sulpice 1680 rue St-Denis (at Ontario) **514/844-9458** • 11am-3am, till midnight Sun • gay/ straight • karaoke • WiFi • large terrace

NIGHTCLUBS

Apollon 1450 rue Ste-Catherine Est • 10pm-3am clsd Mon-Wed • mostly gay men • dancing/DJ

Circus After Hours 915 rue Ste-Catherine Est **514/844-3626** • 2am-8am Th & Sun, 1am-10pm Fri-Sat • gay/ straight • dancing/DJ

Cirque du Boudoir **514/789-9068** • quarterly • gay/ straight • opulent theme parties • dancing/DJ • performance

Complexe Sky 1474 rue Ste-Catherine Est **514/529-6969, 514/529-8989** • noon-3am • lesbians/ gay men • rooftop pool & spa • cabaret & dance club Fri-Sat

Pink 28 • monthly events for professional gay women • check www.pink28montreal.com for details

Red Lite (After Hours) 1755 rue de Lierre, Laval **450/967-3057** • Fri-Sun only 2am-10am • popular • gay-friendly

Stéréo 858 rue Ste-Catherine Est (at St-Andre) **514/658-2646** • after-hours Fri-Sun only • gay/ straight • cover • popular

Unity II 1171 rue Ste-Catherine Est (at Montcalm) **514/523-2777** • 9pm-close Fri-Sat only • lesbians/ gay men • dancing/DJ • great rooftoop terrace • live shows

CAFES

Cafe Santropol 3990 St-Urbain (at Duluth) **514/842-3110** • 11:30am-12am, from 9am during summer • unique sandwiches • wheelchair access

Cafe Titanic 445 St-Pierre (in Old Montréal) **514/849-0894** • 8am-4:30pm, clsd wknds • popular • salad & soup • WiFi

Kilo 6744 rue Hutchison **514/270-3024, 877/270-3024** • 9am-5pm, clsd wknds • cakes, coffee & light meals

RESTAURANTS

L' Anecdote 801 rue Rachel Est (at St-Hubert) **514/526-7967** • 7:30am-10pm, from 9am wknds • gay-owned

Après le Jour 901 rue Rachel Est (at St-Andre) **514/527-4141** • 5pm-9pm, clsd Mon • Italian/ French • seafood • BYOB • wheelchair access

Au Pain Perdu 4489 rue de la Roche **514/527-2900** • 7am-3pm • charming brunch spot in renovated garage

Bangkok 1616 rue Ste-Catherine Ouest **514/935-2178** • 9am-9pm • wheelchair access

Beauty's 93 Mont-Royal Ouest **514/849-8883** • 7am-3pm, 8am-4pm wknds• diner/ Jewish deli • worth the wait

La Binerie 367 Mt-Royal **514/285-9078** • 6am-8pm, 8am-3pm wknds

Le Cagibi 5490 boul St-Laurent 514/509–1199 • 9am-1am, from 10:30am wknds, 6pm-midnight Mon • vegetarian • also live music & events

La Colombe 554 Duluth Est 514/849–8844 • 5:30pm-midnight, clsd Sun-Mon • BYOB • French

Commensal 1720 rue St-Denis (at Ontario) 514/845–2627 • 11am-10:30pm, till 11pm Fri-Sat • vegetarian • beer/ wine • wheelchair access

Ella Grill 1237 Amherst 514/523–5553 • upscale Mediterranean/Greek • lesbian-owned

L' Exception 1200 rue St-Hubert (at Réné-Lévèsque) 514/282–1282 • 11am-8pm, fill 10pm Sat • terrace

L' Express 3927 rue St-Denis (at Duluth) 514/845–5333 • 8am-2am, from 10am Sat-Sun • full bar • great pâté • reservations recommended • wheelchair access

Fantasie 1355 rue Ste-Catherine Est 514/523–3466 • dinner only • sushi • gay-owned

La Strega 1477 rue Ste-Catherine Est 514/523–6000 • 11am-midnight, from 5pm wknds • inexpensive Italian • some veggie • wheelchair access

Le Nouveau Palais 281 rue Bernard W 514/273–1180 • open till 3am wknds, clsd Mon, old school diner

La Paryse 302 rue Ontario Est (near Sanguinet) 514/842–2040 • 11am-11pm, clsd Mon • lesbians/ gay men • '50s-style diner • lesbian-owned

Le Planète 1451 rue Ste-Catherine Est (at Plessis) 514/528–6953 • 5pm-10:30pm, brunch only Sun • global cuisine • beer/ wine

Resto du Village 1310 rue Wolfe 514/524–5404 • 24hrs • "cuisine canadienne" • WiFi • gay-owned

Saloon Cafe 1333 rue Ste-Catherine Est (at Panêt) 514/522–1333 • dinner nightly, lunch wknds only • plenty veggie • big dishes & even bigger drinks

Schwartz's Deli 3895 boul St-Laurent 514/842–4813 • 8am-12:30am, till 1:30am Fri, till 2:30am Sat

Thai Grill 5101 boul St-Laurent (at Laurier) 514/270–5566 • lunch Mon-Fri, dinner nightly • one of Montréal's best Thai eateries

ENTERTAINMENT & RECREATION

Ça Roule 27 rue de la Commune Est 514/866–0633, 877/866–0633 • join the beautiful people skating & biking up & down Ste-Catherine

Prince Arthur Est at boul St-Laurent, not far from Sherbrooke Métro station • closed-off street w/ many outdoor restaurants & cafés • touristy but oh-so-European

RETAIL SHOPS

Cuir Mont-Royal 826-A Mont Royal Est (at St-Hubert) 514/527–0238, 888/333–8283 • leather • fetish

Priape 1311 Ste-Catherine Est (at Visitation) 514 /521–8451, 800/461–6969 • 10am-9pm, till 11pm Fri-Sat, noon-9pm Sun • clubwear • leather • books • toys & more

Screaming Eagle 1424 boul St-Laurent 514/849–2843 • leather shop

PUBLICATIONS

2B 514/521–3873 • English-language LGBT publication covering Québec

Fugues 514/848–1854, 888/848–1854 • glossy LGBT bar/ entertainment guide

EROTICA

Il Bolero 6846 St-Hubert (btwn St-Zotique & Bélanger) 514/270–6065 • fetish & clubwear emporium • ask about monthly fetish party

Québec City

ACCOMMODATIONS

ALT Hotel Québec 1200 av Germain des Prés (at Laurier Blvd), Sainte-Foy 418/658–1224, 800/463–5253 • gay-friendly • non-smoking • WiFi • kids ok • restaurant • wheelchair access • women-owned

Auberge Place D'Armes 24 rue Ste-Anne (at St-Louis) 418/694–9485, 866/333–9485 • gay-friendly • nonsmoking • WiFi • restaurant

Le Château du Faubourg 429A rue St-Jean (at Claire Fontaine) 418/524–2902 • gay-friendly • B&B in château • nonsmoking • also beauty salon • gay-owned

Gite TerreCiel 113 rue Sainte Anne, Baie-Saint-Paul 418/435–0149 • gay/ straight • WiFi • gay-owned

Hotel Le Clos Saint-Louis 69 St-Louis (at St-Ursule) 418/694–1311, 800/461–1311 • gay/ straight • boutique hotel located in historic district • nonsmoking • WiFi

Hôtel Le Germain Dominion 1912 126 rue St-Pierre (at Marché Finlay) **418/692–2224, 888/833–5253** • gay-friendly • boutique hotel in city's 1st skyscraper • pets ok • wheelchair access

Hôtel-Motel Le Voyageur 2250 boul Ste-Anne (at Estimauville) **418/661–7701, 800/463–5568** • gay/ straight • pool • kids/ pets ok • restaurant & bar • WiFi

Le Moulin de St-Laurent Chalets 754 chemin Royal, St Laurent, Ile d' Orleans **418/829–3888, 888/629–3888** • gay/ straight • cottages • pool • kids/ pets ok • also restaurant • nonsmoking

BARS

Bar Le Drague 815 rue St-Augustin (at St-Jean) **418/649–7212** • 10am-3am • popular • mostly gay men • neighborhood bar • dancing/DJ Th-Sun • food served • karaoke • cabaret • drag shows • terrace • wheelchair access

Bar St Matthew's 889 côte Ste-Geneviève (at St-Gabriel) **418/524–5000** • 11am-3am • lesbians/ gay men • neighborhood bar • patio

RESTAURANTS

Le Commensal 860 rue St-Jean **418/647–3733** • 11am-9pm, till 10pm Th-Sat • vegetarian/ vegan

Le Hobbit 700 rue St-Jean (at Ste-Geneviève) **418/647–2677** • 9am-10pm • some veggie

La Piazzetta 707 rue St-Jean **418/529–7489** • 11am-10:30pm

Le Poisson d'Avril 115 quai St-André (at St-Thomas) **418/692–1010, 877/692–1010** • 5pm-close • name is French for "April Fools"

Vertige 540 Ave Duluth E **514/842–4443** • 5:30pm-10pm, till 11pm Fri-Sat, clsd Sun-Mon

ENTERTAINMENT & RECREATION

Fairmont Le Château Frontenac 1 rue des Carrières **418/692–3861, 800/257–7544** • this hotel disguised as a castle remains the symbol of Québec, come & enjoy the view from outside

Ice Hotel /Hôtel de Glace 75, Montée de l'Auberge, Pavillon Ukiuk, Sainte-Catherine-de-la-Jacques-Cartier **418/875–4522, 877/505–0423** • sometimes getting put on ice isn't a bad thing—check this gay-friendly hotel out before it melts away, 9 km E of Québec City in Montmorency Falls Park (Jan-March only)

PUBLICATIONS

2B 514/521–3873 • English-language LGBT publication covering Québec

EROTICA

Importation André Dubois 46 côte de la Montagne (at Frontenac Castle) **418/692–0264** • transgender-friendly • wheelchair access

St-Georges-de-Beauce

BARS

Le Planet 8450 Blvd Lacroix **418/228–1322** • 2pm-3am, till 10pm Sun, clsd Mon-Tue • gay/ straight • neighborhood bar

SASKATCHEWAN

Provincewide

PUBLICATIONS

Perceptions 306/244–1930 • covers the Canadian prairies

Ravenscrag

ACCOMMODATIONS

Spring Valley Guest Ranch 306/295–4124 • gay/ straight • 1913 character home • also cabin • full brkfst • kids/ pets ok • nonsmoking • also restaurant • gay-owned

Regina

INFO LINES & SERVICES

The Gay & Lesbian Community of Regina 2070 Broad St (at Victoria) **306/569–1995** • 7am-3pm

NIGHTCLUBS

The OUTside 2070 Broad St (at Victoria, at Gay Center) **306/569–1995** • 7pm-3am • lesbians/ gay men • dancing/DJ

RESTAURANTS

Abstractions Cafe 2161 Rose St **306/352–5374** • 9am-6pm, from 11am Sat, clsd Sun • live music

The Creek in Cathedral Bistro 3414 13th Ave **306/352–4448** • lunch & dinner, clsd Sun

Saskatoon

INFO LINES & SERVICES

Avenue Community Centre 201-320 21st St W **306/665–1224, 800/358–1833** • 10am-5pm, till 9pm Wed-Fri,4:30pm-9:30pm Sat • many social/ support groups • queer gift store

Circle of Choice Gay/ Lesbian AA 505 10th St E (at Grace Westminster United Church) **306/665–6727** • 8pm Wed

NIGHTCLUBS

302 Lounge 302 Pacific Ave **306/665-6863** •
7am-2am, till 3am Fri-Sat, clsd Sun-Tue •
lesbians/ gay men • dancing/DJ

Diva's 220 3rd Ave S #110 (alley entrance)
306/665-0100 • 8pm-2am, till 5am Sat, clsd
Mon-Tue • lesbians/ gay men • dancing/DJ •
drag shows • karaoke • WiFi • private club
(guests welcome)

RESTAURANTS

2nd Ave Grill 10-123 2nd Ave S
306/244-9899 • 11am-10pm, till 11pm Fri-Sat

The Berry Barn 830 Valley Rd **306/978-9797**
• open daily • seasonal • home-style eatery w/
views of river

The Ivy Dining & Lounge 24th St E &
Ontario Ave **306/384-4444** • lunch & dinner
Mon-Fri, dinner only Sat-Sun

Prairie Ink 3130 8th St E **306/955-3579** •
9am-10pm, till 11pm Fri-Sat, till 6pm Sun •
also bookstore

ENTERTAINMENT & RECREATION

AKA Gallery 424 20th St W **306/652-0044** •
noon-6pm, till 4pm Sat, clsd Sun-Mon •
contemporary art & performance

BOOKSTORES

Turning the Tide 525 11th St E
306/955-3070 • noon-8pm, till 10pm Th-Sat •
Saskatoon's alternative bookstore

BAHAMAS

Nassau

NIGHTCLUBS

Club Waterloo E Bay St (1/2 mile E of
Paradise Island Bridge) **242/393-7324** • 4pm-
close • gay-friendly • more women Th •
indoor/ outdoor complex w/ 5 bars •
dancing/DJ • live music • restaurant •
swimming

BARBADOS

Bridgetown

RESTAURANTS

The Waterfront Cafe The Careenage
246/427-0093 • 10am-midnight, clsd Sun •
also bar • live music • outdoor seating

BRITISH VIRGIN ISLANDS

Tortola

ACCOMMODATIONS

Fort Recovery Villa Beach Resort Road
Town, Tortola **284/495-4467, 800/367-8455**
(WAIT FOR RING) • gay-friendly • private
beachfront villas • pool • kids ok • wheelchair
access • women-owned

DOMINICAN REPUBLIC

Puerto Plata

ACCOMMODATIONS

Tropix Hotel **809/571-2291** • gay-friendly •
full brkfst • garden setting near center of town
& beach • pool • kids/ pets ok • lesbian & gay-
owned

Santiago

BARS

Monaco Bar 40 Av 27 de Febrero, Santo
Domingo **809/226-1589** • lesbians/ gay men
• dancing/DJ

Santo Domingo

ACCOMMODATIONS

Caribe Colonial Hotel Isabel Catolica 159
809/688-7799 • gay-friendly • boutique hotel
• WiFi

Foreigners Club Hotel 102 Calle Canela (at
Estrelleta) **809/689-3017** • lesbians/ gay men
• in Zona Colonial • nonsmoking • WiFi •
wheelchair access • gay-owned

Hotel Aida Calle El Conde 464
809/685-7692 • gay-friendly

BARS

Amazonia 71 Delgado Dr (Gazcue)
809/412-7629 • from 8pm Th-Sun • mostly
women

Amazonia Dr Delgado 71 • mostly women

Click 3 Vicente Celestino Duarte (Zona
Colonial) **829/449-5154** • mostly women
• men very welcome • karaoke

Colonial Bar & Disco 109 Mella Ave (nr
Calle Arzobispo Nouel) **809/205-1970** • open
Th-Sun • mostly gay men • karaoke

Esedeku **809/869-6322** • 8pm-close, from
5pm Sun, clsd Mon • lesbians/ gay men • food
served

Fogoo Discotec 67 Calle Arzobispo Nouel (btw Espaillat & Santome) **809/205–1970** • mostly gay men • dancing/DJ • drag shows

Jay Dee's Jose Reyes 10, Zona Colonial **809/335–5905** • 9pm-4am • mostly gay men • neighborhood bar • strippers • videos

NIGHTCLUBS

Pure Disco Club 365 George Washington Ave (at Hotel Meliá) **809/221–6666** • gay/ straight • open till 6am, no shorts or flip flops

Sunev Bar & Lounge 203 Calle 19 de Marzo (nr Calle El Conde) **809/221–5167** • 9pm-midnight, till 2am Fri-Sat from 6am Sun, clsd Mon-Tue • mostly gay men • dancing/DJ

RESTAURANTS

El Conuco 152 Casimiro de Moya (behind Jaragua Hotel) **809/686–0129** • touristy local landmark

Green Light Cuisine 20 Heriberto Pieter, Naco **809/732–7719** • sandwiches & salads, fresh & light

Mamajuana 451 Avenida Roberto Pastoriza **809/547–1019** • Nuevo Latino

Onno's Bar 157 Calle Hostos (at El Conde) **809/689–1183** • DJ on the wknds

ENTERTAINMENT & RECREATION

Parque Duarte Calle Duarte (at Calle Padre Billini) • Th-Sun nights, this park is the gathering place for young gay Dominicans

DUTCH & FRENCH WEST INDIES

Aruba

BARS

Jimmy's Place Windstraat 32, Oranjestad **297/582–2550** • 5pm-2am, till 4am Fri-Sat, from 8pm Mon • lesbians/ gay men • neighborhood bar • dancing/DJ • food served

The Paddock LG Smith Blvd #13, Oranjestad **297/583–2334, 297/583–2606** • 10am-2am • gay/ straight • neighborhood bar • food served

RESTAURANTS

Cafe the Plaza Seaport Marketplace, Oranjestad **297/583–8826** • 8am-1am, patio

Barbados

ACCOMMODATIONS

Gemini House B&B 70 Plover Court, Inch Marlow, Christ Church **246/428–7221** • gay-friendly • WiFi

Inchcape Seaside Villas **246/428–7006** • private villa rentals • WiFi

Curacao

INFO LINES & SERVICES

Pink House Charlottestraat 6, Willemstad **5999/462–6616** • LGBT community center, health & rights organization • events

ACCOMMODATIONS

The Avila Beach Hotel 130 Penstraat, Willemstad **800/747–8162** • gay-friendly

Floris Suite Hotel Piscadera Bay **5999/462–6111, 800/411–0170** • mostly gay men • pool • WiFi • wheelchair access • gay-owned

Kura Hulanda Langestraat 8, Willemstad **888/264–3106 , 5999/434–7700** • gay-friendly • also Jacob's Bar

Papagayo Beach Resort Willemstad **800/652–2962 (FROM US), 5999/747–4333** • gay-friendly

BARS

Grand Cafe De Heeren Zuikertuintjeweg 1 **5999/736–0491** • 9am-1am, till 2:30am Th-Fri, clsd Sun • gay/ straight • live shows • also restaurant

Mundo Bizarro Nieuwestraat 12 (in the Pietermaai quarter) **5999/461-6767** • gay-friendly • weird & wonderful eatery & café • live shows

Rainbow Lounge at Floris Suite Hotel, Piscadera Bay **5999/462–6111** • 5pm-midnight • lesbians/ gay men

NIGHTCLUBS

Bermuda Disco Scharlooweg 72-76 (at the Waaigat, behind the movies), Willemstad **5999/461–4685** • 10pm-4am, popular Fri-Sat • gay-friendly • ladies night Th (mostly straight) • dancing/DJ

Cabana Beach at Seaquarium Beach **599/946–5158** • open Wed-Sat • gay-friendly • dancing/DJ • also restaurant

Tu Tu Tango Plasa Mundo Merced, Punda **5999/465–4633** • 11pm-4am • more gay Fri • also restaurant

RESTAURANTS

Mambo Beach Bapor Kibra, Seaquarium Beach **5999/461–8999** • 9am-midnight, till 4am Sat • full bar • more gay Sat

O Mundo Zuikertuintje Shopping Mall, Willemstad • lunch & dinner • also gay party 2nd Sat

ENTERTAINMENT & RECREATION

Cas Abao Beach • gay-friendly • popular local beach

Dolphin Academy Curaçao Sea Aquarium, Bapor Kibra z/n (east of Willemstad, at Sea Aquarium Park) **5999/465-8900, 5999/465-8300** • swim w/ dolphins!

Jan Thiel Beach • good people-watching

Museum Kura Hulanda Klipstraat 9, Willemstad **5999/434-7765** • African history & culture • Antillean art

South Caribbean Pride 5999/462-6111, 800/411-0170 • April/May

Saba

ACCOMMODATIONS

Juliana's Hotel Dutch West Indies, Windwardside **599/416-2269, 866/783-3319** • gay/ straight • pool • hot tub • full brkfst • ocean & garden views • also Saban-style cottages & restaurant • kids ok • WiFi

Shearwater Resort Cliff Side (Booby Hill) **589/416-2498** • gay-friendly • full brkfst • pool • nonsmoking • WiFi • also restaurant • gay-owned

RESTAURANTS

Rainforest Restaurant Windwardside (Dutch WI) **599/416-3888** • brkfst, lunch & dinner • full bar

Restaurant Eden The Road (Windwardside), Windwardside **599/416-2539** • 5:30pm-9:30pm, clsd Tue

St Barthelemy

ACCOMMODATIONS

Hotel le Village St-Jean St-Jean Hill **590-590/27-61-39, 800/651-8366** • gay-friendly • hotel & cottages • pool

Hotel Normandie Quartier Lorient **590-590/27-61-66** • gay-friendly • WiFi

Hotel St-Barth Isle De France Plage des Flamands **508/528-7727, 800/421-3396** • gay-friendly • ultraluxe hotel

NIGHTCLUBS

Le Sélect Gustavia **590-590/27-86-87** • gay-friendly • more gay after 11pm

RESTAURANTS

Le Grain de Sel Grand Saline Beach **590/524-605** • lunch & dinner • clsd Mon • relaxing setting • ideal before & after sunbathing

ENTERTAINMENT & RECREATION

Anse Gouverneur St-Jean Beach • nudity

Anse Grande Saline Beach • nudity • gay section on the left side of Saline

Orient Beach • gay beach

St Maarten

ACCOMMODATIONS

Blue Ocean Villas 352/505-2805 • private villa rentals

Holland House 43 Front St, Philipsburg **599/542-2572** • gay-friendly • on the beach • restaurant • bar

RESTAURANTS

Cheri's Cafe Rhine Rd #45 (Maho Reef) **599/54-53-361** • 11am-1:30am, clsd Tue • full bar • dancing • live music • touristy • wheelchair access

St Martin

BARS

Tantra Rhine Road, Maho Bay, Marigot (at the Marina Royale) **599/545-2861** • 11pm-close Wed, Fri-Sat • gay/ straight

NIGHTCLUBS

Eros Rue Victor Maurasse, Marigot **590/690-881-930** • Sat night • mostly gay men • dancing/DJ • spectacular view from top of the club

RESTAURANTS

L' Escapade 94 Blvd de Grand Case **590-590/87-75-04** • French • some veggie • reservations recommended

Le Pressoir 30 Blvd de Grand Case **590-590/87-76-62** • dinner nightly, clsd Sun • French

ENTERTAINMENT & RECREATION

Orient Beach on the northeast side of the island • gay-friendly nude beach

JAMAICA

Montego Bay

ACCOMMODATIONS

Half Moon 877/956-625, 866/648-6951 • gay-friendly • upscale resort

Negril

ACCOMMODATIONS

Seagrape Villas The Cliffs, West End Rd 831/625–1255 (US#) • gay/ straight • 3 seafront villas • excellent sunsets

Ocho Rios

ACCOMMODATIONS

Golden Clouds Villa North Coast Rd, Oracabessa 941/922–9191, 888/625–6007 • gay-friendly • private estate • full brkfst • fully staffed • jacuzzi • pool • kids ok • wheelchair access • gay-owned

Port Antonio

ACCOMMODATIONS

Hotel Mocking Bird Hill 876/993–7267, 876/993–7134 • gay-friendly • eco-friendly inn • fresh local food served • pool • massage • kids ok • wheelchair access • lesbian-owned

Westmoreland

ACCOMMODATIONS

Moun Tambrin Retreat set in the mtns 28 miles from Montego Bay 876/437–4353 • gay/ straight • art deco estate • pool

MARTINIQUE

Les Trois Ilets

ACCOMMODATIONS

Le Carbet B&B 18 rue des Alamandas (in Anse Mitan district) 596/596–66–0331 • mostly men • full brkfst • jacuzzi • nude sunbathing • gay-owned

PUERTO RICO

Please Note: For those with rusty or no Spanish, "carretera" means "highway" and "calle" means "street."

Baja Sucia

ENTERTAINMENT & RECREATION

Playa Sucia/ La Playuela S of Cabo Rojo Nat'l Wildlife Refuge, Guanica • beautiful, secluded beach

Bayamon

BARS

Start Night Club 31 Ongay St (behind Clendo lab) 787/536–3579 • open Th-Sat • lesbians/ gay men • drag shows

Boqueron

BARS

El Schamar Bar at corner of Muñoz Rivera & Jose de Diego 787/851–0542 • 11am-midnight • gay/ straight • drag shows • also hotel

Sunset Sunrise 65 Calle Barbosa 787/255–1478 • 10am-close • gay/ straight • older crowd

RESTAURANTS

The Fish Net & Roberto's Villa Playera Calle de Diego 787/254–3163 • best seafood in town

Camuy

BARS

Distortion Carr 119 Norte, KM 7.6 (Barrio Membrio) 787/614–3404 • 10pm Sat only • lesbians/ gay men • dancing/DJ • swimming

Ceiba

ACCOMMODATIONS

Ceiba Country Inn Carretera 977 787/885–0471, 888/560–2816 • gay-friendly • dramatic ocean views • also bar • 15 minutes to Vieques/Culebra ferry • WiFi • gay-owned

Guanica

ENTERTAINMENT & RECREATION

Gilligan's Island take Rd 333 to Copamarina Resort, then take ferry to island 787/821–5706 (FERRY INFO) • beautiful beach located in a biosphere on Southern coast of PR

Ponce

BARS

Wejele's Cafe 8 Leon St 787/603–8095 • 9pm-3am Wed-Sat • lesbians/ gay men • neighborhood bar

Rincon

ACCOMMODATIONS

Horned Dorset Primavera Hotel Apartado 1132 800/633–1857 • gay/ straight • swimming pool • kids 12+ ok

Lemontree Oceanfront Cottages Carr 429, km 4.1 (at Carr 115) 787/823–6452, 888/418–8733 • gay/ straight • kids ok • nonsmoking • WiFi • wheelchair access

San Juan

INFO LINES & SERVICES

Centro Communitario LGBTT/ LGBT Community Center 37 Calle Mayaguez **787/294–9850** • 1pm-10pm, clsd wknds • resources, events, AIDS testing • also cyber cafe

ACCOMMODATIONS

Casa del Caribe Guest House Calle Caribe 57, Condado (at Magdalena) **787/722–7139, 877/722–7139** • gay-friendly • B&B in heart of Condado • kids ok • nonsmoking • WiFi

La Concha 1077 Ashford Ave, Condado **787/721–7500** • gay/ straight • retro urban showcase & architectural landmark • restaurants & bar

Coqui del Mar Guesthouse 2218 Calle General del Valle (at General Patton, Ocean Park) **787/220–4204** • gay-friendly • studios & apts • gay-owned

Hotel El Convento Calle Cristo 100, Old San Juan (btwn Caleta de las Monjas & Calle Sol) **787/723–9020, 800/468–2779** • gay-friendly • 17th-c former Carmelite convent • pool • WiFi

San Juan

LGBT PRIDE:
June.

ANNUAL EVENTS:
January - San Sebastian Street Festival 787/724-4788.
February - Ponce Carnival.
February/ March - Festival Casals, web: www.festcasalspr.gobierno.pr.
March-April - Heineken Jazz Fest 787/272-8877, web: www.prheinekenjazz.com.
June - San Juan Bautista Day. San Juan celebrates Puerto Rico's own saint w/ week-long music, dance, religious processions, parties. On midnight of the eve before June 24th (the official saint's day), revelers walk/jump backwards into the sea 3 to 7 times to ward off evil spirits & renew good luck for the coming year.

CITY INFO:
Puerto Rico Tourism Company, 800/866-7827, web: www.topuertorico.org

WEATHER:
Tropical sunshine year-round, with temperatures that average in the mid-80°s from November to May. Expect more rain on the northern coast.

BEST VIEW:
From El Morro or alternatively, one of the harbor cruises that depart from Pier 2 in Old San Juan.

ATTRACTIONS:
Cathedral de San Juan 787/722–0861, web: www.catedralsanjuan.com.
Condado Beach.
La Fortaleza 787/ 721–7000, web: www.fortaleza.gobierno.pr.
Historic Old San Juan.
El Morro Fortress & Fort San Cristobal (San Juan National Historic Site) 787/729-6777, web: www.nps.gov/saju.
La Casita weekly festival 787/721–2891.
Pablo Casals Museum 787/723-9185.
Paseo de la Princesa.
Quincentennial Plaza.
San José Church.
San Juan Museum of Art & History 787/724-1875.
Santurce Marketplace.

TRANSIT:
TaxiVan, 787/645-8294, web: www.taxivansanjuan.com.
American Taxi, 787/982-3466, web: www.americantaxipr.com.
Santana Taxi Service, web: www.taxituristico.com.
Metropolitan Bus Authority (AMA, its Spanish initials, and Metrobus) 787/767-7979, web: www.dtop.gov.pr.
Also look for the free trolley that winds through Old Town.

Miramar Hotel 606 Ave Ponce de Leon (at Miramar) **787/977-1000** • gay-friendly • WiFi • also restaurant & bar

Numero Uno on the Beach Calle Santa Ana 1, Ocean Park (near Calle Italia) **787/726-5010, 866/726-5010** • gay/ straight • pool • also Pamela's, full bar & grill • kids ok • wheelchair access

The San Juan Water & Beach Club Hotel 2 Tartak St (Isla Verde), Carolina **787/728-3666, 888/265-6699** • gay-friendly • boutique hotel on the beach • restaurant & lounge • kids ok • rooftop pool • nonsmoking • WiFi • wheelchair access

BARS

Angelu's Cafe Calle Eleanor Roosevelt 239, Hato Rey • clsd Sun-Mon • mostly women • neighborhood bar

Batucada 15 Ave Carlos Chardon, Hato Rey **787/993-1291** • gay-friendly • neighborhood sports bar & grill • karaoke

Esechys 478 Calle Jose Canals (near Calle Rodrigo de Triana, Placita Roosevelt), Hato Rey **787/607-3939** • open Tue-Sun • mostly women • live music Fri

Splash Av Condado 6 (in Condado, next to the San Juan Marriot) **787/721-7145** • 1pm-close • mostly gay men • near beach

Tia Maria's 326 Ave Jose de Diego, Parada 22 (at Ponce de León), Santurce **787/724-4011** • 11am-midnight, till 2am Fri-Sat • lesbians/ gay men • neighborhood bar • also liquor shop

NIGHTCLUBS

Circo Bar Calle Condado 650, Parada 18, Santurce **787/725-9676** • 9pm-5am • mostly men • dancing/DJ • karaoke • beware of the neighborhood

CAFES

Cafe Berlin Calle San Francisco 407, Plaza Colón, Old San Juan (btwn Calles Norzagary & O'Donnel) **787/722-5205** • 11am-11pm • popular • espresso bar • plenty veggie

Kasalta Bakery 1966 McLeary Ave (at Teniente Matta) **787/727-7340** • 6am-10pm • bakery & deli

RESTAURANTS

Aguaviva 364 Calle La Fortaleza, Old San Juan (at Calle O'Donnell) **787/722-0665** • dinner nightly • fresh seafood & ceviche • wheelchair access

Ajili Mojili 1052 Ashford Ave, Condado (at Aguadilla) **787/725-9195** • local specialties • live music • great ambiance

Al Dente 309 Calle Recinto S, Old San Juan **787/723-7303** • lunch & dinner, clsd Sun • Italian • also wine bar

Bebo's Cafe 1600 Calle Loiza (at Del Parque) **787/268-5087** • cheap & delicious • cafeteria-style Puerto Rican favorites

Cafe Puerto Rico 208 O'Donnell, Old San Juan **787/724-2281** • noon-11pm • great mofongo • outdoor seating

La Casita Blanca 351 Calle Tapia (off Ave Eduardo Conde, near Laguna Los Corozas) **787/726-5501** • 11am-4pm, till 6pm Th, till 9pm Fri-Sat • amazing local cuisine • best reached by car • no English spoken • beware of neighborhood

Dieguito & Markito's Kiosk 44 in Luquillo **787/355-0875** • 2pm-9pm, open late wknds • also bar • karaoke

Dragonfly 364 S Fortaleza St, Old San Juan (across from Parrot Club) **787/977-3886** • opens 5:30pm daily • full bar • Latin/ Asian fusion

Fleria 1754 Calle Loiza, Santurce **787/268-0010** • lunch & dinner, clsd Sun-Mon • Greek • some veggie

El Jibarito Calle Sol 280 **787/725-8375** • Puerto Rican/ criolla • also bar

Oceano Restaurant & Lounge 2 Calle Vendig, Condado **787/724-6400** • great beach location • Sun gay party

The Parrot Club Calle Fortaleza 363, Old San Juan (btwn Plaza Colón & Callejón de la Capilla) **787/725-7370** • lunch & dinner • chic Nuevo Latino bistro & bar • live music

Perla 1077 Ashford Ave, at La Concha Resort, Condado **787/721-7500** • enjoy an upscale dining experience inside a gigantic conch shell • swank!

Pura Vida 1853 McLeary Ave, Condado (at Calle Atlantic Pl) **787/728-8119** • noon-10pm • WiFi

Vidy's Cafe Ave Universidad 104 (Rio Piedras) **787/767-3062** • 10am-1am • plenty veggie • karaoke

ENTERTAINMENT & RECREATION

Atlantic Beach in front of Atlantic Beach Hotel • very gay-friendly beach

Nuyorican Cafe San Francisco 312 (by El Callejon) **787/977-1276, 787/366-5074** • live music & arts venue

Ocean Park Beach E of Condado • gay/ straight beach • adult-oriented (less kids)

La Placita/ Plaza del Mercado Santurce • open-air market by day, street-party by night • lots of bars & restaurants

PUBLICATIONS

Conexion G 787/607–3939 • LGBT paper, in Spanish

Vieques Island

ACCOMMODATIONS

Bravo! North Shore Rd (at Lighthouse) 787/741–1128 • gay/ straight • pool • gay-owned

Casa de Amistad 27 Benitez Castano 787/741–3758 • gay/ straight • guesthouse in heart of Isabel Segunda • WiFi • gay-owned

Crow's Nest Inn 787/741–0033, 877/276–9763 • gay-friendly • small inn • pool • nonsmoking • restaurant

Inn on the Blue Horizon 787/741–3318 • gay-friendly • country inn & cottages • pool • beach access • restaurant • nonsmoking • WiFi

TRINIDAD & TOBAGO

Tobago

ACCOMMODATIONS

Grafton Beach Resort 868/639–0191, 888/790–5264 • gay-friendly • pool • food served

Kariwak Village Hotel & Holistic Haven Store Bay Local Rd, Crown Point 868/639–8442, 868/639–8545 • gay-friendly • holistic hotel • kids ok • pool • restaurant • wheelchair access

US VIRGIN ISLANDS

St Croix

ACCOMMODATIONS

King Christian Hotel 59 Kings Wharf, Christiansted 340/773–6330, 800/524–2012 • gay-friendly • pool • also restaurant

The Palms at Pelican Cove 4126 La Grande Princesse 340/778–8920, 888/790–5264 • lesbians/ gay men • beachfront resort • food served • pool

Sand Castle on the Beach 127 Smithfield, Frederiksted 340/772–1205, 800/524–2018 • lesbian, gay & straight-friendly • hotel • solar heated pool • WiFi • also restaurant & bar • lesbian & gay-owned

St John

ACCOMMODATIONS

Gallows Point Suite Resort Cruz Bay 340/776–6434, 800/323–7229 • gay-friendly • beachfront resort • pool • kitchens • also restaurant • full bar • wheelchair access

Hillcrest Guest House 340/776–6774, 340/998–8388 • gay-friendly • WiFi • nonsmoking • kids ok

St John Inn 800/666–7688, 340/693–8688 • gay-friendly • kids ok • pool • nonsmoking

RESTAURANTS

Asolare Rte 20, Cruz Bay 340/779–4747 • 5:30pm-9:30pm • Asian/ French fusion • hip & elegant

ENTERTAINMENT & RECREATION

Salomon Bay • 20-minute hike on Salomon Beach Trail

St Thomas

ACCOMMODATIONS

Hotel 1829 Government Hill 340/776–1829, 800/524–2002 • gay-friendly • pool • also full bar & restaurant

Magen's Point Resort 6200 Magen's Bay Rd 340/777–6000, 877/850–4465 • gay-friendly • pool • wheelchair access

Pavilions & Pools Hotel 6400 Estate Smith Bay 340/775–6110, 800/524–2001 • gay-friendly • 1-bdrm villas each w/ own private swimming pool

RESTAURANTS

Mafolie Hotel & Restaurant 7091 Estate Mafolie 340/774–2790 • great place for lunch with a view

Oceana Restaurant & Wine Bar Historic Pointe at Villa Olga 340/774–4262 • on the water's edge • owned by renowned chef Patricia LaCorte

Virgilio's 18 Dronningens Gade 340/776–4920 • great Italian, full bar

ENTERTAINMENT & RECREATION

Beach at Emerald Beach Resort up hill (near airport runway) • walking distance from cruise ship dock

Morning Star Beach • popular gay beach

MEXICO

Please Note: Mexican cities are often divided into districts or "Colonias," which we abbreviate as "Col." Please use these when giving addresses for directions.

Acapulco

ACCOMMODATIONS

Casa Condesa Bella Vista 125 52–744/484–1616, 800/816–4817 (US & CANADA) • mostly gay men • full brkfst • near beach • pool

Hotel Boca Chica Punta Caletilla (Fraccionamiento las Playas) 800/337–4685 • gay-friendly • pool • also restaurant

Hotel Encanto Jacques Cousteau 51 (Fraccionamiento Brisas Marques) 52–744/446–7101 • gay-friendly • pool • WiFi • also restaurant

Las Brisas Carretera Escenica 5255 52–744/469–6900, 866/221–2961 (US#) • popular • gay-friendly • luxury resort • private pools • kids ok • wheelchair access

NIGHTCLUBS

Baby 'O 52–744/484–7474 • 10:30pm-5am, till midnight Sun • gay/ straight

Cabaré-Tito Beach Privada de Piedra Picuda 17 PA (nr Torres Gemelas) 52–744/1–24–89–29 • 6pm-3am, from 4pm Th-Sat • lesbians/ gay men • dancing/DJ

Relax Calle Lomas de Mar 4 (Zona Dorada) 52–744/482–0421 • 10pm-late, clsd Mon-Wed • popular • lesbians/ gay men • dancing/DJ • drag & strip shows wknds • videos • young crowd

RESTAURANTS

100% Natural Av Costera Miguel Alemán 200 (near Acapulco Plaza) 52–744/485–3982 • 24hrs • fast (healthy) food • plenty veggie

Becco al Mare 52–744/446–7402 • lunch & dinner • Italian • nice views

Beto's Restaurant Av Costera Miguel Alemán 99 (at Condesa Beach) 52–744/484–0473 • 11am-midnight • lesbians/ gay men • full bar • seafood • palapas

El Cabrito Av Costera Miguel Alemán 1480 (near Convention Center) 52–744/484–7711 • 2pm-midnight, till 11pm Sun • local favorite • try the roasted goat

Carlos & Charlie's Blvd de las Naciones #1813 (in La Isla Shopping Village) 52–744/462–2104 • lunch & dinner • entertainment

Kookaburra 3 Fracc (at Marina Las Brisas) 52–744/446–6039 • lunch & dinner • int'l • expensive

La Cabaña de Caleta Playa Caleta Lado Oriente s/n (Fracc. las Playas) 52–744/469–8553, 52–744/469–7919 • 9am-9pm • seafood • right on Playa Caleta • great magaritas

La Tortuga Calle Lomas del Mar 5 52–744/484–6985 • noon-midnight, clsd Mon • full bar • good Mexican • seafood • patio • gay-owned

Shu 52–744/462–2001 • Japanese

Su Casa Angel & Shelly Av Anahuac 110 52–744/484–1261, 52–744/484–4350 • seafood • tasty margaritas • great views

Suntory de Acapulco Costera Miguel Alemán 36 52–744/484–8088 • 2pm-midnight • Japanese • gardens

El Zorrito's Av Costera Miguel Alemán (at Anton de Alaminos) 52–744/485–3735 • traditional Mexican • several locations along Costera • some all night

Aguascalientes

NIGHTCLUBS

Mandiles Av Lopez Mateos Poniente 730 W (btwn Agucate & Chabacano) 52–449/153–281 • 10pm-3am Fri-Sat only • lesbians/ gay men • dancing/DJ

Cabo San Lucas

ACCOMMODATIONS

Cabo Villas Beach Resort Callejon del Pescador s/n (Col. El Medano) 52–624/143–9199 • gay-friendly • resort on Medano Beach • pool

Solmar Suites Av Solmar 1 800/344–3349, 310/459–9861 (US#) • gay-friendly • oceanfront suites at southernmost tip • 2 pools • hot tub

NIGHTCLUBS

Las Varitas Calle Vallentin Gomez Farias (at Camino Viejo a San Jose) 52–624/143–9999 • 9pm-3am, clsd Mon • gay-friendly • dancing/DJ • live shows • rock 'n' roll bar • Ladies Night Fri

RESTAURANTS

Mi Casa Av Cabo San Lucas (at Lazarus Cardenas) **52-624/143-1933** • clsd Sun • lunch & dinner • great chicken mole • reservations recommended

Cancún

see also Cozumel & Playa del Carmen

ACCOMMODATIONS

Rancho Sak Ol Puerto Morelos **52-998/871-0181** • gay-friendly • beachfront palapa-style B&B • 30 minutes from Cancún

BARS

Picante Bar Av Tulúm 20, Centro (E of Av Uxmal, next to Plaza Galerías) • 9pm-5am • popular • mostly gay men • dancing/DJ • young crowd • drag shows & strippers Wed-Sat

NIGHTCLUBS

Karamba Av Tulúm 9 (Azucenas 2nd flr, SM 22) **52-998/884-0032** • 10:30pm-close, clsd Mon • popular • lesbians/ gay men • dancing/DJ • karaoke • drag shows • go-go boys Fri

Sexy's Club Av Tulum Plaza Safa Planta Alta **52-998/280-3943** • 10pm-8am, clsd Mon-Tue • mostly gay men • dancing/DJ • cover charge

RESTAURANTS

100% Natural Sunyaxchen 62 **52-998/884-0102** • healthy fast food

Perico's Av Yaxhilan 61 **52-998/884-3152** • noon-1am • traditional Mexican served up w/ huge theatrical flare

ENTERTAINMENT & RECREATION

Chichén Itza • the must-see Mayan ruin 125 miles from Cancún

Playa Delfines in the Hotel Zone (next to Hilton's beach) • gay beach

Chihuahua

ACCOMMODATIONS

Hacienda Huiyochi Copper Canyon **51–1/625-121-8101** • first & only hotel in Copper Canyon that caters to the LGBT community • full brkfst • kids/ pets ok

Ciudad Juárez

see also El Paso, Texas, USA

BARS

Club La Escondida Calle Ignacio de la Peña 366 W • gay/ straight • neighborhood bar

Copala

ACCOMMODATIONS

La Caracola Antelmo Ventura 68 (2 1/2 hrs from Acapulco) **52-741/101–3047** • gay/ straight • pool • WiFi • women-run

Cordoba

BARS

Salon Bar El Metro Av 7 no. 117–C (btwn Calles 1 & 3) • lesbians/ gay men • dancing

Cozumel

see also Cancún & Playa del Carmen

ACCOMMODATIONS

Flamingo Hotel Calle 6 Norte #81 (at Ave 5) **954/351-9236, 800/806-1601** • gay-friendly • WI • pets ok

Cuernavaca

ACCOMMODATIONS

Casa del Angel Calle Clavel 18, Col. Satelite (at Begonia) **52-777/512–6775** • gay/ straight • contemporary guesthouse on hill overlooking Cuernavaca • hot tub • nonsmoking • full brkfst • gay-owned

Las Mañanitas Ricardo Linares 107 **52-777/312-8982 & 314-1466, 888/413-9199 (US ONLY)** • gay-friendly • gardens • pool • restaurant • peacocks!

La Nuestra Calle Mesalina 18 (at Calle Neptuno) **52-777/315-2272, 404/806-9694** • gay/ straight • B&B • full brkfst • pool • kids ok • WiFi • lesbian-owned

BARS

Barecito Comonfort 17 (at Morrow) **52-777/314-1425** • 10am-1am, clsd Sun-Mon • lesbians/ gay men • food served • lesbian-owned

NIGHTCLUBS

Oxygen Av Vincente Guerrero 1303 (near Sam's Club) **52-777/317-2714** • 10pm-close, Fri-Sat only • mostly gay men • dancing/DJ • food served • live shows • drag shows • videos • 18+ • young crowd

RESTAURANTS

La India Bonita Dwight Morrow 15 (btwn Morelos & Matamoros) **52-777/312-5021** • 9am-9pm, till 5pm Sun-Mon

La Maga Calle Morrow #9 Altos **52-777/310-0432** • clsd Sun, popular lunch buffet • plenty veggie • live music

Marco Polo Calle Hidalgo 30 (in front of cathedral, 2nd flr) 52–777/312–3484, 52-777/318–4032 • 1pm-close • Italian (pasta & pizza) • overlooking cathedral

ENTERTAINMENT & RECREATION

Diego Rivera Murals Plaza de Museo (in Cuauhnáhuac Regional Museum)

Ensenada

NIGHTCLUBS

Sublime Plaza Blanca , 3rd Fl 52–646/128–8798 • 9pm-close • mostly gay men • dancing/DJ

RESTAURANTS

Casamar Blvd Costero 987 52–646/174–0417 • 8am-10:30pm • popular • seafood • also bar • Ensenada landmark for 30 years

Guadalajara

ACCOMMODATIONS

Casa Alebrijes Hotel Libertad 1016, Zona Centro 52–33/3614–5232 • mostly gay men • boutique hotel in historic center • two blocks from gay nightlife area • WiFi • gay-owned

Casa de las Flores B&B Santos Degollado 175, Tlaquepaque 52–33/3659–3186, 888/582–4896 • gay-friendly • 15 minutes from Guadalajara • great brkfsts & margaritas

Casa Venezuela Calle Venezuela 459 (at Col. Americana) 52–33/3826–6590 • gay/ straight • B&B in 100-year-old colonial house • full brkfst • nonsmoking • WiFi • gay-owned

Hostel Lit Degollado 413 52–33/1200–5505 • gay-friendly • WiFi

Hotel San Francisco Degollado 267 52–33/3613–3256 • gay-friendly • hotel w/ Old World charm • close to gay bars • also restaurant

Old Guadalajara B&B Belén 236 (Centro Histórico) 52–33/3613–9958 • gay/ straight • nonsmoking • gay-owned

Orchid House B&B Juan de Ojeda 75 (at Ave La Paz) 52–33/3335–19 21 • gay/ straight • gay-owned

La Perla B&B Prado 128, Col. Americana (Vallarta y Lopez Cotilla) 52–33/3825–1948 • gay/ straight • full brkfst • nonsmoking • WiFi • gay-owned

La Villa del Ensueño Florida St 305, Tlaquepaque 52–33/3635–8792 • gay/ straight • full brkfst

BARS

Caudillos Bar Calle Prisciliano Sánchez 305, Centro (at Ocampo) 52–33/3613–5445 • 5pm-3am • popular • mostly gay men • dancing from 9pm • friendly bar • also restaurant

Club YeYe Prisciliano Sánchez 395 (Zona Centro) 52–33/1337–5253 • 5pm-3am • lesbians/ gay men • chic video lounge • food served

Dona Diabla Colon 530 • 7pm-3am Wed-Sun • gay/ straight • shows

Equilibrio Restaurant & Bar Ocampo 293 (at Miguel Blanco)

Maskaras Calle Maestranza 238 (at Prisciliano Sánchez) 52–33/3614–8103 • noon-3am • lesbians/ gay men • neighborhood bar • colorful atmosphere • live music • food served

La Minerva 8 de Julio #73 52–33/3613–5167 • mostly gay men • karaoke • strippers • theme nights

NIGHTCLUBS

7 Sins Pedro Moreno 532 (at Donato Guerra, Zona Centro) 52–33/3658–0713 • mostly gay men • dancing/DJ

Black Cherry Grand Popocatepetl 40 (at Adolfo Lopez Mateos Sur) 52–33/3647–9024 • 10pm-5am Sat only • mostly gay men • dancing/DJ

El Botanero Calle Javier Mina 1348 (at Calle 54, Sector Libertad) 52–33/3643–0545 • 6pm-3am, till 1am Sun, clsd Mon-Tue • mostly gay men • dancing/DJ • food served • karaoke • drag shows • T-dance Sun • cover charge

Circus Galeana 277 (at Prisciliano Sánchez, Centro Histórico) 52–33/3613–0299 • 9pm-5am • popular • lesbians/ gay men • dancing • live shows

Mónica's Av Álvaro Obregón 1713 (btwn Calles 68 & 70, Sector Libertad; no sign, look for canopy under a big palm tree) 52–33/3643–9544 • 9pm-5am, clsd Mon-Tue • popular after midnight • mostly gay men • dancing/DJ • drag & strip shows wknds • young crowd • cover charge • take a taxi to & from

Om Club Ocampo 270 52–33/3121–9547 • 9am-4pm Th-Sat, 5pm-10pm Sun • mostly gay men • dancing/DJ

Velvett 52–33/3830–4165 • 9pm-5am • lesbians/ gay men • dancing/DJ

CAFES

Dolce Veele Enrique González Martínez 177 52–33/1523–9593 • 4pm-1am • lesbians/gay men • WiFi

Queer Nation López Cotilla 611 • 5pm-midnight, clsd Sun • souvenirs

Vida Caffe Av Hidalgo 907 52–33/1181–1834 • 4:30pm-close • lesbians/gay men

RESTAURANTS

Sanborns Av 16 de Septiembre 127 52–33/3613–6264 • many locations • WiFi

PUBLICATIONS

GAYGDL • online magazine at www.gaygdl.com

Urbana Revista • gay lifestyle magazine w/ bars & clubs for Guadalajara & Puerto Vallarta

Isla Mujeres

ACCOMMODATIONS

Casa Sirena Av Miguel Hidalgo, Centro (at Bravo y Allende) • gay-friendly • Isla Mujeres is a short, 20-minute ferry ride from Cancun • gay-owned

La Paz

ACCOMMODATIONS

La Casa Mexicana Inn Calle Nicolas Bravo 106 (btwn Madero & Mutualismo) 52–612/125–2748 • open Nov-June • gay/straight • Spanish/Moorish retreat • 1 block from La Paz Bay • nonsmoking • WiFi • wheelchair access • woman-owned

Hotel Mediterrane Allende 36 (at Malecón) 52–612/125–1195 • gay/straight • WiFi • nonsmoking • bar & restaurant • sun terrace • gay-owned

BARS

Cafe La Pazta Allende 36 (at Hotel Mediterrane) 52–612/125–1195 • 7am-11pm • gay/straight • neighborhood bar • also restaurant • young crowd • gay-owned

NIGHTCLUBS

Las Varitas Calle Independencia 111 (at Malecón) 52–612/123–1590 • 9pm-3am, clsd Mon • gay-friendly • dancing/DJ • live shows • rock 'n' roll bar • Ladies Night Fri

León

BARS

G*bar Madero 226 (at Gante, Centro Histórico) 52–477/740–8863 • 6pm-2am • café-bar w/ terrace • young crowd

NIGHTCLUBS

La Madame Blvd A López Mateos 1709 Oriente (in front of Torre Banamex) 52–477/763–3086 • 10pm-3am, clsd Mon-Wed • mostly gay men • dancing/DJ • drag shows • go-go boys

Nation 52–477/716–3695 • gay/straight • dancing/DJ

Manzanillo

ACCOMMODATIONS

Las Hadas Av Vista Hermosa s/n (Fracc. Península de Santiago) 52–314/331–0101, 888/559–4329 • gay-friendly • great resort & location

Red Tree Melaque Inn Primaveras 32 (30 miles N of Manzanillo), Melaque-Villa Obregon 52–315/355–8917, 480/389–5786 (US) • gay-friendly • bungalows • near ocean • pool • kids/pets ok • nonsmoking • gay-owned

Mazatlán

ACCOMMODATIONS

El Cid Resort 866/306–6113, 52–669/913–3333 • gay-friendly

Hotel Los Sábalos Av Playa Gaviotas 100 (Zona Dorada) 52–669/983–5333, 800/528–8760 (US#) • gay-friendly • resort • swimming • beach • health club • also popular Joe's Oyster Bar

Old Mazatlan Inn 52–520/366–8487, 866/385–2945 • gay-friendly • swimming • WiFi • gay-owned

The Pueblo Bonito Emerald Bay Ave Ernesto Coppel Compaña 201 52–669/989–0525, 800/990–8250 • gay-friendly • resort on 20 acres • jacuzzi • pool • restaurant • piano bar • gym

BARS

La Alemana Calle Zaragoza 16 (at Benito Juarez & Serdan) • gay/straight • sports bar

Pepe Toro Av de las Garzas 18 (1 block W of Av Camarón Sábalo, Zona Dorada) 52–669/914–4176 • 9:30pm-4am, clsd Mon-Th • popular • mostly gay men • dancing/DJ • drag & strip shows

Vitrolas Bar Heriberto Frías 1608 (in Centro Historico) 52–669/985–2221 • 3pm-1am, clsd Mon • lesbians/gay men • lunch menu • karaoke • drag shows & strippers Sun

RESTAURANTS

Panamá Restaurant & Pastelería at Avs de las Garzas & Camarón Sábalo (Zona Dorada) **52-669/913-6977**

Roca Mar Av del Mar (at Calle Isla de Lobos, Zona Costera) **52-669/981-6008** • till 2am • popular • seafood • full bar • lesbian-owned

Mérida

ACCOMMODATIONS

Angeles de Mérida Calle 74-A, #494-A (at Calle 57 & Calle 59) **52-999/923-8163** • gay-friendly • B&B in 18th-c home on quietest streets of Mérida • full brkfst • nonsmoking • pool • spa services available

Los Arcos B&B Calle 66 **52-999/928-0214** • gay-friendly • pool • gay-owned

Casa Ana B&B Calle 52 #469 (btwn 51 & 53) **52-999/924-0005** • gay-friendly • pool • nonsmoking • women-owned

La Casa Lorenzo Calle 41 #516 A (btwn 62 & 64) **52-999/139-0423, 866/515-4105** • gay-friendly • pool • nonsmoking • WiFi • gay-owned

Casa San Juan B&B 545-A Calle 62 (btwn Calle 69 & Calle 71) **52-999/986-2937, 866/979-6753** • gay/ straight • nonsmoking • kids ok • wheelchair access • gay-owned

Casa Santiago B&B Calle 63 #562 (btwn Calles 70 & 72) **52-999/928-9375** • gay/ straight • colonial restored house • pool • nonsmoking • WiFi • wheelchair access • gay-owned

Gran Hotel Calle 60 #496 (nr Parque Cepeda Peraza) **52-999/924-7730 & 923-6963** • gay-friendly • historic turn-of-the-century hotel • pets ok • also restaurant

Las Arecas Guesthouse Calle 59 #541 (btwn Calle 66 & Calle 68) **52-999/928-3626** • gay-friendly • guesthouse • garden • gay-owned

Posada Santiago Guesthouse Calle 57 No 552 (between Calle 66 & 68, Centro Historico) **52-999/928-4258** • gay/ straight • pool • nonsmoking • WiFi • wheelchair access • gay-owned

BARS

El Establo Calle 60 #482 (btwn Calle 56 & 58) **52-999/924-2289** • gay-friendly • dancing/DJ • food served • popular w/ tourists & locals

NIGHTCLUBS

Pride Disco Campeche A (200 meters del Puente de Ulman), Anillo Periferico **52-999/946-4401** • mostly gay men • dancing/DJ • strippers • south of town, all taxi drivers know where it is located

RESTAURANTS

Cafe La Habana Calle 59 #511-A (at Calle 62) **52-999/928-6502** • 24hrs • also bar & café

Cafeteria Pop Calle 57 (btwn Calle 60 & 62) **52-999/928-6163** • brkfst, lunch & "light dinner" • beer & wine

La Bella Época Calle 60 #447 (upstairs in the Hotel del Parque) **52-99/928-1928** • 4pm-1am • Yucatécan cuisine • try to get one of the balcony tables

Mexico City

Note: M°=Metro station

Note: Mexico City is divided into "Zonas" (ie, Zona Rosa) & "Colonias" (abbreviated here as "Col."). Remember to use these when giving addresses to taxi drivers.

INFO LINES & SERVICES

Cálamo (LGBT AA) Av de Chapultepec 465, desd 202 (Col. Juárez) **52-55/5574-1210** • 8pm Mon-Fri, 7pm Sat, 6pm Sun

Centro Cultural de la Diversidad Sexual Colima 267 (Col. Roma Norte) **52-55/5514-2565, 52-55/1450-9511** • Mexico City's LGBT center • also cafe

Jovenes La Villa AA Calle 521 #248 (nr Ave 510) **52-55/2603-7696**

ACCOMMODATIONS

Best Western Majestic Hotel Ave Madero 73, Col. Centro **52-55/5521-8600** • gay-friendly • on the Zócalo Plaza • rooftop restaurant • wheelchair access

Condesa Haus Cuernavaca 142 (at Campeche) **52-55/5256-2494, 310/622 4825 (US)** • gay-friendly • WiFi • full brkfst • gay-owned

Downtown México 30 Isabel la Catolica **52-55/5130-6830** • gay-friendly • magnificent 17th century building, rooftop bar & pool

Hostal Central Historico Regina 5 de Febrero #53 (Col. Centro) **52-55/5709-4192** • gay-friendly • also cafe • WiFi

Hotel Casa Blanca Lafragua 7 (Col. Tabacalera) **52-55/5096-4500, 800/905-2905** • gay-friendly • pool • restaurant & bar

Hotel Gillow Isabel la Católica 17 (Col. Centro) **52–55/5518-1440, 52–55/5510-2636** • gay-friendly • also restaurant & bar

Hotel Principado Londres 42 (Col Juarez) **52–55/5533-2944** • gay-friendly

El Patio 77 Icazbalceta 77 (Col. San Rafael) **52–55/5455-0332, 52–55/5592-8452** • gay-friendly • eco-friendly B&B • WiFi

The Red Tree House Culiacan 6 (at Avenida Amsterdam) **52–55/5584-3829** • gay-friendly • gay-owned

W Mexico City Campos Eliseos 252 **52–55/9138-1800** • gay-friendly • in trendy Polanco • 2 restaurants & bar • WiFi

BARS

42 Bar Amberes 4 (Zona Rosa) **52–55/5208-0352**

Bar Lili Calle 65 #7 (Col. Puebla) **52–55/4551-0414** • lesbians/ gay men • neighborhood bar

Black Out Amberes 11 (Zona Rosa) **52–55/5511-9247** • gay/ straight • upscale lounge • also restaurant

Cafeína Nuevo Leon 73 (in Condesa) **52–55/5212-0090** • 7pm-4am, 6pm-10pm Sun • gay-friendly • dancing/DJ • co-owned by Diego Luna of Y Tu Mama También fame

Enigma Calle Morelia 111, Col. Roma (4 blocks from Mº Niños Héroes, Zona Rosa) **52–55/5207-7367** • 9pm-3:30am, 6pm-2am Sun, clsd Mon • lesbians/ gay men • dancing/DJ • shows for women Th • live shows • cover charge

La Gayta/ Pussy Bar Amberes 18 (Zona Rosa) **52–551/055-5873** • lesbians/ gay men • neighborhood bar • young crowd

Lipstick Amberes 1 (at Paseo de la Reforma, Zona Rosa) **52–55/5514-4920** • clsd Sun-Wed • gay/ straight • more lesbian Th • lounge • videos • live shows

El Marrakech Salón Republica de Cuba 18 (Col. Centro) • lesbians/ gay men • neighborhood bar

Oasis República de Cuba 2 (Centro Historico) **52–55/5511-9740** • 3pm-1am, till 3am Fri-Sat • mostly gay men • drag shows • cover charge

Papi Fun Bar Amberes 18 (Zona Rosa) **52–55/5208-3755** • lesbians/ gay men • neighborhood bar • young crowd

Pride Restbar Alfonso Reyes 281 (Col. Condessa) **52–55/5516-2368**

Tom's Leather Bar Av Insurgentes 357 (Col. Condesa) **55–84/5564-0728** • 9pm-4am, clsd Mon

Mexico City

CITY INFO:
Mexican Tourism 800-446-3942, web: www.visitmexico.com.

ATTRACTIONS:
Frida Kahlo House.
Metropolitan Cathedral.
Diego Rivera Web Museum, web: www.diegorivera.com.
Museo Dolores Olmedo (largest collection of Kahlo's works) 52–55/5555-0891, web: www.museodoloresolmedo.org.mx.
Museum of Anthropology 52–55/4040-5300, web: www.mna.inah.gob.mx.
Museum of the Palace of Fine Arts 800/904-4000, web: www.bellasartes.gob.mx.
Shrine to Our Lady of Guadalupe.
Teotihuacan Pyramids.

WEATHER:
Temperate and dry most of the year, with most of the annual rainfall coming in May-Oct. When the smog gets unbearable, head for a museum or other indoor activity.

TRANSIT:
Official Radio Taxis 52–55/1495-3545, web: www.taxi-mexico.com.
Don't hail a taxi on the street. It costs more to call an official taxi, but it's worth it.
Mexico City Metrobus. Hop on hop off bus 800/702-8000, web: www.turibus.com.mx.

Viena Bar República de Cuba 3 (Centro Historico) 52–55/5512–0929 • 11am-11pm, clsd Mon-Tue • mostly gay men • beer & tequila only

NIGHTCLUBS

Butterflies Calle Izazaga 9 (at Av Lazaro Cárdenas S, Centro Historico) 52–55/5761–1861 • 9pm-3am, till 4:30am Fri-Sat, clsd Mon • popular • lesbians/ gay men • dancing/DJ • 2 flrs • lavish drag shows Fri-Sat • cover charge

Cabaré-Tito Fusion Londres 77 (Zona Rosa) 52–55/5511–1613 • open 4pm, clsd Mon-Tue • lesbians/ gay men • more women Th • 18+

Cabaré-Tito Neón Calle Londres 161, Local 20-A, Plaza del Angel (Zona Rosa) 52–55/5514–9455 • 6pm-close • mostly gay men • dancing/DJ • go-go dancers

Club 24 Santa María La Ribera # 24 Del Cuauhtémoc 52–55/2198–2580 • 9am-4am Fri-Sat only • mostly gay men • dancing/DJ

Envy Av Las Palmas 500 (Sierra Gamon) • gay/ straight • dancing/DJ

Hibrido Calle Londres 161, Plaza del Angel, 2nd flr (Zona Rosa) 52–55/5511–1197 • Th-Sun • lesbians/ gay men • dancing/DJ • strippers

Liverpool 100 Liverpool 100 (Col. Juarez) 52–55/5208–4507 • 9pm-close Wed, Fri-Sat only • mostly gay men • dancing/DJ

Living Bucareli 144 (Col. Juarez) 55–55/5512–7281 • 10pm-close Fri-Sat only • popular • mostly men • popular • theme nights

CAFES

B Gay B Proud Amberes 12-B (Zona Rosa) • food served

RESTAURANTS

12:30 Amberes 13 (Zona Rosa) 52–55/5514–5971 • popular before-clubbing hangout

La Antigua Cortesana Chiapas 173-A (Col. Roma) 52–55/5584–4678 • 1pm-11pm, till midnight Fri-Sat, till 7pm Sun • popular Mexican cuisine • also bar

Cafe 22 Montes de Oca 22 (Col. Condesa) 52–55/5212–1533 • 6pm-2am • Mexican & Italian • also shows

El Cardenal Calle de Palma 23 52–55/5521–8815 • incredible pastries

Casa Merlos Victoriano Zepeda 80 (at Obsevatoria) 52–55/5277–4360 • traditional poblano food • definitely try the molé

Cote Sud Orizaba 87 (Col. Roma) 52–55/5219–2981 • 8am-11pm, till midnight Fri, 10am-6pm Sun • French/ tapas

Fonda San Ángel Plaza San Jacinto 3, Col. San Ángel (across from Bazar San Ángel) 52–55/5550–1641 & 1942 • popular after 7pm Fri-Sat • classic Mexican dishes

Ligaya Nuevo Leon 68 (in Condesa) 52–55/5286–6268 • nouvelle Mexican • dinner nightly • outdoor seating

La Nueva Opera Ave Cinco de Mayo 10 (Centro Historico) 52–55/5512–8959 • 1pm-midnight, clsd Sun • legendary cantina since Pancho Villa fired a bullet into the ceiling

Sanborns Madera 4 (in Casa de los Azulejos) 52–55/5518–6676 • brkfst, lunch & dinner • superstore

Xel-Ha 52–55/5553–5968 • traditional cuisine of the Yucatan

ENTERTAINMENT & RECREATION

El Hábito Madrid 13 (Coyacán District) 52–55/5659–1139 • avant-garde theater & bar

Museo de Arte Carrillo Gil Av Revolución 1608 (Col San Angel) 52–55/5550–6260, 52–55/5550–3983 • 10am-6pm, clsd Mon • contemporary art

Museo de Frida Kahlo Calle Londres 247 (Coyacán) 52–55/5554–5999 • 10am-5:45pm, clsd Mon • original paintings, furniture, letters & Frida's dresses • also garden & café

Museo Templo Mayor Calle Seminario 8 (at República de Guatemala, enter on plaza, near Cathedral) 52–55/4040–5600 • 9am-5pm, clsd Mon • artifacts from the central Aztec temple at Tenochtitlán

BOOKSTORES

El Armario Abierto Agustín Melgar 25 (Col. Condesa) 52–55/5286–0895 • Mexico's only bookstore specializing in sexuality • some LGBT titles

Voces en Tinta Niza 23A (A Entre Reforma y Hamburgo) 52–55/5533–7116 • 10am-9pm • lesbian bookstore & cafe

RETAIL SHOPS

Rainbowland Estrasburgo 31 (Zona Rosa) 52–55/5525–9066

PUBLICATIONS

LeS VOZ Magazine • "The magazine of Mexico's lesbian feminist culture, by & for women"

Ser Gay 52–55/1450–9511 • quarterly magazine • covers all Mexico nightlife

Monterrey

ACCOMMODATIONS

Holiday Inn Monterrey Centro Av Padre Mier 194 N (at Garibaldi, Centro) 52-81/8228-6000 • gay-friendly • near Zona Rosa • pool • also restaurant

BARS

Akbal Abasolo 870B, 2nd flr, Casa del Maíz 52-81/1257-2986 • 9pm-2am, clsd Mon • gay/ straight • more gay Sun

Casa de Lola 52-81/8343-6210 • Th-Sat only • mostly gay men • dancing/DJ • karaoke

NIGHTCLUBS

Baby Shower Ocampo 433 Puente (btwn Rayon & Aldama Centro) 52-81/8881-5632 • 9pm-close, clsd Mon-Tue • lesbians/ gay men • dancing/DJ • strippers • videos

Bizù Disco 1355 Miguel Hidalgo y Costilla 52-81/8994-4676

Parking Allende 120 Ote (btwn Juarez & Guerrero) 52-81/8343-2624 • 10pm-close Wed-Sat • mostly gay men • dancing/DJ

Vongole & Between Bar 2121 Eugenio Garza Sada Ave 52-81/8358-7035

Morelia

ACCOMMODATIONS

Casa Camelinas B&B Jacarandas 172 (Col. Nueva Jacarandas) 52-433/324-5194, 707/942-4822 (US#) • gay-friendly • mostly women • 3 1/2 hours from Mexico City • nonsmoking • also Spanish classes

Hotel de la Soledad Ignacio Zaragoza 90 52-443/312-1888 • gay-friendly • in charming old hotel in converted convent • also restaurant & bar

NIGHTCLUBS

Con la Rojas Calle Aldama 343 (Centro) 52-443/312-1578 • 10pm-2:30am, clsd Sun-Tue • mostly gay men • dancing/DJ • cover charge

Mamá no lo sabe Aldama 116 (at García Obeso) 52-44/3189-9447 • 10pm-3am • mostly gay men • karaoke

RESTAURANTS

Fonda Las Mercedes Calle Leon Guzmán 47 52-443/312-6113 & 313-3222 • popular • inside beautiful colonial home

Oaxaca

ACCOMMODATIONS

Casa Adobe B&B Independencia 801 (at Matamoros), Tlalixtac de Cabrera 52-951/517-7268 • gay/ straight • 15 minutes from center of Oaxaca • WiFi • gay-owned

Casa Colonial Calle Miguel Negrete 105 (Division Poniente) 52-951/516-5280 • gay-friendly • WiFi • kids/pets ok • wheelchair access

La Casa de Don Pablo Hostel Melchor Ocampo 412, Centro (at Rayon St) 52-951/516-8384 • gay/ straight • nonsmoking

Casa Machaya Oaxaca B&B Sierra Nevada 164, Col. Loma Linda 52/951-1328203 • gay-friendly • kids ok • private level w/ patio & valley views

Casa Sol Zipolite 6 Arco Iris, Col. Arroyo Tres 52-95/8100-0462 • mostly gay men • pool • WiFi • gay-owned • 300 meters from famous Playa Zipolite

Posada Arigalan 52-958/111-5801, 956/280-2165 (US) • gay/ straight • perched above the Pacific Ocean • women-run

NIGHTCLUBS

Club Privado 502 (aka El Número) Calle Porfirio Díaz 502 (Centro, ring to enter) • 10pm-close, clsd Sun-Tue • gay/ straight • dancing/DJ • cover charge

Elefante 20 de Noviembre 52-951/164-8637

Gavana Dance Club Calzada Porfirio Diaz #216 (Col. Reforma) • 9pm-close Th-Sat • gay/ straight

CAFES

B Proud Morelos 1107-A • open 9am & 4pm Sun • WiFi

RESTAURANTS

El Asador Vasco Portal de Flores 10-A (Centro) 52-951/514-4755 • popular • great views • authentic Oaxacan cuisine (can you say ¡mole!)

Casa Crespo Allende 107 52-951/516-0918 • lunch & dinner, also cooking classes

Playa del Carmen

see also Cancún & Cozumel

ACCOMMODATIONS

Acanto Boutique Hotel 16th St N (btwn 5th Ave & the beach) 631/882-1986 • gay-friendly • pool • nonsmoking • full brkfst based on package

Aventura Mexicana Hotel Av 10 (at Calle 24) **52–984/873–1876, 800/455–3417** • gay-friendly • pool • also restaurant & bar

Hotel Copa Cabana 5ta Av Norte **52–984/873–0218** • gay-friendly • WiFi • wheelchair access

Luna Blue Hotel & Bar Calle 26 (at 5th Av) 415/839–8541

Reina Roja Hotel 22 Street (btwn 5th & 10th Ave) **52–984/877–3800** • gay/ straight • pool • WiFi • pets ok

NIGHTCLUBS

Playa 69 Av 5 (btwn Calle 4 & Calle 6, ground flr) • 9pm-4am wknds • mostly gay men • dancing/DJ • gay-owned

Playa Palms 1st Avenue Bis (btwn 12 & 14th N St) **52–984/803–3908, 888/676–4431** • gay/ straight • directly in front of a pristine, white sandy beach in downtown Playa del Carmen • pool

RESTAURANTS

100% Natural Av 5 (btwn 10th & 12th) **52–984/73–2242** • vegetarian

Puebla

BARS

La Cigarra Ave 5 Poniente 538 (at Calle 7, Centro) **52–222/246–6356** • 6pm-3am • mostly gay men • beer bar • videos

Franco's Bule Bar 5 Oriente 402 (Los Sapos) **52–222/232–3409** • 10pm-3am, till 6am Th-Sat, clsd Mon-Tue • mostly gay men • live shows • drag shows • strippers

Mono Avenia Juarez 2505 (Colonia La Paz) • gay/straight • small bar in front, dance club in back • food served

NIGHTCLUBS

Cabaré-Tito VIP Av Juarez 2309 Local B (Colonia La Paz), Mexico City • 9pm-close wknds only • lesbians/ gay men • theme nights • dancing/DJ • go-go dancers • drag shows

Garotos 22 Orient E 602 (close to Blvd 5 de Mayo, Xenenetla) **52–222/242–4232** • 9pm-3am Fri-Sat only • gay-friendly • dancing/DJ • cover charge

Puerto Vallarta

INFO LINES & SERVICES

Community Center GLBT SETAC 427 Constitucion (at Manuel M Diéguez) **52–322/224–1974** • AA meetings, movie nights, HIV testing & Spanish classes

ACCOMMODATIONS

Blue Chairs Beach Resort **52–322/222–5040, 888/302–3662** • lesbians/ gay men • pool & beach • WiFi • wheelchair access

Boana Torre Malibu Condo Hotel Calle Amapas 325 **52–322/222–0999, 52–322/222–6695** • gay/ straight • food served • pool • poolside bar • gay-owned

Casa Andrea Calle Francisca Rodriguez 174 **52–322/222–1213** • gay/ straight • WiFi

Casa Cúpula Callejon de la Igualdad 129, Col. Amapas **52–322/223–2484, 866/352–2511** • lesbians/ gay men • swimming • nonsmoking • WiFi • wheelchair access • gay-owned

Casa de las Flores Calle Santa Barbara #359 503 /314-444(US), 52–3222/120–5242 • condos overlooking Los Muertos Beach • gay-owned

Casa Fantasía Pinot Suarez 203, Col. Emiliano Zapata (near the Rio Cuale) **52–322/223–2444** • gay/ straight • B&B made up of 3 traditional haciendas • full brkfst • terrace • pool • nonsmoking • wheelchair access • gay-owned

Los Cuatro Vientos Matamoros 520 **52–322/222–0161** • gay-friendly • El Nido rooftop bar & restaurant • annual Women's Getaway • pool • WiFi

Hotel Emperador Amapas 114 **52–322/222–1767 , 800/523–1158** • gay/ straight • located right on "Los muertos" beach • WiFi

Hotel Mercurio **52–322/222–4793, 866/388–2689** • popular • lesbians/ gay men • 1 1/2 blocks from beach • pool • WiFi • gay-owned

The San Franciscan Resort & Gym Calle Pilitas #213 (at Playa Los Muertos) **52–322/222–6473 x0** • gay/ straight • pool • WiFi

Villa Safari Condo Francisca Rodriguez 203 269/469–0468 (US #) • gay/ straight • condos • nonsmoking • gay-owned

BARS

Los Amigos Bar Calle Venustiano Carranza 237 (upstairs, next to Paco's Ranch) **52–322/222–7802** • 6pm-4am • lesbians/ gay men • Mexican cantina • patio

Apaches Olas Altas 439 (at Rodriguez) **52–322/222–4004** • 5pm-2am, till 1am Sun-Mon • gay/ straight • classy martini bar • tapas • great outdoor seating area • lesbian-owned

Frida 301-A Insurgentes (at Venustiano Carranza) **52-322/222-3668** • 1pm-2am, from 7pm Mon-Tue • gay/ straight • Mexican cantina • bears • more gay later in evening • food served • gay-owned

Garbo Pulpito 142 (at Olas Altas) **52-322/223-5753** • 6pm-2am • gay/ straight • upscale martini lounge • live music • gay-owned • 18+

La Noche Lázaro Cárdenas 257 (Zona Romantica) **52-322/222-3364** • 7pm-2am • lesbians/ gay men

The Palm/ Viva Olas Altas 508 (at Rodolfo Gomez) **52-322/223-4818** • 4pm-4am • mostly gay men • dancing/DJ • cabaret

Reinas Lazaro Cardenas 361 **52-322/125-9532** • 5pm-2am • mostly gay men • neighborhood bar

Sama Olas Altas 510 (at Rodolfo Gomez) **52-322/223-3182** • 4:30pm-2am • lesbians/ gay men • small martini bar w/ sidewalk seating

NIGHTCLUBS

CC Slaughter's Lazaro Cardenas 254 Emiliano (Zapata) **52-322/222-3412** • bar and disco

Club Mañana Venustiano Carranza #290 (at Col Emiliano Zapata) • 10pm-6am, clsd Sun-Tue • mostly gay men • dancing/DJ

No Borders 221 Libertad **52-322/136-8775** • 1pm-2am • lesbians/ gay men • neighborhood bar • rooftop patio

Paco's Ranch 237 Ignacio Vallarta **52-322/222-1899** • 10pm-6am • popular • lesbians/ gay men • dancing/DJ • also rooftop terrace • drag shows • cover charge • gay-owned

CAFES

A Page in the Sun 179 Plaza Lázaro Cárdenas (in Zona Romantica) **52-322/222-3608** • 7am-11pm coffee shop & English bookstore

Cafe San Angel Olas Altas 449 (at Francisco Rodriguez) **52-322/223-1273** • 7am-1am • sidewalk cafe

The Coffee Cup Rodolfo Gómez 146-A (at Olas Altas) **52-322/222-8584** • 7am-10pm, clsd Sun in summer • gay-owned

Uncommon Grounds Buddha Lounge Lazaro Cardenas 625 **52-322/223-3834** • 5pm-close, clsd Mon-Tue • also aromatherapy & gifts

Xocodiva Rodolfo Gomez 118 **52-322/113-0352** • artisinal chocolate • women-owned

RESTAURANTS

El Arrayan Allende #344 (at El Centro) **52-322/222-7195** • 6pm-11pm, clsd Tue • lesbian-owned

The Blue Shrimp Olas Altas 366 (Zona Romantica) **52-322/222-4246** • 11am-midnight

El Brujo Venustiano Carranza 510 (at Naranjo) **52-322/223-3026** • 1pm-9:30pm, clsd Mon • Mexican/ seafood • worth the wait

Cafe Bohemio Rodolfo Gómez 127 (at Olas Altas) **44-322/134-2436** • 5pm-2am, clsd Sun • lesbians/ gay men • open-air cafe • late-evening happy hour • gay-owned

Cafe de Olla Calle Basilio Badillo 168 **52-322/223-1626** • 10am-11pm, clsd Tue • popular • Mexican • wait list an hour

Cafe des Artistes Calle Guadalupe Sánchez 740 (at Leona Vicario) **52-322/222-3228** • 6pm-11:30pm • popular • upscale French w/ a Mexican twist • reservations required

Chez Elena Matamoros 520, Centro (at Los Quatro Vientos Hotel) **52-322/222-0161** • 6pm-11pm • seasonal • garden restaurant • also rooftop bar • woman-owned

Daiquiri Dick's Olas Altas 314 (on Playa Los Muertos) **310/697-3799** • 8:30am-1:30pm & 5:30pm-11pm, clsd Tue & clsd Sept

El Dorado Pulpito 102, Playa de los Muertos **52-322/222-4124** • beach club & restaurant • evening shows

Le Bistro Jazz Cafe Isla Rio Cuale 16-A (on the island, at the East Bridge) **52-322/222-0283** • 9am-midnight, clsd Sun • gay-owned

Lido Beach Club Malecon 1 Esq Abedul Col Emiliano Zapata **813/855-0190** • 10am-6pm

Memo's Casa de los Hotcakes Calle Basilio Badillo 289 **52-322/222-6272** • 8am-2pm • popular • long lines for cheap & good brkfst • indoor patio

Mezzogiorno Ristorante Italiano Avenida del Pacifico 33 (North Beach Bucerias Nayarit) **52-329/298-0350** • 6pm-11pm (clsd Mon off-season)

El Mole de Jovita 220B Basillo Badillo • 3pm-10pm, clsd Sun, authentic mole

La Palapa Pulpito 103, Col Emiliano Zapata **52-322/222-5225** • brkfst, lunch & dinner, beachside dining

La Piazzetta Rodolfo Gomez #143 (at Olas Atlas, Romantic Zone) 52–322/222–0650 • 4pm-11pm • Italian

Planeta Vegetariano Iturbide 270 (Centro) 52–322/222–3073 • 8am-10pm, clsd Sun • buffet-style

Red Cabbage Calle Rivera del Rio 204-A (at Basilio Badillo) 52–322/223–0411 • 5pm-11pm • on Rio Cuale w/ great kitschy decor • lesbian-owned

The Swedes/ Crows Nest Bar Púlpito 154 (at Olas Altas) 52–322/223–2353 • 4pm-2am • lesbians/ gay men • Swedish/ European • bar upstairs • gay-owned

Trio Guerrero 264 (Centro) 52–322/222–2196 • 6pm-midnight, clsd Sun • patio • live music • reservations advised

ENTERTAINMENT & RECREATION

Boana Tours Calle Amapas 325 (at Casa Boana Torre Malibu) 52–322/222–0099, 52–322/222–6695 • horseback tours daily

Diana's Cruise the Bay Tour meet at Los Muertos pier • 9:30am-5pm Th • lesbians/ gay men • cruise on 33-ft trimaran • food served • open bar

Ladies Outdoor Club Adventures 52–322/223–9538 • walking tours and day trips • lesbian-owned

Ocean Friendly Paseo del Marlin 510-103, Col. Aralias 52–322/225–3774, 044–322/294–0385 (CELL) • whale-watching tours • Dec 15-March 31

Playa Los Muertos/ Playa del Sol S of Rio Cuale • popular • the gay beach • now spans "Blue Chairs" & "Green Chairs"

PUBLICATIONS

Gay PV 52–322/113–0224 • great gay magazine for PV

Urbana Revista 52–333/844–6471 • gay lifestyle magazine

GYMS & HEALTH CLUBS

Acqua Day Spa & Gym Calle Constitución 450 (F Rodriguez) 52–322/223–5270 • 7am-9pm, till 5pm Sat, clsd Sun • spa services • also small gym

Total Fitness Gym Calle Timon 1 (Marina Vallarta) 52–322/221–0770 • 6:30am-9:30pm, Sat 8am-2pm, clsd Sun • women only • wide variety of classes

EROTICA

The Closet Lazaro Cardenas 230 52–322/223–3030 • noon-9pm

Querétaro

NIGHTCLUBS

Con la Rojas Ave Constituyentes Pte 42A (Centro) 52–442/212–4795 • 10pm-2:30am, clsd Sun-Wed • mostly gay men • dancing/DJ • cover charge

San Jose del Cabo

ACCOMMODATIONS

El Encanto Inn 210/858-6649, 52–614/142–0388 • gay-friendly • spa & restaurant • swimming

One & Only Palmilla Apartado Postal 52, 23400 52–624/146–7000, 866/829–2977 (US#) • gay-friendly • upscale resort w/ golf course • swimming

RESTAURANTS

Voila Bistro & Catering 1705 Comonfort (Plaza Paulina) 52–624/130–7569 • noon-10pm, from 4pm Sun • popular • Mexican w/ French twist • full bar • patio

San Miguel de Allende

ACCOMMODATIONS

Casa de Sierra Nevada Calle Hospicio 35 (Centro) 52–415/152–7040, 800/701–1561 (US#) • gay-friendly • horseback riding • also spa • swimming • patios

Casa Schuck Boutique B&B Garita 3, Centro 52–415/152–6618, 937/684–4092 • gay-friendly • boutique hotel • full brkfst • pool • WiFi

Dos Casas Calle Quebrada 101 (Guanajuato) 52–415/154–4073 • gay-friendly • full brkfst

Las Terrazas San Miguel Santo Domingo 3 52–415/152–5028, 707/534–1833 (US#) • gay/ straight • 4 rental homes • nonsmoking • WiFi • gay-owned

RESTAURANTS

La Azotea Umaran 6 52–415/152–4977 • delicious tapas & drinks

Mezzanine Bistro Cuna de Allende 11 (at Hotel Vista Hermosa) 52–415/152–2799 • lunch & dinner, clsd Sun • gay-owned

Tijuana

BARS

Gay Bar Endless Summer Km 29.5 Carretera Libre Ensenada-Tijuana, Rosarito 52/611–006–832 • 10:30am-2am, 5pm-5am Fri-Sat, 2pm-2am Sun, clsd Mon • mostly gay men

Luna Sol Lounge Av Pacifico 640, Playas de Tijuana 52-664/609-4977 • 2pm-midnight • gay/ straight • beach bar • gay-owned

NIGHTCLUBS

Club Fusion Calle Larroque 213 52-664/345-8817 • 8pm-3am Fri-Sun • mostly gay men • dancing/DJ • karaoke • drag shows

Extasis Larroque 213 (in Plaza Viva Tijuana, next to the border) 52-664/682-8339 • 8pm-late, clsd Mon-Wed • popular • mostly gay men • women's night Th • dancing/DJ • strippers • cover charge

Mike's Disco Av Revolución 1220 (at Calle 6A) 52-664/685-3534 • 8pm-5am, till 3am Th, clsd Wed • lesbians/ gay men • dancing/DJ • drag shows • videos

Sin Tabu Av Sanchez Taboada 10291-7 52-664/681-8138 • gay/ straight

Terraza 9 Calle 5a (at Av Revolución) 52-664/685-3534 • 5pm-2am, till 5am Fri-Sat, clsd Mon • gay-friendly • dancing/DJ

CAFES

D'Luna Cafe Calle 8 #8380 52-664/321-9735

Todos Santos

ACCOMMODATIONS

The Todos Santos Inn Calle Legaspi #33 (Topete) 52-612/145-0040 • gay/ straight • in historic district • pool • nonsmoking • also bar • gay-owned

Tulúm

ACCOMMODATIONS

Adonis Tulum Riviera Maya Gay Resort & Spa Carretera Tulum Boca Paila Km 3.8 800/233-5162, 52-984/871-1000 • mostly gay men • pool

Casa de las Olas 10.6km Tulum Beach Rd 52-984/807-3909 • gay-friendly • WiFi • sustaianable beach villa, very secluded that has 5 beautiful ocean front suites

EcoTulum Resorts & Spa Carretera Tulum Ruinas Km 5 54-115/5918-6400, 877/301-4666 • gay-friendly • WiFi

Om Tulum Caraterra Ruinas Punta -Allen Km 9.5 521-98/4114-0538 • gay-friendly • WiFi

Posada Luna del Sur Calle Luna Sur 5 52-984/871-2984 • gay-friendly

Veracruz

ACCOMMODATIONS

Hotel Villa del Mar Blvd Miguel Ávila Camacho 2431 (across street from Playa del Mar beach) 52-229/989-6500 • gay-friendly • hotel w/ separate motel & bungalows • near aquarium

ENTERTAINMENT & RECREATION

San Juan de Ulua Fortress • 9am-4:30pm, clsd Mon • impressive early colonial-era floating fortress

Veracruz Aquarium Blvd Avila Camacho (at Xicolencat) 52-229/932-7984 • 10am-7pm • one of the largest & best in the world • don't miss it!

Zacatecas

ACCOMMODATIONS

Quinta Real Zacatecas Av Ignacio Rayón 434 (Col. Centro) 52-492/1105-1010, 866/621-9288 • gay-friendly • 5-star hotel built into grandstand of bullfighting ring

Zihuatanejo

ACCOMMODATIONS

Hotel Las Palmas Calle de Aeropuerto (at lot 5) 52-755/557-0634, 888/527-7256 • gay-friendly • full brkfst • pool

NIGHTCLUBS

Mydori Disco Bar Calle La Laja s/n (Col. Centro) 52-755/104-5670 • 8pm-4am • lesbians/ gay men • dancing/DJ • drag shows

Tequila Town Cuauhtemoc 3 (Col Centro) 52-755/553-8587 • 8pm-4am • gay-friendly • more gay after 11pm • karaoke • videos

COSTA RICA

Alajuela

BARS

Rick's Bar & Restaurant 500 mts Este Casino Fiesta, carretera Heredia, en Río Segundo de Alajuela 506-2/441-3213 • 6pm-close, from 4pm Sun • lesbians/ gay men

Chirripó Nat'l Park

ACCOMMODATIONS

Monte Azul Contiguo al puente de Chucuyo, Chirimol 506/2742-5222 • gay/ straight • boutique resort, nature preserve & artist colony, less than 2 hrs from Manuel Antonio • restaurant on-site • gay-owned

Dominical

ACCOMMODATIONS

Paradise Costa Rica Escaleras (at San Martin Sur) 800/708-4552 • gay/ straight • vacation villas • lap size pools • nonsmoking • gay-owned

Guanacaste

ACCOMMODATIONS

Villa Decary Nuevo Arenal, 5717 Tilaran 506-2/694-4330, 800/556-0505 (FROM US & CANADA) • gay-friendly • former coffee farm overlooking Lake Arenal • gay-owned

Malpais

ACCOMMODATIONS

Kelea Surf Spa 949/492-7263 • women-only • surf spa

Manuel Antonio, Quepos

ACCOMMODATIONS

Casa Antonio Enter at Arboleda Hotel 506/8639-1085 • lesbians/ gay men • luxury rental house in the jungle • nonsmoking • gay-owned

Casa de Frutas 506-8/825-3257 (CELL), 800/936-9622 • gay/ straight • luxury villa in Tulemar Gardens

Casa Mono Titi in the hills 800/282-3680 • gay-friendly • vacation home • pool • near beaches & bars • kids ok • nonsmoking • WiFi • gay-owned

Casa Romano 404/290-6919 • gay/ straight • pool • near gay beach • WiFi • wheelchair access • gay-owned

Casitas Eclipse KM 5 Manuel Antonio Rd 506-2/777-0408 • gay/ straight • detached casitas

Costa Verde 506-2/777-0584, 866/854-7958 (FROM US & CANADA) • gay/ straight • bungalows, studios & apts • pool • gay-owned

Gaia Hotel & Reserve km 2.7 Carretera Quepos a Manuel Antonio 506-2/777-9797, 800/226-2515 • gay-friendly • boutique hotel • surrounded by wildlife refuge • full brkfst • pool • WiFi • gay-owned

Hotel Parador 506-2/777-1414, 877/506-1414 • gay-friendly • large luxury resort • swimming • also gourmet restaurant • WiFi

Hotel Villa Roca 506-2/777-1349 • mostly gay men • great ocean views • near beaches • pool • nonsmoking • gay-owned

La Mansion Inn 506-2/777-3489, 800/360-2071 • gay/ straight • luxury hotel • pool • also restaurant • bar • ocean views • gay-owned

La Posada 506-2/777-1446 • gay-friendly • 4 bungalows & 2 guest rooms • pool • full brkfst • gay-owned

Si Como No 506-2/777-0777, 888/742-6667 • gay-friendly • 25-acre wildlife refuge • also spa • pool • wheelchair access

BARS

Tutu/ Gato Negro KM 5 Manuel Antonio Rd (at Casitas Eclipse) 506-2/777-0408 • 4pm-close • popular • gay/ straight • also restaurant • great view

NIGHTCLUBS

Liquid Lounge 506-2/777-5158 • 9pm-3am Tue & Th-Sun • mostly men • dancing/DJ • drag shows

RESTAURANTS

El Barba Roja Carretera al Parque Nacional 506-2/777-0331 • 7am-10pm, from 4pm Mon • American • popular • great sunset location

El Gran Escape & Fish Head Bar Quepos Centro 506-2/777-0395 • brkfst, lunch, dinner, clsd Tue • seafood • full bar

La Hacienda Restaurante Plaza Yara 506-2/777-3473 • 10:30am-10:30pm • live shows

Rico Tico in Hotel Si Como No • brkfst, lunch & dinner • Tex/ Mex • includes use of pool bar • popular • live shows • also Claro Que Sí (seafood restaurant)

Osa Peninsula

ACCOMMODATIONS

Blue Osa Yoga Sanctuary & Spa 506/8704-7006 • gay/ straight • all meals included • kids/ ok • nonsmoking • WiFi • gay-owned

Pavones

ACCOMMODATIONS

Casa Siempre Domingo B & B 506/2776-2185 • gay/ straight • pool • WiFi • lesbian-owned

Playa Sámara

ACCOMMODATIONS

Casitas LazDívaz B&B 506/2656-0295 • gay-friendly • full brkfst • beachfront • wheelchair access • lesbian diva-owned

Puerto Viejo

ACCOMMODATIONS

Banana Azul 200 meters N of Perla Negra Hotel **506–2/750–2035, 506–2/351–4582 (CELL)** • mostly men • full brkfst • nonsmoking • WiFi • gay-owned

RESTAURANTS

Koki Beach Restaurant Bar & Lounge Main St (town center across from water) **506/8305–0747** • 5pm-11pm, clsd Mon • Latin fusion cuisine • WiFi

Puntarenas

ACCOMMODATIONS

Villa Caletas Garabito **506/2630–3000** • gay/ straight • restaurant on site • pool • a luxury boutique hotel, 1 hour from San Jose airport

San José

ACCOMMODATIONS

Colours Oasis Resort El Triangulo Noroeste, Blvd Rohrmoser (200 meters before end of blvd) **506–2/296–1880, 866/517–4390 (US & CANADA)** • lesbians/ gay men • pool • also bar & restaurant • WiFi • gay-owned

Hotel El Mirador Bello Horizonte, Escazú **506/2289–3981** • mostly men • swimming • conveniently located in Escazú, a suburb of San José

Hotel Kekoldi Av 9 (btwn Calles 5 & 7, Barrio Amón) **506–2/248–0804, 786/221–9011 (FROM US)** • gay/ straight • in art deco bldg in downtown • secluded garden • WiFi • gay-owned

Secret Garden B&B 506–2/290–3890 • gay/ straight • in historic Rohrmoser district • WiFi • gay-owned

BARS

Bar Al Despiste in front of Mudanzas Mundiales (W of Universal Zapote) **506–2/234–5956** • 6pm-2am, 5pm-10pm Sun, clsd Mon • gay/ straight • theme nights • karaoke

Buenas Vibraciones Ave 14 (btw Calle 7 & 9, in Paseo de los Estudiantes) **506–2/223–4573** • lesbians/ gay men • lesbian-owned

Casa Vieja 400 metros al este de la capilla religiosa de Montserrat, Alajuela **506/2440–8525** • 6pm-2am, noon-midnight Sun • lesbians/ gay men • food served

Zona Rosa 250m norte del Correo Central • lesbians/ gay men • dancing/DJ • karaoke

NIGHTCLUBS

La Avispa 834 Calle 1 (pink house btwn Avs 8 & 10) **506–2/223–5343** • 8pm-2am, popular T-dance from 5pm Sun, clsd Mon-Wed • lesbians/ gay men • women's night 2nd & 4th Fri • dancing/DJ

Azotea Uruca, de Capris 300 Norte (Plaza Rohrmoser) **506–2/220–2506** • gay/ straight • dancing/DJ

El Bochinche Calle 11 (btwn Avs 10 & 12, Paseo de los Etudiantes), San Pedro **506–2/221–0500** • 7pm-2am, till 5pm Fri-Sat, clsd Sun-Tue • also full restaurant • Mexican • dancing/DJ after 10pm • videos

Club Energy Paseo Colon (near 30th, by Pizza Hut) **506/2223–7594** • from 7:30pm Th-Sun • lesbians/ gay men • dancing/DJ • also restaurant

Club Oh! Calle 2 (btwn Avs 14 & 16) **506–22/221–9341** • 9pm-close Fri-Sat • gay/ straight • dancing/DJ • take taxi to avoid bad area

Club Oh Calle 2 (btwn Ave 14 & 16) **506–2/221–9341** • 9pm-2am Fri-Sat • mostly gay men • dancing/DJ

Puchos Calle 11 & Av 8 (knock to enter) **506–2/256–1147, 506–2/222–7967** • 8pm-2:30am, clsd Sun • mostly gay men • strippers

RESTAURANTS

Ankara San José de la Montaña (Heredia, San Antonio de Belén, S of church) **50/8326 6646** • clsd Mon-Tue • live music

Cafe Mundo Av 9 & Calle 15 (200 meters E of parking lot for INS, Barrio Amón) **506–2/222–6190** • 11am-11pm, 5pm-midnight Sat, clsd Sun • Italian • garden seating • also cafe/ bar • gay-owned

La Cocina de Leña in El Pueblo complex **506–2/255–1360** • 11am-11pm • 5 minutes from downtown • reservations recommended

Machu Picchu Calle 32 (btwn Aves 1 & 3) **506–2/283–3679** • Peruvian

Mirador Ram Luna from center of Aserrí, go 4 kilometers on the road toward Tabarca, Aserri **506–2/230–3060** • dinner nightly, lunch & dinner wknds, clsd Mon • hillside restaurant w/ amazing views

Olio Escalante, Bario California (N of Baselman's, San Pedro/ Los Yoses) **506–2/281–0541** • lunch & dinner, clsd Sun • Spanish • also full bar

Vishnu Vegetarian Restaurant Av 1 (btwn Calles 3 & 1) 506-2/256-6063 • 8am-9:30pm

ENTERTAINMENT & RECREATION

Gay Tours Costa Rica 309-2200 Coronado 506-2/305-8044 • LGBT daily events & excursions

Mercado Central/ Central Market Central Avenida (btwn Calles 6 & 8) • bustling market selling food, clothing, souvenirs & more

San Ramon

ACCOMMODATIONS

Angel Valley Farm B&B 200m N & 300m E of Iglesia de Los Angeles (at Autopista to Arenal Volcano) 506-2/456-4084, 910/805-0149 (US#) • gay/ straight • full brkfst • kids over 5 & small pets ok • nonsmoking • WiFi • wheelchair access

Santa Clara

ACCOMMODATIONS

Tree Houses Hotel Costa Rica 506-2/475-6507 • gay/ straight • private treehouses in canopy of trees on wildlife refuge • full brkfst • nonsmoking • lesbian-owned • kids/ pets ok

Tamarindo

ACCOMMODATIONS

Cala Luna Hotel & Villas Playa Langosta (at Playa Tamarindo) 506-2/653-0214, 800/503-5202 • gay-friendly • pools • kids ok

Hotel Sueño del Mar Playa Langosta 506-2/653-0284 • gay-friendly • private hacienda on the beach • full brkfst • pool • nonsmoking • WiFi

ARGENTINA

Buenos Aires

INFO LINES & SERVICES

La Casa del Encuentro/ Lesbian Feminist Cultural Center Rivadavia 3917 54-1/4982-2550

Comunidad Homosexual Argentina Tomas Liberti 1080 54-11/4361-6382

La Fulana Callao 339, 5th fl 54-1/6548-9542

Pink Point Avenida de Mayo 1370, 10th flr (at Palacio Barolo) 54-1/4382-8227 • LGBT tourist info

ACCOMMODATIONS

1555 Malabia House Malabia 1555, Palermo Viejo (at Honduras) 54-11/4833-2410 • gay-friendly • pets ok • WiFi

The Cocker Av Juan de Garay 458 (at Defensa) 54-1/4362-8451 • WiFi • full brkfst • pets ok • gay-owned

Faena Hotel & Universe 445 Martha Salotti St 54-11/4010-9000 • gay/ straight • luxury hotel • WiFi • live shows at The Universe

Home Hotel Honduras 5860 54-11/4778-1008 • gay-friendly boutique hotel • pool • loft apts available • WiFi

Hotel Axel Venezuela 649 54-11/4136-9393 • lesbians/ gay men • luxury gay hotel • WiFi • also restaurant

Hotel Intercontinental Buenos Aires Moreno 809 888/424-6835 (US#), 54-11/4340-7100 • gay-friendly • WiFi • gym • bar • restaurants

Hotel Vitrum 5641 Gorriti 54-1/4776-5030 • gay-friendly • stylish boutique hotel

Palermo Viejo B&B Niceto Vega 4629 (at Av Scalabrini Ortiz) 54-11/4773-6012 • gay/ straight • nonsmoking • WiFi • near shopping & gay nightlife • gay-owned

Rooney's Boutique Hotel Sarmiento 1775, Piso 3 54-11/5252-5060 • gay/friendly • exceptional location & free tango classes • WiFi

Solar Soler B&B Soler 5676 (at Bonpland) 54-11/4776-3065 • gay-friendly • kids ok • nonsmoking

Telmho Hotel Boutique 1086 Defensa St (at Humberto Primo) 54-11/4116-5467 • gay-friendly • WiFi

BARS

Bach Bar Antonio Cabrera 4390 54-11/5184-0137 • 11pm-close, clsd Mon • lesbians/ gay men • live shows Th-Fri • karaoke • videos

Bar Jolie Scalabrini Ortiz 1398 • 9pm-5am Wed only • mostly women • dancing/DJ

Bulnes Class Bulnes 1250 (Palermo) 54-11/4861-7492 • from 7pm Th & 11pm Fri-Sat • lesbians/ gay men • dancing/DJ

Cero Consecuencia Cabrera 3769 • 10pm-close, clsd Mon-Tue • lesbians/ gay men

Flux Bar Marcelo T de Alvear 980 (at 9 de Julio) 54-11/5252-0258 • 7pm-close, from 8pm wknds, clsd Sun • lesbians/ gay men • dancing/DJ • art • English, Portuguese, & Russian spoken

Inside Bartolomé Mitre 1571 54-11/4372-5439 • 6pm-close • mostly men • also restaurant • live shows • older crowd

Just For Us Armenia 1744 (at Tazz restaurant) 54-1/5512-3781 • 10:30pm Th only • mostly women • dinner, drinks & dancing

KM Zero Av Santa Fe 2516 54-11/4822-7530 • 7pm-close, clsd Sun • also restaurant • lesbians/ gay men • dancing/DJ • drag shows • strippers • videos

Mundo Bizarro 1222 Serrano 54-11/4773-1967 • gay-friendly • 1950s American-style cocktail lounge • food served

Sitges Córdoba 4119 54-11/4861-3763 • 10:30pm-4am, till 6am Fri-Sat, clsd Mon-Tue • lesbians/ gay men • women go earlier

NIGHTCLUBS

Ambar La Fox Av Federico Lacroze 3455 (at Alvarez Thomas, at El Teatro) • Sat only • lesbians/ gay men • dancing/ DJ • young, alternative mixed crowd

Amerika Gascón 1040 (at Cordoba) 54-11/4865-4416 • open late • mostly gay men • dancing/DJ • cruisy

Angel's Viamonte 2168 • midnight-7am Th-Sat • lesbians/ gay men • dancing/DJ

Bahrein Lavalle 345 • 6pm-7am Wed & Fri, from 10pm Sat, from midnight Tue • gay/ straight • dancing/DJ • also restaurant

Club 69 Niceto Vega 5510 (btwn Humboldt & Fitzroy, Palermo) 54-1/4779-9396 • 11:30pm Th only • gay/ straight • dancing/DJ • drag shows • performance • over-the-top theme parties

Club Namunkura Niceto Vega 5699 (Palermo, at Club M) • 1st Fri only • lesbians/ gay men • dancing/DJ • transgender-friendly

Cocoliche Rivadavia 878 • gay/ straight • dancing/DJ

Fiesta Dorothy Alsina 940 (near Plaza de Mayo, at Palacio Alsina) 54-11/4334-0097, 54-11/4334-0098 • huge dance bi-monthly dance party • lesbians/ gay men

Fiesta Eyeliner Sarmiento 1272 (at Salon Real) • monthly queer/ alternative dance party • check www.fiestaeyelinertk for dates

Fiesta Oliver Cordoba 543 (at Sub Club) • 1am Fri only (Fri night) • lesbians/ gay men • dancing/DJ

Fiesta Plop Av Federico Lacroze 3455 (at Alvarez Thomas, at El Teatro) • Fri only • lesbians/ gay men • dancing/ DJ • young, alternative mixed crowd

Glam Cabrera 3046 54-11/4963-2521 • midnight-close wknds • mostly gay men • popular • dancing/DJ

Human Av Costanera Norte Rafael Obligado (at Av Sarmiento, at Mandalay Complex) • midnight Fri only • mostly gay men • huge dance party

Juana 775 Av 44 54-1/557-6807 • from 11:30pm Fri-Sat only • lesbians/ gay men • dancing/DJ

Pacha Av Costanera y Pampa 54-11/4788-4280 • popular dance club • gay-friendly

Rheo Marcelino Freyre S/N, Arco 17 (at Crobar) 54-1/3430-2711 • midnight Sat only • mostly gay men • dancing/DJ

Sub Club Cordoba 543 • Fri-Sat only • lesbians/ gay men • dancing/DJ

Unna Fiesta at Glam Disco • mostly women • dancing/DJ • check www.fiestaunna.com.ar for dates

CAFES

Gout Cafe Juncal 2124 54-11/4825-8330 • sandwiches, pastries • gay-owned

Pride Cafe Balcarce 869 (in San Telmo) 54-11/4300-6435 • 10am-10pm • live show Th night

Pure Vida Reconquista 516 (btwn Tucuman & Lavalle) 54-11/4393-0093 • 8:30am-7pm, 10am-5:30pm Sat, clsd Sun • juice bar • food served • plenty veggie

RESTAURANTS

Arevalito Arevalo 1478 54-11/4776-4252 • 9am-midnight • vegetarian

Bio Humbolt 2192 (Palermo Viejo) 54-11/4774-3880 • lunch & dinner • vegetarian • organic market

La Cabana Alicia Moreau de Justo 380 54-11/4314-3710 • brkfst, lunch & dinner • popular • upscale steak house

Casa Cruz 1658 Uriarte 54-11/4833-1112 • 8:30pm-3am, later Fri-Sat • upscale, trendy restaurant • also bar

Cumana Rodriguez Pena 1149 (at Arenales) 54-11/4813-9207 • popular • regional cuisine

El Palacio de la Papa Frita Lavalle 735 (at Maipu) 54-11/4393-5849 • popular • hearty traditional meals • also Av Corrientes 1612, 11/4374-8063

Filo San Martin 975 54-11/4311-0312, 54-11/4311-1871 • 8pm-close • Italian • trendy • also art gallery

Lobby Nicaragua 5944 **54–11/4770–9335** • 8am-1am, till 8pm Sun-Mon, wine bar, cafe & restaurant

Mark's Deli & Coffeehouse El Salvador 4107 (in Palermo) **54–11/4832–6244** • 11am-8pm, till 9pm Sun, clsd Mon • popular

Milion Parana 1048 **54–11/4815–9925** • popular • swank lounge/ restaurant spread over 3-flr mansion • garden

Naturaleza Sabia Balcarce 958 (at Carlos Calvo) **54–11/4300–6454** • clsd Mon • vegetarian

Rave Gorriti 5092 **54–11/4833–7832** • lunch Tue-Sun & dinner nightly • popular

Sucre Sucre 676 **54–11/4782–9082** • upscale contemporary

Verde Llama Jorge Newbery 3623 **54–11/4554–7467** • 11am-6pm, till midnight Th-Sat • organic vegetarian cafe

ENTERTAINMENT & RECREATION

Casa Brandon Luis Maria Drago 236 (at Lavalleja) **54–11/4858–0610** • LGBT events, dance parties, poetry readings, art & more • also bar/ restaurant

Espanol al Sur Pichincha 1031 #2 (at Carlos Calvo) **54–11/4942–9582, 54–11/6449–5447** • gay-friendly • Spanish language & tango classes • lesbian-owned

La Marshall Maipu 444 **54–11/4912–9043** • 8:30pm Wed • exclusively gay tango lessons

Museo Evita Peron Lafinur 2988 (in Palermo) **54–11/4807–9433** • 2pm-7:30pm, clsd Mon

Out & About Pub Crawl **54–911/3036–1361** • lesbians/ gay men • make new friends on a tour of the local gay bars

BOOKSTORES

Otras Letras Soler 4796, Palermo **54–1/2060–2942** • 2pm-8pm, from 3pm Sat, clsd Sun • LGBT books & culture

PUBLICATIONS

Actitud

G-Maps Buenos Aires Franklin 1463, Florida Oeste **54–11/4730–0729** • free pocket-size gay map of Buenos Aires

The Ronda • gay pocket guide w/ local listings • www.theronda.com.ar

BRAZIL

Rio de Janeiro

Note: M°=Metro station

INFO LINES & SERVICES

Grupo Arco-Iris Rio de Janeiro Rua do Senado 230 **55–21/2222–7286** • 1pm-7pm, till 11pm Sat, clsd Sun • LGBT community center

Rainbow Kiosk/ Quiosque Atlantic Av (in front of Copacabana Palace Hotel) **55–21/2275–1641** • popular • 24hrs • lesbians/ gay men • tourist info • drag shows

ACCOMMODATIONS

Casa Cool Beans Rua Laurinda Santos Lobo 136 **55–21/2262–0552** • gay/ straight • pool • WiFi • gay-owned

Casa Dois Gatos Rua Rosalina Terra 6, Cabo Frio **561/282–0023, 55–22/2645–5806** • mostly gay men • free transportation from Rio airport • pool • WiFi • gay-owned

Ipanema Plaza Rua Farme Amoedo (at Rua Prudente de Morais) **55–21/3687–2000** • gay/ straight • near gay beach • rooftop pool • also restaurant

MyRioCondo.com 3150 Avenida Atlantica, Apt 901 (Copacabana) **215/847–2397 (US#)** • gay/ straight • WiFi • kids ok • gay-owned

Rio Penthouse **55–21/2541–3882** • gay-friendly • beachfront apts & penthouse suites

BARS

Melt Rua Rita Ludolf 47 **55–21/2249–9309** • gay-friendly • lounge • also restaurant • live music

TV Bar Av Nossa Senhora de Copacabana 1417 **55–21/2267–1663** • 10pm-5am, 9pm-3am Sun, clsd Mon-Wed • television-themed bar • mostly men • theme nights

NIGHTCLUBS

Boite 1140 1140 Rua Capitao Menezes **55–21/7830–8867** • 11pm-5am Th-Sun • lesbians/ gay men • dancing/DJ • drag shows

Casa da Matriz Rua Henrique de Novaes 107 **54–11/2226–9691, 54–11/2266–1014** • 11pm-close, clsd Tue • gay/ straight • dancing/DJ • 18+

Cine Ideal Rua da Carioca 64 **55–21/2252–3460** • gay/ straight • dancing/DJ • huge club w/ visting big-name DJs

Fosfobox Rua Siqueira Campos 143
55–21/2548–7498 • open Th-Sun • gay/
straight • underground techno

Galeria Cafe Rua Teixeira de Melo 31
(Ipanema) **55–21/2523–8250** • 10:30pm-close,
clsd Sun-Tue • gay/ straight • dancing/DJ • also
gallery

La Girl Club Rua Raul Pompeia 102
(Copacabana) **55–21/2247–8342** • 9pm-3am,
clsd Mon-Wed • popular • mostly women •
dancing/DJ • strippers • young crowd

Papa G 42 Almerinda Freitas
55–21/2450–1253 • lesbians/ gay men
• dancing/DJ • drag shows • theme nights

Up Turn 2000 Av das Americas
55–21/3387–7957 • lesbians/ gay men
• dancing/DJ • food served • outdoor seating

The Week 154 Rua Sacadura Cabral
55–21/2253–1020 • gay-friendly • dance club

CAFES

Cafeína Rua Farme de Amoedo 43
(Ipanema) **55–21/2521–2194** • 8am-11:30pm

Copa Cafe Av Atlantica 3056
55–21/2235–2947

Expresso Carioca Rua Farme de Amoedo
76 **55–21/2267–8604**

RESTAURANTS

Bar d'Hotel Av Delfim Moreira 696 (2nd flr,
inside Marina All Suites Hotel, Leblon)
55–21/2172–1112 • food served all day, bar till
late • Mediterranean • see & be seen

Boox Rua Br Torre 368 (in Ipanema)
55–21/2522–3730 • upscale restaurant &
nightclub

Cafe del Mar Av Atlantica 1910
55–21/7857–8681 • gay-friendly • upscale
lounge

Caroline Cafe 10 Rua JJ Seabra
55–21/2540–0705 • steak & burgers • full bar

Gringo Cafe Rua Barao da Torre 240
55–21/3813–3972 • American classics

Maxim's Av Atlantica 1850 **55–21/2255–7444**

Pizzaria Guanabara 1228 Ave Ataulfo de
Paiva, Leblon **55–21/2294–0797**

To Nem Ai Rua Farme de Amoedo 57
55–21/2247–8403 • lesbians/ gay men
• popular bar w/ outdoor seating

Via Sete **55–21/2512–8100** • noon-midnight
• plenty veggie

Zero Zero Av Padre Leonel Franca 240
(inside planetarium) **55–21/2540–8041** • gay/
straight • more gay Sun • dancing/DJ • upscale
restaurant & nightclub

ENTERTAINMENT & RECREATION

Copacabana Beach at Rua Rodolfo Dantas
• gay across from Copacabana Palace Hotel

Farme de Amoedo/ Farme Gay Beach
across from Rua Farme de Amoedo • see &
be seen at this popular gay beach

Ipanema Beach • gay E of Rua Farme
Amoedo

PUBLICATIONS

Rio For Partiers **55–21/2523–9857** • great
guide book

CHILE

Santiago

Note: M°=Metro station

ACCOMMODATIONS

The Aubrey Hotel Constitución 299-317,
Bellavista **56–2/940–2800** • gay-friendly • hip
boutique hotel

Casa Moro Corte Suprema 177 (at Padre
Gomez Vidaurre) **56–2/2696–9499** • lesbians/
gay men • full brkfst • gay-owned

Lastarria Hotel Coronel Santiago Bueras
188 **56–2/840–3700** • gay-friendly • luxury
boutique hotel

Le Reve Hotel Orrego Luco 023,
Providencia **56–2/757–6000, 56–2/757–6011** •
gay-friendly • luxury boutique hotel

BARS

Amor del Bueno Ernesto Pinto Lagarrigue
106 **56–2/737–2790** • 5pm-1am, till 4am Fri-
Sat • clsd Sun • mostly women • also
restaurant • lesbian-owned

Bar 105 Bombero Nuñez 105 **56–2/403–2990**
• 9pm-late Th-Sat • lesbians/ gay men

Bar de Willy Av 11 de Septiembre 2214
(Común Providencia) **56–2/381–1806** •
10pm-4am, till 5am wknds • lesbians/ gay men
• live shows

El Closet Santa Filomena 138 (at Bombero
Nuñez) • lesbians/ gay men • karaoke

Farinelli Bombero Nuñez 68 (Recoleta)
56–2/732–8966 • 5pm-2am • food served •
live shows • drag shows • strippers

Pub Friend's Bombero Nuñez 365 (at
Dominica, barrio Bellavista) **56–2/777–3979** •
9:30pm-4am, till 5am Fri-Sat • lesbians/ gay
men • drag shows

Vox Populi Ernesto Pinto Lagarrigue 364 (Bellavista) **56-2/671-1267** • 9:30pm-3am, clsd Sun-Mon • mostly gay men • also restaurant • garden patio

NIGHTCLUBS

Blondie Alameda 2879, loc 104 **56-2/681-7793** • gay/ straight • alternative • dancing/DJ • theme nights

Bokhara Discoteque Pio Nono 430 (at Constitución, barrio Bellavista) **56-2/732-1050, 56-2/735-1271** • 10pm-6am, till 7am wknds • popular • mostly gay men • dancing/DJ • food served • strippers • drag shows

Bunker Bombero Nuñez 159 (Bellavista) **56-2/738-2301, 56-2/738-2314** • 11pm-close Fri-Sat • lesbians/ gay men • dancing/DJ • food served • live shows

Club Ignorancia Ernesto Pinto Lagarrigue 282 **56-2/8216-3857**

Club Principe Pio Nono 398 **56-2/777-6381** • mostly gay men • dancing/DJ • drag shows • strippers

Nueva Cero Euclides 1204 par 2 Gran Avenida • mostly gay men • dancing/DJ • drag shows

CAFES

Tavelli Andrés de Fuenzalida 34 (Providencia) **56-2/231-5830** • 8:30am-10pm, from 9:30am Sat • popular

RESTAURANTS

Ali Baba 102 Santa Filomena (Barrio Bellavista, Recoleta) **56-2/732-7036** • Middle Eastern

Capricho Español Purisima 65 (barrio Bellavista) **56-2/777-7674** • dinner only • lesbians/ gay men • Spanish • full bar

La Pizza Nostra Av Providencia 1975 & Pedro de Valdivia **56-2/231-8941** • Italian

Santo Remedio 152 Roman Diaz, Providencia **56-2/235-0984** • 6:30pm-close, from 10:30pm wknds • global cuisine • full bar • live DJs

El Toro Loreto 33 **56-2/737-5937** • noon-midnight

EROTICA

Japi Jane Luis Thayer Ojeda 059, Oficina 11 **56-2/234-4917** • 11am-8pm, till 4pm Sat, clsd Sun • women-owned

AUSTRIA

Vienna

INFO LINES & SERVICES

Gay & Lesbian AA 43-1/799-5599, 43-665/490-5603 (ENGLISH) • call for info

Hosi Zentrum Heumuhlgasse 14 43-1/216-6604 • LGBT political organization • many groups & events • cafe • news magazine

Rosa Lila Villa Linke Wienzeile 102 (near Hofmühlgasse, U4-Pilgramgasse) 43-1/586-8150 (WOMEN), 43-1/585-4343 (MEN) • LGBT center • staffed 5pm-8pm Mon, Wed, Fri • info • gay city maps • also meeting place for various groups • also cafe-bar

ACCOMMODATIONS

Altstadt Kirchengasse 41 43-1/522-6666 • gay-friendly • located centrally in ancient artist quarter Spittelberg • WiFi

Arcotel Wimberger Neubaugürtel 34-36 (at Goldschlagstr) 43-1/521-650 • gay-friendly • restaurant & bar on premises • also fitness club

Art Hotel Brandmayergasse 7-9 43-1/544-5108 • gay-friendly • modern, art-filled hotel

Boutique Hotel Stadthalle Hackengasse 20 43-1/982-4272 • gay/ straight • eco-friendly boutique hotel

Designapartment Vienna Glockengasse 25/9 43-650/592-8941 • gay-friendly • full kitchen • terrace • WiFi • gay-owned

Gay At Home 43-1/586-1200 • lesbians/ gay men • rental apts around Vienna • gay-owned

Le Méridien Wien Opernring 13-15 43-1/588-900, 800/543-4300 • gay-friendly • pool • sauna • hot tub • also restaurant & bar

Pension Wild Lange Gasse 10 (off Lerchenfelder Str) 43-1/406-5174 • mostly gay men • rooms & apts • also restaurant • gay sauna & bar in basement • gay-owned

Das Tyrol Mariahilfer Str 15 43-1/587-5415 • gay-friendly • small luxury hotel

BARS

Cafe Cheri Franzensg 2 43-650/208-1471 • 10pm-4am • mostly gay men • also cafe

Cafe Savoy Linke Wienzeile 36 (at Köstlergasse) 43-1/581-1557 • 8am-2am • popular • lesbians/ gay men • upscale cafe-bar

Felixx Gumpendorferstr 5 43-1/920-4714 • 7pm-3am, from 10am Sat, 7pm-1am Sun • lesbians/ gay men • food • WiFi

Frauencafé Lange Gasse 11 43-1/406-3754 • 7pm-midnight, till 2am Fri-Sat (sometimes clsd Sun-Mon) • mostly women • transgender-friendly • cafe-bar

Frauenzentrum Bar Währingerstr 59 (enter on Prechtlgasse) 43-1/402-8754 • 7pm-midnight Th-Sat • women • dancing/DJ

Labris Bar Biberstrasse 12 43-1/945-6921 • 6pm-2am, till 4am wknds • mostly women

Marea Alta Gumpendorferstr 28 43-699/1159-7131 • 7pm-2am, till 4am Fri-Sat, clsd Sun-Mon • mostly women • young crowd

Merandy Lounge Mollardgasse 17 • 7pm-2am Th, 8pm-6am Fri-Sat • lesbians/ gay men • dancing/DJ

Peter's Operncafé Hartauer Riemergasse 9 (at Singer) 43-1/512-8981 • 6pm-2am, clsd Sun-Mon • gay/ straight • food served • terrace

Red Carpet Magdalenenstr 2 43-1/676-782-2966 • lesbians/ gay men • dancing/DJ • younger crowd • theme nights

Schik Schikanedergasse 5 • 7pm-2am, till 4am Fri-Sat, clsd Sun • lesbians/ gay men • WiFi

Studio 67 Gumpendorferstr 67 43-1/966-7182 • 10am-4am Th-Sat • gay/ straight • dancing/DJ • also upscale lounge

Village Bar Stiegengasse 8 (near Naschmarkt) 43-1/676-3848977 • 8pm-3am • mostly men • young crowd

Wiener Freiheit Schönbrunner Str 25 (U4-Kettenbrückengasse) 43-1/931-9111 • 8pm-midnight, till 4am Fri-Sat, clsd Sun-Mon • lesbians/gay men • transgender-friendly • 3 flrs • disco 10pm-4am Fri-Sat • also cafe

NIGHTCLUBS

BallCanCan Schwarzenberg Platz 10 (at Ost Klub) • lesbians/gay men • dancing/DJ • monthly queer Balkan club

g.spot Neubaugasse 2 (at Camera Club) 43-1/523-3063 • 9pm 1st Fri • mostly women • dancing/DJ • monthly parties • call for info

Heaven Gay Night 43-1/523-3063 • 10pm-6am Sat • mostly men • dancing/DJ • transgender-friendly • strippers • young crowd

Inside Bar Schikanedergasse 12 43-1/581-2184 • 9pm-4am, clsd Sun • mostly gay men • dancing/DJ

Las Chicas Lederergasse 11 (at Gerard) • check for dates • women only • dancing/DJ

Meat Market • queer electro dance party • check local listings

Queer Beat Landstr Hauptstr 38 (at the Viper Room) • 2nd & 4th Sat only • mostly gay men • dancing/DJ

Up! Mariahilfer Str 3 (at Lutz Club) • 2nd Fri only • mostly gay men • uplifing house music

Why Not? Tiefer Graben 22 (at Wipplinger, U-Schottentor) 43-1/925-3024 • 10pm-close Fri-Sat & before public holidays • mostly gay men • dancing/DJ • live shows • videos

CAFES

Bakul Margaretenstr 58 • 9am-2am • also guesthouse

Cafe Berg Berggasse 8 (at Wasagasse, U2-Schottentor) 43-1/319-5720 • 10am-1am • popular • lesbians/ gay men • cafe-bar

Cafe Central Herrengasse 14 (at Strauchgasse) 43-1/533-3763 • 7:30am-10pm, from 10am Sun & public holidays • "world's most famous coffeehouse"

Cafe Standard Margaretenstr 63 43-1/581-0586 • 8am-midnight, from 11am wknds

Cafe Stein Währinger Str 6-8 (near U-Schottentor) 43-1/319-7241 • 7am-1am, from 9am Sun • gay-friendly • cafe-bar • internet access • terrace

Das Möbel Burggasse 10 (Spittelberg) 43-1/524-9497 • 10am-1am • trendy • also art gallery • WiFi

Point of Sale Schleifmuhlgasse 12 43-1/941-6397 • 7am-1am • cafe & deli • also vegan items • WiFi • also bar

SMart Cafe Kostlergasse 9 43-1/585-7165 • 6pm-2am, till 4am Fri-Sat, clsd Sun-Mon • gay/ straight • S/M & fetish cafe

RESTAURANTS

Andino Münzwardeingasse 2 (U4-Pilgramgasse) 43-1/587-6125 • 11am-2am, from 10am Sat, 11am-midnight Sun • Latin American • live music • full bar

Aux Gazelles Rahlgasse 5 43-1/585-6645 • French/ Moroccan restaurant 6pm-midnight • Arabian-style lounge, cafe & deli 11am-2am • also Turkish steam baths noon-10pm

Bin Im Leo Servitengasse 14 43-1/391-7763 • 4pm-midnight, from noon wknds • beer/ wine • plenty veggie

Cafe-Restaurant Willendorf Linke Wienzeile 102 (near Hofmuhlgasse, U4-Pilgramgasse) **43–1/587–1789** • 6pm-2am, food served till midnight • lesbians/ gay men • plenty veggie • full bar • terrace

Halle Museumsquartier 1 **43–1/523–7001** • 10am-2am • modern bistro • artsy crowd

Kantine Porzellangasse 19 **43–1/319–5918** • 6pm-2am • Thai

Motto Schönbrunner Str 30 (enter on Rüdigergasse) **43–1/587–0672** • 6pm-2am, till 4am Fri-Sat • popular • trendy • also bar • patio • reservations recommended

Santo Spirito Kumpfgasse 7 **43–1/512–9998** • 6pm-11pm, bar till 2am • classical music

Schon Schön Lindengasse 53 (Ecke Andreasgasse) • lunch & dinner • fashionable restaurant • also bar • also clothing & hair salon

Sly & Arny Lothringerstrasse 22 **43–1/405–0458** • lunch Mon-Fri, dinner nightly, bar till late

Stöger Ramperstorffergasse 63 **43–1/544–7596** • 11am-midnight, clsd Sun, from 5pm Mon • Viennese

Zum Roten Elefanten Gumpendorferstrasse 3 **43–1/966–8008** • lunch & dinner, open late Fri-Sat, clsd Sun (lunch only in summer)

ENTERTAINMENT & RECREATION

Haus der Musik/ House of Music Seilerstätte 30 **43–1/516–4810** • 10am-10pm • interactive museum of sound • also cafe

Kunsthistorisches Museum Maria Theresien-Platz (enter Heldenplatz) **43–1/525–240** • 10am-6pm, till 9pm Th, clsd Mon • not to be missed • works from Ancient Egypt to the Renaissance to Klimt

BOOKSTORES

American Discount Rechte Wienzeile 5 (at Paniglgasse) **43–1/587–5772** • 9:30am-6:30pm, till 5pm Sat, clsd Sun • int'l magazines & books • also Neubaugasse 39, 43–1/523–37–07

Löwenherz Berggasse 8 (next to Cafe Berg, enter on Wasagasse, U2-Schottentor) **43–1/317–2982** • 10am-7pm, till 8pm Fri, till 6pm Sat, clsd Sun • LGBT • large selection of English titles

PUBLICATIONS

Vienna Gay Guide **43–1/789–1000** • city map & guide

Xtra • gay magazine

EROTICA

Art-X Percostr 3 **43–1/25804–4413** • 10am-8pm, till 9pm Th, till 6pm Sat, clsd Sun • leather, latex, rubber • toys • music • videos • magazines

Sexworld XXL Store Mariahilfer Str 49 **43–1/587–6656** • upscale sex shop

Tiberius Lindengasse 2 (at Stiftgasse, U3-Neubaugasse) **43–1/522–0474** • clsd Sun • wheelchair access • designer fetish-wear

CZECH REPUBLIC

PRAGUE (PRAHA)

Note: M°=Metro station

Prague is divided into 10 city districts: Praha—1, Praha—2, etc.

Praha—Overview

ACCOMMODATIONS

Apartments in Prague **420/775–588–508, 303/800–0858** • gay/ straight • WiFi • kids/ pets ok

ENTERTAINMENT & RECREATION

Letna Park & Beer Garden • great view of the city

Praha—1

ACCOMMODATIONS

Buddha Bar Hotel Jakubská 649/8 **420 /221–776–300** • gay/ straight • WiFi • small sexy hotel • pets ok

Hotel Leonardo Karollny Svetle 27 **420 /239–009–239** • gay/ straight • restaurant • WiFi • great location

Hotel Metropol Narodni 33 (at Na Perstyne) **420/246–022–100** • gay/ straight • design hotel • all-glass facade

The ICON Boutique Hotel V Jame 6 (at Vodickova) **420/221–634–100** • gay/ straight • restaurant & bar • WiFi • wheelchair access

The Palace Road Hotel Prague Nerudova 7 (at Malostranske Namesti) **420/257–531–941** • gay/ straight • located in city center • WiFi

BARS

Café Bar Flirt Martinská 5/419 **420/224–248–592** • cafe open 10am-2am, bar open 10pm-2am Fri-Sat • mostly gay men • dancing/DJ Fri-Sat • karaoke

Friends Bar Bartolomejská 11
420/226–211–920 • 7pm-6am • popular •
mostly men • dancing/DJ • neighborhood bar
• DJ Wed-Sat • videos • WiFi

K.U. Bar Rytiřská 13 (at Perlová, near
Oldtown Square) 420/724-695-910 • 7pm-
4am • gay/ straight • upscale & trendy •
dancing/DJ • live shows

Kafirna U Ceského Pána Kozí 13, Stare
Mesto 420/222–328–283 • 1pm-11pm, mostly
gay men • small bar popular w/ locals

Loca Cafe Bar Smetanovo nabrezi24
420/6049–01188 • 5pm-2am, till 3am Wed-Th,
4am Fri-Sat • lesbians/gay men, more women
Wed • dancing/DJ • food served

NIGHTCLUBS

Stage Stepanska 23 (at Reznicka)
420/252–548–683 • mostly gay men • cafe/
restaurant from 4pm • nightclub opens 9pm •
karaoke Tue

CAFES

Cafe Cafe Rytiřská 10 (at Perlová, near
Oldtown Square) 420/224–210–597 • 10am-
11pm • WiFi

Cafe Erra Konviktská 11 420/222–220–568 •
10am-midnight • salads, sandwiches &
entrées

Cafe Louvre Národni 22 (M° Narodni Trida)
420/224-930-949 • 9am-11:30pm • the
favorite hangout of Albert Einstein & Franz
Kafka

Cafe Muzeum Mezibranska 19
420/222–221–312 • 10am-11pm, from 1pm
wknds

Q Cafe Opatovická 166/12 420/776-856-361
• noon-midnight

RESTAURANTS

Campanulla Cafe Restaurant
Velkoprevorske namesti 4 420/257–217–736 •
set in the beautiful garden of The Grand Priory
of Bohemia Palace

Farrango Dusni 15 420/224-815-996 • 4pm-
midnight, clsd Sun • Thai

Maitrea Tynska 6/1064 (nr Old Town Square)
420/221–711–631 • noon-11:30pm •
vegetarian

Noi Ujezd 19 420/257-311-411 • 11am-1am •
Thai

Petrinské Terasy Seminarská Zahrada 393,
Malá Strana 420/257–320–688 • noon-11pm
• in a former monastery • great view • gay-
owned

Restaurant Dlouhá Dlouhá 23 (basement)
420/222–329–853 • 11am-11pm

Staromestska Restaurace Staromestske
namesti 19 420/224–213–015 • 11am-
midnight • local Czech specialties

ENTERTAINMENT & RECREATION

NoD Gallery/ Roxy Dlouhá 33 •
experimental theater, dance & performance •
also cafe & live music venue

Sex Machines Museum Melantrichova 18
420/227–186–260 • 10am-11pm

BOOKSTORES

Globe Patrossova 6 420/224-934-203 •
English-language bookstore • also cafe

EROTICA

Erotic City Zitna 43 420/737-221-264

Praha—2

ACCOMMODATIONS

Balbin Penzion Balbinova 26 (near
Wenceslaus Square) 420/222–250–660 • gay/
straight • located in city center • full brkfst •
WiFi

Prague Saints Polska 32 (office location) (at
Trebizkeho, at Saints Bar) 420/775-152-041,
420/775-152-042 • lesbians/ gay men • apts
in gay Vinohrady district • gay-owned

BARS

Angels Cafe Vinohradská 30 • 6pm-
midnight, from 2pm Sat • 10am-10pm Sun •
lesbians/ gay men • cafe & lounge • WiFi

Club Strelec Anglicka 2 420/224-941-446 •
5pm-2am, till midnight Sun • mostly gay men
• bear bar on Wed & Sat

Fan Fan Club Dittrichova 5 (at Trojanova)
420/776-360-698 • 5pm-2am • mostly gay
men • karaoke

FenoMan Club Blanická 28 (at Vinohradska)
420/603-740-263 • 5pm-5am, till 9am Fri-Sat
• mostly gay men • dancing/DJ • food served •
WiFi

JampaDampa V Tunich 10 (at Zitna)
420/603-260-678 • 6pm-2am, till 4am Wed,
6pm-6am Fri-Sat, clsd Sun-Mon • popular •
mostly women • dancing/DJ • karaoke

Klub 21 Rimska 21 420/222-364-720 • 7pm-
close, clsd Sun • lesbians/ gay men • cellar
bar/ gallery • food • young crowd • mostly
Czechs

Saints Polska 32 (at Trebizkeho)
420/222-250-326 • 7pm-2am, till 4am wknds
• lesbians/ gay men

NIGHTCLUBS

Freedom Night Trojická 10 (at PM Club) • monthly women's party • check www.djhenriette.cz for details

Lollypop Belehradska 120, Vinohrady (at Radost FX) **420/224-254-776, 420/603-193-711** • mostly gay men • huge, bi-monthly party • dancing/DJ

On Vinohradska 40 (at Blanicka) **420/222-520-630, 420/776-360-698 (CELL)** • noon-5am • lesbians/ gay men • dancing/DJ • video • 3 levels • darkroom

Termix Trebizskeho 4 (at Vinohradska) **420/222-710-462** • 10pm-5am, clsd Sun-Tue • popular • lesbians/ gay men • dancing/DJ • karaoke

RESTAURANTS

Celebrity Cafe Vinohradska 40 (in Vinohrady) **420/222-511-343** • 8am-2am, noon-3am Sat, noon-midnight Sun • also bar

Céleste Restaurant & Bar Rasalnovo nabrezi 1981/80 (at Dancing House) **420/2219-84160** • lunch & dinner, clsd Sun • French dining with great views of the river

Radost FX Belehradska 120, Vinohrady **420/224-254-776, 420/603-193-711** • fabulous wknd brunch • vegetarian cafe • also straight nightclub w/ popular bi-monthly gay party Lollypop

Sahara Cafe & Lounge Namesti Miru 6 **420/222-514-987** • 11am-midnight • live music

Praha—3

BARS

Latimerie Club Cafe Slezska 74 (at Nitranska) **420/224-252-049** • 4pm-close, from 6pm wknds • lesbians/ gay men • drag shows

Piano Bar Milesovská 10 (at Ondrickova) **420/775-727-496** • 5pm-close • lesbians/ gay men • mostly Czech older crowd • food served

CAFES

Blaze Husitska 43 **420/777-102-028** • 5pm-close • live music, art & more

RESTAURANTS

Restaurant Mozaika Nitranská 13 **420/224-253-011** • contemporary take on international cuisine • non-smoking

ENTERTAINMENT & RECREATION

TV Tower Mahlerovy sady 1 **420/724-251-286** • get a bird's-eye view of the city from the top of this tower

Praha—4

GYMS & HEALTH CLUBS

Plavecky Stadion Podoli Podolská 74 **420/241-433-952** • 6am-9:45 pm • gay/ straight • public baths • restaurants • women's sauna Th-Fri & Sun

Praha—5

ACCOMMODATIONS

Andel's Hotel Stroupeznickeho 21 (at Pizenska) **420/296-889-688** • gay-friendly • restaurant & bar

Praha—7

NIGHTCLUBS

OMG/ Oh My Gay Party U Pruhonu 3 (at Mecca) • 3rd Sat only • mostly gay men • dancing/DJ

CAFES

Duhova Cajovna Milada Horáková 73 (at Ovenecka) **420/775-269-699** • 3pm-midnight • "Rainbow Tearoom" • food served • WiFi

Praha—10

ACCOMMODATIONS

Ron's Rainbow Guest House Bulharska 4 (at Finská) **420/271-725-664, 420/731-165-022 (CELL)** • gay/ straight • quiet & friendly • near city center • gay-owned

DENMARK

Copenhagen

INFO LINES & SERVICES

Kafe Knud Skindergade 21 **45/3332-5861** • 4pm-10pm Tue & Th only • HIV resource center • cafe open Tue & Th only

Sabaah Onkel Dannys Plads 1 • community center for LGBT ethnic minorities • events • meetings

Wonderful Copenhagen Convention & Visitors Bureau Vesterbrogade 4A **45/7022-2442 (TOURIST INFO)**

ACCOMMODATIONS

Carstens Guesthouse Christians Brygge 28, 5th flr **45/3314-9107, 45/4050-9107 (CELL)** • lesbians/ gay men • B&B, hostel & apts • shared baths • kids/ pets ok on request • WiFi • 5 minutes from gay area

Copenhagen Admiral Hotel Toldbodgade 24-28 **45/3374-1414** • gay-friendly • great views • WiFi

First Hotel Kong Frederik Vester Voldgade 25 45/3312–5902

First Hotel Skt. Petri Krystalgade 22 45/3345–9100 • hotel embodying the ultra-coolest of Scandinavian design • great bar • WiFi • wheelchair access

First Hotel Twentyseven Løngangstræde 27 45/7027–5627

Hotel Fox Jarmers Plads 3 45/3395–7755, 45/3313–3000 • gay/ straight • nonsmoking • artistic rooms • central location • roof terrace • also lounge & restaurant

Hotel Kong Arthur Norre Sogade 11 45/3311–1212

Hotel Windsor Frederiksborggade 30, 1360 45/3311–0830 • mostly gay men • near gay scene • shared baths • gay-owned

Radisson Blu Royal Hotel Hammerichsgade 1 45/3342–6000

The Square Rådhuspladsen 14 45/3338–1200

BARS

Amigo Bar Schønbergsgade 4, Frederiksberg 45 5/3321–4915 • 10pm-6am • lesbians/ gay men • neighborhood bar • karaoke

Cafe Intime Allegade 25, Frederiksberg 45/3834–1958 • 6pm-2am • gay-friendly • cafe-bar • piano bar

Can-Can Mikkel Bryggers Gade 11 45/3311–5010 • 2pm-2am, till 5am Fri-Sat • mostly gay men • friendly neighborhood bar

Centralhjørnet Kattesundet 18 45/3311–8549 • noon-2am • mostly gay men • WiFi

Copenhagen

LGBT PRIDE:
August. www.copenhagenpride.dk.

ANNUAL EVENTS:
July - Queer Festival, web: www.queerfestival.org.
October - Gay & Lesbian Film Festival 45/3313-0766, web: www.cglff.dk.

CITY INFO:
Copenhagen Visitors Bureau 45/7022-2442, web: www.visit-copenhagen.com.

BEST VIEW:
From the dome of Marble Church, or from the spiral tower of Our Savior's Church.

TRANSIT:
Kobenhavns Taxa 3535–3535, web: www.4x35.dk.
Metro 45/3311-1700, www.m.dk. Ask about the Copenhagen Card, which offers bargains on museums and public transportation.
Bycyklen 45/3616–4233, web: www.bycyklen.dk. 110 racks around the city center offering free bicycle rental!

ATTRACTIONS:
Botanisk Have (Botanical Garden) 45/3532–2222, web: www.botanik.snm.ku.dk.
Dansk Design Center 45/3369–3369, web: www.ddc.dk.
Latin Quarter.
The Little Mermaid.
Marmorkirken (Marble Church) 45/3315–0144, web: www.marmorkirken.dk.
Nationalmuseet (National Museum) 45/3313–4411, web: www.natmus.dk.
Statens Museum for Kunst (Royal Museum of Fine Arts) 45/3374–8494, web: www.smk.dk.
Strøget shopping district.
Tivoli 45/3515–1001, web: www.tivoli.dk.
Vor Frelsers Kirke (Our Savior's Church), web: www.vorfrelserkirke.dk.

WEATHER:
Winters are cold & wet, with temperatures in the upper 30°s. Early summer is the best time to visit, when locals enjoy long days and temperatures around 70°.

Cosy Bar Studiestræde 24 (in Latin Quarter) 45/3312–7427 • 10pm-6am, till 8am Fri-Sat • popular • mostly gay men

Heaven Radhuspladsen 75 45/3333–0806 • 10am-2am, till 5am wknds • lesbians/gay men • food served

Lesbisk Kaffe Enghavevej 56 • 10am-10pm, till 1am wknds • mostly women • cafe & bar • food served • performances • WiFi

Masken Studiestræde 33 45/3391–0937 • 2pm-3am, till 5am Fri-Sat • popular • lesbians/gay men • cafe-bar • WiFi

Never Mind Nørre Voldgade 2 45/3311–8886 • 10pm-6am • mostly gay men

Oscar Bar Cafe Radhuspladsen 77 45/3312–0999 • noon-2am • mostly men • lesbians welcome • food served • great happy hour • WiFi

Vela Viktoriagade 2-4 45/3331–3419 • 8pm-midnight Wed, till 2am Th, till 5am Fri-Sat, clsd Sun-Tue • mostly women • neighborhood bar

NIGHTCLUBS

Christopher Club Knabrostræde 3 • midnight-5am Fri-Sat only • lesbians/gay men • dancing/DJ

CAFES

Jernbanecafeen • 7am-2am • WiFi • patio

RESTAURANTS

Jailhouse Restaurant & Bar Studiestraede 12 45/3315–2255 • 3pm-2am, till 5am Fri-Sat • popular • mostly gay men • bears

Laekkerier Borgergade 17F • 8:30am-5pm, till 10pm Th, from 10am wknds • organic take-out

Luna's Diner Vesterbrogade 42 45/3322–4757 • 10am-midnight, till 1am Fri-Sat

Tight Hyskenstraede 10 45/3311–0900 • 5pm-10pm, from noon wknds • Canadian, French & Australian

ENTERTAINMENT & RECREATION

Amager Strandpark • beach 5 km from city center

Bellevue Beach • mostly gay beach • left end is nude

Kifak Staldgade 8 • venue for LGBT special events

Warehouse 9 Bygning 66 (enter from parking lot in front of Oksnehallen, in the meatpacking district) 45/3322–2847 • queer art, music, performance & more

PUBLICATIONS

Out & About 45/4093–1977

EROTICA

Lust Mikkel Bryggersgade 3A 45/3333–0110 • erotica for women

ENGLAND

LONDON

London is divided into 6 regions:
London—Overview
London—Central
London—West
London—North
London—East
London—South

London—Overview

BARS

Glass Bar • women's parties around London • check www.theglassbar.org.uk for events

NIGHTCLUBS

Exilio 44–(0)79/5698–3230 • 9:30pm-2:30am twice a month on Sat, call for location • lesbians/gay men • dancing/DJ • Latino/a

Torture Garden 44–020/7700–1441 • the worlds largest fetish/body art club • check www.torturegarden.com for events

ENTERTAINMENT & RECREATION

The Women's Library, London Metropolitan University Old Castle St 44–020/7320–2222 • clsd Sun • also cafe • museum • cultural center • call for events • nonsmoking

PUBLICATIONS

Diva 44–020/7424–7400 • glorious glossy magazine for lesbians & bisexual women

g3 44–020/7724–9898 • free monthly lesbian glossy

London—Central

London—Central includes Soho, Covent Garden, Bloomsbury, Mayfair, Westminster, Pimlico & Belgravia

ACCOMMODATIONS

Dover Hotel 42/44 Belgrave Rd 44–020/7821–9085 • gay-friendly • WiFi

Fitz B&B 15 Colville Place (btwn Charlotte & Whitfield) 44–(0)78/3437–2866 • lesbians/gay men • 18th-c townhouse • nonsmoking • WiFi • gay-owned

George Hotel 58–60 Cartwright Gardens (N of Russell Square) 44–020/7387–8777 • gay-friendly • full brkfst • some shared baths • kids ok

Hazlitt's 6 Frith St (Soho Sq) 44–020/7434–1771 • gay-friendly • WiFi

Lincoln House 33 Gloucester Pl, Marble Arch (at Baker St) 44–20/7486–7630 • gay/straight • B&B • full brkfst • WiFi • wheelchair access

Marble Arch Inn 49-50 Upper Berkeley St 44–020/7723–7888 • gay-friendly

Z Hotel 17 Moor St 44–020/3551–3700 • gay/straight • WiFi • great Soho location

BARS

The Admiral Duncan 54 Old Compton St (Soho) 44–020/7437–5300 • pub hours • popular • lesbians/gay men • neighborhood bar • transgender-friendly

Bar Soho 23-25 Old Compton St (at Frith St) 44–020/7439–0439 • noon-1am, till 3am Fri-Sat, from 2pm Sun

Candy/ Ku Bar 4 Carlisle St, S (at Dean) 44–020/7287–5041 • 5pm-11:30pm, till 2am Fri-Sat • women only (men welcome as guests) • dancing/DJ • food served • karaoke • strippers

Circa 62 Frith St 44–020/7734–6826 • 4pm-1am • mostly gay men • dancing/DJ

Compton's of Soho 51-53 Old Compton St (at Dean St) 44–020/7479–7961 • noon-midnight, till 10:30pm Sun • mostly gay men • food served Sun • wheelchair access

London

LGBT PRIDE:
June-July www.prideinlondon.org.

ANNUAL EVENTS:
March-April - Lesbian & Gay Film Festival 44–(0)20/7928-3232, web: www.llgff.org.uk.

CITY INFO:
44–(0)20/7292-2333, web: www.visitlondon.com, www.londoninformation.org.

BEST VIEW:
London Eye, 44-(0)87/0990-8883, web: www.londoneye.com

WEATHER:
London is warmer and less rainy than you may have heard. Summer temperatures reach the 70ºs and the average annual rainfall is about half of that of Atlanta, GA or Hartford, CT.

TRANSIT:
Freedom Cars 44-(0)20-7734-1313, Minicabs 44-(0)20-8888-4444, web:www.eminicabs.co.uk.
London Travel Information (Tube & buses) 44-(0)20/7222-1234, 24hr info, web: www.tfl.gov.uk.

ATTRACTIONS:
British Museum 44–(0)20/7323–8299, web: www.britishmuseum.org.
Buckingham Palace 44–(0)20/7766-7300, web: www.royal.gov.uk.
Globe Theatre 44–(0)20/7902–1400, web: www.shakespearesglobe.com.
Kensington Palace 44–(0)87/0751-5170.
Madame Tussaud's 44–(0)87/0999–0046, web: www.madame-tussauds.co.uk.
National Gallery 44–(0)20/7747-2885, web: www.nationalgallery.org.uk.
Oscar Wilde's house (34 Tite Street)
St Paul's Cathedral 44–(0)20/7236–4128, www.stpauls.co.uk.
Tate Gallery 44–(0)20/7887-8008, web: www.tate.org.uk.
Tower of London 44–(0)87/0756–6060.
Westminster Abbey 44–(0)20/7654-4900, www.westminster-abbey.org.

Dog & Duck 18 Bateman St (at Frith St) 44–020/7494–0697 • 10am-11:30pm • gay/ straight • neighborhood bar • food served

Duke of Wellington 77 Wardour (Soho) 44–020/7439–1274 • pub hours • gay/ straight • snacks

The Edge 11 Soho Square (at Oxford St) 44–020/7439–1313 • 3pm-1am, till 3am Fri-Sat, till 11:30pm Sun • popular • dancing/DJ • live music • good food • outdoor seating • wheelchair access

The Escape 10-A Brewer St (at Rupert) 44–020/7734–3040 • 5pm-3am, clsd Sun-Mon • popular • mostly gay men • dancing/DJ • videos • theme nights

Freedom Bar 66 Wardour St (off Old Compton St) 44–020/7734–0071 • 4pm-3am, from 2pm Fri-Sat, 2pm-11:30pm Sun • lesbians/ gay men • dancing/DJ • food served • young crowd

Friendly Society 79 Wardour St (the basement at Old Compton, enter Tisbury Ct) 44–020/7434–3805 • 4pm-11pm, till 10:30pm Sun • lesbians/ gay men • young crowd

G-A-Y Bar 30 Old Compton St (at Frith) 44–020/7494–2756 • noon-midnight • lesbians/ gay men • basement women's bar

Green Carnation 4-5 Greek St (Soho Sq) 44–020/8123–4267 • 4pm-2am • inspired by the time & life of Oscar Wilde

Ku Bar/ Ku Klub 30 Lisle St (Leicester Sq) 44–020/7437–4303 • noon-3am, till 10:30pm Sun • lesbians/ gay men • karaoke • young crowd • WiFi • also Soho bar at 25 Frith St

Madam JoJo's 8-10 Brewer St (at Rupert) 44–020/7734–3040 • mostly gay men • live shows • Tranny Shack Wed

The New Bloomsbury Set 76 Marchmont St (at Tavistock Pl) 44–020/7383–3084 • 4pm-11pm, 2pm-10:30pm Sun • gay/straight

Note: "Pub hours" usually means 11am-11pm Mon-Sat and noon-3pm & 7pm-10:30pm Sun

The Retro Bar 2 George Ct (at Strand) 44–020/7321–2811 • pub hours • lesbians/ gay men • neighborhood bar • dancing/DJ • karaoke

Ruby Tuesday 30 Lisle St (at Ku Bar, Leicester Sq) 44–020/7437–4303 • 2nd Tue only • mostly women • dancing/DJ • entertainment

Rupert Street 50 Rupert St (off Brewer) 44–020/7292–7141 • pub hours • popular • lesbians/ gay men • upscale "fashiony-types" • food served • wheelchair access

Star at Night 22 Great Chapel St (at Hollen St) 44–020/7494–2488 • 6pm-11:30pm, clsd Sun-Mon • lesbians/ gay men • dancing/DJ • relaxed cafe/ bar • live shows

The Village Soho 81 Wardour St (at Old Compton) 44–020/7478–0530 • 4pm-1am, till 11:30pm Sun • popular • mostly gay men • 18+ • young crowd • wheelchair access

The Yard 57 Rupert St (off Brewer) 44–020/7437–2652, 871/426–2243 • pub hours • popular • mostly gay men • 2 levels • young crowd • food served • wheelchair access

NIGHTCLUBS

Code 5 Greek St (at Green Carnation, Soho) 44–079/5652–9649 • last Fri only • mostly women • dancing

G-A-Y Club Under the Arches, Villers St (at Heaven) 44–020/7734–6963 • 11pm-3am • popular • mostly gay men • dancing/DJ • live shows • young crowd • Camp Attack Fri • cover charge

Heaven 9 The Arches (off Villiers St) 44–020/7930-2020 • the mother of all London gay clubs • call for hours/ events • mostly gay men • dancing/DJ

KU Bar Frith St 25 Frith St (at Old Compton St, Soho) 44–020/7287–7986 • noon-11pm, till midnight wknds • mostly men • dancing/DJ

The Shadow Lounge 5-7 Brewer St (Soho) 44–020/7317–9270 • 10pm-3am, clsd Sun • mostly gay men • dancing/DJ • private club

CAFES

Balans Cafe 34 Old Compton St 44–020/7439–3309 • 24hrs • popular • lesbians/ gay men • all-day brkfst • terrace

Caffe Nero 43 Frith St 44–020/7434–3887 • 7am-2am, till 4am Sat

Flat White 17 Berwick St 44–020/7734–0370 • 8am-7pm, 9am-6pm wknds • Australian-style cafe

LJ Coffee House 3 Winnett St (at Rupert) 44–020/7434–1174 • 7:30am-7pm, 10am-8pm Sat, from 1pm Sun • cozy cafe • street views

Milk Bar 3 Bateman St 44–020/7287–4796 • 8am-7pm, till 5pm wknds • wheelchair access

RESTAURANTS

Cha Cha Moon 15-21 Ganton St 44–020/7297–9800 • noon-11pm, till 10pm Sun • inexpensive Chinese

Food for Thought 31 Neal St, downstairs (Covent Garden) 44–020/7836–0239 • noon-8:30pm, till 5:30pm Sun • vegetarian • inexpensive hole-in-the-wall • BYOB

The Gay Hussar 2 Greek St (on Soho Square) 44-020/7437-0973 • lunch & dinner, clsd Sun • Hungarian • wheelchair access

Mildred's 45 Lexington 44-020/7494-1634 • noon-11pm, clsd Sun • popular • vegetarian • plenty vegan

Randall & Aubin 16 Brewer St (at Walkers Court) 44-020/7287-4447 • noon-11pm • casual French • good people-watching

Wagamama Noodle Bar 10-A Lexington St 44-020/7292-0990 • noon-11pm • Japanese • nonsmoking • chain w/ locations throughout city

BOOKSTORES

Gay's the Word 66 Marchmont St (near Russell Sq Underground) 44-020/7278-7654 • 10am-6:30pm, 2pm-6pm Sun

RETAIL SHOPS

Prowler Soho 5-7 Brewer St (behind Village Soho bar) 44-020/7734-4031 • 11am-10pm, noon-8pm Sun • popular • large gay department store

London—West

London—West includes Earl's Court, Kensington, Chelsea & Bayswater

ACCOMMODATIONS

Cardiff Hotel 5, 7, 9 Norfolk Sq (Hyde Park) 44-020/7723-9068 • gay-friendly • B&B hotel in 3 Victorian townhouses • some shared baths • WiFi

Millennium Bailey's Hotel 140 Gloucester Rd (at Old Brompton Rd, Kensington) 44-020/7373-6000 • located in the heart of Kensington • also restaurant & bar

Myhotel Chelsea 35 Ixworth Place (at Elystan St, Chelsea) 44-020/7225-7500, 44-020/7637-2000 • gay-friendly • stylish boutique hotel in Chelsea

Parkwood Hotel 4 Stanhope Pl (Marble Arch) 44-020/7402-2241 • gay-friendly • full brkfst • nonsmoking

BARS

Richmond Arms 20 The Square (at Princes, Richmond) 44-020/8940-2118 • pub hours • lesbians/ gay men • dancing/DJ • professional crowd • karaoke • drag shows • cabaret

West Five (W5) 6 Popes Ln (South Ealing) 44-020/8579-3266 • 7pm-close, clsd Mon-Tue • lesbians/ gay men • cabaret • lounge • piano bar • garden

RESTAURANTS

The Churchill Arms 119 Kensington Church St 44-020/7727-4242 • inexpensive, fantastic Thai • also pub

The Gate 51 Queen Caroline St, Hammersmith • lunch & dinner, clsd Sun, vegetarian

Star of India 154 Old Brompton Rd 44-020/737-2901 • lunch & dinner • upscale

ENTERTAINMENT & RECREATION

Walking Tour of Gay SOHO 56 Old Compton St (at Admiral Duncan Pub) 44-020/7437-6063 • 2pm Sun • world-famous historical walking tour covering over 600 years of gay history in London's "square mile of sin"

London—North

London—North includes Paddington, Regents Park, Camden, St Pancras & Islington

ACCOMMODATIONS

Ambassadors Bloomsbury 12 Upper Woburn Pl (at Euston Rd, Bloomsbury) 44-020/7693-5400 • gay-friendly • near Kings Cross St Pancras & Euston Stations • Italian restaurant on-site • nonsmoking

Ossian Guesthouse 20 Ossian Rd (at Mt Pleasant Villas, Crouch Hill) 44-020/8340-4331 • gay-friendly • Victorian house on quiet street in quiet suburb

The Royal Park Hotel 3 Westbourne Terr (Hyde Park) 44-020/7479-6600 • gay-friendly • intimate luxury hotel • sauna & gym • WiFi

BARS

Blush 8 Cazenove Rd (Stoke Newington) 44-020/7923-9202 • 5pm-midnight, 1pm-midnight Sun, clsd Mon • mostly women • friendly cafe-bar • beer garden • live music Sun • karaoke Fri • lesbian-owned

Duke of Wellington 119 Balls Pond Rd 44-020/7275-7640 • 3pm-midnight, till 1am Fri-Sat • gay/ straight • popular w/ lesbians • food served

G-A-Y Late 5 Goslett Yard (Camden Town) • 11pm-3am • mostly gay men

The George Music Bar 114 Twickenham Rd (Isleworth) 44-020/8560-1456 • 5pm-close, from noon wknds • transgender-friendly • cabaret • gay-owned

King William IV (KW) 77 Hampstead High St (Hampstead) 44-020/7435-5747 • pub hours • lesbians/ gay men • food served • beer garden

NIGHTCLUBS

Club Kali 1 Dartmouth Park Hill (at The Dome) 44-020/7272-8153 (DOME #) • 10pm-3am 3rd Fri • popular • lesbians/ gay men • dancing/DJ • mostly Asian • transgender-friendly • South Asian music • cover charge

Dream Bags Jaquar Shoes 32-36 Kingsland Rd 44-020/7729-5830 • noon-1am • jam-packed club in a former shoe shop • also art exhibts

East Bloc 217 City Rd (at Shepherdess Walk, Old Street) 44-020/7253-0367 • 10pm-4am, till 6am Fri-Sat, clsd Mon-Wed • mostly men • electro dance club in funky basement space

Egg 200 York Way (Kings Cross) 44-020/7871-1111 • 10pm-6am Sat, until late afternoon Sun • gay/ straight • dancing/DJ

Habibi London 99-100 Turnmills (Farringdon) • 10:30pm last Fri only • lesbians/ gay men • Middle Eastern

RESTAURANTS

Manna 4 Erskine Rd (at Ainger Rd, Camden) 44-020/7722-8028 • lunch Tue-Sun, dinner nightly • vegetarian • reservations recommended

Providores and Tapa Room 109 Marylebone High St (at New Cavendish St) 44-020/7935-6175 • lunch & dinner • Asian fusion

ENTERTAINMENT & RECREATION

Rosemary Branch Theatre 2 Shepperton Rd 44-020/7704-2730 (BAR), 44-020/7704-6665 (THEATRE) • gay/ straight • also restaurant & bar • many gay-themed plays

London—East

London—East includes City, Tower, Clerkenwell & Shoreditch

ACCOMMODATIONS

Andaz Liverpool Street 40 Liverpool St (near Bishopsgate, at Liverpool Street Station) 44-020/7961-1234 • restaurants, bars, gym

The Hoxton 81 Great Eastern St 44-020/7550-1000 • gay-friendly • also restaurant • nonsmoking • WiFi

BARS

Bar Music Hall 134 Curtain Rd (Shoreditch) 44-020/7729-7216 • 11am-midnight, till 3am Fri-Sat • gay-friendly • great wknd brunch • dancing/DJ • live shows

Bethnal Green Working Men's Club 42-44 Pollard Row (at Squirries St, Bethnal Green) 44-020/7739-7170 • lesbians/ gay men • performance art • cabaret • drag shows • transgender-friendly

Dalston Superstore 117 Kingsland High St (at Sandringham Rd) 44-020/7254 2273 • noon-2am • gay/ straight • neighborhood bar • food served • WiFi

The Macbeth 70 Hoxton St (at Crondall St, Old St) 44-020/7749-0600 • 8pm-1am • gay/ straight • live shows • terrace

The Old Ship 17 Barnes St (Stepney) 44-020/7790-4082 • from 4pm Mon, from 7pm Wed-Sat, from 6pm Sun, clsd Tue • lesbians/ gay men • neighborhood bar • cabaret • wheelchair access

NIGHTCLUBS

Kaos at Stunners 566 Cable St (at Butcher Row, Cable St Studios, Limehouse) • monthy parties • check www.kaoslondon.com • transgender • dancing/DJ • private club

Pelucas y Tacones 6 Shoreditch High St (at Concrete/ Pizza East) • 9pm-2am 2nd Sat only • queer disco party

Pout 2-3 Old Change Court (at Yager Bar) • 8pm 2ndSat only • mostly women • dancing/DJ

Rumours 64-73 Minories (at The Minories) 44-(0)79/4947-7804 • 1st Sat • popular • women only • dancing/DJ

Unskinny Bop 42-44 Pollard Row (Bethnal Green Club) • 9pm 3rd Satonly • mostly women • dancing/DJ • live music

Urban Desi 18-20 Houndsditch (at Dukes) • 11pm-5am 2nd Sat • lesbians/ gay men • dancing/DJ • mostly South Asian

Way Out Club 14 New London St (at Gilt Bar, corner of Crutched Friers and Seething Ln) 44-(0)20/7264-1910 • 9pm-4am Sat only • transsexuals & their friends • dancing/DJ • live shows • private club • cover charge

CAFES

Pogo Cafe 76 Clarence Rd 44-020/8533-1214 • 12:30pm-9pm, from 11am Sun • vegan • volunteer-run • queer social space

RESTAURANTS

Bistrotheque 23-27 Waderson St 44-020/8983-7900 • expensive & glamorous • also cabaret shows after dinner

Bonds Restaurant & Bar 5 Threadneedle St 44-020/7657-8090 • lunch & dinner Mon-Fri, just bar service & snacks wknds, space formerly a bank lobby

Cafe Spice Namaste 16 Prescott St 44-020/7488-9242 • lunch Mon-Fri, dinner nightly, clsd Sun • Indian

Canteen 2 Crispin Pl (Spitalfields) 44-(0)84/5686-1122 • place to be for brkfst

Hoxton Square Bar & Kitchen 2-4 Hoxton Square 44-020/9613-1171 • great dark spot for brkfst • live music

Les Trois Garçons 1 Club Row (at Bethnal, Shoreditch) 44-020/7613-1924 • 6pm-midnight, clsd Sun • eclectic decor • reservations recommended

Lounge Lover 44-020/7012-1234 • fancy cuisine in a posh lounge • reservations required • wheelchair access

Royal Oak 73 Columbia Rd (at Hackney Rd, Old St) 44-020/7729-2220 • 4pm-11pm, from noon Fri-Sun • popular Sun for the Columbia Rd Flower market

Saf 63-97 Barkers Building, High Street (in Kensington, at Wholefoods Market) 44-020/7368-4555 • lunch & dinner, also bar till midnight • upscale vegan/ raw food

EROTICA

Expectations 75 Great Eastern St (Shoreditch) 44-020/7739-0292 • 11am-7pm, till 8pm Sat, noon-5pm Sun • leather/ rubber store • also mail order

Sh! Women's Erotic Emporium 57 Hoxton Sq (off Old St, Shoreditch) 44-020/7613-5458 • noon-8pm • men very welcome when accompanied by a woman

London—South

London—South includes Southwark, Lambeth, Kennington, Vauxhall, Battersea, Lewisham & Greenwich

ACCOMMODATIONS

Griffin House 22 Stockwell Green 44-020/7096-3332 • lesbians/ gay men • 2 rental apts near Vauxhall Gay Village & West End • WiFi • gay-owned

BARS

Bar Wotever 372 Kennington Ln (at Royal Vauxhall Tavern) • 6pm-midnight Tue • dancing/DJ • genderqueers & their admirers

Battersea Barge Riverside Walk Nine Elms Ln (Vauxhall) 44-020/7498-0004 • call for events • gay-friendly • cabaret • comedy • food served • gay-owned

The Cambria 40 Kemerton Rd (Denmark Hill) 44-020/7737-3676 • upmarket eclectic pub • gay/straight • food served • beautiful back garden

George & Dragon 2 Blackheath Hill (Greenwich) 44-020/8691-3764 • 6pm-2am, till 4am Fri-Sat • mostly gay men • live shows • cabaret

Kazbar 50 Clapham High St (Clapham) 44-020/7622-0070 • 5pm-midnight, till 1am Fri-Sat, from 1pm Sun • lesbians/ gay men

The Little Apple 98 Kennington Ln 44-020/7735-2039 • noon-midnight, till 3am Sat • lesbians/ gay men • dancing/DJ • transgender-friendly • food served • terrace • wheelchair access

Prince of Greenwich 72 Royal Hill (Greenwich) • 4pm-11pm, from noon Fri-Sat • mostly gay men • neighborhood bar • food served • drag shows

The Star & Garter 227 High St (Bromley) 44-020/8466-7733 • pub hours • lesbians/ gay men • karaoke • WiFi • wheelchair access

The Two Brewers 114 Clapham High St (Clapham) 44-020/7819-9539 • 4pm-2am, till 4am Fri-Sat, from 2pm Sun • lesbians/ gay men • dancing/DJ • karaoke • cabaret

NIGHTCLUBS

Black Sheep Bar 68 High St (at S Norwood Hill, Croydon) 44-020/8680-2233 • gay/straight • theme nights • alternative club

Bootylicious 1 Nine Elms (at Club Colosseum) • 11pm 3rd Sat • popular black gay club

Fire 47B S Lambeth Rd (Vauxhall) 44-020/3242-0040 • after-hours, Sat mornings & Sun afternoons • gay/ straight • dancing/DJ • cover charge

Hard On 66 Albert Embankment (at Union, in Vauxhall) 44-020/7533 402 985 • 3rd Sat only • mLesbians/gay men • fetish party • large play area with equipment • private club

Horse Meat Disco 349 Kennington Ln (at the Eagle) 44-020/7793-0903 • 8pm Sun only • lesbians/ gay men • dancing/DJ • popular queer dance party

Popstarz 100 Tinworth St (at Hidden bar, Vauxhall) 44-020/7240-1900 • popular • 10pm-6am Fri • lesbians/ gay men • dancing/DJ • cover charge

Royal Vauxhall Tavern 372 Kennington Ln (Vauxhall) **44-020/7820-1222** • 8pm-late, 9pm-3am Fri-Sat, 2pm-midnight Sun • mostly gay men • popular wknds • more women Sat for Duckie • dancing/DJ • transgender-friendly • food served • wheelchair access

CAFES

Glow Lounge 6 Cavendish Parade (Clapham Common S Side) **44-020/8673-4471** • noon-11pm, 9:30am-1am Fri-Sat, 10am-7pm Sun • WiFi

ENTERTAINMENT & RECREATION

Oval Theatre Cafe Bar 52-54 Kennington Oval **44-020/7582-0080** • 6pm-11pm Tue-Sat (cafe) • inquire about current theatre & art

FRANCE

PARIS

Note: M°=Métro station

Paris is divided by arrondissements (city districts); 01=1st arrondissement, 02=2nd arrondissement, etc

Paris—Overview

Note: When phoning Paris from the US, dial the country code + the city code + the local phone number

INFO LINES & SERVICES

Centre Gai et Lesbien 63 rue Beaubourg **33-1/4357-2147** • drop-in evenings • call for other events/groups

Gay AA 7 rue Auguste Vacquerie (at St George's Anglican) **33-1/4634-5965** • 7:30pm Tue, see calendar for other times

ACCOMMODATIONS

Gay Accommodation Paris 271, rue du Faubourg Saint Antoine **33-1/4348-1382** • studios for rent in central Paris • gay-owned

NIGHTCLUBS

Womexx • mostly women • dancing/DJ • lesbian parties in cool spaces • www.womexx.fr

PUBLICATIONS

Têtu **33-1/5680-2080** • stylish & intelligent LGBT monthly (en français)

Paris—01

ACCOMMODATIONS

Hotel Louvre Richelieu 51 rue de Richelieu (M° Palais-Royal) **33-1/4297-4620** • gay/ straight • nonsmoking • WiFi

Hotel Louvre Saint-Honoré 141 rue Saint-Honoré (at rue du Louvre) **33-1/4296-2323** • gay/straight • full brkfst • kids ok • WiFi • wheelchair access

BARS

Le Banana Cafe 13–15 rue de la Ferronnerie (near rue St-Denis, M° Châtelet) **33-1/4233-3531** • 6pm-dawn • lesbians/gay men • dancing/DJ • theme nights • piano bar • live shows • young crowd • wheelchair access • terrace

Bar du Kent'z 2-4 rue Vauvilliers (M° Chatelet-Les Halles) **33-1/4221-0116** • mostly gay men • 1920s style cocktail lounge

Le Tropic Cafe 66 rue des Lombards (M° Châtelet) **33-1/4013-9262** • 4pm-5am • lesbians/gay men • dancing/DJ Fri-Sat • transgender-friendly • kitschy, fun bar • tapas served • terrace • wheelchair access

NIGHTCLUBS

Le Klub 14 rue St-Denis (at rue des Lombards, M° Châtelet) **33-1/4508-9625** • 8pm-11pm, till 6am Fri-Sat, clsd Wed & Sun • gay/straight • rock & electro club • multiracial • cover charge

RESTAURANTS

L' Amazonial 3 rue Ste-Opportune (at rue Ferronnerie, M° Châtelet) **33-1/4233-5313** • lunch & dinner, brunch wknds • lesbians/gay men • Brazilian/int'l • cabaret • drag shows • heated terrace • wheelchair access

Au Diable des Lombards 64 rue des Lombards (at rue St-Denis, M° Châtelet) **33-1/4233-8184** • 8am-1am • American • full bar • terrace

Marc Mitonne 60 rue de l'Arbre-Sec (M° Les Halles) **33-1/4261-5316** • 6pm-2am, clsd Sun-Mon • live shows • cabaret

La Poule au Pot 9 rue Vauvilliers (M° Les Halles) **33-1/4236-3296** • 7pm-5am, clsd Mon • clsd Aug • bistro • traditional French

Le Velvet 43 rue Saint Honore • Thai restaurant & small gay bar

ENTERTAINMENT & RECREATION

Forum des Halles 101 Porte Berger (M° Châtelet-Les Halles) **33-1/4476-9656** • underground sports/entertainment complex w/ museums, theater, shops, clubs, cafes & more

GYMS & HEALTH CLUBS

Club Med Gym 147 rue St–Honoré (M° Louvre) **33-1/4020-0303** • gay/straight • day passes available • many locations throughout the city

Paris—02

BARS

La Champmeslé 4 rue Chabanais (at rue des Petits Champs, M° Pyramides) 33-1/4296-8520 • 4pm-3am, till 7am Fri-Sat, clsd Sun • popular • mostly women • theme nights • older crowd • WiFi • wheelchair access • a lesbian landmark, in business for over 20 years

NIGHTCLUBS

Rex Club 5 blvd Poissonière (M° Bonne Nouvelle) 33-1/4236-1096 • gay-friendly • call for events • clsd August • cover

CAFES

Stuart Friendly 16 rue Marie Stuart 33-1/4233-2400 • noon-11pm, till midnight Fri-Sat, till 5:30pm Sun • "straight-friendly" cafe • food served

RESTAURANTS

Le Lezard Cafe 32 rue Etienne Marcel 33-1/4233-2273 • full bar • terrace year round

Le Loup Blanc 42 rue Tiquetonne (M° Etienne-Marcel) 33-1/4013-0835 • 7:30pm-midnight, till 1am Sat, also brunch 11am-4:30pm Sun • popular • lesbians/gay men

Paris—03

ACCOMMODATIONS

Absolu Living 236 rue St Martin 33-1/4454-9700 • lesbians/ gay men • fully furnished apts in central Paris • short & long-term stays • gay-owned

Adorable Apartment in Paris (M° Rambuteau) 415/287-0306 (US#) • gay-friendly • in heart of Marais • nonsmoking • lesbian & gay-owned

Paris

LGBT PRIDE:
June. web: www.gaypride.fr.

ANNUAL EVENTS:
May-June - French Open tennis championship, web: french.open-tennis.com.
July - Tour de France, web: www.letour.fr.
July 14 - Bastille Day.
November - Paris Lesbian & Gay Film Festival, web: www.cheries-cheris.com.

CITY INFO:
Pyramides Welcome Center 3308/9268-3000, 25 rue des Pyramides, web: en.parisinfo.com.

BEST VIEW:
Eiffel Tower (but of course!) and Sacre Coeur.

TRANSIT:
Alpha Taxi 33-1/4585-8585, web: www.alphataxis.fr.
Taxi Bleu 33-8/9170-1010, web: www.taxis-bleus.com.
RATP (bus and Métro) web: www.ratp.fr.

ATTRACTIONS:
Arc de Triomphe 33-1/5537-7377, web: www.monuments-nationaux.fr.
Notre Dame Cathedral 33-8/9270-1239, web: www.notredamedeparis.fr.
Eiffel Tower (up in lights for 10 minutes each hour from sunset till past midnight!) 33-1/4411-2323, web: www.tour-eiffel.fr.
Louvre 33-1/4020-5760, web: www.louvre.fr.
Musée d'Orsay 33-1/4049-4814, web: www.musee-orsay.fr.
Picasso Museum 33-1/4271-2521, web: www.musee-picasso.fr.
Rodin Musuem 33-1/4418-6110, web: www.musee-rodin.fr.
Sacre-Coeur Basilica 33-1/5341-8900, web: www.sacre-coeur-montmartre.com.
Sainte-Chapelle 33-1/5340-6096, web: www.monuments-nationaux.fr.

WEATHER:
Paris really *is* beautiful in the springtime. Chilly in the winter, the temperatures reach the 70°s during the summer.

Hôtel du Vieux Saule 6 rue de Picardie 33–1/4272–0114 • gay-friendly

Hotel Jules & Jim 11 rue des Gravilliers 33–1/4454–1313 • gay/straight • gay-owned

BARS

Le CUD Club 12 rue des Haudriettes 33–1/4277–4412 • 11pm-6am, till 7am wknds • mostly men • dancing/DJ • young crowd

Le Duplex 25 rue Michel-Le-Comte (at rue Beaubourg, M° Rambuteau) 33–1/4272–8086 • 8pm-2am, till 4am Fri-Sat • lesbians/gay men • neighborhood bar • bohemian types • live shows • WiFi

La Mutinerie 176–178 rue St-Martin (near rue Réaumur, M° Rambuteau) 33–1/4272–7059 • 4pm-2am • mostly women • neighborhood bar • young crowd

Le Tango/ La Boite à Frissons 13 rue au Maire (M° Arts-et-Métiers) 33–1/4272–1778 • 10:30pm-5am, clsd Mon • lesbians/gay men • food served

RESTAURANTS

La Fontaine Gourmande 11 rue Charlot 33–1/4278–7240 • noon-2pm Tue-Fri, 7:30pm-close Tue-Sun, clsd Mon • women-owned

EROTICA

Rex 42 rue de Poitou (at rue Charlot, M° St-Sébastien-Froissard) 33–1/4277–5857 • 1pm-8pm, clsd Sun • new, custom & secondhand leather & S/M accessories

Paris—04

ACCOMMODATIONS

Historic Rentals 800/537–5408 (US#) • gay-friendly • 1-bdrm apt • full kitchen • nonsmoking • WiFi

Hôtel Beaubourg 11 rue Simon le Franc (btwn rue Beaubourg & rue du Temple, M° Hôtel-de-Ville) 33–1/4274–3424 • gay/straight • next to Centre Pompidou • WiFi

Hôtel de la Bretonnerie 22 rue Ste-Croix-de-la-Bretonnerie (M° Hôtel-de-Ville) 33–1/4887–7763 • gay-friendly • 17th-c hotel w/ Louis XIII decor

Hôtel du Vieux Marais 8 rue du Plâtre (M° Hôtel-de-Ville) 33–1/4278–4722 • gay-friendly • centrally located • WiFi

Paris At Home 33–06/1991–5828 • lesbians/gay men • B&B & apts • gay-owned

BARS

3W Kafe 8 rue des Ecouffes (M° St Paul) 33–1/4887–3926 • 5pm-2am, till 4am Fri-Sat • popular • mostly women • dancing/DJ • live shows • young crowd

Au Mange Disque 15 rue de la Reynie (at Boule de Sebastopol) 33–1/4804–7817 • 11am-2am, from 5pm Sun-Mon • mostly gay men • theme nights • colorful, modern decor

Le Carrefour 8 rue des Archives (at rue de la Verrerie) 33–1/4029–9005 • 6am-2am • mostly gay men • neighborhood bar • good location & terrace

Cox 15 rue des Archives (at rue Ste-Croix-de-la-Bretonnerie, M° Hôtel-de-Ville) 33–1/4272–0800 • 5:30pm-2am, from 4:30pm Fri-Sun • mostly gay men • dancing/DJ • huge terrace

Dandy's Cafe 9 rue Nicolas Flamel 33–1/4271–4582 • 2pm-2am • mostly gay men

L' Enchanteur 15 rue Michel Lecomte (M° Rambuteau) 33–1/4804–0238 • 6pm-6am, clsd Mon • lesbians/gay men • karaoke

Les Filles de Paris 57 rue Quincampoix 33–1/4271–7220 • 10pm-5am Wed-Sat, also restaurant from 7pm, clsd Sun-Mon • gay/straight • dancing/DJ • drag shows, burlesque & cabaret

Le Freedj 35 rue Ste-Croix-de-la-Bretonnerie (at rue du Temple, M° Hôtel-de-Ville) 33–1/4029–4440 • 6pm-4am • lesbians/gay men • bar upstairs, club downstairs

Gossip Cafe 16 rue des Lombards (at bd de Sébastopol, M° Châtelet) 33–1/4271–3683 • 2pm-6am • lesbians/gay men • food served • terrace

L' Imprevu Cafe 9 rue Quincampoix 33–1/4278–2350 • 3pm-2am, from 1pm Sun • mostly gay men • low key neighborhood cafe/bar • food served

Les Jacasses 5 rue des Ecouffes (M° St Paul) 33–1/4271–1551 • 5pm-2am • mostly women • men welcome

Morgan Bar 25 rue du Roi de Sicile 33–1/4277–0666 • lesbians/gay men • dancing/DJ • WiFi

L' Oiseau Bariolé 16 rue Saint-Croix-de-la-Bretonnerie (M° Hotel de Ville) 33–1/4272–3712 • lesbians/gay-men • 5pm-close • quiet

Okawa 40 rue Vieille du Temple (at rue Ste-Croix-de-la-Bretonnerie, M° Hôtel-de-Ville) 33–1/4804–3069 • 10am-2am, till 4am Fri-Sat • gay/straight • trendy cafe-bar in 12th- & 13th-c caves • cabaret • piano bar Tue-Wed • also restaurant from 7pm

L' Open Cafe 17 rue des Archives (at rue Ste-Croix-de-la-Bretonnerie, M° Hôtel-de-Ville) • 11am-2am, till 4am Fri-Sat • popular • lesbians/gay men • sidewalk cafe-bar

Le Pur Bar/ Titi's Bar 12 rue de Plâtre (btwn rue du Temple & rue des Archives, M° Hôtel-de-Ville) **33-1/4887-0259** • 5pm-2am • lesbians/ gay men • neighborhood cafe-bar

Le Raidd 23 rue du Temple (M° Hotel de ville) **33-1/4277-0488** • 5pm-5am • mostly men • dancing/DJ • go-go boys

Sly Bar 22 rue des Lombards **33-1/8253-2781** • mostly gay men • neighborhood bar • dancing/DJ

Le So What 30 rue du Roi de Sicile (M° Hôtel-de-Ville) • 9pm-2am, 10pm-4am Fri-Sat, clsd Sun-Tue • lesbians/ gay men • stylish new bar • dancing/DJ • lesbian-owned

Les Souffleurs 7 rue de la Verrerie (M° Hôtel-de-Ville) **33-1/6421-8133** • lesbians/ gay men • artsy younger crowd • events in the basement

Le Troisieme Lieu 62 rue Quincampoix **33-1/4804-8564** • 6pm-2am, clsd Sun • mostly women • also restaurant & nightclub

Le Voulez-Vous 18 rue du Temple (M° Hôtel-de-Ville) **33-1/4459-3857** • 11am-2am • lesbians/ gay men • lounge & restaurant • terrace

Yono 37 rue Vieille du Temple **33-1/4274-3165** • 6pm-2am, 4:30pm-11pm Sun, clsd Mon • lesbians/ gay men • dancing/DJ • cozy basement bar • also restaurant

Ze Baar 41 rue des Blancs Manteaux (at rue du Temple) **33-1/4271-7508** • 5pm-2am • mostly gay men • neighborhood bar • also restaurant

CAFES

Le Kofi du Marais 54 rue Ste-Croix-de-la-Bretonnerie (M° Hôtel de Ville) **33-1/4887-4871** • 7pm-midnight, clsd Sun • lesbians/ gay men • coffee & light meals

RESTAURANTS

4 Pat 4 rue St Merri **33-1/4277-2545** • noon-2am • dancing/DJ • Italian menu

Les Agités 15 rue de la Reijny (at Boule de Sebastopol) **33-1/8389-5309** • 7pm-2am, clsd Sun-Mon

L' Alimentari 6 Rue des Ecouffes **33-1/4277-2459** • very good small trattoria

Le Chant des Voyelles 4 rue des Lombards (M° Châtelet) **33-1/4277-7707** • 11:30am-3pm & 6:30pm-midnight, open all day in summer • traditional French • terrace

Etamine Cafe 13 rue des Ecouffes (at rue des Rosiers, M° Hotel de Ville) **33-1/4478-0962** • noon-midnight, clsd Mon • also bar

Le Gai Moulin 10 rue St-Merri (at rue du Temple, M° Hôtel-de-Ville) **33-1/4887-0600** • noon-midnight • lesbians/ gay men • French/ int'l

HD Diner 6-8 Square Ste-Croix de la Bretonnerie **33-1/4277-6934** • 11am-midnight • 50's style diner

La Pas-Sage-Oblige 29 rue du Bourg-Tibourg (M° Hôtel-de-Ville) **33-1/4041-9503** • lunch & dinner • vegetarian

Les Piétons 8 rue des Lombards (M° Châtelet) **33-1/4887-8287** • noon-2am • Spanish/ tapas • also bar

Who's 14 rue Saint Merri (M° Rambuteau) **33-1/4272-7597** • noon-6am

Woo Bar 3 rue Pierre au Lard (M° Rambuteau) **33-1/4272-7597** • noon-6am

BOOKSTORES

Les Mots à la Bouche 6 rue Ste-Croix-de-la-Bretonnerie (near rue du Vieille du Temple, M° Hôtel-de-Ville) **33-1/4278-8830** • 11am-11pm, 1pm-9pm Sun • LGBT • English titles

RETAIL SHOPS

Abraxas 9 rue St-Merri **33-1/4804-3355** • tattoos • piercing • large selection of body jewelry

EROTICA

Dollhouse 24 rue du Roi de Sicile (at Ferdinand Duval) **33-9/5074-5974** • women's erotica store

Paris — 05

RESTAURANTS

L' AOC **33-1/4354-2252** • lunch & dinner, clsd Sun

Le Petit Prince 12 rue de Lanneau (M° Maubert-Mutualité) **33-1/4354-7726** • 7:30pm-midnight • popular • French

ENTERTAINMENT & RECREATION

Open-Air Sculpture Museum Quai Saint-Bernard • along the Seine btwn the Jardin des Plantes & the Institut du Monde Arabe

Paris — 06

ACCOMMODATIONS

The Hotel Luxembourg Parc 42 rue de Vaugirard **33-1/5310-3650** • gay/ straight • great location

Bars

La Venus Noire 25 rue de l'Hirondelle (M°
St-Michel) • 6pm-1am, till 2am Fri-Sat, clsd
Sun • mostly women • neighborhood bar •
live music

Nightclubs

Le Rive Gauche 1 rue du Sabot (M° St-
Sulpice) 33-1/4020-4323 • 11pm-dawn Fri-
Sat only • mostly women • dancing/DJ • cover
charge

Bookstores

Les Amazones 68 rue Bonaparte
33-1/4046-0837 • specializes in antique,
lesbian & feminist books

Paris—08

Accommodations

François 1er 7 rue Magellan
33-1/4723-4404 • gay-friendly • boutique
hotel near les Champs-Elysées • also bar

Hôtel le Lavoisier 21 rue Lavoisier
33-1/5330-0606, 866/376-7831 (US#) • gay-
friendly • 19th-c townhouse • WiFi

Prince de Galles 33 Avenue George V
33-1/5323-7777 • gay-friendly • legendary
jewel of the Parisian Art Deco movement near
les Champs-Elysées • WiFi

Bars

Le Day Off 10 rue de l'Isly (M° Gare-St-
Lazare) 33-1/4522-8790 • 5pm-3am Mon-Fri
only • food served • woman-owned

Nightclubs

Escualita 128 rue de la Boetie (at Club
"MadaM") • midnight Sun only • mostly men
• transgender-friendly • fab tranny dance party
• all are welcome

Le Queen 102 av des Champs-Élysées (btwn
rue Washington & rue de Berri, M° Georges-
V) 33-8/5389-0890 • midnight-dawn, more
gay Sun • popular • gay/ straight • dancing/DJ
• drag shows • young crowd • selective door •
cover charge

Paris—09

Accommodations

The Grand 2 rue Scribe 33-1/4007-3232,
888/424-6835 (US#) • gay-friendly • ultraluxe
art deco hotel • WiFi

Bars

Rosa Bonheur 1 rue Botzaris
33-1/4200-0045 • gay-friendly • more gay
Sun, arrive before 6pm to avoid the line

Nightclubs

Folies Pigalle 11 place Pigalle (M° Pigalle)
33-1/4878-5525, 33-1/4280-1203 (BBB INFO
LINE) • midnight-dawn • gay/ straight •
dancing/DJ • theme nights • transgender-
friendly • multiracial • cover charge

Fox Club 9 rue Frochot 33-1/4281-0923 •
6pm-2am, 7pm-5am Fri-Sat, clsd Sun-Tue •
mostly women • dancing/DJ

Glass 7 rue Frochot (in Pigalle)
33-9/8072-9883 • 7pm-2am • gay/straight •
dancing/DJ • popular with locals Mon

Paris—10

Bars

L' Okubi 219 rue St-Maur (M° Goncourt)
33-1/4201-3508 • 6pm-2am, clsd Sun •
lesbians/ gay men • dancing/DJ

Paris—11

Accommodations

Le 20 Prieure Hotel 20 rue du Grand
Prieuré 33-1/4700-7414 • gay/ straight •
WiFi

Le General Hotel 5/7 rue Rampon
33-1/4700-4157 • gay-friendly • WiFi •
wheelchair access

HI Matic 71 rue de Charonne • gay-friendly
• a new urban eco-lodging concept • WiFi •
wheelchair access • gay-owned

Hôtel Beaumarchais 3 rue Oberkampf
(btwn bd Beaumarchais & bd Voltaire, M°
Filles-du-Calvaire) 33-1/5336-8686 • gay/
straight • beautiful hotel • WiFi

Bars

Le Bataclan 50 blvd Voltaire (at Bataclan
club, M° Saint Ambroise) 33-1/4314-0030 •
gay-friendly • live music venue • more gay for
the Follivores & Crazyvores • call for events

Follivores/ Crazyvores 50 blvd Voltaire (M°
Saint Ambroise) 33-1/4314-0030 • lesbians/
gay men • monthly sing-along dance parties •
Follivores is 1960s-1990s French pop •
Crazyvores is English-speaking • kitsch factor
very high!

In Out 241 rue du Fbg St Antoine
33-9/5241-0037 • 5pm-2am, clsd Sun • gay/
straight • dancing/DJ • young crowd

Nightclubs

Les Disquaires 6 rue des Taillandiers (M°
Bastille) 33-1/4021-9460 • gay/ straight •
dance bar • live bands

CAFES

Cannibale Café 93 Rue Jean-Pierre Timbaud 33-1/4929-0040 • an old-fashioned Parisian café in Belleville • WiFi

Le Pause Cafe 41 rue de Charonne 33-1/4806-8033 • 8am-2am, 9am-8pm Sun • food served

RESTAURANTS

Le Tabarin 3 rue Amelot 33-1/4807-1522 • lunch Sun-Fri, dinner Sun-Sat • lesbians/ gay men • full bar • piano bar

ENTERTAINMENT & RECREATION

L' ArtiShow 3 cite Souzy 33-1/4002-1803 • cabaret • also lunch & dinner served

BOOKSTORES

Violette & Co 102 rue de Charonne (at boulevard Voltaire, M° Charonne) 33-1/4372-1607 • 11am-8pm, 2pm-7pm Sun, clsd Mon • LGBT & feminist • English titles • art shows • lesbian-owned

EROTICA

Démonia 22 ave Jean Aicard (at rue Oberkampf, M° St-Maur) 33-1/4314-8270 • clsd Sun • BDSM shop • lingerie • videos • toys

Paris—12

SEX CLUBS

Atlantide 13 rue Parrot (M° Gare de Lyon) 33-1/4342-2243 • gay/ straight sauna w/ sexual atmosphere • men, women, transgender-friendly • private cabins • also bar

Paris—14

ENTERTAINMENT & RECREATION

Friday Night Fever Place Raoul Dautry (btwn Montparnasse office tower & Montparnasse train station) • 10pm-1am Fri (weather-permitting), meet 9:30pm • rollerblade through the city • gay/ straight

GYMS & HEALTH CLUBS

Amphibi 73 rue Hallé (at rue Bézout, M° Alesia) 33-1/4047-5090 • sauna where everyone is welcome: gay, straight, bisexual, transgendered

Paris—15

ACCOMMODATIONS

Platine Hotel 20 rue Ingénieur Robert Keller 33-1/4571-1515 • gay/ straight • Marilyn Monroe and 1950's theme • WiFi • wheelchair access

Paris—16

ACCOMMODATIONS

Keppler 10 rue Keppler 33-1/4720-6505 • gay-friendly • near major tourist stops • also bar • kids/ pets ok • WiFi

Paris—17

RESTAURANTS

Sans Gêne 112 rue Legendre 33-1/4627-6782 • 5pm-2am, Sun brunch, clsd Mon • also bar

Paris—18

BARS

Karambole Cafe 10 rue Hegesippe Moreau (M° Place de Clichy or La Fourche) 33-1/4293-3068 • 9am-2am, from 6pm Sat, clsd Sun • gay/ straight • artsy cafe by day • DJs by night

Le Tagada Bar 40 rue Trois-Frères (M° Abesses) 33-1/4255-9556 • 6pm-2am, clsd Mon • mostly gay men • upscale food

ENTERTAINMENT & RECREATION

Michou 80 rue des Martyrs (at Blvd de Clichy, M° Pigalle) 33-1/4606-1604 • infamous drag cabaret • dinner show

Paris—19

CAFES

Cafe Cherie 44 Blvd de la Villette (M° Belleville) 33-1/4202-0205 • 8am-2am • gay/ straight • live music & DJs starting at 10pm • WiFi

Paris—20

ACCOMMODATIONS

Mama Shelter 109 rue de Bagnolet 33-1/ 4348-4848 • gay/ straight • great location on the Right Bank • kichenettes • also restaurant & cool local bars • WiFi

ENTERTAINMENT & RECREATION

Père Lachaise Cemetery bd de Ménilmontant (M° Père-Lachaise) • perhaps the world's most famous resting place, where lie such notables as Chopin, Gertrude Stein, Oscar Wilde, Sarah Bernhardt, Isadora Duncan, Edith Piaf & Jim Morrison

GERMANY

BERLIN

Berlin is divided into 5 regions:
Berlin—Overview
Berlin—Kreuzberg
Berlin—Prenzlauer Berg–Mitte
Berlin—Schöneberg-Tiergarten
Berlin—Outer

Berlin — Overview

INFO LINES & SERVICES

Gay AA for English Speakers at Mann-O-Meter 49–30/787–5188 • 5pm Tue, also Gay AA 8pm Th

Lesbenberatung (Lesbian Advice) Kulmer Str 20a (in Kreuzberg) 49–30/215–2000 • switchboard & center • staffed 10am-5pm, till 7pm Tue & Th

Mann-O-Meter Bülowstr 106 (at Nollendorfplatz) 49–30/216–8008 • 5pm-10pm • gay switchboard & center • also cafe • also B&B referral service

Sonntags Club Greifenhagener Str 28 (S/U-Schönhauser Allee) 49–30/449–7590 • info line 10am-6pm daily • LGBT info • also cafe-bar • 5pm-midnight • women's night Fri 8pm

Spinnboden Lesbian Archive & Library U-Bahn 8, Bernauerstr (in 2nd courtyard, 2nd flr) 49–30/448–5848 • call for hours • also by appt

NIGHTCLUBS

MegaDyke Productions 49–30/179 59 12 738 • popular parties & events for lesbians, including L-Tunes at SchwuZ & annual pride events for lesbians in other locations • see www.megadyke.de for more details

RESTAURANTS

Paris Bar Kantstrasse152 49–30/313–8052 • bistro & bar

ENTERTAINMENT & RECREATION

Fritz Music Tour 49–30/3087–5633 • visit the haunts of David Bowie, Nina Hagen, Iggy Pop & Rammstein, among other popular musical acts

The Jewish Museum Berlin Lindenstr 9-14 49–30/2599–3300 • 10am-8pm, till 10pm Mon • German-Jewish history & culture

Schwules (Gay) Museum U6/U7 Mehringdamm 61 49–30/6959–9050 • 2pm-6pm, till 7pm Sat, clsd Tue • guided tours 5pm Sat (in German) • exhibits, archives & library

PUBLICATIONS

Siegessäule 49–30/235–5390 • free monthly LGBT city magazine (in German) • awesome maps

Berlin — Kreuzberg

ACCOMMODATIONS

Hotel Transit Hagelberger Straße 53–54 49–30/789–0470 • gay-friendly • loft-style hotel in 19th-c factory • also bar

The Mövenpick Hotel 49–30/230–060 • gay-friendly • convenient location • also space-agey bar

BARS

Barbie Bar Mehringdamm 77 (at Kreuzbergstr) 49–30/6956–8610 • 3pm-close • lesbians/ gay men • lounge • terrace

Bierhimmel Oranienstr 183 (U-Kottbusser Tor) 49–30/615–3122 • 9am-3am, from 1pm wknds • gay/ straight • young crowd

Galander Grossbeerenstr 54 (nr Mehringdamm) 49–30/2850–9030 • 6pm-2am • gay/ straight • lovely 20's cocktail bar • small snacks served

Mobel Olfe Reichenbergerstrasse 177 (at Skalitzer) 49–30/2327–4690 • 8pm-close Tue-Sun • popular • lesbians/ gay men

Rauschgold Mehringdamm 62 (U-Mehringdamm) 49–30/7895–2668 • 8pm-close • lesbians/ gay men

Roses Oranienstr 187 (at Kottbusser Tor) 49–30/615–6570 • 10pm-close • popular • lesbians/ gay men • transgender-friendly • young crowd

Sofia • open 9am, from 11am Sat & 8pm Sun • lesbians/ gay men

NIGHTCLUBS

L-tunes Mehringdamm 61 (at SchwuZ) 49–30/179 59 12 738 • 10pm last Fri only • mostly women, queer friends welcome • dancing/DJ • events

SchwuZ (SchwulenZentrum) Mehringdamm 61 (enter through Café Sundstroem) 49–30/629–088 • from 11pm Fri-Sat • mostly gay men • more women last Fri • dancing/DJ • live/ drag shows • young crowd • wheelchair access

Serene Bar Schwiebusser Str 2 49–30/6904–1580 • lesbians/ gay men • popular Girls Bar Th • Girls Dance 10pm Sat

SO 36 Oranienstr 190 (at Kottbusser Tor) **49–30/6140–1306, 49–30/6140–1307** • popular • gay/straight • dancing/DJ • transgender-friendly • live shows • videos • young crowd • wheelchair access • theme nights include Café Fatal (ballroom dancing) & Gayhane (Turkish night)

CAFES

Drama Mehringdamm 63 **49–30/6746–9562** • opens 2pm • also bar & terrace

Melitta Sundström Mehringdamm 61 (at Gneisenaustr, U-Mehringdamm) **49–30/692–4414** • 10am-11pm • lesbians/gay men • terrace • wheelchair access • also LGBT bookstore

Berlin

LGBT PRIDE:

Christopher Street Day, 3rd or 4th Saturday in June, web: www.csd-berlin.de.

ANNUAL EVENTS:

February - Berlinale: Berlin Int'l Film Festival w/ Queer Teddy Award 49-30/259-200, web: www.berlinale.de.

April - Verzaubert Int'l Queer Film Festival, web: www.verzaubertfilmfest.com.

June - Lesbian & Gay City Festival/ Stadtfest, web: www.regenbogenfonds.de.

Sept- Folsom Europe, web: www.folsom-europe.info.

October - Wigstoeckel transgender/ drag festival, web: www.wigstoeckel.com.

November - Jazz Fest Berlin, www.berlinerfestspiele.de.

CITY INFO:

Berlin-Tourism, web: www.visitberlin.de/en.

Europa Center 49–30/2649-7940, web: www.europa-center-berlin.de.

TRANSIT:

Taxifunk Berlin 49–800/443–322, web: www.taxifunkberlin.de.

Jet Express-Bus X9 from Tegel Airport to central Berlin 49–30/19449.

U-Bahn (subway) and bus 49–30/19449, web: www.bvg.de.

S-Bahn (elevated train) 49-30/2974–3333, web: www.s-bahn-berlin.de.

ATTRACTIONS:

Bauhaus Design Museum 49–30/254–0020, web: www.bauhaus.de.

Brandenburg Gate.

Charlottenburg Palace 49–30/2655-7656.

Egyptian Museum 49–30/2090–5544, web: www.egyptian-museum-berlin.com.

Gay Museum 49–30/6959–9050, web: www.schwulesmuseum.de.

Homo Memorial (at Nollendorfplatz station).

The Jewish Museum Berlin 49-30/2599–3300, web: www.juedisches-museum-berlin.de.

Kaiser Wilhelm Memorial Church, web: www.gedaechtniskirche-berlin.de.

Käthe-Kollwitz Museum 49–30/882–5210, web: www.kaethe-kollwitz.de.

Museuminsel (Museum Island) 49–30/266–424-242, web: www.smb.spk-berlin.de.

Reichstag 49–30/2273–2152, web: www.bundestag.de.

WEATHER:

Berlin is on the same parallel as Newfoundland, so if you're visiting in the winter, prepare for snow and bitter cold. Summer is balmy while spring and fall are beautiful, if sometimes rainy.

Sudblock Admiralstrasse 1-2 • 10am-7pm • lesbians/ gay men • live entertainment

RESTAURANTS

Amrit Oranienstr 202 49–30/612–5550 • noon-1am • Indian

Kaiserstein Mehringdamm 80 49–30/7889–5887 • 9am-1am

Little Otik Graefestrasse 71 49–30/5036–2301 • 7pm-11pm, clsd Sun-Tue • gay-owned

Locus Marheinekeplatz 4 49–30/691–5637 • 10am-1:30am • popular • lesbians/ gay men • Mexican • full bar • lesbian-owned

Restaurant Z Friesenstr 12 49–30/692–2716 • 5pm-1am • Greek/ Mediterranean

SEX CLUBS

Be Cunt Görlitzer Str 71 (at Club Culture Houze) 49–30/6170–9669 • 2nd Tue of the month • trans, dykes, genderfucks, femmes, tomboys & female queers

Club Culture Houze Görlitzer Str 71 (off Skalitzer Str) 49–30/6170–9669 • 2nd Tue lesbian night, gay male theme nights Mon, Th & Sun, gay/ straight other nights

EROTICA

Altelier Dos Santos Mehringdamm 119 (U Platz der Luftbrucke) 49–30/5059–9919 • noon-6pm, till 4pm Sat • high quality custom leather & fetish wear • lesbian-owned

Playstixx Heimstrasse 6 49–30/6165–9500 • makers & sellers of silicone toys for women & lovers

Sexclusivitäten Fürbringer Str 2 49–30/693–6666 • lesbian sex shop • Open Salon sex party noon-8pm Fri • also escort service

Berlin—Prenzlauer Berg-Mitte

ACCOMMODATIONS

Andel's Hotel Landsberger Allee 106 49–30/453–053 • gay-friendly • WiFi • also restaurant • wheelchair access

Arte Luise Kunsthotel Luisenstr 19 (Mitte) 49–30/284–480 • gay-friendly • former palace near River Spree

Intermezzo Hotel for Women Gertrud-Kolmar Str 5 (at Brandenburger Tor) 49–30/2248–9096 • women only • wheelchair access

Schall & Rauch Pension Gleimstr 23 (at Schönhauser Allee) 49–30/339–723 • lesbians/ gay men • also bar & restaurant

BARS

Besenkammer Bar Rathausstr 1 (at Alexanderplatz, under the S-Bahn bridge) 49–30/242–4083 • 24hrs • lesbians/ gay men • tiny "beer bar"

Betty F*** Mulackstrasse 13 (at Gormannstrasse) • from 10pm • lesbians/ gay men • tiny neighborhood bar

Cafe Amsterdam Gleimstr 24 (at Schönhauser Allee) 49–30/448–0792, 49–30/231–6796 • 9am-3am, till 5am Fri-Sat • food served • gay/ straight • transgender-friendly • terrace • wheelchair access • also pension

Marietta Stargarder Str 13 49–30/4372–0646 • 10am-2am, till 4am Sat-Sun • lesbians/ gay men

Perle Sredzkistrasse 64 • 7pm-close, clsd Sun-Mon • lesbians/ gay men • innovative lighting & electronica

Privatleben Rhinowerstr 12 (at Gleimstra) 49–30/4320–5851 • from 6pm • lesbians/ gay men • small friendly bar

Reingold Novalisstr 11 (U-Oranienburger Str) 49–30/4985–3450 • from 7pm, clsd Sun-Mon • gay/ straight • more gay Th • food served • lesbian-owned cocktail lounge

Sanatorium 23 Frankfurter Allee 23 49–30/4202–1193 • from 3pm • gay/ straight • trendy cafe/ bar • also guesthouse

Sharon Stonewall Kleinen Präsidentenstr 3 (at Hackeschen Market) 49–30/2408–5502 • 8pm-2am, till 4:30am Fri-Sat, clsd Mon • lesbians/ gay men • WiFi

Zum Schmutzigen Hobby/ Nina's Bar Revalerstrasse 99 • 6pm-close • lesbians/ gay men • dancing/DJ • drag shows • transgender-friendly

NIGHTCLUBS

Berghain Am Wrietzener Bahnhof (off Strasse der Pariser Kommune, near Ostbahnhof station) 49–30/2936–0210 • lesbians/ gay men • converted power station is now popular dance club

Chantals House of Shame • 11pm Th & Bad Girls club monthly parties

Girls Town Karl-Marx-Allee 33 (at Kino International, U-Schillingstr) 49–30/2475–6011 • 2nd Sat every other month • mostly women • dancing/DJ • huge, popular lesbian club

GMF Alexanderstrasse 7 (at Week End, U-Alexanderplatz) 49–30/2809–5396 • mostly gay men • Sun only 11pm-close

Irrenhouse Am Friedrichshain 33 (at Geburtstagsklub) • 3rd Sat • lesbians/ gay men • dancing/DJ • drag shows • transgender-friendly • Nina Queer's monthly drag party

KitKat Club Kopenickerstrasse 76 (enter on Bruckenstrasse) **49–30/2173–6841** • 8pm-close Th, 11pm-8am Fri-Sat • gay/ straight • also S/M club • cabaret

Klub International Karl-Marx-Allee 33 (at Kino International, U-Schillingstr) **49–30/2475–6011** • 11pm-close, 2nd Sat lesbian night • mostly gay men • dancing/DJ • cover charge

Milkshake Warschauer Str 34 (at Monstrer Ronson's) • check milkshakegirls.de for events • mostly women • dancing/DJ • transgender-friendly

Spy Club Friedrichstr/ Unter den Linden (at Cookies) **49–30/2809–5396** • last Sat only • lesbians/ gay men • dancing/DJ

CAFES

Anna Blume Kollwitzstrasse 83 **49–30/4404–8749** • 8am-2am • great brkfst

Café Berger Senefelderstr 4 (btwn Helmholtzplatz & Kollwitz area) **49–30/4320–5851** • 10am-7pm • popular • WiFi

Cafe Seidenfaden Dircksenstr 47 (U-Alexanderplatz) **49–30/283–2783** • 10am-6pm, noon-8pm Sat, clsd Sun • women only • drug- & alcohol-free cafe • info board • nonsmoking

November Husemannstr 15 (at Sredzkistr) **49–30/442–8425** • 10am-2am • lesbians/ gay men • cafe-bar • terrace • brkfst buffet wknds

RESTAURANTS

Anda Lucia Savignyplatz 2 **49–30/5471–0271** • 6pm-10pm • tapas bar

The Kosher Classroom Auguststrasse 11-13 **49–30/3300–6070** • traditional Jewish cuisine, vegan meals and specialties from the sea

Rice Queen Danziger Str 13 (U-Eberswalder Str) **49–30/4404–5800** • 5pm-11pm, from 2pm wknds • Asian fusion

Schall & Rauch Wirtshaus Gleimstr 23 (at Schönhauser Allee) **49–30/443–3970** • 10am-close • lesbians/ gay men

Thüringer Stuben Stargarder Str 28 (at Dunckerstr, S/U-Schönhauser Allee) **49–30/4463–3339** • 4pm-1am, from noon Sun • full bar

BOOKSTORES

Ana Koluth Schönhauser Allee 124 **49–30/8733–6980** • 10am-8pm, till 6pm Sat, clsd Sun • lesbian-owned

EROTICA

Blackstyle Seelower Str 5 (S/U-Schönhauser Allee) **49–30/4468–8595** • clsd Sun • latex & rubber wear

Berlin—Schöneberg-Tiergarten

ACCOMMODATIONS

Arco Hotel Geisbergstr 30 (at Ansbacherstr, U-Wittenbergplatz) **49–30/235–1480** • gay/ straight • centrally located • kids/ pets ok • wheelchair access • gay-owned

Axel Hotel Berlin Lietzenburger Str 13/15 **49–30/2100–2893** • mostly gay men • WiFi

Bananas Berlin Geisbergstr 41 **49–30/2196–1768** • mostly gay men • WiFi • central location in a quiet area • gay-owned

Berlin B&B • lesbians/ gay men • apt rentals, 2 locations • WiFi • gay-owned

Hotel California Kurfürstendamm 35 (at Knesebeckstr, U-Uhlandstr) **49–30/880–120** • gay-friendly • cafe/ bar • nonsmoking flr • kids ok

Hotel Hansablick Flotowstr 6 (at Bachstr, off Str des 17 Juni) **49–30/390–4800** • gay-friendly • full brkfst • kids/ pets ok • WiFi

Hotel Zu Hause Kleiststrasse 35 (at Eisenacher Str) **49–(0)30/2362–6522** • gay/ straight • WiFi • gay-owned

BARS

Blond Eisenacher Str 3a (at Fuggerstr, U-Nollendorfplatz) **49–30/6640–3947** • 10am-2am • gay/ straight • food served • WiFi

Eldorado Motzstr 20 (U-Nollendorfplatz) **49–30/8431–6901** • 24hrs • mostly gay men • food served • music bar • terrace

Green Door Winterfeldstr 50 **49–30/152–515** • 6pm-3am, till 4am Fri-Sat * gay/straight • cute decor

Hafen Motzstr 19 (at Eisenacher Str, U-Nollendorfplatz) **49–30/211–4118** • 8pm-close • mostly gay men • transgender-friendly • live shows

HarDie's Kneipe Ansbacherstr 29 (in Wittenberplatz) **49–30/2363–9841** • noon-midnight, till 2am wknds • mostly gay men • cafe/ pub

Heile Welt Motzstrasse 5 **49–30/2191–7507** • 6pm-4am • popular • lesbians/ gay men

Incognito Hohenstauffenstr 53 (off Luther Str, U-Viktoria Luise Platz) **49–30/2191–6300** • 6pm-4am • lesbians/ gay men • trangender-friendly

Kumpelnest 3000 Lützowstr 23 (at Potsdamer Str, U-Kurfürstenstr) **49–30/261–6918** • 5pm-5am, till 8am Fri-Sat • popular wknds • gay-friendly • cocktail bar • dancing/DJ • transgender-friendly • young crowd

Nah-Bar Kalkreuthstr 16 **49–30/3150–3062** • open 6pm Fri-Sat, Mon-Tue • mostly women • games nights & DJ some nights

Neues Ufer Haupstrasse 157 (U-Bahn Kleistpark) **49–30/7895–7900** • 11am-2am, clsd wknds • lesbians/ gay men • older crowd

Prinz Knecht Fuggerstr 33 (U-Nollendorfplatz) **49–30/236–27444** • 3pm-2am • popular • mostly gay men

Pussy-Cat Kalckreuthstr 7 (U-Nollendorfplatz) **49–30/213–3586** • 6pm-6am • lesbians/ gay men

Storks Kleiststrasse 7 **49–30/2362–4700** • 10pm-late, 24hrs wknds • mostly gay men • small bar & bistro

Vielharmonie **49–30/3064–7302** • 6pm-close • mostly gay men • food served

NIGHTCLUBS

Propaganda Nollendorfplatz 5 (at Goya Theater) • 2nd Sat only • mostly gay men • dancing/DJ • drag shows

CAFES

Begine Potsdamer Str 139 (at Bülowstr) **49–30/215–1414** • meeting point for women

Cafe Berio Maaßenstr 7 (at Winterfeldtstr, U-Nollendorfplatz) **49–30/216–1946** • 7am-midnight, from 8am wknds • popular • brkfst all day • also bar • seasonal terrace • wheelchair access

Cafe Savigny Grolmanstr 53–54 (at Savignyplatz) **49–30/4470–8386** • 9am-midnight • artsy crowd • full bar • terrace

RESTAURANTS

Café des Artistes Fuggerstr 35 **49–30/2363–5249** • noon-midnight • great food & nice staff

Diodata Goltzstrasse 51 **49–30/2191–7884** • 11am-11pm, 10am-3pm Sun • Viennese

Fritz & Co Wittenbergplatz • organic snack bar • look for the rainbow flags

Gnadenbrot Martin-Luther-Str 20a **49–30/2196–1786** • 3pm-1am • cheap & good

Hamburger Mary's Lietzenburger Str 15 (in theAxel Hotel) **49–30/2100–2895** • brkfst & dinner, full bar • mostly gay men • drag shows • karaoke • wheelchair access • gay-owned

More Motzstrasse 28 (at Martin-Lutherstrasse) **49–30/2363–5702** • 9am-midnight • popular

Sissi Motzstr 34 **49–30/2101–8101** • great Austrian food, terrace & location

ENTERTAINMENT & RECREATION

Xenon Kino Kolonnenstr 5-6 **49–30/7800–1530** • gay & lesbian cinema

Berlin—Outer

ACCOMMODATIONS

Artemisia Women's Hotel Brandenburgischestr 18 (at Konstanzerstr) **49–30/873–8905, 49–30/869–9320** • the only hotel for women in Berlin • a real bargain • quiet rooms • bar • sundeck w/ view • some shared baths • nonsmoking rooms available

Charlottenburger Hof Stuttgarter Platz 14 (at Wilmersdorfer Str) **49–30/329–070** • gay-friendly • centrally located • also cafe & bar open 24hrs

BARS

Himmelreich Simon Dach Str 36 (off Warschauer Str, in Friedrichshain, U-Frankfurter Tor) **49–30/2936–9292** • from 7pm Mon-Fri, 2pm-close wknds • lesbians/ gay men • women's night Tue

Monster Ronsons Warschauerstr 34 **49–30/8975–1327** • 7pm-4am • lesbians/ gay men • popular karaoke bar

Silver Future Weserstr 206 (Neukölln) **49–30/7563–4987** • 2pm-2am, till 3am Th-Sat

NIGHTCLUBS

Die Busche Warschauer Platz 18 **49–30/296–0800** • 10pm-5am, tiill 7am Fri-Sat, clsd Tue & Th • popular • lesbians/ gay men • dancing/DJ • live shows • terrace • cover charge

Mermaids Falckensteinstr 47 (at Comet Club) • 10pm 3rd Sat, May-Oct only • mostly women • dancing/DJ • also between parties on the 2nd Fri at Hafenbar Marianne Mariannenstr 6

CAFES

Schrader's Malplaquetstr 16b (at Utrechter Str, Wedding) **49–30/4508–2663** • also bar • gay-owned

RESTAURANTS

Cafe Rix Karl-Marx-Str 141 (in Neükolln) **49–30/686–9020** • 9am-midnight • Mediterranean • plenty veggie • also bar

Kurhaus Korsakow Grunbergrestrasse 81 (in Friedrichshain) **49–30/5473–7786** • 5pm-close, from 9am wknds, clsd Mon

IRELAND

Dublin

INFO LINES & SERVICES

AA 105 Capel St (at Outhouse) **353–1/873–4999** • 6pm Tue & 7:45pm Fri

Dublin Lesbian Line **353–1/872–9911** • 7pm-9pm Mon & Th

Gay Switchboard Dublin **353–1/872–1055** • 6:30pm-9:30pm, 4pm-6pm wknds

Outhouse 105 Capel St **353–1/873–4999** • LGBT community center, cafe, library, meetings

ACCOMMODATIONS

The Arlington Hotel Temple Bar 16 Lord Edward St **353–1/670–8777** • gay/ straight • conveniently located with restaurant & bar

The Clarence 6-8 Wellington Quay **353–1/407–0800** • gay-friendly • owned by Bono & The Edge of U2 • kids ok • WiFi • wheelchair access

The Dylan Eastmoreland Place **353–1/660–3000** • gay/ straight • restaurant & bar

Fitzwilliam Hotel St Stephen's Green **353–1/478–7000** • gay-friendly • bar & restaurant

Inn On the Liffey 21 Upper Ormond Quay **353–1/677–0828** • lesbians/ gay men • WiFi • gay-owned

The Merchant House 8 Eustace St (Temple Bar Area) **353–1/633–4477** • gay/ straight • WiFi • gay-owned

Waterloo House 8-10 Waterloo Rd **353–1/660–1888** • 5-star hotel • gay/ straight • restaurant & bar

BARS

The Dragon 64-45 S Great Georges St **353–1/478–1590** • 8pm-3am, clsd Sun, Tue & Wed • lesbians/ gay men • dancing/DJ

Front Lounge 33 Parliament St **353–1/670–4112** • noon-11:30pm, till 2am Sat • popular • lesbians/ gay men • dancing/DJ • transgender-friendly • karaoke

The George aka Bridies 89 S Great George St **353–1/478–2983** • 2pm-2:30am, till 11:30pm Mon-Tue, till 1am Sun • popular • lesbians/ gay men • dancing/DJ • drag shows • karaoke

Panti Bar 7-8 Capel St **353–1/874–0710** • 5pm-close • lesbians/ gay men • dancing/DJ • food • drag shows • wheelchair access

NIGHTCLUBS

Mother Exchange St (at Copper Alley, Arlington Hotel) • 10:30pm Sat only • lesbians/ gay men • dancing/DJ

Nimhneach • gay/ straight • fetish & BDSM party • strict dress code • see www.nimhneach.ie for dates & location

Prhomo 6 Wicklow St (at Base Ba) • 10:30pm Th only • lesbians/ gay men • dancing/DJ

CAFES

3Fe 54 Middle Abbey St (Twisted Pepper Bldg) **353–1/661–9329** • 10am-7pm, noon-6pm Sun • run by barista champion

Irish Film Institute Bar & Restaurant 6 Eustace St (in Temple Bar) **353–1/679–5744** • lunch & dinner • next to independent cinema • light meals • plenty veggie

Lovinspoon Cafe 13 N Frederick St **353–1/804–7604** • 7am-6pm, clsd Sun (except summers)

RESTAURANTS

Brasserie Sixty6 66 S Great Georges St **353–1/400–5878** • brkfst, lunch, dinner, wknd brunch • WiFi

La Cave 28 S Anne St **353–1/679–4409** • 12:30pm-close, from 6pm Sun • French

The Chameleon 1 Lower Fownes St **353–1/671–0362** • 5pm-11pm, from 3pm Sun, clsd Mon • Indonesian

Cornucopia 19 Wicklow **353–1/677–7583** • 8:30am-9pm, till 10:30pm Sat, from noon Sun • affordable vegetarian

DavyByrnes 21 Duke St **353–1/677–5217** • 11am-11pm • famous pub frequented by James Joyce

L' Ecrivain 109A Lower Baggot St **353–1/661–1919** • lunch Mon-Fri, dinner Mon-Sat, clsd Sun • also piano bar • reservations recommended

Eden 7 South William St **353–1/670–6887** • lunch & dinner, wknd brunch • patio dining

F.X. Buckley 2 Crow St **353–1/671–1248** • 5:30pm-close • steak & seafood

Fire Restaurant Mansion House, Dawson St 353–1/676–7200 • 5:30pm-close, noon-3pm jazz lunch Sat, clsd Sun

Gruel 68A Dame St 353–1/670–7119 • lunch & dinner

Odessa 14 Dame Court 353–1/670–7634 • lunch & dinner, wknd brunch • local hot spot • also nightclub w/ drag shows

Shack 24 E Essex St 353–1/679–0043 • lunch & dinner

Town Bar & Grill 21 Kildare St 353–1/662–4800 • lunch & dinner, clsd Sun-Mon • modern Irish brasserie

Trocadero 4 Saint Andrew St 353–1/677–5545 • 5pm-midnight, clsd Sun

The Winding Stair Restaurant 40 Lower Ormond Quay 353–1/872–7320 • lunch & dinner • Irish • young crowd • also bookshop

ENTERTAINMENT & RECREATION

Irish Queer Archive 2 Kildare St (National Library of Ireland)

BOOKSTORES

Chapters Bookstore Ivy House, Parnell St 353–1/872–3297 • LGBT section

The Winding Stair Bookshop 40 Lower Ormond Quay 353–1/872–7320 • 10am-6pm, till 7pm Th-Sat, from noon Sun • also restaurant

PUBLICATIONS

GCN (Gay Community News) Unit 2 Scarlet Row, Essex St W, Temple Bar, 8 353–1/675–5025 • monthly LGBT newspaper • many resources

ITALY

Rome

Note: M°=Metro station

INFO LINES & SERVICES

Circolo di Cultura Omosessual Mario Mieli Via Efeso 2a (M° San Paolo) 800/110–611 • 4pm-7pm Mon-Fri • switchboard, meetings & discussion groups

Gay Help Line 800/713–713 • 4pm-8pm, clsd Sun

ACCOMMODATIONS

2nd Floor B&B via San Giovanni in Laterano 10 39–06/9604–9256 • lesbians/gay men • in the heart of Rome's gaylife • WiFi • gay-owned

58 Le Real de Luxe Via Cavour 58, 4th flr (near Colosseum) 39–06/482–3566, 0039/347–182–9387 (CELL) • gay/ straight • B&B inn • kids ok • nonsmoking • WiFi • wheelchair access

Albergo Del Sole al Pantheon Piazza della Rotonda 63 39–06/678–0441 • gay-friendly • 4-star hotel • jacuzzi • kids ok

Ares Rooms Via Domenichino 7 39–06/474–4525, 39–340/278–1248 (CELL) • gay-friendly • some shared baths

B&B In And Out Rome Via Arco del Monte (at Viale Trastevere) 39–339/784–0653 • gay/ straight • in 18th-c palace • kids/ pets ok • nonsmoking • WiFi • wheelchair access • lesbian-owned

Best Place Via Turati 13 39–329/213–2320 • lesbians/ gay men • reservations required

Claridge Hotel Via Liegi 62 39–06/845–441 • gay-friendly • near Borghese park • gym w/ sauna & Turkish bath

Daphne Veneto Via di San Basilio 55 39–06/8745–0086 • gay-friendly • small, cozy inn in heart of historical Rome • kids ok • nonsmoking • also Daphne Trevi at Via degli Avignonesi 20

Discover Roma Via Castelfidardo 50 39–06/4470–3154 • lesbians/ gay men • woman-owned

Domus Valeria B&B Via del Babuino 96, Apt 14 (Spanish Square) 39–339/232–6540 • lesbians/ gay men • shared baths • WiFi • gay-owned

Franklin Via Rodi 29 39–06/3903–0165 • gay-friendly • music-themed hotel w/ CD library

Gayopen B&B Via dello Statuto 44, Apt 18 (at Via Merulana, Piazza Vittorio) 39–06/482–0013 • gay/ straight • B&B • full brkfst • kids/ pets ok • lesbian & gay-owned

Hotel Altavilla Via Principe Amedeo 9 39–06/474–1186 • gay-friendly • pets ok • also bar

Hotel Edera Via A Poliziano 75 39–06/7045–3888 • gay-friendly • WiFi

Hotel Labelle Via Cavour 310 39–06/679–4750 • lesbians/ gay men • near the Roman Forum

Hotel Malu Via Principe Amedeo 85/a 39–06/9603–1250 • gay-friendly • WiFi • near Termini Station

Hotel Scott House Via Gioberti 30 39–06/446–5379 • gay-friendly

Hotel Welcome Piram Via Amendola 7 **39–06/4890–1248** • lesbians/ gay men • hot tubs

Nicolas Inn Via Cavour 295 (at Via dei Serpenti) **39–06/9761–8483, 39–338/937–8387** • gay-friendly • near the Colosseum & Roman Forum • nonsmoking • WiFi • native English speaker

Orsa Maggiore for Women Via San Francesco di Sales 1/a (at Via della Lungara) **39–06/689–3753** • women only • inside 16th-c former convent • nonsmoking

Pensione Ottaviano Via Ottaviano 6 **39–06/3973–8138** • gay-friendly • in quiet area near St Peter's Square • hostel

The Rainbow B&B Viale Giulio Cesare 151 **39–06/347–507–0344 (CELL), 39–06/348–3343689** • lesbians/ gay men • WiFi

Relais Conte di Cavour de Luxe B&B Via Farini 16 (at Via Cavour) **39–06/482–1638** • gay-friendly • great location • WiFi

Relais le Clarisse Via Cardinale Merry del Val 20 (at Viale Trastevere) **39–06/5833–4437** • gay/ straight • nonsmoking • WiFi • on historic site in central Rome • lesbian-owned

Scalinata di Spagna Piazza Trinità dei Monti 17 (M° Piazza di Spagna) **39–06/6994–0896, 39–06/679–3006 (BOOKING #)** • gay-friendly • roof garden • kids/ pets ok • nonsmoking • WiFi

Valadier Via della Fontanella 15 **39–06/361–1998** • gay-friendly • kids ok • 2 restaurants & piano bar • WiFi

BARS

Coming Out Via San Giovanni in Laterano 8 (near Colosseum) **39–06/700–9871** • 7:30pm-2am • popular • lesbians/ gay men • dancing/DJ • transgender-friendly • food served • live music Th • karaoke • lesbian-owned

Garbo Vicolo di Santa Margherita 1a (in Trastevere, Tram 8) **39–06/581–2766, 39–34/9815–1446** • 10pm-3am, clsd Mon • lesbians/ gay men • cocktail bar • food served • gay-owned

Il Giardino dei Ciliegi Via dei Fienaroli 4 **39–06/580–3423** • 5pm-2am, from 1pm Sun • lesbians/ gay men • tea salon & bar

NIGHTCLUBS

L' Alibi Via di Monte Testaccio 40–44 (M° Piramide) **39–06/574–3448** • 11pm-4am, clsd Mon-Tue • popular • lesbians/ gay men • dancing/DJ • theme nights • live shows • rooftop garden in summer • young crowd

Amigdala Via delle Conce 14 (at Rising Love) • Sat only • check site for dates: www.amigdalaqueer.it • lesbians/ gay men • dancing/DJ • electronica & queer culture

Frutta e Verdura Via Placido Zurla 68-70 (in Casilina) **39–347/244–6721 (ENGLISH), 39–348/879–7063 (ITALIAN)** • 4:30am-10am Sun & public holiday evenings • lesbians/ gay men • dancing/DJ

Gorgeous Via del Commercio 36 (at Alpheus) **39–06/574–7826** • 11pm-5am Sat • lesbians/ gay men • dancing/DJ

Muccassassina via di Portonaccio 212 (at Qube) **39–06/541–3985** • 10:30pm-5am Fri only (Sept-June) • popular • lesbians/ gay men • dancing/DJ • live shows • young crowd • cover charge

Venus Rising Via Libetta 13 **39–06/574–8277** • last Sun only • special events for women • check www.venusrising.it for upcoming parties

CAFES

Oppio Caffè Via delle Terme di Tito 72 **39–06/474–5262, 39–347/510–8594 (CELL)** • brkfst, lunch & dinner • open 24hrs in Aug • popular • lesbians/ gay men • full bar • live shows • terrace w/ great view

RESTAURANTS

Asino Cotto Ristorante Via dei Vascellari 38 (in Travestere, Tram 8) **39–06/589–8985** • lunch & dinner, clsd Mon • creative gourmet Mediterranean • reservations required • gay-owned

La Carbonara Via Panisperna 214 **39–06/482–5176** • lunch & dinner, clsd Sun • classic Roman cuisine since 1906

Città in Fiore Via Cavour 269 **39–06/482–4874** • lunch Th-Mon, dinner nightly • lesbians/ gay men • Chinese

Ditirambo Piazza della Cancelleria 74-75 (near Campo dei Fiori) **39–06/687–1626**

La Focaccia Via della Pace 11 **39–06/6880–3312** • 11am-2am • pizza

Gelateria San Crispino Via Panetteria 42 (near Trevi Fountain) **39–06/679–3924** • noon-12:30am, till 1:30am Fri-Sat, clsd Tue • gelato!

Mater Matuta Via Milano 47 (basement) **39–06/4782–5746** • lunch Mon-Fri, dinner nightly • also wine bar

Osteria del Pegno Vicolo Montevecchio 8 (Plaza Navona) **39–06/6880–7025** • lunch & dinner, clsd Wed winter • large pizza selection • wheelchair access

Ristorante da Dino Via dei Mille 10 (at Piazza Indipendenza) **39–06/491–425** • clsd Wed • family-run Roman food at reasonable prices • near Termini Station

La Taverna di Edoardo II Vicolo Margana 14 **39–06/6994–2419** • 7:30pm-midnight, clsd Tue • lesbians/ gay men • full bar • wheelchair access

ENTERTAINMENT & RECREATION

Gay Village **39–06/753–8396** • gay summer festival

RETAIL SHOPS

Hydra II Via Urbana 139 **39–06/489–7773** • leather, vinyl, clubwear, western, vintage & more

Souvenir Rainbow via San Giovanni in Laterano 26 **39–06/7720–4593** • 9am-9pm • gay gifts

EROTICA

Alcova Piazza Sforza Cesarini 27 (at Corso Vittorio Emanuele II) **39–06/686–4118** • fetish shop

TRAVEL AGENTS

Through Eternity Tours Italy Via Astura 2/B **39–06/700–9336** • walking tours of Rome • get 10% off by using the code "Damron10" • gay-owned

NETHERLANDS

AMSTERDAM

Amsterdam is divided into 5 regions:
Amsterdam—Overview
Amsterdam—Centrum
Amsterdam—Jordaan
Amsterdam—Rembrandtplein
Amsterdam—Outer

Amsterdam—Overview

INFO LINES & SERVICES

COC-Amsterdam Rozenstraat 14 (at Prinsengracht, in the Jordaan) **31–20/626–3087** • info line 10am-5pm, also cafe 8pm-11:30pm Wed-Fri • also sponsors women's parties at clubs around town • www.cocamsterdam.nl for info

Gay/ Lesbian Switchboard **31–20/623–6565** • noon-10pm, 4pm-8pm wknds • English spoken

Pink Point Westermarkt (Raadhuisstraat & Keizersgracht, in the Jordaan by Homomonument) **31–20/428–1070** • 10am-6pm • info on Homomonument & general LGBT info • friendly volunteers • queer souvenirs & gifts

NIGHTCLUBS

Fuckin' Pop Queers/ Ultrasexi/ Multisexi • lesbians/ gay men • monthly queer dance parties at different clubs around the city • check ultrasexi.com for details

Girlesque • mostly women (cool gay guys welcome) • huge quarterly dance parties • check www.girlesque.nl for info

UNK Admiraal de Ruijterweg 56 B (at Club 8) **31–20/685–1703** • 4th Sat only • lesbians/ gay men • electro/ queer dance party

ENTERTAINMENT & RECREATION

The Anne Frank House Prinsengracht 263-267 (in the Jordaan) **31–20/556–7105** **(RECORDED INFO)**, **31–20/556–7100** • the final hiding place of Amsterdam's most famous resident

Boom Chicago Leidseplein 12 (Leidseplein Theater) **31–20/423–0101** **(TICKETS)** • English-language improv comedy • distributes free Boom! guide to Amsterdam

Gay and Lesbian History Walks **31–20/628–689–775** • mention Damron & you get 10% off

MacBike Stationsplein 12 (next to Centraal Station) **31–20/620–0985** • rental bikes & map for self-guided tour of Amsterdam's gay points of interest, also 4 other locations

The van Gogh Museum Paulus Potterstr 7 (on the Museumplein) **31–20/570–5200** • under renovations, check www.vangoghmuseum.nl for updates

PUBLICATIONS

Gay News Amsterdam **31–20/679–1556** • bilingual paper • extensive listings

Gay & Night **31–20/788–1360** • free monthly bilingual entertainment paper w/ club listings

Amsterdam—Centrum

ACCOMMODATIONS

Amsterdam B&B Barangay **31–6/2504–5432** • gay/ straight • 1777 town house • near tourist attractions • full brkfst • nonsmoking • WiFi • gay-owned

Amsterdam Central B&B Oudebrugsteeg 6-II (at Warmoesstraat) 31–62/445–7593 • lesbians/gay men • B&B apts in 16th-c guesthouse • WiFi • full brkfst • gay-owned

Crowne Plaza Amsterdam City Centre NZ Voorburgwal 5 31–20/620-0500, 877/227-6963 (US#) • gay-friendly • pool • restaurant & bar • wheelchair access

Hotel The Exchange Damrak 50 31–20/523-0080 • gay/straight • an independent design hotel in central Amsterdam that playfully weaves together fashion and architecture in unique rooms

Mauro Mansion Geldersekade 16 (at OZ Kolk) • gay/straight • 9-room boutique-style hotel, set in a 16th century canal house

NH City Centre Hotel Spuistraat 288–292 31–20/420-4545 • gay-friendly • kids/pets ok • WiFi • wheelchair access

NH Grand Hotel Krasnapolsky Dam 9 (at Warmoesstraat) 31–20/554-9111 • gay-friendly • full-service hotel • in the city center opposite Royal Palace • WiFi • wheelchair access

Palace B&B Spuistraat 224 31–6/3169-3878 • gay/straight • 1794 bldg w/ indoor garden • nonsmoking • WiFi • gay-owned

Victoria Hotel Amsterdam Damrak 1-5 (opposite Centraal Station) 31–20/623-4255, 800/777-1700 (US#) • gay-friendly • 4-star hotel • pool • gym • restaurants & bar • WiFi • wheelchair access

Amsterdam

LGBT Pride:
1st wknd in August, web: www.amsterdampride.nl.

Annual Events:
April 30 - Queen's Birthday/ Roze Wester Festival, web: www.gala-amsterdam.nl.
May - Memorial Day & Liberation Day.
June - Holland Festival, web: www.hollandfestival.nl.
October - Leather Pride, web: www.leatherpride.nl.

City Info:
Amsterdam Tourism & Convention Board 31-20/201-8800, web: www.iamsterdam.com. Visit their office directly opposite Centraal Station. Netherlands Board of Tourism, web: www.holland.com.

Transit:
31–20/677-7777.
Can also be found at taxi stands on the main squares.
KLM Bus 31–20/653-4975.
GVB 31-20/460-6060, web: www.gvb.nl, or visit their office across from the Centraal Station (Stationsplein 10). Trams, buses & subway.

Attractions:
Anne Frank House 31–20/556-7105, web: www.annefrank.org.
Hermitage Amsterdam 31-20/530-7488, web: www.hermitage.nl.
Homomonument
Jewish Historical Museum 31–20/531-0310, web: www.jhm.nl.
Rembrandt House 31–20/520-0400, web: www.rembrandthuis.nl.
Rijksmuseum 31–20/674-7000, web: www.rijksmuseum.nl.
Stedelijk Museum of Modern Art 31–20/573-2911, web: www.stedelijk.nl.
Vincent van Gogh Museum 31–20/570-5200, web: www.vangoghmuseum.nl.
Red District Tour, web: www.amsterdamredlightdistricttour.com.

Weather:
Temperatures hover around freezing in the winter and rise to the mid-60ºs in the summer. Rain is possible year-round.

Winston Hotel Warmoesstraat 129 31–20/623-1380 • gay-friendly • hipster hotel • rockers & artists • popular bar • live DJs • gallery • some shared baths

BARS

De Barderij Zeedijk 14 (at OZ Kolk) 31–20/420-5132 • noon-1am, till 3am Fri-Sat • mostly gay men • large neighborhood bar/ brown café • older crowd

Cafe Mandje Zeedijk 63 (at Stormsteeg) 31–20/622-5375 • gay/ straight • originally opened in 1927 as Amsterdam's first gay bar by dyke-on-bike Bet van Beeren

Cozy Bar Sint Jacobsstraat 8 31–20/420-8321 • 4pm-1am • mostly gay men • neighborhood • DJ

De Engel Next Door Zeedijk 23-25 (at OZ Kolk) 31–20/427-6381 • 1pm-1am, till 3am Fri-Sat, clsd Mon-Tue • mostly gay men

De Engel van Amsterdam Zeedijk 21 (at OZ Kolk) 31–20/427-6381 • 1pm-1am, till 3am Fri-Sat • mostly gay men • patio

Getto Warmoesstraat 51 (at Niezel) 31–20/421-5151 • 4pm-1am, till 2am Fri-Sat, till midnight Sun, clsd Mon • popular • lesbians/ gay men • live DJs • also restaurant till 11pm

Prik Spuistraat 109 31–20/320-0002 • 4pm-1am, till 3am Fri-Sat • lesbians/ gay men • food served • patio

NIGHTCLUBS

Club Stereo Jonge Roelensteeg 4 (at Kalvertstraat) 31–20/770-4037 • 7pm-1am, till 3am Fri-Sat • gay/ straight • dancing/DJ • live shows

CAFES

Dampkring Haarlemmerstraat 44 31–20/638-0705 • smoking coffeeshop • great fresh OJ

Gary's Late Night TT Vasumweg 260 31–20/637-3643 • noon-3am, till 4am Fri-Sat • popular • fresh muffins & bagels • organic fair-trade coffee

Puccini Bomboni Staalstraat 17 31–20/626-5474 • If you love chocolate, do we have a cafe for you!

RESTAURANTS

Cafe de Jaren Nieuwe Doelenstraat 20-22 31–20/625-5771 • 10am-1am, till 2am Fri-Sat • some veggie • full bar • terrace

Cafe de Schutter Voetboogstraat 13-15 (upstairs) 31–20/622-4608 • noon-1am, till 3am Fri-Sat • popular local hangout • plenty veggie • full bar • terrace

Cafe Latei Zeedijk 143 (in Red Light District) 31–20/625-7485 • 8am-6pm, from 9am Sat, from 11am Sun • Indian food • great coffee hangout • WiFi

Greenwoods Singel 103 (near Dam Square) 31–20/623-7071 • English-style brkfst & tea snacks

Hemelse Modder Oude Waal 11 31–20/624-3203 • 6pm-10pm • popular • lesbians/ gay men • French/ int'l • also full bar • wheelchair access • gay-owned

Japans Restaurant An Weteringschans 76 (at Vijzerstraat) 31–20/624-4672 • lunch & dinner, clsd Sun-Mon • Japanese • patio • cash only

Krua Thai Staalstraat 22 31–20/622-9533 • 5pm-10:30pm • terrace • wheelchair access

Het Land van Walem Keizersgracht 449 31–20/625-3544 • lunch & dinner • int'l • inexpensive • local crowd • canalside terrace • wheelchair access • lesbian-owned

Maoz Muntplein 1 31–20/420-7435 • 11am-1am, till 3am wknds • vegetarian

't Sluisje Torensteeg 1 31–20/624-0813 • 6pm-close, clsd Mon-Tue • popular steak house • lesbians/ gay men • transgender-friendly • full bar (open later) • drag shows nightly

Song Kwae Kloveniersburgwal 14 (near Nieuwmarkt & Chinatown) 31–20/624-2568 • 1pm-10:30pm • Thai • full bar • terrace

BOOKSTORES

The American Book Center Spui 12 31–20/625-5537 • 10am-8pm, till 9pm Th, 11am-6:30pm Sun • large LGBT section • wheelchair access

Boekhandel Vrolijk Gay & Lesbian Bookshop Paleisstraat 135 (at Spuistraat, near Dam Square) 31–20/623-5142 • 11am-6pm, 10am-5pm Sat, from 1pm Sun

RETAIL SHOPS

Gays & Gadgets Spuistraat 44 31–20/330-1461 • gifts, gadgets, clothing, cards

Magic Mushroom Spuistraat 249 31–20/427-5765 • 11am-7pm, till 8pm Fri-Sat • "smartshop": magic mushrooms & more • also Singel 524

GYMS & HEALTH CLUBS

Splash Looiersgracht 26-30 31–20/624-8404 • gym & wellness center

EROTICA

Absolute Danny Oudezijds Achterburgwal 78 (in the Red Light District) **31–20/421–0915** • 11am-9pm • upscale erotica • woman-owned

Black Body Spuistraat 44 **31–20/626–2553** • clsd Sun • rubber clothing specialists • leather • toys • DVDs • wheelchair access

Christine Le Duc Spui 6 **31–20/624–8265**

DeMask Zeedijk 64 **31–20/423–3090** • 11am-7pm, clsd Sun • rubber & leather clothing

Female & Partners Spuistraat 100 **31–20/620–9152** • 11am-6:30pm, from 1pm Mon,till 9pm Th, 1pm-6pm Sun • fashions & toys for women

Amsterdam—Jordaan

ACCOMMODATIONS

Chic and Basic Amsterdam Herengracht 13-19 (at Brouwersgr) **31–20/522–2345** • gay-friendly • "the quiet hotel"

The Dylan Keizersgracht 384 (at Runstraat) **31–20/530–2010** • gay-friendly • sleep in high style • also restaurant

Hotel Acacia Lindengracht 251 (at Lijnbaansgr) **31–20/622–1460** • gay-friendly • "homey hotel in heart of Jordaan" • WiFi

Hotel Pulitzer Prinsengracht 315–331 (at Reestraat) **31–20/523–5235** • gay-friendly • occupies 24 17th-c buildings on 2 of Amsterdam's most picturesque canals

Hotel Rembrandt Centrum Herengracht 255 (at Hartenstraat) **31–20/622–1727** • gay/straight • canalside hotel near Dam Square

Maes B&B Herenstraat 26 (at Keizersgr) **31–20/427–5165** • gay/ straight • nonsmoking • WiFi • gay-owned

Marnixkade Canalview Apartments **31–6/1012–1296** • lesbians/ gay men • fully furnished apts in 17th-c canal house on a quiet canal in heart of Jordaan • nonsmoking • WiFi • gay-owned

Sunhead of 1617 Herengracht 152 (at Leliegracht & Raadshuisstraat) **31–20/626–1809** • gay/ straight • full brkfst • kids/ pets ok • nonsmoking • also several canal apts • WiFi • gay-owned

BARS

Cafe de Gijs Lindengracht 249 (at Lijnbaansgr) **31–20/638–0740, 31–6/2537–3674** • 4pm-1am • 1st Wed of month social gathering for transvestites & transsexuals, from 6pm

Saarein 2 Elandsstraat 119 (at Hazenstraat) **31–20/623–4901** • 4pm-1am, till 2am Fri-Sat, clsd Mon • mostly women • food served • brown cafe

NIGHTCLUBS

Jet Lounge Groen van Prinstererstraat 41 (3 blks W of Westerpark) **31–20/684–1126** • 6pm-1am, till 3am Fri-Sat, clsd Sun-Mon • gay/staright • dancing/DJ • live music

de Trut Bilderdijkstraat 165 (at Kinkerstraat) **31–20/612–3524** • 10pm-3am Sun only • lesbians/ gay men • hip underground dance party in legalized squat • alternative • young crowd

CAFES

Cafe 't Smalle Egelantiersgracht 12 **31–20/623–9617** • 10am-1am, till 2am wknds • brown cafe • full bar • outdoor seating

Lab111 Arie Biemondstrat 111 **31–20/616–9994** • noon-1am, till 3am Fri-Sat, lab turned cafe • lab turned cafe • live music

RESTAURANTS

Bojo Lange Leidsedwarsstraat 49–51 (near Leidseplein) **31–20/622–7434** • 11am-9pm, from 4:30pm wknds • popular • Indonesian

De Bolhoed Prinsengracht 60 (at Tuinstr) **31–20/626–1803** • noon-10pm, from 11am Sat • vegetarian/ vegan

Burger's Patio 2e Tuindwarsstr 12 **31–20/623–6854** • 6pm-1am • Italian • plenty veggie

Foodism Nassaukade 122 (at Hugo de Grootstraat) **31–20/486–8137** • 5pm-10pm • good Mediterranean food • funky & fun

Freud Spaarndammerstraat 424 **31–20/688–5548** • lunch & dinner, clsd Sun-Mon

Granada Leidsekruisstraat 13 **31–20/625–1073** • 5pm-close • Spanish • tapas • also bar • live music wknds

De Vliegende Schotel Nieuwe Leliestraat 162 **31–20/625–2041** • 4pm-11:30pm • vegetarian/ vegan

ENTERTAINMENT & RECREATION

Homomonument Westermarkt (Raadhuisstraat/Keizersgracht) • moving sculptural tribute to lesbians & gays killed by Nazis

BOOKSTORES

Xantippe Unlimited Prinsengracht 290 **31–20/623–5854** • 1pm-6pm, from 10am Sat, noon-5pm Sun • women's bookstore • lesbian section • English titles • lesbian-owned

RETAIL SHOPS

Dare to Wear Buiten Oranjestraat 15
31–20/686–8679 • piercing, jewelry &
accessories

House of Tattoos Haarlemmerdijk 130c
31–20/330–9046 • 11am-6pm, from 1pm Sun
• great tattoos, great people

SEX CLUBS

Sameplace Nassaukade 120
31–20/475–1981 • gay/ straight • men only
Mon • transgender-friendly • dancing/DJ •
theme nights • darkroom

Amsterdam—Rembrandtplein

ACCOMMODATIONS

Amsterdam House 's Gravelandseveer 7 (at
Kloveniersburgwal) 31–20/626–2577 (OFFICE),
31–20/624–6607 (HOTEL) • gay-friendly • hotel,
apts & houseboats

Dikker & Thijs Fenice Hotel Prinsengracht
444 (at Leidsestraat) 31–20/620–1212 • gay-
friendly • great location • nonsmoking rooms
• bar & restaurant

Eden Hotel Amstel 144 31–20/530–7878 •
gay-friendly • 3-star hotel • nonsmoking
rooms • brasserie overlooking River Amstel •
WiFi • wheelchair access

Hotel de l'Europe Nieuwe Doelenstraat 2-8
31–20/531–1777 • gay-friendly • grand hotel
on the River Amstel • fitness center • pool

Hotel Monopole Amstel 60 (at
Kloveniersburgwal) 31–20/624–6271 • gay-
friendly • centrally located • nonsmoking
rooms available • kids ok • also Cafe Rouge

Hotel Orlando Prinsengracht 1099 (at
Amstel River) 31–20/638–6915 • gay-friendly
• beautifully restored 17th-c canal house •
gay-owned

Hotel The Golden Bear Kerkstraat 37 (at
Leidsestraat) 31–20/624–4785 • lesbians/ gay
men • best place to stay in central
Amsterdam • WiFi • gay-owned

Hotel Waterfront Singel 458 (at
Koningsplein) 31–20/421–6621 • gay-friendly
• rooms & studios • brkfst • located in city's
center

ITC Hotel Prinsengracht 1051 (at
Utrechtsestraat) 31–20/623–0230,
31–20/623–1711 • lesbians/ gay men • 18th-c
canal house • great location • also bar &
lounge • WiFi • lesbian- & gay-owned

Seven Bridges Reguliersgracht 31 (at
KeizersGracht) 31–20/623–1329 • gay-friendly
• small & so elegant • canalside w/ view of 7
bridges (surprise!) • brkfst brought to you

BARS

Cafe Rouge Amstel 60 (at
Kloveniersburgwal) 31–20/420–9881 • 4pm-
1am, till 3am wknds • mostly gay men •
neighborhood bar

Chez Rene Amstel 50 (at Kloveniersburgwal)
31–20/420–3388 • 8pm-3am, till 4am Fri-Sat
• lesbians/ gay men • lesbian-owned

Het Dwarsliggertje Cafe
Reguliersdwarsstraat 105 31–61/677–8599 •
3pm-1am, till 3am Fri-Sat • mostly gay men •
neighborhood bar

Entre Nous Halvemaansteeg 14 (at
Reguliersbreestr) 31–20/623–1700 • 9pm-
3am, till 4am Fri-Sat • lesbians/ gay men •
neighborhood bar

Eve Reguliersdwarsstraat 44 (at
Geelvinckssteeg) 31–20/689–7070 • 4pm-
1am, till 3am Fri-Sat • gay/ straight •
dancing/DJ • hip 20-something crowd • also
restaurant

Habibi Ana Lange Leidsedwarsstraat 93
31–06/2192–1686 • 7pm-1am, till 3am Fri-Sat,
clsd Mon-Tue • lesbians/ gay men • Arabian
clientele • Arabian & int'l music • bellydancing
shows wknds

Hot Spot Cafe Amstel 102 (at Bakkersstr)
31–20/622–8335 • 9pm-3am, from 8pm Fri-
Sun • mostly gay men • neighborhood bar

Ludwig Reguliersdwarsstraat 37 (at St
Jorisstraat) 31–20/625–3661 • 7pm-1am, till
3am Fri-Sat, clsd Mon-Tue • mostly gay men •
dancing in the back • terrace

Mankind Weteringstraat 60 (at
Weteringschans) 31–20/638–4755 • noon-
11pm, clsd Sun • mixed crowd • canalside
terrace • food served till 8pm • Dutch/ English
• WiFi

Reality Girlz Reguliersdwarsstraat 125
31–20/639–3012 • 8pm-1am, till 3am Fri-Sat,
clsd Mon-Tue • mostly women •
neighborhood bar • mixed crowd

Soho Reguliersdwarsstraat 36 (at St
Jorisstraat) 31–20/422–3312 • 5pm-3am, till
4am Fri-Sat • popular • lesbians/ gay men •
young crowd • British pub 1st flr • lounge
upstairs • happy hour 10pm-11pm

Taboo Reguliersdwarsstraat 45
31–20/775–3963 • 5pm-3am, from 4pm
wknds • lesbians/ gay men • neighborhood
bar

Vivelavie Amstelstraat 7 (at Rembrandtplein) **31–20/624-0114** • 3pm-3am, till 4am Fri-Sat • mostly women

Het Wapen van Londen Amstel 14 (at Vijzelstraat) **31–6/1539-5317** • 4pm-1am, till 2am Fri-Sat • popular cafe-bar • mostly gay men • terrace

NIGHTCLUBS

Club Roque Amstel 178 (at Wagenstraat) • 11pm-5am, clsd Sun-Tue • lesbians/ gay men • dancing/DJ

F*cking Pop Queers Korte Leidsedwarsstraat 18 (at Jimmy Woo) • 2nd Sat • mostly gay men • dancing/DJ

Studio 80 Rembrandtplein 17 (at Amstelstraat) **31–20/521-8333** • 9pm-5am Th-Sat • gay/ straight • dancing/DJ

CAFES

Betty, Too Reguliersdwarsstraat 29 (at Leidsestraat) • 10am-1am • occasional gay events

Happy Feelings Kerkstr 51 **31–20/423-1936** • 11am-midnight, till 1am Fri-Sat • smoking coffeeshop • publisher's choice

Lunchroom Reguliersdwarsstraat 31 (at Koningsplein) **31–20/622-9958** • 10am-7pm • terrace open in summer • gay-owned

The Other Side Reguliersdwarsstraat 6 (at Koningsplein) **31–72/625-5141** • 11am-1am • mostly gay men • smoking coffeeshop • gay-owned

RESTAURANTS

Garlic Queen Reguliersdwarsstr 27 **31–20/422-6426** • 6pm-close, clsd Mon-Tue • even the desserts are made w/ garlic!

Golden Temple Utrechtsestr 126 **31–20/626-8560** • 5pm-9:30pm • mix of Indian, Mexican & Mediterranean • oldest vegetarian & vegan restaurant in city • nonsmoking

De Huyschkaemer Utrechtsestraat 137 **31–20/627-0575** • noon-1am, till 3am wknds

Rose's Cantina Reguliersdwarsstr 40 (near Rembrandtplein) **31–20/625-9797** • 5pm-11pm • popular • Tex-Mex • full bar

Saturnino Reguliersdwarsstr 5 **31–20/639-0102** • noon-midnight • Italian • full bar • gay-owned

EROTICA

Mail & Female Nieuwe Vijzelstraat 2, 1017 HT **31–20/623-3916** • erotic fashions & toys for women

Amsterdam—Outer

ACCOMMODATIONS

Amsterdam B&B Roeterstraat 18 (at Nieuwe Achtergracht) **31–20/624-0174** • gay-friendly • full brkfst • powered by green energy • kids ok • nonsmoking • WiFi • gay-owned

Between Art & Kitsch Ruysdaelkade 75-2 (at Daniel Stalpertstraat) **31–20/679-0485** • gay-friendly • near museums • WiFi

Blue Moon B&B Weteringschans 123A (at Weteringstraat) **31–20/428-8800** • gay/ straight • WiFi • directly opposite the famous Rijksmuseum • gay-owned

The Collector B&B De Lairessestr 46 hs (in museum area) **31–6/1101-0105** (CELL), **31–20/673-6779** • gay-friendly • B&B • full brkfst • WiFi • kids ok • gay-owned

Conscious Hotel Vondelpark Overtoom 519 **31–20/820-3333** • gay/straight • WiFi • wheelchair access

Freeland Hotel Marnixstraat 386 (at Leidsegracht) **31–20/622-7511** • gay-friendly • 2-star hotel • full brkfst • WiFi • gay-owned

Hemp Hotel Frederiksplein 15 (at Achtergracht) **31–20/625-4425** • only in Amsterdam: sleep on a hemp mattress, eat a hemp roll (THC-free) for brkfst or drink hemp beer in the Hemp Temple bar

Hotel Arena Gravesandestraat 51 (at Mauritskade) **31–20/850-2400** • gay-friendly • huge hotel in former orphanage • popular nightclub in former chapel • WiFi • also restaurant & cafe-bar

Hotel Kap Den Texstraat 5 **31–20/624-5908** • gay/ straight • bikes available to rent • also self-catering apt • gay-owned

Hotel Rembrandt Plantage Middenlaan 17 (at Plantage Parklaan) **31–20/627-2714** • gay-friendly • beautiful brkfst room w/ 17th-c art • near Rembrandtplein • nonsmoking

Lloyd Hotel Oostelijke Handelskade 34 **31–20/561-3636, 31–20/561-3604** • gay-friendly • hip hotel for all budgets in cool Eastern Harbor area • WiFi

NL Hotel Nassaukade 368 (at B Toussaintstraat) **31–20/689-0030** • gay/ straight • WiFi • gay-owned

Prinsen Hotel Vondelstraat 36-38 (near Leidseplein) **31–20/616-2323** • gay-friendly • also bar

Bars

Garbo Amsteldijk 223 (at Miranda Paviljoen & Brasseriede Lakey) **31–20/644-5768** • 4pm-midnight 1st Sat only • women only • dancing/DJ • dinner also served

Nightclubs

Flirtation Oostelijke Handelskade 4 (at Piet Heinkade, at Club Panama) • bi-monthly women's dance party • check local listings for next event

Melkweg Lijnbaansgracht 234 (at Leidseplein) **31–20/531-8181** • gay/ straight • popular live-music venue • restaurant • theater • cinema • gallery

Restaurants

De Peper Overtoom 301 **31–20/412-2954** • 7pm-close Sun, Tue & Th-Fri • sliding scale, volunteer-run vegan cafe • also monthly queer & women's parties

De Waaghals Frans Halsstraat 29 **31–20/679-9609** • 5pm-9:30pm • int'l vegetarian

SCOTLAND

Edinburgh

Info Lines & Services

The Edinburgh LGBT Centre 58A & 60 Broughton St **44–0131/556-9471**

The Edinburgh LGBT Centre 58A & 60 Broughton St **44–0131/556-9471**

LGBT Centre for Health & Wellbeing 9 Howe St **44–0131/523-1100**

Accommodations

94DR 94 Dalkeith Rd **44–131/662-9286** • gay/ straight • guesthouse central location • full brkfst • WiFi • gay-owned

Ardmor House 74 Pilrig St (at Leith Walk) **44–0131/554-4944** • lesbians/ gay men • Victorian • kids/ pets ok • nonsmoking • wheelchair access • gay-owned

Averon Guest House 44 Gilmore Pl **44–0131/229-9932** • gay-friendly • comfortable guesthouse in city center • full brkfst • nonsmoking

Ayden Guest House 70 Pilrig St **44–0131/554-2187** • gay/ straight • guesthouse in quiet, central location • in-house chef cooks fabulous brkfst • WiFi • lesbian-owned

Garlands 48 Pilrig St (off Leith Walk) **44–0131/554-4205** • gay/ straight • Georgian town house • full brkfst • nonsmoking • WiFi • gay-owned

Sheraton Grand Hotel and Spa 1 Festival Sq **44–131/229-9131** • gay-friendly • newly-renovated • gym & pool

Tigerlily 125 George St **44–131/225-5005** • gay-friendly • glamorous bar & restaurant • WiFi

The Witchery by the Castle Castlehill (The Royal Mile) **44–0131/225.5613** • gay-friendly • B&B • full brkfst • theatrical suites at the gates of Edinburgh castle • also restaurant

Bars

The Auld Hoose 23-25 St Leonards St **44–0131/668-2934** • noon-1am, from 12:30pm Sun • gay/ straight • neighborhood bar • food served

Cafe Habana 22 Greenside Pl **44–0131/558-1270** • 1pm-1am • lesbians/ gay men • theme nights • popular pre-clubbing • WiFi

Cafe Nom de Plume 60 Broughton St **44–0131/478-1372** • 11am-11pm, till 1am Fri-Sat • food served

CC Bloom's 23 Greenside Pl (at Leith Walk) **44–0131/556-9331** • 6pm-3am, from 7pm Sun • mostly gay men • dancing/DJ • live shows • theme nights

Elbow 133-135 E Claremont St **44–0131/556-5662** • 11am-1pm • gay/straight • bar & bistro

LAGRAD (Lesbian and Gay Real Ale Drinkers) 2 Montrose Terrace (at the Regent) **44–0131/661-8198** • first Monday of the month

Newtown Bar 26-B Dublin St **44–0131/538-7775** • noon-1am, till 2am Fri-Sat • lesbians/ gay men • dancing/DJ • food served • WiFi

Planet 6 Baxter's Pl (at Leith Walk) **44–0131/556-5551** • 4pm-1am • lesbians/ gay men • popular • food served

The Regent 2 Montrose Terrace **44–0131/661-8198** • noon-1am, from 12:30pm Sun • mostly gay men • food served • WiFi

The Street 2 Picardy Pl **44–0131/556-4272** • noon-1am • gay/ straight • dancing/DJ • food served • patio

Theatre Royal Bar 25-27 Greenside Pl **44–0131/557-2142** • noon-midnight • gay-friendly • good ale • food served

Woodland Creatures 260 - 262 Leith Walk
44–0131/629–5509 • 11am-1pm • gay/straight
• cool café bar • live music

NIGHTCLUBS

GHQ 4 Picardy Pl **44–0131/550–1780** • 9pm-
3am • lesbians/ gay men • dancing/DJ • theme
nights

CAFES

Cafe Lucia 13–29 Nicolson St (next to
Edinburgh Festival Theatre)
44–0131/662–1112 • 10am-10pm

Filmhouse Cafe 88 Lothian Rd
**44–0131/229–5932, 44–0131/228–2688
(CINEMA)** • 10am-11:30pm, till 12:30am • beer/
wine • also cinema

RESTAURANTS

Blue Moon 1 Barony St **44–0131/556–2788** •
11am-midnight, from 10am wknds • popular •
lesbians/ gay men • famous for macaroni
cheese • gay-owned

Henderson's 94 Hanover St
44–0131/225.2131 • organic vegetarian • also
deli & cafe • beer/ wine

Tower Restaurant & Terrace National
Museum of Scotland, Chambers St (at
George IV Brigde) **44–0131/225–3003** • lunch
& dinner • panoramic views of Edinburgh's
castle & historic skyline • wheelchair access

Valvona & Crolla 19 Elm Row
44–0131/556–6066 • clsd Sun • oldest Italian
deli in Scotland

ENTERTAINMENT & RECREATION

Black Kilt Tours 125b Grange Loan
44–786/416–5362 • tailor-made driver/guided
tours of Scotland for the LGBT community and
friends, gay-owned

BOOKSTORES

Bobbie's Bookshop 220 Morrison St
44–0131/538–7069 • 10am-5pm, clsd Sun

Word Power Books 43-45 W Nicolson St
44–0131/662–9112 • 10am-6pm, noon-5pm
Sun • independent & radical • events

RETAIL SHOPS

Q Store 5 Barony St **44–0131/477–4756** •
11am-7pm Sat-Wed, till 6pm Sat, 1pm-5pm
Sun • pride store

NATIONAL PUBLICATIONS

ScotsGay **44–0131/539–0666** • Scotland's
premier magazine for lesbians, gays, bisexuals
& friends • published monthly

EROTICA

Fem 2 Dom 25 Easter Rd **44–0131/623–6969**
• 10am-9pm, from noon Sun • toys, clothing &
videos

SPAIN

Barcelona

Note: M°=Metro station

INFO LINES & SERVICES

Casal Lambda c/ Verdaguer y Callís 10 (M°
Drassanes) **34/93–319–5550** • 5pm-9pm •
community center • cafe • archives • library •
also publish magazine

Col-Lectiu Gai de Barcelona (CGB)
34/934–534–125 • staffed 7pm-9pm Mon-Sat
• also publishes Info Gai

Coordinadora Gai Lesbiana Vicant
d'Hongria 156, E–08014 **34/900–601–601** •
7pm-9pm Mon-Fri, 6pm-8pm Sat • nat'l gay
group

ACCOMMODATIONS

Agua Alegre c/ Roger de Lluria 47 (M°
Catalunya) **34/93–487–8032** • gay/ straight •
garden terrace

Barcelona City Centre **34/653–900–039** •
mostly gay men • in Eixample District • kids/
pets ok • WiFi • gay-owned

California Hotel Rauric 14 (at Ferran, M°
Liceu) **34/93–317–7766** • gay/ straight

Casa de Billy Barcelona Rambla Catalunya
85, Piso 5, Puerta 1 (at Mallorca)
34/93–426–3048 • gay/ straight • shared baths
• full brkfst • nonsmoking • WiFi

Catalonia Diagonal Centro Balmes
142–146 **34/93–415–9090** • gay-friendly • kids
ok • food served • WiFi • wheelchair access

Catalonia Portal de l'Àngel Avenida Portal
de L'Angel 17 **34/93–318–4141** • gay-friendly •
WiFi • pool

Éos Gran Via de los Corts Catalanes 575 (M°
Universitat) **34/93–451–8772, 34/617–931–439**
• lesbians/ gay men • B&B in gay district •
gay-owned

Fashion House Bruc 13 Principal
34/63–790–4044 • lesbians/ gay men • shared
baths

GayStay BCN C / Piquer 15, Pral 3 (at Carrer
de Mata) **34/676–145–909** • mostly men •
WiFi • gay-owned

HCC Regente Rambla de Catalunya 76 **34/93–487–5989** • gay-friendly • in 1913 art nouveau bldg • pool • WiFi • wheelchair access

HCC Taber Arago 256 **34/93–487–3887** • gay-friendly • in art nouveau bldg designed by Doménech i Montaner • WiFi

Hostal Baires **34/93–319–7774** • gay-friendly • in Barrio Gótico

Hostal Que Tal Mallorca 290 (at Bruch) **34/93–459–2366** • mostly gay men

Hotel Axel Aribau 33 (at Consell de Cent) **34/93–323–9393** • lesbians/ gay men • full brkfst • pool • WiFi • also restaurant • also Skybar • wheelchair access

Hotel Catalonia Fira Av. Gran Via N 50 (Plaza Europa) **34/93–236–0000** • gay-friendly • WiFi • new 4-star hotel in the heart of old Barcelona

Hotel Colon Avenida Catedral 7 **34/93–301–1404** • gay-friendly

Hotel Majestic Barcelona Paseo de Gracia 68 (in city center) **34/93–488–1717** • gay-friendly • 5-star hotel • rooftop pool • wheelchair access

Room Mate Emma Carrer Rosselló 205 **34/932–385–606** • gay-friendly • nighclub vibe • WiFi

Bars

Aire/ Sala Diana Valencia 236 (btwn Enriq. Granados & c/ Balmes) **34/93–451–8462** • 11pm-3am, clsd Sun-Wed • seasonal • gay/ straight, more women Sun • dancing/DJ • cafe-bar

Al Maximo Assaonadora 25 • clsd Sun-Mon • lesbians/ gay men • neighborhood bar

El Balcon des Aquiles Lleo 9 • 7pm-3am • mostly gay men • neighborhood bar • theme nights

Bar Plata Consejo de Ciento 233 (at Urgell) • 5pm-3am • mostly gay men

BimBamBum Casanova 48 • 11pm-3am, clsd Mon-Tue • mostly gay men • dancing/DJ

Black Bull Muntaner 64 **34/934–515–104** • 8pm-2:30am • mostly gay men

El Cangrejo Villarroel 86 • 10:30pm-3am, clsd Mon-Tue • popular • lesbians/ gay men • dancing/DJ

La Chapelle Muntaner 65 • mostly gay men • cafe by day

Chiringuito GayLorenzo Ed Dulce Deseo de Lorenzo (Playa de la Mar Bella) • summer gay beach bar

La Cueva Calàbria 91 • open 4pm, clsd Mon • lesbians/ gay men • drag shows

Dacksy Consell de Cent 247 **34/934–519–925** • 5pm-3am • lesbians/ gay men • trendy cocktail lounge • dancing/DJ

Lust Casanova 75 (at Consell de Cent) • 9pm-2:30am, clsd Mon, pre-clubbing bar • lesbians/ gay men

La Madame Ronda Sant Pere 19-21 (M° Urquinaona) **34/93–426–8444** • from midnight Sun only • gay/ straight • dancing/DJ

Moeem Muntaner 11 **34/659–229–033** • 6pm-3am • lesbians/ gay men • cheap drinks

Museum Cafe & Club Sepulveda 178 (at Urgell) • 6:30pm-3am • mostly gay men

People Lounge Villarroel 71 (M° Urgell) **34/93–451–5986** • 7pm-3am • mostly gay men • food served

Punto BCN Muntaner 63–65 (at Y Aragón, Metro, M° Universitat) **34–93/451–9152** • 6pm-2:30am • popular • mostly gay men • upscale cafe-bar • wheelchair access

Zelig **34/93–441–5622** • 7pm-2am, till 3am wknds, clsd Mon • gay/ straight • dancing/DJ • food served

Nightclubs

Arena Classic Diputació 233 (at Balmes, M° Universitat) **34/93–487–8342** • 12:30am-5am Fri-Sat only • popular • mostly gay men • dancing/DJ • Spanish music • live shows • cover charge

Arena Sala Madre Balmes 32 (at Diputació, M° Universitat) **34/93–487–8342** • 12:30am-5am, clsd Mon (except in Aug) • popular • mostly gay men • dancing/DJ • food served • live shows • cover charge

Centrik Weekend Bar Aribau 30 • 11pm-3am Fri-Sat • mostly gay men

Les Fatales • mostly women • dancing/DJ • parties around Barcelona • check lesfatales.org for details

Metro Sepúlveda 185 (M° Universitat) **34/93–323–5227** • midnight-5am, from 1am Mon • popular • mostly gay men • dancing/DJ • leather • drag shows • cover charge

Souvenir Barcelona Noi del Sucre 75 (Viladecans) • after-hours club 6am-1pm Sat-Sun & holidays

Cafes

La Concha del Barrio Chino Guardia 14 (M° Liceu) **34/93–302–4118** • 4pm-3am • gay/ straight • dancing/DJ • transgender-friendly

RESTAURANTS

7 Portes Passeig d'Isabel II, 14 **34/93-319-3033, 34/93-319-2950** • 1pm-1am • Catalan • upscale • over 150 years old!

El Berro Diputació 180 **34/933-236-956** • 7am-3am, from 9am wknds • inexpensive diner-style restaurant • also bar

Botafumeiro El Gran de Gràcia 81 **34/93-218-4230, 34/93-217-9642** • 1pm-1am • Galician seafood • full bar • reservations recommended

Castro Casanova 85 (M° Urgell) **34/93-323-6784** • 1pm-4pm & 9pm-midnight, clsd Sun • Catalan • full bar • live shows

dDivine Balmes 24 (M° Universitat) **34/93-317-2248** • 9:30pm-1am, clsd Sun-Tue • dinner show hosted by "Divine" • lesbians/gay men • reservations recommended

Eterna Consell de Cent 127-129 (at Villarroel) **34/93-424-2526** • 1pm-4pm Mon-Fri, 9:30pm-midnight Th-Sat, clsd Sun • lesbians/gay men • drag shows

La Flauta Magica c/ de Banys Vells 18 (M° Jaume I) **34/93-268-4694** • dinner nightly • vegetarian/ organic • wheelchair access

Iurantia Casanova 42 (M° Urgell) **34/93-454-7887** • lunch Mon-Fri, dinner Mon-Sat, clsd Sun • pizzeria • reservations recommended

Barcelona

LGBT PRIDE:
July.

ANNUAL EVENTS:
February - Carnival web: barcelona.de/en/barcelona-carnival.html.

July - Grec Summer Festival 34-93/316-1000, web: www.grec.bcn.cat/en.

July - Gay/Lesbian Film Festival, 34-93/319-5550, web: www.cine-malambda.com.

August - Festa Major de Gràcia (huge street party) 34-93/459-3080, web: www.festamajorde-gracia.cat.

CITY INFO:
34-93/285-3834, web: www.barcelonaturisme.com.

WEATHER:
Barcelona boasts a mild Mediterranean climate, with summer temperatures in the 70°s-80°s, and 40°s-50°s in winter. Rain is possible year-round, with July being the driest month.

BEST VIEW:
Torre de Collserola, 34-93/406-9354.
Giant glass elevator takes you 944 ft into the air to a platform.

ATTRACTIONS:
Barcelona Museum of Contemporary Art 34-93/412-0810, web: www.macba.es.

Barrì Gotic.

Boqueria Market 34-93/318-2584 , web: www.boqueria.info.

Catedral de Barcelona 34-93/310-7195, web:catedralbcn.org

Fundació Joan Miró 34-93/443-9470, web: www.bcn.fjmiro.es.

Museu Picasso 34-93/256-3000

National Museum of Catalan Art 34-93/622-0376, web: www.mnac.es.

Parc Güell.

La Sagrada Familia 34-93/207-3031, web: www.sagradafamilia.org.

TRANSIT:
Radio Taxi 34-93/303-3033, web: www.radiotaxio33.com.

Aerobus to Plaza de Cataluña 34-93/223-5151 , web: www.emt-amb.com.

Transports Metropolitans de Barcelona 34-90/207-5027, web: www.tmb.net.

Little Italy Carrer del Rec 30 (near Passeig del Born) **34/93-319-7973** • 1pm-4pm & 9pm-midnight • live jazz

Madrid-Barcelona Carrer d'Arago 282 (M° Passeig de Gracia) **34/93-215-7027** • lunch & dinner, clsd Sun • located on old railway line • Catalan

Marquette Diputació 172 (M° Universitat) **34/93-162-3905** • 6pm-3am • Italian food •

Sazzerak **34/93-451-1138** • full bar

Tafino Consejo de Ciento 193 • 1pm-4pm Mon-Fri, 8:30pm-midnight Tue-Sat

Tu Sabes **34/615-999-282** • 7pm-midnight Th, 9pm-3am Fri-Sat

La Veronica Rambla de Raval 2-4 **34/93-329-3303** • 1pm-1am, clsd Mon • popular pizzeria • terrace

ENTERTAINMENT & RECREATION

Chernobyl Beach take the Metro to Sant Roc • popular gay beach

Mar Bella • popular gay beach

Museu Picasso Montcada 15-23 **34/93-256-3000** • early Picasso works

Parc Guell Mount Tibidado • mosiacs & sculpture by Gaudi

Sant Sebastiàn • popular gay beach

BOOKSTORES

Antinous Josep Anselm Clavé 6 (btwn Las Ramblas & Ample, M° Drassanes) **34/93-301-9070** • clsd Sun • LGBT • books • gifts • also cafe • wheelchair access

Cómplices Cervantes 2 (at Avinyó, M° Liceu) **34/93-412-7283** • 10:30am-8:30pm, from noon Sat, clsd Sun • LGBT • Spanish & English titles

Nosotr@s Casanova 56 (M° Urgell) **34/93-451-5134** • LGBT books • magazines • gifts • videos • DVDs

PUBLICATIONS

Gay Barcelona Av Roma 152 **34/93-454-9100** • monthly gay magazine

EROTICA

Erotic Museum of Barcelona Ramblas 96 **34/93-318-9865** • 10am-midnight (seasonal hours)

Harmony Love **34/93-405-3300**

Kitsch Muntaner 17-19 (at Gran Vía) **34/93-453-2052** • 10am-10pm, from 5pm Sun

Madrid

Note: M°=Metro station

INFO LINES & SERVICES

COGAM (Colectivo de Lesbianas, Gays, Transexuales, y Bisexuales de Madrid) Puebla 9 (Bajo) **34/91-522-4517** • LGBT center • groups • library • also cafe-bar

ACCOMMODATIONS

Camino de Soto Puente de la Reine 18, Soto del Real **34-66/744-1351** • gay/ straight • located 40 minutes from Madrid • full brkfst • pool • WiFi • gay-owned

Chueca Pension Gravina 4 **34/91-523-1473** • mostly gay men • hostel • kids ok • WiFi

Hostal CasaChueca Calle San Bartolomé 4 (at San Marcos) **34/91-523-8127** • mostly gay men • WiFi • gay-owned

Hostal La Fontana Valverde 6, 1° (M° Gran Vía) **34/91-521-8449, 34/91-523-1561** • lesbians/ gay men • WiFi

Hostal la Zona Calle Valverde 7, 1 & 2 (at Gran Vía) **34/91-521-9904** • mostly gay men • full brkfst • all rooms w/ private baths & balconies • WiFi • gay-owned

Hotel Catalonia Gaudí Gran Vía 7-9 (at Alcalá) **34/91-531-2222** • gay-friendly • WiFi • kids ok • wheelchair access

Hotel Urban Madrid Carrera de San Jerónimo 34 **34/91-787-7770** • gay-friendly • upscale hotel w/ 3 restaurants & rooftop pool • WiFi

Pensión Madrid House Barbieri 1 **34/651-387 535** • gay/ straight • one block from Chueca Square • WiFi • gay-owned

BARS

El 51 Hortaleza 51 (in Chueca) **34/91-521-2564** • 6pm-3am, from 4pm wknds • popular • mostly gay gay men • upscale cocktail lounge

Ambienta2 22 San Bartolome (at Figueroa) **34/606-939592** • 6pm-2am, till 2:30am wknds, from noon Sun • lesbians/ gay men • dancing/DJ • drag shows • live entertainment • theme nights

Bar Lio Pelayo 58 • 7pm-2am • lesbians/ gay men • karaoke • drag shows • transgender-friendly

Enfrente Infantas 12 (M° Gran Vía) **34/68-779-1462** • 8pm-3am • mostly gay men • leather • DJs Th & Sun

Fulanita de Tal Calle del Conde de Xiquena 2 (at Prim) • mostly women • stylish & hip • dancing/DJ

El Gallinero San Carlos 6 (in Lavapies area) • 7:30pm-midnight, till 2:30am Th-Sat, clsd Mon • mostly women • lesbian-owned

Gris • 10pm-3am, from 9pm Th-Sat, clsd Sun-Mon • lesbians/ gay men • reduced drink prices until 11:30pm • music bar

LL Pelayo 11 (M° Chueca) 34/91–523–3121 • 5pm-close • popular • mostly gay men • neighborhood bar • dancing • strippers • drag shows • videos

El Mojito Olmo 6 (in Lavapies area) 34/91–531–1141 • 9pm-3am, till 3:30am Fri-Sat • lesbians/ gay men • cocktail bar • great music

Museo Chicote Calle Gran Via 12 34/915–326–737 • 9pm-3am • gay/ straight • '50s style lounge • food served • live shows

La Ochenta (80) Calle de la Sombrerería 8 (in Lavapies area) • 80's music

Rick's Calle del Clavel 8 (at Infantas, M° Gran Vía, ring to enter) 34/91–531–9186 • 11pm-6am, open later Fri-Sat, 9pm-2am Sun • popular • mostly gay men • dancing/DJ

Rimmel Calle de Luis de Góngora 2 (M° Chueca) • 7pm-3am • mostly gay men • 2 for 1 drinks till 11:30pm

El Rincón Guay Embajadores 62 (Lavapiés quarter) 34/914–68–37–00 • 9am-2am • lesbians/ gay men • neighborhood bar/ cafe • WiFi

Sacha's Plaza de Chueca 1 (M° Chueca) • 8pm-3am • lesbians/ gay men • dancing/DJ • drag shows • terrace

Sixta Calatrava 15 (M° La Latina) 34/913–663–018 • 10pm-2am, 3pm-midnight Sun, clsd Mon-Wed • packed on Sun afternoon • gay/ straight • gay-owned

Studio 54 Madrid Barbieri 7 (btwn San Marcos & Infantas, M° Chueca) 34/615–126–807 • 11:30pm-3:30am, clsd Mon-Tue • lesbians/ gay men • dancing/DJ • live shows

Tántalo Libertad 14 34/915–213–127 • 6pm-2:30am • mostly gay men • WiFi

Truco Calle de Gravina 10 (at Plaza de Chueca) 34/91–532–8921 • 8pm-close, clsd Mon-Tue • popular • mostly women • dance bar • great parties • seasonal terrace

---

Madrid

LGBT Pride:
June, web: orgullolgtb.org.

Annual Events:
October/November - International Gay & Lesbian Film Festival, web: www.lesgaicinemad.com.

City Info:
Oficina Municipale de Turismo 34/91-308-0400, web: www.esmadrid.com.

Best View:
From the funicular in the Parque des Atracciones.

Weather:
Winter temps average in the 40°s (and maybe even a little snow!). Summer days in Madrid are hot, with highs well into the 80°s.

Attractions:
Chueca.
El Rastro (flea market).
Museo del Prado 34/91–330–2800, web: www.museodelprado.es.
Museo Thyssen-Bornemisza 34/91–369–0151, web: www.museothyssen.org.
Museo de Reina Sofia (home of Picasso's 'Guernica') 34/91–774–1000, web: www.museoreinasofia.es.
El Retiro (park).
Royal Palace 34/91–454–8700, web: patrimonionacional.es.

Transit:
Taxi 34/64-436-6461, web: taxi24madrid.com.
Aerocity 34/91-747-7570, web: www.gomadrid.com/aerocity.
Metro 34/90–244-4403, web: www.metromadrid.es.

Why Not San Bartolomé 6 (M° Gran Vía) • 9pm-3am, till 5am Fri-Sat • mostly gay men • dancing/DJ

NIGHTCLUBS

Boite Calle Tetuan 27 (Plaza del Carmen) 34/91-522-9620 • gay/ straight • dancing/DJ • check listings for gay club nights

Club 33 Cabeza 33 (M° Antón Martín) 34/91-369-3302 • midnight-6am, from 6pm Sun, clsd Mon-Wed • popular wknds • women only • men welcome as guests • dancing/DJ • cabaret • cover charge

Dark Hole Pelayo 80-82 • 1am -6am Sat, gay goth club

Escape Gravina 13 (at Plaza de Chueca) 34/91-532-5206 • 10pm-5am Wed-Sun • mostly women • dancing/DJ • live shows

Griffin's Marqués de Valdeiglesias 6 (M° Banco de España) 34/91-522-2079 • 11pm-late • mostly gay men • dancing/DJ • drag shows • entertainment

Joy Eslava Arenal 11 (M° Sol) 34/91-366-3733 • 11:30pm-6pm Sat only • popular • fabulous crowd • converted theater

Long Play Plaza de Vázquez de Mella 2 • midnight-6am wknds only • lesbians/ gay men • dancing/DJ

Ohm Plaza de Callao 4 (at Sala Bash, M° Callao) 34/91-531-0132 • midnight-close Fri-Sat • popular • gay/ straight • dancing/DJ • go-go dancers

Tábata Vergara 12 (next to Teatro Real, M° Opera) 34/91-547-9735 • 11:30pm-late Wed-Sat • lesbians/ gay men • dancing/DJ • young crowd • cover charge

Week-end Plaza de Callao 4 (at Ohm Club) 34/91-541-3500 • midnight-6am Sun • popular • lesbians/ gay men • dancing/DJ • alternative • cover charge

CAFES

El Apolo Barco 18 34/915-210-830 • 8am-3pm & 6pm-2am, 10am-2am Sat, from 5pm Sun

Cafe Acuarela Gravina 10 (M° Chueca) 34/91-522-2143, 34/91-570-6907 • 3pm-3am, from 11am Sat-Sun • lesbians/ gay men • bohemian cafe-bar • cocktails

Cafe Figueroa Augusto Figueroa 17 (at Hortaleza, M° Chueca) 34/91-521-1673 • 4pm-midnight, till 2:30am wknds • lesbians/ gay men • also bar

Cafe la Troje Pelayo 26 (at Figueroa, M° Chueca) 34/91-531-0535 • 5pm-2am • lesbians/ gay men • full bar

D'Mystic Gravina 5 (M° Pelayo) 34/91-308-2460 • 9:30am-close • gay/ straight • popular • hot food served • hip cafe-bar in Chueca area

Mama Inés Hortaleza 22 (M° Chueca) 34/91-523-2333 • 10am-2am • sandwiches • pies

XXX Cafe Clavel 2 (M° Gran Vía) 34/91-532-8415 • 1pm-1am • mostly gay men • food served • cabaret wknds

RESTAURANTS

Al Natural Zorrilla 11 (M° Sevilla) 34/91-369-4709 • lunch & dinner, no dinner Sun • vegetarian

Antigua Taqueria Calle Cabestreros 4 (in Lavapies area) 34/915-308-270 • 11am-midnight, till 2am Fri-Sat • Tex-Mex • lesbian-owned

El Armario San Bartolomé 7 (btwn Figueroa & San Marcos, M° Chueca) 34/91-532-8377 • lunch & dinner • lesbians/ gay men • Mediterranean

Artemisa Ventura de la Vega 4 (at Zorrilla) 34/91-429-5092 • lesbians/ gay men • vegetarian • also Tres Cruces 4 location

La Berenjena Calle Marqués de Toca,7 (in Lavapies area) 34/914-675-297 • 8pm-2am, from 1:30pm wknds, till midnight Sun, clsd Mon • lesbian-owned

La Berenjena Calle Marqués de Toca 7 (in Lavapies area) 34/914-675-297 • 8pm-2am, from 1:30pm wknds, till midnight Sun, clsd Mon • lesbian-owned

Botin 34/91-366-4217 • one of the oldest restaurants in the world (open since 1725) & an old Hemingway haunt

Colby 34/91-521-2554 • 9:30am-close, from 11:30am Sun

Divina La Cocina Colmenares 13 (at San Marcos, M° Chueca) 34/91-531-3765 • lunch & dinner • lesbians/ gay men • elegant & trendy

Ecocentro Esquilache 2, 4, y 6 (at Pablo Iglesias, M° Rios Rosas) 34/91-553-5502 • open till midnight • vegetarian • natural foods • also shop • herbalist school

El Chambao Manuel Malasana 16 (at Calle de Monteleon) • tapas restaurant • also bar

La Gastrocroqueteria de Chema Calle Segovia 17 34/913-642-263 • dinner nightly from 9pm, lunch wknds from 2pm, romantic space serving traditonal tapas

Gula Gula Gran Via 1 (M° Gran Via)
34/91–522–8764 • lunch & dinner • popular
• lesbians/ gay men • buffet/ salad bar • drag
shows • reservations required

Marsot Pelayo 6 (M° Chueca)
34/91–531–0726 • lunch & dinner

Mercado de la Reina Calle Gran Vía 12
34/915 –213–198 • 9am-2am, hip and
happening with high quality food

Momo Calle de la Libertad 8 **34/91–532–7162**
• lunch & dinner • nonsmoking • charming
staff • gay-owned

Paris Tokyo Plaza Vázquez de Mella 12
34/915–216–128 • noon-2am • fine dining
with a disco vibe • gay-owned

El Rincón de Pelayo Pelayo 19 (M° Chueca)
34/91–521–8407 • lunch & dinner • lesbians/
gay men

Sama-Sama San Bartolomé 23 (M° Chueca)
34/91–521–5547 • lunch & dinner, clsd Sun •
Balinese decor • also Infante 5 location

Taberna el Olivar Calle Olivar 54 (in
Lavapies area) • 7pm-midnight, from 1pm
Fri-Sun, clsd Tues • lesbian-owned

Vegaviana Pelayo 35 **34/913–080–381** •
lunch & dinner, clsd Sun-Mon • vegetarian

BOOKSTORES

A Different Life Pelayo 30 (M° Chueca)
34/91–532–9652 • 11am-10pm • LGBT •
books • magazines • music • videos • sex
shop downstairs

Berkana Bookstore Hortaleza 64
34/91–522–5599 • 10:30am-9pm, from noon
Sat-Sun • LGBT • ask for free gay map of
Madrid • wheelchair access

PUBLICATIONS

Shangay Express **34/91–445–1741** • free
bi-weekly gay paper • also publishes
Shanguide

GYMS & HEALTH CLUBS

Gimnasio V35 Valverde 35 (M° Gran Via)
34/91–523–9352 • 8:30am-11pm, 10am-10pm
Sat, clsd Sun

Holiday Gym Princesa Serrano Jover 3 (M°
Argüelles) **34/91–547–4033** • central location
• pool

EROTICA

Amantis Pelayo 46 **34/91–702–0510**

La Jugueteria Travesia de San Mateo 12
34–91/308–7269 • 11am-3pm & 5pm-9pm,
clsd Sun • very lesbian friendly

Los Placeres de Lola Doctor Fourquet, 34
34/91–468–6178 • noon-10pm, clsd Sun •
women & their companions only • toys,
leather, books & videos • also cafe

Sitges

ACCOMMODATIONS

Antonio's Guesthouse Passeig Vilanova 58
34/93–894–9207 • mostly men • WiFi • also
apts • gay-owned

B My Guest B&B Ctra Sant Pere de Ribes
34/639–534–979 • women-only penthouse
apt • WiFi • lesbian-owned

Los Globos Avda Ntra Sra de Montserrat 43
34/93–894–9374 • lesbians/ gay men • kids/
pets ok • also bar • brkfst buffet • WiFi •
wheelchair access • gay-owned

Hotel Antemare Verge de Montserrat 48-50
34/93–894–7000 • gay-friendly • pool • 1
block from beach

Hotel Liberty Isla de Cuba 45 (at Artur
Carbonell) **34/93–811–0872** • lesbians/ gay-
men • seasonal • nonsmoking • WiFi •
wheelchair access • gay-owned

Hotel Renaixença Illa de Cuba 13 , 08070
34/93–894–8375 • mostly gay men • some
shared baths • hotel bar

Hotel Romàntic Sant Isidre 33
34/93–894–8375 • gay/ straight • full brkfst •
some shared baths • seasonal • kids/ pets ok •
also full bar

Hotel Santa Maria Paseo de la Ribera 52
34/93–894–0999 • gay/ straight • clean &
modest • great restaurant

Medium Sitges Park Hotel Calle Jesus 16
34/938–940–205 • gay/ straight • pool,
restaurant, bar & garden • WiFi • wheelchair
access

Parrot's Hotel Joan Tarrida 16
34/93–894–1350 • lesbians/ gay men • WiFi •
also bar & restaurant

San Sebastian Playa Port Alegre 53
305/538–9697 (US#), 866/376–7831 (IN US) •
gay-friendly • pool • also bar/ restaurant •
nonsmoking • wheelchair access

Sitges Royal Rooms **34/64–998–1148** •
mosty gay men • WiFi • gay-owned

BARS

Azul Sant Bonaventura 10 **34/93–894–7634** •
9pm-3am • mostly gay men • neighborhood
bar

Dark/ DSB Bonaire 14 • 5pm-3am • mostly
men • sleek lounge

Mojito & Co Plaza Industrial 1 • 5pm-3am • mostly men • breezy lounge w/ outdoor seating

Parrot's Pub Plaza Industria 2 (at Primero de Mayo) 34/93-894-7881 • 5pm-close, seasonal • popular • lesbians/ gay men • live shows • patio • also restaurant

Ruby's Terrace Joan Tarrida Ferratges 14 • from 8pm • mostly gay men • drag shows • terrace

XXL Joan Tarrida Ferratges 7 • 11pm-3:30am (wknds only off-season) • popular • mostly gay men • dancing/DJ

NIGHTCLUBS

Bourbon's Sant Bonaventura 13 34/93-894-3347 • 10:30pm-3:30am (Sat only off-season) • popular • mostly gay men • dancing/DJ • videos • young crowd

Comodín Tacó 4 34/93-894-1698 • 10pm-3am,,mostly gay men • dancing/DJ • drag shows

Mediterraneo Sant Bonaventura 6 34/93-894-3347 • 11pm-3:30am • popular • mostly gay men • dance bar • patio

Orek's Bonaire 13 • 10pm-3am (only Fri-Sat in winter) • mostly gay men • dancing/DJ • strippers • darkroom

Organic Bonaire 15 34/93-894-2230 • opens 2:30am (wknds only off-season) • mostly gay men • transgender-friendly • dancing/DJ • singles party Th • darkroom • cover charge

El Piano Bonaventura 37 34/93-814-6245 • 10pm-3am • lesbians/ gay men • piano bar • cabaret

Queenz Bonaire 17 • 10pm-3:30am, seasonal • mostly men • DJs • drag shows • cabaret

Ricky's • midnight-6am, clsd Mon • gay/ straight, more gay Fri

Trailer Angel Vidal 36 • 1am-6am, seasonal • popular • mostly gay men • dancing/DJ

CAFES

Cafe Al Fresco Carrer Major 33 34/93-811-3307 • 9am-midnight

Cine Cafe Jesus 55 34/662-560-050 • 10am-midnight, clsd Tue • mostly gay men • Anglo-American • gay-owned

Mont Roig Cafe Marques de Montroig 11-13 34/93-894-8439 • 9am-3am • patio • WiFi • also full bar

RESTAURANTS

Air Coco Paseo Maritim 2 34/93-894-2445 • clsd Mon • popular • patio seating • water views • reservations recommended

Alma Tacó 16 34/93-894-6387 • 8pm-close (clsd Tue-Wed off-season) • lesbians/ gay men • French • terrace

Beach House Sant Pau 34 34/93-894-9029 • brkfst & dinner , friendly service from the owners themselves • full bar • patio • gay-owned

El Celler Vell 34/93-811-1961 • dinner nightly, lunch Fri-Sun, clsd Wed • traditional Catalan

Ma Maison Bonaire 28 34/93-894-6054 • lunch & dinner • popular • lesbians/ gay men • French • full bar • terrace

Mezzanine Espalter 8 34/93-894-9940 • dinner only • French

Pic Nic Paseo de la Ribera 34/93-811-0040 • in front of gay beach • also internet cafe

Sitthai Bonaire 29 34/938-111-6 58 • 8pm-midnight, clsd Mon

So Ca/ Southern California Sant Gaudenci 9 34/93-894-3046 • 1pm-close • also bar

El Trull Mossèn Felix Clará 3 (off Major) 34/93-894-4705 • dinner only, clsd Wed • popular • lesbians/ gay men • French/ int'l

ENTERTAINMENT & RECREATION

Gay Beach Party La Playa De La Bossa Rodona • midnight-6am Tue in season

Gay Beach (Platja de la Bassa Rodona) • in front of Calipolis Hotel & Picnic cafe

Playa De Las Balmins • turn left then pass a long beach strip & then climb a hill past a cemetery

Playa del Muerto • exclusively gay beach 50 minutes walk from the center of Sitges • also beach bar

RETAIL SHOPS

Laguna Beach Shop Sant Josep 25 34/938-947-204 • 10:30am-2pm, 5pm-9pm

Oscar Marqués de Montroig 2 (at Plaza Industria) 34/93-894-1976 • designer clothing

JAPAN

Tokyo

ACCOMMODATIONS

Capitol Tokyu 10-3 Nagata-cho 2-chome (Chiyoda-ku) 81–3/3581-4511, 800/428-6598 • gay-friendly • near the Diet

Four Seasons Hotel 10-8 Sekiguchi 2-chome (Bunkyo-ku) 81–3/3943-2222 • gay-friendly • wheelchair access • pool • surrounded by historic Japanese garden

HI Tokyo Central Hostel 18F Central Plaza (1-1 Kagurakashi, Shinjuku-ku) 81–3/3235-1107 • gay-friendly • 11pm curfew

Hotel Century Southern Tower 2-2-1 Yoyogi (Shibuya-ku) 81–3/5354-0111 • gay-friendly • near gay district

Hotel Sunroute Plaza Shinjuku 2-3-1 Yoyogi (Shibuya-ku) 81–3/3375-3211 • gay-friendly • near gay district

Keio Plaza Hotel 2-2-1 Nishi Shinjuku 81–3/3344-0111 • gay-friendly • swimming • restaurants & bars

Park Hyatt 3-7-1-2 Nishi Shinjuku 81–3/5322-1234 • gay-friendly • kids ok • restaurant & lounge • luxury hotel featured in Lost in Translation • pool • spa

Shinjuku Prince Hotel 30-1 Kabuki-cho 1-chome (Shinjuku-ku) 81–3/3205-1111, 800/542-8686 (US) • gay-friendly • WiFi

Shinjuku Washington Hotel 3-2-9 Nishi-Shinjuku (Shinjuku-ku) 81–3/3343-3111 • gay-friendly

Tokyu Stay 5-9-8 Nishi Shinjuku 81–3/3370-1090 • gay-friendly • great location

BARS

Advocates Cafe 1-F, Dai-7 Tenka Bldg (Shinjuku 2-18-1) 81–3/3358-3988 • 6pm-4am, till 1am Sun • cafe-bar • lesbians/ gay men • young crowd

Tokyo

LGBT PRIDE:
August.

ANNUAL EVENTS:
September - Tokyo International Lesbian & Gay Film Festival, web: www.tokyo-lgff.org.

CITY INFO:
Japan National Tourist Organization 81–3/3201–3331 or 212/757–5640 (US), web: www.jnto.go.jp.
Tokyo Convention & Visitors Bureau, web: www.tcvb.or.jp.

BEST VIEW:
From any of 3 major observation decks: Tokyo Metropolis Observatories, Bunkyo Civic Center of Edogawa City Office.

TRANSIT:
Nihon Kotsu 81–3/5755–2151 (English), web: www.nihon-kotsu.co.jp.
Toei, web: www.kotsu.metro.tokyo.jp.
Tokyo Metro, web: www.tokyometro.jp/en.

ATTRACTIONS:
Edo-Tokyo Museum 81–3/3626–9974, web: www.edo-tokyo-museum.or.jp.
Grand Sumo Tournaments, web: www.sumo.or.jp.
Imperial Palace, web: sankan.kunaicho.go.jp.
Kabuki-za Theater 81–3/3541-3131, web: www.kabuki-bito.jpr.
Meiji Jingu Shrine 81–3/3379-5511, web: www.meijijingu.or.jp.
Roppongi Kingyo 81–3/3478-3000, web: www.kingyo.co.jp.
Sensoji Temple 81–3/3842-0181.
Shinjuku Gyoen National Garden
Tokyo National Museum 81–3/3822-1111, web: www.tnm.jp.
Tsukiji Market, web: www.tsukiji-market.or.jp.
Ueno Park.

WEATHER:
Hot & rainy in the summer, cool (though rarely freezing) in the winter. Spring & fall are clear, mild & gorgeous.

Alamas Cafe 1/F Garnet Bldg, Shinjuku 2-12-1 81–3/6457–4242 • 6pm-2am, till 5am Fri-Sat, 3pm-midnight Sun • lesbians/ gay men • dancie club at night

Arty Farty 2F, #33 Kyutei Bldg (Shinjuku 2-11-7), Shinjuku-ku 81–3/5362–9720 • 6pm-5am, from 7pm Fri, from 5pm wknds, till 3am Sun • mostly gay men • dancing/DJ • young crowd

DNA 81–3/3341–4445 • 3pm-5am • gay/ straight • neighborhood bar

GB B1, Shinjuku Plaza Bldg (Shinjuku 2-12-3), Shinjuku-ku 81–3/3352–8972 • 8pm-2am, till 3am Fri-Sat • mostly gay men

Hug Shinjuku 2-15-8 81–3/5379–5085 • 9pm-5am, clsd Sun • women only • karaoke • cover charge

Keivi 4F Yoshino Bldg, 17-10 Sakuragaoka 81–3/3496–0006 • 6pm-midnight • mostly gay men • neighborhood bar

Kinsmen 2F Shinjuku 2-12-16 (near Shinjuku Sanchome Station) 81–3/3354–4949 • 7pm-1am, till 3am Fri-Sat, clsd Mon • lesbians/ gay men

Kinswomyn 3F, Dai-Ichi Tenka Bldg (Shinjuku 2-15-10) 81–3/3354–8720 • 8pm-4am, clsd Tue • popular • women only

Kusuo 3F Sunflower Bldg (Shinjuku 2-17-1) 81–3/3354–5050 • 8pm-4am, till 5am wknds • mostly men • dancing/DJ

Lamp Post 201 Yamahara Heights (Shinjuku 2-12-15) 81–3/3354–0436 • 7pm-3am • mostly men • piano bar

Monsoon Shimazaki Bldg 6F (2-14-9 Shinjuku) 81–3/3354–0470 • 3pm-6am • mostly gay men • small, inexpensive bar

Peach 1F (Shinjuku 2-15-8) 81–3/3351–7034 • 11pm-2am, clsd Sun-Mon • women only • in a brick building next to 'Hug' & across from 'Agit' • look for the peach mark on the door • cover charge

Sunny 2F Nakabayashi Tenpo (Shinjuku 2-15-8) 81–3/3356–0368 • 8pm-5am • one of the oldest lesbian bars in Tokyo • karaoke • neighborhood bar • piano bar

Tac's Knot 2F, Rm 202 (Shinjuku 3-11-12) 81–3/3341–9404 • 8pm-2am • lesbians/ gay men • also art exhibitions

Tamago 1F Yamahara Heights Bldg (Shinjuku 2-12-15) 81–3/3351–4838 • 9pm-5am • women only • drag king shows

Town House Ginza 6 Shinbashi, Bldg 1-11-15 (Minato-ku) 81–3/3289-8558 • 6pm-midnight, from 4pm Sat, clsd Sun • mostly gay men • karaoke

Usagi on lock U facing block V, 5th Fl (up the narrow stairs) • mostly gay men • great balcony

Warai-Tei 301 Nakae Bldg III, 2F (2-15-13 Shinjuku) 81–3/3226-0830

Wordup Bar 2-10-7 2F TOM Bld Shinjuku 81–3/3353–2466 • mostly gay men • dancing/DJ

NIGHTCLUBS

Agit 81–3/3350–8083 • 8pm-6am • lesbians/ gay men • karaoke • lesbian-owned

Arch B1F Hayakawa Bldg (Shinjuku 2-14-6) 81–3/3352–6297 • lesbians/ gay men • dancing/DJ • check www.clubarch.net for info on men-only & women-only nights

Club Zinc Shinjuku 2-14-6 (across from Shinjuku Park) 81–3/3352–6297 • 8pm-4am • lesbians/ gay men • 1st Th women's party called Bar Monalisa

Diamond Cutter B1F Hayakawa Bldg (Shinjuku 2-14-6, at Club Arch) 81–3/3352–6297 (ARCH) • 9pm-5am 1st Fri only • women only • dancing/DJ • cabaret

Motel #203 81–3/6383–4649 • 8pm-5am, till 2am Sun, clsd Tue • popular happy hour 8pm-9pm • women only • dancing/DJ

Rehab Lounge 81–3/3355–7833 • 7pm-2am, till 3am Fri-Sat • popular happy hour 7pm-9pm • mostly gay men • dancing/DJ

Shangri-La 2-2-10, Shinkiba (at ageHa, Studio Coast) 81–3/5534–2525 • bi-monthly • mostly men • popular • dancing/DJ

Warehouse Fukao Bldg B 1-4-5 (exit 7 Azabu Juban station) 81–3/6230 0343 • gay/ straight • large underground club host Red gay nights

RESTAURANTS

Angkor Wat 1-38-13 Yoyogi (Shibuya-ku) 81–3/3370–3019 • lunch & dinner • Cambodian

Ban Thai 1-23-14 Kabuki-cho, 3rd flr (Shinjuku) 81–3/3207–0068 • lunch & dinner

Chin-ya 1-3-4 Asukusa 81–3/3841–0010 • lunch & dinner • serving shabu-shabu & sukiyaki since 1880

Edogin 4-5-1 Tsukiji (Chuo-ku) 81–3/3543–4401 • 11am-9:30pm, till 8pm Sun • popular • sushi

Gonpachi 1-13-11 Nishi Azabu, 1F, 2F (Minato-ku) **81–3/5771-0170** • 11:30am-5am • multiple locations

Kakiden 3-37-11 Shinjuku, 8th flr **81–3/3352-5121** • lunch & dinner • upscale Japanese

Kitchen Five 4-2-15 Nishi-Azabu (Minato-ku) **81–3/3409-8835** • 6pm-9:45pm • Mediterranean • woman chef

Kozue 3-7-1-2 Nishi Shinjuku (at the Park Hyatt) **81–3/5323-3460** • lunch and dinner daily, on a clear day you can see Mount Fuji from the hotel's exquisite contemporary Japanese restaurant , dress code

Las Chicas Jingumae 5-47-6 (off Shibuya), Shibuya-ku **81–3/3407-6865** • 11:30am-11pm • English spoken

Maisen 4-8-5 Jingu-mae (Shibuya-ku) **81–3/3470-0071** • specializes in tonkatsu

Moti 3F Roppongi Hama Bldg (6-2-35 Roppongi) **81–3/3479-1939** • noon-10pm • Indian

New York Grill 3-7-1-2 Nishi Shinjuku (at Park Hyatt hotel, 52nd flr) **81–3/5322-1234** • lunch & dinner • reservations recommended

The Pink Cow 1-3-18 Shibuya, Shibuya-ku (Villa Modernuna B-1, across from Aoyama Park Tower) **81–3/3406-5597** • 5pm-late, clsd Mon

Sasa-no-yuki 2-15-10 Negishi (Taito-ku) **81–3/3873-1145** • 11am-9pm, clsd Mon • serving homemade tofu for 300 years

Tenmatsu 1-6-1 Dogen-zaka (Shibuya-ku) **81–3/3462-2815** • tempura

Teyandei 2-20-1 Nishi Azabu (Minato-ku) **81–3/3407-8127** • a cozy izakaya in a 2 story house on a quiet discrete street with more residences than businesses, also other locations

Yuian 2-6-1 Nishi-Shinjuku 52nd Fl (in the Shinjuku Sumitomo Bldg) **81–3/3342-5671** • 5:30-1030pm, upscale Japanese pub (Izakaya) on the 52nd floor and the window tables have amazing views

Retail Shops

Isetan Men's 3-14-1 Shinjyuku 1-11-15 **81–3/3352-1111**

Gyms & Health Clubs

Gold's Gym Harajuku 6-31-17 Jingumae (Shibuya-ku) **81–3/5766-3131** • 24 hrs, except Sun, many gay members

Travel Agents

Magnet Tours 2-11-14 Nishishinbash Bldg 2F (Minato-ku) **81–3/3500-4819** • tour operator in Japan to focus specifically on LGBT travelers

Thailand

Bangkok

Info Lines & Services

Gay AA 12/3 Silom Rd (at the Coffee Society) **66–2/231-8300** • 7pm Th

Accommodations

Baan Saladaeng 69/2 Soi Saladaeng 3, Saladaeng Rd (Silom, Bangrak) **66–2/2636-3038** • gay-friendly • upscale • near gay scene

Bangkok Rama Place, City Resort & Hotel 1546 Pattanakarn Rd (in Suan-Luang District) **66–2/722-6602-10** • gay-friendly • full brkfst • pool • kids ok • also restaurant • WiFi • wheelchair access • lesbian-owned

D&D Inn 68-70 Khaosan Rd (Phranakorn) **66–2/629-0526** • gay-friendly • central location • pool • "life's little luxuries at a price you can afford"

Elephantstay Royal Elephant Kraal & Village (74/1 M3 Tumbol Suanpik), Phra Nakhon Si Ayutthaya **66–81/668-7727, 66-87/116-3307** • gay/ straight • live w/, care for & learn about elephants • near Lopburi River • 1 hour to Bangkok • lesbian-owned

Furama Silom 59 Silom Rd **66–2/237-0488** • gay-friendly • pool • sauna • gym • restaurant • bar

Heaven@4 Hotel Sukhumvit Soi 4 **66–2/656-9450** • gay/ straight • WiFi • also bar

Hotel de Moc 78 Prajatipatai Rd, Pra-Nakorn **66–2/282-2831-3, 66-2/629-2100-5** • gay-friendly • pool • WiFi • wheelchair access

Lub d 4 Decho Rd (Silom, Bangrak) **66–2/634-7999** • gay-friendly • hostel w/ some private rooms • WiFi

Luxx 6/11 Decho Rd **66–2/635-8800** • gay-friendly • style-conscious, minimalist design hotel • full brkfst • WiFi

Old Bangkok Inn 607 Pra Sumen Rd (at Rajdamnern Ave, in Pra Nakhon) **66–2/629-1787** • environmentally-friendly • full brkfst • kids/ pets ok • nonsmoking

Omyim Lodge 72-74 Naratiwat Rd Silom 66-2/635-0169 • gay/ straight • full brkfst • nonsmoking • kids ok • WiFi • lesbian & gay-owned

Pinnacle Hotel 17 Soi Ngam Duphli, Rama 4 Rd, Sathorn 66-2/287-0111 • gay/ straight • fitness center

Regency Park Hotel 12/3 Sukhumvit 22, Soi Sainamthip 66-2/259-7420 • gay-friendly • located in heart of Bangkok • full brkfst • pool

Sheraton Grande Sukhumvit 250 Sukhumvit Rd 66-2/649-8888 • gay-friendly • tropical garden • pool WiFi • wheelchair access • also Thai & Italian restaurant

Tarntawan Place Hotel 119/ 5-10 Surawong Rd 66-2/238-2620 • centrally located • kids ok • discount for gays • WiFi • wheelchair access

Wow Bangkok 3/16 Sukhumvit Soi 31 66-2/260-3560 • gay-friendly • small boutique hotel serenely hidden in a blind alley • WiFi

BARS

70's Bar 231/16 Sarasin (Chitlom) 66-2/253-4433 • lesbians/ gay men • dancing/DJ • retro lounge

The Balcony Pub & Restaurant 86-88 Silom Soi 4 (off Silom Rd) 66-2/235-5891 • 5:30pm-close • popular • mostly gay men • karaoke • terrace

Bed Supperclub 26 Soi Sukhumvit 11, Sukhumvit Rd, Klongtoey-nua, Wattana 66-2/651-3537 • 7:30pm-close • gay/ straight • dancing/DJ • dinner served in bed

Club Love Remix Ramkhamhaeng Soi 89/2 66-2/378-4345, 66-1/987-4946 • gay/ straight • dancing/DJ • young crowd • also restaurant

@Diamond 10/17 Silom Soi 2/1 66-2/234-0459 • 6pm-2am • mostly men • neighborhood bar • food served

Expresso 8/10-11 Silom Rd, Soi 2 (Bang Rak) • mostly gay men • relaxed café-bar

Golden Dome 252/5 Ratchadapisek Rd Soi 18 (Huay Kwang) 66-2/692-8202 • lesbians/ gay men • cabaret • shows nightly at 5pm, 7pm & 9pm

JJ Park 8/3 Silom Rd, Soi 2 (Bang Rak) 66-2/235-1227 • 10:30pm-2am • gay/ straight • food • live music

Maxi's Bar & Restaurant 38/1-2 Soi Pratoochai Suriwong Rd 66-2/2266-4225 • 6pm-2am • mostly gay men

MTV Remix Ramkhamhaeng Soi 24 66-2/319-8340 • gay/ straight • dancing/DJ

One Night Only Silom Soi 4, 74-1 66-89/499-0303 • 6pm-3am • mostly gay men • small bar on the first floor, also lounge & outside area

Telephone Pub & Restaurant 114/ 11 Silom Rd, Soi 4 66-2/234-3279 • 6pm-1am • lesbians/ gay men • karaoke • WiFi • food served

NIGHTCLUBS

DJ Station 8/6-8 Silom Rd, Soi 2 (Bang Rak) 66-02/266-4029 • 10:30pm-2am • lesbians/ gay men • dancing/DJ

G-Star Ratchada Rd, Soi 8 (Din Daeng) 66-2/643-8792 • 7pm-2am • mostly gay men • dancing/DJ

Happen 8/14 Silom Soi 2 • 8pm-late, busy after 11pm • mostly gay men • karaoke

Pharaoh's Music Bar 104 Silom Soi 4 (above Sphinx) 66-2/234-7249 • 7pm-2am • gay/ straight • food • karaoke

X Boom Soi Anuman Ratchathon, Suriwong, Bangkok • opens at 8pm • popular 'after-hours' place • mostly gay men • dancing/DJ • go-go dancers

Zeta 29/67-69 Soi Soonvijai (aka Royal City Ave, or RCA) (Block C, Rama 9) 66-2/203-1043 • 9pm-2am • women only • live music

CAFES

Bug & Bee 18 Silom Rd, Suriyawong (Bang Rak) 66-2/233-8118 • 24hrs

Coffee Society 12/3 Silom Rd (Suriyawong, Bang Rak) 66-2/235-9784 • 24hrs • WiFi • also art gallery

Dick's Cafe Bangkok 894/7-8 Soi Pratuchai (Duangthawee Plaza, off Surawong Rd) 66-2/637-0078 • 11am-2am • European-style cafe in the heart of the action

RESTAURANTS

Cabbages & Condoms 6 Soi 12 Sukhumvit Rd (at Birds & Bees Resort) 66-2/229-4611 • 11am-10pm • Thai food w/ safe-sex education

Coyote on Convent 1/2 Sivadon Bldg Convent (Silom Bangrak) 66-2/631-2325 • 11am-midnight • Mexican • ladies night 6pm-8pm Th & 10pm-midnight Sat

Crêpes & Co 59/4 Langsuan Soi 1 (Ploenchit Rd, Lumpini) 66-2/653-3990 • 9am-11pm • lounge • full bar

Eat Me Soi Pipat 2 (off Soi Convent) 66-2/238-0931 • 3pm-1am • upscale • also gallery • live music

Food Loft 1027 Ploenchit Rd, Lumpini, Pathumwan (Central Chisholm, 7th flr) **66-2/655-7777** • upscale in'tl food

Full Moon 144/2 Silom Soi 10 **66-2/634-0766** • Thai food • gay-owned

Hemlock 56 Phra Arthit Rd, Chanasongkram **66-2/282-7507** • 5pm-midnight, clsd Sun • traditional Thai food • more lesbian wknds

Indigo 6 Convent Rd (off Silom Rd) **66-2/235-3268** • noon-1am, clsd Sun • patio • full bar • French

Loy Nava Dinner Cruises 37 Charoen Nakorn Rd, Klongsan **66-2/437-4932** • traditional Thai cuisine on rice barge on Chao Phraya River • reservations required

Mali 43 Sathorn Soi 1 **66-2/679-8693** • 8am-11pm • Thai & int'l • gay-owned

Mango Tree 37 Soi Tantawan (off Suriwong Rd) **66-2/236-2820** • popular • reservations recommended • traditional Thai food • live music nightly

May Kaidee 111 Tanao Rd, Bang-lam-phu (behind Burger King) **66-9/137-3173** • 9am-11pm • innovative vegetarian • also 33 Samen Rd (Soi 1)

O...Ho... 2/8 Soi Sri Bumphen **66-2/286-5292** • 9am-midnight • Thai & Western menu • gay-owned

Once Upon a Time 32 Soi Petchaburi 17, Pratunam **66-2/252-8629** • 11am-11pm • Thai

Sphinx 100 Silom Soi 4 **66-2/234-7249** • 6pm-1am • popular • Thai & Western • mostly gay men • full bar • karaoke • terrace

Sweet Basil 1 Srivieng Rd (Si Lom, Bang Rak) **66-02/234-1889** • 11:30am-9pm • popular • Vietnamese food

Zup Zip 674 Soi 101, Lad Prao Rd **66-081/734-2759** • 6pm-2am • popular w/ local lesbians • lesbian-owned

ENTERTAINMENT & RECREATION

Calypso Cabaret 296 Phaya Thai Rd, Pathumwan (at Asia Hotel) **66-2/261-6355** • lesbians/ gay men • cabaret • drag shows nightly at 8:15pm & 9:30pm

Mambo 59/28 Sathu-phararam 3 Rd **66-2/294-7381-2** • cabaret • shows nightly at 7:15pm & 10pm

Bangkok

ANNUAL EVENTS:
Jan/Feb - Chinese New Year Festival. April 13-15 Songkran (Thai New Year or Water Festival). May - Royal Ploughing Ceremony. Aug 12 - Queen Sirikit's birthday.

CITY INFO:
Tourism Authority of Thailand 1672, web: www.tourismthailand.org.

ATTRACTIONS:
The Grand Palace 66-2/224-3328, web: palaces.thai.net. The Jim Thompson House 66-2/216-7368, web: www.jimthompsonhouse.com. Lumphini Park. National Museum 66-2/224-1333. Wat Arun 66-2/891-1149, web: www.watarun.org. Wat Benchamabophit 66-2/282-7413. Wat Pho 66-2/222-5910. Wat Phra Kaeo 66-2/222-8181.

BEST VIEW:
Baiyoke Sky Hotel observation deck.

WEATHER:
Tropical, with heavy rains throughout the summer & drier weather Jan-Feb. Temperatures can dip as low as the 60ºs Nov-Dec, and rise as high as the 90ºs March-May.

TRANSIT:
SkyTrain 66-2/617-6000, web: www.bts.co.th.

AUSTRALIA
Sydney

INFO LINES & SERVICES

The Gender Centre 61-2/9569-2366 • 9am-4:30pm Mon-Fri, free services for transgender/ transsexual people & their partners/ friends/ families

Lesbian & Gay Counselling Service 61-2/8594-9596, 1-800/18-4527 (OUTSIDE SYDNEY) • 5:30pm-10:30pm • info & support

ACCOMMODATIONS

Best Western Hotel Stellar 4 Wentworth Ave (at Oxford St) 61-2/9264-9754 • gay/ straight • kitchenette in each room • WiFi • cafe & bar

Brickfield Hill B&B Inn 403 Riley St (at Foveaux), Surry Hills 61-2/9211-4886 • gay/ straight • Victorian terrace-house in gay district • near beaches & downtown • WiFi • gay-owned

Chelsea Guest House 49 Womerah Ave (at Oswald Ln), Darlinghurst 61-2/9380-5994 • gay/ straight • Victorian w/ Italianate courtyard • nonsmoking • gay-owned

Kirketon Boutique Hotel 229 Darlinghurst Rd (at Farrell Ave) 61-2/9332-2011, 800/332-920 (AUSTRALIA ONLY) • gay-friendly • also restaurant & bars • kids ok • WiFi

Medusa 267 Darlinghurst Rd (at Liverpool), Darlinghurst 61-2/9331-1000 • gay-friendly • modern boutique hotel • WiFi

Nomads Westend 412 Pitt St (at Goulburn St) 61-2/9211-4588, 1800/013-186 • gay-friendly • budget/ backpacker's accommodations • cafe • wheelchair access

Pensione Hotel 631-635 George St (at Goulburn St) 61-2/9265-8888, 800/885-886 • gay-friendly • close to the Capital theatre

Victoria Court Hotel Sydney 122 Victoria St (at Orwell), Potts Point 61-2/9357-3200, 1800/630-505 (IN AUSTRALIA) • gay-friendly • historic B&B-inn in elegant Victorian • full brkfst • WiFi

BARS

Bar Cleveland/ Hershey Bar 433 Cleveland St (at Bourke), Surry Hills 61-2/9698-1908 • 11am-4am • noon-midnight Sun • gay/ straight • cocktail lounge • DJ • young crowd

The Beauchamp 265 Oxford St (at S Dowling), Darlinghurst 61-2/9331-2575 • noon-2am popular • gay/ straight • neighborhood bar • food served • pronounced "Bee-chum" • gay-owned

Beresford Sundays 354 Bourke St (at Albion St), Surry Hills 61-2/9357-1111 • from noon Sun • lesbians/ gay men • fun in the sun

The Colombian 117-123 Oxford St (at Crown St), Darlinghurst 61-2/9360-2151 • 9am-6am • lesbians/ gay men • dancing/DJ • theme nights

The Flinders Hotel 63-65 Flinders St (at Hill St), Darlinghurst 61-2/9356-3622 • 5pm-3am, clsd Sun-Mon • gay/ straight • dancing/DJ

Green Park Hotel 360 Victoria St (at Liverpool), Darlinghurst 61-2/9380-5311 • 10am-2am, noon-midnight Sun • more gay Sun • stylish bar

The Imperial Hotel 35 Erskineville Rd, Newtown 61-2/9519-9899 • lesbians/ gay men • dancing/DJ • food served • drag shows

Lava Bar 2 Oxford St (top flr of Burdekin Hotel), Darlinghurst 61-2/9331-3066 • 11am-1am, 4pm-4am Sat • gay/ straight • popular w/ lesbians Fri till 4am • live shows

The Oxford 134 Oxford St (at Bourke St, Taylor Square), Darlinghurst 61-2/8324-5200 • 10am-close • popular • lesbians/ gay men • 3 bars include the Polo Lounge, Supper Club & Gilligans

The Palms On Oxford 124 Oxford St (at Bourke St, Taylor Square), Darlinghurst 61-2/9357-4166 • 8pm-late, clsd Mon-Wed • dancing/DJ

Phoenix Bar 34 Oxford St (at Exchange Hotel), Darlinghurst 61-2/9331-2956 • 10am-5am, till 7am Fri-Sun, clsd Mon-Tue • gay/ straight • sweaty downstairs dance den • 5 other bars in complex

The Stonewall 175 Oxford St (at Bourke), Darlinghurst 61-2/9360-1963 • noon-6am, from 9am wknds • popular • mostly gay men • dancing/DJ • drag shows

ZanziBar 323 King St (at Phillips St), Newtown 62-2/9519-1511 • gay-friendly • food served

NIGHTCLUBS

ARQ 16 Flinders St (at Taylor Square), Darlinghurst 61-2/9380-8700 • 9pm-late Th-Sun, clsd Mon-Wed • popular • mostly gay men • dancing/DJ • drag shows Th • cover charge

Bitch 61-2/439-430-428 • hot weekly women's parties • also big events on long wknds • www.bitchnews.com.au

Chicks With Picks 20 Broadway Rd (at Kensington St, at Clare Hotel), Ultimo • 2nd Sun only • women's open mic

Hellfire 16-18 Oxford Square (on corner of Riley, at The Gaff), Darlinghurst • 9:30pm-late 4th Fri • gay/ straight women-oriented fetish party • dancing/DJ • alternative • leather • burlesque • live shows • cover charge

Sydney

LGBT PRIDE:
June - Sydney Gay & Lesbian Pride. 61-2/9383-0900

ANNUAL EVENTS:
January - Sydney Festival, web: www.sydneyfestival.org.au.
February/March - Sydney Gay & Lesbian Mardi Gras Festival. Nearly a month of events and parties. 61-2/9383-0900, web: www.mardigras.org.au.
July - Sydney Leather Pride Week, web: www.sydneyleatherpride.org.
September - Manly Jazz Festival 61-2/9976-1430, web: www.manly.nsw.gov.au.

CITY INFO:
Sydney Tourist Information, web: www.discoversydney.com.au.
Sydney Visitors Centre, 61-2/9240-8788, web: www.sydneyvisitorcentre.com.

WEATHER:
Temperate—in the 50°s-70°s year-round. The summer months (January-March) can get hot and humid. Spring (September-December) sees the least rain. It's sunny most of the year. Bring a hat and lots of sunscreen!

TRANSIT:
61-2/133-300, web: www.taxiscombined.com.au.
Airport Connect 02/9557-7615, web: www.airportconnect.com.au.
State Transit Authority 61-2/131-500, web: www.sta.nsw.gov.au.
Monorail 61-2/8584-5288, web: www.metrolightrail.com.au.

ATTRACTIONS:
Art Gallery of New South Wales 61-2/9225-1700, web: www.artgallery.nsw.gov.au.
Bondi Beach.
Chinatown.
Darling Harbour.
Featherdale Wildlife Park 61-2/9622-1644, web: www.featherdale.com.au.
Manly beaches 61-2/9976-1430, web: www.manlyaustralia.com.au.
Museum of Contemporary Art 61-2/9245-2400, web: www.mca.com.au.
Queen Victoria Building, web: www.qvb.com.au.
The Rocks.
Royal Botanical Gardens 61-2/9231-8111, web: www.rbgsyd.nsw.gov.au.
Sydney Harbour Bridge.
Sydney Jewish Museum 61-2/9360-7999, web: sydney-jewishmuseum.com.au.
Sydney Opera House 61-2/9250-7111, web: www.sydneyoperahouse.com.
The Women's Library 61-2/9557-7060, web: www.thewomenslibrary.org.au.

BEST VIEW:
From the AMP Centrepoint Tower or Mrs Macquarie's Chair.

Home Tenancy 101, Cockle Bay Wharf (at Wheat Rd, Darling Harbour) 61-2/9266-0600 • open Fri-Sun • popular • gay-friendly • hosts Homesexual (www.homesexual.com.au)

Kitty Bar 35 Erskineville Rd (at The Imperial Hotel), Erskineville 61-2/9380-8700 • last Fri only • popular • mostly women • dancing/DJ • live shows • cover charge

The Midnight Shift 85 Oxford St (at Riley), Darlinghurst 61-2/9358-3848 • 10pm-late Fri-Sat • also Saddle Bar • popular • mostly gay men

Nevermind 163 Oxford St, Darlinghurst • Fri-Sun only • gay/ straight • theme nights • cutting edge electronic music

Pussycat Club 134 Oxford St (at The Oxford Hotel), Darlinghurst 61-2/9331-3467 • 3rd Sat only • mostly women • trans-friendly • dancing/DJ • cabaret & burlesque shows • all queers welcome

Queer Central 199 Enmore Rd (at Sly Fox Hotel), Enmore 61-2/9557-1016 • 9pm Wed only • mostly women • dancing/DJ • live performances

Rising Day Club 34 Oxford St (at Phoenix bar), Darlinghurst • recovery club starts at 4am Sat-Sun • mostly gay men • dancing/DJ

Slide 41 Oxford St (at Pelican) 61-2/8915-1899 • 6pm-3am, 5pm-4am Fri, 7pm-4am Sat-Sun, clsd Mon-Tue • lesbians/ gay men • dancing/DJ • also restaurant • live music • cabaret

Sly Fox 199 Enmore Rd, Enmore 61-2/9557-1016 • lesbians/ gay men • karaoke

Velvet Wednesdays 324 King St (at the Bank Hotel), Newtown • 8pm Wed only • mostly women • dancing/DJ

Cafes

Fratelli Fresh Waterloo 7 Danks St 61-2/9699-3161 • 9am-6pm, 8am-4pm Sat, 10am-4pm Sun • Italian vegetarian

Victoire 285 Darling St 61-2/9818-5529 • great bread

Vinyl Lounge Cafe 17 Elizabeth Bay Rd, Elizabeth Bay 61-2/9326-9224 • 7am-4pm, from 8am wknds, clsd Mon • lesbians/ gay men • light menu • plenty veggie • cash only

Restaurants

Bentley Restaurant & Bar 320 Crown St (Surry Hills) 61-2/9332-2344 • noon-late, clsd Sun- Mon • tapas & small plates • excellent wine

Bertoni Casalinga 281 Darling St 61-2/9818-5845 • 6am-6:30pm • Italian

Bills Surry Hills 359 Crown St (Surry Hills) 61-2/9360-4762 • 7am-10pm • great ricotta pancakes

Billy Kwong 3/355 Crown St (Surry Hills) 61-2/9332-3300 • sustainable local & organic Chinese from 6pm daily • reservations recommended • wheelchair access

The Boathouse on Blackwattle Bay End of Ferry Road (Glebe) 61-2/9518-9011 • lunch & dinner Tue-Sun • gourmet seafood • some veggie • great view • reservations required

Bright N Up 77 Oxford St (at the Brighton Hotel), Darlinghurst 61-2/9361-3379 • 4:30pm-midnight

Chu Bay 312a Bourke St, Darlinghurst 61-2/9331-3386 • 5:30pm-11pm • Vietnamese • some veggie

Fu Manchu 249 Victoria St, Darlinghurst 61-2/9360-9424 • lunch & dinner • chic noodle bar • plenty veggie • nonsmoking • cash only

Iku Wholefood Kitchen 25a Glebe Point Rd, Glebe 61-2/9692-8720, 800/732-962 • lunch & dinner • creative vegan/ macrobiotic fare • nonsmoking • outdoor seating • cash only

Kujin 41b Elizabeth Bay Rd, Elizabeth Bay 61-2/9331-6077 • lunch & dinner, clsd Mon • Japanese

Pink Peppercorn 122 Oxford St (near Taylor Square), Darlinghurst 61-2/9360-9922 • 6pm-late, clsd Mon • Laotian & Thai • gay-owned

Queen Victoria Hotel/ Razors Bistro 167 Enmore Rd, Enmore 61-2/9517-9685 • Modern Australian

Sean's Panorama 270 Campbell Parade, Bondi Beach 61-2/9365-4924 • open 6pm , from noon Sat-Sun, clsd Mon-Tue

Thai Kanteen 541 Military Rd (at Harbour St), Mosman 61-2/9960-3282 • dinner nightly, clsd Sun • modern Thai • gay-owned

Thai Pothong 294 King St (Newtown) 61-2/9550-6277 • lunch & dinner • Thai • wheelchair access

Entertainment & Recreation

Bondi Beach Bondi Beach • Sydney's most popular beach • more gay at north end

Lady Jane Beach/ Lady Bay Beach Watsons Bay • crowded nude beach • mostly men

McIver Baths/ Coogee Pool Beach St, Grant Reserve, Coogee • pool for women & children only

Obelisk Beach Middle Head Rd (at Chowder Bay Rd) • mostly men • gay beach • nudity permitted

Sydney by Diva departs from Oxford Hotel (in Taylor Square), Darlinghurst 61–2/9310-0200 • tour Sydney w/ drag queen host

Sydney Gay/ Lesbian Mardi Gras 94 Oxford St, Darlinghurst 2010 61–2/9383-0900 • the wildest party under the rainbow on this planet (see www.mardigras.org.au)

The Women's Library 8-10 Brown St 61–2/9557-7060 • "books, journals, ephemera, & art by, for, & about women"

BOOKSTORES

The Bookshop Darlinghurst 207 Oxford St (near Darlinghurst Rd), Darlinghurst 61–2/9331-1103 • 10am-10pm • Australia's oldest LGBT bookstore • staff happy to help w/ tourist info

Gertrude & Alice 46 Hall St (Bondi Beach) 61–2/9130-5155 • second-hand books • also coffee shop

RETAIL SHOPS

House of Priscilla 47 Oxford St, Darlinghurst 61–2/9286-3023 • wigs, costumes & more

PUBLICATIONS

LOTL Magazine 61–2/9332-2725 • Lesbians on the Loose • monthly magazine

SX Weekly 61–2/9360-8934 • free gay/ lesbian weekly

Sydney Star Observer 61–2/8263-0500 • weekly newspaper w/ club & event listings

GYMS & HEALTH CLUBS

City Gym 107–113 Crown St (at William St), E Sydney 61–2/9360-6247 • day passes available

Gold's Gym Sydney 58 Kippax St (level 1), Surry Hills 61–2/9211-2799 • 5:30am-9pm, 8am-6pm Sat, till 5pm Sun

SEX CLUBS

Aarows 17 Bridge St (at Pitt St), Rydalmere 61–2/9638-0553 • 24hrs • lesbians/ gay men • transgender-friendly • 18+

EROTICA

House of Fetish 288 Crown St, Darlinghurst 61–2/9380-9042 • clsd Mon-Tues

CRUISES

Women Only

➤ **Olivia Travel 800/631–6277** 434 Brannan St, San Francisco, CA 94107 • exclusive cruise, resort & escape vacations for lesbians" • see ad in front color section • *www.olivia.com*

Gay/Lesbian

Aquafest 800/592–9058 4801 Woodway #400-W, Houston, TX 77056 • LGBT groups mingle w/ mixed clientele on major cruise lines • *www.aquafestcruises.com*

Gayribbean Cruises 877/560–8318 Dallas, TX • gay & lesbian group cruise organizer • fabulous destinations • annual Halloween cruise from Galveston, TX • *www.gayribbeancruises.com*

Port Yacht Charters 516/883–0998, 877/DO-A-BOAT 9 Belleview Ave, Port Washington, NY 11050 • custom charters worldwide, specializing in the Caribbean • commitment ceremonies • gourmet cuisine • *www.portyachtcharters.com*

R Family 917/522–0985 5 Washington Ave, Nyack, NY 10960 • family-friendly vacations designed especially for the LGBT community • *www.rfamilyvacations.com*

Rainbow Charters 808/347–0235 Kewalo Basin, Honolulu, HI 96814 • gay & lesbian weddings • custom sailing cruises • whale-watching • snorkeling • sunset cruises • *www.RainbowChartersHawaii.com*

RSVP Vacations 800/328–7787 gay & lesbian cruise vacations • *www.rsvpvacations.com*

Sailing Affairs 917/453–6425 58 E 1st St #6-B, New York City, NY 10003 • gay sailboat charters, day trips, sunset sails & sailing vacations on 47-foot Beneteau • East Coast, Caribbean, Europe & Mediterranean • *www.sailingaffairs.com*

LUXURY TOURS

DavidTravel 949/427–0199 310 Dahlia Pl, Ste A, Corona del Mar, CA 92625-2821 • full-service travel agency & tour operator • small luxury group departures & customized travel for individuals & groups • milestone events, including honeymoons! • *www.DavidTravel.com*

Steele Luxury Travel 646/688–2274 New York City, NY 10011 • unique & top-rated travel experiences to exotic destinations worldwide • *www.steeletravel.com*

GREAT OUTDOORS ADVENTURES

Women Only

Adventure Associates of WA 206/932–8352 PO Box 16304, Seattle, WA 98116 • worldwide eco-adventures for women • cruises, cultural immersion, history & ruins, treks, safaris, hiking, kayaking & biking • *www.adventureassociates.net*

Adventures in Good Company 410/435–1965, 877/439–4042 5913 Brackenridge Ave, Baltimore, MD 21212 • outdoor & adventure travel for women of all ages & abilities • *www.adventuresingoodcompany.com*

Bushwise Women /61 266840178 PO Box 5417, Lismore, NSW 2480, Australia • international escapes & adventures for women • wilderness & cultural trips in New Zealand, Australia, Egypt & Europe • also hosts The Women's Accomodation Network • *www.bushwise.co.nz*

Call of the Wild Adventure Travel 650/265–1662, 888/378–1978 20834 Solstice Dr, Bend, OR 97701 • hiking, camping & cultural trips for all levels in Western US, Alaska, Mexico, New Zealand & Peru • longest-running adventure travel company for women • *www.callwild.com*

Chicks with Picks & Chicks Rock 970/626-4424 PO Box 486, Ridgway, CO 81432 • ice climbing & rock climbing for women • all levels welcome • www.chickswithpicks.net

Equinox Wilderness Expeditions 206/462-5246 2440 E Tudor Rd, Anchorage, AK 99507 • wilderness trips in Alaska, British Columbia & the Southwest US by raft, canoe, sea kayak & backpack • also ski tours near Whistler, BC • www.equinoxexpeditions.com

Grand Canyon Field Institute 928/638-2485, 866/471-4435 PO Box 399, Grand Canyon, AZ 86023 • women's educational backpacking classes in the Grand Canyon • also co-ed trips • custom classes/ tours for groups • www.grandcanyon.org/fieldinstitute

Herizen™ Life Adventures Int'l Inc SKYPE:/VALMA - HERIZEN 101-5170 Dunster Rd #176, Nanaimo, BC V9T 6M4, Canada • women-only retreats • sailing, yoga, riding & more in Baja, Mexico, Belize, British Columbia & British Virgin Islands • www.herizenlifeadventures.com

Mariah Wilderness Expeditions 530/626-6049, 800/462-7424 PO Box 1160, Lotus, CA 95651 • unique vacations for women on roads less traveled • multi-sport adventures • unique cultural & eco-explorations • www.mariahwe.com

National Women's Sailing Association 401/682-2064 146 South Great Rd, Lincoln, MA 01773 • sailing seminars & workshops • www.womensailing.org

Nurture Through Nature 207/595-8260 77 Wilton Warren Rd, Denmark, ME 04022 • holistic personal retreats • solar-powered eco-cabin rentals • wood-fired sauna • yoga • canoe tours • hiking & camping • www.ntnretreats.com

Octopus Reef Dive Training & Tours 808/875-0183 Maui, HI • experienced instructors teaching & guiding SCUBA divers in Maui • www.OctopusReef.com

Sea Sense: The Women's Sailing & Powerboating School 727/289-6917 PO Box 1961, St Petersburg, FL 33731 • US & worldwide sailing & powerboating courses • custom courses • also private, "on your own boat" courses • www.seasenseboating.com

Tethys Offshore Sailing for Women 206/789-5118 2442 NW Market St #498, Seattle, WA 98107 • join Capt Nancy Erley as learning crew for a week in the Pacific Northwest aboard the 38' Tethys • www.tethysoffshore.com

WalkingWomen 0114/241-2774 York, United Kingdom • women's walking vacations for all levels • England, Scotland, Ireland, Wales, Europe, & as far as Nepal & South Africa! • www.walkingwomen.com

Wild Women Expeditions 888/993-1222 PO Box 264, Woody Point, NF A0K 1P0, Canada • Canada's outdoor adventure company for women • kayaking • hiking • cycling • yoga & more • decidedly dykey! • wildwomenexp.com/lesbianbi-trips

Wildlotus Adventures 844/715-2440 43 Nghi Tam Rd, Tay Ho, Hanoi, Vietnam • tailor made tours & off the beaten path experiences for women in Vietman, Laos, Cambodia & Thailand • www.wildlotusadventures.com

Winter Moon Summer Sun 218/848-2442 3388 Petrell, Brimson, MN 55602 • dogsledding trips in winter • kayaking Lake Superior in summer • rustic accommodations w/ meals provided • www.wintermoonsummersun.com

Womanship 410/267-6661 137 Conduit St, Annapolis, MD 21401 • daily or live-aboard learning cruises for women • sail & "see" adventures in the Greek Isles, Turkey, Florida Keys & more • www.womanship.com

WomanTours 585/424-2124, 800/247-1444 3495 Winton Place, Bldg E-245, Rochester, NY 14623 • fully supported bicycle tours for women • call for a free catalog • www.womantours.com

Women On A Roll 310/839-2500 3842 Main Street #B, Culver City, CA 90232 • travel, sporting, cultural & social club for women • wide range of events & trips • largest lesbian organization in Southern California • www.womenonaroll.com

Women's Flyfishing® 907/274-7113 PO Box 243963, Anchorage, AK 99524 • women-only fly-fishing schools & guided trips for women & couples in Alaska, Argentina & Mexico • we provide all gear & equipment • beginners welcome! • www.womensflyfishing.net

Mostly Women

Venus Charters 305/304–1181 Garrison Bight Marina, Key West, FL 33040 • snorkeling & dolphin-watching • light-tackle fishing • commitment ceremonies • www.venuscharters.com

Gay/Lesbian

Alyson Adventures, Inc 305/296–9935, 800/825–9766 626 Josephine Parker Dr #206, Key West, FL 33040 • award-winning adventure travel & active vacations • hiking, biking & multi-sport activities • www.hetravel.com

Journeyweavers 607/277–1416 313 Washington St, Ithaca, NY 14850 • group & individual outdoor adventure & birding trips in Costa Rica & beyond • www.journeyweavers.com

Out in Alaska 907/339–0101 1819 Dimond Dr, Anchorage, AK 99507 • adventure travel throughout Alaska for LGBT travelers • your best bet for a fun & authentic Alaska vacation! • www.outinalaska.com

OutWest Global Adventures 406/446–1533, 800/743–0458 PO Box 2050, Red Lodge, MT 59068 • specializing in gay/ lesbian active & adventure travel • worldwide • www.outwestadventures.com

South American Journeys, LLC Cuzco, Peru • yoga, writing workshops, hiking, camping, out-reach programs & more in Peru & South America • women-only & men-only trips available • www.southamericanjourneys.com

Undersea Expeditions 858/270–2900, 800/669–0310 758 Kapahulu Ave #100-1188, Honolulu, HI 96816 • gay & lesbian scuba adventures worldwide • www.UnderseaX.com

Gay/Straight

Atlantis Yacht Charters 415/332–0800 Schoonmaker Pt Marina, 85 Liberty Ship Way #110-A, Sausalito, CA 94965 • group charters • www.yachtcharter.com

GoNorth Alaska Adventure Travel Center 907/479–7271, 855/236–7271 3713 South Lathrop St, Fairbanks, AK 99709 • guided tours throughout Alaska & the Arctic • air taxis & transportation • www.GoNorth-Alaska.com

Himalayan High Treks 415/551–1005, 800/455–8735 241 Dolores St, San Francisco, CA 94103 • experience indigenous Buddhist & Hindu cultures • www.hightreks.com

Natural Habitat Adventures 303/449–3711, 800/543–8917 PO Box 3065, Boulder, CO 80307 • up-close encounters w/ the world's most amazing wildlife in its natural habitat • www.nathab.com

Open Eye Tours 808/572–3483 PO Box 324, Makawao, HI 96768 • customized private land tours of Maui & other islands • visit popular spots or places seldom seen, walking or not • sharing Maui's best-kept secrets since 1983 • www.openeyetours.com

Pacific Yachting & Sailing 831/423–7245, 800/374–2626 790 Mariner Park Way, Santa Cruz, CA 95062 • international & local yachting vacations for gays, lesbians & mixed groups • also sailing instruction • www.pacificsail.com

Paddling South & Saddling South 707/942–4550, 800/398–6200 PO Box 827, Calistoga, CA 94515 • horseback, mountain-biking & sea-kayak trips in Baja • also women-only trips • call for complete calendar • www.tourbaja.com

Puffin Fishing Charters 907/224–4653, 800/978–3346 PO Box 1169, Seward, AK 99664 • guided charter fishing • almost 30 years of experience • halibut, salmon & rockfish on vessels custom-built for Alaskan waters • www.puffincharters.com

Voyageur North Outfitters 218/365–3251, 800/848–5530 1829 E Sheridan, Ely, MN 55731 • canoe outfitting & trips • www.vnorth.com

Whitewater Connection 530/622–6446, 800/336–7238 PO Box 270, Coloma, CA 95613 • whitewater rafting adventures • www.whitewaterconnection.com

SPIRITUAL/HEALTH VACATIONS

Women Only

Les Be Well 610/966–9668 4840 Beck Rd, Emmaus, PA 18049 • vacation adventures & retreats for mind, body & spirit for lesbians, bisexuals and other women of acceptance • *www.lesbewell.com*

Sounds & Furies 604/253–7189 PO Box 21510, 1424 Commercial Dr, Vancouver, BC V5L 5G2, Canada • concerts featuring lesbian performers • annual Women's Arts Faire • events for older lesbians • *www.soundsandfuries.com*

Gay/Lesbian

Spirit Journeys 201/483–3111, 800/754–1875 134 River Rd, New Milford, NJ 97646 • spiritual retreats, workshops & adventure trips throughout the US & abroad • *www.spiritjourneys.com*

THEMATIC TOURS

Mostly Men

Hawaii Gay Tours 808/234–9260 Honolulu, HI 96821 • experience Hawaii as the locals do • customizable tours • *www.hawaiigaytours.com*

Women Only

Canyon Calling Adventures for Women 928/282–0916 200 Carol Canyon Dr, Sedona, AZ 86336 • worldwide multi-activity adventure trips for moderately fit women, including the premiere trip to New Zealand w/ Kiwi company founder • *www.canyoncalling.com*

Driftwood Dreamers 64–7/315–6627 93 Armstrong Rd, Opotiki, Bay of Plenty 3198, New Zealand • women's adventures in New Zealand • rugged landscapes, gorgeous beaches, fascinating Maori culture • *www.driftwooddreamers.com*

Ela Brasil Tours 203/840–9010 14 Burlington Dr, Norwalk, CT 06851 • custom trips to Brazil • promoting responsible travel & cultural diversity • EcoVolunteer programs • *www.elabrasil.com*

Mouriscastours 351/963–857–776 Faro, Portugal • private tours in Portugal • *www.mouriscastours.com*

Sights & Soul Travels 240/750–0597, 866/737–9602 13610 Chrisbar Ct, Germantown, MD 20874 • small group, upscale, women-only trips to 32 destinations in Europe, Africa, South America & Asia • *www.sightsandsoul.com*

Tours of Exploration 604/886–7300, 800/690–7887 PO Box 1503, Gibsons, BC V0N 1V0, Canada • eco-cultural journeys to Ecuador & Bolivia for women • *www.toursexplore.com*

Towanda Women Motorcycle Tours 64–3/314–9097 PO Box 4437, Christchurch, New Zealand • motorcycle tours for women by women in Alaska, Europe, New Zealand & Australia • ride the best motorcycling roads in the world w/ like-minded women • *www.towanda.org*

Women's Motorcyclist Foundation 7 Lent Ave, LeRoy, NY 14482 • works to improve the sport of motorcycling • also raises money for breast cancer • *www.womensmotorcyclistfoundation.org*

Mostly Women

French Escapade 510/483–5713, 888/483–5713 2389 Blackpool Pl, 94577 San Leandro • discover France, Belgium, Spain & Switzerand in small groups • sightseeing, painting, cooking tours • some women-only trips • lesbian owned/run • *www.frenchescapade.com*

Robin Tyler International Tours for Women 818/893-4075 15842 Chase St, North Hills, CA 91343 • upscale int'l five-star lesbian travel founded in 1990 • specializes in Africa, Asia, Galapagos & other exotic locations • www.robintylertours.com

Gay/Lesbian

Africa Outing 27-21/671-4028 5 Alcyone Rd, Claremont, Capetown 7708, South Africa • gay/ lesbian safaris & more • tours customized to your needs • www.afouting.com

Brazil Fiesta Visa Service 415/986-1134, 800/200-0582 268 Bush St #3531, San Francisco, CA 94104 • expedited Brazilian visa service • www.brazilfiesta.net

CM by Carlos Melia 917/754-5515 630 5th Ave #2207, 10011 New York City • boutique gay travel to Argentina, Uruguay & New York City • all services tested by me • "Been There Done That" • www.carlosmelia.com

Gay Bali Tours 62-361/736-818, 62-361/788-6627 Jl. Braban No. 67, Seminyak, 80361 Bali, Indonesia • premier & professional tour operator permanently based in Bali • www.baligay.net

Go Pink China 86/1366-124-6689 Beijing, China • adding queer elements to city tours & national trips in China • www.gopinkchina.com

Kuyay Travel 56-652/438-990, 56-97/519-3259 Puerto Rosales 46, 5550000 Puerto Varas, Los Lagos, Chile • gay-owned/run travel planner & tour host in Patagonia • www.gaypatagonia.com

MexGay Vacations 213/383-9491, 866/639-4299 355 S Grand Ave #2450, Los Angeles, CA 90071 • specializing in gay travel to Mexico • www.mexgay.com

National Gay Pilots Association 214/336-0873 PO Box 1652, San Jose, CA 95109 • several annual gatherings • call for more info • www.ngpa.org

Pacific Ocean Holidays 808/923-2400 Honolulu, HI • Hawaii vacation packages • www.gayhawaiivacations.com

Planetdwellers 61-2/8667-3336 Shop 47 Elizabeth Bay Rd, Elizabeth Bay, NSW 2011, Australia • LGBT tours of Australia • come to OZ! • www.planetdwellers.com.au

Venture Out 415/626-5678, 888/431-6789 575 Pierce St #604, San Francisco, CA 94117 • high-end, escorted, small-group tours for gay & lesbian travelers to countries around the world • www.venture-out.com

Gay/Straight

Alaska Railroad 907/265-2494, 800/544-0552 (RESERVATIONS) 431 W 1st Ave, Anchorage, AK 99501 • rail & tour packages • www.alaskarailroad.com

Aria Tours 866/686-1288 PO Box 159, Little Bridge St, Almonte, ON K0A 1A0, Canada • luxury travel for opera & the arts to the most spectacular destinations in the world • www.aria-tours.com

Asian Pacific Adventures 818/881-2745, 800/825-1680 6065 Calvin Ave, Tarzana, CA 91356 • custom tours to Asia, including India, Thailand, China, Tibet, Vietnam, Japan & more • festivals, tribes, safaris & art • hiking & biking • www.asianpacificadventures.com

Brazil Ecojourneys 55-48/3389-5619 Estrada Rozalia Paulina Ferreira 1132, Armação, 88063-555 Florianopolis, Brazil • lesbian-owned Brazil tour operator • www.brazilecojourneys.com

Ecotour Expeditions, Inc 401/423-3377, 800/688-1822 PO Box 128, Jamestown, RI 02835 • small group boat tours of the Amazon & more • call for color catalog • www.nature-tours.com

Heritage Tours Private Travel 212/206-8400, 800/378-4555 121 W 27th St #1201, New York, NY 10001 • custom private trips to Morocco, Spain, Portugal, Turkey, Southern & East Africa • www.HTprivatetravel.com

Holbrook Travel 800/451–7111 3540 NW 13th St, Gainesville, FL 32609 • natural history tours in Central America, South America & Africa • small groups • www.holbrooktravel.com

Lima Tours 51-1/619–6900 Jr De la Union 1040, Lima, Peru • personalized, gay-friendly tours to Peru • www.limatours.com.pe

New England Vacation Tours 802/464–2076, 800/742–7669 PO Box 560, West Dover, VT 05356 • gay/ lesbian tours (including fall foliage) conducted by a mainstream tour operator • www.newenglandvacationtours.com

Pacha Tours 800/722–4288 36 W 44th St # 1208, New York City, NY 10036 • trips to Turkey, Spain, France & Greece • www.pachatours.com

Shop Around Tours 212/684–3763 305 E 24th St #2-N, New York City, NY 10010 • for people who live to shop & love to travel • www.shoparoundtours.com

Sublime Journeys 800/830–7142 Albrook Plaza, no. 31, Panama City, Panama • progressive, diverse & extraordinary travel experiences in South & Central America • www.discoversublime.com

Wild Rainbow African Safaris 800/423–1945 308 Jones St, Ukiah, CA 95482 • bespoke African safaris lead by Jody Cole • www.wildrainbowsafaris.com

CUSTOM TOURS

Costa Rica Experts 773/935–1009, 800/827–9046 3166 N Lincoln Ave #424, Chicago, IL 60657 • www.costaricaexperts.com

Travel & Culture Dubai 971/5287–38211 201 Al Habbai Building (opposite Deira city center), Dubai, United Arab Emirates • tours, safaris & hotel reservations in Dubai • www.dubai.travel-culture.com

Travel & Culture Pakistan 92-321/242–4778 702 Panorama Center Office Plaza, 75530 Karachi, Pakistan • tours, safaris & hotel reservations in Pakistan • www.travel-culture.com

Travel & Culture Sri Lanka 94/777-864-479 07-1B, E Tower, World Trade Ctr, Colombo, Sri Lanka • tours, safaris & hotel reservations in Sri Lanka • www.srilanka.travel-culture.com

VARIOUS TOURS

Women Only

Thanks Babs, the Day Tripper 702/370–6961 Las Vegas, NV • outdoor tours, shows & attractions • Grand Canyon getaways • full service concierge for Las Vegas, state of NV & the Southwest • it's like having a lesbian aunt in Las Vegas! • also tours in San Francisco, CA • www.thanksbabs.com

Gay/Lesbian

Footprints 416/962–8111, 888/962–6211 19 Madison Ave #300, Toronto, ON M5R 2S2, Canada • custom-designed, private tours arranged to worldwide destinations • www.footprintstravel.com

Friends of Dorothy Travel® 415/864–1600, 800/640–4918 1177 California St #B, San Francisco, CA 94108 • unique gay & lesbian adventures • individual & group arrangements • www.fodtravel.com

Out & About Travel 800/842–4753 161 Federal St, Providence, RI 02903 • full-service travel agency specializing in gay & lesbian tours, cruises, adventure travel, ski trips, honeymoons, customized packages & more • serving the GLBT community since 1999! • www.gaytravelpros.com

Zoom Vacations 773/772–9666, 866/966–6822 Chicago, IL • takes gay group travel to the next level • experience the best of a destination w/ surprises, insider events & a sense of magic • www.zoomvacations.com

EVENTS

January

12-19: Aspen Gay Ski Week   *Aspen, CO*
LGBT • 5000+ attendees • 970/925-4123 • **www.gayskiweek.com**

12-Feb 2: Midsumma Festival   *Melbourne, Australia*
arts, culture & community • LGBTQ • 61-3/9415-9819 • **www.midsumma.org.au**

16-21: Sin City Shootout   *Las Vegas, NV*
LGBT athletes compete in softball, basketball, wrestling, body building & more • LGBT • 6,750
attendees • 909/227-1794 • **www.sincityshootout.com**

22-26: Winter Rendezvous   *Stowe, VT*
annual gay ski week • skiing, winter sports & entertainment • 587/445-7198 •
www.winterrendezvous.com

26-Feb 2: WinterPRIDE: Whistler Gay Ski Week   *Whistler, BC, Canada*
annual gay/ lesbian ski week • parties for boys & girls! • top-notch DJs & venues • popular destination 75 miles N of Vancouver • LGBT • 3,000+ attendees • 604/288-7218, 866/787-1966 •
www.gaywhistler.com

March

2-9: Lake Tahoe WinterFest Gay & Lesbian Ski Week   *Lake Tahoe, NV*
world-class skiing • gay comedy • Lake Tahoe dinner/dance cruise • LGBT • 800 attendees •
www.LakeTahoeWinterfest.com

4: Mardi Gras   *New Orleans, LA*
mixed gay/ straight • 800/672-6124 • **www.neworleanscvb.com**

21-30: Winter Music Conference   *Miami, FL*
huge annual EDM conference • workshops, seminars, IDMA & of course dance
parties • mixed gay/ straight • 100,000 attendees • /954 • **www.WinterMusicConference.com**

25-30: OutBoard   *Steamboat Springs, CO*
annual lesbian/ gay snowboarding festival • 300+ attendees • 877/38-BOARD •
www.outboard.org

31-April 6: Kraft Nabisco Golf Championship   *Palm Springs, CA*
previously known as the Dinah Shore Golf Championship • mostly women • 760/324-4546 •
www.nabiscochampionship.com

TBA: Chicago Takes Off   *Chicago, IL*
burlesque show to fight HIV/AIDS in the Chicagoland area • LGBT • 1400 attendees •
773/989-9400 • **www.chicagotakesoff.org**

April

13: AIDS Walk Miami   *Miami Beach, FL*
5K walk-a-thon fundraiser benefiting Care Resource • LGBT • 305/576-1234 •
www.aidswalkmiami.org

20-27: Philadelphia Black Gay Pride   *Philadelphia, PA*
a weekend of social & cultural activities • films, BBQ, spoken word, parties & more • LGBT •
877/497-7247 • **www.phillyblackpride.org**

30: Queensday   *Amsterdam, Netherlands*
huge street festival to celebrate what was originally the birthday of the Queen Mother • LGBT •
www.queensdayamsterdam.eu

TBA: Boybutante Ball   *Athens, GA*
LGBT • 1000+ attendees • **www.boybutante.org**

AQUA GIRL®

15-YEAR ANNIVERSARY

CELEBRATION

BENEFITING & PRODUCED BY

aqua foundation for women

5 DAYS OF SPECTACULAR EVENTS FOR WOMEN WHO LOVE WOMEN

MAY 14-18, 2014 | MIAMI BEACH

WWW.AQUAGIRL.ORG

May

1-4: Equality Forum   *Philadelphia, PA*
largest nat'l & int'l LGBT civil rights summit w/ panels, parties & special events • 215/732-3378
x116 • www.equalityforum.com

3: Down & Derby   *Louisville, KY*
official LGBT event of the Kentucky Derby • LGBT • www.louisvilledownandderby.com

5-18: Int'l Dublin Gay Theatre Festival   *Dublin, Ireland*
353-87/657-3732 • www.gaytheatre.ie

8-11: Splash: Houston Black Gay Pride   *Houston, TX*
LGBT • 832/443-1016 • www.houstonsplash.com

10-16: OutGames   *Darwin, Australia*
gay sport & cultural festival • LGBT • 32 475/541 247 • www.glisa.org

12-14: Annual Gay Bowling Tournament   *Tucson, AZ*
check site for local tournaments throughout the year • www.igbo.org

14-18: Aqua Girl   *Miami Beach, FL*
a weekend of hot women's parties in Miami • mostly women • 305/576-AQUA •
www.aquagirl.org

18: AIDS Walk New York   *New York City, NY*
AIDS benefit • mixed gay/ straight • 212/807-9255 • www.aidswalk.net

18: Minnesota AIDS Walk   *Minneapolis, MN*
enjoy a 10K walk from Minnehaha Park & raise money for MN AIDS Project • mixed gay/ straight •
10,000 attendees • 612/373-2410 • www.mnaidsproject.org

22-25: Int'l Association of Country Western Dance Clubs
Annual Convention   *Denver, CO*
also semi-annual conventions in March (Fort Lauderdale, FL) & October (San Francisco, CA) • LGBT
• 400-600 attendees • www.outcountrydance.com

22-26: Pensacola Memorial Day Weekend   *Pensacola, FL*
many parties on beaches & in bars • LGBT • 35,000+ attendees • 850/433-9491 •
www.memorialweekendpensacola.com

23-June 8: Spoleto Festival USA   *Charleston, SC*
one of the continent's premier avant-garde cultural arts festivals • 140+ performances of dance,
theater & music from around the world • mixed gay/ straight • 843/579-3100 (tickets), 843/722-
2764 (office) • www.spoletousa.org

TBA: DC Black Pride   *Washington, DC*
LGBT • 202/347-0555 • www.dcblackpride.org

June

1-7: AIDS LifeCycle   *San Francisco to Los Angeles, CA*
bike from San Francisco to Los Angeles to raise money for HIV/AIDS services • 415/581-7077 •
www.aidslifecycle.org

ongoing: LGBT Pride   *Cross-country, USA*
celebrate yourself & attend one – or many – of the hundreds of Gay Pride parades & festivities
happening in cities around the world • www.interpride.org

ongoing: Music in the Mountains   *Grass Valley, CA*
summer music festival • mixed gay/ straight • 530/265-6173 • www.musicinthemountains.org

ongoing: National Queer Arts Festival   *San Francisco, CA*
performances & exhibitions in the San Francisco Bay Area highlighting artists from around the
country • year-round events • LGBT • 415/935-5948 • www.QueerCulturalCenter.org

3-9: Gay Days Orlando
Orlando, FL
including Gay Day at Disney • 7 days of parties & fun for boys & girls alike! • LGBT • 407/896-8431 • www.gaydays.com

5-8: Girls in Wonderland
Orlando, FL
Pandora events presents the biggest women's week celebration on the East Coast with 4,000 women taking over the Sheraton Lake Buena Vista Resort at Disney World for non-stop dance parties, comedy, pool parties, celebrity hosts, awesome girl DJs, live women's music, theme parks and so much more • mostly women • 954/288-8691 • www.girlsinwonderland.com

6-8: PrideFest
Milwaukee, WI
celebrate LGBT pride at Henry W Maier Festival Park • 414/272-3378 • **www.pridefest.com**

13-15: Black Gay Pride
Memphis, TN
LGBT • 901/522-8459 • **www.memphisblackpride.org**

15: Unofficial Gay Day at Cedar Point
Sandusky, OH
wear red to show your support on the unofficial Gay Day at this popular amusement park • mixed gay/ straight •

18-22: South Carolina Black Pride
Columbia, SC
• www.southcarolinablackpride.com

28-29: San Francisco LGBT Pride Parade/ Celebration
San Francisco, CA
LGBT • 415/864-0831 • www.sfpride.org

TBA: AIDS Walk Boston & 5K Run
Boston, MA
mixed gay/ straight • 12,000 attendees • 617/424-9255 • www.aidswalkboston.org

TBA: Howl Festival
New York City, NY
a cabaret from the underworld • outdoor murals • hip hop howl • all in Tompkins Square Park • mixed gay/ straight • 212/243-3413 • **www.howlfestival.com**

TBA: Idapalooza Fruit Jam
Dowelltown, TN
queer music festival in backwoods TN • camping • vegetarian feasts • 615/597-4409 • www.planetida.com

TBA: IGLFA World Championship
TBA, Worldwide
Int'l Gay & Lesbian Football Association's annual soccer tournament • www.iglfa.org

TBA: Juneteenth Jamboree of New Plays
New York City, NY
annual theater festival • new works about the African American experience & its legacy • mixed gay/ straight • 212/964-1904 • www.juneteenthlegacytheatre.com

TBA: Paris Circuit Party
Paris, France
gay culture festival • film • performance • political discussions • dance parties & more • LGBT • www.pariscircuitparty.com

TBA: PDX Black Pride
Portland, OR
films, workshops, parties & more • LGBT • pflagpdx.org

TBA: UK Black Pride
London, England
44 020/8257 5358 • www.ukblackpride.org.uk

TBA: Windy City Black Pride
Chicago, IL
a weekend of parties, seminars & more • LGBT • 888/922-7244 • www.windycityblackpride.org

July

2-6: At the Beach/ LA Black Pride Weekend
Los Angeles, CA
celebrate a weekend of diversity & LGBT-QS/SGL pride at the beach & across Los Angeles • LGBT • 323/285-4225 • www.atbla.com

3-6: Int'l Gay Square Dance Clubs Convention
Salt Lake City, UT
303/722-5276 • www.iagsdc.org

11-13: GaymerCon
San Francisco, CA
gaming & geek lifestyle convention w/ a focus on LGBT culture • www.gaymercon.org

12-13: Ride for AIDS Chicago   *Chicago, IL*
2-day bike ride to fight HIV/ AIDS in the Chicagoland area • LGBT • 500 attendees •
773/989-9400 • rideforaids.org

14: Joining Hearts   *Atlanta, GA*
at Piedmont Park Pool • open bar, catered hors d'oeuvres, live entertainment, dancing under the
stars & a grand finale fireworks spectacular • 100% donated to beneficiaries • 678/318-1446 •
www.joininghearts.org

21: AIDS Walk San Francisco   *San Francisco, CA*
mixed gay/ straight • 27,000+ attendees • 415/615-9255 • www.aidswalk.net

26: Crape Myrtle Festival   *Raleigh-Durham, Chapel Hill, NC*
yearlong fundraising events for HIV/LGBT concerns culminating in a grand gala the last Saturday of
July • mixed gay/ straight • 500+ attendees • 919/656-4205 • **www.crapemyrtlefest.org**

TBA: Charlotte Black Gay Pride   *Charlotte, NC*
art & performances, community forums, dance parties & more • 704/953-8813 • **www.cbgp.org**

TBA: EuroPride 2014   *Oslo, Norway*
parties, politics, performance & more • there is something for everyone at this massive celebration
of gay pride • **www.europride.info**

TBA: Gaylaxicon   *Boston, MA*
LGBT science fiction, fantasy, horror & gaming convention • **www.gaylacticnetwork.org**

TBA: Hotter Than July Weekend   *Detroit, MI*
the Midwest's oldest black same-gender-loving pride celebration • LGBT • 888/755-9165 •
blackpridesociety.org

TBA: Triangle Black Pride   *Raleigh-Durham, Chapel Hill, NC*
celebrate & honor the diversity of the African American LGBTQ community in the Triangle •
919/233-2044 • triangleblackpride.org

August

1-25: Edinburgh Fringe Festival   *Edinburgh, Scotland*
the largest arts festival in the world • dance, theater, music, comedy, events & more • mixed gay/
straight • 44-131/226-0026 • www.edfringe.com

6-9: Rendezvous 2014   *Medicine Bow Nat'l Forest, WY*
5-day camping festival to celebrate LGBT pride • 400+ attendees • 307/778-7645 •
www.wyomingequality.org

8-10: Fire Island Black Out (FIBO)   *Fire Island, NY*
3-day beach event for the LGBT community & friends • all are invited to attend & enjoy, regardless
of race, gender or orientation • LGBT • 215/751-0808 • **www.fireislandblackout.com**

9-16: Gay Games 2014   *Cleveland, OH*
8 days of sports, cultural events, arts & ceremonies • LGBT • 49-221/925 2607 • **www.gg9cle.com**

22-27: National Gay Softball World Series   *Dallas, TX*
LGBT • 412/362-1247 • **www.gaysoftballworldseries.com**

24-31: 'Camp' Camp   *Porter, ME*
summer camp for LGBT adults • sports, pottery, theater, yoga & more • LGBT • 347/453-5257 •
www.campcamp.com

27-Sept 1: Atlanta Black Pride Weekend   *Atlanta, GA*
celebrate Black Pride over Labor Day weekend in Atlanta • LGBT • 678/799-8526 •
www.inthelifeatlanta.com

30-Sept 6: Gay Ski Week QT   *Queenstown, New Zealand*
64 21/033-6270 • www.gayskiweekqt.com

TBA: AIDS Walk Colorado   *Denver, CO*
303/962-5302 • www.aidswalkcolorado.org

TBA: Black Pride NYC   *New York City, NY*
multicultural LGBT festival w/ a wide array of entertainment, forums, workshops & events • LGBT •
www.nycblackpride.com

TBA: Blackout: Oakland Black & Brown Pride   *Oakland, CA*
celebrate w/ a weekend of conferences, awards ceremonies & parties • 510/621-3553 •
www.oaklandpride.org

TBA: Inferno Dominican Republic   *Punta Cana, Dominican Republic*
the premier Labor Day pride celebration • deluxe, all-inclusive accommodations • LGBT •
305/891-7536 • www.infernodr.com

TBA: Northalsted Market Days   *Chicago, IL*
a good ol' summer block party on Main St of Boys' Town, USA • LGBT • 773/883-0500 •
www.northalsted.com

TBA: St Louis Black Pride   *St Louis, MO*
314/531-2284 • www.st-louisblackpride.org

September

2-8: Gay Days Las Vegas   *Orlando, FL*
including Gay Day at Disney • 7 days of parties & fun for boys & girls alike! • LGBT • 407/896-
8431 • www.gaydays.com

21: Out in the Park   *Springfield, MA*
unofficial gay day at Six Flags New England • wear red to show your support • LGBT • 1000+
attendees • www.outinthepark.info

TBA: Braking the Cycle   *Boston, MA to New York City, NY*
3-day fully-supported bike ride from Boston to New York • benefiting the HIV/AIDS related services of the LGBT Community Center in NYC • mixed gay/ straight • 212/989-1111 •
www.brakingthecycle.org

TBA: Get Wet Weekend   *Curaçao, Netherlands Antilles, Caribbean*
discover the Caribbean Dutch Paradise of Curaçao! • gay/ lesbian • 599/9510-6479,
599/9510-6499 • www.gaycuracao.com

TBA: Out On The Mountain   *Valencia, CA*
gay day at Six Flags Magic Mountain • LGBT • www.outonthemountain.com

TBA: Pink Season   *Hong Kong, China*
2-month festival featuring speakers, plays, dance parties, pageants & more • LGBT •
www.pinkseason.hk

TBA: Seattle AIDS Walk   *Seattle, WA*
mixed gay/ straight • 4000+ attendees • 206/957-1606 • www.SeattleAIDSWalk.org

October

1-6: Dallas Black Pride   *Dallas, TX*
LGBT • 214/440-9300 • dfwpridemovement.org

ongoing: October is Breast Cancer Awareness Month *Cross-country, USA*
check local listings for fund-raising events in your area to fight breast cancer •

3-5: Gay Days Anaheim   *Anaheim, CA*
"join 30,000 GLBT mouseketeers as we turn the happiest place in earth into the gayest!" •
www.GayDaysAnaheim.com

5: Castro Street Fair   *San Francisco, CA*
performance, arts & community groups street fair • co-founded by Harvey Milk • 800/853-5950 •
www.castrostreetfair.org

11: National Coming Out Day *Cross-country, USA*
check local listings for events in your area or visit www.hrc.com/ncop • 202/628-4160, 800/777-4723 • **www.hrc.org/comingout**

16-19: Sundance Stompede *San Francisco, CA*
San Francisco's annual country/ western dance weekend • LGBT • 415/820-1403 • **www.stompede.com**

19: AIDS Walk LA *Los Angeles, CA*
annual AIDS fundraiser in West Hollywood • mixed gay/ straight • 213/201-9255 • **www.aidswalk.net**

TBA: Glasgay! *Glasgow, Scotland*
UK's largest lesbian & gay multi-arts festival • 44-141/552-7575 • **www.glasgay.com**

TBA: AIDS Walk Atlanta & 5k Run *Atlanta, GA*
mixed gay/ straight • 10,000+ attendees • 404/876-9255 • **WWW.aidswalkatlanta.com**

TBA: Black Pride *Nashville, TN*
gay/ lesbian • 615/974-2832, 800/845-4266x269 • **www.brothersunited.com**

TBA: Taiwan LGBT Pride *Taipei, Taiwan*
• www.twpride.org

November

1-2: Greater Palm Springs Pride *Palm Springs, CA*
free entertainment, dance parties, lots of people & a parade on Sunday • 760/416-8711 • **www.PSPride.org**

TBA: Transgender Film Festival *San Francisco, CA*
films that promote the visibility of transgender & gender variant people • **www.trannyfest.com**

December

15-18: Utah Gay & Lesbian Ski Week *Salt Lake City, UT*
ski at Alta, Snowbird, Solitude, Brighton, Snow Basin & The Canyons • 877/429-6368 • **www.gayskiing.org**

31: Mummer's Strut *Philadelphia, PA*
big New Year's Eve party • followed by New Year's Day Parade • mixed gay/ straight • $40-50 • 215/336-3050 • **www.mummers.com**

TBA: Holly Folly *Provincetown, MA*
lesbian/ gay holiday celebration • fabulous parties • holiday concert • open houses • 1st wknd in December • **www.ptown.org**

TBA: IAGLBC Annual Bridge Tournament *Palm Springs, CA*
Int'l Association of Gay & Lesbian Bridge Clubs • **www.GayBridge.org**

WOMEN'S FESTIVALS, PARTIES & GATHERINGS

January

16-20: Silver Threads Celebration *St Petersburg Beach, FL*
4 day celebration for lesbians over 50 & their younger friends • women only • **www.silverthreadscelebration.org**

March

5-10: Winter Party for Women *Miami/ South Beach, FL*
check the schedule for hot women's events all weekend long • mostly women • **www.winterparty.com**

April

2-6: Club Skirts Dinah Shore Weekend   *Palm Springs, CA*
women only • 415/596-8730 • www.thedinah.com

3-6: Palm Springs Women's Jazz Festival   *Palm Springs, CA*
a women's jazz festival during Dinah Shore Weekend • presented by Lucy & Gail • women only •
760/416-3545 • www.dinahincolor.com

11-13: Fling   *Miami/ South Beach, FL*
the official women's events of Miami Beach Pride • Pandora & Icandee events join forces to bring
you an entire weekend of women's dance parties and pool parties at the hippest spots on Miami
Beach during the HOTTEST gay pride celebration in America • mostly women • 954/288-8691 •
www.pandoraevents.com

24-27: Girl Bar Dinah Vegas   *Las Vegas, NV*
huge gathering of lesbians for mega dance parties, huge pool parties, comedy, national recording
artists & yes, some golf watching • 5,000-8,000 attend • see website for ticket info • also
www.girlbar.com • dinahshorevip@aol.com • women only • 310/659-4551 •
www.dinahshoreweekend.com

TBA: Queer Eye Festival   *Prague, Czech Republic*
alternative music & culture festival • www.queerEye.cz

May

5-8: Women of Color Weekend   *Provincetown, MA*
3 days of comedy, wine tasting, dance parties & more • mostly women •
www.womenofcolorweekend.com

16-18: Single Women's Weekend   *Provincetown, MA*
3 days of comedy, music, dance parties & more • mostly women •
www.singlewomensweekend.com

21-25: Womonwrites   *1 hr SE of Atlanta, GA*
annual conference of Southeastern lesbian writers • also a fall event (October) •
womonwrites.wordpress.com

22-27: Int'l Ladies Weekend   *Cancun, Mexico*
welcome reception, luau party, concert, dance party and more! • mostly women • 877/604-8192 •
www.internationallgbtladies.com

23-26: Women Outdoors National Gathering   *Hancock, NH*
camping • hiking • workshops • women only • 110+ attendees • $120-285 •
www.womenoutdoors.org

29-June 1: Silver Threads North   *Rehoboth Beach, DE*
4 day celebration for lesbians over 50 & their younger friends • women only • 516/342-6026 •
www.silverthreadsnorth.com

TBA: Herland Bi-Annual Retreats   *Oklahoma City, OK*
music, workshops, campfire events & potluck • girls of all ages & boys under 10 welcome • also in
October • women only • 405/521-9696 • www.herlandsisters.org

TBA: Russian River Women's Wknd   *Guerneville, CA*
this village is packed w/ dykes for a weekend of pool parties, bumpin' night life, comedy, sports,
outdoor activities & more • 75 miles north of San Francisco • mostly women •
www.russianriverwomensweekend.org

TBA: Women's Fun Weekend   *County Cork, Ireland*
entertainment, sports, dance parties & more! • women only • www.corkwomensfunweekend.ie

June

4-8: Deaf Lesbian Festival *Phoenix, AZ*
a celebration & global gathering of culturally identified deaf & lesbian women • www.deaflesbianfestival.org

5-8: Ontario Womyn's Drum Camp *35 miles N of Kingston, ON, Canada*
all levels welcome • women only • 180 attendees • 613/599-4274 • www.drumcamps.ca

26-29: National Women's Music Festival *Middleton, WI*
check website for details • mostly women • 317/713-1144 • www.wiaonline.org

28: San Francisco Dyke March *San Francisco, CA*
join thousands of dykes of all shapes, colors & sizes for music, marching & more through the streets of the Mission & the Castro • www.thedykemarch.org

July

22-26: Girl Splash *Provincetown, MA*
4 days of comedy, music, dance parties & more • mostly women • www.womeninnkeepers.com

23-27: OLOC (Old Lesbians Organizing for Change) Nat'l Gathering *Oakland, CA*
lesbians 60+ gather for workshops, guest speakers & entertainment to promote Old Lesbian pride & fight ageism • women only • 888/706-7506 • www.oloc.org

TBA: Fabulosa *Sonoma, CA*
women-centered music wknd • healing arts, film & crafts • mostly women • 415/624-9390 • www.fabulosa.org

August

5-10: Michigan Womyn's Music Festival *near Hart, MI*
theater, music & dance performances • workshops, film festival & craft fair • ASL interpreting & differently-abled resources • child care • camping • women only • 3,000-5,000 attendees • 231/757-4766 • www.michfest.com

12-17: Girlie Circuit *Barcelona, Spain*
water park events • club nights • pool parties • films, discussions & more • gay/ lesbian • www.circuitfestival.net

15-17: Womyn's Gathering *Louisa, VA*
last wknd in Aug • camping, music & workshops • mixed gay/ straight • $40-140 • 540/894-5126 • www.womensgathering.org

21-24: Women in the Woods *Portland, OR*
rustic cabins • natural hot springs • all meals included • women only • 300-400 attendees • 503/284-0722 • www.womeninthewoods.com

29-31: Festival of Babes *Pacific Northwest, USA*
fun, frivolous & flirtatious soccer tournament • Int'l Babes play hard & party harder • rotates btwn Vancouver, Seattle, Portland & San Francisco • women only • www.festivalofthebabes.com

September

4-7: BOLDFest *Vancouver, BC, Canada*
Bold Old(er) Lesbians & Dykes meet up for the annual West Coast gathering • 604/253-7189 • www.boldfest.com

4-7: WomenFest *Key West, FL*
live music • film festival • pool parties • comedy show • dance parties • golf tournament • women only • 800/535-7797 • www.womenfest.com

5-7: Sisterspace Wknd *Darlington, MD*
sliding scale • women only • 888/294-1110 • www.sisterspace.org

19-21: Ohio Lesbian Festival   *Kirkersville (E of Columbus), OH*
women only • 2000-3000 attendees • www.ohiolba.org

TBA: Iowa Women's Music Festival   *Iowa City, IA*
mostly women • 319/335-1486 • www.prairievoices.net

TBA: Shedonism   *Las Vegas, NV*
the official Women's Weekend of Las Vegas Pride! • a weekend long celebration of SIN, in none
other than SIN CITY! Day parties, nightclub parties, pop stars, singers, dancers, performers, DJ's,
comedians, show girls, poker tournaments & a parade (just to name a few) • women only •
954/288-8691 • www.shedonismvegas.com

October

13-19: Provincetown Women's Week   *Provincetown, MA*
very popular – make your reservations early! • mostly women • 5,000+ attendees • www.wom-
eninnkeepers.com

TBA: Peach Atlanta   *Atlanta, GA*
Pandora Events & Curve Personals present The Women's events of Atlanta Pride • join over 2,000
women for the sexiest party of the year w/ superstar DJs, go-go girls galore & Real L Word host as
they party the night away & celebrate in Southern style • mostly women • 954/288-8691 •
www.pandoraevents.com

TBA: WomynSpirit Festival   *Orangeville, ON, Canada*
celebrate Samhain at this queer-friendly womyn's pagan weekend • women only • 416/481-7634
• womynspiritfestival.weebly.com

November

19-30: Women's White Party   *Miami, FL*
join Pandora Events on the beautiful sun-drenched shores of South Beach for an unforgettable
weekend of stylish women's parties, shopping, dinning & more • mostly women • 954/288-8691 •
www.womenswhiteparty.com

TBA: Nia Gathering   *Petaluma, CA*
lesbians of African descent gather to reflect on the past & build a postive future • women only •
510/869-4403 • www.niacollective.org

FILM FESTIVALS

January

20-26: Zinegoak   *Bilbao, Spain*
LGBT film & performing arts festival • 34-94/415-6258 • www.zinegoak.com

30-Feb 8: Reelout Queer Film & Video Festival   *Kingston, ON, Canada*
celebrating the best of queer independent film & video • 613/549-7335 • www.reelout.com

February

13-23: Mardi Gras Film Festival   *Sydney, Australia*
Sydney film festival corresponds with massive Mardi Gras event • 61-2/9332-4938 • www.queer-
screen.com.au

March

13-24: Melbourne Queer Film Festival   *Melbourne, Australia*
613/9662-4147 • www.mqff.com.au

20-30: London Lesbian & Gay Film Festival *London, England*
grab your tickets for the largest LGBT film fest in Europe • 44 (0)20/7928-3232 • **www.llgff.org.uk**

TBA: Outfest Fusion LGBT People of Color Film Festival *Los Angeles, CA*
213/480-7088 • **www.outfest.org**

April

3-12: Boston LGBT Film Festival *Boston, MA*
617/369-3300 • **www.bostonlgbtfilmfest.org**

13-17: QFest *St Louis, MO*
314/289-4152 • **www.cinemastlouis.org/qfest**

25-27: London Lesbian Film Festival *London, ON, Canada*
women only Fri-Sat, open to all on Sunday • **www.llff.ca**

25-May 4: Miami Gay & Lesbian Film Festival *Miami, FL*
305/751-6305 • **www.MGLFF.com**

TBA: Brisbane Queer Film Festival *Brisbane, Australia*
61 7/3358 8600 • **www.bqff.com.au**

TBA: Out in Africa *Cape Town, South Africa*
the only film festival of its kind on the African continent • three 10-day festivals throughout the year • also August & October • also in Johannesburg • 27 21/461 40 27 • **www.oia.co.za**

May

22-June 1: Inside Out: Toronto LGBT Film & Video Festival *Toronto, ON, Canada*
416/977-6847 • **www.insideout.ca**

23-31: Fairy Tales Int'l LGBT Film Festival *Calgary, AB, Canada*
403/244-1956 • **www.fairytalesfilmfest.com**

29-June 11: Out Takes LGBT Film Festival *Wellington, New Zealand*
week-long festival in Auckland, Wellington & Christchurch • 64-4/972-6775 • **www.outtakes.org.nz**

30-June 1: FilmOut San Diego *San Diego, CA*
LGBT film festival • 619/512-5157 • **www.filmoutsandiego.com**

30-June 7: Connecticut Gay & Lesbian Film Festival *Hartford, CT*
gay & lesbian film festival at Cinestudio • 860/586-1136 • **www.outfilmct.org**

TBA: Translations: Transgender Film Festival *Seattle, WA*
206/323-4274 • **www.threedollarbillcinema.org**

June

3-13: Rio Gay Film Festival *Rio de Janeiro, Brazil*
LGBT • **www.riofgc.com**

7-14: TLVFest: The Tel Aviv LGBT Film Festival *Tel Aviv, Israel*
films will also show in Jerusalem & Haifa • 972-52/2767404 • **www.tlvfest.com**

1-15: Honolulu Rainbow Film Festival *Honolulu, HI*
808/675-8428 • **www.hglcf.org**

13-15: Queer Women of Color Film Festival *San Francisco, CA*
festival focus: SWANA/AMEMSA queer women of color & transgender/genderqueer people of color • 415/752-0868 • **www.qwocmap.org**

18-22: Provincetown Int'l Film Festival *Provincetown, MA*
mixed gay/ straight • 508/487-3456 • **www.ptownfilmfest.org**

frameline

SAN FRANCISCO INTERNATIONAL LGBT FILM FESTIVAL

JUNE 19 - 29, 2014 & JUNE 18 - 28, 2015

The world's first & largest queer film festival
(and so much more)

EXHIBITION

FILMMAKER SUPPORT

DISTRIBUTION

 frameline    @framelinefest

frameline.org

19-29: Frameline: San Francisco Int'l LGBT Film Festival *San Francisco, CA*
get your tickets early for a slew of films about us • LGBT • 65,000+ attendees • 415/703-8650 •
www.frameline.org

TBA: Identities Queer Film Festival   *Vienna, Austria*
43-1/524-6274 • www.identities.at/index/en/

TBA: Mix Milano Int'l LGBT Film Festival   *Milan, Italy*
• www.cinemagaylesbico.com

July

10-20: Outfest Los Angeles LGBT Film Festival   *Los Angeles, CA*
Los Angeles' lesbian/ gay film & video festival in mid-July • 213/480-7088 • www.outfest.org

TBA: Mostra Lambda Barcelona   *Barcelona, Spain*
LGBT film festival • www.cinemalambda.com

TBA: Philadelphia QFest   *Philadelphia, PA*
267/765-9800 • www.qfest.com

TBA: Tokyo Int'l Lesbian & Gay Film Festival   *Tokyo, Japan*
• www.tokyo-lgff.org

August

5-10: Flickers: Rhode Island Int'l Film Festival   *Providence, RI*
don't miss the Gay & Lesbian Film Fest • mixed gay/ straight • 401/861-4445 • **www.film-festi-val.org**

TBA: Birmingham Shout   *Birmingham, AL*
LGBT film festival • 205/324-0888 • www.bhamshout.com

TBA: Gaze Dublin Int'l LGBT Film Festival   *Dublin, Ireland*
0872/709700 • www.gaze.ie

TBA: North Carolina Gay & Lesbian Film Festival   *Durham, NC*
919/560-3030 (box office), 919/560-3040 • festivals.carolinatheatre.org/ncglff

TBA: Vancouver Queer Film & Video Festival   *Vancouver, BC, Canada*
LGBT • 604/844-1615 • www.queerfilmfestival.ca

September

12-14: Q Film Festival   *Long Beach, CA*
showcasing films of interest to the queer community • 562/434-4455 •
www.qfilmslongbeach.com

TBA: Fresno Reel Pride   *Fresno, CA*
annual lesbian & gay film festival in central California • 559/999-7971 • www.reelpride.com

TBA: Hong Kong Lesbian/ Gay Film Festival   *Hong Kong, China*
LGBT • 852/2311 8081 • www.hklgff.hk

TBA: NewFest: New York LGBT Film Festival   *New York City, NY*
646/290-8136 • www.newfest.org

TBA: Outflix   *Memphis, TN*
LGBT film festival • www.outflixfestival.org

TBA: Queer Lisbon   *Lisbon, Portugal*
Portugal's only LGBT film festival • 351 91/335-8603 • www.queerlisboa.pt

three
dollar bill
cinema

Coming to Seattle? We want to show you a good time.

Keeping audiences entertained since 1996, Three Dollar Bill Cinema promotes and produces LGBT film events throughout the year, including free outdoor movies every summer, our Spring Film Series of vintage queer classics, the Seattle Lesbian & Gay Film Festival in October, and other unique events.

Check out our website or find us on Facebook and Twitter to see what's happening on your next visit to Seattle.

three
dollar bill
cinema

October

2-9: Out on Film *Atlanta, GA*
LGBT • 678/237-7206 • www.outonfilm.org

10-19: Reel Q Int'l Lesbian & Gay Film Festival *Pittsburgh, PA*
412/422-6776 • www.plgfs.org

10-19: Southwest Gay & Lesbian Film Festival *Albuquerque, NM*
also in Santa Fe, NM • 505/243-1870 • www.swglff.com

14-18: St John's International Women's Film Festival *St John's, NL, Canada*
mixed gay/ straight • 4500 attendees • 709/754-3141 • www.womensfilmfestival.com

14-19: Hamburg Int'l Lesbian & Gay Film Festival *Hamburg, Germany*
49-40/348-0670 • www.lsf-hamburg.de

16-26: Barcelona Int'l LGTIB Film Festival *Barcelona, Spain*
gay/ lesbian • 973/664-421 • www.barcelonafilmfestival.org

16-26: Seattle Lesbian & Gay Film Festival *Seattle, WA*
206/323-4274 • www.threedollarbillcinema.org

TBA: Cheries-Cheris: Paris Gay, Lesbian & Trans Film Festival *Paris, France*
• www.cheries-cheris.com

TBA: Berlin Lesbian Film Festival *Berlin, Germany*
49-172/381-2883 • www.lesbenfilmfestival.de

TBA: Cineffable: Paris Int'l Lesbian & Feminist Film Festival *Paris, France*
• www.cineffable.fr

TBA: Madrid LGBT Film Festival *Madrid, Spain*
34-91/593-0540 • www.lesgaicinemad.com

TBA: Milwaukee LGBT Film/ Video Festival *Milwaukee, WI*
414/229-4758 • www4.uwm.edu/psoa/film/lgbtfilmfestival/

TBA: Mix *Copenhagen, Denmark*
45/2843-4217 • www.mixcopenhagen.dk

TBA: Polari *Austin, TX*
512/302-9889 • www.polarifest.com

TBA: Portland Lesbian & Gay Film Festival *Portland, OR*
• www.plgff.org

TBA: Q Cinema *Fort Worth, TX*
annual celebration of LGBT-themed movies • 817/723-4358 • www.qcinema.org

TBA: Reel Affirmations: The Nation's LGBT Film Festival *Washington, DC*
lesbian/ gay films • 202/349-7358 • www.reelaffirmations.org

TBA: Sacramento Int'l Gay & Lesbian Film Festival *Sacramento, CA*
916/304-3456 • www.siglff.org

TBA: Tampa Bay Int'l Gay & Lesbian Film Festival *Tampa Bay, FL*
813/879-4220 • www.tiglff.com

November

6-13: Reeling: Chicago Lesbian & Gay Int'l Film Fest *Chicago, IL*
773/293-1447 • www.reelingfilmfestival.org

7-10: Long Island Gay & Lesbian Film Festival *Huntington, NY*
• www.liglff.org

TBA: image+nation: Montréal Int'l LGBT Film Festival *Montréal, QC, Canada*
LGBT • 514/285-4467 • www.image-nation.org

TBA: Mezipatra *Prague & Brno, Czech Republic*
Czech LGBT film festival • www.mezipatra.cz

**TBA: Mix: New York Lesbian & Gay
Experimental Film Fest** *New York City, NY*
film, videos, installations & media performances • write for info • 212/742-8880 •
www.mixnyc.org

LEATHER

January

17-20: Mid-Atlantic Leather Weekend *Washington, DC*
LGBT • 703/863-7295 • www.leatherweekend.com

23-25: Southwest Leather Conference *Phoenix, AZ*
workshops, vendors & fetish ball • MASTER/slave, Bootblack & Daddy/boy contests • LGBT •
www.southwestleather.org

April

4-6: Rubbout *Vancouver, BC, Canada*
annual party weekend of rubber & fetish for men • men only • 604/345-1357 •
www.rubbout.com

11-13: Leather Leadership Conference *Philadelphia, PA*
join us to develop & strengthen problem-solving & camaraderie in the leather community • LGBT
• www.leatherleadership.org

24-27: International Ms Bootblack Contest *San Jose, CA*
workshops • parties • vending • contest takes place the weekend of International Ms Leather
weekend • mixed gay/ straight • www.IMsL.org

24-27: International Ms Leather Contest *San Jose, CA*
contest • workshops • parties • vending • mixed gay/ straight • www.IMsL.org

May

16-18: Northwest Leather Celebration (NWLC) *San Jose, CA*
host of the NW regional Master/slave contest • LGBT • www.northwestleathercelebration.com

June

19-22: Southeast Leatherfest *Atlanta, GA*
LGBT • www.seleatherfest.com

TBA: Desire: Leather Women Unleashed *Palm Springs, CA*
weekend retreat for leather- & kinky women • women only • www.desireleatherwomen.org

TBA: Folsom Street East *New York City, NY*
New York City's answer to the famous San Francisco fetish street fair • LGBT • www.folsom-streeteast.org

July

11-13: Thunder in the Mountains *Denver, CO*
weekend of pansexual leather events & seminars • kinky comedy revue • talent show • LGBT •
800+ attendees • 303/698-1207 • www.thunderinthemountains.com

25-27: International Deaf Leather *Providence, RI*
weekend of events, including Mr & Ms Deaf Leather Contest •
www.internationaldeafleather.org

TBA: TransCampOUT   *Walton, WV*
presentations • games • auctions • outdoor dungeon • swimming • trans-oriented • everyone welcome regardless of sexual orientation or gender identity • LGBT • 971/295-6106 • **www.transcampout.org**

August

9-11: Rocky Mountain Olympus Leather   *Salt Lake City, UT*
leather competition • participants from Utah, Colorado, Wyoming, Idaho & Montana • mixed gay/straight • 200 attendees • 415/409-9447 • **www.rockymountainolympus.com**

September

13-14: Folsom Europe   *Berlin, Germany*
49 30/23 62 86 32 • **www.folsomeurope.info**

21: Folsom Street Fair   *San Francisco, CA*
huge SM/ leather street fair, topping a week of kinky events • LGBT • thousands of local & visiting kinky men & women attendees • 415/777-3247 • **www.folsomstreetevents.org**

October

TBA: Pantheon of Leather   *Atlanta, GA*
annual leather/ SM/ fetish community service awards & int'l Mr & Ms Olympus Leather • mixed gay/ straight • **www.TheLeatherJournal.com/pantheon**

November

TBA: Santa Clara County Leather Weekend   *San Jose, CA*
leather fellowship in the San Jose area • LGBT • www.SCCLeather.org

CONFERENCES & RETREATS

January

29-Feb 2: Creating Change Conference   *Houston, TX*
for lesbians, gays, bisexuals, transgender people & allies seeking positive & enduring political & social change • 2500+ attendees • 617/492-6393 • **www.creatingchange.org**

March

21-23: Together We Can   *Detroit, MI*
annual LGBT substance abuse conference • 248/838-9905 • **www.twcdetroit.com**

May

15-18: Saints & Sinners   *New Orleans, LA*
LGBT writers & readers from around the country gather for a hot weekend of readings, panels & performance • 300 attendees • $100 • 504/581-1144 • **www.sasfest.com**

June

TBA: Lambda Literary Awards   *New York City, NY*
the Lammies are the Oscars of LGBT writing & publishing • LGBT • 323/366-2104 • **www.lambdaliterary.org**

July

9-13: GCLS Annual Literary Convention   *Portland, OR*
The Golden Crown Literary Society (GCLS) annual gathering for the enjoyment, discussion & enhancement of lesbian literature • 513/457-5126 (9am-5pm EST) • **www.goldencrown.org**

TBA: NGLCC Conference   *TBA, USA*
anual gathering of Nat'l Gay & Lesbian Chamber of Commerce • 202/234-9181 • **www.nglcc.org**

August

14-17: Gender Odyssey   *Seattle, WA*
4 days of panels, workshops & meetings • entertainment & art • focus on transmen, transwomen & families with transgender children & teens • open to all • 206/306-8383 • **www.genderodyssey.org**

TBA: Nat'l Lesbian & Gay Journalists Assoc Convention   *TBA, USA*
workshops • keynote speakers • entertainment • 202/588-9888 x10 • **www.nlgja.org**

September

1-7: Southern Comfort Conference   *Atlanta, GA*
entertainers & leaders from the entire spectrum of the transgender community offering 5 days of learning, networking & fun • 910/443-3659 • **www.sccatl.org**

October

2-4: National LGBT MBA Conference   *San Francisco, CA*
career fair & discussions of sexual orientation, gender & leadership in the workplace by MBA students & out Fortune 500 company leaders • LGBT • 800+ attendees • **www.reachingoutmba.org**

November

TBA: Transgender Leadership Summit   *TBA, USA*
join transgender activists to help create a unified voice to advance the movement for transgender equality • 200+ attendees • 415/865-0176 • **www.transgenderlawcenter.org**

SPIRITUAL

February

14-17: PantheaCon   *San Jose, CA*
pagan convention • mixed gay/ straight • 510/653-3244 • **www.pantheacon.com**

May

16-18: A Gathering of Priestesses & Goddess Women *Wisconsin Dells, Southwestern WI*
women's spirituality conference • also Hallows Gathering in October • women only • 608/226-9998 • **www.rcgi.org**

June

15-22: Pagan Spirit Gathering   *Earlville, IL*
summer solstice celebration • primitive camping • workshops • rituals • advance registration required • mixed gay/ straight • 608/924-2216 • **www.circlesanctuary.org/psg**

August

TBA: BC Witchcamp   *near Vancouver, BC, Canada*
weeklong Wiccan intensive at Evans Lake • mixed gay/ straight • 250/598-9229 • **www.bcwitchcamp.ca**

TBA: Elderflower Womenspirit Festival   *Mendocino, CA*
earth-based spirituality retreat for women and girls • honoring the feminine through the Goddess • women & girls only • 415/339-8000 • **elderflower.org**

BREAST CANCER BENEFITS

January

ongoing throughout the year: Susan G Komen Race for the Cure Series
Cross-country, USA
5K & 1-mile run/fitness walks in cities around the country to fight breast cancer • call for local city dates • organized by local affiliate offices • 877/GO-KOMEN • **www.komen.org**

TBA: Boarding for Breast Cancer Board-a-thon   *TBA, USA*
help raise money & awareness for breast cancer • live music & pro exihibitions at ski resorts around the country • also other events during the year • mixed gay/ straight • 323/467-2663 • **www.b4bc.org**

KIDS' STUFF

February

14-17: Camp It Up! LGBT Family Camp Winter Session   *Quincy, CA*
swimming • horseback riding • arts & crafts • music, dance & theater • family spa & salon! • at Feather River Camp • since 1990 • 250+ attendees • 510/338-0370 • **www.campitup.org**

July

26-Aug 3: Camp It Up! LGBT Family Camp   *Quincy, CA*
swimming • horseback riding • arts & crafts • music, dance & theater • family spa & salon! • at Feather River Camp • since 1990 • 250+ attendees • 510/338-0370 • **www.campitup.org**

27-Aug 2: Camp Ten Oaks   *Ottawa, ON, Canada*
summer camp for LGBTQ kids & kids from LGBTQ families • ages 8-17 • also Project Acorn leadership retreat for ages 16-24 • 613/321-2824 • **www.camptenoaks.org**

August

11-24: Camp Ten Trees   *Western WA*
residential summer camp • one week for LGBTQA youth ages 13-17 • one week for kids ages 8-17 of LGBTQA/ non-traditional families • 206/288-9568 • **www.camptentrees.org**

TBA: Keshet Camp: Jewish Family Camp   *Yosemite, CA*
a rainbow camp for LGBT families & their friends • sports, music, arts & crafts & more • 415/543-2267 • **www.tawonga.org**

TBA: Family Week   *Provincetown, MA*
join hundreds of LGBT parents, kids & allies for a week of workshops, boat rides, campfires, sandcastle competitions & more • LGBT • 617/502-8700 • **www.familyequality.org**

dattch

The best way to meet